# Guide to Real Estate Licensing Examinations

# Guide to Real Estate Licensing Examinations

## for Salespersons and Brokers
## ASI, ETS, ACT

## Fifth Edition

*William B. French*
Attorney, REALTOR®, Real Estate Consultant, and Educator,
University of Notre Dame, Notre Dame, Indiana

*Stephen J. Martin*
Director, Real Estate Certification Program,
Center for Real Estate Education and Research,
Bloomington, Indiana

*Thomas E. Battle, III*
Coordinator, Statewide Prelicensing Courses for
Salespersons and Brokers, Real Estate Certification Program
and Lecturer, School of Business, Indiana University

WILEY

**JOHN WILEY & SONS**

**New York • Chichester • Brisbane • Toronto • Singapore**

*Library of Congress Cataloging in Publication Data*

French, William B.
   Guide to real estate licensing examinations for
salespersons and brokers. ASI, ETS, ACT

   Bibliography: p.
   Includes index.
   1. Real estate business—United States. 2. Real
estate business—United States—Examinations, questions,
etc. 3. Real estate agents—Licenses—United States.
I. Martin, Stephen John, 1948-    . II. Battle,
Thomas E. III. Title.

HD1375.F74 1988        333.33'0973        88-5493
ISBN 0-471-85354-2

*Printed in the United States of America*

10   9   8   7   6   5   4   3   2   1

# PREFACE

The fifth edition of the *Guide to Real Estate Licensing Examinations* is designed to prepare prospective salespersons and brokers for state real estate licensing examinations. The text has been carefully written to assist with examinations administered by the Educational Testing Service (ETS), American College Testing (ACT), and Assessment Systems, Inc. (ASI). It can be used by students as a fundamental classroom text or by individuals for independent study.

The Fifth Edition covers a complete body of real estate knowledge, including detailed coverage of the legal, economic, mathematical, and ethical considerations of the real estate business. The combination text and workbook format has proven to be extremely helpful in preparing students for the licensing examination. Each chapter contains a series of review questions designed to test the student's knowledge of basic principles. In addition, Chapter 18 presents examinations similar in content and format to the licensing examinations administered by ETS, ACT, and ASI. Chapter vocabularies and a glossary at the end of the text help the student become familiar with real estate terminology. The appendix includes answers to all review questions; all mathematical solutions are shown completely worked out.

The book covers all the topics required by students studying for the licensing examinations. Information about a particular state's licensing laws may be obtained by contacting the appropriate state agency for its bulletin and, in some states, by consulting the special supplement published by John Wiley & Sons.

It would have been impossible to have completed the task of writing and organizing earlier editions of this book had it not been for the most capable assistance of Suzann M. Owen, whose help is still apparent and whose editing skills are still appreciated.

William B. French
Stephen J. Martin
Thomas E. Battle, III

# CONTENTS

# Guide to Real Estate Licensing Examinations

# Part I
# Preparing To Use the Text

# Chapter 1
# Use of the Guide

This book covers all major areas of the field of real estate in a format designed to be used in preparation for the uniform Real Estate License Examinations (RELE), the ACT Multistate Examination (ACT), or Assessment Systems, Inc. (ASI) Examinations.

Each chapter on real estate topics contains a vocabulary list, text discussion, suggested readings, and review questions. You should pay particular attention to the vocabulary sections. The authors have selected those words that play a key role in understanding real estate. Real estate has its own vocabulary, as does any discipline, and success or failure in the business and on the licensing examination depends on your ability to apply the proper terms to the situation presented. The vocabulary lists provide an excellent source of review material. A complete listing of words and their definitions appears in the Glossary.

The text discussion in each chapter provides an in-depth explanation of the topics presented. These sections are the key to understanding each major area, and they contain the source material for preparation for the uniform licensing examination.

The review questions for the chapters covering real estate topics are designed to give you feedback on your own understanding of the materials just studied, and should help you identify your strengths and weaknesses. The answers are in Appendix B.

This guide includes a chapter (Chapter 16) on real estate mathematics which contains problems and instructions as to how the math functions should be performed. Solutions to all math problems appear in Appendix B.

The listing, offer, and settlement practice problems in Chapter 17 should be of major concern to all students, since questions on these topics constitute a significant portion of the uniform examination for both salespersons and brokers. There are six problems depicting different listing, offer, and settlement situations. The first problem has been worked out as a guide for you to follow in completing the other five. Each problem should be done in its entirety. This is good preparation for both brokers and salespersons. The solutions to the problems appear in Appendix B.

The practice examinations in Chapter 18 follow the format of the uniform examinations you will be taking. The questions are similar in difficulty and structure to those that appear on the RELE, ACT, and ASI examinations, though they are not actual questions from examinations administered by the Testing Services. The answers and math solutions to the test questions appear at the end of each test. These tests should not be taken until you have completed study of all the topics presented in the text. They are the final preparation for the uniform tests.

You will note that no sample State Test has been provided. Since each licensing agency is responsible for developing its own State Test, it is not possible to create a uniform sample. However, the subject areas normally covered on the state examinations are outlined in detail in Chapter 4. In the same chapter, the authors have provided a list of addresses of licensing agencies so that you can contact them for specific information about a State Test. This will also serve as a reference source for the future.

# Chapter 2

# The Real Estate Licensing Examinations

## UNIFORM EXAMINATIONS

In order to establish a program to provide examinations for salespersons and brokers that are professionally prepared and of a consistently high quality, four jurisdictions—the District of Columbia, Maryland, North Carolina, and Virginia—sponsored development of the Real Estate Licensing Examinations (RELE) program in 1970. The representatives of the jurisdictions worked with examination specialists from the Educational Testing Service (ETS) in Princeton, New Jersey, to construct examinations that could be used in all four jurisdictions for real estate licensing.

As a result of the similarity of many facets of real estate nationally, the Uniform Test of the RELE evolved. This test measures the general knowledge and skills required uniformly among the various jurisdictions that participate in the examination program. There are two different versions of the Uniform Test, one for salesperson license candidates and one for broker license candidates.

Similar nationally administered examinations have been developed by American College Testing (ACT) and by Assessment Systems, Inc. (ASI). The ASI exam is referred to as the Real Estate Assessment for Licensure (REAL) Program. The questions on both exams are based on pools of test items on general practices and principles in real estate.

Each testing organization provides examination candidates with a booklet describing their examination, application process, and scoring procedures.

## THE STATE TESTS

Those who desire licenses as brokers or salespersons must also be examined on the laws, rules, regulations, and practices unique to their own jurisdictions. This portion of the examinations is known as the State Test. It differs in content from jurisdiction to jurisdiction, according to practice and procedure.

## EXAMINATION APPLICATION

Each jurisdiction's licensing agency determines an individual's eligibility for licensing. You should contact your particular licensing agency (see Chapter 4) for the specific requirements, which vary from jurisdiction to jurisdiction. In some instances prelicensing education is required for an extended period prior to examination. This information may be obtained through your agency, real estate education program, or jurisdiction's licensing agency or commission.

## LOCATIONS OF EXAMINATIONS

Some jurisdictions have several examination locations. If this is the case in your jurisdiction, you will be allowed to state your preference. If you are not placed at the location of your choice, then you will be placed at the location nearest to the one you prefer.

## EXAMINATION DATES

Not all jurisdictions give the examinations on the same date. You should check with your jurisdiction's licensing agency for the dates on which it offers the examination. Most states schedule examinations several times a year.

## ADMISSION TO THE EXAMINATION

If you have registered to take the uniform examinations, you should receive an admission ticket no later than one week prior to the examination. (The admission ticket for salesperson applicants may be sent to the sponsoring broker if that is required in a particular jurisdiction.) If you are taking some other form of test being administered by the state licensing agency, you should check with your licensing agency about admission requirements.

Your admission ticket will list the name of the examination (salesperson or broker) for which you have registered, the name and address of the assigned test center, and the time at which you should appear for your examination.

You must have your admission ticket with you at the test center. If you do not receive an admission ticket one week prior to the examination, or if you lose your ticket, you should contact your licensing agency or testing agency, which will handle the problem according to predetermined policy.

### EXAMINATION CENTER ADMISSION

Report to the examination center to which you have been assigned as indicated on the admission ticket. You must have the proper admission ticket or authorization, or your name must appear on the attendance roster for the center, before you will be admitted to the examination.

In addition to the admission ticket, you should bring at least three No. 2 pencils and an eraser. And you *must* have with you at least two pieces of identification, such as a driver's license and an employment or student identification card.

### INSTRUCTIONS

Instructions will be read by an examination supervisor from the manual prepared by the testing agency. These instructions are to guide you and to ensure that the proper information is placed on the answer sheet. This also allows uniform testing conditions to prevail from center to center.

### CALCULATORS AND SLIDE RULES

Not all jurisdictions permit the use of a slide rule or calculator. If they are permitted in your jurisdiction, it will be indicated on your admission ticket. If you are uncertain about this prior to receiving the admission ticket, contact your licensing agency for clarification.

The rules concerning the use and types of instruments permitted are:

☐ The candidate may use only hand-held, silent, battery-operated instruments that *do not* have a paper tape printing capacity. If the instrument does not meet the above requirements, this will be grounds for immediate dismissal from the examination. If the testing supervisor determines prior to admission to the examination that the instrument does not meet the described standards, the candidate will be permitted to take the examination upon surrender of the instrument to the supervisor for the duration of the examination.

☐ If the candidate's instrument should not function

during the examination, this will not be grounds for challenging examination results or demanding extended time for completion of the examination.

*Note:* It is the opinion of the testing agencies that calculators or slide rules are not necessary to complete the calculations needed for the examination questions. Any figuring can be done by pencil and paper in the time allotted.

### EXAMINATION CENTER REGULATIONS

Each examination center adheres to the same set of examination guidelines and rules so as to ensure equality in the examination process. The basic rules are:

☐ No books, dictionaries, or papers of any kind (including scratch paper) will be permitted in the examination room. Any candidate found with any of these items will not be allowed to continue the examination.

☐ The candidate will *not* be permitted to work beyond the prescribed time under any circumstances.

☐ Any scratch work must be done in the margins of the examination booklet and not on the answer sheet. The answer sheet should contain only the candidate's identifying information and his or her responses to the questions.

☐ If a candidate desires to leave the room for any purpose, permission must be obtained from the test supervisor.

☐ Any candidate engaging in any form of misconduct will be reported to the licensing agency. Disciplinary action will be the responsibility of the licensing agency.

### TAKING THE EXAMINATION

The examinations for both salespersons and brokers consist entirely of multiple-choice questions. Upon receipt of the examination booklet the candidate should read the directions carefully so as not to miss anything which might be of importance to the examination and would cause loss of credit.

The candidate should use the allotted time carefully and economically by not wasting time in any one area. Take the questions in order and return to difficult ones later.

As indicated, the answers to the questions are to be recorded on a separate answer sheet. No credit is given for answers recorded in the question booklet. The answer sheets are numbered and lettered to correspond to the questions and possible responses given in the booklet. The candidate will choose the one best response from the four listed and darken the appropriate circle on the answer sheet. If the candidate marks more than one response to a single question, the question will be scored as incorrect. If you want to change an answer, be sure the erasure is complete.

The score is based upon the percentage of questions the candidate answers correctly. Do not be overly concerned if there are a few questions you cannot answer. If you feel reasonably certain, do not be afraid to guess.

Detailed outlines of the subjects covered in the examinations appear in Chapter 18.

## EXAMINATION SCORES AND SCORE REPORTS

Each examination consists of two parts, the Uniform portion and the State portion. The examinee must pass both tests to pass the entire examination. The individual licensing agencies will determine the passing or failing percentage for each test.

The candidate's scores are reported to the licensing agency, and an individual report is sent to the candidate. In some jurisdictions, the sponsoring broker may receive the salesperson's score report.

If the candidate passes the examination, the report will indicate PASS only. The actual numerical score will not be given, to avoid the possibility of misuse. The report may also contain certain important information from the licensing agency.

If the candidate fails the examination, separate scores will be reported for the individual parts of the examination. This will enable the candidate to see which areas gave him or her difficulty.

## NEW ETS TEST-TAKING DEVICE

The Educational Testing Service has recently made available in a number of states in its RELE testing program a new on-site score reporting system known as KEYWAY™. This is an electronic device similar to a calculator or small computer that records the examinee's responses to the test questions for immediate grading. Instead of recording the responses to the test questions on the usual optical scanning answer sheet, the examinee enters the answers into the KEYWAY™ answerpad.

The device is given to the examinee at check-in for the examination along with the test question booklet. In order to use the system, the examinee enters the proper identification sequence, which includes such items as test identification number, social security number, and birth date.

The system comes equipped with a series of practice exercises to familiarize the examinee with the functions of the KEYWAY™ answerpad before he or she begins to take the actual test. The examinee follows a series of prompts displayed on an LCD panel in order to have the answerpad perform the required function. Once comfortable with the operations of the KEYWAY™ answerpad, the examinee may begin to take the examination and enter the answers into the KEYWAY™ answerpad.

The answerpad has provisions for the examinee to review previously entered answers, to check for skipped questions, and to erase and change answers. The system is designed to prevent the accidental erasure of answers.

Once the examinee has entered all the answers into the KEYWAY™ answerpad and made any desired changes, the examinee locks the answers into the machine for grading. Precautions have been taken to prevent the locking in of answers before the examinee is finished. After the answers are locked in, the answerpad is returned to the test proctor. The test answers can now be graded at the test site, and the examinee can receive the results prior to leaving.

The new KEYWAY™ system allows the examinee to have almost immediate feedback about the test results; it also shortens the time between the examination and the issuance of the license.

## REVIEWING THE EXAMINATION

No provisions are made for either passing or failing candidates to review the examination results with the licensing agency or with the staff of the testing agency. This is necessary in order to maintain test security.

# Part II
# Understanding Real Estate Concepts

# Chapter 3
# The Real Estate Business

REAL estate could well be considered the most important factor in today's world. No everyday activity goes unaffected by real estate. It allows the production of food and provides the natural resources for domestic and commercial shelters. The study of real estate therefore involves all the aspects of land and the structures that might be built on it.

The marketing of land and its improvement must be handled in a responsible manner, for land cannot be replenished. Also, much of it cannot be considered fit for human habitation because of its location, topography, or quality. Although some specialists have emerged, the real estate professional must have a broad understanding of all aspects of the real estate business beyond brokerage—land development, construction, sale of property, property management, and finance—if he or she is to act responsibly in dealing with this precious resource.

## REAL ESTATE RESOURCES

Individuals interested in the real estate business must start by learning about the basic resources of the business itself. Obviously, the most important resource is raw land. The primary utilization of land has always been for the cultivation of crops or the pasturage of livestock. Because it is so important in producing food, great care must be exercised when introducing a new use, such as the development of residential, commercial, or industrial buildings or recreational facilities.

Second only to its use for food production is the use of land for shelter, more commonly called housing. Housing can take all forms, from luxury single-family homes to the most modest low-income housing. Other types of improvements involve such commercial enterprises as retail stores, shopping centers, industrial concerns, warehouses, and office buildings. Our everyday lives also involve the use of real estate for schools, churches, hospitals, and recreational facilities.

The basic definition of real estate is simple and must be mastered by all who enter the business:

*Real estate* is land and all things permanently attached to it as improvements.

The term *real property* is often used interchangeably with *real estate,* although it has a slightly expanded meaning that includes the legal rights to land and its improvements. This important difference is discussed in Chapter 6.

## REAL ESTATE RESOURCES AND THEIR CHARACTERISTICS

### Characteristics of Land

Each plot of land is unique; that is, it has its own special physical characteristics: (1) Its location is fixed; (2) no two plots are identical; (3) it is indestructible.

These three points must be considered for all plots of land. In addition, land has other characteristics which are primarily economic in nature: (1) Usable land is relatively scarce; (2) all usable land can be improved or have its value increased when structures are built on it; (3) its location to a great extent determines its value.

**Characteristics of Improvements**

Over one-half of the national wealth is represented by real estate resources, that is, land and improvements. The real estate business consists primarily of individuals utilizing such resources to meet the demands of the marketplace. Perhaps the greatest demand for real estate resources lies in housing. Residential property goes beyond the single-family residence to include duplexes, triplexes, quadriplexes, apartment buildings, cooperatives, condominiums, and mobile homes. The existing supply of residential structures is great, but the demand for more housing keeps the residential construction business expanding at a rapid pace. It is the residential market where most individuals enter the real estate industry today. But this industry was not always so active. It might be helpful for you to have a basic historical perspective of what has made the industry what it is today.

## ORIGINS OF REAL ESTATE AS WE KNOW IT TODAY

Ever since human beings developed a desire to own and control the use of real estate, the laws which protect rights of ownership and restrictions on the power to exercise these rights have been in the process of evolution.

The history of real estate in this country developed through a combination of two different systems. The *feudal system* recognizes the sovereign power of the king or the designated feudal lord as the legal owner of the property. The *allodial system* recognizes that property interests are vested in the person possessing the title to the land. Obviously, the allodial system had the greater effect on our nation's development of real estate resources.

Our nation was the first to be built on the precept of private ownership of land and the right to transfer such land. To accomplish this, a method was required by which the transfer could be made with as few problems as possible. Those who saw the need to facilitate transfers from those owning land to those who wanted to own land created colonization companies, became land agents, speculators, or auctioneers, and thus formed the beginning of the American real estate business.

In recognition of the increasing trade in land, the federal government passed the *Ordinance of 1785,* which contained these primary contributions to our land system:

- ☐ The rectangular survey of land
- ☐ Allowance for the transfer of public land to private ownership
- ☐ Provisions for private ownership of land
- ☐ Establishment of the process of transfer of property by deed or government patent

While the federal government tried to have a major impact on creating a new real estate system, it could not ignore the influence that other nations had on our nation's early settlers, including the method by which they took title to property. Robert Kevin Brown, in *Essentials of Real Estate,* tells us that, for the purpose of establishing the source of title to a parcel of land anywhere in the United States, the country as a whole may be divided into two categories:

- ☐ Titles to land in Maine, Vermont, New Hampshire, Massachusetts, Rhode Island, Connecticut, New York, New Jersey, Pennsylvania, Delaware, Maryland, Virginia, North Carolina, South Carolina, and Georgia are found in the following sources: (a) grants made to individuals and corporations by the local proprietary owners who had ownership by virtue of charters or patents issued by the English and Dutch governments; (b) grants by the state that succeeded to that ownership; or (c) grants by the respective states of any land not so granted or conveyed and which the states acquired as successors to these governments at the close of the American Revolution.
- ☐ Titles to land in all other states are found in the grants and patents made to individuals, corporations, states, and municipalities by the federal government, which obtained ownership of the land by virtue of concession, purchase, or discovery; or by grants and patents from any state in the United States now the owner of any ungranted or unpatented land.

From such beginnings, the real estate business experienced hampered growth for many years because of the limited number of transactions and their simplicity. Eventually the number of transactions taking place rose, and they became increasingly more complicated. Such factors led to the growth of today's real estate market.

## THE MODERN REAL ESTATE MARKET

The real estate market is influenced by many factors, but *supply* and *demand* are responsible for its existence. This market is somewhat different from the markets for other goods. Since real estate is immovable, its market must be a local one. If houses are selling well in California, the demand may exceed the supply. At the same time, a small midwestern town may have an oversupply of housing. However, housing cannot be moved across the country to an area where a greater demand exists.

It must also be noted that building new structures to meet demand takes time; thus supply cannot respond quickly to increased demand for real estate. Furthermore, large sums of money are needed. Funds invested in real estate are called *capital*. The availability or lack of such capital limits the market for real estate by controlling the effective demand.

The sophistication of the modern real estate market causes a number of specialists to become involved in the marketplace. Perhaps one of the most difficult choices the newcomer to real estate must make involves deciding which area of the business is the most interesting.

## Human Resources

Because of the high cost of purchasing real estate and the complexity involved in transferring ownership from one party to another, the most commonly found expert in real estate is the broker or salesperson who markets residential or commercial real estate. The real estate *broker* or *salesperson* is the individual who brings the parties together and negotiates the transaction, whether it be buying, selling, renting, or exchanging real estate. This is done for a fee known as a *commission*. The brokerage relationship is governed by the law of agency and involves two parties, the *agent* (broker) and the *principal* (buyer or owner).

In most states the real estate business operates with a two-tier system of licensing. On the first tier is the broker, the individual responsible for the transaction that takes place. On the second tier is the salesperson, who must be affiliated with a particular broker who holds his or her license, and brokers who are not principals in real estate firms but who perform the same sales role as salespersons. (Such a broker is usually called a broker associate.) These distinctions will be discussed in later chapters, and the concept of agency will also be discussed in detail.

## Types of Real Estate Service

Many areas of expertise exist in the real estate business. The following listing of the major categories of the business describes the function, compensation, and opportunities in each area.

*Brokerage (a service function)*

☐ *Function.* The primary function of brokers and salespersons is to bring buyers and sellers together. The most common function that an agent performs is to list a seller's residence for sale. Commercial and industrial brokers perform this service for commercial sellers.

☐ *Compensation.* A broker's compensation is a com-

mission that is a percentage of the *gross selling price* of the property.

☐ *Opportunities.* Since compensation is a percentage of the sales results, it can be virtually unlimited. Commission rates vary greatly from community to community, as does the division of an earned commission between the broker and the salesperson.

*Property Management (a service function)*

☐ *Function.* The property manager attempts to direct the owner's real estate resources in such a way as to produce for the owner the desired objectives. The manager handles the day-to-day problems of the real property, collects rent, arranges for repairs, pays bills, supervises custodial help, rents vacant space, renders a periodic accounting to the owner, and conserves the property and surroundings.

☐ *Compensation.* Managers are compensated in two ways. They receive a fee for management services and a commission for leasing or renting. For example, a manager might earn a set percentage on each new lease signed, as well as a fee for management services.

☐ *Opportunities.* Opportunities in this field are expanding as a result of the increase in absentee ownership and the need for specialists in operating complex properties.

*Financing (a service function)*

☐ *Function.* This service function brings together a lender and a purchaser who needs to borrow money. Individuals in real estate finance must understand the policies that determine what loans lenders will make. Considerations involve the borrower's creditworthiness, the value of the property as security for the loan, and economic trends affecting the property.

☐ *Compensation.* Individuals who work for a lending institution such as a bank, savings and loan association, or insurance company are usually salaried. A *mortgage broker,* who acts in an agency capacity between the lender and the borrower, earns a commission. The mortgage broker may also receive a fee for servicing the loan. Most mortgage brokers are independent agents who place loans with financial institutions as the representative of the borrower.

☐ *Opportunities.* With financial arrangements becoming more and more complex, opportunities for skilled specialists are growing. In many respects, financing today is the determining factor in planning a new development, marketing existing property, or determining the future use of real property.

*Appraising (a service function)*

☐ *Function.* This is generally regarded as the most respected professional area in the real estate field. An appraiser is employed by a client to render an opinion about the value of a property. The buyer wants to know whether the seller's asking price is reasonable; the seller wants to know whether the buyer's offer is fair; the lender wants to know whether the property is adequate collateral for the loan.

☐ *Compensation.* The appraiser is paid on the basis of time, knowledge, and skill and usually receives a predetermined fee. In *no* event is the fee based on a percentage of the appraised value, for that might influence the appraiser's conclusion.

☐ *Opportunities.* Most appraisers are independent fee appraisers, and their opportunities are limited only by their development of a professional standing in the community. Other appraisers are staff appraisers employed by financial institutions, insurance companies or corporations. They receive salaries.

### Development (a production function)

☐ *Function.* A developer plans and produces improvements. Whether the developer is building an industrial park or creating a subdivision or an apartment complex, he or she is helping to mold the future character of the community.

☐ *Compensation.* The developer can be a firm or an individual entrepreneur who takes raw land, adds services such as streets and utilities, and, in effect, creates a development. The developer's ability to market the completed package at a profit over and above acquisition and development costs determines the amount of compensation earned.

☐ *Opportunities.* In a dynamic economy where the need for housing, and for retail, commercial, and industrial development, is accelerated by an expanding population, the opportunities are good and profits are related primarily to the developer's resourcefulness and ability to finance within the current market.

### Building and Construction (a production function)

☐ *Function.* Some building contractors are developers; others offer services to developers. This production function creates new units or rehabilitates old structures, altering the character of the community.

☐ *Compensation.* The contractor may accept a job on a fixed-fee basis or for a percentage of the final cost of the project. When the builder is also the developer, the profit is the difference between the builder's cost and the selling price on a *speculative* (*spec*) house.

☐ *Opportunities.* Opportunities are good for the builder who can plan and organize the operation within the framework of the local market and who has access to financing.

### Real Estate Investing and Operation (service and production functions)

☐ *Function.* Real estate investors and operators act for themselves, not as agents for others. They buy, sell, rent, and renovate their own real estate holdings.

☐ *Compensation.* Their remuneration is the profit they derive from the operation of their own business.

☐ *Opportunities.* Fortunes have been built in real estate through the operation of a business in which an individual's own energy and initiative can create a very great profit.

### Special Services (advisors)

Other experts involved in the private section of the real estate business include:

☐ *Consultants.* Trained persons who advise individuals, industry, business, and governmental units on real estate matters.

☐ *Land use planners.* Specialists, such as metropolitan and city planners, involved in planning for the use of real estate resources.

☐ *Engineers.* Specialists who concentrate in an area of real estate—for example, engineers, who design structural features of buildings, and civil engineers, who are responsible for utility design and layout of subdivisions and other major projects.

☐ *Lawyers.* Many attorneys are involved in the demanding but rewarding category of real estate specialization.

☐ *Title abstractors and insurers.* Companies involved in bringing abstracts up to date and issuing title insurance. These are vital services in assisting the transfer of real property.

☐ *Architects.* Trained individuals who design and plan new structures and may also provide inspection and construction supervision for new buildings.

☐ *Tax and accounting experts.* Individuals who advise investors and others about the impact and growing importance of taxes on real estate.

### Public (governmental) Real Estate Specialists

☐ *Federal employees.* The federal government is directly involved in the real estate business through such agencies as the Veterans' Administration (VA), the Department of Housing and Urban Development (HUD), and the General Services Administration (GSA).

☐ *State employees.* The state is responsible for protecting the health, safety, and welfare of its citizens and their property. This is important to the maintenance of stable real estate values. The state also participates in the planning of real estate resources and governs the real estate industry through regulatory agencies.

☐ *Local officials.* Local government affects real estate activity through the administration of zoning ordinances, building codes, and planning regulation. Local governments also own substantial amounts of real estate, such as streets, parks, playgrounds, and municipal buildings.

## Real Estate as a Profession

The general public views real estate practitioners as business people rather than as professionals. Even though real estate practitioners do not have the same standing as doctors or lawyers, they must conduct a client's business in a responsible, professional manner. Although brokers compete with each other for new properties to list and sell, all the brokers in a community should work together to establish and maintain ethical standards for dealings with clients, fellow brokers, and the general public.

High standards of ethical conduct are very important in the real estate business because clients often do not have a good understanding of the services they are entitled to receive. Clients rely on the broker to guide them through the complicated maze of activities involved in buying or selling a home. It is most important, then, that the client be able to have the utmost confidence in the individual performing this critical service.

## Real Estate Organizations

The real estate industry has organized several associations that operate on national, state, and local levels. These organizations promote the general interest of the real estate community, and they advocate the high standards of ethical conduct desired by those in the industry.

By far the largest of the real estate trade associations is the *National Association of REALTORS®(NAR).* The NAR functions at local, state, and national levels. To be eligible to use the designation *REALTOR®,* a broker must be a member of NAR. This is accomplished by joining a local board that is affiliated with a state association and the national association. According to publications of NAR:

> *A REALTOR® is a professional in real estate who subscribes to a strict code of ethics as a member of the local and state boards and of NAR.*

Two important aspects of NAR are its code of ethics and its special institutes that promote professionalism in real estate activities through educational programs and the publication of information regarding their areas of specialization.

A code of ethics was first adopted by the *National Association of Real Estate Boards (NAREB)* in 1913, five years after it was organized. All members of NAR, the successor to NAREB, subscribe to the code that appears at the end of this chapter.

## NAR Affiliate Organizations

The following affiliates of NAR play an important role in the development of REALTOR® members. (See Figure 3-1)

### American Institute of Real Estate Appraisers (AIREA)

Purpose: Conducts educational programs, publishes materials, and promotes research on real estate appraisal.

Designations conferred: MAI (Member, Appraisal Institute), RM (Residential Member).

Requirements: A combination of experience and education, as well as written and oral examinations on course work and performance on demonstration appraisals. RM requirements are similar but less strenuous.

### American Society of Real Estate Counselors (ASREC)

Purpose: Conducts educational programs for counselors and advisors on real estate problems.

Designation conferred: CRE (Counselor of Real Estate).

Requirements: Experience, education, and professionalism. A minimum of ten years' experience prior to application.

### REALTORS® Land Institute (RLI)

Purpose: To bring together specialists in the sale, development, planning, management, and syndication of land and to establish professional standards through educational programs for members.

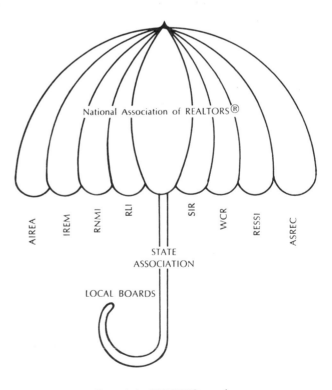

*Figure 3-1—REALTOR® members.*

Designation conferred: AFLM (Accredited Farm and Land Member). This designation, formerly known as Accredited Farm and Land Broker, was revised in 1975.

Requirements: A set number of points to be earned according to a scale established by the institute and based on experience, education, and completion of written and oral examinations.

### International Real Estate Federation (IREF), American Chapter

Purpose: To promote understanding of real estate among those involved in the real estate business throughout the world.

Designation conferred: None.

Requirements: Invitation to join based on membership in a local board of REALTORS® and a demonstrated interest in real estate on an international level.

### Institute of Real Estate Management (IREM)

Purpose: To professionalize members involved in all elements of property management through standards of practice, ethical considerations, and educational programs.

Designations conferred: CPM (Certified Property Manager), AMO (Accredited Management Organization), ARM (Accredited Resident Manager).

Requirements: All designations awarded according to a point system based on experience, education, and examinations.

### Realtors National Marketing Institute (RNMI)

Purpose: To provide educational programs for REALTORS® in the area of commercial and investment properties, residential sales, and real estate office administration.

Designations conferred: CRB (Certified Residential Broker), CCIM (Certified Commercial and Investment Member), CRS (Certified Residential Specialist).

Requirements: Experience, education, and completion of a GRI program.

### Society of Industrial and Office Realtors® (SIR)

Purpose: To provide educational opportunities for REALTORS® working with industrial property transactions.

Designation conferred: SIR (Society of Industrial REALTORS®).

Requirements: Ethical, educational, and experience achievements.

### Real Estate Securities and Syndication Institute (RESSI)

Purpose: To provide educational opportunities in the field of marketing securities and syndication of real estate.

Designation conferred: None.

Requirements: Membership open to REALTORS® with an interest in the area of syndication or real estate securities.

### Women's Council of Realtors (WCR)

Purpose: To provide educational programs, training, and publications for women REALTORS® whose primary interest is in residential brokerage.

Designation conferred: None.

Requirements: An interest in furthering the role of women in real estate brokerage.

One other important designation is awarded by state associations of REALTORS® throughout the nation. The GRI (Graduate Realtors® Institute) is a program designed to help the REALTOR® gain more insight and expertise in the real estate business. It involves a lengthy series of courses and examinations. While the designation itself is awarded by the state association, the program was established and is monitored by NAR to insure continuity from state to state.

Other organizations active in the real estate industry but not a part of NAR include groups representing the multi-faceted aspects of the real estate industry. For example, *The National Association of Real Estate Brokers (Realtists)* represents another segment of brokers and real estate licensees who follow a strict code of ethical practice and professional standards which are designed to protect the public as well as other members of the industry.

The *National Association of Real Estate License Law Officials (NARELLO)*, the *Society of Real Estate Appraisers (SREA)*, *Building Owners and Managers Association International (BOMA)*, the *National Association of Home Builders (NAHB)* and the *National Association of Review Appraisers (NARA)* are but a few of the other associations which play an important role in the real estate industry. Though this list is far from inclusive, it does provide the reader with some idea of the number of professional associations which are available to real estate professionals.

### SUMMARY

While real estate is not a true profession, social policy demands that its members conduct themselves in a professional manner, in part because of the large amounts of capital involved in real estate transactions. It is a career demanding great knowledge, and specialists are found in the many different areas of the real estate business. The immobility of real estate and the fact that each parcel is unique causes the real estate market to be a local and therefore a highly specialized one.

# Code of Ethics and Standards of Practice

of the
## NATIONAL ASSOCIATION OF REALTORS®

**Where the word REALTOR® is used in this Code and Preamble, it shall be deemed to include REALTOR-ASSOCIATE®. Pronouns shall be considered to include REALTORS® and REALTOR-ASSOCIATE®s of both genders.**

## Preamble...

Under all is the land. Upon its wise utilization and widely allocated ownership depend the survival and growth of free institutions and of our civilization. The REALTOR® should recognize that the interests of the nation and its citizens require the highest and best use of the land and the widest distribution of land ownership. They require the creation of adequate housing, the building of functioning cities, the development of productive industries and farms, and the preservation of a healthful environment.

Such interests impose obligations beyond those of ordinary commerce. They impose grave social responsibility and a patriotic duty to which the REALTOR® should dedicate himself, and for which he should be diligent in preparing himself. The REALTOR®, therefore, is zealous to maintain and improve the standards of his calling and shares with his fellow REALTORS® a common responsibility for its integrity and honor. The term REALTOR® has come to connote competency, fairness, and high integrity resulting from adherence to a lofty ideal of moral conduct in business relations. No inducement of profit and no instruction from clients ever can justify departure from this ideal.

In the interpretation of this obligation, a REALTOR® can take no safer guide than that which has been handed down through the centuries, embodied in the Golden Rule, "Whatsoever ye would that men should do to you, do ye even so to them."

Accepting this standard as his own, every REALTOR® pledges himself to observe its spirit in all of his activities and to conduct his business in accordance with the tenets set forth below.

## Articles 1 through 5 are aspirational and establish ideals the REALTOR® should strive to attain.

## ARTICLE 1
The REALTOR® should keep himself informed on matters affecting real estate in his community, the state, and nation so that he may be able to contribute responsibly to public thinking on such matters.

## ARTICLE 2
In justice to those who place their interests in his care, the REALTOR® should endeavor always to be informed regarding laws, proposed legislation, governmental regulations, public policies, and current market conditions in order to be in a position to advise his clients properly.

## ARTICLE 3
The REALTOR® should endeavor to eliminate in his community any practices which could be damaging to the public or bring discredit to the real estate profession. The REALTOR® should assist the governmental agency charged with regulating the practices of brokers and salesmen in his state. (Revised 11/87)

## ARTICLE 4
To prevent dissension and misunderstanding and to assure better service to the owner, the REALTOR® should urge the exclusive listing of property unless contrary to the best interest of the owner. (Revised 11/87)

## ARTICLE 5
In the best interests of society, of his associates, and his own business, the REALTOR® should willingly share with other REALTORS® the lessons of his experience and study for the benefit of the public, and should be loyal to the Board of REALTORS® of his community and active in its work.

## Articles 6 through 23 establish specific obligations. Failure to observe these requirements subjects the REALTOR® to disciplinary action.

## ARTICLE 6
The REALTOR® shall seek no unfair advantage over other REALTORS® and shall conduct his business so as to avoid controversies with other REALTORS®. (Revised 11/87)

### • Standard of Practice 6-1
"The REALTOR® shall not misrepresent the availability of access to show or inspect a listed property. (Cross-reference Article 22.)" (Revised 11/87)

## ARTICLE 7
In accepting employment as an agent, the REALTOR® pledges himself to protect and promote the interests of the client. This obligation of absolute fidelity to the client's interests is primary, but it does not relieve the REALTOR® of the obligation to treat fairly all parties to the transaction.

### • Standard of Practice 7-1
"Unless precluded by law, government rule or regulation, or agreed otherwise in writing, the REALTOR® shall submit to the seller all offers until closing. Unless the REALTOR® and the seller agree otherwise, the REALTOR® shall not be obligated to continue to market the property after an offer has been accepted. Unless the subsequent offer is contingent upon the termination of an existing contract, the REALTOR® shall recommend that the seller obtain the advice of legal counsel prior to acceptance. (Cross-reference Article 17.)"

### • Standard of Practice 7-2
"The REALTOR®, acting as listing broker, shall submit all offers to the seller as quickly as possible."

### • Standard of Practice 7-3
"The REALTOR®, in attempting to secure a listing, shall not deliberately mislead the owner as to market value."

### • Standard of Practice 7-4
(Refer to Standard of Practice 22-1, which also relates to Article 7, Code of Ethics.)

### • Standard of Practice 7-5
(Refer to Standard of Practice 22-2, which also relates to Article 7, Code of Ethics.)

### • Standard of Practice 7-6
"The REALTOR®, when acting as a principal in a real estate transaction, cannot avoid his responsibilities under the Code of Ethics."

## ARTICLE 8
The REALTOR® shall not accept compensation from more than one party, even if permitted by law, without the full knowledge of all parties to the transaction.

## ARTICLE 9
The REALTOR® shall avoid exaggeration, misrepresentation, or concealment of pertinent facts relating to the property or the transaction. The REALTOR® shall not, however, be obligated to discover latent defects in the property or to advise on matters outside the scope of his real estate license.

### • Standard of Practice 9-1

"The REALTOR® shall not be a party to the naming of a false consideration in any document, unless it be the naming of an obviously nominal consideration."

### • Standard of Practice 9-2

(Refer to Standard of Practice 21-3, which also relates to Article 9, Code of Ethics.)

### • Standard of Practice 9-3

(Refer to Standard of Practice 7-3, which also relates to Article 9, Code of Ethics.)

### • Standard of Practice 9-4

"The REALTOR® shall not offer a service described as 'free of charge' when the rendering of a service is contingent on the obtaining of a benefit such as a listing or commission."

### • Standard of Practice 9-5

"The REALTOR® shall, with respect to the subagency of another REALTOR®, timely communicate any change of compensation for subagency services to the other REALTOR® prior to the time such REALTOR® produces a prospective buyer who has signed an offer to purchase the property for which the subagency has been offered through MLS or otherwise by the listing agency."

### • Standard of Practice 9-6

"REALTORS® shall disclose their REALTOR® status when seeking information from another REALTOR® concerning real property for which the other REALTOR® is an agent or subagent."

### • Standard of Practice 9-7

"The offering of premiums, prizes, merchandise discounts or other inducements to list or sell is not, in itself, unethical even if receipt of the benefit is contingent on listing or purchasing through the REALTOR® making the offer. However, the REALTOR® must exercise care and candor in any such advertising or other public or private representations so that any party interested in receiving or otherwise benefiting from the REALTOR®'s offer will have clear, thorough, advance understanding of all the terms and conditions of the offer. The offering of any inducements to do business is subject to the limitations and restrictions of state law and the ethical obligations established by Article 9, as interpreted by any applicable Standard of Practice."

### • Standard of Practice 9-8

"The REALTOR® shall be obligated to discover and disclose adverse factors reasonably apparent to someone with expertise in only those areas required by their real estate licensing authority. Article 9 does not impose upon the REALTOR® the obligation of expertise in other professional or technical disciplines. (Cross-reference Article 11.)"

## ARTICLE 10

The REALTOR® shall not deny equal professional services to any person for reasons of race, creed, sex, or country of national origin. The REALTOR® shall not be party to any plan or agreement to discriminate against a person or persons on the basis of race, creed, sex, or country of national origin.

## ARTICLE 11

A REALTOR® is expected to provide a level of competent service in keeping with the standards of practice in those fields in which the REALTOR® customarily engages.

The REALTOR® shall not undertake to provide specialized professional services concerning a type of property or service that is outside his field of competence unless he engages the assistance of one who is competent on such types of property or service, or unless the facts are fully disclosed to the client. Any person engaged to provide such assistance shall be so identified to the client and his contribution to the assignment should be set forth.

The REALTOR® shall refer to the Standards of Practice of the National Association as to the degree of competence that a client has a right to expect the REALTOR® to possess, taking into consideration the complexity of the problem, the availability of expert assistance, and the opportunities for experience available to the REALTOR®.

### • Standard of Practice 11-1

"Whenever a REALTOR® submits an oral or written opinion of the value of real property for a fee, his opinion shall be supported by a memorandum in his file or an appraisal report, either of which shall include as a minimum the following:

1. Limiting conditions
2. Any existing or contemplated interest
3. Defined value
4. Date applicable
5. The estate appraised
6. A description of the property
7. The basis of the reasoning including applicable market data and/or capitalization computation

"This report or memorandum shall be available to the Professional Standards Committee for a period of at least two years (beginning subsequent to final determination of the court if the appraisal is involved in litigation) to ensure compliance with Article 11 of the Code of Ethics of the NATIONAL ASSOCIATION OF REALTORS®."

### • Standard of Practice 11-2

"The REALTOR® shall not undertake to make an appraisal when his employment or fee is contingent upon the amount of appraisal."

### • Standard of Practice 11-3

"REALTORS® engaged in real estate securities and syndications transactions are engaged in an activity subject to regulations beyond those governing real estate transactions generally, and therefore have the affirmative obligation to be informed of applicable federal and state laws, and rules and regulations regarding these types of transactions."

## ARTICLE 12

The REALTOR® shall not undertake to provide professional services concerning a property or its value where he has a present or contemplated interest unless such interest is specifically disclosed to all affected parties.

### • Standard of Practice 12-1

(Refer to Standards of Practice 9-4 ad 16-1, which also relate to Article 12, Code of Ethics.)

## ARTICLE 13

The REALTOR® shall not acquire an interest in or buy for himself, any member of his immediate family, his firm or any member thereof, or any entity in which he has a substantial ownership interest, property listed with him, without making the true position known to the listing owner. In selling property owned by himself, or in which he has any interest, the REALTOR® shall reveal the facts of his ownership or interest to the purchaser.

### • Standard of Practice 13-1

"For the protection of all parties, the disclosures required by Article 13 shall be in writing and provided by the REALTOR® prior to the signing of any contract."

## ARTICLE 14

In the event of a controversy between REALTORS® associated with different firms, arising out of their relationship as REALTORS®, the REALTORS® shall submit the dispute to arbitration in accordance with the regulations of their Board or Boards rather than litigate the matter.

- **Standard of Practice 14-1**

"The filing of litigation and refusal to withdraw from it by a REALTOR® in an arbitrable matter constitutes a refusal to arbitrate."

- **Standard of Practice 14-2**

"The obligation to arbitrate mandated by Article 14 includes arbitration requests initiated by the REALTOR®'s client."

## ARTICLE 15

If a REALTOR® is charged with unethical practice or is asked to present evidence in any disciplinary proceeding or investigation, he shall place all pertinent facts before the proper tribunal of the Member Board or affiliated institute, society, or council of which he is a member.

- **Standard of Practice 15-1**

"The REALTOR® shall not be subject to disciplinary proceedings in more than one Board of REALTORS® with respect to alleged violations of the Code of Ethics relating to the same transaction."

- **Standard of Practice 15-2**

"The REALTOR® shall not make any unauthorized disclosure or dissemination of the allegations, findings, or decision developed in connection with an ethics hearing or appeal."

- **Standard of Practice 15-3**

"The REALTOR® shall not obstruct the Board's investigative or disciplinary proceedings by instituting or threatening to institute actions for libel, slander or defamation against any party to a professional standards proceeding or their witnesses." (Approved 11/87).

## ARTICLE 16

When acting as agent, the REALTOR® shall not accept any commission, rebate, or profit on expenditures made for his principal-owner, without the principal's knowledge and consent.

- **Standard of Practice 16-1**

"The REALTOR® shall not recommend or suggest to a principal or a customer the use of services of another organization or business entity in which he has a direct interest without disclosing such interest at the time of the recommendation or suggestion."

## ARTICLE 17

The REALTOR® shall not engage in activities that constitute the unauthorized practice of law and shall recommend that legal counsel be obtained when the interest of any party to the transaction requires it.

## ARTICLE 18

The REALTOR® shall keep in a special account in an appropriate financial institution, separated from his own funds, monies coming into his possession in trust for other persons, such as escrows, trust funds, clients' monies, and other like items.

## ARTICLE 19

The REALTOR® shall be careful at all times to present a true picture in his advertising and representations to the public. The REALTOR® shall also ensure that his status as a broker or a REALTOR® is clearly identifiable in any such advertising.

- **Standard of Practice 19-1**

"The REALTOR® shall not submit or advertise property without authority, and in any offering, the price quoted shall not be other than that agreed upon with the owners."

- **Standard of Practice 19-2**

(Refer to Standard of Practice 9-4, which also relates to Article 19, Code of Ethics.)

- **Standard of Practice 19-3**

"The REALTOR®, when advertising unlisted real property for sale in which he has an ownership interest, shall disclose his status as both an owner and as a REALTOR® or real estate licensee."

- **Standard of Practice 19-4**

"The REALTOR® shall not advertise nor permit any person employed by or affiliated with him to advertise listed property without disclosing the name of the firm."

- **Standard of Practice 19-5**

"The REALTOR®, when acting as listing broker, retains the exclusive right to represent that he has 'sold' the property, even if the sale resulted through the cooperative efforts of another broker. However, after the transaction has been consummated, the listing broker may not prohibit a successful cooperating broker from advertising his 'participation' or 'assistance' in the transaction, or from making similar representations provided that any such representation does not create the impression that the cooperating broker had listed or sold the property. (Cross-reference Article 21.)"

## ARTICLE 20

The REALTOR®, for the protection of all parties, shall see that financial obligations and commitments regarding real estate transactions are in writing, expressing the exact agreement of the parties. A copy of each agreement shall be furnished to each party upon his signing such agreement.

- **Standard of Practice 20-1**

"At the time of signing or initialing, the REALTOR® shall furnish to the party a copy of any document signed or initialed."

- **Standard of Practice 20-2**

"For the protection of all parties, the REALTOR® shall use reasonable care to ensure that documents pertaining to the purchase and sale of real estate are kept current through the use of written extensions or amendments."

## ARTICLE 21

The REALTOR® shall not engage in any practice or take any action inconsistent with the agency of another REALTOR®.

- **Standard of Practice 21-1**

"Signs giving notice of property for sale, rent, lease, or exchange shall not be placed on property without the consent of the owner."

- **Standard of Practice 21-2**

"The REALTOR® obtaining information from a listing broker about a specific property shall not convey this information to, nor invite the cooperation of a third party broker without the consent of the listing broker."

- **Standard of Practice 21-3**

"The REALTOR® shall not solicit a listing which is currently listed exclusively with another broker. However, if the listing broker, when asked by the REALTOR®, refuses to disclose the expiration date and nature of such listing; i.e., an exclusive right to sell, an exclusive agency, open listing, or other form of contractual agreement between the listing broker and his client, the REALTOR®, unless precluded by law, may contact the owner to secure such information and may discuss the terms upon which he might take a future listing or, alternatively, may take a listing to become effective upon expiration of any existing exclusive listing."

- **Standard of Practice 21-4**

"The REALTOR® shall not use information obtained by him from the listing broker, through offers to cooperate received through Multiple Listing Services or other sources authorized by the listing broker, for the purpose of creating a referral prospect to a third broker, or for creating a buyer prospect unless such use is authorized by the listing broker."

- **Standard of Practice 21-5**

"The fact that a property has been listed exclusively with a REALTOR® shall not preclude or inhibit any other REALTOR® from soliciting such listing after its expiration."

### • Standard of Practice 21-6

"The fact that a property owner has retained a REALTOR® as his exclusive agent in respect of one or more past transactions creates no interest or agency which precludes or inhibits other REALTORS® from seeking such owner's future business."

### • Standard of Practice 21-7

"The REALTOR® shall be free to list property which is 'open listed' at any time, but shall not knowingly obligate the seller to pay more than one commission except with the seller's knowledgeable consent." (Revised 11/87)

### • Standard of Practice 21-8

"When a REALTOR® is contacted by an owner regarding the sale of property that is exclusively listed with another broker, and the REALTOR® has not directly or indirectly initiated the discussion, unless precluded by law, the REALTOR® may discuss the terms upon which he might take a future listing or, alternatively, may take a listing to become effective upon expiration of any existing exclusive listing."

### • Standard of Practice 21-9

"In cooperative transactions a REALTOR® shall compensate the co-operating REALTOR® (principal broker) and shall not compensate nor offer to compensate, directly or indirectly, any of the sales licensees employed by or affiliated with another REALTOR® without the prior express knowledge and consent of the cooperating broker."

### • Standard of Practice 21-10

"Article 21 does not preclude REALTORS® from making general announcements to property owners describing their services and the terms of their availability even though some recipients may have exclusively listed their property for sale or lease with another REALTOR®. A general telephone canvass, general mailing or distribution addressed to all property owners in a given geographical area or in a given profession, business, club, or organization, or other classification or group is deemed 'general' for purposes of this standard.

Article 21 is intended to recognize as unethical two basic types of solicitation:

First, telephone or personal solicitations of property owners who have been identified by a real estate sign, multiple listing compilation, or other information service as having exclusively listed their property with another REALTOR®; and

Second, mail or other forms of written solicitations of property owners whose properties are exclusively listed with another REALTOR® when such solicitations are not part of a general mailing but are directed specifically to property owners identified through compilations of current listings, 'for sale' signs, or other sources of information required by Article 22 and Multiple Listing Service rules to be made available to other REALTORS® under offers of subagency or cooperation."

---

Form No. 166-288-1 (11/87)

### • Standard of Practice 21-11

"The REALTOR®, prior to accepting a listing, has an affirmative obligation to make reasonable efforts to determine whether the property is subject to a current, valid exclusive listing agreement."

## ARTICLE 22

In the sale of property which is exclusively listed with a REALTOR®, the REALTOR® shall utilize the services of other brokers upon mutually agreed upon terms when it is in the best interests of the client.

Negotiations concerning property which is listed exclusively shall be carried on with the listing broker, not with the owner, except with the consent of the listing broker.

### • Standard of Practice 22-1

"It is the obligation of the selling broker as subagent of the listing broker to disclose immediately all pertinent facts to the listing broker prior to as well as after the contract is executed."

### • Standard of Practice 22-2

"The REALTOR®, when submitting offers to the seller, shall present each in an objective and unbiased manner."

### • Standard of Practice 22-3

"The REALTOR® shall disclose the existence of an accepted offer to any broker seeking cooperation."

## ARTICLE 23

The REALTOR® shall not publicly disparage the business practice of a competitor nor volunteer an opinion of a competitor's transaction. If his opinion is sought and if the REALTOR® deems it appropriate to respond, such opinion shall be rendered with strict professional integrity and courtesy.

**The Code of Ethics was adopted in 1913. Amended at the Annual Convention in 1924, 1928, 1950, 1951, 1952, 1955, 1956, 1961, 1962, 1974, 1982, 1986, and 1987.**

## EXPLANATORY NOTE CONCERNING THE STANDARDS OF PRACTICE

The reader should be aware of the following policy which has been approved by the Board of Directors of the National Association:

"In filing a charge of an alleged violation of the Code of Ethics by a REALTOR®, the charge shall read as an alleged violation of one or more Articles of the Code. A Standard of Practice may only be cited in support of the charge."

The Standards of Practice are not an integral part of the Code but rather serve to clarify the ethical obligations imposed by the various Articles. The Standards of Practice supplement, and do not substitute for, the Case Interpretations in *Interpretations of the Code of Ethics*.

Modifications to existing Standards of Practice and additional new Standards of Practice are approved from time to time. The reader is cautioned to ensure that the most recent publications are utilized.

# REVIEW QUESTIONS

1. The residential real estate business can best be described as

   (A) localized and disorganized in nature
   (B) national in scope
   (C) regional in make-up but disorganized
   (D) well structured but localized

2. Which of the following combinations of characteristics makes real estate different from other commodities?

   (A) Fixed location, standardization, high unit cost
   (B) Fixed location, long life, high unit cost
   (C) Mobility, indestructibility, low unit cost
   (D) Short life, indestructibility, low unit cost

3. The typical real estate broker earns the majority of commissions from the sale of

   (A) commercial properties
   (B) investment properties
   (C) residential properties
   (D) industrial properties

4. What is the relationship between the broker and the client?

   (A) Agent and principal
   (B) Client and principal
   (C) Agent and customer
   (D) No legal relationship is present

5. Which of the following would **not** be considered part of the public sector affecting real estate?

   (A) General Services Administration (GSA)
   (B) Federal Housing Authority (FHA)
   (C) Housing and Urban Development (HUD)
   (D) A local real estate brokerage firm

6. Each plot of land is unique for all of the following reasons except

   (A) its location is fixed
   (B) no two plots are identical
   (C) it is indestructible
   (D) its legal rights are always the same as those of all other plots

7. The most important impact of the Ordinance of 1785 has been

   (A) total governmental control of real estate
   (B) the rectangular survey of land
   (C) transfer of all state real property to federal control
   (D) a revocation of all private rights to land

8. A house that is built with the anticipation that the builder can sell the house at a profit is a

   (A) custom house
   (B) stick-built house
   (C) spec house
   (D) pre-fab house

9. According to NAR, a REALTOR® is

   (A) any real estate salesperson who sells residential real estate
   (B) only a real estate broker who owns a brokerage firm
   (C) any real estate licensee in a state
   (D) a real estate professional who is a member of a local Board of REALTORS®

10. The MAI designation is awarded by

    (A) SIR          (C) ASREC
    (B) RMNI         (D) AIREA

11. Which of the following is considered to be an area of real estate that concentrates on production?

    (A) Brokerage
    (B) Property management
    (C) Development
    (D) Appraisal

12. According to the NAR Code of Ethics, in regard to exclusive listings, the REALTOR®

    (A) is required by state laws to take only exclusive listings
    (B) must avoid exclusive listings and use other forms of listings
    (C) should urge the exclusive listing type
    (D) should take the listing regardless of type

13. The practice of combining personal funds with those of a client is

    (A) standard practice
    (B) a form of escrow account
    (C) unethical by the NAR Code of Ethics
    (D) not in violation of state laws

14. How is the amount of commissions to be received by the broker determined?

    (A) A predetermined percentage of the gross sales price
    (B) The difference between the gross sales price and net at closing
    (C) A percentage of the net sales price at closing
    (D) A percentage of the listed price

15. As a real estate licensee, you should **not**

    (A) provide legal advice on contract questions
    (B) explain the closing statement to the seller
    (C) take exclusive listings
    (D) introduce buyers to lenders

16. According to the NAR Code of Ethics, a REALTOR® may

    (A) accept rebates on expenditures made for a principal
    (B) pay directly to a salesperson of another REAL-TOR® a portion of the commission
    (C) collect a fee from both buyer and seller with full disclosure
    (D) discriminate based on a person's sex in the service provided

17. A property manager is responsible for all of the following EXCEPT

    (A) renting vacant space
    (B) periodic accounting to the owner
    (C) conserving the property
    (D) reinvesting any profit

18. Which of the following designations is awarded by the Institute of Real Estate Management?

    (A) MAI          (C) CRE
    (B) SIR          (D) CPM

19. Local governmental officials affect real estate activity through

    (A) zoning ordinances
    (B) mortgage rates
    (C) license laws
    (D) none of the above

20. An appraiser is paid on what basis?

    (A) Predetermined fee for the work required
    (B) A percentage of appraised value
    (C) Net listed price minus gross sales price
    (D) A percentage of mortgage value

# Chapter 4
# Regulation of the Real Estate Business

---

## VOCABULARY

*You will find it important to have a complete working knowledge of the following terms, concepts, and abbreviations found in the text or the glossary.*

| | | |
|---|---|---|
| Affirmative Marketing Agreement | Federal Fair Housing Law (Title VIII, | police powers |
| blockbusting | Civil Rights Act of 1968) | racial steering |
| Civil Rights Act of 1866 | FHA | reciprocity |
| Code for Equal Opportunity | HUD | Regulation Z |
| commingling of funds | misrepresentation | RESPA |
| Consumer Protection Act of 1968 | NAR | truth in lending |
| discriminatory practices | NARELLO | undisclosed principal |
| | panic selling | |

---

BECAUSE of its importance and because of the large amounts of capital involved, the real estate business is highly regulated. All levels of government have laws concerning real estate transactions. Federal regulations are extensive, but they have their greatest impact in two areas, finance and civil rights. State regulations primarily affect the licensing of real estate practitioners and the establishment of codes that protect the public in many areas of construction and development. Real estate controls by local governments are discussed in Chapter 5.

## FEDERAL INFLUENCES

The federal government's influence on real estate extends into federal subsidies, through governmental housing programs, civil rights, and fair housing, and into consumer protection through the *Truth-in-Lending Act,* the *Consumer Protection Act of 1968,* and, most recently, the *Real Estate Settlement Procedures Act (RESPA).*

Formation of the Public Housing Administration in 1937 was the first major step in increasing the federal government's role in real estate. This role has continued to grow, and today the head of the major regulatory body, the *Department of Housing and Urban Development (HUD),* occupies a presidential cabinet position in the federal government.

HUD was created in 1965 by combining the Public Housing Administration, the *Federal Housing Administration (FHA),* the *Federal National Mortgage Association*

*(Fannie Mae),* and Urban Renewal. HUD's primary purpose is to coordinate, with state and local governments, the use of federal resources to solve housing problems facing the nation.

One thrust of HUD is in the area of fair housing. The basis of fair housing in the United States is not new but stems from the *Civil Rights Act of 1866* and has since been strengthened considerably.

### Fair Housing Laws

*Civil Rights Act of 1866*

After the Civil War, Congress passed a Civil Rights Act prohibiting racial discrimination in housing as well as in ownership of land. It allowed the complainant to go directly to a federal court in a case involving racial discrimination.

*Federal Fair Housing Law (Title VIII, Civil Rights Act of 1968)*

This law is the most comprehensive of the federal fair housing statutes. It prohibits discrimination in the sale or rental of housing because of race, color, religion, national origin, or sex. Federal agencies must administer their programs "in a manner affirmatively to further the purpose of this Title." About 80 percent of the nation's private housing stock is covered by Title VIII, and the rest is covered by the Civil Rights Act of 1866.

The following acts are prohibited under Title VIII:

☐ Refusing to sell or rent to or deal or negotiate with any person

☐ Discriminating in terms or conditions for buying or renting housing

☐ Discriminating by advertising that housing is available to persons of a certain race, color, religion, national origin, or sex

☐ Denying that housing is available for inspection, sale, or rent, when it is available

☐ Blockbusting for profit, that is, persuading owners to sell or rent housing by telling them that minority groups are moving into the neighborhood

☐ Denying or naming different terms or conditions for home loans by commercial lenders

☐ Denying to anyone the use of or participation in any real estate service, such as multiple-listing services or other facilities for selling a house

Title VIII applies to single-family housing owned by private individuals when a broker or other person in the business of selling or renting is used and/or discriminatory advertising is used. It also applies to single-family homes when owned by a private individual who owns three such houses or who, in any two-year period, sells more than one in which he was not the most recent resident. Title VIII covers multifamily dwellings of five or more units and four or fewer units, provided, in the latter case, that the owner does not reside in one of the units.

Title VIII does not apply to

☐ The sale or rental of single-family homes owned by the owner of fewer than three such units as long as neither a broker nor discriminatory advertising is used

☐ Rentals of rooms or units in owner-occupied multifamily dwellings for two to four families if discriminatory advertising is not used

☐ The sale, rental, or occupancy of dwellings that a religious organization owns or operates for other than a commercial purpose as long as membership in that religion is not restricted by race, color, or national origin

☐ The rental or occupancy of lodgings owned or operated by a private club that are limited to its own members

Title VIII allows an aggrieved party to file a complaint with the Department of Housing and Urban Development (HUD), which then must investigate and resolve the complaint by eliminating the discriminatory practice. HUD is obligated to refer complaints to state agencies if their fair housing laws are "substantially equivalent" to Title VIII. In either case, the complainant can go to court if either the state agency or HUD fails to end the discrim-

inatory practice. Complainants can also, without filing a complaint with HUD, go to a U.S. district court within 180 days of the alleged act.*

The notice of the Federal Fair Housing Law usually posted in a broker's office is shown in Figure 4-1.

### Blockbusting

The illegal practice of introducing a nonconforming user or use to an area for the purpose of causing an abnormally high turnover of property ownership.

### Panic Selling

The illegal practice of introducing fear among property owners in a particular neighborhood that an abnormally high turnover might occur as a result of the introduction of a nonconforming use or user in the area. Frequently a result of blockbusting activities.

### Racial Steering

A broker or salesperson must not "steer" a client toward a property for discriminatory reasons. The prospect, not the broker, must pick the location. To steer the client away from property in a particular neighborhood or to limit the choice of housing based on any of the reasons listed in Title VIII is prohibited by law. Clients must choose from the properties listed the ones they wish to visit and consider for purchase.

### Fair Housing Practices Today and Tomorrow

The real estate business is continuing its efforts to make Title VIII work. These efforts include equal opportunity in hiring policies, training regarding discriminatory practices, utilization of nonracist advertising, and the clearly established policy regarding the nonacceptance of listings that are discriminatory in nature and therefore illegal.

NAR is gaining support for its affirmative marketing plan in housing. The plan, which has been developed in conjunction with HUD to assure all minority groups equal access to housing, has helped local boards to clarify their position on open housing. The NAR Code for Equal Opportunity, shown in Figure 4-2, stresses the REALTOR® role.

In addition, HUD and the National Association of REALTORS® have executed a formal *Affirmative Marketing Agreement* which signifies the REALTOR®'s concern for fair housing practices. Members of the local board pledge to deal fairly with all prospects for housing, regardless of race, creed, color, national origin, sex, or age. The agree-

*From *The Arnold Encyclopedia of Real Estate,* by Alvin L. Arnold and Jack Kusnet. Boston: Warren, Gorham & Lamont, 1978.

**U.S. DEPARTMENT OF HOUSING AND URBAN DEVELOPMENT**

# Federal Fair Housing Law

(Title VIII of the Civil Rights Act of 1968)

It Is Illegal To Discriminate Against Any Person
Because Of Race, Color, Religion, Sex,
Or National Origin

- In the sale or rental of housing or residential lots

- In advertising the sale or rental of housing

- In the financing of housing

- In the provision of real estate brokerage services

    Blockbusting is also illegal

*Those who feel they have been discriminated against
should send complaint to
U.S. Department of Housing and Urban Development,
Assistant Secretary for Equal Opportunity
Washington, D.C. 20410*

Figure 4-1—*Federal Fair Housing Law. A topical outline of what is illegal under the Federal Fair Housing Law (Title VIII of the Civil Rights Act of 1968), usually posted in a broker's office.*

**NATIONAL ASSOCIATION OF REALTORS** ®

# Code for Equal Opportunity

subscribes to the policy that equal opportunity in the acquisition of housing can best be accomplished through leadership, example, education, and the mutual cooperation of the real estate industry and the public. In the spirit of this endeavor, this board proclaims the following provisions of its Code for Equal Opportunity to which each member is obligated to adhere:

1. In the sale, purchase, exchange, rental, or lease of real property, REALTORS® and their REALTOR®-ASSOCIATES have the responsibility to offer equal service to all clients and prospects without regard to race, color, religion, sex, or national origin. This encompasses:

   A. Standing ready to enter broker-client relationships or to show property equally to members of all racial, creedal, or ethnic groups.

   B. Receiving all formal written offers and communicating them to the owner.

   C. Exerting their best efforts to conclude all transactions.

   D. Maintaining equal opportunity employment practices.

2. Members, individually and collectively, in performing their agency functions have no right or responsibility to volunteer information regarding the racial, creedal, or ethnic composition of any neighborhood or any part thereof.

3. Members shall not engage in any activity which has the purpose of inducing panic selling.

4. Members shall not print, display, or circulate any statement or advertisement with respect to the sale or rental of a dwelling that indicates any preference, limitations, or discrimination based on race, color, religion, sex, or ethnic background.

5. Members who violate the spirit or any provision of this Code of Equal Opportunity shall be subject to disciplinary action.

*Those who feel they have been discriminated against*
*may contact the management of this office*
*or the Board of REALTORS®*

*Figure 4-2—The NAR Code for Equal Opportunity outlines the obligations of a REALTOR® under the 1968 law.*

ment, which is voluntary on the part of state associations, local boards, and individual REALTORS®, was originally formulated in December 1975 and is now being adopted at the local level throughout the country.

The equal housing opportunity publisher's notice shown in Figure 4-3 signifies the compliance of newspapers that carry advertisements for housing for rent, lease, or sale. It must be displayed in every edition containing real estate advertisements.

## Consumer Protection Laws

Consumer concern about underlying terms and conditions in mortgages spurred the federal government to pass the *Consumer Credit Protection Act of 1969.* Included as part of this act was the *Truth-in-Lending Act,* which empowered the Federal Reserve Board to implement *Regulation Z.* Its objective is to let the purchaser of real property know exactly what credit charges are being

# EQUAL HOUSING OPPORTUNITY

All real estate advertising in this newspaper is subject to the Federal Fair Housing Act of 1968 which makes it illegal to advertise "any preference, limitation or discrimination based on race, color, religion, sex or national origin, or an intention to make any such preference, limitation or discrimination."

This newspaper will not knowingly accept any advertising for real estate which is in violation of the law. Our readers are hereby informed that all dwellings advertised in this newspaper are available on an equal opportunity basis.

*Figure 4-3—Federal Fair Housing publisher's notice.*

paid to the lender and the exact terms of the loan. The regulation also covers advertising. A complete statement of the Truth-in-Lending Act can be found in Chapter 11.

### RESPA

The Real Estate Settlement Procedures Act *(RESPA),* passed in 1975, requires lending institutions to inform loan applicants of approximate settlement costs for the closing of the prospective loan. The applicant who has this information in advance will then be able to compare the costs of different avenues of finance. More can be found on this topic in Chapter 11.

### The Magnuson-Moss Warranty/Federal Trade Commission Act

This federal warranty legislation appears to be aimed at controlling certain abuses with respect to the warranties extended to buyers of automobiles and appliances. It is administered by the Federal Trade Commission, which published rules under this act, which became effective December 31, 1976. The act clearly has an impact upon both builders and sellers of new homes that include built-in items which would clearly be covered by the act if they were sold separately to the consumer. The act does not require that a warranty be given; however, if a warranty of any kind is given (and this is the normal case today in the home building field), it must meet the highly technical terms of the act.

The act and its legislative history provide little assistance in trying to apply the act properly to the building and selling of new houses. In addition, the act tends to blur the traditional distinction between real and personal property as affected by the common law of fixtures. Undoubtedly it will take some time for the practical meaning of the act to the real estate industry to be developed through test cases in the courts. Meanwhile, anyone active in either building or selling new housing must be aware that federal warranty provisions are in effect. The need for legal counsel should be apparent.

## REAL ESTATE LICENSE LAW

All the states and the District of Columbia have license laws to regulate real estate practitioners. The purpose of such laws is twofold: first, to protect the public by setting up specific requirements regarding standards of practice on the part of real estate practitioners and, second, to protect the licensee from improper business practices. The laws (and any rules or regulations passed by the regulatory body) control entry into the real estate business by requiring the real estate practitioner to hold a license in order to practice. The laws also provide for suspension and revocation of that license when violations occur.

The state license law must be created through an act or statute passed by the state's legislature. Once passed, it becomes an extension of the state's constitution, as do all state laws. The state creates a commission or licensing board and authorizes the commission to interpret, administer, and enforce the laws. It also authorizes the commission to establish the rules and regulations used to clarify and interpret the laws passed by the legislature which relate to real estate licenses.

The power to establish such license laws stems from the *police powers* of the state, that is, the right of the state to protect the general public in areas of public interest such as real estate. More information about police powers appears in Chapter 5.

A real estate license, then, is a privilege, not a right. It informs the public that the individual holding such a license is knowledgeable and has acquired the skills to act in the capacity of a real estate salesperson or broker. A real estate broker is authorized to operate his or her own real estate brokerage concern. The individual who holds a salesperson's license is held responsible by a broker who has indicated to the real estate commission his or her willingness to be responsible for the salesperson's actions.

Most state license laws fit the pattern of the model license law written by the *National Association of Real Estate License Law Officials (NARELLO)*. Yet each state has specific portions of its license law which differ from those of other states. Later in this chapter is an outline of the kinds of provisions contained in your state's license law, rules, and regulations.

It is *essential* that prospective licensees know the laws of their states. You should study in detail the license law guide for your jurisdiction and any additional material your licensing agency provides to obtain a full understanding of this information.

### Acquiring State Materials

If you have not already obtained a copy of the license laws for the state in which you are applying for licensure, write immediately to the state licensing agency at the address listed at the end of this chapter. Application forms for licensing examinations and other materials should be available from the same address.

### TYPICAL LICENSING REQUIREMENTS

Even though the requirements for obtaining a real estate license vary from state to state, a number of similarities exist among them. The following list is intended only to aid in understanding the broad spectrum of real estate licensing regulations. The outline at the end of this chapter provides space for you to write in the requirements pertaining to your state. You will find these requirements listed in the materials you obtain from the real estate commission in your jurisdiction.

1. *License.* An individual must be licensed before a transaction is initiated and, in almost all cases, prior to receiving a commission for the sale of property.
2. *Education.* State requirements vary from none at all to a college or university degree for a broker. Most states require a high school diploma and/or a specific number of hours of classroom real estate education.
3. *Experience.* The most common requirement for a broker is two years' experience in real estate prior to application for licensure and/or classes at an accredited college or university in real estate subjects.
4. *Examination.* All states require salesperson and broker candidates to pass examinations (a different examination for each license.)
5. *Sponsorship.* Some state laws require that salesperson candidates be sponsored by a licensed broker who will be the holder of the individual's license when it is issued.
6. *Minimum age.* This is usually the age of majority in the state in which you are applying. The most common minimum age is 18. Some states have different requirements for brokers and salespersons.
7. *Citizenship.* Some states still require United States citizenship, but the legality of this requirement has been challenged.
8. *Fair housing.* All states have some requirement in their license law that deals with discrimination and the licensee.
9. *Application.* Applicants for licensure must apply on the specific form provided by the state. This application must be filled out completely and delivered to the real estate commission, usually 30 to 60 days prior to the examination date. A common requirement is that the applicant list references attesting to personal character. Such references are usually given by either landowners or licensed real estate brokers in the particular state.
10. *Convictions.* Almost all states have some restriction for licensure when the applicant has been convicted of a felony. Many states have a statute of limitations that specifies the length of time a license can be denied on this basis.
11. *Fees.* Two categories of fees exist, for the original licensing of the individual and for periodic renewals. The license law usually includes a statement regarding the disbursement of fees collected.
12. *Reciprocity.* Many states have reciprocal licensing agreements that allow credit for experience or for licensure in another state.
13. *Administration of the law.* All license laws indicate how the commission is appointed or elected, what

paid employees are allowed, and what their duties are.

14. *Advertising.* In all states, advertising must include the broker's name.

15. *Display of license.* All licenses must be displayed in the broker's place of business. In many states, pocket cards indicating that the individual is a licensee must also be carried.

16. *Placement of license.* When employment or affiliation is terminated by a salesperson, his or her license must be returned to the real estate commission until it is requested by a new broker.

17. *Suspension and revocation of license.* All state license laws specify fraudulent activities that can result in suspension or revocation of licenses. Other penalties may include fines.

18. *Real estate definition.* All states define what constitutes real estate and what types of transactions require licensing.

## TYPICAL EXEMPTIONS FROM LICENSING REQUIREMENTS

It is common practice for states to exempt certain categories of individuals from licensure. Those most commonly exempted are:

☐ Any individual selling or offering real estate for himself

☐ Attorneys acting on behalf of clients as part of their law practice

☐ Court-appointed administrators, executors, or trustees

☐ Public officials, when involved as part of their official duties

☐ Officials of regulated utilities or their employees whose real estate activities are directly related to the firm's business

☐ In some states, resident managers of apartments who show vacant units

## TYPES OF VIOLATIONS THAT RESULT IN LICENSE SUSPENSION OR REVOCATION

☐ *Discriminatory practices.* A refusal to show, sell, or lease real estate to any individual because of race, color, national origin, or sex can result in the suspension or revocation of a license.

☐ *Misrepresentation.* Any substantial misstatement of fact may be considered misrepresentation and may be grounds for suspension or revocation.

☐ *Commingling of funds.* All states require the keeping of clients' and brokers' funds in separate accounts, usually called escrow or trust accounts.

☐ *Advertising.* Advertising which misrepresents a property is a violation in all states. Certain methods of advertising can also result in license suspension or revocation. In many states, the placement of a "For Sale" or "For Rent" sign on a property without prior written consent of the owner is a violation.

☐ *Notification as a license holder.* It is essential that the licensee serve notice to any individual with whom he or she is dealing that he or she holds a real estate license. This is especially important in personal transactions, where it provides the other party with notice that a knowledgeable real estate person is participating in the transaction.

☐ *Guaranteeing future profits.* The licensee may not guarantee profits from the future sale of a property being considered for purchase.

☐ *Personal benefits from expenditures made for a principal.* No licensee is allowed to receive a commission, rebate, or profit from any such expenditures.

☐ *Sharing commissions with an unlicensed individual.* Only licensees may share in real estate sales fees (commissions).

☐ *Conviction.* Conviction for a felony is usually grounds for the revocation or suspension of a license.

☐ *Failure to deliver copies of required documents.* All states have requirements regarding the delivery of listing and purchase agreements as well as closing statements.

☐ *Undisclosed principal.* It is a violation for a licensee to represent more than one party or himself in a transaction without the full knowledge of all parties involved.

☐ *Bonds.* Many states require the posting and regular renewal of a bond.

☐ *Failure to submit all offers.* A licensee who does not sumbit all bona fide written offers to an owner for consideration commits a violation. This includes all offers received prior to written acceptance of a previous offer. All written offers must be submitted to the owner regardless of the licensee's opinion of any offer.

☐ *Unethical conduct.* This category, found in all state license laws, covers such areas as committing unworthy or incompetent acts, inducing parties to break a contract in order to enter into another, and conducting real estate transactions which demonstrate dishonesty.

Since license law varies from state to state, it is essential that you now review your own state's requirements and record your understanding of the rules and regulations as well as the license law in the appropriate places in the outline which follows.

## LICENSING REQUIREMENTS OUTLINE

The following outline has been provided for your use in conjunction with the appropriate materials obtained from the state licensing agency for the jurisdiction in which you will be tested. Take those materials and carefully research these topics.

1. License

_____
_____
_____
_____
_____

2. Education

_____
_____
_____
_____
_____

3. Experience

_____
_____
_____
_____
_____

4. Examination

_____
_____
_____
_____
_____

5. Sponsorship

_____
_____
_____

6. Minimum age

_____
_____

7. Citizenship

_____
_____

8. Fair housing

_____
_____
_____
_____
_____

9. Application

_____
_____
_____

10. Convictions

_____
_____

11. Fees

_____
_____
_____
_____

12. Reciprocity

_____
_____
_____
_____

13. Administration of the law

_____
_____
_____

14. Advertising

_____
_____
_____

15. Display of license

_____
_____

16. Placement of license

_____
_____
_____

17. Suspension and revocation of license

_____
_____
_____
_____

18. Real estate definition

_____
_____
_____
_____
_____

## STATE COMMISSIONS

*Alabama.* Real Estate Commission, c/o State Capitol, Montgomery 36130. Phone: (205) 261-5544.

*Alaska.* Real Estate Commission, 3601 "C" St. 798, Anchorage 99503. Phone: (907) 563-2169.

*Arizona.* Real Estate Commissioner, 1645 W. Jefferson St., Phoenix 85007. Phone: (602) 255-4670.

*Arkansas.* Real Estate Commission, 1 Riverfront Pl., Suite 660, North Little Rock 72114. Phone: (501) 371-1247.

*California.* Department of Real Estate, P.O. Box 160009, Sacramento 95816. Phone: (916) 739-3600.

*Colorado.* Real Estate Commission, 1776 Logan St., 4th Floor, Denver 80203. Phone: (303) 866-2633.

*Connecticut.* Real Estate Division, 165 Capitol Ave., Room G8A, Hartford 06106. Phone: (203) 566-5130.

*Delaware.* Real Estate Commission, Post Office Box 1401, Dover 19901. Phone: (302) 736-4186 or 4670.

*District of Columbia.* D.C. Real Estate Commission, 614 H St., N.W., Room 923, Washington 20001. Phone: (202) 727-7468.

*Florida.* Division of Real Estate, P.O. Box 1900, Orlando 32802. Phone: (305) 423-6053.

*Georgia.* Real Estate Commission, 40 Pryor St., Atlanta 30303-3184. Phone: (404) 656-3916.

*Guam.* Real Estate Commissioner, Department of Revenue & Taxation, Division of Insurance, Banking & Real Estate, P.O. Box 2796, Agana, Guam 96910.

*Hawaii.* Real Estate Commission, P.O. Box 3469, Honolulu 96801. Phone: (808) 548-7464.

*Idaho.* Real Estate Commission, Statehouse Mail, Boise 83720. Phone: (208) 334-3285.

*Illinois.* Department of Registration & Education, 320 West Washington St., Springfield 62786. Phone: (217) 785-0890.

*Indiana.* Real Estate Commission, 100 N. Senate Ave., Room 1021, Indianapolis 46204. Phone: (317) 232-3888.

*Iowa.* Real Estate Commission, Executive Hills, Suite 205, Des Moines 50319. Phone: (515) 281-3183.

*Kansas.* Real Estate Commission, 217 East 4th, Topeka 66603. Phone: (913) 296-3411.

*Kentucky.* Real Estate Commission, 222 S. First St., Suite 300, Louisville 40202. Phone: (502) 588-4462.

*Louisiana.* Real Estate Commission, P.O. Box 14785, Baton Rouge 70808. Phone: (504) 925-4800.

*Maine.* Real Estate Commission, State House, State 35, Augusta 04333. Phone: (207) 289-3735.

*Maryland.* Real Estate Commission, 501 St. Paul Place, Room 804, Baltimore 21202. Phone: (301) 659-6230.

*Massachusetts.* Board of Registration of Real Estate Brokers and Salesmen, 100 Cambridge St., Room 1525, Boston 02202. Phone: (617) 727-3055.

*Michigan.* Board of Real Estate Brokers & Salespersons, P.O. Box 30018, Lansing 48909. Phone: (517) 373-0490.

*Minnesota.* Director of Licensing, Department of Commerce, 500 Metro Square Building, St. Paul 55101. Phone: (612) 296-6319.

*Mississippi.* Real Estate Commission, 1920 Dunbarton St., Jackson 39216. Phone: (601) 982-6300.

*Missouri.* Real Estate Commission, P.O. Box 1339, Jefferson City 65102. Phone: (314) 751-2334.

*Montana.* Board of Realty Regulation, 1424 9th Ave., Helena 59601. Phone: (406) 449-2961.

*Nebraska.* Real Estate Commission, 301 Centennial Mall South, Lincoln 68509. Phone: (402) 471-2004.

*Nevada.* Real Estate Division, Department of Commerce, 201 South Fall St., Carson City 89710. Phone: (702) 885-4280.

*New Hampshire.* Real Estate Commission, 3 Capitol St., Concord 03301. Phone: (602) 271-2701 or 2702.

*New Jersey.* Real Estate Commission, 201 E. State St., Trenton 08625. Phone: (609) 292-7656.

*New Mexico.* Real Estate Commission, 4000 San Pedro, N.E., Suite A, Albuquerque 87110. Phone: (505) 841-6524.

*New York.* Department of State, 162 Washington Ave., Albany 12231. Phone: (518) 474-7936.

*North Carolina.* Real Estate Commission, 1200 Navaho Dr., P.O. Box 17100, Raleigh 27619. Phone: (919) 733-9580.

*North Dakota.* 314 East Thayer Ave., P.O. Box 727, Bismarck 58502. Phone: (701) 224-2749 or 2737.

*Ohio.* Division of Real Estate, Department of Commerce, Two Nationwide Plaza, Columbus 43215. Phone: (614) 466-4100.

*Oklahoma.* Real Estate Commission, 4040 N. Lincoln Blvd., Suite 100, Oklahoma City 73105. Phone: (405) 521-3387.

*Oregon.* Real Estate Commission, 158 12th St., N.E., Salem 97310. Phone: (503) 378-4170.

*Pennsylvania.* Administrative Officer, P.O. Box 2649, Room 611, Transportation & Safety Building, Commonwealth Avenue & Forester Street, Harrisburg 17105-2649. Phone: (717) 783-1293.

*Rhode Island.* Real Estate Division, 100 North Main St., Providence 02903. Phone: (401) 277-2255.

*Saskatchewan.* Supt. of Insurance, Consumer and Commercial Affairs, 1871 Smith St., Regina S4P 3V7. Phone: (306) 565-2957.

*South Carolina.* Real Estate Commission, P.O. Box 210189, Columbia 29221. Phone: (803) 758-6736.

*South Dakota.* Real Estate Commission, P.O. Box 490, Pierre 57501.

*Tennessee.* Real Estate Commission, Doctor's Building, Room 428, 706 Church St., Nashville 37219-5322. Phone: (615) 741-2273.

*Texas.* Real Estate Commission, P.O. Box 12188, Capitol Station, Austin 78711. Phone: (512) 459-1123.

*Utah.* Real Estate Division, Heber M. Wells Building, 160 East 300 South, P.O. Box 45802, Salt Lake City 48145. Phone: (801) 530-6747.

*Vermont.* Real Estate Commission, 7 East State St., State Office Building, Montpelier 05602. Phone: (802) 828-3228.

*Virginia.* Department of Commerce, 3600 West Broad St., Richmond 23230. Phone: (804) 275-8516.

*Virgin Islands.* Division of Licensing, P.O. Box 2515, St. Thomas 00801. Phone: (809) 774-6336.

*Washington.* Real Estate Division, P.O. Box 247, Olympia 98504. Phone: (206) 753-6681.

*West Virginia.* Real Estate Commission, 1033 Quarrier St., Suite 400, Charleston 25301. Phone: (304) 348-3555.

*Wisconsin.* Department of Regulation and Licensing, P.O. Box 8936, Madison 53708. Phone: (608) 266-5514.

*Wyoming.* Director of Real Estate, Herschler Building, Cheyenne 82002. Phone: (307) 777-7141.

# REVIEW QUESTIONS

1. You are an apartment manager for Colonial Apartments, Inc., which rents apartments to people of many different nationalities. A Soviet immigrant who has become a U.S. citizen wishes to rent an apartment from you, but because of the political differences between the United States and the Soviet Union, you refuse. Which is true?

   (A) You are within your rights as a property owner
   (B) You have violated the 1968 Civil Rights Act
   (C) You have violated the NAR Code of Equal Opportunity
   (D) You are violating the Civil Rights Code

2. In your jurisdiction, who is considered to be an associate broker?

   (A) A member of a real estate association
   (B) A licensed broker working for a principal broker
   (C) A salesperson training to obtain a broker's license
   (D) A broker from another firm participating in a transaction

3. Which of the following is **not** usually a state license law requirement?

   (A) Salespersons must have their own escrow accounts
   (B) Salespersons must be supervised by licensed brokers
   (C) Salespersons are required to complete prelicensing education courses
   (D) Salespersons must hold a broker's license first

4. Real estate license laws originate with

   (A) state legislatures
   (B) state real estate commissions
   (C) a state's governor
   (D) NAR

5. The agency of the federal government that administers fair housing laws is

   (A) VA           (C) NARELLO
   (B) HUD          (D) AIREA

6. To receive a commission, a real estate salesperson must be all of the following EXCEPT

   (A) a REALTOR®
   (B) licensed in the jurisdiction
   (C) affiliated with a principal broker
   (D) the receiver of a commission from the principal broker

7. The main purpose of the license law is to

   (A) protect the public
   (B) protect the licensee from unethical brokers
   (C) restrict competition
   (D) restrict entry of new salespersons

8. You, as an apartment manager for Brightwood Apartments, receive a telephone inquiry regarding a vacancy. On the telephone you indicate that you have several vacant apartments. When the callers arrive, you discover that they are an interracial married couple. You inform them that all the apartments have been rented (when, in fact, you know they have not been). Which is true?

   (A) You are protecting the interest of your principal
   (B) You have violated the 1968 Civil Rights Act
   (C) You have violated RESPA
   (D) You are in compliance with the Magnuson-Moss Act

9. A real estate salesperson is responsible for his or her actions to the

   (A) mortgagor        (C) employing broker
   (B) mortgagee        (D) seller

10. Under federal law, a salesperson must

   (A) show listed property to any interested party
   (B) steer buyers to ethnic neighborhoods
   (C) work with lenders in red-lining areas
   (D) assist in blockbusting of all white neighborhoods

11. Who may sell real estate without a license?

   (A) Appraisers
   (B) Property managers
   (C) Owners
   (D) A friend of the owner

12. A real estate licensee is required to do all of the following EXCEPT

   (A) display the license properly
   (B) refrain from discriminatory practice
   (C) decline certain listings
   (D) pass an examination for licensure

13. If one state accepts the requirements for licensure of another state and grants a license on that basis, that state is practicing

   (A) discrimination    (C) sponsorship
   (B) reciprocity       (D) revocation

14. You are a homeowner who is concerned that your neighborhood may be entering a racially transitional state. A broker whom you have contacted informs you that Haitian refugees are in fact purchasing a home in your neighborhood. The broker indicates also that prices will decline because of this influx of refugees. The broker has

   (A) violated the Civil Rights Act of 1968 through blockbusting
   (B) violated the Civil Rights Act of 1968 through racial steering
   (C) violated the Civil Rights Act of 1968 through panic selling
   (D) not violated the Civil Rights Act of 1968 in any sense

15. To become a licensed broker one must usually

   (A) pass a licensing examination
   (B) open his or her own office
   (C) employ salespeople
   (D) have 10 years' experience

16. The Federal Fair Housing Law of 1968 does not forbid

   (A) racial steering of buyers
   (B) panic selling in neighborhoods in transition
   (C) redlining in financially distressed areas
   (D) discrimination based on marital status

17. When may discrimination **not** be covered by the Federal Fair Housing Law of 1968?

   (A) When a single-family home is sold without use of a broker and without discriminatory advertising
   (B) When an owner, broker, or salesperson denies that housing is available for sale when it is
   (C) When different rental terms are established for racial reasons
   (D) When a person is denied the use of a particular property that is available to others

18. The major federal agency that regulates the real estate industry is

   (A) FHA    (C) HUD
   (B) VA     (D) GSA

19. A discrimination complaint may be filed directly with all of the following EXCEPT the

   (A) Supreme Court
   (B) Board of REALTORS®
   (C) State Real Estate Commission
   (D) Civil Rights Commission

20. Broker A deposits buyer K's earnest money check in his personal account. Broker A has committed

   (A) misrepresentation    (C) commingling
   (B) reciprocity          (D) fraud

# Chapter 5
# Legal Aspects of Real Estate

---

## VOCABULARY

*You will find it important to have a complete working knowledge of the following terms and concepts found in the text or the glossary.*

| | | |
|---|---|---|
| ad valorem taxes | escheat | nuisance |
| affirmative easement | estate in land | police powers |
| allodial ownership | fee simple absolute | probate homesteads |
| assessment | fee simple determinable | profit |
| bundle of rights | fee tail | profit à prendre |
| commercial easements in gross | feudal tenure | redeem |
| condemnation | feuds | remainder |
| conditional fee | freehold estates | restrictive covenants |
| corporeal rights | homestead exemption | reversion |
| covenants | incorporeal rights | rezoning |
| curtesy | intestate | seisin |
| determinable fee | judgment liens | servient tenement |
| dominant tenement | leasehold estate | tax liens |
| dower | license | taxation of real estate |
| easement | lien | trespass |
| easement appurtenant | life estate | urban planning |
| easement in gross | mechanic's lien | valuation and appraisement law |
| eminent domain | municipal improvements | variance |
| encroachment | negative easement | waste |
| equity of redemption | nonconforming use | zoning |

---

WHILE many believe that the law pertaining to the ownership of real estate changes so slowly that it is almost static, quite the contrary is true. Basic rights of ownership and interests in real estate do indeed change slowly, and in the United States today true and absolute ownership of land is recognized. In the discussion that follows we compare the origin of real estate ownership with the present-day concept of ownership.

### THE FEUDAL SYSTEM OF LAND TENURE

The *feudal system* of land ownership had its origins in the law of England as it developed after the Norman conquest in 1066 A.D. Under this system, only the ruling monarch, the king, really owned real estate as we think of ownership today. Instead of granting outright ownership to others, the king created *feuds,* which were the equiv-

alent of today's leases of real estate. The owner of the feud held it only so long as he enjoyed the king's favor and performed the duties imposed by the king—the furnishing and support of military personnel and money to support the king (the government) being among the most important. This system of ownership is commonly called *feudal tenure* because continued ownership depended upon continuous performance of the duties imposed.

Even though this form of ownership was ultimately recognized as inheritable, inheritance was surrounded with so many restrictions that *absolute* ownership could not be achieved; ownership was always conditional in nature. Although this system of ownership had changed dramatically by the time of the American Revolution, it was nevertheless an important cause of the revolution. The dream of Americans was absolute ownership of the land.

## THE ALLODIAL SYSTEM OF LAND TENURE

Under the *allodial system* of land ownership, which prevails today in the United States, we feel that we own real estate absolutely, without being dependent upon the whims of a ruling monarch and without having the burdensome duties which existed under the feudal system. In truth, we do own land allodially today, and our system of government clearly recognizes that fact. But in order to retain this right of ownership and to protect it, we make certain concessions. They include eminent domain, police powers, property taxation, and escheat.

### Eminent Domain

The power of *eminent domain* is an inherent right reserved by the government. It is the power of governmental units literally to take private property when it is concluded that such action is in the best interests of the general public. The method by which this power is exercised is called *condemnation.* Privately owned property may be taken by condemning it to a public use.

Several general rules apply in this area:

☐ The taking or condemning of private property must be done in accordance with specific legislative authority and within the limitations of the owner's constitutional rights, both federal and state.

☐ Generally, payment must be made to the landowner based upon the fair value of the property taken, and the landowner may also collect payments for damages (in terms of loss of value) to the property remaining. The question of damages to the property not taken depends upon state law. Consider the taking of land for a new highway as shown in Figure 5-1.

Clearly the property owner is entitled to be paid for the strip taken, but what is the impact on the 4 acres that are "landlocked," having no access? This acreage has been substantially diminished in value, and so has the remaining farmland. State law will determine whether or not the property owner can recover an amount for this damage.

☐ The power of eminent domain can be delegated to others, even to private companies such as public utilities, so that they can condemn property that is needed to make their services available. Generally, these actions take the form of easements (discussed later in the chapter) rather than outright ownership. An easement (for power lines, for example) carries with it the right to enter upon the property in order to maintain the utility. Extensive damage to the crop of corn may be caused when heavy equipment is moved through a field to repair a power or gas line; such damages are not the responsibility of the person committing the damage unless specified by previous agreement.

☐ Once there has been a legitimate determination that private property is needed for a public purpose (that is, that the taking is not arbitrary or capricious), the landowner can only dispute the *value* of the property being taken. Such litigation may take years to resolve, but the taking of the property may be as immediate as is necessary for the public purpose to be served.

### Police Powers: Zoning

The inherent power of government to police the conduct of its citizens is well established. To the extent that it affects the use of prviately owned real estate, it may impose limitations on the concept of allodial ownership of real estate.

Perhaps the most important application of police powers occurs in the area of zoning. Each state, through laws known as enabling statutes, delegates to local communities the authority to create and enforce zoning laws or ordinances. These ordinances are established by a zoning board or commission, or by an area planning board or commission whose task it is to guide real estate development in a specific community.

In general, the intent of zoning is to control growth and to force it to follow an orderly plan. Zoning attempts to maintain or enhance the quality of life of a community by promoting the safety, health, and general well-being of its residents. Each zoning ordinance is based on the need to provide protection to the general public from fire and other hazards, to guard against an excessive concentration of population, and to preserve property values.

Some typical zoning controls are:

☐ Setback requirements specifying distances from lot lines for the construction of buildings

☐ Limits to the percentage of a ground area that may be covered by a building

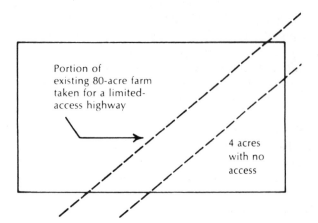

*Figure 5-1—Situation resulting from power of eminent domain.*

☐ Limits on the number of families that may be housed per acre

☐ Restrictions on the use of property by category, such as residential, light manufacturing, and heavy industry

Obviously, the decisions of zoning boards and commissions can have a dramatic impact on the value of a given piece of real estate. For example, a 5-acre tract limited to a single-family residence may have a value of $40,000. However, if it were zoned for heavy industrial use, it might be worth $200,000. Clearly the zoning powers of government are very important to anyone involved in the real estate field.

Three specific zoning provisions should be noted here.

### The Preexisting Nonconforming Use

Suppose that a legally constituted zoning board decides that in a particular area only single-family residences of a maximum height of 40 feet will be allowed. Assume further that in the middle of this zone stands a six-story hotel. Must the hotel be demolished or cease operation?

Normally, the answer is no because the hotel was already in existence and presumably did not violate earlier laws or zoning ordinances. If the zoning ordinance were to require the hotel's demolition, it would be considered an act of condemnation, a taking, and the owner would be entitled to be paid for the economic loss suffered. Vacant lots in the area, however, would be subject to the ordinance and would not be entitled to compensation for any loss suffered.

### The Variance

When a large area of a city is zoned exclusively for single-family residential purposes, this fact alone might make it desirable to establish there a convenience shopping center for the benefit of the residents. To accomplish this, it would be necessary to apply to the appropriate zoning body and request permission to vary the use from the existing zoning ordinance. Normally, such action would require a public hearing, with prior notice given to all nearby property owners whose property values might be affected by the outcome. Following the hearing, the board or commission would decide to permit or deny the proposed variance.

### Rezoning

It frequently happens that so many violations of existing zoning rules have been allowed to occur (either because residents do not object or governmental agencies are not responsive) that, for all practical purposes, the general usage of the property in the neighborhood has in fact changed. Typically, this is seen in older neighborhoods that have been zoned for single-family residential

usage but in fact have become either multifamily, commercial, or even light industrial in actual usage. When this occurs, it is possible to seek rezoning of the entire area so that remaining single-family residential properties can be sold or used for a more appropriate purpose.

### Real Estate Taxation

It is obviously necessary that we pay for our governmental system which makes it possible to have absolute ownership of real estate. All of us are familiar with the concept of income taxes, both federal and state. In addition, most states and local governmental units impose a tax on real estate, which includes houses or other improvements located upon the land. These taxes pay for a wide variety of local services, among them police protection, fire departments, schools, and libraries.

Since the purpose of this form of taxation is to provide benefits to the property owner, these taxes are usually based upon the value of the property (ad valorem) as appraised or assessed. While this system has some built-in inequities, some arbitrary and easy to administer system is necessary in order to avoid the high costs of administration. Under this system, all property in a given tax unit is periodically revalued and a uniform tax rate is applied equally to all properties. Failure to pay such taxes may result in a forced sale (a tax sale) of the property, the proceeds going to pay the delinquent taxes.

### Escheat

The doctrine of escheat has remained a part of real property law for centuries. Its basic concept has not changed, but its application has been modified.

Under early English common law, even after the right to inherit real estate was recognized, only close family members could acquire real estate by inheritance. Today, individuals who have no legal heirs who would have a statutory right to inherit their property may leave their property to others simply by executing a valid will. As a result, the doctrine of escheat is seldom seen in action even though it still exists.

Under modern real estate law, the rule that has developed is this: If the owner of real estate dies without a valid will (intestate) by which he or she disposes of his or her real estate and there are no legal heirs entitled to inherit the property under state law, then the real estate escheats to the state in which it is located. That is, the state is a potential "heir" of all owners of real estate, and it takes their property unless someone else succeeds to its ownership either by virtue of disposition by a valid will or by the state rules of inheritance.

### Assessments for Municipal Improvements

Very often improvements are made by municipalities that benefit all property owners in the area and presumably increase the value of their property. Paved streets, sewers, water, sidewalks, and streetlights are common examples.

The cost of making these improvements is generally charged to the benefited property owners on some sort of pro rata basis, such as feet of frontage or amount of acreage. As a general rule, the affected property owners are first notified of the proposed improvement, its anticipated cost, and the method of prorating this expense. They then have the opportunity to decide, by majority vote, whether or not they want the improvement.

This is not, however, universally true; more often the improvement is forced upon the property owners because it is essential to the health or safety of all of them—in effect, the police power of government is exercised. For example, the population density and the soil conditions in a particular subdivision may make it mandatory that city water and sewage disposal facilities be installed in order to avoid a potential water pollution problem. In such a case the property owners may have no voice in deciding whether they need or want the proposed improvements. And they may nevertheless be compelled to pay for them.

## Urban Planning

In recent years the recognized power to zone areas for limited use has been greatly expanded to include the concept of urban planning or area planning. This concept is much broader than zoning, both in terms of the area that may be included—frequently an entire county or city—as well as in its application, which may include requirements for so-called green belts of open space or the limited use of properties in a specified portion of the area. Urban or area planning can have an important impact on the value of land when that land might otherwise be more intensively (and more profitably) used.

This broadened exercise of the inherent police powers of government may be entirely at odds with the plans of the landowners in the affected areas. Since such controls are not consistent with common law concepts of real estate ownership, there must normally be some form of enabling legislation. The growth of urban planning has created new career opportunities for those knowledgeable in real estate and social development.

## Other Limitations

If all the foregoing limitations on the uses to which individually owned real estate may be put appear to cast some doubt on the actuality of absolute or allodial ownership today, then our point has been made.

Even without all these restrictions on the use and ownership of one's own property, however, there still remain the classic common law doctrines of *trespass* and *nuisance,* which provide private remedies for adjoining property owners as well as individual property owners. Any owner of real estate is entitled to protect his or her own property from and is restricted from the commission of trespass and nuisance.

### Trespass

Any property owner is entitled to maintain a civil suit against a neighbor or a stranger who enters upon his property without permission. This is true whether the trespass is occasional or continuous, and the law presumes that some damage, which can be measured in dollars, always occurs when there has been a trespass. For example, a neighbor who occasionally trespasses by driving across one's property, or does it as a matter of habit, may be sued for money damages or enjoined (ordered) to refrain from doing so again.

### Nuisance

Regardless of what the zoning laws *do not* prohibit, owners of real estate are entitled to insist that a neighbor refrain from using his or her property in a way that is injurious to them. For example, even though no law prohibits it, an owner of a residential lot can be sued for damages or prohibited from using the lot as an open trash dump. While this doctrine protects the rights of individual property owners, it also restricts their own property rights in the same manner.

## Concepts of Ownership

In concluding our review of absolute ownership as we recognize it today, we might well ask whether or not the concept of ownership of real estate has really changed, as we perhaps thought when we first compared feudal and allodial tenure. It is true that the basic character of ownership of real estate has changed, but it is also true that the cost of achieving allodial ownership has required the surrender of many rights that we may have thought of as inherent in the definition of *ownership.* In the next chapter we shall consider the *bundle of rights* concept of ownership, always keeping in mind the foregoing limitations on the rights of ownership.

## INTERESTS IN LAND

### Estates in Land

An *estate in land,* as distinguished from a lesser (temporary or limited) interest, is *ownership.* Estates are further divided into freeholds and leaseholds. The essential characteristic in each case is the fact that the owner of a freehold estate or the lessee of a leasehold estate has an estate which gives to him or her the rights of ownership (whether unlimited or limited), as opposed to the simple right to use the property of another for a specific purpose. The important estates in land are shown in the chart in Figure 5-2. These interests are also called *corporeal rights.*

### Freehold Estates (Estates for an Indefinite Period of Time)

When we define a *freehold estate* as an estate for an indefinite period of time, we do not imply that the length of the estate is vague and therefore cannot be defined. The word *indefinite* is used here quite literally: theoretically, it can last forever—as opposed to having some definite termination date that can be accurately predicted at the outset. Certainly the owner of such an interest will not live forever, but the concept allows that owner the power to control ownership indefinitely.

☐ *Fee simple absolute.* This is the highest and most complete form of ownership known under our law. It includes all rights recognized by law, including the right to create lesser estates or interests. However, these rights may be subordinated to the rights of other members of society protected by the same law as the property owner. Thus the owner may not maintain a nuisance, may have property taken for a public purpose, and may be restricted, for the public benefit, in the use of property even though he or she owns it absolutely.

☐ *Fee tail.* This is a fee simple absolute estate which is restricted to inheritance by direct descendants of the holder. Used in England at one time but held to be an unreasonable restraint in almost all states today, it is in fact outlawed by statutes that convert it to a fee simple absolute.

☐ *Fee simple determinable.* Sometimes referred to as a *conditional fee,* this contains all the elements of the fee simple absolute except that the interest is subject to possible termination in the event that a specified condition is broken. Since the condition may never be broken or the time at which it will be broken cannot be determined at the time the interest is created, it is potentially absolute. When (and if) the condition is broken, the fee simple absolute reverts to its creator, his or her heirs, or whoever else might be named in the deed which created it. This potential interest is known as the *reversion.* For example:

I hereby convey (certain property) to the Izaac Walton League of America for so long as the property is used as a conservation club. In the event such use shall cease the property is to go to the State of Michigan for use as a public park.

In this example, since no limitation is expressed on the scope of the interest being conveyed, it is presumed to be a fee simple absolute; however, the transfer is clearly conditional upon its continued use for a specific purpose. When that condition is broken, the fee simple interest is *determined,* hence the name *fee simple determinable.* In practice, the clarity with which such interests are created frequently leaves something to be desired, so caution should be exercised in dealing with them.

### Life Estates

A *life estate* is an estate in land that is limited to the lifetime of the holder (or, occasionally, the lifetime of another).

☐ *Conventional life estates.* A life tenant has legal title and an estate, but these rights are limited to the holder's lifetime. Basically, they are rights to income as opposed to principal, for the remainderman or reversioner holds the balance of all rights to the fee. The basic duty of the life tenant is to refrain from encroaching upon the rights of remainder interests by committing *waste:* abusing, destroying, or consuming the property beyond his immediate needs. The life tenant could, for example, cut down trees for his or her own use as firewood but not for sale to others. The life tenant does not have the duty to insure the property for the remainderman, to pay taxes beyond income produced by the property, or to pay more than the interest on existing mortgages and liens.

☐ *Legal life estates.* These are created by statute and are dependent on the law of the state where the real estate is located. Historically, the most important legal life estates recognized by our law have been *dower* and *curtesy. Dower* is the interest that a wife has in real estate owned by her husband at his death and that was owned by him during the marriage. *Curtesy* is the interest of the husband in real estate owned by his wife during the marriage.

For most of the history of this country, this interest has been a life estate in all or part of such real estate (depending upon what other legal heirs survived the deceased owner) but normally not less than one-third. The limitations on the life estate of the surviving spouse were the same as those outlined above for conventional life estates.

Since modern probate codes, the homestead exemption, and the popularity of some form of joint ownership between husbands and wives seem to provide adequate protection to each spouse against the irresponsible or unfair dispositions of real estate by the other, many states have completely eliminated dower and curtesy. In other states a statutory substi-

# CORPOREAL RIGHTS — ESTATES IN LAND

## PRESENTLY POSSESSORY

CLASSIFIED AS TO DURATION

### FUTURE ESTATES

**Remainder**
balance to others after limited estate
A to B for life of B, with remainder to C

**Reversion**
balance reverts to grantor after limited estate
A to B for life of B

**Possibility of Reverter**
retained by grantor upon a conveyance of a fee on limitation
A to B, until . . . .

**Right of Reacquisition**
retained by grantor upon a conveyance of a fee on condition
A to B, provided . . .

(Formerly Freehold)

**Estates in Fee**
uncertain or unlimited duration; perpetual; inheritable

*Fee Simple Absolute*
generally inheritable; maximum rights of ownership
A to B, or A to B and his heirs

*Fee Tail*
lineally inheritable; now outlawed
A to B and the heirs of his body

*Fee on Condition*
may terminate if condition is broken and reentry made; grantor has right to repossess
A to B, but if . . .

*Fee on Limitation*
(Fee Simple Determinable)
continues until a certain condition occurs and then terminates automatically
A to B, so long as . . .

**Life Estates**
measured by a life or lives; terminates upon expiration of said life

*Conventional* (created purposely)
life tenant has right to income, rent, profits generally responsible for all current carrying charges and expenses
may not commit waste
A for life;
A to B for life;
A to B for life of C

*Legal* (created by law)
curtesy or dower
homestead
community property

(Formerly Nonfreehold Estates)

**Leaseholds**
of limited duration

*Estate for Years*
specific termination date
L to T from 1/1/Y1 to 12/31/Y3

*From Period to Period*
renewable without termination
L to T, with rent payable monthly in advance on the first day of the month

*Estate at Will*
indefinite unless terminated
L to T, so long as L wishes

*Estate at Sufferance*
tenant's continued possession without landlord's consent

40

tute has been created which makes the interest of the spouse a fee interest rather than a life estate. Almost all states have modified the interest in some way. Where the traditional legal life estates of dower and curtesy are still recognized, however, the holder of the life estate has the limited rights discussed above under conventional life estates.

### Homestead Exemption

Dower and curtesy were created in order to protect against the disposition of real estate by one spouse without the concurrence of the other. In addition, there is in the United States some protection of the family from the rights of creditors of the head of the household acting alone.

The *homestead exemption,* as the name implies, is designed to exempt the home from creditors' claims incurred solely by the head of the household—traditionally, the husband—without the concurrence of the wife. In the absence of such concurrence, under a typical homestead exemption the homestead may not be reached by creditors. The one generally recognized exception to this is the debt incurred for the purchase of the homestead in the first place.

The rules in those states that recognize the homestead exemption are not uniform, and in many states a formal declaration of the claim of the homestead exemption may be necessary to obtain its benefits. In states which recognize the homestead, it does not generally have the status of a true estate in land, but it is rather an exception of the particular property from creditors' claims. There are exceptions to this generalization, and local laws must be consulted.

In some states the exemption of certain property is not called a homestead exemption but is instead referred to as a *valuation and appraisement law.* Therefore many documents used in real estate (particularly those, such as a promissory note, that evidence a debt) will include both terms to avoid the application of such exemptions. A typical clause will read, "without relief from homestead or valuation and appraisement laws."

The extent of property that may be claimed to be exempt as a homestead may vary widely, depending on whether the home is a house on a residential lot or whether it is a farm, in which case substantial acreage and the home on it can still qualify for the homestead exemption.

In many states the right is limited by some dollar amount of value that may be claimed under the exemption. Various definitions of what constitutes a family or household are also found from state to state. Some states have abolished the homestead exemption during a person's lifetime and recognize only a limited homestead right for surviving family members. These are frequently referred to as *probate homesteads.*

In view of the widespread recognition of some form of homestead (even though in some jurisdictions it is very limited), the practice of requiring the execution by both spouses of all documents transferring or creating interests in real estate is fortified. This is true even in those states that have liberalized or expanded the rights of married individuals to own real estate individually.

### Leasehold Estates

Rights to the possession of real estate granted by its owner for a specified period or periods of time are called *leasehold estates.* We discuss them in detail in Chapter 9. The types of leases include:

☐  *Estates for years,* which create rights in the tenant in the estate for a definite period of time.
☐  *Estates from year to year (or period to period),* which are distinguished from estates for years in that they continue for successive periods until one of the parties gives notice of termination.
☐  *Estates at will,* which give the tenant the right to possession with the consent of the landlord, but the term of the estate is indefinite and either party may terminate it by giving proper notice.
☐  *Estates at sufferance,* which arise when the tenant comes into possession of the real property lawfully and then, after his or her rights have expired, holds possession of the premises without the consent of the person entitled to possession.

## OTHER INTERESTS, LESS THAN ESTATES

### Easements

The fact that estates in land are recognized creates the power in the holder of an estate to create lesser interests in the land. The important interests that can be created are easements, licenses, and profits.

An *easement* is a nonpossessory interest in land owned by another, that is, a right in the land of another which is less than the right of possession. It is an intangible right and creates no right of ownership of the land itself. Easements are categorized, and the categories must be understood because they are a benefit to the holder and represent a restriction on the rights of the owner of the property subject to the easement—and therefore affect the value of each property. The major categories recognized today are discussed below and are illustrated in Figure 5-3.

### Easements Appurtenant

The owner of one piece of land has the right to certain uses of or restrictions on the use of the land owned by another under an easement appurtenant. When such an easement exists, the *dominant tenement* is the land

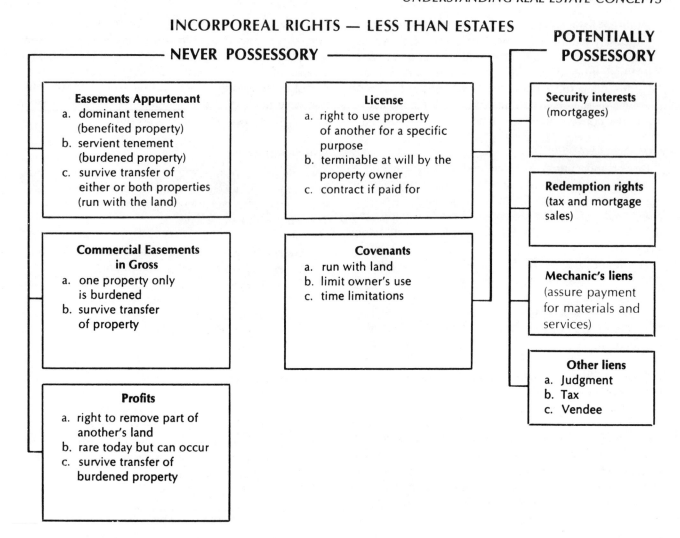

## INCORPOREAL RIGHTS — LESS THAN ESTATES

### NEVER POSSESSORY

**POTENTIALLY POSSESSORY**

**Easements Appurtenant**
a. dominant tenement (benefited property)
b. servient tenement (burdened property)
c. survive transfer of either or both properties (run with the land)

**License**
a. right to use property of another for a specific purpose
b. terminable at will by the property owner
c. contract if paid for

**Security interests** (mortgages)

**Commercial Easements in Gross**
a. one property only is burdened
b. survive transfer of property

**Covenants**
a. run with land
b. limit owner's use
c. time limitations

**Redemption rights** (tax and mortgage sales)

**Mechanic's liens** (assure payment for materials and services)

**Profits**
a. right to remove part of another's land
b. rare today but can occur
c. survive transfer of burdened property

**Other liens**
a. Judgment
b. Tax
c. Vendee

*Figure 5-3—Interests that are less than estates. (From Guide to the New York Real Estate Salespersons' Course 3E by Norman Weinberg, Paul J. Colletti, William A. Colavito, and Frank A. Melchior. Copyright © 1985 by John Wiley & Sons, Inc. Reprinted by permission of John Wiley & Sons, Inc.)*

benefited by the easement, and the *servient tenement* is the land encumbered by or subject to the easement (see Figure 5-4).

Most important is the fact that an easement appurtenant is not merely a personal right but a right that attaches to the dominant tenement and passes with it to a new owner, *and* the servient tenement is encumbered or restricted by the easement when it is transferred to a new owner. Such an easement is said to "run with the land." This has the effect of enhancing the value of the dominant tenement and decreasing the value of the servient tenement.

An easement appurtenant may be either *affirmative* or *negative*. That is, the servient tenement may be subject to the use of some of it by the owner of the dominant tenement (such as a right of way), or the owner of the servient tenement may be required to refrain from making certain uses of land for the benefit of the owner of the dominant tenement (such as restrictions on building

structures that would cut off light and air to the dominant tenement).

### Easements in Gross

The right of the holder of an easement to use the property of another is created by an easement in gross. It is not related to the ownership of any adjoining property. The original *personal* easement in gross has largely disappeared in modern real estate practice. It is so rare that

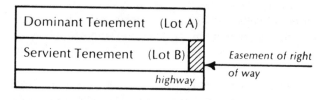

*Figure 5-4—Dominant vs. servient tenement.*

many lawyers believe that it would not be recognized by a modern court.

The important easement of this type is the *commercial* easement in gross, which is assignable and can be both conveyed and inherited. People active in the real estate business need to be aware of this type of easement, which in the past has been used for railroad rights of way, pipelines, and electrical and telephone lines. Serious title problems often arise because of the scope of the easement granted by an earlier owner of the property. Two common problems indicate the importance of the commercial easement in gross.

Electrical power line easements in the early days of the expansion of the power industry were often broadly written. It is not unusual to find in an abstract a grant of a commercial easement in gross in such terms as "the right to install electrical power lines over, under, or through any and all property which I presently own in Any County, This State." At the time that such easements were taken, much of the land to which they applied was farmland, but this same land today may be either residential, industrial, or commercial. The existence of such broad easements is frequently a problem because holders of the easement have the legal right to place power lines wherever they choose. Obviously, the owner of the property cannot build under such conditions, for he or she may incur a loss if the easement is later used. The practical solution to this problem is to obtain from the utility involved a deed that releases from the easement the land which is not actually needed and limits what may be used.

Railroad rights of way that have been abandoned by companies which have long since gone out of business pose a similar problem. Generally, case law provides that upon abandonment of such a commercial easement in gross, the easement is terminated and the owner of the fee simple then owns the property free of the encumbrance of the easement. Unfortunately, the creation of such easements was often done by deeds that are ambiguous to the point that it is sometimes difficult to tell whether they were intended to convey a fee interest or an easement. Occasionally, the owner of such an easement has made a conveyance of it under the false notion that he or she owns the fee. Clearing the title to such a piece of property and proving ownership can be difficult and costly.

## Profits

A *profit* in land is the right to take part of the soil or produce of land owned by someone else. This includes the right to take soil, gravel, minerals, oil, gas, and the like from the land of another. It is not an important interest in land today but, like the overly broad commercial easement in gross, its existence in the chain of title to a piece of real estate can be troublesome. The legal term used to express this concept is *profit à prendre*.

Like the personal easement in gross, the profit à prendre is seldom used in modern real estate practice because of the highly technical rules that govern it and the fact that a carefully drafted contract can more clearly express the true intentions of the parties. The true profit, for example, might be indefinite with respect to time or quantity. In practice, the owner of the ground will desire limitations on both points, and the common law profit is not precise enough to accommodate a modern business transaction.

## Licenses

A *license* is merely the privilege to go upon land owned by another for a specific purpose. It does not create in the holder of the license any interest in the land of the owner. Because of this limitation, the license is neither assignable (saleable) nor inheritable. It may be revoked at any time by the landowner without rendering him liable for damages to the holder of the license *unless* it was created by contract and the license was paid for by the licensee. Two examples will illustrate the difference:

*Example*   A permits B to hunt upon A's property without receiving payment from B. A may revoke this license at any time.

*Example*   A stadium sells a ticket to a ball game, which grants the fan who buys it a license to be present for a sports event. The stadium arbitrarily ejects the fan before the event is complete. The fan has paid for the license and is entitled to be paid for this breach of contract.

## Restrictive Covenants

In addition to the public law limitations on the rights of ownership already discussed, it is also possible to impose further limitations on the private use of real property. The use of *restrictive covenants* in deeds limits the use of the property by subsequent owners. These are very important to subdivision development in which such covenants (promises) determine how the property can be used by all owners in the subdivision. They cover such items as: minimum setback lines for buildings, minimum house size, and limits on the number of families per house. If there is a conflict between zoning laws and private restrictive covenants, which prevails? The answer is that they *both* do. That is, the property owner must comply with both sets of limitations, so the more restrictive one will apply. Where property is zoned for commercial use but limited to residential use by covenant there is an obvious impact upon property value.

## Encroachments

Occasionally the buildings or other improvements erected by the owner of one parcel of real estate will extend beyond that owner's property line and be wholly or partially placed on the adjoining parcel of real estate. Fences, driveways, garages, and other outbuildings are frequently placed with less care than a residence. When this occurs, the structure or improvement is an *encroachment* on the adjoining property and on its owner's rights.

In most cases the encroachment is the result of an honest error, not deliberate action. Regardless of the intent of the encroaching party, however, the resulting problem can be troublesome. In some cases the encroaching party may acquire title to part of the adjoining property under the doctrine of adverse possession (to be discussed later); in other cases the encroaching party may be compelled to remove the encroaching structure. In either situation it may take expensive litigation to resolve the matter.

## SECURITY INTERESTS AND LIENS

The fact of ownership of real estate gives the owner the power to create security interests in lenders who have loaned money to the owner. In effect, the owner is *pledging* the real estate and making it available to be sold for the payment of a debt he or she fails to pay. This pledge of real estate may be voluntary or involuntary. It is voluntary when the owner borrows money, often for the purpose of buying the real estate in the first place, and gives the lender a *mortgage* or *deed of trust*. These devices specifically authorize the sale of the property if the owner does not repay the loan. The pledge is involuntary when state law authorizes the sale of the owner's property for a variety of other obligations, including payment of real estate taxes; payment of judgments against the owner; and payment to contractors for work done on the property. In each of these cases the real estate may be sold if the owner fails to pay these obligations.

By the same token, in most states there is a limited period of time within which the defaulting borrower may redeem the property, the *equity of redemption,* which usually permits the defaulting borrower to remain in possession of the property for a limited period of time in order to pay the debt and thus redeem the property from the possibility of foreclosure. Mortgages are discussed in Chapter 10.

## Mechanic's Liens

While there is no uniformity among the states and no such interest existed under common law, some protection is afforded by local statutes to the contractor who improves the property of another. A contractor is generally entitled to file a lien upon the property for the value of the work or materials furnished if unpaid at the end of the time period specified by local statute, and the lien may be enforced by an action quite similar to a mortgage foreclosure. Ultimately the property may even be sold to pay such claims.

## Local Law

Each state has its own body of law to define the various interests in real estate that it will recognize and the extent of the rights created in the owner of each right. For this reason it is essential that brokers and salespersons be familiar with local property law. The following specific areas should be independently verified for each jurisdiction:

☐ Governmental limitations such as zoning and planning
☐ State and local real estate taxes and the important role they play in the marketability of real estate
☐ Legal life estates if dower and/or curtesy are recognized in the state

## Mortgages (Deeds of Trust)

The use of mortgages or deeds of trust as financing devices creates potentially possessory interests in real estate in both the lender and the borrower. The lender's rights to the property are dependent on a default (failure to pay the debt) by the borrower and are governed by local law. In general, when there is a default by the mortgagor (borrower), the mortgagee (lender) has the right to bring legal proceedings to force the sale of the property to pay the debt.

## Tax and Judgment Liens

Real estate taxes usually become a lien against the real estate by statute. Failure to pay these taxes when due can result in the sale of the property against the owner's will. Since real estate taxes are seldom permitted to accumulate up to the value of the property, the owner is usually given some time after the sale to pay the taxes and redeem the property, which effectively sets the sale aside. Local law in each state will determine the procedure that must be followed for the sale and possible redemption.

Judgment liens may arise under local law when the owner is successfully sued by another for any reason; the lawsuit may be completely unrelated to the real estate. The property may be seized and sold to pay the judgment debt. Again, local law must be studied to see when such a lien may arise, how it is established, and the owner's powers to protect property from such a sale.

Figure 5-5 summarizes the interests recognized by the various states.

**Ownership interests** (Total)

| Interest | Total |
|---|---|
| Fee simple | 50 |
| Fee simple determinable | 48 |
| Life estate | 51 |
| Dower | 22 |
| Curtesy | 11 |
| Homestead | 42 |

**Forms of ownership** (Total)

| Form | Total |
|---|---|
| Individual | 50 |
| Joint tenancy | 47 |
| Tenancy in common | 50 |
| Community property | 8 |
| Tenancy by the entirety | 27 |
| Trust | 51 |
| Condominium | 51 |

*Figure 5-5—Summary of the interests recognized by the states.*

## REVIEW QUESTIONS

1. The most complete form of ownership the law recognizes today is the

   (A) fee simple determinable
   (B) fee simple conditional
   (C) life estate
   (D) fee simple absolute

2. The holder of a life estate measured by his or her own life

   (A) has the duty to refrain from committing waste to the property
   (B) is not entitled to the net income the property produces
   (C) must insure the property for the remainderman
   (D) may not convey the property to a third party

3. The owner of a fee simple interest in real estate can do all of the following EXCEPT

   (A) create a life estate in A with the remainder in fee to B
   (B) sell the property on land contract to A and mortgage the property to B
   (C) exercise a limited right of eminent domain to gain an easement from B
   (D) lease the property to A and permit a sublease to B

4. A transfer of real estate to "the ABC Church for so long as it is used for church purposes" creates

   (A) a determinable fee, a fee simple absolute, and a possible reversion interest
   (B) a determinable fee, a possible reversion interest, and a long-term lease
   (C) a determinable fee and a possible reversion interest
   (D) a determinable fee, a fee simple absolute, and a long-term lease

5. Which of the following reflects the concept of nuisance?

   (A) Title transferred under fee tail within a family
   (B) Insistence by one neighbor that another neighbor not use his property in an injurious manner
   (C) The government's condemning a property for the public good
   (D) Entering the property of another without permission from the owner

6. If a person dies intestate and without an heir to inherit the property, the property will

   (A) be foreclosed and sold at public auction
   (B) be condemned and sold under eminent domain
   (C) escheat to the state
   (D) be sold at a tax sale

7. A deed to "A for as long as B shall live and then to C in fee simple" creates a

   (A) life estate to A and a reversion to B
   (B) life estate to A and a remainder to C
   (C) reversion to B, a remainder to C, and a life estate to B
   (D) life estate to A and a life estate to B

8. The life estate created when two people are married and own property is considered a

   (A) conventional life estate
   (B) legal life estate
   (C) fee tail estate
   (D) conditional fee estate

9. A license to use another's real estate

   (A) is less than an estate in land
   (B) may be sold to another party
   (C) will be inherited by the license holder
   (D) may be sublicensed to others

10. The duration of the life estate created by A with B as the life tenant will be

    (A) a fixed period of years
    (B) for the extent of the life of A
    (C) for the extent of the life of B
    (D) a maximum of 50 years

11. The absolute power held by the government to take private property for a public purpose is

    (A) escheat            (C) fee tail
    (B) adverse possession  (D) eminent domain

12. A wishes to build a small, strip shopping center in an area that is zoned residential. To do this, A must

    (A) ask that the property be condemned and rezoned
    (B) seek a variance from the zoning board
    (C) request the planning commission to escheat the property
    (D) get permission from all adjoining residential land owners

13. When the owner of real estate erects improvements that extend onto adjoining property, there exists

    (A) a license   (C) a nuisance
    (B) a profit     (D) an encroachment

14. To protect a family from the financial irresponsibility of the head of the household, most states provide some form of relief from creditors called

    (A) credit insurance
    (B) homestead exemption
    (C) moratorium on all debt repayment
    (D) low interest rate debt consolidation loans

15. The right to enter upon the property of another and to take from it sand, gravel, or the like is called

    (A) a trespass          (C) a license
    (B) a nuisance          (D) a profit à prendre

16. An easement for light and air is given to *A* and restricts the height of a building that *B* wishes to construct on a lot. This easement is

    (A) illegal because of the burden on *B*
    (B) positive to *B*
    (C) negative to *A*
    (D) positive to *A* and negative to *B*

17. The right of whoever is the owner of lot *A* to cross lot *B*, regardless of who owns lot *B*, is

    (A) a positive easement, an easement of right of way, and appurtenant to lot *A*
    (B) an easement appurtenant to lot *B* and an easement that runs with the land
    (C) an easement appurtenant to lot *B*, an easement that runs with the land, and an easement of right of way
    (D) an easement appurtenant to lot *B*, a positive easement, an easement that runs with the land, and an easement of right of way

18. Which of the following is a key element in recognizing if an estate in land exists?

    (A) The right of exclusive possession of the property
    (B) The right to transfer title
    (C) The freedom from any government influence
    (D) The ability to inherit an interest

19. Which of the following is **not** a freehold estate?

    (A) Fee simple absolute
    (B) Determinable fee
    (C) Life estate
    (D) Leasehold estate

20. *A* establishes an easement with *B* to use a portion of *B*'s lot as access to *A*'s lot. This would be a true easement appurtenant if

    (A) the two pieces of property adjoined and one is burdened and the other is benefitted
    (B) the easement is extinguished when either property is sold
    (C) it is purely a personal right of *B*
    (D) it is created by escheat

# Chapter 6
# Ownership of Real Property

Broadly defined, ownership of real property is the holding of rights or interests in real estate. But certain clear-cut limitations exist. As we saw in Chapter 5, the exercise of the exclusive right of ownership of private property is subject to at least four reservations placed on it by the state. Thus ownership is never complete in the absolute sense of the word. Certain other reservations may be placed on property from both the public and private sectors. Real estate professionals must be aware of these reservations, since they significantly affect the use, marketability, and value of real property. In review, these reservations are:

☐ Public controls
- *Eminent domain.* The right of government to take private property for public use.
- *Property taxation.* Taxes imposed on owners of property (nonpayment of which can affect the ownership thereof).
- *Zoning and building codes.* Limits on the use of property.
- *Escheat.* The reversion of private property to the state at the death of an owner without heirs.

☐ Nonpublic (private) controls
- *Deed restriction.* Limitations placed upon the use of real property in the deed by which ownership is transferred.

- *Easement.* The right to make limited use of real property owned by another without taking actual possession of it.
- *Profit.* The right to take part of the soil or produce of land owned by someone else.
- *License.* The privilege of going upon the land of another for some specific purpose.

## REAL PROPERTY

### The Law of Fixtures

We have said that there is a technical difference between the terms *real estate* and *real property*. Now it is important to emphasize this difference. As we noted, *real estate* includes land and all things permanently attached to it. Here the *law of fixtures* comes into play. Simply stated, items of personal property that would otherwise be governed by the laws relating to personal property ownership undergo a change when they are permanently attached to land. From that point on they are governed by the laws of real estate ownership and are no longer considered personal property.

The obvious example of this is the construction of a residence upon a plot of land. Because it is intended that the various components of a house are to be permanently attached to the land, they become legally a part of the land. In short, they become what the law calls *fixtures*, in order to distinguish them from the land itself.

It is important to recognize this transformation in character because from the time of permanent attachment to the land, ownership of the land includes ownership of the fixtures. Once permanently attached, fixtures may not be removed without following the laws relating to ownership of the underlying real estate. The lumber, nails, windows, and furnace that were personal property before they became essential elements of a house have become real estate by virtue of the permanent attachment intended.

### Trade Fixtures

One exception to the law of fixtures applies to *trade fixtures* used in commercial or industrial real estate. When trade fixtures such as commercial refrigerators necessary to the business purposes for which the real estate is used are attached, they do not become part of the real estate and ownership of them does not pass with the transfer of ownership of the underlying real estate. Such trade fixtures can generally be *severed* and removed, provided their removal does no structural damage to the building.

It is important to be aware of the problem of fixtures when one is dealing with the sale of business properties. When such a sale covers the business itself, including goodwill and inventory as well as fixtures, then the distinction between fixtures, trade fixtures, and personal property is very important. Creditors may have perfected rights against either personal property or trade fixtures. The law surrounding such "bulk sales" is quite technical and complex, and qualified legal advice should be sought before such a sale is attempted.

The term *real property* is more comprehensive than the term *real estate* because it includes the legal rights which flow from the ownership of real estate or land and attachments. These ownership rights may be all-inclusive in the fee simple absolute or may be very limited in, for example, a short-term lease. In an effort to sort out the various elements of real property, or ownership of real estate, the law has come to recognize the bundle of rights concept of ownership.

## Riparian Rights

With houses and other buildings frequently being built along natural streams and rivers, it is important to be aware of the *riparian rights* of the owners of such properties, as well as certain limitations on these rights. These property owners are entitled to have other owners upstream from them refrain from using their properties in ways that might interfere with the enjoyment of the downstream owner. (One such duty is to refrain from polluting the stream or river.) In turn, the protected downstream owner has the corresponding duty to do the same for the benefit of owners still further downstream.

Natural water courses may from time to time change their course. When this occurs, one property owner's parcel may receive the benefit of additional ground (known as *accretion* of *alluvion* soil) while other owners may lose part of their property (known as *avulsion*) for the same reason.

## Bundle of Rights

We suggested earlier the concept of ownership of real estate as the ownership or control of a *bundle of rights.* Now that we have seen the wide variety of interests or rights that can exist in the same piece of real estate, the concept may be clearer. For example, when an individual holds the fee simple absolute title to a piece of real estate and there are no outstanding mortgages, life estates, leases, licenses, or any of the other lesser interests we have discussed, it should be clear that the individual owns all the possible rights our law recognizes. He or she owns the whole bundle and consequently has the power to "unbundle" this package of rights as desired (within the limitations imposed by our legal system).

The owner of the fee simple can do any or all of the following to create interests in the same property:

- ☐ Mortgage the property to secure a debt
- ☐ Grant an easement of right of way to a neighbor
- ☐ Give a license to another to hunt upon the property
- ☐ Convey a life estate in the property to A and retain the reversionary interest or convey the remainder to B
- ☐ Lease the property to a tenant for a period of years

In so doing, the owner unbundles the bundle of rights which constituted the fee simple absolute originally held. Of course, the order in which these transfers are made makes a great deal of difference, for the owner can never transfer more than he or she owns. For example, should the owner mortgage the property and then convey a life estate to A with the remainder to B, the interests of A and B would be subject to the rights of the mortgagee. By the same token, if the property were leased prior to conveyance, the rights of the tenant would not be cut off and the conveyance would be subject to the tenant's rights. This is frequently referred to as one's *sole and separate* property, particularly when the owner happens to be married but owns the property in severalty and separately from his or her spouse.

## Ownership in Severalty

Even though the term *severalty* seems to indicate some form of ownership shared by two or more persons, such is not the case. The term is a technical one meaning *sole* ownership. Therefore, when we say that A owns an estate in land *in severalty,* we mean that *A* owns the property outright, in *A's* name alone, without a co-owner.

## CO-OWNERSHIP

Joint tenancies, tenancies by the entirety, and tenancies in common are forms of the co-ownership of real estate. Co-ownership of personal property, such as joint bank accounts and the joint ownership of stocks, is familiar to most people. Co-ownership of real estate, however, is much more sophisticated in that several different forms are recognized, and the rights of the co-owners and their creditors vary depending upon the type of co-ownership involved.

Co-ownership of real estate may be chosen by purchasers to control the transfer from one owner to the other upon the death of one, to permit the pooling of resources by several individuals in order to buy real estate as a unit that no one of them could afford individually, and for a variety of other reasons. Co-ownership can also result without the co-owners intending it to happen. This frequently occurs as the result of inheriting real estate from a person who dies intestate. Also, the form of co-ownership may change by law, as it does when the tenancy by the entireties of a husband and wife is converted upon divorce to a tenancy in common.

The owner of real estate may not be fully aware of the types or consequences of co-ownership with another. However, someone active in the real estate business must be aware of the differences between the forms of co-ownership and the rights of a co-owner of real estate. It should be a broker's standard practice to urge the parties contemplating co-ownership to seek competent legal counsel in order to determine in advance the legal results of various forms of co-ownership within the local jurisdiction. There are subtle but important differences from state to state.

### The Three Forms of Co-ownership

Three common forms of co-ownership are widely recognized: (1) joint tenancy with right of survivorship, (2) tenancy in common, and (3) tenancy by the entireties.

☐ *Joint tenancy.* Because of the preference of our law for tenancy in common, joint tenancies must be specifically created. A deed must clearly express the intent to create a joint tenancy; the co-owners in a joint tenancy each own an undivided interest in the whole parcel which is *necessarily* equal; when one joint tenant dies, his or her interest terminates and passes automatically to the surviving tenant or tenants.

☐ *Tenancy in common* is preferred generally by statute. Tenants in common each own an undivided frac-

tional interest in the real estate which is *not necessarily* equal, and there is no survivorship feature.

☐ *Tenancy by the entireties* is created automatically by a conveyance to a husband and wife. (To avoid this tenancy the deed must express a contrary intent.) The marriage owns the property and neither the husband nor the wife can convey any part of it individually, nor can either one individually encumber the property; by law, the survivor succeeds to the entire title upon the death of either one.

Each of these tenancies has important characteristics.

### Joint Tenancy

The creation of a joint tenancy never happens by accident. The four unities of time, title, possession, and interest must exist *in addition to* the clearly expressed intent to create it before a joint tenancy with right of survivorship can arise. By the four unities we mean that each joint tenant must have acquired an equal *interest,* at the same *time,* with the same degree of ownership or *title,* as well as the right to *possession* of the whole property in question. Only then, along with the intent to create it, can the true joint tenancy with the right of survivorship arise. The highly technical common law rules for its creation are met in a deceptively simple fashion by a deed which simply recites that the real estate is "hereby conveyed to A, B, & C, equally, as joint tenants with right of survivorship and not as tenants in common." From such a conveyance the four unities, because they are not limited in any fashion, will necessarily follow.

The right of survivorship under a true joint tenancy is one of its most important features. Upon the death of one joint tenant, the entire interest passes to the surviving tenant(s). The deceased tenant has no estate to survive him or her, and the property does not go to his or her heirs. However, when one tenant severs the joint tenancy by sale of his or her interest to another, the buyer takes the seller's share as a tenant in common. The buyer does not purchase the right of survivorship.

### Tenancy in Common

The creation of a tenancy in common frequently happens by accident—for example, the "accident" of dying without a will and leaving several descendants. It also happens in a divorce when no definite arrangements are made in connection with real estate held by the husband and wife during the marriage as tenants by the entirety.

The tenants in such a tenancy each own an undivided interest in the real estate—an interest that can be sold, mortgaged, or left to heirs without affecting the tenancy or the rights of other tenants.

The tenant in common has an interest that can be legally terminated individually by *partition.* This is an absolute right of such a tenant, and in an appropriate action the court will divide the property physically or sell it and divide the proceeds. The partition of real estate held as tenants in common results when one or more of them desires to have the undivided interest of each tenant specifically segregated and set off in severalty. Where the property can be easily divided on a fair and equitable basis the court will order such division, and the tenants will thereafter own their shares (which are now *divided* as opposed to *undivided*) individually and free of the rights of the other tenants to possession and use of the whole property. It frequently happens, however, that an equitable physical segregation of shares is not practicable; in such cases the court will order a sale of the whole property and then order a division of the net proceeds of sale among the tenants in accordance with the fractional interests owned by each of them prior to the sale.

*Tenancy by the Entireties*

In states which recognize it, this tenancy arises from any conveyance to a man and woman who are husband and wife at the time of conveyance. It is generally not necessary that the deed express an intent to create it (as is necessary for a joint tenancy).

Tenancy by the entireties, while it has some of the characteristics of a joint tenancy, is not a joint tenancy in all respects. The most important difference is that neither the husband nor the wife may sell his or her interest, encumber it, or sever the tenancy (except, of course, by divorce), nor can either alone enter into a binding contract to sell or mortgage the property. The rules of tenancy by the entireties are so strict and unyielding that property cannot even be reached by creditors of either the husband or wife alone. Termination of a tenancy by the entireties occurs:

☐ *By sale.* Termination of tenancy by the entireties can be achieved through sale if (and only if) both husband and wife consent to the sale.
☐ *By death.* Upon the death of either the husband or the wife, the survivor succeeds to the entire interest held by the entirety. To this extent, this tenancy is similar to the joint tenancy.
☐ *By divorce.* In the event of the divorce of tenants by the entirety, the real estate is subsequently held by them as tenants in common. This frequently poses serious problems for the real estate broker or salesperson dealing with the property subsequent to the divorce because all the rules applicable to tenancy in common apply. That is, each divorced spouse owns an undivided half of the property without a legal partition proceeding. The problem is particularly acute with residential property. Figure 6-1 summarizes the three forms of co-ownership.

## Community Property

The community property concept is recognized in several southwestern and far western states. In each state the rules are statutory, and there is very little uniformity among states. The concept is best characterized as a marital "partnership" form of ownership. This aspect becomes particularly important in the event of divorce because it often results in a division of property that is not encountered under other systems of husband-and-wife ownership of real estate. Local law must be carefully investigated when property located in a community property state is to be acquired by a husband and wife.

# CONDOMINIUMS

## Creation of a Condominium

A true condominium is foreign to common law. The estate interests in land which we recognize and the varieties of co-ownership that we discussed are simply not flexible enough to permit the creation of a true condominium. Consequently it was necessary to create one by statute as a recognized form of tenancy in real estate. This was done by states passing *Horizontal Property Acts.* The basic steps are spelled out in detail in the statute, which describes the creation of a condominium as a declaration of *horizontal property regime* on the property.

The declaration of a horizontal property regime on certain real estate must be made by all owners who have an interest in the property. The declaration must include a detailed description of the land, a complete description of the proposed building, and a set of floor plans indicating the dimensions of each "apartment." In addition, the declaration must describe the common areas that may be used by all apartment owners and any and all limited common areas. It must list the percentage of common area ownership belonging to each apartment owner. This percentage of ownership is the basis upon which each owner will be entitled to vote on matters relating to the whole property. By-laws must accompany the declaration to specify the procedures for election of officers and property management.

The declaration and related plans, by-laws, and other documents must be recorded with the recorder of the county in which the land is situated. The declaration is not valid unless it has been properly recorded. That is, the steps described below must be taken to impose a different set of rules for ownership of the property. This new set of rules is called a *regime.*

The establishment of a condominium is similar in many respects to the formation of a corporation. It requires the establishment of by-laws and voting rights for each apartment owner in proportion to the percentage of his or her ownership. The establishment of a condominium is not absolutely irrevocable, and the property on which a horizontal property regime has been declared may be removed from the regime. The statute specifically provides for such removal; however, such removal requires that all apartment owners (and their creditors) consent to it. When the property is removed from the regime, the apartment owners become tenants in common and their share is determined by the percentage of the common areas and facilities of the condominium they previously owned.

## Rights of the Unit Owners

Each unit owner in the condominium has the fee simple title to his or her property and the right to exclusive ownership and possession of one unit. The owner also has an undivided interest in common areas and facilities. Since the owner has, by statute, an estate in land, the Horizontal Property Act gives that owner the right to deal with it as with any other estate. It can be sold, mortgaged, given away, or left to heirs. In addition, the act specifically provides that any form of co-ownership of land recognized by state law may be applied to the unit. Therefore unit ownership may be held in tenancy by the entireties, joint tenancy with right of survivorship, or tenancy in common.

The rights and duties of each owner concerning property operation and maintenance are specified in the by-laws of the condominium. They may be tailored as desired; however, the act specifies that certain minimums must be covered. These include provisions for the election of a board of directors; for a method of perpetuating the board, its duties, and compensation; for meetings of owners, how they are to be called, and the requirement for a quorum; for the election of a president, secretary, and treasurer; for the maintenance and repair of common areas, the method of collection of expenses paid by owners, and the hiring of maintenance personnel; for the method of adopting and amending administrative sales to govern the operation and use of the common areas and facilities; and for the percentage of votes required to amend the by-laws.

The rights of unit owners in common areas and provisions for maintenance and repair of the condominium may be complex and may change from time to time in accordance with the by-laws. Therefore a prospective buyer of such an interest should be thoroughly familiar with the by-laws before purchasing a unit.

## Rights of Creditors of the Unit Owner

Each unit is an estate characterized as real property. The owner therefore has a distinct interest that may be used as security for a loan, and an owner has the power to mortgage this interest to secure a creditor. In the event that foreclosure of a mortgage is made necessary by a default on the part of an owner, the purchaser at the foreclosure sale does not become liable for any common expenses or assessments against the interest which occurred prior to his or her acquisition. But the purchaser will be liable for expenses arising after acquisition. If the defaulting owner is in arrears in paying his or her share of expenses and assessments, this unpaid share becomes the liability of all the owners in common. The new purchaser will be liable as well, but only for his or her proportionate share.

> *Example* A, who is one of 40 unit owners, defaults on his mortgage. The mortgage is foreclosed, and the unit is sold. At the time of the sale A also owed $400 in expenses and assessments. The purchaser at the foreclosure sale does not become liable for the entire $400 but only for his or her share, which is $10. Each of the other 39 owners also becomes liable for $10.

Real estate taxes and assessments by local government units are assessed against each unit individually. That is, each unit in a condominium is taxed as though it were a separate parcel of real estate and is carried separately on the tax rolls. In the event of delinquency, the lien of taxes and assessments can be enforced only against the unit to which it applies.

Any charge or assessment levied against a unit by the owners' association becomes a lien against the unit. This lien is given priority over all other liens except those for taxes and any unpaid first mortgages on record. It is enforceable as though it were a mechanic's lien, and by the same procedure any purchaser of the unit takes title subject to any liens which exist, including the lien for unpaid charges or assessments by the owners' association. Such a purchaser is entitled to a statement from the association which specifies the amounts due at the time he or she takes title, and the purchaser cannot be held liable for an amount in excess of the amount shown on that statement. This statement must be obtained separately because it is not a matter of public record, as real estate taxes and the existence of a mortgage would be.

By accepting a conveyance, the purchaser becomes jointly liable with the sellers for all unpaid charges. As a practical matter, the new owner will have to pay them in order to remove the lien against the unit. The purchaser is of course entitled to a contribution from the seller, but it is far better to have the statement in advance of the closing and handle the matter at the closing as a deduction from the purchase price.

## Condominium Conversion

The attractions of condominium ownership have encouraged the conversion of existing buildings to condo-

# FORMS OF CO-OWNERSHIP

| | Joint Tenancy With Rights of Survivorship | Tenancy in Common | Tenancy by the Entireties |
|---|---|---|---|
| **Characteristics** | Always equal interests<br>□ each has right to possession of the whole<br>□ this is the tenancy of co-executors, co-trustees, or co-guardians<br>□ at death, interest of decedent passes to surviving tenants automatically<br>□ necessary for each co-tenant to sign deed, mortgage, contract, lease, etc., to cover entire interest in property | Not necessarily equal interests<br>□ each entitled to possession of the whole<br>□ each interest inheritable<br>□ a will may pass title to share owned by decedent<br>□ necessary for each co-tenant to sign deed, mortgage, contract, lease, etc., to cover entire interest in property | Equal interests of husband and wife<br>□ each spouse entitled to possession of the whole<br>□ divorce converts to a tenancy in common<br>□ on death, interest of decedent passes automatically to surviving tenant<br>□ necessary for each co-tenant to sign deed, mortgage, contract, lease, etc., to cover entire interest in property |
| **Creation** | Must be created on purpose<br>□ one deed<br>□ equal interests<br>□ survivorship must be specified<br>□ four unities—time, title, possession, and interest—must exist | May happen accidentally<br>□ inheritance by more than one heir<br>□ purchase in shares which may or may not be equal<br>□ failure to specify joint tenancy with rights of survivorship | Created automatically by a deed to a husband and wife<br>□ fact of marriage critical<br>□ description as husband and wife not necessary<br>□ other tenancy to avoid entireties must be specified |

| Rights and obligations | Each tenant has an undivided share in the whole property; is ratably responsible for expenses and ratably entitled to rents and profits | Each tenant has an undivided share in the whole property; is ratably responsible for expenses and ratably entitled to rents and profits | Marriage owns the whole property; is responsible for expenses and entitled to rents and profits |
|---|---|---|---|
| **Termination** | Terminated by sale of one co-tenant<br>☐ unities destroyed<br>☐ new owner is tenant in common<br>☐ partition available | Sale by one co-tenant does not terminate<br>☐ buyer succeeds to interest<br>☐ substitution is result<br>☐ partition available | One member cannot sell his interest<br>☐ right of survivorship not defeated by attempted sale<br>☐ divorce converts to tenancy in common<br>☐ partition not available |
| **Creditors Rights** | ☐ debtor's rights limited<br>☐ creditor can become tenant in common | ☐ debtor's rights survive him<br>☐ creditor can become tenant in common | ☐ creditor cannot levy against husband or wife singly<br>☐ creditor can reach for joint debts of husband and wife |

Figure 6-1—Forms of co-ownership. (From Guide to the New York Real Estate Salesperson's Course 3 E by Norman Weinberg, Paul J. Colletti, William A. Colavito, and Frank A. Melchior. Copyright © 1985 by John Wiley & Sons, Inc. Reprinted by permission of John Wiley & Sons, Inc.)

miniums. It is possible in many states today for the owner of a rental building to convert it into a condominium and *sell* rather than rent the units. Accomplishing such a conversion is generally an involved legal process. Tenants frequently complain that the process is more beneficial to the building owner than it is to them, for they are faced with the difficult decision whether to buy their units or move. So many abuses have occurred in this area that there are frequently stringent local laws that must be consulted to determine whether and how such conversions will be permitted.

### Timesharing and Interval Ownership

Closely tied to the increasing popularity of condominium ownership, particularly in resort areas, are the concepts of *timesharing* and *interval ownership* of units. Each requires local enabling legislation because the concepts are as foreign to existing legal systems as is the condominium concept.

The time-share ownership creates a tenancy in common among many owners of the same unit and includes the exclusive right of each of them to use it for specified periods. Interval ownership, on the other hand, creates sole title to the unit and therefore the exclusive right to use it for a specified period each year. Under either approach the buyer purchases the right of use for, say, "the 22nd and 23rd weeks of each year." Thus far the development of these devices has been intended for the sale of recreation time, not for creating an investment for each owner.

## COOPERATIVES

### Creation of the Cooperative

Cooperative apartment projects are difficult to define in specific terms because they can be created in a variety of ways with substantially different rights and duties created in the apartment owners. The characteristic which distinguishes a cooperative apartment building is the fact that the owner-builders usually construct the building for the purpose of occupancy by themselves rather than for investment purposes. However, even this generalization is subject to exception, for frequently portions of the building are rented out to commercial users.

While the typical vehicle used for construction and operation is usually a corporation, it is not essential to use this form of ownership. The various forms of co-ownership discussed above could be used, as could a partnership or trust. Even when a corporation is used, the obligations of the stockholders may differ drastically from those of stockholders in a business corporation. Typically the risk of the owner of a share of corporate stock is limited to the purchase price, and the stock is freely transferable and can be bought or sold readily. But

stock in a corporation formed for the purpose of building and owning a cooperative may provide for the possibility of further assessment and may have severe restrictions upon its transferability.

Regardless of the vehicle used to build, own, and operate the building, there is another step in the acquisition of an apartment in a cooperative building: a long-term lease on an apartment from the building corporation to its shareholder. The ownership of stock does not normally carry with it the right to occupy a particular apartment in the building. The right to possession of an apartment and the conditions which surround it are covered by the lease agreement (called a *proprietary lease*), which usually has terms that would otherwise appear extraordinary. The lease is generally for a relatively long term (often in order to satisfy the lender who is financing the construction of the building) and usually has severe restrictions on its assignability and on subletting. Typically the sale (or, more accurately, the assignment) of the tenant's rights under the lease is subject to the prior approval of the corporation-landlord. This degree of control protects the other owner-tenants. It requires tenants to be financially responsible because there is a definite risk that all tenants may be assessed to help pay the share of expenses left by a defaulting tenant.

### Rights of Owners

The rights of the owner of a cooperative apartment are specified in the stock certificate (which defines the extent to which the owner can affect the management of the property) and in the lease (which describes in detail the rights the owner has acquired and the obligations assumed). These rights and duties vary from one project to another. The typical terms of a lease can perhaps be best illustrated by considering the advantages and disadvantages the apartment owner will have. (The individual is of course an owner of stock and a tenant under a lease, which gives a limited estate in land; but he or she is not, legally at least, an owner of the real estate itself.)

Some of the advantages offered by the cooperative apartment are:

☐ The lease is typically for a long term because the tenant has actually paid the cost of the apartment he or she is occupying. This feature assures tenants of continuous occupancy.

☐ The long-term nature of the lease permits the tenant a wide degree of latitude with regard to modifications made to the apartment. The tenant is allowed to customize the apartment, since he or she will have use of it for an extended period.

☐ The apartment owner pays no rent as such. Instead, a monthly assessment is paid, representing costs of maintenance, real estate taxes, and debt service on the mortgage (when there is one). No landlord profit is involved. This cost may be offset by rental income earned from any commercial space included in the building.

☐ The tenancy in a cooperative apartment tends to be stable. This is dictated by the investment of each apartment owner, and it can be controlled at least to a limited extent by the tenants because they are shareholders of the corporation that owns and manages the building. The tenants, by exercising their rights as shareholders, can control the policies established with regard to the acceptability of new tenants.

In order to have the advantages outlined above, sacrifices must be made by the tenants in the cooperative project. Some of the more important are:

☐ The apartment owner does not in fact own real estate, and even though the lease creates an estate under tax law, he or she does not have an interest acceptable to lenders as loan security. Consequently the tenant must pay cash for his interest or must borrow on personal credit or by using the cooperative stock as security (and pay higher interest as a result).

☐ The degree of control exercised by the operating corporation, which benefits the tenants, creates serious problems of marketability for an individual tenant's interest. The tenant may have difficulty in finding an acceptable replacement and may not be able to sublet his or her apartment.

☐ The actual occupancy expense is unpredictable. Since it is not rent but a sharing of common maintenance costs as well as the cost of maintenance of the individual apartment, this expense varies from year to year and tends to increase from year to year.

☐ There is always the danger that some tenants will default in their obligations to maintain the building. The other tenants will then be called on to bear proportionate shares of the unpaid expense. While they may ultimately recover it upon a sale of the defaulting tenant's interest or by suing that person,

during the interim the other tenants will have this burden.

### Rights of Creditors

The typical cooperative apartment venture includes a corporation that owns and operates the building. The shareholders are the tenants not by virtue of their stock ownership but by virtue of their leases of individual apartments. As a result there can be two different kinds of creditors, creditors of the corporation itself and creditors of the individual tenants.

Creditors of the corporation have the rights they would normally have against other corporations. Typically, the major creditor of the corporation is the mortgage lender who has financed the construction of the project and holds the long-term mortgage loan on the property. The mortgage lender will be looking to the leases and their quality as underlying security for the repayment of the loan. Technically, the lender's security is a mortgage on the whole project, and for this reason individual apartment purchasers will have difficulty obtaining additional long-term financing. The rights of the lender who finances the project are the same as those of any mortgagee.

Creditors of the individual owner-tenants have a rather unusual and awkward interest to look to for security. As a result they do not normally lend money on the strength of the individual owner-tenant's interest. This fact makes financing difficult to obtain for these individuals to purchase their ownership interests. In the event that a creditor must look to the individual's interest in the cooperative apartment, he or she must take it subject to all its limitations and may even have to contribute to the continuing expense of ownership of the interest.

### Insurance

As noted earlier in connection with condominiums, the insurance requirement for co-ops is twofold because the "owner" of the apartment is, in reality, a tenant under a long-term lease of space. Therefore, insurance on the building itself must be carried by the corporation for the benefit of the tenant as a shareholder.

## REVIEW QUESTIONS

1. To convey the entire title to property owned in a true joint tenancy,

    (A) the signature of any of the joint tenants may be used
    (B) the signature of a majority of the joint tenants are needed
    (C) the signatures of all the joint tenants are required

    (D) a death must occur, and then title is transferred by inheritance

2. If the tenants in common cannot agree on a division of their shares or on a sales price, any one of them may bring a partition proceeding under which the court can

    (A) have the property escheated

    (B)  order a physical division of the property between the tenants in common

    (C)  have the property condemned and sold at public auction

    (D)  not interfere with the owners and the property division

3. Which of the following is **not** a right of a joint tenant?

    (A)  The right to possession and use of the entire property

    (B)  The right to sell the interest to a nonmember of the tenancy

    (C)  The right to leave the interest to heirs in a will

    (D)  The right of equal shares of ownership

4. Among the following limitations placed on absolute ownership of real property, which is a private control?

    (A)  The power of eminent domain, under which private property may be taken for a public use

    (B)  A zoning ordinance that restricts the property to a residential use

    (C)  A building code that restricts use of a certain insulation

    (D)  A deed restriction requiring a minimum number of square feet in a house

5. To mortgage a property where the title is held in tenancy by the entireties, the lender

    (A)  would require both the husband and the wife to sign the mortgage

    (B)  would allow either the husband or the wife to sign the mortgage

    (C)  may not issue a mortgage on a property owned this way

    (D)  would ask for an executed land contract

6. If two individuals hold title to a property as joint tenants with right of survivorship, which of the following statements is true?

    (A)  Each has the right to use the entire property

    (B)  One may have a larger ownership interest than the other

    (C)  Each may will his or her interest to an heir upon death

    (D)  Either may sell his or her interest, and the new owner will also become a joint tenant

7. Tenants in common

    (A)  always have identical shares in the property

    (B)  all have the right to the use of the whole property

    (C)  lose their interest at death to the surviving tenants

    (D)  have interests that may not be reached by creditors

8. Under the tenancy by the entireties, the interest of a deceased spouse

    (A)  goes to the surviving spouse

    (B)  passes by will to the children

    (C)  would undergo escheat

    (D)  will be divided between the spouse and the children

9. When owners of a tenancy by the entireties are divorced

    (A)  they become tenants at sufferance

    (B)  they become joint tenants with right of survivorship

    (C)  they become tenants in common

    (D)  they remain tenants by the entireties

10. When the course of a river shifts naturally and adds property through accretion, the new land belongs to the owner as a result of

    (A)  joint tenancy rights

    (B)  riparian rights

    (C)  profit à prendre

    (D)  prescriptive easements

11. The creditors of a tenant in common in a property

    (A)  may pursue the interest of that tenant and force the sale of the property to satisfy the debt

    (B)  may become a joint tenant and take title to the property through license

    (C)  can foreclose the entire property to get satisfaction

    (D)  have no recourse because of the tenancy and its structure

12. When commercial real estate is sold, what happens to the trade fixtures owned by the seller?

    (A)  They become the property of the buyer under the law of fixtures

    (B)  They are the property of the seller and may be removed

    (C)  They are held in a joint tenancy until payment is made

    (D)  They must be severed and sold under separate contract to the buyer

13. The apartment owner–tenant in a cooperative

    (A)  may not be evicted for nonpayment of assessments

    (B)  pays no rent because he or she owns shares in the cooperative

    (C)  receives a deed to the apartment

    (D)  may not sublease the apartment

14. Under the tenancy in common form of ownership, the tenant

    (A) must have an equal share with other owners
    (B) may have unequal ownership shares
    (C) may not own more than half of the property
    (D) must own over 10 percent of the property

15. Which of the following would create a tenancy in common as the necessary form of ownership?

    (A) Transferring the rights of a joint tenant to a third party
    (B) A husband and wife holding title jointly in the name of the marriage
    (C) A person owning property in his or her own name
    (D) A corporation owning a property

16. In the establishment of the condominium form of ownership, which of the following is **not** true?

    (A) Each unit owner receives a deed
    (B) The unit owners are also co-owners of the common areas
    (C) The regime must meet local and state statutes
    (D) Proprietary leases and stock are issued to unit owners

17. A wife wishes to sell the home that is owned by the entireties. Which of the following is true?

    (A) She may execute the deed and transfer title on her signature
    (B) She must also have the husband's signature to convey title
    (C) She may convey one-half of the title upon her signature
    (D) She may execute through a power of attorney

18. If the taxes on a unit in a condominium project are not paid, who is liable?

    (A) Unit owner
    (B) Developer
    (C) Homeowners' Association
    (D) Cooperative Association

19. Which of the following is not essential in the creation of a joint tenancy with the right of survivorship?

    (A) Equality of shares of ownership
    (B) Unity of time
    (C) A marriage must exist
    (D) Unity of title

20. Which of the following forms of co-ownership does not permit the creditor to levy against property of the individual co-owner?

    (A) Joint tenancy
    (B) Tenancy in common
    (C) Tenancy by the entireties
    (D) None of the above

# Chapter 7
# Transfer of Real Property

## VOCABULARY

*You will find it important to have a complete working knowledge of the following terms and concepts found in the text or the glossary.*

acceptance of deed
acknowledgment
adjudged incompetent
administrator
adverse possession
bargain and sale deed
commissioner's deeds
conveyance
corporate deeds
decedent's estate
delivery of deed
descent of real estate
description
devise of real estate

execution of deed
executor
executor's deeds
fiduciary deed
general warranty deed
gift deed
grantee
grantor
guardian's deeds
incompetent
intestate
judicial deed
legal capacity
livery of seisin

minors' deeds
partnership deeds
personal representative
probate deeds
quiet title proceedings
quitclaim deed
recital of consideration
sheriff's deeds
special warranty deed
testate
trustee's deeds
void deeds
voidable deeds
will
words of conveyance

Now that we have studied the various interests in land recognized by modern law and the various forms of ownership by which these interests may be held, it is appropriate to discuss the various methods by which ownership can be transferred. In addition we will take up the question of the quality of each ownership interest transferred and how this quality is ascertained.

One rule must be kept in mind: An owner of real estate cannot transfer more than he or she owns. If, for example, the owner of real estate has only a conditional fee, she may not transfer, by sale or otherwise, more than the conditional fee. This is true even though she may execute a deed which warrants or guarantees that she owns the fee simple absolute or that the degree of ownership is *assured* by an attorney's opinion or title insurance.

By far the most common method of transferring ownership of real estate is the deed, which is the culmination of a contract to sell the real estate. But title (ownership) of real estate may be transferred in other ways as well: inheritance, right of survivorship, mortgage or trust deed foreclosure, or even by a legal form of theft called *adverse possession*. Even when the property is *conveyed* (transferred by deed), several types of deeds are commonly used, ranging from the *general warranty deed*, which includes guarantees of ownership and the quality of the title, to the *quitclaim deed*, which transfers only what the seller has—from the fee simple absolute to nothing.

## TYPES OF DEEDS

### The General Warranty Deed

Most propositions call for execution by the seller of a general warranty deed. As the name indicates, the deed contains several warranties and covenants on the part of the seller. In many states, a so-called short form warranty deed is used. This deed includes the word "warrant," which in effect makes it a general warranty deed. In executing such a deed the *grantor* (seller) makes the following warranties:

☐ That the grantor possesses an indefeasible fee simple title to the real estate. (A fee simple title is the highest title under the law, involving full and complete rights of ownership to the exclusion of all others.)
☐ That there are no encumbrances against the real estate other than those specifically expressed in the deed.

☐ That the *grantee* (purchaser) shall have quiet enjoyment of the real estate *and* that the grantor (seller) will warrant and defend the title to the real estate against any and all claims, from the beginning of time to the execution of the deed of conveyance.

Where there is an unbroken chain of general warranty deeds, each grantor in the chain may be liable to all subsequent grantees for any claim arising prior to the date of conveyance by that particular grantor. When the chain is broken by the execution of a deed other than a general warranty, subsequent grantees may not look for redress to any grantors who may have executed warranty deeds prior to the date when the chain was broken.

The sample deed shown in Figure 7-1 shows how deceptively simple such an important document may in fact be.

### The Special Warranty Deed

The special warranty deed is a deed of limited warranty, and the warranty contained therein is limited to any claim arising out of the period of ownership of the grantor executing the deed. Thus an owner who held title from January 1 to October 31 could execute a special warranty deed that would warrant only against any claims arising out of that particular period. The new owner's warranty would not extend back to the beginning of time.

Trustees will normally be willing to execute a special warranty deed for property purchased from a trust. They are unwilling to warrant the quality of the title which they received from the creator of the trust because they usually receive it in the form of a gift and pay nothing that would serve as consideration to enforce any warranties made by the creator of the trust. Therefore, they are unable to enforce any warranties against earlier owners. Unless a special warranty deed is contracted for, the trustee will prefer to use a *trustee's deed,* which contains no warranties at all. Such deeds are similar to *probate deeds,* discussed in detail later in this chapter.

### The Quitclaim Deed

The quitclaim deed is a deed of release. It conveys without warranty whatever right, claim, title, or interest the grantor may have in the real estate conveyed. If the grantor has a fee simple title, the quitclaim deed will convey the same. If the grantor has no title, nothing will be conveyed by the quitclaim deed.

Quitclaim deeds are generally used to convey lesser interests in real estate, such as life estates or minor interests, and are widely used to correct prior conveyances that have been improperly executed.

### Bargain and Sale Deeds

Deeds of bargain and sale are used occasionally. Like warranty deeds, they purport to transfer title; like the quitclaim deed, they make no warranties as to the *quality* of that title.

### Judicial Deeds

Many titles to real estate are conveyed by judicial deeds. As the name implies, judicial deeds are deeds executed pursuant to a court order. Examples of such conveyances are deeds of executors and administrators, guardians, and trustees; *sheriff's* deeds executed by virtue of foreclosure proceedings; and *commissioner's* deeds executed in partition proceedings. Such deeds, assuming that the judicial proceedings in the particular case have been legally pursued, are effectual to convey good title to real estate—*but without warranties.*

### Gift Deeds

Where a gift of real estate is made by deed, the deed form may be either a general warranty deed or a quitclaim deed. Regardless of the form used, any warranties that may be included are unenforceable because, by definition, no payment was made, and without payment they cannot be sued upon. When one receives a gift, one accepts it with whatever defects it may contain.

## BASIC REQUIREMENTS OF A VALID DEED

When there is a transfer of title to real estate by *conveyance* (by a deed from the seller to the buyer), certain minimum legal requirements must be met to make the transfer of ownership effective.

### The Grantor Must Have Legal Capacity

The grantor (seller or owner) must have the legal power to make a deed or a transfer of ownership. The matter of legal capacity varies with the nature of the grantor. That is, the grantor may be an individual, a partnership, a trust, a corporation, a unit of government, or any other legally recognizable entity. The requirements of legal capacity are different for each one.

#### Individuals as Grantors

*Individuals* must be competent in terms of age and mental capacity. Generally, an individual is a minor until he or she reaches the age of 18. If one is under the age of majority, his or her deed will be *voidable* and may be set aside when the age of majority is reached. The same is true for those who are *in fact* mentally incompetent to make a deed. In both cases, there is a presumption of legal capacity that may be set aside by proof of incapacity. Nevertheless, such deeds are not *void* (meaningless) at the outset; there must be proof of incompetency, and affirmative action must be taken to set such deeds aside. There is therefore an element of risk in dealing with young persons and those who appear to be unstable at the time of the transaction.

## GENERAL WARRANTY DEED

This indenture witnesses that: John S. Brown and Mary A. Brown, husband and wife, of Any County, State of XYZ, hereby convey and generally warrant to Robert J. Smith, an adult male, of Some County, State of XYZ, for and in consideration of the sum of Ten Dollars ($10.00) and other good and valuable consideration, the receipt of which is hereby acknowledged, the following described real estate located in Any County, State of XYZ:

    Lot numbered Fifty-one (51) in Eden Gardens, Mooresville, XYZ, as per plat thereof recorded in Plat Book 61, page 21, in the Office of the Recorder of Any County, XYZ.

Subject to: all real estate taxes becoming due and payable after the date hereof; and also subject to all restrictions, conditions, easements, rights of way and covenants of record.

Dated this 15th day of February, 198X

_____
John S. Brown                <u>seal</u>

_____
Mary A. Brown              <u>seal</u>


State of XYZ  ⎱
            ⎰ SS:
Any County  ⎱

Before me, the undersigned, a Notary Public in and for said County and State, this 15th day of February, 198X, personally appeared John S. Brown and Mary A. Brown, husband and wife, and acknowledged the execution of the foregoing deed. In witness whereof I have hereunto subscribed my name and affixed my official seal. My commission expires November 19, 198X.


_____
James Barner, Notary Public

My county of residence is: Any County
This instrument prepared by: John Doe, attorney at law

*Figure 7-1—A sample general warranty deed.*

A different rule applies when the grantor has been *adjudged incompetent* by a local court. In such cases the finding of incompetency is a matter of record, and all persons are bound to know what the public records reveal even though they do not in fact have this knowledge. Once there has been a formal adjudication finding that an individual is incompetent and a guardian (or conservator) is appointed by the court, deeds signed by the individual become void and no transfer of title can result. Only the legally appointed guardian can deal with the property of the incompetent. Sales from the guardianship usually utilize a guardian's deed, which normally includes no warranties whatever. The fact that the deed has been approved by the court does nothing to improve the quality of the title. The guardian cannot convey better title than the ward had. Such deeds should only be accepted when there is some other assurance of title, as discussed in Chapter 8.

### Partnerships as Grantors

Under the Uniform Partnership Act (UPA), *partnerships* may hold title to real estate in the partnership name, and any *general partner* may bind the partnership by a deed of real estate owned by it. Proof of the fact that the person executing the deed is a general partner should be shown. An attorney's opinion should always be sought before accepting the validity of a partner's deed.

### Corporations as Grantors

*Corporations* are legal entities solely by virtue of statutes that permit their formation and permit them to conduct business—including the ownership and sale of real estate. A corporation may conduct business only through its authorized officers, and evidence of the authority of particular officers to convey the corporation's real estate is of crucial importance in determining the validity of the deed. This is especially true when the deed transfers real estate which represents all or substantially all of the assets of the corporation. In such cases it may be necessary to show not only that the board of directors has authorized the sale but also that a majority (or more in some states) of the shareholders have approved the transaction. There is obviously no substitute for legal counsel in such situations.

### Government Units as Grantors

*Government units* have no inherent power or capacity to sell real estate, and they must therefore follow very strictly the statutes and necessary public proceedings to permit the sale of public property. In the absence of statutory authority, exercised in accordance with very technical requirements, the deeds of government units may be absolutely void. Again, legal counsel should pass upon the question of the validity of such deeds.

### Fiduciaries as Grantors

*Fiduciaries* (trustees, administrators, executors, agents, guardians) have severe limitations upon their authority to convey title to real estate. These limitations may be imposed by the agreements under which they operate or the courts who appoint them. A safe rule to follow is that whenever *anyone* purports to convey title to real estate which the records show he or she does not own, strict proof of the authority to sell it must be produced. That is, there must be positive evidence of this authority in the form of either a written and recorded agreement or a court order; there must be *actual* (as opposed to apparent) authority; and there must be recorded (or recordable) evidence of such authority. The limitations on the authority of fiduciaries can hardly be overemphasized.

## The Grantee(s) Must Be Named with Reasonable Certainty

More than just good business practice dictates that the grantees (buyers) be named with accuracy. It is also important to the effectiveness of the recording systems by which the validity of titles to land is determined. The accuracy of the names of the grantees is important to the indexing systems used to make public records accessible and useful.

It is also important that the grantee(s) be further described in terms of the form of ownership that will result. For example, in most states it is essential to create clearly a joint tenancy with right of survivorship. Careful attorneys do not rely upon shortcuts in this area and do not use such phrases as "to John and Mary Jones, jointly." Instead the deed should read, "to John Jones and Mary Jones, as joint tenants with right of survivorship and not as tenants in common." If the creation of a tenancy in common were desired, that should be so stated and the fractional share of each of the grantees indicated: "to John Jones and Mary Jones as tenants in common in the following shares: as to an undivided one-third to John Jones and as to the remaining two-thirds to Mary Jones."

Care must be exercised in this portion of the deed whenever something less than the entire fee simple absolute is being transferred. The presumption is that the entire fee is being conveyed (or whatever other interest is being transferred) unless the deed clearly states a contrary intent. If the owner of the fee simple wishes, for example, to reserve a life estate to himself, the deed must clearly say so: ". . . convey and warrant all of my right, title, and interest in and to (the property described) reserving, however, to myself a life estate in said property."

In some states a deed to two people who are husband and wife automatically creates a tenancy by the entireties even though the parties are not identified as husband and wife. Once again a careful attorney will describe the relationship and may even go further and specify the tenancy intended. Such a deed might read, "to John Jones and Mary Jones, husband and wife, as tenants by the entirety."

In the naming of the grantees, one should remember that today's buyers may be tomorrow's sellers. The certainty of their identity and their interests in the real estate will be important in determining the quality of their title and the effectiveness of their deed to pass good title.

### There Must Be Words of Conveyance

Without some clearly expressed intent to transfer the ownership of real estate, a deed may be ineffective in accomplishing its purpose or may at best create ambiguity as to just what its purpose is. This portion of the deed should clearly state any limitations or reservations that are intended. The standard form deeds in use today utilize terms such as "convey and warrant" in general warranty deeds, "convey and specially warrant" when a deed of limited warranty is intended, or "release and quit-claim" when no warranties of any kind are intended.

### There Must Be a Recital of Consideration

The matter of consideration is a technical requirement. Most deeds do not show the full purchase price paid so that the information will remain private and not be made a matter of public record. To meet the requirement of consideration, the deed must include a statement to the effect that there was paid "$10 and other valuable consideration, the receipt of which is hereby acknowledged by the seller." One might argue that the signing and delivery of a deed to valuable real estate would not be done by the grantor without payment and that therefore it is unnecessary to include such a statement. Nevertheless its inclusion is crucial as evidence that there was payment in order that suit might be brought against the seller upon any warranties made in the deed. It is far easier to introduce the deed as evidence of payment than to attempt to prove payment by other evidence.

The use of a nominal sum in the recital of consideration satisfies the technical requirement of contract law that there be *some* consideration. It is not necessary to the validity of the deed that the amount expressed be the fair value of the property.

### The Real Estate Being Conveyed Must Be Accurately Described

To identify correctly the property being conveyed, it must be described with a reasonable degree of accuracy. Great emphasis is placed on precision in the preparation of legal descriptions, and this is usually the job of an expert, the surveyor. It is beyond the scope of this book to provide detailed coverage of this highly technical area; however, certain fundamentals are discussed below.

Almost all of the United States has been subjected to a survey by the federal government, the so-called rectangular survey. Even though there are various ways to describe real estate, in almost all cases they depend upon the rectangular survey to establish a starting point, some specific point on the surface of the earth. Additional material on this subject can be found in Chapter 8.

### The Deed Must Be Executed by the Grantor(s)

To transfer title effectively by a deed, it must be *executed by the grantor*. That is, it must be signed by the grantor with the intent that ownership of some interest in land be transferred to the grantee. In the event that there are co-owners of the property and the agreement is to transfer the interests of each of them, all the owners must sign the deed. Married couples generally hold title to their residential property in some form of joint tenancy with right of survivorship. In the case of such property, both husband and wife must sign the deed so that their entire interest will be effectively conveyed. Even where it is apparent that only one of them owns the property, in many states it is still necessary that both husband and wife sign the deed to cut off the rights of dower and curtesy or their statutory substitutes. Even in states that have in recent years eliminated the necessity of the other spouse signing deeds to property owned solely by one spouse, it is still required by careful practitioners. The rule in practice should be to require the signatures of both husband and wife on any deed to property owned by only one of them (unless legal counsel is sought and a contrary opinion obtained).

The execution of a deed to property owned by a partnership can be accomplished by any general partner's signature on the deed. It is of course necessary to verify that the signer is a general partner, and an attorney's approval of the effectiveness of the execution should be obtained. Much the same is true for the execution of deeds by a corporation, and a resolution of the board of directors authorizing certain officers to execute deeds should be obtained. Again, an attorney's opinion should be sought.

### The Deed Should Be Acknowledged

We say that a deed *should* be acknowledged because in most states acknowledgment of the deed is not required to make the deed effective between the parties. As a practical matter, however, without acknowledgment the deed cannot be recorded so as to provide notice of the transfer to the general public. The acknowledgment of a deed is more than a mere witnessing of the signatures; only certain publicly appointed officials (usually notaries public) can take acknowledgments. *The acknowledgment of a deed is the appearance before the notary public by the signers and their declaration to the notary that their signatures were free and willful.* The notary then countersigns and seals the deed after stating upon it the above facts. Typically, this statement reads as follows:

State of _____

County of _____

_____, 19_____

   Then and there personally appeared John Jones and Mary Jones, signers and sealers of the foregoing instrument and they acknowledge the same to be their free act and deed before me.
                 (Notary Public) _____

   When the deed has been properly acknowledged, it is eligible for recording in the public records, which constitutes a notice of its contents to all persons subsequently dealing with the property conveyed.

## The Deed Must Be Delivered to and Accepted by the Grantee(s)

   The final steps necessary to make the deed legally operate to transfer the title to real estate are its delivery by the grantor to the grantee and the grantee's acceptance of it. In the majority of cases these steps are easily recognized and are quite straightforward. They are accomplished by a simple exchange of the deed for payment of the purchase price. Acceptance of the deed by the grantee is presumed in all but the most unusual circumstances.

   It is important, however, to recognize that delivery of the deed is crucial to its legal effectiveness and that occasionally it is not clear and in still other instances it is legally ineffective.

☐ The intent of the grantor to transfer title by delivery of the deed is a crucial element. Therefore, when the deed is handed to the grantee (or his or her lawyer, broker, or other agent) for the purpose of inspecting it for adequacy and accuracy, this does not constitute delivery even though the grantee or his or her agent has physical possession of the deed.

☐ If the deed is placed in escrow, delivered to an independent third party, to be held until all the conditions of the sale are met (the most significant condition being payment), there again has been no legally effective delivery because the escrowee is not the agent of either party. Even though the grantor has parted with the deed, there has been no delivery because of the missing element of intent.

☐ Yet delivery and acceptance of the deed can be accomplished by delivery to a third party who is the agent of the grantee. Frequently this is the grantee's attorney, his lender, or even his broker.

☐ Ill-advised individuals have been known to execute deeds to real estate to various relatives and to place them in a safe deposit box so that they will be found after the death of the grantor. This is usually done as a will substitute in order to avoid the expense of probate. It is almost universally found that these deeds are ineffective for lack of delivery because they never left the control of the grantors—and of course the grantees could hardly accept them if they did not even know of their existence.

   As a general rule, the fact that a deed has been executed, acknowledged, and recorded (as discussed below) creates a *presumption* that the deed has been delivered and accepted. This presumption may be rebutted upon proof that neither delivery nor acceptance was actually intended by the party so claiming; however, legal action would be required to set the record straight.

## TRANSFER BY DESCENT OR DEVISE

   While real estate is most commonly transferred between owners by a deed that is the result of a negotiated contract of sale, it frequently happens that the title to real estate is transferred as a result of the owner's death. It should be recalled that certain interests in land do not survive the owner at death (for example, the life estate measured by his or her life, the license which is personal to the holder, and, as we shall see in Chapter 9, the tenant in a tenancy at will). There is no transfer of these interests; they expire when the owner expires.

   We should also recall that certain interests by law pass to survivors: joint tenancy with right of survivorship and tenancy by the entireties. In each of these two categories of interest in land, expiration of the interest or its transfer are automatic and the question of inheritance is not involved.

   Generally speaking, all other interests in land (along with some obligations attached to ownership) descend or survive the death of the owner. For example, if the decedent owned the entire fee simple absolute, this interest is theoretically perpetual and survives the death of the owner.

   In this section we review the general rules which apply to interests that are inheritable, what happens to them at the owner's death, and how they may be sold during the administration of the estate.

### Alternative Dispositions of Real Property at Death

   When an individual dies, some disposition of his or her property must be made in accordance with prevailing state law, a valid will, or both. This is done through an individual (or a bank) who becomes an officer of the court for this purpose. This officer is usually referred to as the *personal representative* of the decedent. This generic term is used to identify either an *executor* under a valid will or an *administrator* appointed by the court when there is no valid will.

There are two basic methods by which title to real estate may be transferred at the death of the owner. If the owner makes a valid will which disposes of the real estate, it will go to the *devisees* (those named as recipients by the will); if there is no will, the property will *descend* to the legal heirs in accordance with state laws of descent and distribution. It is frequently said that, when an individual makes no will, the state makes one for him. Generally speaking, these statutes result in the inheritance of real estate by immediate family members (spouse, children, grandchildren) if they survive and, if they do not survive, by other close family members (parents, brothers, sisters) or, failing their survival, by more remote relatives.

In the event that a valid will is executed, it must be proven to be valid (admitted to probate). The right to make a will is a privilege that is subject to limitations imposed by state law that create some restrictions on the individual's freedom to leave his property to whomever he chooses. As a general rule, these limitations favor the surviving spouse and children to whom the decedent had a legal obligation of support. As might be expected, the decedent's creditors (including death tax collectors) occupy a favored position under the maxim, *A person must be just before he or she may be generous.*

With this in mind, let us outline some of the limitations that must be kept in mind in dealing with a decedent's real estate.

## Limitations on Title Transfer

In general, the title to any interest in land vests immediately in *heirs* or *devisees* under the will. At the moment of death, the decedent's interest passes immediately to the legal heirs if the person dies *intestate* (without a will) or to the named devisees if he or she dies *testate* (with a valid will). While this is legally and theoretically true, such transfer of title is not final; it is subject to limitations.

The limitations on the title passed to heirs or devisees are:

☐ The transfer is subject to the right of the personal representative (executor or administrator) to possession of the real estate. The personal representative not only has the right to possession of the decedent's real estate but frequently has a positive duty to take possession of the property for the benefit of the estate. This possession may be constructive rather than actual when, for example, there is a tenant in possession under a valid lease. In such cases the personal representative of the estate is entitled to receive the rents. But the rights of the personal representative

are not personal rights, and they may be exercised only for the benefit of the estate of the decedent.

☐ The title that passes to the heirs or devisees is subject to any and all valid claims against the decedent. The primary purpose of estate administration is to protect creditors. That is, an individual's debts must be paid before gifts can be made after death to heirs or beneficiaries named in his or her will. The benefits which may flow to the heirs or devisees are therefore subject to the possibility that creditor's claims may compel sale of the property and application of the proceeds to payment of the decedent's debts.

☐ The title of the heirs or devisees is subject to the surviving spouse's rights to take his or her statutory share of the estate. The surviving spouse is generally entitled by statute to a specified share of the deceased spouse's estate. This share depends on who else survives the decedent, but it is usually at least one-third of the net estate. The surviving spouse is normally entitled to this share absolutely as a matter of right, and this right may not be defeated by a will that makes a different disposition of the estate.

☐ The title of the heirs or devisees is subject to all liens and encumbrances on the real estate that exist at the time of the decedent's death. Thus any mortgages or other liens pass with the property. The decedent's will may specify that debts are to be paid from some other source, such as other assets of the estate; but if the will makes no such provision, title passes subject to all liens and encumbrances.

☐ When real estate is devised by will to named devisees, there is always the possibility that the will may be challenged. The validity of a will may be questioned for several reasons. A claim may be made that the decedent was mentally incompetent to make a will at the time it was executed; that he or she was subjected to fraud, duress, or undue influence at the time of its execution; or that the will was not executed and witnessed according to law. If any of these charges can be sustained, the will will be set aside and thus will be ineffective for the purpose of passing title to the named devisees. Finding a will invalid normally results in an intestate situation in which only the legal heirs can take any interest in the decedent's real estate and other property. Such a challenge is more likely when the decedent makes a property disposition to persons outside the immediate family.

☐ The title of the heirs and devisees is subject to a death tax, imposed upon the decedent's estate as a result of the transfer of ownership. This estate and inheritance tax lien attaches to all property, including real estate, owned by the decedent at the time of death. The death tax lien represents a serious defect in the title of the heirs or devisees until the tax liability is determined and discharged by the estate's personal representative.

The foregoing limitations make it apparent that, during administration of the estate, the title of the heirs and devisees is tenuous at best and requires further action to make it saleable. This action is the final decree of distribution by which the court having jurisdiction over the estate enters its judgment that all debts, taxes, and expenses of administration have been paid, that the claims of all parties have been settled or the time for filing them has passed without action being taken to perfect them, and that title is confirmed in the heirs or devisees.

The quality of the decedent's title at the time of death generally is unaffected by estate administration. Certainly it is not improved by virtue of his or her death. The title that descends to the heirs or devisees is only as good as the title the decedent had during his or her lifetime. Since the passage of title through a decedent's estate is essentially a gift, no guarantee or warranty is made by the personal representative. In the absence of directions to do so in the will, liens or encumbrances on the property are not required to be cleared by the personal representative.

In the event that they are not cleared during administration of the estate, the heirs or devisees take the real estate subject to them. However, typical probate codes allow the personal representative to begin a quiet title action (see below) in order to clear defects or adverse claims to the title. It may be necessary to do this if the property is to be sold during administration, since a buyer is entitled to insist upon a merchantable title. Heirs and devisees are not entitled to a merchantable title because they are not parting with consideration; they are receiving a gift, and they take it with whatever defects exist.

## Purchases from Decedent's Estate

The general public often assumes that the personal representative of a decedent's estate has complete authority to sell any of the decedent's assets, including real estate. Yet this is frequently not the case. With regard to real estate, the personal representative must find authority from one of two sources: the will itself or the court having jurisdiction over the estate. Each of these sources can be looked to when there is a valid will, but when the decedent dies without a will, only the court can be looked to for the necessary authority.

When there is clear authority in the will, the legally appointed executor may proceed to sell the decedent's real estate without a court order so long as he or she stays within any limitations specified in the will. When the will does give the executor clear authority (or even directions) to sell real estate, he or she can either rely on that authority or seek a court order to sell the property.

Many lawyers do not rely on an authority given in the will when they represent the executor. It is far safer for the executor to obtain a court order authorizing the sale of the real estate, in order to be protected by that court order from later claims that he or she failed to follow the terms in the will.

When there is no will, the personal representative (the administrator) has no alternative but to seek a court order to authorize sale of the property. The administrator cannot merely desire to sell the property. Typical probate codes spell out certain conditions under which the sale of real estate may be approved and ordered by the court. These include: (1) to pay debts, taxes, and expenses of administration; (2) to make an equitable and fair distribution of the estate; and (3) for convenience in making ultimate distribution. Unless the administrator can show that one or more of these reasons exist for sale of the decedent's real estate, the court will not authorize the sale.

When court authority is sought for the real estate sale, either by the administrator of an intestate estate or by the executor under a will who either has no authority to sell or elects not to rely upon it, the procedure that must be followed is cumbersome and usually time consuming.

There are three essential steps in the procedure:

☐ Before authority is sought to sell it, the property must be appraised and inventoried. The appraisal is incorporated into a formal inventory that is signed by the appraisers and the personal representative and filed with the court.

☐ When the personal representative's petition for authority to sell is filed, the court sets a hearing date on which to decide the question and orders that notice be given to interested parties, allowing them the opportunity to appear and contest the matter. In the event that all interested parties agree to the sale proposed by the personal representative, they may waive this notice and the matter can be heard immediately. The petition spells out the proposed basis for the property sale. The significance of the appraisal and inventory becomes apparent at this point. If the sale is to be a private sale—the usual negotiated transaction—the sales price may not be less than the appraised value. However, if the sale is to be a public sale—formally advertised and in strict accordance with the statutes—the sales price must be the minimum established by law.

☐ Once the personal representative has the necessary authority from the court, he or she may enter into a contract to sell, subject to the court's approval, within the limits of his or her authority. The personal representative may list the property with a broker or attempt to sell it personally. As an officer of the court, the personal representative need not be a licensed broker or salesperson. When a sale has been negotiated, he or she must file with the court a *report of sale,* along with the proposed deed. The report of sale states that the personal representative has successfully negotiated a sale in accordance with the court's order and requests an order approving the report of sale and the deed itself. The report of sale also indicates the amount of commission to be paid to the broker who sold the property (if one is employed) so that the court's order will clearly authorize payment of this commission. When the transaction is approved, the court will enter an order approving the report of sale and the proposed deed. At this point the personal representative is in a position to complete the closing of the sale. It is not unusual for a careful personal representative to wait until the closing has been partially completed and "the money is on the table" before obtaining the order approving the report of sale and the deed.

The foregoing procedure can be time consuming, particularly if it is not possible to obtain waivers of notice of the hearing on the petition for authority to sell. More important, if the statutes are strictly followed, there can be several undesirable consequences:

☐ The appraisal and inventory are a matter of public record and, in some communities, are published in local newspapers as a news item. The availability of this information tends to establish the best price at which the property can be sold and makes it difficult for the personal representative to obtain a more favorable price.

☐ Until the court enters its order authorizing the sale, the personal representative does not have final authority even to enter into an unconditional listing contract. Since this order is entered after the appraisal and inventory, the broker is also hampered in his or her efforts to obtain a favorable sale because of the public nature of the court's records.

One solution to the above problems requires the personal representative to obtain the court's approval to delay the filing of the appraisal and inventory. At the same time, the listing broker must be willing to work under a listing contract, recognizing the fact that court approval of any sale will ultimately be required before he or she can earn a commission. When these steps can be accomplished prior to any sales effort, the listing price can be established on a more businesslike basis rather than be dictated by the appraisal. If, in addition, waivers of notice of the hearing on the petition to sell can be obtained, it is not impossible to accomplish all the above steps requiring court action in a very short time. This preserves the confidential nature of the price-appraisal relationship

and makes it possible to obtain the most favorable price for the real estate.

## Probate Deeds

The term *probate deeds* is frequently used to describe all deeds that may be used for the sale of property from a decedent's estate by the estate's personal representative, whether executor or administrator.

There are certain important limitations on sales of real property by a personal representative. It is important for persons in real estate to recognize these limitations, whether they represent the seller (the estate) or more important, the buyer.

The form of deed given by the personal representative of an estate is usually specified by local probate law. The typical words in such a deed are:

*AB,* as Executor of the last will of *CD* (or *AB* as Administrator of the estate of *CD*), by order of the _____ Court of _____ County, State of _____, entered in order book _____, on the records of said court, on page _____, for and in consideration of the sum of $_____, conveys to *EF* the following real estate, to wit: (insert legal description)

The important point to be noted about this form of deed is that it contains no warranties. It is in effect a quitclaim deed. Because the administration of a decedent's estate is not designed to improve the quality of title to the property, the lack of warranties is especially significant. In all purchases from estates it is important that the quality of the title be carefully examined (or insured) and that the technical steps required to sell property from an estate be complied with.

Competent legal counsel should be consulted in connection with purchases of real estate from a decedent's estate. Even though an attorney may represent the personal representative of the estate, the buyer should not expect the estate's attorney to represent his or her own interests. To do so would create a conflict of interest for the estate's attorney. The estate's attorney is obligated to represent the estate to the best of his or her ability and cannot be expected to represent the buyer in the same transaction.

The buyer's attorney inspects the necessary papers leading up to the sale to verify that they are in proper order and that the personal representative does in fact have the necessary authority to sell the property. In view of the lack of warranties in the personal representative's deed (and the fact that they might be meaningless even if they were made), his or her authority should be clearly ascertained before giving value for the deed.

It is usually unnecessary to record all the documents

(other than the deed) because the estate proceedings are a permanent record and the final decree shows that the estate was ultimately settled without objections. Where the real estate is located in a county other than the county of administration, however, the personal representative must record the final decree in the county in which the real estate is located.

## TRANSFER OF OWNERSHIP BY ADVERSE POSSESION

The doctrine of adverse possession is an antique of the Middle Ages that continues to be useful even today. Prior to the advent of recording systems, it was essential that the owner of real estate carefully preserve each and every document that evidenced claim of ownership to land. Inevitably, an important document would be lost, such as the deed to the individual who was in possession and claimed ownership. When the time came for that owner to sell the real estate, he or she would be unable to prove ownership because the deed was lost. To resolve this problem, the common law developed the doctrine of *adverse possession*.

In its simplest terms the doctrine provided that, if the purported owner had been in complete and absolute possession of the property, with an obvious claim of ownership, for a lengthy period of time, and if he or she could prove these essential points, the court would conclude that he or she was in fact the owner even though he or she lacked the necessary documentary evidence to prove it.

In its earliest days, this doctrine—which was much more technical than the foregoing statement suggests—resulted from the necessity for establishing legal ownership to real estate without the possibility of litigation long after the actual facts could be shown by testimony or other evidence. A typical rule was that if the owner had been in actual possession that was open and notorious (obvious), exclusive (unshared), continuous, and uninterrupted, and with the claim of right of ownership for 21 years, then this individual became the owner of the legal title. When there was no recording system, communications were slow at best, and surveys were poor or unavailable, the practicality of this method of acquiring title and its need were obvious. The doctrine continued to be important in the early years of the development of the United States.

### Early Use in the United States

When the United States was first settled, the doctrine of adverse possession was important in establishing titles to real estate, even though the theory of the lost deed became irrelevant because of the development of recording systems under which the deed, even though

lost, was not needed to prove legal title. The doctrine remained viable and important because large tracts of land might be owned by an individual who did not even know the boundaries of his property. Frequently, through mistake or otherwise, one individual might take possession of another's property, improve it or otherwise utilize it, openly and notoriously, for many years without objection by the true legal owner. Thus the doctrine of adverse possession found a new use: to settle disputes regarding legal title to such land. Title could be established by adverse possession on the theory that, if the true owner did not oppose the claim for a lengthy period, he or she lost the right to assert claim of ownership.

The typical length of the period of possession required to maintain a claim of ownership by adverse possession was 21 years. The justification for this "legalized stealing" of another's real estate was (and still is) that, if the true owner chose to take no action for such a long period of time, the law would not help him or her to regain lost ownership. This is consistent with the basic policy expressed in statutes of limitations that apply in many areas other than real estate: There must be an end to the possibility of litigation. There is a practical reason for this rule; the matter of preserving evidence for a lengthy period, the lack of memory of witnesses (or even the lack of surviving witnesses at all), and the accuracy of old evidence all make any legal determination after a long period highly questionable.

The doctrine is still recognized and is useful in establishing the ownership of real estate, though the length of time has been modified in many jurisdictions. Ten years is now more common than 21 years, in view of the increased efficiency of communications and the general shortening of statutes of limitations. Whenever the doctrine is relied on to establish title to real estate, legal counsel should be consulted.

### Modern Use in the United States

Today the lack of vacant land, the ease of communications, and the fact that property values have increased to the extent that owners are less likely to ignore their interests in real estate have resulted in far less reliance on the doctrine of adverse possession to establish the right of ownership of real estate. Nevertheless, adverse possession remains an important part of real estate law in the correction of boundaries between adjoining properties. It is frequently relied on by surveyors and title insurance examiners to resolve questions of ownership when long-standing buildings in fact encroach upon neighboring properties.

When, for example, an existing building has been encroaching upon adjoining property for many years, the title to this property may be made marketable by relying on the doctrine of adverse possession.

One cautionary note is necessary here: While the doctrine applies against individual owners, it does not apply against governmental units. If a private building encroaches upon public property, such as an alley or street, the owner of the private property cannot acquire title to the publicly owned property no matter how long the encroachment may have existed without objection. Such a problem, when it occurs, must be resolved under local law, usually by obtaining a license to encroach, which may be a very lengthy and expensive process. Usually these problems result from the inaccuracy of early surveying techniques.

## Quiet Title Proceedings

Whenever title to real estate depends on a claim by virtue of adverse possession, it may be necessary to obtain a judicial determination that acquisition of title has in fact occurred. The common name of such a proceeding is a *quiet title* suit. The individual who claims title brings legal action in a local court against anyone and everyone who may have or may ever have had any claim against the property, no matter how remote, to prove the validity of his or her title. Such suits typically name everyone even remotely connected with the property and "the rest of the world" as defendants. A lengthy public notice of the hearing is generally required, and the suit is a legal determination that the claimant (the plaintiff) in the proceeding is in fact the true owner of the property. Even though such a suit is expensive and time-consuming, it may be the only way in which good legal title may be established so that the property can be sold.

## Exception under the Torrens System

Under title registration systems (to be discussed later), the fact of registration, and the judicial character of the proceedings by which title is established and registered, the doctrine of adverse possession does not operate to transfer ownership. In states utilizing title registration systems, the inapplicability of the doctrine is part of the statutory law. When someone other than the registered owner is in possession at the time of sale, this fact may or may not be constructive notice of a claim to the title, depending on local law. The stranger in possession may be there under an unregistered deed or an unrecorded land contract (contract for a deed).

In this chapter we covered the general rules with respect to the transfer of ownership. It must be emphasized that these rules are *general* and that they vary from state to state. Therefore a thorough review and understanding of local law are necessary for all persons engaged in the real estate business. Whenever there is any doubt, the services of an attorney should be utilized.

# REVIEW QUESTIONS

1. The most protection afforded a purchaser in terms of warranty of title is that provided by a

   (A) general warranty deed
   (B) special warranty deed
   (C) quitclaim deed
   (D) executor's deed

2. A deed that is voidable because a grantor was a minor

   (A) may not be recorded
   (B) may be set aside later by legal proceedings
   (C) did not ever transfer title to the grantee
   (D) may only be valid upon the death of the grantor

3. The deed that creates a joint tenancy with the right of survivorship requires all of the following EXCEPT

   (A) the naming of two or more grantees
   (B) no statement of the survivorship
   (C) conveyance of equal interests
   (D) a recital of consideration

4. A valid general warranty deed need **not** contain

   (A) a recital of consideration
   (B) an execution by the grantor
   (C) a written statement of the warranties
   (D) a granting clause

5. Before the executor of an estate can sell a property in the estate, all of the following are necessary EXCEPT

   (A) an appraisal and inventorying of the property
   (B) petition for authority to sell is filed
   (C) enter into a contract to sell subject to court approval
   (D) title must be deeded to the executor first, and then sold

6. A deed that is not acknowledged

   (A) may be recorded in any county
   (B) may not be recorded
   (C) will not be in writing but will be valid
   (D) is not valid and will not convey title

7. When a deed does not specify the estate that is being conveyed, it is presumed to transfer

    (A) a fee simple absolute
    (B) a life estate
    (C) a determinable fee
    (D) an estate for years

8. Which of the following deed forms may convey no ownership rights at all?

    (A) Special warranty deed
    (B) General warranty deed
    (C) Bargain and sale deed
    (D) Quitclaim deed

9. An interest in land that can be inherited is the

    (A) fee simple absolute
    (B) decedent's life estate
    (C) decedent's personal license
    (D) decedent's interest held with another as joint tenants with right of survivorship

10. If a deed is executed by a single individual, the form of ownership being conveyed by the deed is

    (A) severalty
    (B) tenants in common
    (C) joint tenancy
    (D) tenancy by the entirety

11. When title to real estate is inherited, which of the following is true?

    (A) Heirs take title subject to whatever defects might exist at the time of death
    (B) Heirs get possession immediately after death
    (C) Heirs receive equal shares in the property
    (D) None of the above

12. In receiving title to property from a partnership

    (A) all limited and general partners must execute the deed
    (B) any limited partner may fully execute the deed
    (C) a general partner may execute the deed by his or her single signature
    (D) all general partners are required to execute the deed

13. Caution should be exercised in purchasing property from an estate because

    (A) an administrator's or executor's deed usually contains no warranties
    (B) a quitclaim deed is used
    (C) a general warranty deed may not be used
    (D) a special warranty deed is generally used

14. To acquire title under adverse possession, all of the following are true EXCEPT

    (A) it cannot be accomplished in states using the Torrens system
    (B) open and notorious possession must be present
    (C) the statutory period of time of use is continuous
    (D) a special warranty deed is given by the owner

15. A person who has real property devised to her through a will is said to have acquired title by

    (A) adverse possession     (C) reversion
    (B) escheat                (D) inheritance

16. A quiet title proceeding develops when

    (A) questions arise regarding the validity of the title
    (B) the purchaser buys a property with land tenants
    (C) family members purchase a property
    (D) the property is inherited

17. The maximum number of grantees that can be named in a deed is

    (A) two        (C) four
    (B) three      (D) any number

18. One who acquires property under a deed is a

    (A) vendee      (C) trustee
    (B) lessee      (D) grantee

19. Title to real property passes to the grantee at the time the deed is

    (A) delivered    (C) signed
    (B) written      (D) acknowledged

20. Full and complete ownership of land as we recognize it today exists in

    (A) an absolute
    (B) a fee simple absolute
    (C) a leasehold
    (D) an estate

# Chapter 8

# Evidence and Assurance of Title

---

**VOCABULARY**

*You will find it important to have a complete working knowledge of the following terms and concepts found in the text or the glossary.*

abstract
abstractor's certificate
bona fide mortgagee
bona fide purchaser
chain of title
constructive notice
dedication
escrow
governmental survey
marketable title

meridians
metes and bounds
mortgagee
opinion of title
owner of record
owner's policy
parallel
patent
preliminary binder
record plat

recording system
rectangular survey
registration system
section of land
subrogation
tier
title insurance
Torrens system
township
vendor's affidavit

---

## RECORDING SYSTEMS

To understand recording systems and how they work, and to appreciate their value, it is helpful to consider first the concept of the *chain of title*. This simply says that the various transfers of ownership of a particular piece of real estate down through the years, each of them a "link" between a pair of successive owners, together constitute a "chain" that creates a history of the title to the property. In determining who owns the property today, we *prove* the ownership by examining the "chain" to see that it is unbroken, that there are no "missing links." Before purchasing real estate, we expect and demand that the seller demonstrate that he or she is the owner by proving that the chain of title is unbroken from the time the first private owner received title from the government.

This initial transfer from the government to the first private owner was usually by a unique form of conveyance called a *patent,* though property in many areas was transferred to the first private owner through a grant, and still other property from the states themselves because the initial transfer of title was from the federal government to new state governments as they were formed and admitted to statehood.

Since we demand proof of the chain of title through such a lengthy period of time, the present owners would have to have literally hundreds of documents in their possession to prove a chain of title. Under early common law in England (and to a large extent even today) this

is exactly what was required. The seller kept all the documents that formed the chain of title so as to be able to prove his or her ownership by permitting the buyer to inspect them. Fortunately, in the United States the difficulty of this was anticipated and dealt with by the establishment of a system for *recording* important documents and maintaining public records of laws, legal proceedings, and other governmental actions having an impact on property rights. Our modern recording systems were based on the need to have reliable records available to the general public.

### How Recording Systems Work

Two different types of records must be consulted in constructing the complete chain of title: those which are *governmental,* or mandatory, in nature, and those which are *private,* or voluntary, in nature.

### Public Records

Certain matters become *public record* whether the individuals affected by them desire it or not. All state laws and local ordinances are matters of public record. So are court decisions regarding such matters as the formal appointment of guardians or conservators; the administration of decedents' estates, including any will and all final court orders; divorce decrees; judgments in civil cases for damages that may create judgment liens on the defendant's property; assessments for municipal improvements that also create liens on the property benefited; proceedings of local zoning boards or commissions; liens for delinquent real estate taxes; and liens for federal estate taxes which may exist even though unrecorded. This body of public records exists quite apart from the recording system discussed below, and these public records have an impact on the chain of title to the extent that they affect the quality of the title of the present owner.

### Private Records

In addition to its public records, each state has established a separate system for recording documents that represent essentially private transactions between parties. While there are minor variations among the states, there is basic uniformity in the purposes and general workings of all recording systems.

Under these systems, properly prepared and acknowledged instruments are *entitled* to be recorded with the county recorder (or registrar), who is charged with the duty of preserving them, indexing them, and making them available to the general public. A document that is *entitled* to be recorded is one that *may* be recorded but need not be if the parties choose not to record it. Generally, all documents which affect the title to real estate may be recorded, such as deeds, mortgages, deeds of trust, land contracts, leases, mechanic's liens, *lis pendens* (notice that a lawsuit is pending against the present owner of the real estate), powers of attorney, and declarations of trust.

The process of recording does not affect the rights between the parties. A deed that is unrecorded is still effective to convey title in most states. What the recording process does is to make the transaction a matter of public record. The most important aspect of this voluntary recording system is that, once the document is recorded and becomes part of the public records, all persons dealing with the property are *bound* to know of its contents. That is, whether or not they *actually* know that there has been a deed of property from A to B, they are legally *obligated* to know of it. This is called *constructive notice.* It is this element of the system that is so important in establishing the links in the chain of title. Once a document is recorded, it becomes a permanent part of the chain of title.

### Who Is Protected by the Recording System?

In addition to having constructive notice of everything that is a matter of public record, persons dealing with real estate are entitled to rely on the accuracy and completeness of public records, and they are protected in dealing with the property after consulting these records. This protection—that the status of title as shown by the records in the recording system is correct—does not extend to everyone. The protection generally is available only to a *bona fide purchaser* or *mortgagee for value.* By this we mean that the purchaser or mortgagee may rely on the recording system if he or she (1) gives value (money) in reliance on the record and (2) acts in good faith and has no actual knowledge of any *unrecorded* instrument that affects the title.

To illustrate, assume that the *owner of record* (the one who the records show is the true owner of the property) deeds the property to purchaser A on April 1, this year, but A fails to record the deed. On April 10, this year, the owner deeds the same property to purchaser B, who records the deed on that date. Who now owns the legal title? Purchaser B was entitled to rely on the record, and it showed that the seller had legal title; assuming that B gave *value* (and here we mean a realistic price, not just nominal consideration) for the property *and* that he did not *actually* know of the earlier deed, then B is the new owner. Purchaser A is of course entitled to sue the defrauding seller, but he has lost the right to legal title by failing to record promptly. This rule is admittedly arbitrary, but it is justified by the notion that the law helps those who help themselves.

### Registered Title Systems

Several states, in addition to maintaining recording systems, have adopted the *Torrens system* of registration of titles to land. Under this system, generally the title to real estate does not pass until the deed is registered with the registrar pursuant to the controlling statute. As with other recording systems, registration under the Torrens system is not compulsory by law, but it is a practical necessity to obtain the benefits of registration.

The initial registration of property under the Torrens system is accomplished by a court proceeding similar to a quiet title action (see Chapter 7) in which the individual who claims title to a piece of real estate files a claim with the court in the county in which the property is located. Notice to all possible interested parties is given either by personal direct notice or by publication in local newspapers. If no one disputes the claimant's right to ownership within the statutory period specified by state law, the court will order the title to be registered.

After the registration, the owner receives a certificate which he or she transfers to the new owner when the property is sold. The certificate is in addition to the deed. The new owner presents these documents to the registrar, and a new certificate is then issued to the new owner of the property. This system also provides a limited form of title insurance. When the registrar erroneously issues a new certificate, any damages suffered by the injured party are paid from the fund accumulated from the fees charged for registration.

Under the Torrens system the responsibilities of the registrar are much greater than those of the county recorder under the standard recording system. The county recorder usually does not have the responsibility or duty of determining the accuracy or validity of deeds that are recorded. He or she simply checks to see that they are in recordable form and then records and indexes them. Any error made in the recording process which causes damage to anyone must be borne without financial relief from the recorder.

## ASSURANCE OF THE QUALITY OF THE TITLE

It has become customary throughout the United States to require that the seller of real estate furnish satisfactory evidence that he or she is the true owner of the property. All standard contracts for the sale of real estate contain this requirement. In the absence of such a contractual requirement, the seller would have no legal obligation to furnish any evidence that he owns the property. In such a case the buyer must look solely to whatever warranties are contained in the deed and to the seller's financial ability to pay for a breach of warranty. Since the typical contract provides for evidence of title, however, our discussion covers the two most common methods of title assurance in use today: the abstract and opinion method and commercial title insurance.

☐ Under the *abstract* and *opinion* method the abstractor prepares a digest of all the relevant documents and facts that are matters of public record from the earliest history of the property under consideration, and an attorney's opinion is given, based upon these facts, as to where title is currently vested and what defects in its quality may exist.

☐ Under the *title insurance* method, the insurance company, on the basis of its own research of the records, decides that the title of the proposed seller is of sufficient quality that the company will insure that the deed will pass good title to the proposed buyer.

Both systems are dependent upon and limited to the facts disclosed by the recording system which permits (but seldom requires) the filing of documents that can affect the title to real estate with the recorder of the county within which the real estate is located. Other records of fact maintained which can affect title (such as the record of all judgments rendered against the owner that might constitute liens on the property) must also be consulted to verify that all public information has been investigated. Nevertheless, the basic information upon which the quality of the title is based lies in the recording system.

## The Abstract and Opinion Method

Even though the law imposes on all those who deal with real estate an obligation to investigate public records and charges them with notice or knowledge of what such an investigation would yield, it is seldom that an individual purchaser, mortgagee, or lessee undertakes this task. The individual must usually employ others to accomplish this task and normally first employs an abstractor to make a detailed search of the records and to compile a digest of the history of the title to the property. An abstractor is usually necessary because of the tremendous volume of records that must be checked and the complexity of the public records system.

Today the use of an abstractor who is a specialist in the use of this system is essential. Nevertheless, the abstractor's function, though critically important, is one of accumulating information accurately and exhaustively rather than one of interpreting its meaning or legal significance. The latter is the province of the attorney. It is the attorney's function to review the abstract—the history of the title to a piece of real estate—and to reach a decision as to the quality of the present owner's title.

Each of these functions has its protective features and its limitations.

### The Abstract

The *abstract* is the basic tool for establishing who currently owns a given piece of real estate and how good his or her title is.

An abstract is a *digest* of the history of the title to a given parcel of real estate, not a compilation of all recorded documents. That is, the abstractor does not make a copy of each and every document found in the chain of title. To do so would result, in many cases, in a very imposing book. The abstractor is highly trained and knows what portions of each document are significant in terms of ownership. The abstractor therefore abstracts each document and records in the abstract only the essential facts. For example, rather than copy an entire deed, the abstractor simply notes in the abstract:

The location of the deed in the records (the book and page where it can be found)
The date of the deed and the date of its recording
The names of the grantor and grantee
A description of the property
The type of deed
Any conditions or restrictions included in the deed

Wherever it is necessary that the entire contents of a document be included in the abstract to represent the transaction fully, the abstractor includes the entire document.

### Extent and Limitations of Coverage

The extent of the coverage of the abstract is very broad. When it is complete, it includes the history of the title from the earliest known record. As a practical matter, however, most abstracts start with the first private ownership of the property, the patent from the United States to the first individual purchaser. From that point forward the abstract shows all recorded facts that affect the title.

A wide variety of records is consulted, in addition to the deed and mortgage records, in preparing an abstract. For example, the public records of all judgments, marriages, estate proceedings, and tax records, as well as certain others, are searched by the abstractor to be sure that all recorded facts and documents which might affect the quality of title are included in the abstract. It must be emphasized that the abstractor's search is restricted to the public records and does not purport to cover matters that are not in those records.

The areas not covered by the abstract are those the purchaser is expected to investigate personally and those not required to be a matter of record.

Matters that would be revealed by an inspection of the property (but not by an inspection of the record) are not covered by the abstract. That is, the abstractor does not view or inspect the property to determine whether or not there are parties other than the seller who are in possession and claim an interest (such as under an unrecorded short-term lease) or to determine that the physical condition and layout of the property are as represented by the seller (for example, that the buildings are in fact situated on the real estate being purchased). It may require a survey to establish these facts.

The purchaser is also required to satisfy himself that no encroachments or violations of restrictive covenants exist, for the abstractor has no knowledge of these facts and will not be willing to certify that such covenants are not being violated. Again, a survey may be required to establish such facts, and that is the purchaser's responsibility.

Mechanic's liens may have a drastic effect upon the title to real estate, but they may not be recorded at the time of transfer of title, creation of a mortgage, or granting of a leasehold interest. (The notice of intent to hold such a lien need not be recorded until the statutory time after completion of the work.) As a result, the abstract cannot preclude the possibility that such liens may be recorded for some period after the abstract is brought up to date. The abstractor will not accept responsibility for such liens because it cannot be predicted whether or not the possibility of such liens exists.

The *abstractor's certificate* limits his liability for the quality of his work. Typical of the wording used in such certificates is: ". . . hereby certifies, guarantees, and warrants to whoever relies upon this certificate, including present and all future persons in interest, and this certificate runs with the real estate described in the caption hereof that the abstract is complete." Such a certification indicates the willingness of the abstractor to be liable for

any errors and omissions included in his work. However, there is serious question whether or not he can be held liable for a loss suffered by someone who relies upon the accuracy of this work unless that person was the one who paid for it.

### Attorney's Opinion on the Abstract

An attorney's opinion rendered upon the abstract is the second important step of the abstract and opinion method of title assurance. The function of the attorney in the abstract and opinion method of title assurance is critically important. The abstractor makes no determination of the *quality* of the title; the abstractor simply reports what the record shows and who appears to be in title at the time of the abstract continuation. It is the function of the attorney to examine the abstract and determine how good the title is on the basis of the recorded facts. The attorney renders a professional opinion as to the legal effects of the documents and facts reported by the abstractor. The attorney reviews the abstract in detail to determine that the title has in fact passed from each party who has owned it to the next party in the chain of title, whether the transfer was by deed, death, forced sale, or whatever. The attorney also determines that any liens or encumbrances that ever existed against the property have been satisfied so that there are no potential interests in anyone other than the apparent record title holder.

### Extent of Protection Provided by the Abstract and Opinion Method

It is important to understand the extent of the protection obtained by use of the abstract and opinion method of title assurance and its limitations. The entire system is based on public records and the effect of these records on the quality of the title of the present owner. The abstract includes only matters that are in the public records and can be found by a competent and reasonable search of such records; anything not in the records does not go into the abstract.

Since the abstract is the basic information used by the attorney in forming an opinion as to the quality of the title and where it is currently vested, it necessarily follows that the attorney's opinion pertains to the record title only. If the attorney is furnished additional information, his or her opinion can be expanded to include it. For example, if the attorney is provided with a survey which locates the improvements on the property accurately, he or she can expand the opinion to show whether or not there is any violation of restrictive covenants that dictate the location of improvements (such as setback lines).

In the absence of a survey, the obligation of making this determination remains with the proposed buyer, mortgagee, or lessee. The general rule is that the abstract and opinion method covers only matters of record; the buyer is charged with responsibility for matters that would be revealed by an inspection of the property. The buyer is not obligated to have a survey performed if he or she can determine the facts without it, but it has been held that the buyer is bound by what the survey would have shown had it been performed.

In addition to the information about the physical characteristics of the property that an inspection and survey would reveal, two major limitations on this method of title assurance make it essential for the buyer to inspect the property.

The record does not necessarily show the rights of parties other than the owner who may be in possession of the property. The fact that someone other than the record owner is in possession can be established only by inspecting the property, and the law requires the purchaser to make such an inspection on the theory that a reasonable person would do so before parting with value. Since any purchase of the property is subject to the rights of the parties who are in actual possession, it is clearly important that an inspection be performed. If someone other than the owner is in possession, the buyer must determine what rights that person claims.

Certain matters may have a severe effect upon the title and may not be recorded at the time of the sale of the property. Particularly troublesome are mechanic's liens, which can be filed after sale of the property if the work done by the mechanic was completed shortly before the sale. Again, inspection of the property by the buyer just before the closing of the sale may reveal that work has been recently performed. If so, the buyer may be protected from later assertion of a lien by requiring evidence that the work has been paid for. However, even the most careful inspection may not reveal evidence of repair work. In this event the buyer must rely on the protection afforded by the seller's warranties, either in the deed or in a separate document.

The important point here is that the abstract and opinion method of title assurance provides no protection against the possibility of liens that may result from work done or materials supplied shortly before the time the record is checked and the abstract brought up to date.

## Commercial Title Insurance

The business of insuring titles was a natural outgrowth of the abstracting business, since the abstractor is the person most capable of accumulating the necessary information efficiently. Perhaps even more important than the ability to obtain the information available from public records is the fact that, because of the abstractor's familiarity with the system, he or she is best able to judge how good the system is in a given area. The abstractor can evaluate a system's inherent risks, such as misfiled

documents, indexing errors, records not indexed, or documents never recorded.

While most title insurance companies have come about through an expansion of the abstract business, title insurance is also made available by attorneys who have formed such companies to insure titles on the basis of their opinions. The phenomenal growth in the use of title insurance, in metropolitan areas particularly, is due largely to institutional lenders. Many mortgage lenders universally require title insurance, at least to cover their own interest in the property, as a condition for making the loan. This emphasis on insurance of the mortgagee's interest in the property has also made purchasers more aware of its availability and has tended to foster the growth of the title insurance business.

### The Nature of Title Insurance

Essentially, *title insurance* is a single-premium insurance policy that insures the condition of the title to a specified piece of real estate at a precise point in time. It does not insure that the title will not be affected by actions that occur after the date the policy is issued. It simply insures that, as of a certain date and time, the records show that a specific piece of real estate is owned by a particular owner or owners and that the title is good, subject to any exceptions which may be spelled out in the policy.

The cost of the coverage—the premium paid for the policy—is established on the same basis as other casualty insurance: the amount of the coverage in terms of the money involved and the degree of risk being assumed by the insurer. Policies are available that insure owners of property against loss of title or the cost of satisfying a claim or encumbrance against it. Policies are also available for the protection of mortgagees to the extent of the balance owed to them by the borrower; that is, as the loan is amortized, the amount of coverage is correspondingly reduced. Lessees' policies are also available and are popularly used where the tenant intends to make substantial improvements to the property.

### The Preparation of Title Insurance

The preparation and issuance of a title insurance policy is similar in many respects to the procedures of the abstract and opinion method of title assurance, with important exceptions. The first step is inspection of the records to determine the chain of title and to find any defects that may exist, but usually no abstract is prepared. Instead, the title insurer relies on skilled personnel to trace the title and to recognize transactions or facts that may result in a title defect. Rather than digest every document, the title insurer digests only those that appear to pose a problem.

The personnel who perform this function report their

findings to the company's title examiner, usually an attorney skilled in the real estate field. The decision must then be made as to whether the defects found are so significant that the title cannot be insured, that it can be insured only with exceptions, or that it is insurable without exception because the defects found do not represent serious risk of loss.

The insurer then issues a *preliminary binder,* which indicates its willingness to insure the title when acquired by the proposed new owner from the present owner. The preliminary binder is not an abstract and does not show the facts on which the insurer has relied, but it does show any significant defect for which the proposed policy does not provide coverage. If there are serious defects, the parties to the transaction can then take corrective action to cure the defects so that the ultimate policy will be issued without exception.

The final policy is issued after the transaction is completed and the documents recorded, so that the title insurer has the opportunity to see that the record reflects the transfer to the insured.

One disadvantage of title insurance is the fact that the purchaser, mortgagee, or lessee does not receive an abstract and does not have the opportunity to evaluate personally the degree of risk that may exist. If the purchaser, mortgagee, or lessee wants to obtain an abstract in addition to the title insurance policy, there will be the additional expense of preparation. When the property under consideration is very valuable or where a substantial amount will be spent in the construction of improvements, a careful purchaser may obtain both a title insurance policy and an abstract so that the purchaser's attorney can be satisfied that no unusual degree of risk is involved, even if the title insurance company is willing to insure the title.

### Extent and Limitations of Coverage

The extent of coverage provided by the usual title insurance policy and the limitations on that coverage should be clearly understood by anyone active in the real estate business, so as to avoid giving any unintentionally misleading advice to either purchasers or sellers. As a rule, the title insurance policy covers the same matters as the abstract and opinion method. That is, the same records are investigated and the same decisions made as to the quality of the title and its insurability.

One important exception to this generalization provides one of the significant advantages of the system: Title insurance in effect insures the accuracy of the recording system. If, for example, a document affecting the title has been improperly indexed and cannot be found by the most diligent and competent search and there is a resulting loss to the policyholder, typical title insurance policies will cover that loss, even though an abstractor could not have been held liable for failure to find the

document. To this extent title insurance provides broader protection than the abstract and opinion method.

Matters that would be revealed by a survey are not routinely covered by title insurance policies. However, this coverage can be obtained if the title insurer is furnished with a survey that appears to be adequate. Title insurance companies have established certain minimum standards for surveys that they recognize and accept for purposes of insuring titles. Before recommending the procurement of a survey, the broker or salesperson should determine (or caution the client to determine) what kind of survey will be required by the title insurer to induce it to insure such matters as compliance with restrictive covenants.

As with the abstract and opinion method of title assurance, the title insurance policy has certain standard exceptions for the rights of parties in possession, short-term unrecorded leases or land contracts, and mechanic's liens.

### Protected Parties

The parties protected by the title insurance policy are those specified in the policy. The policy is a contract between the insurance company and the purchaser of the coverage. It is important to recognize that a mortgagee's policy, for example, protects only the mortgagee's interest in the property; the owner's interest is not covered. In the event of loss covered by such a policy, the balance due on the loan will be paid to the mortgagee and the owner will be relieved from making further payment; however, the owner will suffer the loss of the property and whatever investment was made in it.

To obtain protection of the owner's interest, an owner's policy must be purchased in addition to any mortgagee's policy. An important point to be aware of in connection with the owner's policy is that it protects only that owner. In the event the property is sold, the protection of the owner's policy does not transfer to the new owner. Subsequent purchasers of insured property must obtain a separate policy to cover their interests.

One person definitely not protected by the title insurance policy is the seller of the real estate. The fact that title insurance is purchased for the benefit of the buyer does not relieve the seller from liability for defects in the title under the owner's warranties in the deed to the purchaser. In fact, it is not unheard of for the title insurer to bring suit against the seller upon his or her warranties when there has been a loss under a policy of title insurance, particularly where the defect in the title was known or should have been known to the seller.

When the insurer is required to pay a claim under the policy, the insurer acquires the *right of subrogation.* That is, the insurer acquires whatever rights the insured party would have had against the seller under his or her warranties. For example, assume that the seller knew of an assessment for sewers and that this fact was not found by the title insurer and not mentioned by the seller at the closing. When the assessment must be paid, the purchaser is entitled to look to either the seller or the title insurer for reimbursement. The simplest procedure for the purchaser is to demand that the insurer pay the assessment under the terms of the insurance policy. The title insurer, upon paying the claim, succeeds to the insured party's rights and may maintain suit against the seller upon his or her warranties. Such suits have been successfully maintained by title insurance companies.

## Supplementary Protection

In special cases supplementary protection may be required in addition to the abstract and opinion method of assurance or commercial title insurance. It is clear that not every problem will be completely covered by either method. This is particularly true in the area of mechanic's liens. Two possible problems may exist at the time of sale in connection with such liens: There may be the strong possibility that such liens will be filed, or such liens may already have been filed and cannot be cleared before the sale is closed. There is a solution for each problem.

### Vendor's Affidavit

When the purchaser believes there is a possibility that mechanic's liens may be filed against the property for work recently done, such as new construction or repairs necessary to qualify the property for the mortgage loan (quite common with FHA-insured loans), the purchaser should insist on evidence that all contractors have been paid. In addition, the purchaser should require a *vendor's affidavit* (sometimes referred to by other names locally, such as a *closing affidavit*) in which the seller makes a sworn statement, under the penalties for perjury, that there are no such liens and that there are no circumstances which would permit such a lien to arise.

### Escrow Fund

When mechanic's liens already exist against the property, there may be good and valid reasons for proceeding with the sale without obtaining releases of the claims. The purchaser may need possession of the property but be unwilling to make payment without some assurance that the lien will be discharged by the seller. At the same time, the seller may be anxious to complete the sale in order to receive the proceeds but may be unwilling to pay the mechanic because of a dispute regarding the value of the work, its quality, or the amount claimed. To be forced to pay the claim at face value would reduce the net price below that which the seller might receive if free to negotiate or litigate the merits of the claim.

A solution in such a case is available in the form of an *escrow,* under which the seller deposits with an independent escrow agent sufficient funds to satisfy the claim at its face value plus any costs which might be chargeable and collectible against the property. The escrow agent is authorized to apply the funds to the satisfaction of the claim when the claim is paid and the lien discharged.

A further provision for the protection of the buyer is a clause that requires resolution of the problem within a specified period of time, so that the buyer is assured of prompt resolution of the matter. Upon failure of the seller to resolve the matter within the specified time limit, the agreement should provide that the escrowee be required to apply the funds to satisfy the lien.

## ACCEPTABLE RESTRICTIONS ON THE TITLE

There are a variety of restrictions on the use of real estate being sold that may in fact be beneficial to the use and enjoyment of the property by the grantee and are therefore quite acceptable and do not constitute defects in the title that would make it unmarketable. Subdivision restrictions are typical; we discuss them later in the chapter.

It is also possible that an existing encumbrance is an asset to the buyer. For example, there may be an outstanding mortgage on the property at a more favorable rate than that available at the time of sale. If this mortgage can be assumed by the buyer, it will be made a condition in the deed itself. The acceptance of the deed which states this condition will not breach the seller's warranty against encumbrances. This matter is fully discussed in Chapter 10.

At this point it is appropriate to note that even though we require evidence of the quality of the seller's title prior to completion of the sale, we are generally not entitled to demand a *perfect* title, for it is unlikely that there is such a title in existence today. What we are entitled to insist on, however, is a *marketable* title. That is, certain limitations on the title are acceptable under modern land title practice, and the buyer must accept the deed to such property. Easements for power lines, sewers, and other utilities which serve the property are examples of technical defects that do not make the title unmarketable.

Every state today has some form of marketable title legislation designed to cure defects in title that are very old. While there are many variations from state to state, particularly as to the length of time they cover, the basic purpose of this legislation is to invalidate any outstanding claim or to correct any error that is so old that it is unlikely to affect the marketability of the title. These statutes generally require clear evidence of an unbroken chain of title for some lengthy period of time. Forty years is typical, but there is no universal standard. Early statutes were of doubtful constitutionality; however, recently such statutes have been updated and have withstood attacks on their constitutionality. In spite of this, careful title examiners always look beyond this statutory period because such statutes frequently do not protect against governmental claims or against people who are incompetent.

## LEGAL DESCRIPTIONS

Because of the dependency of the recording system on an accurate way of identifying and indexing property, it is important to understand the ways in which real estate may be legally described.

### The Rectangular System

The government or *rectangular survey* refers to a grid of north and south lines (meridians) and east and west lines (parallels). The vertical rows of the grid are called *checks* and the horizontal rows are called *tiers*. The distance between principal meridians and guide meridians is 24 miles, the same as the distance between the base line and standard parallels. A single square in the grid, known as a *tract,* is 24 miles square (576 square miles) and is composed of 16 townships. A township is 6 miles square (36 square miles) and is made up of 36 sections (see Figure 8-1).

Each section is 1 mile square (1 square mile) and can be divided easily for platting purposes, as shown in Figure 8-2.

□  A section contains 640 acres and is 1 mile square, 5,280 feet per side.
□  A half section contains 320 acres and is a rectangle, 5,280 feet by 2,640 feet.
□  A quarter section contains 160 acres and is a square, 2,640 feet per side.
□  A quarter-quarter section contains 40 acres and is a square, 1,320 feet per side.
□  A quarter-quarter-quarter section contains 10 acres and is a square, 660 feet per side.

### The Record Plat

Many residential properties are situated in subdivisions that are legally described by means of a *record plat* (sometimes called a description by *lot and block*). It is important that the real estate salesperson become familiar with this type of legal description. An example of a portion of a record plat is shown in Figure 8-3.

The record plat typically utilizes several means of describing real estate. First, the record plat employs the rectangular system (the government system) as a base system of reference. Section corners and section lines are sometimes referred to in the record plat. Second, the record plat typically utilizes the *metes and bounds* (measures and direction) technique to describe the outer boundary of the land included in the record plat. Finally, the record plat includes a pictorial representation of the several lots

(parcels of land intended to be conveyed), streets, easements, rectangular system references, metes and bounds calls, and other information. Once the detailed surveying, calculation, and drafting have been done, it is by virtue of the pictorial illustration, which is a major part of the record plat, that subsequent description of a parcel of real property can be made relatively simple.

It should be kept in mind that, while the technical work associated with the preparation of a record plat is important, it is equally significant that the record plat be recorded and thus made part of the land records in the county in which the land is situated. It is with this recorded information and the representations made in the record plat that a legal description for a particular lot can be generated. For example, Lot 8, as shown in Figure 8-3, would be described as follows:

> Lot 8, in Block 2, of "Brandywine Section One," the plat of which was recorded November 12, this year, as Instrument 4653 in Book 6, pages 52 through 56, in the Office of the Recorder, Your County, Your State.

A metes and bounds description of Lot 8 would be a difficult and time-consuming effort. (See for example Figure 8-5.)

Information typically shown on a record plat, as illustrated in Figure 8-3, includes:

□  Name of the subdivision
□  Lot lines (including directions and distances)
□  Lot numbers
□  Block numbers (a block is usually defined as contiguous lots bounded by streets)
□  Building lines illustrating required setback of all structures from the street right-of-way
□  Area of the lot
□  Easements, such as utility, sewer, and drainage easements
□  Street names, width and longitudinal dimensions of right-of-way
□  North arrow and scale of drawing
□  Location and description of monuments and markers
□  Beginning point and rectangular survey references
□  Adjoining property references
□  Recording information, including time and date of recording, instrument number, book and page number, where recorded, and name of recorder
□  Curve data to be utilized by surveyors in staking particular lots

Other information normally included in the record plat is as follows. This information appears on pages 2 and 3 of Figure 8-4, immediately after the diagram. It is important that the reader be aware that the record

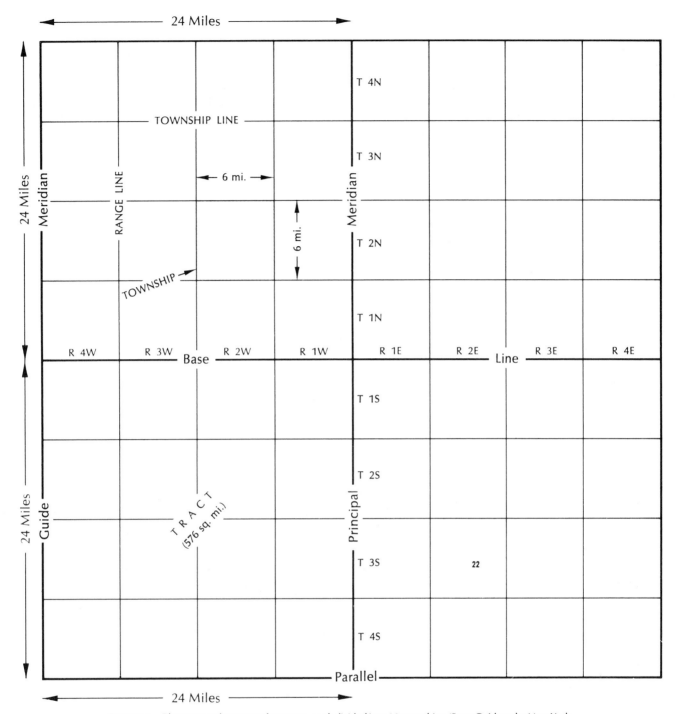

Figure 8-1—The rectangular system: four tracts, each divided into 16 townships. (From Guide to the New York Real Estate Salespersons' Course 3E by Norman Weinberg, Paul J. Colletti, William A. Colavito, and Frank A. Melchior. Copyright © 1985 by John Wiley & Sons, Inc. Reprinted by permission of John Wiley & Sons.)

plat includes both the diagram or map and all of the information shown on pages 2 and 3 of Figure 8-4. In actual practice, the record plat is an oversized document that includes the map of the subdivision and all of the data relating to restrictions and other information shown on pages 2 and 3. In reproducing it for this text, it has been necessary to use three pages, all of which must be considered as one document.

☐ Legal description of the perimeter boundary of the record plat
☐ Land surveyor's certification of plat accuracy
☐ Landowner's dedication of the platted ground as shown on the plat for lots, right-of-way, easements, etc.
☐ Definitions of lots, easements, etc., as shown on the plat

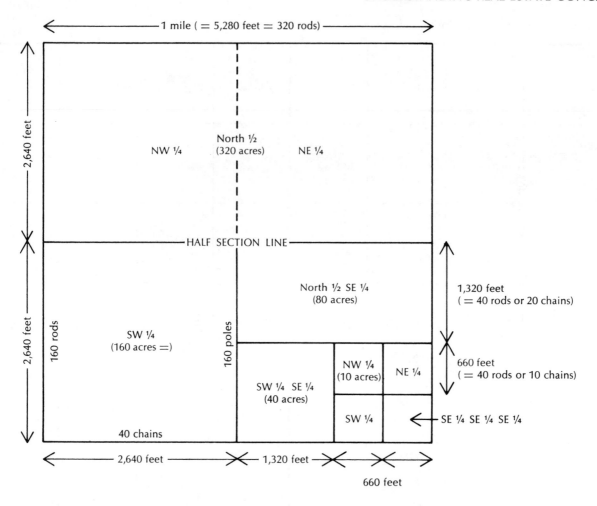

Figure 8-2—One section divided into half, quarter, half-quarter, quarter-quarter, and quarter-quarter-quarter sections.

- ☐ Private restrictions attached to use of land
- ☐ Enforcement provisions for restrictions on use of land
- ☐ Reference to other pertinent recorded instruments made of part of the plat
- ☐ Execution of the record plat by the owners of lands to be platted
- ☐ Acknowledgment of record plat (required for recording)
- ☐ Statements and signatures of approval from government agencies having jurisdiction over the platting process
- ☐ Name of person preparing plat and date of preparation

It should be remembered that, while the record plat is a highly detailed, technical representation of a particular parcel of real property, it does not replace the importance of a thorough search and opinion of title or a title policy. For example, there may be an easement on the real property that does not appear on the record plat. Or an owner may convey a portion of a lot to another person, and thus the ownership of a particular lot may be different from that represented on the record plat.

Nevertheless, while the record plat does not solve all the problems associated with transfer of title, it can make the job of transfer much simpler for the salesperson, lender, attorney, abstractor, title insurance company, land surveyor, owner, prospective purchaser, and other persons involved with the transfer of real property.

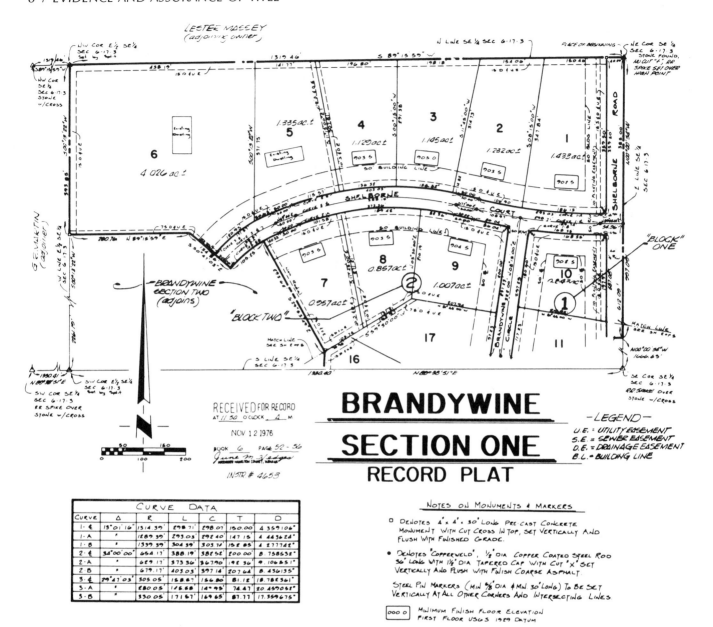

Figure 8-3—This record plat shows a portion of a complete record plat including lot sizes, street layouts, various power and sewer easements, and building lines. Courtesy of Paul I. Cripe, Inc., Indianapolis, Indiana.

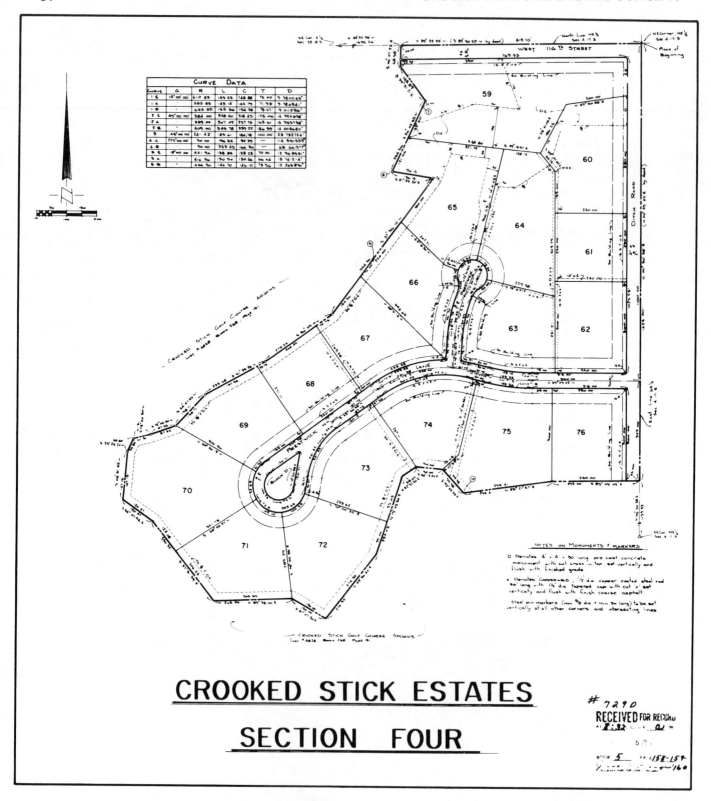

# CROOKED STICK ESTATES

# SECTION FOUR

*Figure 8-4 (page 1 of 3)—A portion of a complete record plat, including lot sizes, street layouts, various power and sewer easements, building lines, land surveyor's certificate, statement of covenants of the development, signature of seller and purchaser, along with acknowledgments necessary for recording. Courtesy of Paul I. Cripe, Inc., Indianapolis, Indiana.*

I, the undersigned, hereby certify that the above plat is true and correct and represents a survey made by me of real estate described as follows:

A part of the Northeast Quarter of Section 4, Township 17 North, Range 3 East in Hamilton County, Indiana, more particularly described as follows: Beginning at the Northeast corner of the said Northeast Quarter; thence South 89 degrees 52 minutes 35 seconds West (assumed bearing) on and along the North line of the said Northeast Quarter, 801.50 feet; thence South 00 degrees 07 minutes 25 seconds East 68.98 feet; thence South 45 degrees 55 minutes 10 seconds East 137.02 feet; thence South 26 degrees 02 minutes 35 seconds West 254.56 feet; thence South 81 degrees 36 minutes 25 seconds East 231.68 feet; thence South 37 degrees 36 minutes 10 seconds West 554.46 feet; thence South 56 minutes 10 seconds West 275.24 feet; thence South 61 degrees 35 minutes 25 seconds West 23.68 feet; thence South 44 degrees 47 minutes 45 seconds West 138.71 feet; thence South 72 degrees 06 minutes 50 seconds West 147.15 feet; thence South 54 degrees 07 minutes 45 seconds East 120.47 feet; thence South 37 degrees 51 minutes 55 seconds East 330.32 feet; thence North 89 degrees 38 minutes 00 seconds East 265.59 feet; thence South 61 degrees 07 minutes 30 seconds East 136.00 feet; thence North 39 degrees 36 minutes 36 seconds East 374.32 feet; thence North 19 degrees 05 minutes 50 seconds East 254.03 feet; thence North 52 degrees 57 minutes 20 seconds East 58.40 feet; thence South 84 degrees 11 minutes 20 seconds East 90.00 feet; thence South 43 degrees 45 minutes 05 seconds East 99.40 feet; thence North 83 degrees 21 minutes 57 seconds East 295.00 feet to the East line of the said Northeast Quarter; thence North 00 degrees 50 minutes 58 seconds East of and along the said East line 1425.00 feet to the Place of Beginning, containing 38.798 acres, more or less.

Between points 7 and 8 and between points 9 and 10 as shown on the plat for "Crooked Stick Estates-Section Four", the boundary herein described is coincident with a corresponding portion of the boundary description of a certain tract set out and recorded as Instrument #1884, Book 267, pages 300-314, in the Office of the Recorder of Hamilton County, Indiana.

This subdivision consists of 18 lots, numbered 59 to 76, inclusively. The size of the lots and widths of the streets are shown in figures denoting feet and decimal parts thereof.

This survey was made by me during the month of MARCH , 1975.

Witness my signature this 17th day of June , 1975.

[signature] , Registered Land Surveyor #1098

The undersigned, Guernsey VanRiper, Jr., Owner of the real estate shown and described herein, being a part of the land described, conveyed and recorded as Instrument #1500A, Plat Book 281, pages 632 to 636, inclusively, in the Office of the Recorder of Hamilton County, Indiana, May 30, 1975 do hereby certify that we have laid off, platted and subdivided said real estate in accordance with the within plat.

This subdivision shall be known and designated as CROOKED STICK ESTATES-SECTION FOUR, an addition to Hamilton County, Indiana.

In order to afford adequate protection to all present and future owners of lots in this subdivision, the undersigned owners hereby adopt and establish the following protective covenants, each and all enuring to the benefit of each and every owner of any lot or lots in said subdivision, their heirs and/or assigns, binding all the same each grantor and their heirs and/or assigns.

1. All streets shown on this plat and not heretofore dedicated are hereby dedicated to the public.

2. All lots in this subdivision shall be known and described as residential lots and no lots will be resubdivided into two or more building lots.

3. No structure shall be erected, altered, placed or permitted to remain on any residential lot other than one single-family dwelling, a private garage, and such other outbuildings usual and incidental to the use of such residential lot.

4. No residence, dwelling house, garage, servant's quarters or other structure of any nature, composition or description shall be constructed or erected on any lot until the building plans, including plot plans, specifications, plans for landscaping and any other data or information which may be requested shall be submitted to the building committee for its approval, said approval to be evidenced by a written instrument and stamped approval executed by the committee and delivered to the person or persons requesting such approval.

5. The building committee shall consist of three members and shall be composed of the following individuals: Guernsey VanRiper, Jr., Eugene Friedmann and Willis Adams. A majority of the said members shall constitute a quorum for approval or disapproval of any plans submitted and the decision of the majority shall control without exception; and their decision shall be final. The committee shall determine whether the proposed structures, plans and specifications show conformity and harmony of external design with existing structures and whether the building and property set-back lines are in conformity. In the event that the building committee does not indicate in writing its approval or disapproval of plans submitted within a period of 15 days after submission, the committee shall be deemed to have approved such plans. No charge shall be made to any purchaser of any lot for examination of plans or giving approval as provided. In the event of death, disability or resignation of any of the above named members, the remaining member or members shall select the successor or successors to fill the vacancy or vacancies created.

6. No residence of dwelling shall be constructed on any lot or part thereof, unless such residence, exclusive of open porches, attached garages and basements shall have a ground floor area of 2,500 square feet if a one-story structure, or 1,500 square feet in case of a building higher than one-story there shall be at least 1,000 square feet in addition to the ground floor area.

7. No trailer, shack, tent, basement, garage or other outbuilding shall be used at any time as a residence, temporary or permanent, nor shall any structure of a temporary character be used as a residence.

8. Easements: There are strips of ground as shown on the within plat marked "Drainage Easements" (D.E.), "Sewer Easements" (S.E.) and "Utility Easements" (U.E.) either separately or in any combination of the three, which are reserved for the use of the public utility companies and governmental agencies as follows: "Drainage Easements" (D.E.) are created to provide paths and courses for area and local storm drainage, either overland or in adequate underground conduit, to serve the needs of this and adjoining ground and/or public drainage system. No structure, including fences, shall be built upon said easement, which will obstruct flow from the area being served. "Sewer Easements" (S.E.) are created for the use of the local governmental agency having jurisdiction over the storm and sanitary waste disposal system of said city and/or county for the purpose of installation and maintenance of sewers that are part of said system. "Utility Easements" (U.E.) are created for the use of all public utility companies, not including transportation companies, for the installation and maintenance of mains, ducts, poles, lines and wires; and also all rights and uses specified for sewer easements above designated. All such easements shall include the right of reasonable ingress to and egress from said strips for the exercise of the other rights reserved.

9. No residence, dwelling house or any other structure whatsoever shall be used for the purpose of carrying on a business, trade, profession or any other calling.

10. "Building lines" (B.L.) are established as shown on this plat between which line and the front lot line no building shall be erected, placed, altered or permitted to remain. No structure or any part thereof shall be built or erected nearer than 20 feet to any side yard line or nearer than 25 feet to any rear lot line.

11. No fence, wall, hedge or shrub planting which obstructs sight lines at elevations between 2 and 6 feet above the street, shall be placed or permitted to remain on any corner lot within the triangular area formed by the street property lines and a line connecting points 25 feet from the intersection of said street lines, or in the case of a rounded property corner, from the intersection of the street lines extended. The same sight line limitation shall apply to any lot within 10 feet from the intersection of a street line with the edge of a driveway pavement. No tree shall be permitted to remain within such distances of such intersection unless the foliage line is maintained at sufficient height to prevent obstruction of such sight lines.

12. The owners of lots 59, 60, 61 shall provide driveway "turn arounds" on their respective lots such that exiting vehicles need not back onto the access road. This covenant shall also apply to the owners of lots 62 and 76 should they elect driveway access directly onto Ditch Road.

Figure 8-4—(page 2 of 3).

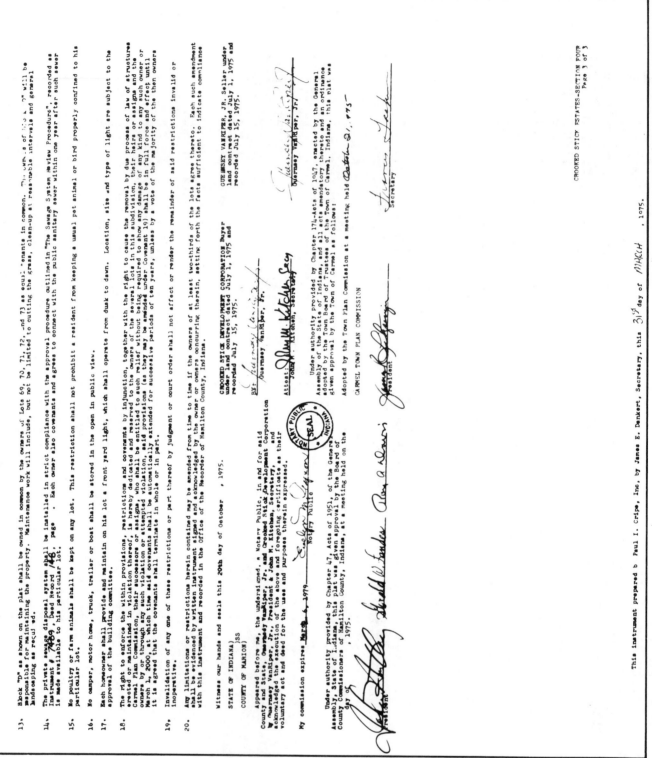

Figure 8-4—(page 3 of 3).

(It should be noted that the 20 provisions listed on pages 2 and 3 of this figure are part of the map that appears on the preceding page. All of these restrictions and limitations are incorporated into the deed by reference to this record plat.)

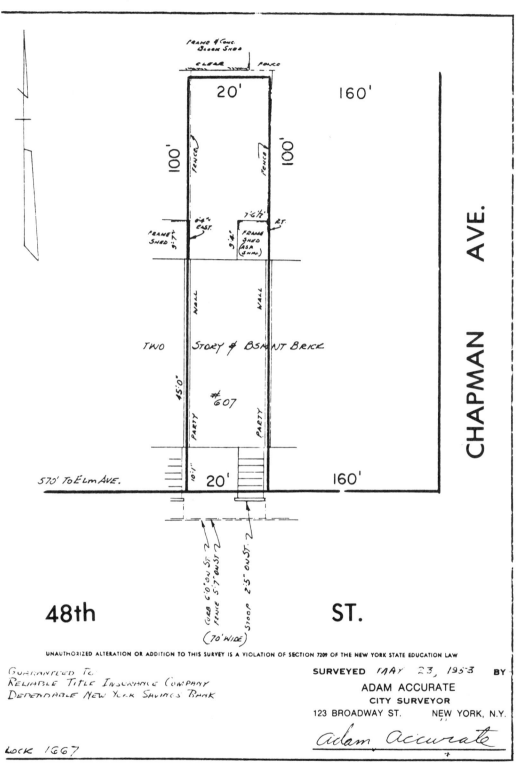

*Figure 8-5—Survey with metes and bounds description. Courtesy Paul J. Colletti.*

ALL that certain lot, piece or parcel of land, situate, lying and being in the Borough of
Brooklyn, County of Kings, City and State of New York, bounded and described as follows:
BEGINNING at a point on the northerly side of 48th Street, distant 160 feet westerly from the
intersection formed by the northerly side of 48th Street and the westerly side of Chapman Avenue;
RUNNING THENCE northerly parallel with Chapman Avenue and part of the distance through a party
wall a distance of 100 feet;
THENCE westerly parallel with 48th Street for a distance of 20 feet;
THENCE southerly parallel with Chapman Avenue and part of the distance through a party wall a
distance of 100 feet to the northerly side of 48th Street,
and THENCE easterly along the northerly side of 48th Street a distance of 20 feet to the point
or place BEGINNING.

# REVIEW QUESTIONS

1. A legal description which conveys the NW ¼ of the NW ¼ of Section 24 of a specified township includes

   (A) 160 acres        (C) 40 acres
   (B) 10 acres         (D) 80 acres

2. Both the abstract and opinion method of assuring title and title insurance

   (A) protect the buyer against encroachments by adjoining property owners
   (B) protect the buyer against the claim of a buyer under an unrecorded land contract
   (C) protect the buyer against defects of record
   (D) protect the buyer against unrecorded mechanic's liens

3. "Lot 452 of Rolling Hills subdivision of the City of Anytown" would be part of what type of legal description?

   (A) Governmental survey
   (B) Metes and bounds
   (C) Platted subdivision
   (D) None of the above

4. A township contains

   (A) 6 miles          (C) 36 sections
   (B) 24 square miles  (D) 640 acres

5. Which of the following items would **not** appear on a subdivision plat?

   (A) Sanitary sewer and electric service line easements
   (B) Building setback lines
   (C) Exact dimensions of each lot
   (D) Names of the owners of the lots

6. J receives an owner's title insurance policy from L at closing. The policy protects

   (A) L from any title defects of which he or she was unaware
   (B) J against any title defects known or unknown by L
   (C) J from boundary problems that should have been found by a survey
   (D) L from loss of title due to a misindexed document in the public record

7. When purchasing an owner's title insurance policy, the premium is paid

   (A) once, at the time of issue of the policy
   (B) annually with the real estate taxes

   (C) every three years with the hazard insurance premium
   (D) each time the owner modifies the property

8. The mortgagee's title insurance policy protects

   (A) the seller from financial loss
   (B) the purchaser from financial loss
   (C) the lending institution from financial loss
   (D) subsequent purchasers from loss

9. Under the Torrens system of land registration,

   (A) an error in recording that causes a loss is not the financial responsibility of the recorder
   (B) the recorder only verifies that the documents are in recordable form
   (C) title may pass prior to registration of the deed
   (D) damages incurred because of a bad certificate of title are paid for out of a special fund

10. The recording system provides the owner with

    (A) title insurance against all defects
    (B) constructive notice of claimed ownership to the public
    (C) building permits
    (D) relief from zoning limitations

11. The abstractor warrants that

    (A) there are no liens against the title to the property
    (B) the seller has good title to convey
    (C) the abstract company will compensate the buyer for any loss of title
    (D) the abstract is complete and all properly recorded documents are digested correctly

12. For the recording system protection to apply to a bona fide purchaser or mortgagee for value, all of the following occur EXCEPT

    (A) they give value (money) in reliance on the record
    (B) they act in good faith
    (C) they pay a premium to the recorder
    (D) they have no actual knowledge of an unrecorded instrument affecting the title

13. Which of the following is **not** required for the recording process?

    (A) The document must be in writing
    (B) The document must be executed and acknowledged
    (C) The document must be recorded in the jurisdiction where the property is located
    (D) The taxes on the property must be current prior to recording

14. The county recorder does which of the following?

    (A) Verifies the accuracy of the legal description on a deed
    (B) Acknowledges the document
    (C) Enters the document into the record
    (D) Verifies the survey

15. If a purchaser of property believes that there might possibly be a mechanic's lien against a property for recent work that has been done, the purchaser would ask for

    (A) a title insurance policy
    (B) a vendor's affidavit
    (C) an acknowledgment
    (D) a patent

16. Under the governmental survey method of land description, a tract of land is

    (A) 24 miles square
    (B) composed of 36 sections
    (C) 6 miles across
    (D) made up of 8 townships

17. In Figure 8-2, a legal description that calls for "220 feet by parallel lines off the SE ¼ of the SE ¼ of the SE ¼ of the section" includes how much land?

    (A) 10 acres      (C) 160 acres
    (B) 40 acres      (D) 3.3 acres

18. The vertical rows of townships are referred to as

    (A) tracts        (C) tiers
    (B) checks        (D) parallels

19. Why is the U.S. Governmental Survey important to legal descriptions for lots in a subdivision that has been platted and recorded?

    (A) Federal law supersedes state law in this area
    (B) Without it, it may be impossible to establish the point of beginning (POB) of the plat
    (C) Recorders carefully check the plat against the governmental survey and will not record the plat without this information
    (D) The governmental survey will show all easements and other restrictions on the use of the land

20. The recorded restrictions for Crooked Stick Estates (Figure 8-4) provide that any two-story home built must include what amount of living area?

    (A) 1,000 square feet    (C) 2,500 square feet
    (B) 1,500 square feet    (D) 3,500 square feet

# Chapter 9

# Landlord and Tenant Relationships

---

## VOCABULARY

*You will find it important to have a complete working knowledge of the following terms and concepts found in the text or the glossary.*

| | | |
|---|---|---|
| assignment of lease | forcible entry and detainer | net-net-net lease |
| burden-shifting clauses | graduated lease | obligation to pay rent |
| condemnation of leased premises | gross lease | percentage leases |
| constructive eviction | ground lease | periodic tenancy |
| economic waste | illegality of purpose | recording leases |
| escalator clause | implied warranty of fitness | self-help |
| estate at sufferance | indexed rent adjustments | step-up leases |
| estate at will | insurable interest | subleases |
| estate for years | invitees | triple net lease |
| estate from year to year | leasehold estate | vacation of premises |
| eviction | net leases | valid lease |
| exculpatory clause | | |

---

DURING much of the history of the United States, the legal rights and duties of both landlords and tenants were relatively unchanged. The common law of leases developed by the courts and supplemented by sparse statutory rules defining terms, rights, and obligations was vague. The result was the development of the standard form lease which spelled out in considerable detail the rights and obligations of both landlord and tenant. Since the landlord historically held the better bargaining position (particularly in the area of residential leasing), the standard forms tended to be "landlord's leases" in that they were heavily weighted in favor of the landlord.

Today the law seems to turn the advantage to the opposite extreme. Courts are now "reading into" leases implied warranties of habitability and "reading out" exculpatory clauses that traditionally relieved the landlord from any and all liability to the tenant for defects in leased property.

The Model Residential Landlord-Tenant Code, which has not yet received wide acceptance by state legislatures, represents a dramatic reversal of the traditional rules favoring the landlord. Tenant rent strikes and the payment of rent to an escrow agent instead of the landlord when the condition of rented property does not

meet health and safety standards are now widespread procedures that have been granted judicial approval even where there was no legal precedent for doing so.

In short, the law governing the rights and duties of landlords and tenants is changing, and the trend is toward an increase in the rights of the tenant with a corresponding increase in the obligations of the landlord. In the discussion that follows, the traditional common law rules are discussed and those that have experienced significant change are noted.

## LEASEHOLD INTERESTS

A *leasehold* is an estate in land created by a contract called a lease. Considerable inconsistency exists in the law of leases and the landlord-tenant relationship. This has come about because the courts have sometimes applied strict property law principles and at other times applied contract law principles in ruling on the various issues before them. Many problems are generated by the characterization of the tenant's interest as an estate in land and the strict application of real property rules, but the application of contract rules in a dispute concerning an estate in land introduces its own problems. Therefore our basic definition is adequate only to the extent that it suggests that both contract law and real property law principles are applicable in this area.

## LEASEHOLD ESTATES GENERALLY RECOGNIZED

Various types of leasehold estates have developed over a period of several hundred years in England and the United States. A wide variety of limited leasehold interests once existed in early English common law. Most of them have long fallen into disuse, and it is unlikely that they would be recognized by a modern court. Yet the few leasehold interests clearly recognized today do not always provide a sufficient range of choices for all situations. No one leasehold estate that we recognize is ideal, and thus many leases in common use today have been so drafted that they do not fit neatly into any of the categories set out below. The parties to the lease, of course, have the right to include almost any modification upon which they can agree. However, the rules governing the leasehold estates recognized by law apply to the extent that the parties do not change them by contract.

### Estate from Year to Year

While *estate from year to year* is technically the correct name for this leasehold estate, it is misleading in that it implies a relatively long-term lease measured in yearly increments. It is more commonly referred to as an *estate from period to period* or as a *periodic tenancy*. This tenancy is an estate that will continue for successive periods of a year, or successive periods of a fraction of a year, unless it is terminated. Thus the period of tenancy may be much shorter than a year. It may be from quarter to quarter, month to month, week to week or, conceivably, day to day.

While the term of the lease is specified as a year or a fraction of a year, the important characteristic of the periodic tenancy is that it renews itself, or is *automatically* extended, for another period without action by either the landlord or the tenant. In fact, it renews itself whether they want it to or not. One or the other must take some positive action in order to terminate it.

The termination of the periodic tenancy must be accomplished by a formal notice of termination from either the landlord or the tenant. The timing of this notice is critical; that is, the party against whom the lease is being terminated is entitled to advance notice. Unless the parties agree to some other time of notice, our statutes impose a highly technical notice provision. Notice of termination must usually be given three months or one full period (whichever is less) prior to the termination date. If, for example, the tenancy is from month to month, the amount of notice must be at least one month. If it is a year-to-year tenancy, notice must generally be given at least three months in advance of the termination date.

The notice of termination is critical to the right to terminate the tenancy, and this technical rule is strictly enforceable.

Certain precautions in the use of the periodic tenancy are warranted by its characteristics, particularly the requirement of notice of termination. The longer the period of the lease, the more severe the consequences of a failure to give timely notice of intent to terminate the lease. For example, failure on the part of the landlord to give timely notice of intent to terminate a year-to-year lease gives the tenant the absolute right to remain for another full year. While the parties may negotiate termination of the lease at the end of the year or at some later point, the bargaining positions of the parties will have changed drastically. At two months and 29 days prior to the end of the period, the landlord may have to buy possession that one day earlier he or she could have had for nothing (where three months' notice is required).

Where there are sufficient administrative controls to ensure that notice dates will not be overlooked, this tenancy may have a stabilizing effect upon occupancy without the necessity of negotiating a new lease at the end of the period. Where these controls are lacking or the lease is an occasional transaction, there is greater danger that the notice date will be overlooked. For leases for relatively short periods, the damage that might result from failure to give timely notice is minimized.

### Estate for Years

An *estate for years* is an estate having a duration fixed in units of a year or multiples or divisions thereof. This definition, like that of periodic tenancy, is of little help and is even misleading. The key element of the estate for years is that it must have a *definite* date of expiration. It makes no difference that the estate is for a period of time measured in terms of days, months, or years; if it has a definite expiration date, it is an estate for years. If the duration of the estate cannot be precisely computed at the outset, it is not an estate for years.

Thus a *determinable date of expiration* is the key to recognizing the estate for years, and it is the most important feature of the leasehold estate it creates. The duration of the lease is precisely stated, and there is no possibility of automatic or accidental renewal of the lease for another term. It terminates upon its expiration date without action on the part of either the landlord or the tenant. In fact, it takes positive action on the part of *both* to continue the relationship beyond the expiration date of the lease.

When the termination date of the estate for years arrives, the leasehold interest of the tenant expires. The tenant is obligated to vacate the property on that date, and the landlord is entitled to retake possession. This type of lease has the advantage of certainty as to the availability of the property (assuming that the tenant does not wrongfully hold over), but it also creates uncertainty as to the continuity of occupancy. The landlord is not entitled to notice from the tenant as to intentions to vacate and may be hesitant to assume the expense of seeking a new tenant when he or she may be able to retain an existing satisfactory tenant. At the same time, the tenant has no assurance that the leasehold estate will continue to be available and does not know what terms may be imposed by the landlord. To this extent the estate for years may introduce a degree of uncertainty that is unacceptable to both landlord and tenant.

The estate for years may be undesirable to both landlord and tenant because of prevailing and anticipated market conditions. When market conditions are unsettled or the landlord anticipates that the market price for the interest being leased is likely to increase, he or she may desire an estate for years because it will provide an opportunity to renegotiate the terms of the lease at its expiration date with either the existing tenant or a new one. The landlord may not want to be "locked in" to the same terms he or she is willing to accept at the onset of the lease. The tenant, for precisely the same reasons, may not be willing to be exposed to a renegotiation of the terms of occupancy at the end of the term of the lease.

Here the relative bargaining strength of the parties becomes a key factor. While the landlord may wish to be in a position to renegotiate the terms of the lease a year hence, he or she may not be able or willing to let the property sit vacant until the market price rises. Moreover, the anticipated rise may not occur. The tenant, however, may not desire exposure to renegotiation of the lease but, assuming the property is attractive to or needed by that person, he or she may not be in a position to pass up the opportunity to guarantee future possession now even though the cost of doing so may be more than the current market seems to dictate. Thus the definite expiration date of the estate for years may become a thorn in the side of both parties.

Frequently the solution to the problem is a combination of two things:

☐ A longer term than was initially contemplated by the tenant. This will assure the landlord of a longer period of "guaranteed" occupancy and perhaps a higher rent than might otherwise be commanded by the property in the current market.

☐ An option permitting the tenant to renew the lease for one or more additional periods of time, usually at an increased rental. This provides some protection to the landlord in the form of increased return if the tenant exercises the option, and it provides protection to the tenant by assuring a continued availability (at a higher price) without the obligation to extend occupancy.

The above arrangement provides some measure of protection to both parties without ruling out the possibility of negotiations leading to a new lease on completely different terms. It does, however, give the tenant an advantage in negotiations, and this advantage usually has to be paid for in the form of higher rent for the initial term.

### Estate at Will

The term of the *estate at will* is unknown at its outset. That is, no period or termination date is specified. It is an estate that is terminable at the will of either party and will continue indefinitely if no action is taken to terminate it by one party or the other. This feature of the tenancy at will introduces an even greater degree of uncertainty as to continued occupancy by the tenant, since he or she is free to vacate at any time after giving notice of termination. The landlord has the same right to terminate the lease at his or her pleasure upon providing proper notice. The lease terminates at the death of either party.

The notice required to terminate the tenancy at will is critical because neither party has any assurance of the continuation of the estate. It is only the length of the notice that gives either party any period of time on which to rely. Local statutes dictate the length of notice, but it may be as short as 30 days. Such notice is referred to as a "notice to quit."

In view of the short period of time provided for the notice to terminate the tenancy at will, this tenancy normally cannot arise by implication or by accident. It usually must be clearly and specifically created by the parties. In addition to this rule, there is also a presumption that a tenancy that is vaguely defined is treated as a month-to-month periodic tenancy. In any event, for property of real continuing value to the tenant, this tenancy should be used only with care and deliberation and with full knowledge of its consequences.

For property of lesser value, a tenancy at will may not present a serious problem for either party. At worst (from the landlord's standpoint), it will be a month-to-month tenancy, and it may eliminate the need for a formal written lease, the expense of which is not justified.

### Estate at Sufferance

The *estate at sufferance* is not an estate in land at all. It is simply a way to distinguish between one who has been rightfully in possession of the land of another under a valid lease and then wrongfully holds over, and one who was wrongfully in possession at the outset. That is, the tenancy at sufferance may be defined as:

an interest in land which exists when a person who had a possessory interest in land by virtue of an effective conveyance wrongfully continues in possession of the land after the termination of such interest but without asserting a claim to a superior title.

Since it is not a true estate in land, it has no termination date. Nor are any mechanics required to work an effective termination of the lease.

The termination of the estate at sufferance does not require notice because it is not a true estate; however, this is not meant to imply that physical removal of the tenant is a simple matter. Even though the landlord is entitled to immediate possession, the taking of it can be quite hazardous in terms of liability for forcible entry and detainer. The problems created by self-help in this area are discussed with respect to the subject of eviction later in the chapter.

## THE SIMPLE LEASE

A *simple lease,* as the term is used here, denotes the simplest kind of agreement between landlord and tenant under which the tenant takes possession of the landlord's property and the parties intend to create the relationship of landlord and tenant. This lease may be written, but it frequently is not. It is the unwritten lease or the written lease that is oversimplified that calls into play the common law and statutory law which exist today.

Just as a person who dies without making a will has a will written for him or her by the statutes of intestate succession, so too will landlord and tenant have their lease written for them by law to the extent that they fail to write it themselves. Knowledge of the rules of law that will be read into the relationship and imposed upon the parties is therefore important. One needs to be aware of their impact and to know what items ought to be agreed upon. Common law and statutory law are in many respects outmoded here and do not agree with the general rules as conceived by the average landlord and tenant.

### Rights and Obligations of the Parties

It is not practical to consider the simple lease an abstract estate in land. Any study of this estate must be made in terms of the rights of the parties because they are the manifestation of the leasehold estate. This is typically the way in which attorneys approach property law. Ownership is equated with a collection or bundle of rights to hold and use the property. So it is with the simple lease; the ownership of the leasehold interest is made up of a group of rights which accrue to the tenant.

### Tenant's Right to Possession

The tenant is entitled to be put in possession of the property by the landlord. Surprisingly, this rule is not universal and has not always been the common law rule. Because the landlord is conveying to the tenant an estate in land with the exclusive right to possession, it was at one time the law that, since the tenant had an estate, he or she had sufficient interest to act to remove parties in possession. However, if the landlord is to receive rent for granting possession to the tenant, the landlord clearly ought to have the burden of removing anyone who is wrongfully (or rightfully) in possession. In short, the landlord ought to be compelled to deliver that for which he or she is accepting payment. Fortunately, this rule of law is clearly established; the landlord has a positive duty to put the tenant in possession.

### Landlord's Right to Inspect

The landlord's right to enter upon the property for purposes of inspection is not clearly established even today. According to the pure estate theory of leases, the landlord has no such right because the landlord has conveyed an estate to the tenant whose consequent right to possession is exclusive with respect to everyone including the landlord. The normal practice is to reserve this right specifically to the landlord in the standard form leases in common use. The inclusion of such a clause has been common for so long that a strong argument could be made to the effect that this custom is so common that it has achieved the status of law. Unfortunately, the only way to prove this would be to try the issue in a local court and obtain a favorable ruling, and to do so may require an appeal to a court having appellate jurisdiction. The expense of this process far outweighs the expense of using a reliable form lease.

### Tenant's Right to Assign Rights

The right of the tenant to enjoy his or her estate in land includes the right to "sell" it by *assigning* his or her rights under the lease. Since the relationship between landlord and tenant is not a personal one, no contract law principle prohibits assignment of the tenant's rights. It is therefore clearly established that the tenant under a valid lease has the right to sell his or her estate. It is just as clear, however, that the tenant cannot sell any more than he or she owns, and the assignee therefore takes the leasehold subject to all restrictions and limitations included in the lease. It is also firmly established that the original tenant cannot escape his or her obligations under the lease by assigning his or her interests under it to another. The tenant remains liable unless and until the landlord agrees to accept the new tenant as a substitute for the initial tenant. This requires a new agreement, however, and the landlord is under no compulsion to enter into one.

### Tenant's Right to Create Lesser Estates

The tenant, unless specifically prohibited by the lease from doing so, has a clearly established right to create lesser estates or interests in the property. That is, the tenant may become a landlord for the term of the leasehold and *sublease* the property to others. He or she can create any interest that does not exceed his or her estate in land. For example, if the tenant has a lease for years which runs for a three-year period, a sublease can be created for any shorter period, such as two years, 11 months, and 29 days. As with the assignment of any leasehold, the tenant cannot create broader rights to the use of the property than that tenant has, and the original tenant remains liable for the performance of all duties imposed upon him or her by the lease.

### Tenant's Obligation to Pay Rent

The obligation of the tenant to pay rent is absolute. This rule follows from the fact that under law the tenant has an estate in land.

Some relief from the obligation to pay rent has come to be recognized today under the contract doctrine of *absolute destruction* of the subject matter of the contract, which relieves both parties from the obligation to perform the contract. Under this doctrine, if the entire subject matter of the contract is accidentally destroyed, neither party is further obligated to perform. The application of this doctrine to the leasehold estate area typically arises when the lease covers office space on an upper floor of an office building that is completely destroyed. This recognizes the reality of a situation in which the use of the land itself was not contemplated by the parties, that the parties actually dealt for something which no longer exists. In the absence of an undertaking on the part of the landlord to replace that which was bargained for, it would be grossly unfair to require the tenant to continue the payment of rent.

### Tenant's Right to Use of the Property

A tenant under a valid lease may use the property for any lawful purpose. Yet it is clearly a matter of some importance to the landlord to know the purpose for which the leased premises will be used. This is particularly true when the lease covers one portion of a shopping center in which the landlord has given to another tenant the exclusive right to conduct a particular business. Should a tenant under an unrestricted lease conduct the same business, it would result in a breach of the right of the tenant under the exclusive lease and would permit that tenant to vacate, perhaps at a serious loss to the landlord. The important point here is that under a lease which has no restrictions as to use, the tenant may use the property for any legal purpose and the landlord is unable to compel the tenant to refrain from using the property for any restricted purpose, no matter how disastrous this might be to other tenants or to the landlord.

While the right of the tenant to use the leased premises for any legal purpose may work to the disadvantage of the landlord, the same right could become a burden on the tenant. This occurs when the tenant leases with a particular purpose in mind that is not specified in the lease and that purpose becomes illegal. The tenant may not avoid his or her obligations under the lease because the tenant still has an estate in land which may be utilized for any *legal* purpose. The risk that the tenant's intended use may later become illegal is the tenant's risk, not the landlord's. While this may appear to be a harsh rule to be applied against the tenant, it must be remembered that inclusion in the lease of a specific clause can be negotiated if the tenant desires this protection. (Some additional consideration may have to be paid to the landlord to obtain this protection.)

While it is true that a tenant who has specified a particular purpose or use for the property may be relieved of his or her obligations under the lease, the rule is highly technical and its application difficult. The illegality of the purpose of the lease must be general rather than specific as to the tenant. For example, if a tenant has leased space for the specific purpose of operating a tavern and because of a change in the laws it becomes illegal to operate a tavern on the premises the tenant has rented, then the tenant will be relieved of obligations under the lease. However, if the tenant is unable to operate a tavern on the premises solely because he or she cannot qualify for a license, that person is not released from his or her obligations. The distinction between the two cases is significant. The risk that the tenant may not be able to qualify for a liquor license is a risk that he or she must take, but the law does not compel the tenant to take the risk of the possible future illegality of a presently legal purpose. While our example may be extreme, the same result can arise from the occurrence of a change in zoning regulations that makes illegal a use which was legal at the time the lease was consummated.

## Condemnation

In the event of condemnation of the leased premises, the tenant, since he or she has an estate in land, is entitled to be compensated for his or her interest. Under the rules which apply to a taking by eminent domain, any interest in land may be taken, but the owner is entitled to be paid for his or her interest. An important point here is that the award is not usually made separately; it is made to the owner of the fee. The tenant is entitled to be paid the value of his or her leasehold interest. This is true even though the tenant may take the bulk of the award because of the value of the leasehold estate. The question of the division of the award is a highly complex legal question that requires representation of the parties by competent counsel.

## Sales of Leased Property

The leasehold estate of the tenant represents an important encumbrance upon the fee interest of the landlord.

Once the leasehold estate is effectively created, it can be extinguished only by termination in accordance with its terms or a default by the tenant. It is not extinguished or in any way affected by a conveyance of the underlying fee interest. There is merely a change in landlords, and the tenant's rights are unaffected by the conveyance. In fact, the purchase may be motivated by the desirability of the tenant and the favorable terms (to the landlord) of the lease.

### Constructive Eviction

A contract doctrine that has been established under the law of landlord and tenant is the doctrine of *constructive eviction*. Under a pure estate theory of leases, there is no such thing as constructive eviction. Either the tenant is in possession or has been ousted from possession by the landlord. If the tenant is evicted, he or she is clearly under no further obligation to pay rent.

Modern law has tended to place more emphasis on the *quality* of possession—whether or not the tenant has received all that was bargained for. A typical case arises in the leasing of apartments in which there is a failure on the part of the landlord to provide housing fit for human habitation. The extent to which the tenant is permitted to treat the lease as being at an end and vacate and discontinue rental payments is far from clear at the present state of development of the law. Each situation must be analyzed on the basis of its own peculiar facts, and the determination then made as to whether constructive eviction has occurred. Whether or not the tenant must actually vacate the premises to have the benefit of the doctrine is also unclear. What is clear is the need for legal counsel before acting in reliance upon this doctrine.

### Risk of Destruction or Damage

The risk of destruction of the leased property is assumed to some extent by both landlord and tenant. Each has an insurable interest in the property, but neither has any obligation to insure the other's interest unless this burden is imposed by the terms of the lease. Since the tenant may have a continuing obligation to pay rent even if some or all of the improvements are destroyed during the term of the lease, he or she clearly needs the protection of casualty insurance.

However, the tenant has no duty to replace improvements that have been destroyed, and as a result the landlord who will receive the property back at the end of the lease term without the improvements that have been destroyed clearly has a need for insurance. At the same time, unless the landlord has agreed to do so in the lease, he or she has no duty to replace improvements that have been destroyed. (The same rules apply for partial destruction or damage to the leased premises.) The solution to

the problem is a well-drafted clause which spells out the duty of the landlord to repair or rebuild and the adjustment that will be made in the tenant's obligation to pay rent while repair or replacement is in process. Such a clause is difficult to draw up and should be written with great care.

### Liability for Personal Injury

The landlord has no liability for personal injuries that may occur to the tenant so long as the defect that causes the injury is obvious. Nor is the landlord liable even if the defect is not obvious and would not be found by reasonable inspection, provided that the landlord warns the tenant of the defect. The landlord's liability to anyone invited upon the premises by the tenant is subject to the same limitations. That is, so long as the defect is obvious or a warning is given to all who can foreseeably use the premises, the landlord will not be liable for personal injuries occurring on the leased premises.

Disputes frequently arise in this area, and as a result the landlord usually insists on a very broad *exculpatory clause* that frees him or her from liability for almost every conceivable injury to anyone. While such clauses may be effective with respect to the tenant, they are of doubtful value where the tenant's invitees are concerned. For the latter can hardly have their rights foreclosed by a private agreement between landlord and tenant of which they are unaware.

Recent case law developments throughout the country suggest that, regardless of the precautions taken by the landlord to avoid liability, there appears to be almost no way to avoid the doctrine of *implied warranty of fitness for habitability* regardless of the nature of the defect. Several states already ignore the exculpatory clause in reading and interpreting a residential lease, and other courts have strongly hinted that they are ready to take the same position when the question is presented.

The tenant, since he or she has an estate in land over which he or she has exclusive dominion, assumes certain obligations to invitees for any personal injury they may suffer. The degree of care the tenant must exercise varies, depending on his or her relationship to the invitee. That is, the tenant obviously owes a higher degree of care to one who has been invited onto the premises than to one who is a trespasser. The tenant owes an even higher degree of care and responsibility to someone who has been invited onto the premises for the profit of the tenant. That is, the business invitee is entitled to a greater degree of protection than the gratuitous or social invitee.

The ramifications of this area of responsibility are highly complex and therefore beyond the scope of this book. The important point is that the tenant has an obligation of reasonable care to invitees, an obligation that may not be able to be passed along to the landlord. The need for adequate insurance is obvious.

## Extent of Tenant's Right to Use Property

Just as self-help on the part of the landlord is looked on with disfavor, so is self-help by the tenant subject to sanction. Clearly, when the tenant uses more property than is included in the leasehold estate, the tenant is to that extent a trespasser and is treated as such by the law. A more difficult question is raised by a wrongful holding over by the tenant after the lease has been terminated either by its terms or by the breach of a condition imposed by the lease. In such a case, the tenant's original entry onto the property was not wrongful and he or she is therefore not a trespasser. However, the tenant's possession is clearly wrongful, and he or she will not be permitted to maintain it against the landlord. This tenant is characterized under the law as a *tenant at sufferance*. He or she may not be forcefully evicted by the landlord, but the tenant's continued possession is at the landlord's sufferance until the landlord can take effective action to evict. The landlord is entitled to be reimbursed by the tenant at sufferance for such damages as the loss of rental income during the period of the wrongful holding over.

## Eviction of Tenant by Landlord

*Eviction*, as used in this section, means complete and absolute dispossession of the tenant from the premises rented. Therefore constructive eviction, as described above, is not considered here. Further, eviction is restricted here to the situation in which it is the landlord who causes dispossession of the tenant. Dispossession as a result of governmental action, such as eminent domain, is not included.

### Grounds in Lease

The grounds on which the landlord may legally evict a tenant and retake possession of the premises must be found in the terms of the lease itself. The terms of the lease include those specifically included by the parties to it, plus the rights and duties imposed by statutory and common law rules, at least to the extent that they are not in conflict with the agreement of the parties.

As we have said, the lease is a contract between the landlord and the tenant. Since a basic policy of our contract law is that competent parties are free to enter into any legal contract they choose, the parties have wide latitude in establishing the terms of their lease. In general, these terms are strictly enforced. However, one must be aware of two points.

The relative strength of the bargaining positions of the parties is not ignored by the courts in considering particularly harsh conditions. This is especially true where the enforcement would work a forfeiture. Therefore, if for some reason the landlord is obviously in a position to dictate the terms of the lease, the terms must be fair.

If they are not, they may be found to be unenforceable even though the tenant agreed to them.

When a form lease is used, if there is any uncertainty in its terms, those terms will be construed against the party who furnished the form. This rule is most important from the residential landlord's point of view. The landlord usually prefers that one standard form of lease be used for all tenants; the uniformity which results promotes efficiency in the management of properties. While it seldom happens that a residential tenant supplies the form, the same is not true in the leasing of commercial space. Frequently the tenant of commercial space insists on the use of his or her own form and is in a strong enough bargaining position to impose its use on the landlord. But the basic rule is the same in either case: The form will be construed against the party who supplied it. Again, essential fairness of the terms, clearly expressed, will make it unnecessary to resort to legal interpretation by a court of law.

The two problems just discussed have a tendency to occur together. That is, frequently the fact that one party or the other is in a stronger bargaining position permits that party to impose a form of lease on the other. Such a situation would give a court two good reasons for finding unduly harsh terms to be unenforceable.

### Typical Grounds for Eviction

While the principal ground for eviction of the tenant is nonpayment of rent (discussed below), it is not unusual for the landlord to provide for other grounds that will terminate the tenant's right to remain in possession and give rise to the landlord's right to evict. The following are typical examples:

- ☐ Noncompliance by the tenant with local ordinances relating to health and safety
- ☐ Bankruptcy or other insolvency of the tenant that results in the right to possession being legally transferred to a receiver or creditor
- ☐ Failure to comply with the exclusive purpose included in the use clause
- ☐ Indulging in immoral or unlawful practices that are prohibited on the premises

The foregoing list is far from being exhaustive. The study of any well-drafted, long-form lease will reveal other conditions and the circumstances existing at the time the lease is negotiated; its purpose and the length of its term will suggest others that it would be desirable to include. The important element is the clause that makes the breach of any condition grounds for terminating the tenant's right to possession and giving rise to the landlord's right to evict the tenant and take possession.

## Nonpayment of Rent

Nonpayment of rent is the typical ground for eviction of the tenant by the landlord. Payment of the agreed rent is the basic consideration provided by the tenant in return for the continued granting of a leasehold estate in the property by the landlord. Statistics show that breach of the tenant's obligation to pay rent is by far the most frequent ground for eviction. It is therefore important to understand the terms under which nonpayment of rent results in the right to evict the tenant and the conditions under which the right to evict must be carried out.

In the absence of an agreement to the contrary in the lease itself, the obligation to pay rent does not arise until the end of the term of the lease. The importance of this feature of the law should not be overlooked from either the practical or the legal standpoint.

With a short-term lease (such as a month-to-month tenancy), the landlord's exposure to loss is minimized because he or she is entitled to rent at the end of the first month and is in a position to take action quickly if it is not received. But the situation is different when the lease is for a longer term (such as a year-to-year lease or an estate for years, which may terminate a year or more after its inception date) because the landlord cannot demand rent until the end of the term. In this case the landlord's exposure to loss is substantially increased.

The usual practice is to require the payment of rent on a monthly basis when the term of the lease is a year or more. The practice of providing for rent on some periodic basis throughout the term of the lease is so common that many persons believe it is the legal obligation of the tenant to pay rent in monthly installments. Yet this is not the case, and failure to provide in the lease for such periodic payments can have serious consequences. A typical clause used in a lease that is an estate for years is: ". . . at the rental of $1,200, which the lessee agrees to pay at the rate of $100 each month during the term of this lease." Such a provision permits the landlord to treat the nonpayment of any one installment as a breach of the tenant's obligation to pay rent and to proceed to evict the tenant.

## Notice of Termination for Nonpayment of Rent

Notice is required to terminate the lease for nonpayment of rent. This provision is usually based on statute, and no eviction proceeding can begin until appropriate notice has been given to the tenant that the lease has been terminated and that he or she must vacate the premises for failure to pay the agreed-upon rent. It must be noted that the expiration of the notice period is critical to the landlord's right to have possession of the property delivered up by the tenant. The notice period must of course be added to the period of time for which the rent was due, since it is not due until the end of the term (un-less the parties agree otherwise). It is therefore clear that the exposure of the landlord to risk is measured by the term of the lease plus the period of notice plus the time it takes to have the tenant physically removed.

The importance of the notice that must be given to terminate the lease for nonpayment of rent lies in the fact that, at the end of the notice period, the landlord has no assurance that the tenant will in fact vacate and surrender possession. At the end of the term of the lease the landlord has the legal *right* to possession; whether the landlord has the *fact* of possession is another matter entirely. If the tenant vacates the premises during the notice period, the landlord may enter and retake possession of the property. However, when the tenant fails to vacate the property, the landlord must take further action (a formal eviction proceeding) to remove the tenant and regain possession. This further delays the retaking of possession and increases the landlord's risk of loss of rent. Yet there is a partial solution to this problem.

Failure to pay rent *due in advance* usually terminates the lease, and no notice of termination is required. While the general rule provides that rent is due at the end of the term, the parties are free to agree to any rental arrangement. If they in fact agree that the rent is payable in advance, the agreement is enforceable and local law comes into play. The significance of this rule should be apparent: It minimizes the landlord's risk of loss of rent when the tenant defaults because the landlord knows of the default at the beginning of the term rather than at the end. In addition, the landlord's risk is further reduced by the fact that he or she need not give notice to terminate; the tenant's right to possession is automatically terminated by failure to pay the rent when it is due. Consequently, the landlord is entitled to demand possession immediately, and if it is not immediately surrendered, he or she may begin the formal eviction process at once.

## Payment of Rent in Advance

The payment of rent in advance has two advantages from the landlord's standpoint. The landlord knows at the beginning of the term if there will be a default and can act to retake possession immediately because no notice to terminate is required. Nevertheless, the landlord is still exposed to the risk of loss of rent for the period of time it takes the tenant to surrender possession either voluntarily or as the consequence of a formal eviction proceeding. To protect against even this risk, many landlords require at the outset of the lease that two months' rent be paid in advance, one covering the first month of the lease and the second covering the last month. This provides protection against loss of rent during the period it takes to remove the defaulting tenant, provided of course that this does not extend beyond one period of the lease, usually one month.

The advance payment should not be confused with the *damage deposit* frequently required by landlords. The damage deposit is earmarked for the cost of extraordinary repairs made necessary by damage caused to the premises by the tenant in addition to *normal wear*. The landlord may be entitled to the damage deposit, even though the tenant does not default in payment of rent, if the tenant commits waste or unreasonable damage to the property during the tenancy. In practice, the damage deposit and the last month's rent collected at the beginning of the term of the lease are frequently confused by both landlord and tenant. It is not at all uncommon for the tenant to forfeit the damage deposit as a penalty for breaking the lease by leaving before the end of its term. Landlords frequently accept the damage deposit in lieu of exercising the right to sue the tenant for the rent due for the balance of the term.

Eviction is not the exclusive remedy of the landlord for a breach of lease by the tenant. The landlord is entitled to pursue other remedies for any damages he or she may suffer as a result of the tenant's breach. That is, the landlord is entitled to sue for all anticipated rents for the entire term, even though the tenant has vacated and surrendered possession prior to the end of the term. Of course the landlord may not sit idly by and let the damages accumulate; the landlord has a duty to mitigate the damages. That is, the landlord must make a reasonable effort to rent the premises to another tenant for the unexpired portion of the term and then deduct the *net* proceeds of such rental (after deducting the expenses involved in obtaining a new tenant) from the amount owed by the defaulting tenant.

### Limitations on Self-Help

Limitations on self-help by the landlord in retaking possession of the leased premises following a default by the tenant are imposed by law and enforced by stern consequences for violation. S lf-help is generally frowned upon by the law on the theory that the available legal system is designed to provide a peaceful means for settling all disputes. This policy is forcefully administered when there is the real possibility of a breach of the peace because of a personal confrontation of the parties in an attempt to regain possession of property wrongfully held. Thus forcible entry by the landlord to regain possession of the property is not tolerated by the law. Nor may the landlord forcefully retain the property, no matter how the landlord obtains possession, unless it be through the legal machinery of a formal eviction proceeding.

Forcible entry into the premises for which the landlord has granted a leasehold estate is the single act most likely to provoke a drastic reaction from our legal system. When the landlord indulges in such action, he or she may be faced with a serious lawsuit that will have equally serious financial consequences. The suit by the dispossessed tenant in such a case proceeds not only upon the *actual* damages he or she has suffered; in addition, punitive or exemplary damages are awarded by the court far in excess of any actual provable damages. As the names suggest, these damages are designed to punish the landlord for taking the law into his or her own hands and to make an example of the landlord for others in the community. It is a rather serious matter when a landlord is charged with forcible entry.

The term *forcible entry* might mislead one to believe that the use of physical force must be involved. However, case law in this area has expanded the definition of the term to include fraud or trickery on the part of the landlord to obtain possession of the property and any subsequent forcible retention of it.

The foregoing rules clearly indicate that precautions should be taken whenever the landlord retakes possession of leased premises following a default by the tenant. Only two situations appear to permit repossession without legal proceedings: (1) when the premises have been abandoned by the defaulting tenant and (2) when, upon being asked to vacate, the defaulting tenant does so. In all other situations, there is serious risk that the landlord will be in violation of the forcible entry and detainer law—with potentially drastic consequences.

### Vacation of the Premises by the Tenant

Just as there are situations in which the landlord may be justified in removing the tenant for a breach of a condition of the lease (such as nonpayment of rent), so are there situations in which the tenant may be justified in vacating the premises. When the tenant is not receiving the benefit of his or her bargain, there should be an opportunity for the tenant to vacate and discontinue the payment of rent. In the event of a failure of consideration (furnishing of the estate under the conditions agreed upon), it is clearly unfair to require the tenant to continue possession and the obligations imposed upon him or her by the lease.

### Rights in Lease

As in the case of the landlord, the tenant's rights must generally be found in the lease itself. That is, just as the tenant may be obligated under the lease to do more than pay rent, so may the landlord be obligated to perform more than mere possession of the premises. If the landlord is to be obligated beyond the furnishing of possession, this obligation must be found in the lease itself. The same rules regarding the rights and duties of the parties under their contract and the interpretation of the form lease that we discussed with regard to eviction by the landlord apply with equal force and effect to the tenant who desires to vacate and avoid obligations before the end of the term of the lease.

In addition to the general rights to exclusive possession for the term of the lease without actual or constructive eviction by the landlord, typical provisions frequently negotiated for the tenant's benefit include

☐ The right to use the property for any lawful purpose
☐ The right to have an exclusive right to use leased premises for a certain purpose, as in a shopping center
☐ Maintenance and repair of the property by the landlord
☐ The right to extend the lease for an additional term at its expiration, upon predetermined conditions and rent

The above list is certainly not conclusive. Many conditions may be imposed by the tenant, including even the option to purchase the property during the term of the lease. The nature and extent of the tenant's rights (in addition to possession) will depend on the circumstances and bargaining positions of the parties at the time the lease is negotiated.

### Eviction

Eviction by the landlord, a physical ouster from possession, is the basic ground that relieves the tenant of his or her obligations under the lease. Even under a pure estate theory of leases, it would be manifestly unfair to require the tenant to perform his or her part of the bargain when the landlord, by his or her own actions, has made it impossible for the tenant to have possession of the leased premises. We have already considered those situations in which something less than a complete ouster is involved—such as constructive eviction, in which there is substantial failure of the landlord to provide the estate agreed upon. In these cases there is, in the eyes of the law, a failure of the tenant's estate that relieves the tenant of the obligation to pay for it. Of course, when governmental intervention either takes the leased premises or makes the sole purpose of the lease illegal, both parties are relieved from further performance of their duties under the lease.

### Breach of a Specific Condition

Additional grounds or conditions may, by the agreement of the parties, be made precedent to the tenant's obligations under the lease. Just as the landlord may restrict the tenant's use of the property to a single purpose, so may a tenant obtain the exclusive right to use the premises for a particular purpose within a prescribed area. Such a condition of exclusivity may or may not be one that the landlord can control, but whether or not the

landlord has control, the parties can agree upon such a continuing state of affairs.

When the condition of exclusivity within a particular area ceases to exist, the tenant is free to vacate and cease payment of rent (or have whatever other relief the lease may provide). Where the parties have clearly established in their lease the conditions under which the tenant is obligated to continue performance of his or her obligations, at least the consequences are predictable. That is, upon a breach of the condition, the tenant may vacate the premises, stop paying rent, and be relieved of other obligations imposed by the lease. However, the lease may require the tenant to accept the breach of the condition for some period of time without being relieved of the lease's obligations. Such provisions are quite common. Also common are provisions that permit modification of the tenant's obligations on a predetermined basis when the landlord is unable to perform his or her obligations completely. Such clauses permit the parties to retain the benefits of their bargain when the breach is not material.

## REQUIREMENTS OF A VALID LEASE

In view of the complexity of the rules relating to leasehold estates and the possibility of misunderstanding between landlord and tenant, any lease should be carefully thought out and should be in writing so that the parties clearly understand their rights and obligations. While such practice is strongly recommended, however, the bare legal requirements are satisfied by a great deal less in most cases. Here we consider the questions of the necessity for formality in establishing the leasehold estate and the relationship of landlord and tenant.

### Requirement of a Written Lease

Since a lease is in effect a legal conveyance of an estate in land and is also frequently a contract that cannot be performed within one year, it is logical to require that it be in writing. Under the statute of frauds, as a general rule, each of the above characteristics requires a written contract in order to make the parties' agreement enforceable. However, the short-term lease of real estate is a major exception to the general rule. Leases for short terms need not be in writing; they may be oral and still be enforceable by both landlord and tenant. If the lease is for an extended period, it must be in writing to comply with the statute.

Two major problems must be considered in deciding whether the lease in a given case should be in writing: enforceability of the lease between landlord and tenant and notice of its existence to third persons.

A lease may be enforceable even though it is not in writing if it is for a short period of time. The terms of the lease, to the extent that the oral agreement of the parties does not change them, are those of a simple common law lease, which we discussed earlier in this chapter. However, except for relatively short-term leases (as in the case of a month-to-month tenancy), the practice of relying on an oral lease is hazardous and invites disputes. Seldom do the parties reach specific agreement on all the points that should be considered.

Where third persons are concerned, the oral lease poses a serious problem. The purchaser of real estate must take it subject to the rights of tenants in possession under a valid lease. It has already been noted that sale of the fee does not cut off the rights of the seller's tenants. Since the short-term lease need not be in writing, it need not be recorded, for an unwritten lease leaves nothing to record. Therefore the prospective purchaser who carefully checks the records maintained by the county recorder will not be aware of the existence of an oral lease. The purchaser must also inspect the property and determine what rights are claimed by whoever is in possession.

While the seller would normally make certain warranties in the deed for the protection of the buyer, these warranties generally provide only for the payment of damages where the true facts are not as represented. Therefore, even though the buyer may have the right to sue the seller for damages resulting from the fact that the fee is encumbered by a short-term lease, this does not affect the tenant's rights to the benefits of the lease. The prudent purchaser of real estate, if he or she is to be a bona fide purchaser, has no choice but to inspect the property immediately prior to closing the sale. If the purchaser finds someone other than the seller in possession, inquiry must be made to determine what rights the party in possession claims. The purchaser who fails to do this may be saddled with a tenant for a relatively long term rather than have the anticipated right to immediate possession.

## Parties to the Lease Must Be Competent

Since the lease of real estate is an important agreement that has characteristics of both a conveyance and a contract, the law requires that landlord and tenant be competent to enter into a binding lease. There is a certain degree of risk in dealing with anyone in a business matter, and it is a practical impossibility to be certain of anyone's legal competence. The real estate business is no exception. The problem may be even more acute here because transactions, including leasing, are not usually entered into out of hand. That is, there is normally discussion and negotiation involved because of the importance of the transaction. Consequently, there is more opportunity to make a judgment as to the competency of the parties and less excuse for not making that judg-

ment. Fortunately, there is a general presumption that all persons are competent. To avoid—that is, to set aside—a contract, the incompetent person generally has the burden of proving that he or she is incompetent.

## Requirement of Consideration

Because the lease is in effect a legal contract between landlord and tenant, it must meet the technical rule that consideration is essential to make it enforceable. Simply stated, the requirement of consideration means that, for a promise to be enforceable, it must be paid for. In the lease of real estate, the basic consideration provided by the landlord is the continued provision of an estate in land; for the tenant the consideration is payment of the agreed rent. However, this is a simplification, for the typical lease imposes additional duties on both landlord and tenant. In each instance the lease itself shows what consideration each party must provide to support the obligations of the other party. The important point here is that some consideration must be provided by each party in order to make the lease enforceable. It is also important to remember that neither party is entitled to more than the agreed consideration. Consider the following situation.

*Example* Landlord and tenant enter into a valid lease of an apartment for one year at a rent of $100 per month. After six months the landlord increases the rent to $125 per month, advising the tenant that the increase is dictated by increased maintenance expenses. The tenant agrees to pay the increased rent but fails to do so. The landlord sues the tenant for the increase. The tenant will prevail.

*Explanation* It is clear that the parties had agreed upon the rent for the entire term of one year. Even though the tenant promised to pay the increased rent, he or she cannot be compelled to do so. The legal reason for this is that the landlord provided no consideration to make the promise binding. That is, the landlord was already legally obligated to provide space to the tenant at $100 per month and has not undertaken or promised to do anything that he or she was not already obligated to do under the lease agreement. The landlord is therefore entitled not to the increased rent but only to the rent agreed upon at the outset.

## Legality of the Purpose of the Lease

As a general rule of contract law, a contract for an illegal purpose is not enforceable. Where the lease of real estate is concerned, this rule makes it impossible for either party to enforce the terms of the lease. A lease entered into for the purpose of conducting a gambling house is illegal today in most states, and either party could avoid the obligations of that lease. A more serious question is raised when the lease is entered into for a purpose that is legal at the time it is negotiated but which later becomes illegal. We discussed this matter earlier in the chapter.

### Requirement of Recording

The statute of frauds does not require that a short-term lease be in writing or that it be recorded. However, when the lease is for a lengthy period, it must be in writing if it is to be enforceable between the parties. In order to provide notice to third parties, such a lease must also be recorded with the recorder of the county in which the real estate is located. Failure to do so may result in the loss of the tenant's rights under the lease if the property is purchased by a bona fide purchaser from the landlord.

It is not usually necessary that an entire lease be recorded. Many statutes provide for the filing of a memorandum of lease, which is sufficient to protect the rights of the tenant without requiring that a public record be made of the entire contents of the lease. The landlord may have little or no interest in seeing that the lease is recorded, since the recording of the lease primarily protects the tenant and in fact creates an encumbrance on the landlord's title. Thus it is quite common for a detailed lease to require that the landlord agree to execute a short form or memorandum of lease in recordable form so that the tenant can protect his or her own interest.

A written lease, even though it need not be recorded because it is for a short term, may nevertheless be recorded if it is in recordable form. As a matter of practice, short-term leases are not recorded, in part because they tend to clutter up the record and, more important, because they are encumbrances on the owner's title. Once they have been recorded they continue to be defects of record and, unless they expire by their terms, evidence must later be provided that they have expired or been terminated. For example, if a lease from year to year is recorded and the tenant defaults after six months, the record will continue to show that the same tenant has an interest in the property. In the event of sale by the landlord, this defect will have to be cleared. If the tenant is not cooperative, this will require litigation by the landlord (such as a quiet title action) to establish as a matter of record that the tenant has no further interest in the property.

There are situations in which the recording of a short-term lease may be important to the tenant. Assume, for example, that the tenant for some reason is not in actual possession of the property, so the tenant's claim of interest in the property will not be apparent to third persons who inspect the property. In such an unusual case the tenant may desire a recordable lease so that the record will protect his or her interest against third parties.

To be recordable, the lease must be in writing. Other formal requirements must also be met. The lease must be acknowledged; if it is not, the county recorder will not accept it for recording. (The requirement of acknowledgment is the same as that for deeds and other documents.) The legal description must be accurate and sufficient to identify the property clearly. This description should be as detailed as it would be in a deed, for if it is not correct, it will not be properly indexed and may not be effective to provide notice to third persons.

### Rent Adjustment Provisions

While the landlord may not arbitrarily increase the rent specified under the agreement with the tenant, and while the tenant is similarly bound to pay the full rent agreed upon, it is frequently in the best interests of both parties to provide for some degree of flexibility, particularly where the term of the lease is lengthy. With significant changes in economic conditions—real estate taxes, casualty insurance costs, maintenance expenses—the party with the obligation to pay them may suffer economic loss. At the same time, the very location of the leased property may be an important factor in determining the fair rental value.

Clauses that provide some measure of protection to both parties can be included in the lease at the outset.

#### Indexed Adjustment of Rent

A commonly used clause in long-term leases is one based on some standard economic indicator maintained by an independent third party. For residential properties it is quite common to provide that the rent will be adjusted annually on the basis of the cost of living statistics maintained and published by the federal government. Since this measure includes a wide variety of items that are unrelated to rents for apartments (such as the cost of food), this clause is frequently tied to only that portion of the cost of living that relates to housing. In this way, even though the trend for the most part has been upward in recent years, theoretically both landlord and tenant are protected from dramatic swings in the value of housing.

Since the lease terms are a matter of private contract between landlord and tenant, there is no reason why this provision could not also include an escalation clause to cover the increasing costs of insurance and rising real estate taxes. Such clauses need to be drafted with considerable care, the primary emphasis being on the certainty of measurement of the indicator and its application to the originally agreed rent.

#### Step-up Leases

Step-up leases attempt to resolve this issue in another way. Indexing the rent to some economic indicator, as discussed above, necessarily includes an element of uncertainty in the amount of rent to be paid in a given year.

Often the parties will agree to some specified increase (step-up) in the rent in terms of dollars rather than another economic indicator. For example, a 5-year lease might provide that the rent is to increase at a rate of 8 percent each year. Inflation may or may not make such an increase each year necessary, or it may make the increase wholly inadequate. It does, however, have the advantage that the tenant can plan ahead based on such a provision. Such *escalator* clauses are not uncommon in leasing office space. *Graduated leases* is another term often used to describe such leases.

### Percentage Leases

In the commercial area it is common to utilize a *percentage lease*. Such a lease includes a relatively low annual rent (but sufficient at least to cover debt service, taxes, and insurance), with a provision that the rent will be increased by a specified percentage of sales volume experienced by the tenant. Such leases are frequently encountered in shopping centers—on the theory that the location in the center and its promotion by the landlord and other tenants have an impact on the volume of sales generated by a particular tenant.

This theory is easier to recognize when it is applied to a franchise type of operation located within a major store. For example, the shoe repair department of a large retail store is frequently operated by someone other than the store itself. In such a case it is far clearer that the traffic generated by the store's general advertising has considerable influence on the volume of traffic and the amount of business done by the independent shoe repair department operator.

Considerable care must be used in drafting this kind of provision, and several difficult questions must be negotiated:

☐ What percentage will be applied? That is, just how much benefit is there to the tenant in terms of increased business?

☐ To what will that percentage be applied? To the gross business done or the net profit earned?

☐ How will determination of the volume of sales be made to the satisfaction of both parties to the lease? An independent audit by a certified public accountant is one method; however, in the case of a relatively small operation, the expense may be prohibitive. Some less precise method may have to be accepted to make the arrangement beneficial to both parties.

### Burden-shifting Clauses (Net leases)

It is not at all uncommon to find leases that require the tenant to pay any increase in insurance costs that results from the use to which the tenant puts the property. However, the lease can go even further and provide that the tenant pay *all* insurance, real estate taxes, and maintenance expenses in addition to the agreed rent. In such a case we have a true *net-net-net lease*. That is, the rent received by the landlord is net of all three expenses assumed by the tenant. Such leases are often used where the tenant will make substantial and expensive improvements upon the property and use it for a long period of time. The price paid by the landlord to obtain such a lease is frequently the surrender of all rights to increase the rent during the term of the lease. The rate of return he receives in such cases is static and may effectively decline during inflationary periods.

Combinations of all the variations discussed above are possible, and any combination of provisions, each of which is complex in itself, is the job of the expert attorney. However, the professional property manager must have a working knowledge of these variations, the ability to recognize the combination that would be most appropriate in a given situation, and the negotiating skills to structure the lease properly.

### Gross Leases

As noted in the discussion of indexed adjustments of rent, the use of net leases introduces an element of uncertainty for the tenant. The total rental cost may vary each year, and the tenant may be unwilling to take this risk. In such a case the rent paid can be purely *gross* rent. Any risk of increased costs for taxes, maintenance, and insurance will then be the burden of the landlord. Obviously, the landlord must be protected to make the gross lease attractive. The answer is to raise the rent high enough to cover any anticipated cost increases during the life of the lease. The higher rental may still be attractive to the tenant because the rental expense is now predictable. For the commercial tenant, this predictability may be a great enough advantage to make the gross lease more attractive than any of the net lease combinations discussed above.

### Ground Leases

Vacant ground which has commercial potential is frequently leased on a long-term basis, even without buildings. At his or her own expense, the tenant will then construct improvements that will enable the property to produce income. In such cases the landlord is not entitled to a return on the value of the buildings because he or she did not furnish them or pay for them. The landlord is entitled to a return based on the value of only the ground itself. Such leases are usually long-term: 40 years or longer. This lengthy period permits the tenant enough time to earn back the cost of the buildings as well as make a profit during the term of the lease. (The buildings will belong to the landlord at the expiration of the lease under the *law of fixtures,* discussed in Chapter 6.) Because insurance, maintenance, and real estate taxes will be determined by the tenant's use of the property as well as the type of buildings the tenant constructs, such leases are almost always triple net leases. Some inflationary pro-tection for the landlord may also be negotiated into such a lease because of its very long term.

## REVIEW QUESTIONS

1. Under a valid lease, the tenant has the right or obligation to do all of the following EXCEPT

   (A) assign his or her entire interest under the lease to another without the landlord's approval
   (B) sublet the premises to third parties without the landlord's permission
   (C) be responsible personally to the landlord for the performance of all tenant's obligations under the lease
   (D) keep the property habitable

2. When the leased premises are taken by the state under eminent domain,

   (A) the landlord and tenant share the payment equally
   (B) the tenants receive no portion of the payment
   (C) the tenants are compensated for their interest
   (D) the tenant must seek separate compensation from the court

3. A lease that has a definite termination date that can be clearly established at the beginning of the lease is called

   (A) an estate for years
   (B) an estate at sufferance
   (C) a determinable lease
   (D) a periodic tenancy

4. If a tenant who had a valid lease holds over after it terminates,

   (A) the landlord may physically remove the tenant and his or her belongings
   (B) the tenant is considered by law to be a trespasser
   (C) the tenant becomes a tenant at sufferance
   (D) the landlord may do nothing until the tenant leaves voluntarily

5. R has leased a property to S for a two-year period. The property is zoned residential. S may

   (A) alter the property to suit his or her needs without R's permission
   (B) sublease the property to a third party
   (C) run a small business from the premises without R's permission
   (D) none of the above

6. A lease that automatically renews itself in the ab-sence of notice of intent to terminate by one party or the other is called

   (A) a tenancy at sufferance
   (B) an estate from year to year
   (C) a tenancy at will
   (D) an estate for years

7. A lease that provides for a base rental plus a per-centage of the gross sales of the tenant is called

   (A) an indexed lease
   (B) a sublease
   (C) a net-net-net lease
   (D) a percentage lease

8. At the end of the period of a ground lease, the fixtures constructed by the tenant

   (A) become the property of the landlord
   (B) are the property of the tenant and may be severed
   (C) must be sold and the money divided equally between the landlord and the tenant
   (D) are considered personal property and are not addressed in the lease

9. G leases office space from D. The building in which the office is located is destroyed by fire. What will be the status of the lease between G and D?

   (A) The lease will continue and the rent will be due as usual
   (B) The lease terminates because there has been destruction of the subject matter of the lease
   (C) The lease will be continued, but rent will be charged against the value of the land only
   (D) The lease will be terminated if repairs cannot be made within 60 days

10. Under the common law of leases, the tenant has been granted an estate in land; therefore,

   (A) the tenant has the right of exclusive possession of the premises for the period of the lease
   (B) the tenant may use the property for any de-sired purpose
   (C) the landlord may freely enter the property to inspect it
   (D) the landlord forgoes any warranty of habitabil-ity

11. Y has leased an office from Z on a month-to-month

basis at $600 per month. The agreement states that either party may terminate the arrangement with 30 days' notice to the other party. Without any notice, the agreement will automatically renew itself each month. This type of lease is

(A)  an estate-for-years lease
(B)  a period-to-period lease
(C)  a tenancy at will
(D)  a tenancy at sufferance

12.  Under a net-net-net lease, the tenant pays

(A)  no expenses of the property
(B)  only maintenance-related expenses
(C)  only taxes charged to the property
(D)  taxes, insurance, and maintenance on the property

13.  When a visitor is invited onto leased premises by the tenant, the tenant

(A)  must warn the visitor of any dangerous condition that is not apparent
(B)  has no duty to the visitor for any injury incurred
(C)  would be obligated to the visitor if the visitor were invited for business purposes
(D)  shares the responsibility for the visitor with the landlord on an equal basis

14.  When a tenant remains in possession after the term of the lease has expired, he becomes

(A)  a trespasser
(B)  a tenant at will
(C)  a tenant at sufferance
(D)  a tenant appurtenant

15.  An indexed lease

(A)  allows for increased space to be taken by the tenant in the future, based on growth
(B)  allows for increases in rent based on an established economic conditions
(C)  makes the tenant liable for all increases in the expenses of the property as they occur
(D)  applies only to ground lease arrangements

16.  When the sole purpose or use as stated in the lease becomes illegal,

(A)  the tenant may vacate and cease paying rent

(B)  the balance of the rent becomes due immediately
(C)  the tenant is liable for rent until a new tenant is found
(D)  the rent is reduced until the tenant puts a legal operation on the premises

17.  The case law on the responsibilities of a landlord has found

(A)  an implied warranty for fitness and habitability in residential leases
(B)  a warranty of fitness and habitability only if it is written in the lease
(C)  no warranty of fitness or habitability if the residential lease is oral
(D)  the tenant assumes the property as is whether the lease is written or oral

18.  A landlord would have grounds to evict a tenant for all of the following reasons EXCEPT

(A)  noncompliance by the tenant with local ordinances relating to health and safety
(B)  failure to comply with the exclusive purpose of the lease
(C)  nonpayment of the agreed-upon rent
(D)  subleasing the premises without the landlord's approval, even though it was not addressed in the lease

19.  J sells an apartment complex he owns to K. All the leases are in force until August of next year. What can K do if he wishes to raise the rents?

(A)  K can ask J to raise the rents before closing so K gets title with new rent
(B)  As soon as K gets title, he can raise the rent
(C)  J should notify all tenants of the sale and the new rents that K will want to charge
(D)  K cannot do anything until August of next year because the purchase is subject to the leases

20.  In the absence of a contrary agreement, rent is due

(A)  for the full term in advance
(B)  in monthly installments on the first day of each month
(C)  monthly on the last day of the month
(D)  at the end of the term of the lease

# Chapter 10

# Mortgages, Deeds of Trust, and Land Contracts

## VOCABULARY

*You will find it important to have a complete working knowledge of the following terms and concepts found in the text or the glossary.*

| | | |
|---|---|---|
| assignment | foreclosure | power of sale |
| assumption of mortgage | forfeiture | priorities of mortgages |
| attachment | free and clear sale | promissory note |
| conditional sales contract | grace period | purchase money mortgage |
| contract for a deed | junior mortgage | release |
| covenants | land contract | rescission |
| deed of trust | lien | satisfaction |
| default | liquidated damages | second mortgage |
| deficiency judgment | mortgage | security device |
| due-on-sale clause | mortgagee | senior mortgage |
| encumbrance | mortgagor | specific performance |
| equitable title | nonrecourse | subject to a mortgage |
| equity | novation | trust deed |
| equity of redemption | penalty clause | trustee |
| execution | personal liability | |

THE legal aspects of financing the purchase of real estate are of obvious importance to real estate salespersons and brokers. Because of the highly technical nature of this area of the law, we do not cover it in great depth in this chapter. It would be impractical to try to do so in any event, for there are many minor variations in the law from state to state. The reader should be aware of the limitations on the scope of the following discussion.

## MORTGAGES

Legally, a *mortgage* is a pledge of the owner's interest in real estate and the improvements on it to secure the repayment of a loan. While different states follow either the *lien* or the *title* theory of mortgage law, the practical difference between them in effect is minimal, and we ignore the distinction in this discussion. The points we make in connection with mortgages are true regardless of the legal theory being applied to determine the rights of the parties.

A mortgage creates a lien on real estate in favor of the lender, but the owner of the real estate retains the usual rights of ownership. All the *mortgagee* (the lender) has is the right to pursue the *mortgagor's* (the borrower's) real estate to satisfy the debt that runs from mortgagor to mortgagee. Since the mortgagor always has title, he or she can sell the property, give it away, mortgage it again, or lease it. The mortgagor retains all rights of ownership (plus duties, such as payment of taxes), subject to the right of the mortgagee to foreclose against and sell the property if the mortgagor fails to pay the debt. Not until there is a default in payment of the debt (or in some other obligation set forth in the mortgage) does the mortgagee have any right to proceed against the mortgagor's real estate.

The mortgage secures the repayment of a *promissory note*. The basic transaction that gives rise to a mortgage is a loan from the mortgagee to the mortgagor which is evidenced by a promissory note (secured by a mortgage of real estate). Thus a mortgage is simply a device that creates a lien on real estate to secure the repayment of a debt. A mortgage agreement sets out the contractual aspects of the loan; such a contract is ineffective without the existence of debt.

The validity of the lien depends on the existence of debt. The life of the mortgage is the debt. Without the existence of debt, there is no purpose for the mortgage and the mortgagee can have no interest in the property.

The mortgagor may or may not be *personally* liable for the debt. In the case of a home mortgage, the borrower is personally liable for repayment of the money he or she has borrowed. The borrower executes a promissory note that personally binds him or her to repay the amount borrowed, separate and distinct from the mortgage. Therefore, if the mortgagor fails to repay the debt, the mortgagee is entitled to foreclose against the realty, have the property sold, and apply the proceeds to the debt. However, if this is insufficient to pay the debt (as is frequently the case), the mortgagor remains personally liable for the balance, called the *deficiency*. This point, which is frequently misunderstood, is crucial to consideration of the subject of sales of mortgaged property.

Loans on commercial property are frequently made on a *nonrecourse* basis; that is, the lender agrees to look solely to the property in the event of a default, with no personal liability on the part of the borrower.

## Requirements for Creating a Mortgage

The formal requirements for the execution of a mortgage are the same as those for a deed, including the requirement of acknowledgment if the mortgage is to be recorded in order to obtain the protection of the recording system.

In addition, the typical form of mortgage used today imposes further duties on the mortgagor, such as the duties to keep the property in good repair, to insure it for the benefit of both borrower and lender, and to pay all taxes and assessments. Failure to keep these *covenants* (promises), which are contractually made, is a breach of the mortgage. These conditions are in addition to the underlying basic promise to pay the debt.

## Sales of Mortgaged Property

Because of the theory of mortgages that generally prevails, under which the mortgagor (owner) of real estate has title to the property and the mortgagee has only a security interest that can be exercised only upon default, it is clear that the owner of mortgaged property may sell it. It is also clear, however, that the rights of the mortgagee cannot be defeated by such a conveyance and that the mortgagor is still personally liable for the debt.

There are three ways in which the mortgagor may sell his or her property.

### Sale Free and Clear

A sale free and clear of the existing mortgage has the following results:

☐ The old mortgage is satisfied at the sale. The buyer provides sufficient cash to permit the seller to pay the debt. The seller pays the debt, and the mortgage that secures it is released by the mortgagee. Since the seller has paid the debt and the mortgage has been released, the seller has no further liability. The property is free and clear of the encumbrance of the mortgage.

☐ A new mortgage may be executed by the buyer. In many cases, the buyer simultaneously borrows money and executes a new mortgage of his or her own so that the property is actually free and clear for only an instant, and it is difficult to recognize legally what has occurred. From a practical standpoint, the property remains subject to a mortgage, but there is a new debt, a new mortgage, and a new mortgagor-owner.

☐ The seller has no further liability for debt by virtue of the *release* by his or her mortgagor.

### Sale Subject to the Mortgage

When the existing mortgage is not *satisfied* at the time of sale (so that the sale will be free and clear), there are the following results:

☐ The seller remains personally liable for the debt. The original mortgagor's note is unpaid, and the mortgagor's obligation to pay it remains; that is, the mortgagor remains personally liable for the whole debt.

☐ The buyer is not liable for the debt. The buyer has no personal obligation to pay the seller's debt because he has not contracted to do so. As a practical matter, he must pay the debt in order to protect his investment; but if he fails to do so, he cannot be compelled to pay it.

☐ The mortgagee's rights against the property are unchanged. Because the mortgage was an existing *encumbrance,* the property is still the security for the original borrower's debt. If the debt is unpaid, the mortgagee can foreclose against the property no matter who owns it. The mortgagee may then sue the original mortgagor for any balance still due, but the mortgagee has no rights against the subsequent purchaser personally for any deficiency. Nor does the original mortgagor have any rights against the purchaser who bought "subject to" the mortgage.

☐ In the event of a default sale and a deficiency, the seller is personally liable and the buyer has no liability to either the seller or the mortgagee. It is important to understand that the seller remains personally liable in such a sale and that the buyer does not become personally liable for the debt. The maximum risk assumed by the buyer is the loss of whatever payments he or she has made to the seller or against the mortgage debt.

*Sale Subject to the Mortgage with the Buyer Assuming and Agreeing to Pay the Mortgage Debt*

When the existing mortgage is not satisfied at the time of sale, but there is an affirmative *assumption* of the debt by the buyer (as opposed to buying "subject to" the mortgage), there are the following results:

☐ The seller remains personally liable for the debt on his or her note to the mortgagee. The underlying obligation of the seller to pay this personal debt is not affected by the fact that the buyer has assumed the obligation to pay it. The seller's note to the lender is unchanged, and the seller is not relieved of the obligation.

☐ The buyer (the grantee) also becomes personally liable to pay the original debt by contracting to do so.

☐ The original mortgagee now has two debtors against whom to proceed. The lender may collect from either or both of them the amount of the debt and the costs of collection to the extent that the proceeds of sale upon foreclosure are insufficient. The lender is entitled to satisfaction only once, no matter how many assuming grantees there are. Each buyer who assumes the mortgage debt (no matter how many there are) becomes liable for the debt. When there is foreclosure and collection of a deficiency judgment by the mortgagee, the last assuming buyer (who can pay it) is liable for the deficiency. The important point here is that, even though a buyer assumes the mortgage debt from the original mortgagor, the original mortgagor remains liable. It is, after all, a personal debt, and liability cannot be avoided by entering into a contract with another who agrees to pay it. If the assuming buyer is unable to pay the debt, the creditor (mortgagee) is still entitled to enforce the obligation against the original borrower. Thus it is important, in selling property that is subject to a mortgage, to determine whether or not the buyer is financially responsible.

Many mortgages written in the 1970s and 1980s include a *due-on-sale* clause. Such a clause allows the lender to call the loan due upon the sale of the property—and therefore the decision of assumption is left to the lender. Commonly one of two things is done: A new loan at the current rate is issued by the lender, or the present loan is assumed at a rate between that of the old loan and the current rate. During times of great fluctuation in interest rates, creating a "blended rate," lenders will almost always exercise their rights under this clause to close out unprofitable loans made at low rates.

## Foreclosure upon Default

*Default* is defined as the failure to pay the debt and to meet other obligations specified in the mortgage (such as paying the taxes and insuring the property). *Foreclosure* must be undertaken by a legal process.

The basic steps in foreclosure are:

☐ Suit is filed in the county where the property is located.

☐ A judgment is obtained on the note in favor of the lender.

☐ *Execution* is obtained—an order to the sheriff to take possession of the property and sell it at public sale.

☐ The property is sold at a public sale at which the lender is generally entitled to bid.

☐ The proceeds of the sale are applied to the mortgage debt, court costs, and attorney's fees.

☐ Any excess of the proceeds after the debt and costs have been met goes to the mortgagor; if the proceeds are insufficient, the mortgagor remains liable for the balance.

☐ Other property of the mortgagor may be *attached* by the sheriff and sold to satisfy any deficiency.

The mortgagor has an *equity of redemption*. That is, the mortgagor has the right to redeem the property after default, but this right is limited.

☐ Execution of a judgment cannot be issued earlier than the statutory period provided by local law. Thus the property cannot be sold immediately even though a judgment has been obtained.

☐ To redeem the property, the mortgagor must pay the entire debt plus the mortgagee's costs. That is, the mortgagor cannot just bring the payments up to date but must pay the entire loan balance.

## PRIORITIES OF MORTGAGES

It is possible for the owner of real estate to incur more than one debt, each secured by a mortgage of his or her property to different creditors. A *second mortgage* on real estate is commonly used.

From the second mortgagee's standpoint, it is essential to recognize that his or her security interest is "junior" to that of the first mortgagee. In the event that neither secured creditor is paid, the second mortgagee must be satisfied with whatever is left from the proceeds of the foreclosure sale after the first mortgagee is completely satisfied and the expenses of sale and collection have been paid—on the theory that the owner-mortgagor can only pledge what he or she has, the net value of the property.

Second mortgages can be important security devices even though they are junior to the first mortgagee's lien on the property. They are frequently used to secure property improvement loans or as additional security for loans unrelated to the property itself. This is possible because the second mortgagee can sue on the note and second mortgage and make the first mortgagee a party. Indeed, the second creditor must do so to force a foreclosure sale. Since under the typical form of mortgage in use today such action may permit the first mortgagee to "deem himself insecure," the first mortgagor also forecloses on the mortgage. This procedure permits the second mortgagee to exert great pressure on the debtor for repayment of the second loan. Nevertheless, if the net proceeds of the sale are insufficient to pay the junior lien holder, the second mortgagee will be compelled to look to other assets of the borrower for repayment.

## PURCHASE MONEY MORTGAGES

In some cases the seller is also the mortgage lender. This may result because the buyer cannot obtain favorable financing through normal sources, because the seller may view the mortgage as a good investment, or for other reasons such as the income tax consequences of the sale. The seller then holds a *purchase money mortgage,* which has priorities over certain other claims against the buyer-mortgagor—for example, liens against the property created by the mortgagor, such as preexisting judgments against the buyer which become a lien against all property owned or acquired by such buyer.

Technically, any mortgage loan made to finance the purchase of real estate is a purchase money mortgage; however, for the commercial mortgage lender to obtain the degree of protection that would be afforded to the seller-lender, great care is taken to see that the proceeds of the loan are disbursed directly to the seller rather than to the purchaser-mortgagor and *then* to the seller. Caution must nevertheless be exercised by the mortgage lender, even if it is the seller, to be sure that the mortgage is promptly recorded since it has no priority over other mortgages or liens recorded in the interim between execution and recording.

## DEEDS OF TRUST

In states that utilize the *deed of trust* in addition to or in lieu of the mortgage for purposes of securing loans on real estate, the differences between the two forms of borrowing are, from a practical standpoint, more apparent than real. Under the deed of trust for security purposes, the basic underlying transaction is the same; that is, there is a loan which is evidenced by a promissory note. To this extent it has no recognizable difference from the mortgage loan transaction. The technical difference is the manner in which the loan is secured by a deed of trust. Here there is a deed to the real estate that transfers legal title to the property to an independent third party *trustee.* This is done under a formal agreement that obligates the trustee to do one of two things: (1) When the loan is paid, the trustee must deed the property to the borrower (buyer); or (2) if the borrower defaults, the trustee must sell the property and pay the proceeds to the lender to the extent necessary to repay the loan; any overage then goes to the borrower.

### Rights of the Parties

To understand the rights of the parties when legal title is held by the trustee, one must first understand a few fundamentals of trust law. Two basic points must be considered.

☐ Under the deed of trust (trust deed) there is a split of the title between the trustee and the beneficiaries of the trust. The trustee takes the *legal* title, and the beneficiaries retain the *equitable* title to the property. That is, the beneficiaries have the power to compel the trustee to carry out the terms of the trust: in this case the positive duty to deed the property back to the borrower when the debt has been paid, and the negative duty to refrain from deeding it to the borrower until full payment has been made to the lender. The term *equitable title* is based on the fact that a court of equity or a court having equity powers will, if petitioned by the beneficiaries, compel the trustee to carry out the duties imposed by the trust agreement.

☐ It is fundamental to the law of trusts that the trustee take only so much of the legal title as is necessary to carry out the terms of the trust. Any action taken by the trustee that exceeds this built-in limitation constitutes a breach of trust and renders the trustee liable to the damaged beneficiary.

### Rights of the Buyer

Because of the development of the law with regard to deeds of trust, either by statute or by case law, the buyer who is not in default has generally the same power to deal with real estate covered by a deed of trust that a mortgagor has with respect to mortgaged property. That is, the property may be sold subject to the deed of trust, with the new buyer assuming the obligations to the lender. The primary obligation to retire the debt remains that of the original borrower. As a practical matter, the rights of the buyer who gives a deed of trust to secure a loan are the same as those of a buyer who uses a mortgage to secure the debt.

### Rights of the Lender

There is a split of authority in the area of lenders' rights under the deed of trust. In many states, as a result of statute or case law, the theory is that any conveyance of real estate intended to secure the payment of a debt is in effect a mortgage, and local foreclosure procedures must be followed just as though it were in fact a mortgage. In these states a deed of trust is seldom used except in connection with major bond issues.

In states that recognize the deed of trust which includes a *power of sale* upon default by the buyer as something other than a mortgage, foreclosure proceedings are not required and the buyer has no equity of redemption. In these states deeds of trust are commonly used and mortgages are seldom seen. A note of caution is in order here: In states that recognize deeds of trust there is no uniform law. Thus local law should be investigated to determine the precise rights of the parties.

## LAND CONTRACTS

The basic transaction involved in a *conditional sales contract* or *land contract* or *contract for deed* is this: The seller retains title to the real estate until it is paid for (which is really no different from the usual agreement to purchase for cash). The distinguishing feature of a land contract, however, is that payment is not immediately made in full but is made over a period of time, usually a number of years. The length of time involved makes it essential that the rights and duties of the parties to the contract be specified in detail.

A particular form of contract has evolved for such sales. In essence, it transfers the rights and burdens of ownership to the buyer during the term of the contract, subject to certain rights retained by the seller so as to provide the seller with a well-developed security interest in the property and empowering the seller to enforce the terms of the contract against the buyer. Of course, the seller retains legal title to the property, and this gives the seller an inherently strong security interest. Nevertheless, during the term of the contract, the buyer has a significant interest called *equitable title,* which gives him or her broad latitude in dealing with the property—plus the absolute right to have the legal title conveyed to him or her upon full payment. This is a significant and substantial legal right that is protected by law. Yet the buyer's rights are limited by whatever terms and conditions are agreed upon by the parties, subject always to the basic rules of law governing contracts.

While land contracts are most frequently used in the sale of relatively inexpensive properties, particularly when conventional methods of financing are unavailable because of the age and condition of the property or because the financial strength of the buyer is questionable, it should be kept in mind that this method of sale can be used to obtain important income tax advantages by spreading a significant capital gain over several tax years. The possibilities for tax savings should be considered whenever a significant capital gain will be incurred by the seller of real estate.

### General Contract Law Rules Apply

While local forms of contracts may vary, general principles of contract law must be observed in conditional sales contracts for real estate. These are reviewed briefly below, and they will be discussed in detail in Chapter 14. Essentially, the basic rules are:

☐ The parties must be legally competent to enter into a contract.
☐ The three fundamental elements of all contracts must be present: *offer, acceptance,* and *consideration.*
☐ The contract must be in writing in order to comply with the statute of frauds, which requires that all contracts relating to the sale of real estate be in writing in order to be legally enforceable.
☐ All the rights and duties of the parties must be included in the contract.
☐ If the parties intend that the contract is to be recorded, then it must be acknowledged (and, in some states, the name of the preparer must be shown).

### The Seller Retains Legal Title as Security

While the normal rules of contract law apply to land contracts, they are nevertheless *security devices.* It is frequently said that the seller under a land contract has the best security device available: legal title to the property. Under a typical land contract, no deed is given to the buyer until the last payment has been made. Only then is the seller obligated to transfer full legal ownership to the buyer.

The following points should be emphasized:

☐ The land contract is generally not treated as a mortgage. That is, the buyer does not have legal title and therefore cannot sell the fee interest. However, in the absence of any prohibition in the contract, the buyer may *assign* his or her rights to a third party. This does not relieve the original purchaser of the obligations assumed in the initial contract. (Most forms of land contract include a clause prohibiting assignment of the buyer's rights without the seller's approval. When the assignment to a new buyer is approved by the seller, there is a *novation,* a new contract, between the seller and the new buyer. In this event the original buyer is relieved of the obligations under the original contract.)
☐ There is generally no equity of redemption available to the defaulting buyer as there is under a typical mortgage. Instead, the contract specifies a *grace period* during which the buyer may "catch

up" past-due payments and cure the default. This provision is purely a matter of negotiation between buyer and seller at the time the contract is entered into. It may be very short (one day) or very liberal (six months or more), depending on the negotiating positions of the parties. However, some courts have begun to conclude that an unreasonably short grace period is inherently unfair and have treated such contracts as though they were mortgages, thus requiring foreclosure proceedings and providing an equity of redemption. Nevertheless, the general rule that the parties are free to make their own contracts remains the fundamental law in the area of land contracts.

☐ During the term of the land contract the buyer has *equitable title* only. This means that when the buyer has completed his or her side of the bargain (made all payments, etc.), he or she is entitled to a deed to the property, and a court of equity will order conveyance of the property to the buyer. Since the seller has legal title during the term of the contract, the seller retains the power to sell the property—subject of course to the rights of the land contract buyer. The new owner of the property becomes entitled to receive payments from the contract buyer and is legally bound to convey the property to the buyer when the buyer's side of the contract is completed.

☐ Along with equitable title and the right to possession of the property during the term of the land contract, the buyer generally has all the burdens and obligations that go with home ownership. Once again, all duties and rights must be found in the land contract itself. The standard contract in use today shifts to the buyer the burdens of ownership such as the duty to pay all real estate taxes and assessments, the duty to insure the property for the benefit of both seller and buyer, and the duty to repair and to refrain from "waste" of the property. Other duties may be included by specific contract provision. One point is clear: If the contract buyer improves the property (by building a house on it, for example) and then defaults, the buyer may not remove these improvements because, under the law of fixtures, they have become part of the real estate.

## Rights of the Parties upon Default

The basic defaults are the failure of the purchaser to make payments under the land contract as agreed and the failure of the seller to convey merchantable legal title after receiving payment of all money due from the purchaser. While a variety of other technical defaults can occur during the term of a land contract sale, these two types of default are significant and common.

### Default by the Seller

Default by the seller, by virtue of his or her inability or unwillingness to convey title to the property to the buyer after all payments have been made, gives rise to several alternative remedies on the part of the buyer.

Since the buyer is entitled to a deed after completing all his or her obligations under the contract, particularly full payment, and since real estate is unique in the eyes of the law, the buyer is entitled to the remedy of *specific performance*. That is, the buyer is entitled to bring action in a court of equity to *compel* the seller to make conveyance of the property to the buyer. The court order to do so is absolute, and failure to comply with it may result in imprisonment for contempt of court until the seller "purges" himself of the contempt by doing what he was ordered to do. This remedy is extreme and is available in only a few cases, one of which is the conveyance of real estate.

Suppose, however, that the seller has no power to convey the property because it has been sold to another. No court can compel a defendant to do that which is impossible. When this occurs, the buyer may *rescind* the contract and obtain recovery of all payments made under the contract. Recovery based on this theory is reduced by the fair rental value of the property for the period during which the buyer was in possession; however, as a practical matter, the values judicially determined are likely to be prejudicial to the defaulting seller, since failure or inability to perform is presumably the result of the seller's own fraud or mistake. If the property has been improved by the buyer in the expectation that the seller would perform his or her obligations, the cost of these improvements is also recoverable.

The purchaser may also elect to pursue the normal remedy for breach of contract: the additional cost of purchasing comparable property. In periods of rising values of real estate and buildings, this remedy may be the most appealing to the buyer. This is particularly true where the value of the property contracted for has actually gone down while the value of comparable properties has gone up. The purchaser may then be content to abandon the right to the extraordinary remedy of specific performance in favor of a suit for money damages.

### Default by the Purchaser

Default by the purchaser, such as the basic failure to make payments when due, gives rise to a variety of remedies for the seller. However, under a typical land contract sale the seller is entitled to be paid for the property sold. As a result, the damages suffered by the seller when the buyer defaults can be measured by a court in terms of money, which is not unique, and the remedy of specific performance, in the strict sense of the term, is not available to the seller. The seller must therefore find relief in the terms of the contract as equated to money or repossession of the property or a combination of the two.

When there is a default by the purchaser under a land contract, and the default is not cured during the grace period written into the contract, the seller typically has the right to retake possession of the property peaceably. The seller is entitled to demand possession of the property from the buyer, and the buyer is obligated to surrender it. But if the buyer does not do so, the seller may not use force to "eject" the buyer. (The limitations are similar to those discussed in the area of landlord-tenant relationships.) Legal action to "foreclose" or set aside the contract and remove the buyer is necessary.

In addition to the right to retake possession of the property, the seller frequently reserves in a land contract the right to retain all payments made by the buyer prior to the default as *liquidated damages*. That is, there is a *forfeiture* of all monies paid out by the buyer during the term of the contract prior to the default. Liquidated damages represents a good-faith effort on the part of both parties to determine in advance what the damages will be in the event of a default during the term of the contract. Where this provision appears to be fair, it will be upheld by the courts. However, where the liquidated damages clause is grossly disproportionate to the damages actually suffered by the seller when the buyer defaults, the courts will label it a *penalty clause*, an economic "club," and will not enforce the provision. Even though the defaulting buyer may commit a civil wrong which damages the seller, the courts will look closely at such a clause to determine that it is essentially fair to both parties. If it is grossly unfair to the defaulting buyer, regardless of his or her breach of contractual duties, the clause will not be enforced and the seller will have to prove what damages have actually been sustained.

### Acknowledgment and Recording of Land Contracts

Since presumably we are considering a contract of sale that is valid between buyer and seller, the question of recording (including the technical requirements to make the contract recordable) would appear to be a matter of mere technicality. This is not the case. The recordability and recording of the land contract have important consequences for both seller and buyer.

From the buyer's standpoint, recording the land contract is of significance because it serves notice of ownership that cannot be ignored by anyone dealing with the owner of record (the seller) without recognizing the rights of the contract buyer. Even without the protection of the recording system, however, if the contract buyer is in obvious possession (that is, living in a residence that is being sold), any third party dealing with the owner of record is bound to know this fact because such a buyer is obligated to inspect the property and determine what claim the resident nonowner has to it.

The decision whether or not to require a contract in recordable form depends on whether or not the contract buyer is in obvious possession of the property. Where the subject property is vacant land, the claim of ownership of the contract buyer is not obvious, and a recordable contract becomes most significant because it may be the only way that the buyer's claim of an interest will be effective notice to the general public. In the event that there is no notice of such a claim, either actual (by virtue of obvious possession) or constructive (by virtue of the recorded land contract), then a *bona fide purchaser for value* can cut off the buyer's equitable title by a direct purchase from the owner of record. (See the discussion in Chapter 7 with regard to the necessary qualifications of a bona fide purchaser.)

From the seller's standpoint, recording the land contract is usually considered a nuisance that "clutters up" or "clouds" the legal title to the property. This occurs when there is a default by the contract buyer. Even though there is an admission of default by the buyer and a surrender back to the seller, these facts are not generally in recordable form so that the record is cleared. (A quitclaim deed from buyer to seller would serve the purpose, but frequently this cannot be obtained.) In the vast majority of cases the unrecorded defaulted land contract poses no problem simply because no one knows of it and because it has been eliminated by virtue of subsequent agreement of the parties that it is null and void. If such a contract is recorded, however, it will take recordable action to clear the owner's record title.

As we said, the quitclaim deed from the defaulting buyer to the seller will clear this defect in the title. If this is not obtainable, however, there must be a legal proceeding that cancels the contract and clears the record title by virtue of a court decree (which is automatically part of the public records) to clear the seller's legal title. There are occasions when the resistance of the seller to entering into a recordable contract proves to be false economy. If, for example, after informal termination of the contract occurs there is a dramatic increase in the value of the property, a subsequent sale by the record owner may be hampered by unfounded claims of the defaulted land contract purchaser. While such claims may have only a nuisance value, they must be settled, and they may be very costly to the owner of the property.

Land contract sales frequently occur during periods of high interest rates for mortgage money. Because the land contract is privately negotiated between seller and buyer, the interest rate can be established at whatever level they agree upon. Often the land contract is being used for high dollar value transactions in which the buyer makes a substantial down payment. In such sales, the

recording of the land contract becomes more significant and is quite common.

## REVIEW QUESTIONS

1. M owns a property that is encumbered by an FHA mortgage. If M wants to sell the property to Q, how may the title be transferred?

   (A) M cannot transfer title to Q until the mortgage is satisfied
   (B) Q may assume the mortgage and agree to pay the debt
   (C) The FHA mortgage is assumable by Q only if he is a qualified veteran
   (D) The FHA will require M to satisfy the old mortgage and will then issue a new mortgage to Q at the present rate of interest

2. The seller will retain title to the property as security until the debt is repaid under what form of financing?

   (A) Deed of trust
   (B) Mortgage
   (C) Land contract
   (D) None of the above

3. All of the following are essential to creating a valid mortgage EXCEPT

   (A) the mortgage must be recorded to create a lien
   (B) the mortgage must be in writing to be valid
   (C) the mortgage must be executed by the mortgagors
   (D) the property must be legally described

4. Under the deed of trust, legal title to the property

   (A) is transferred to the lender until repayment is made
   (B) is held by a third party trustee until satisfaction
   (C) remains with the owner
   (D) is held jointly by the trustee and the lender

5. When the seller takes a mortgage back from the buyer as part payment for the sale

   (A) the seller retains legal title
   (B) the mortgage is a purchase money mortgage
   (C) the seller is entitled to possession of the property until the debt is paid
   (D) no second mortgages may be placed on the property by the buyer

6. In a sale by land contract, the seller

   (A) retains only equitable title in the property until payment is made

   (B) must convey legal title upon the completion of the contract
   (C) has only a security interest in the property until payment is made
   (D) retains no title to the property during the payment period, but may foreclose for nonpayment

7. If the seller defaults under a land contract sale, the buyer may do all of the following EXCEPT

   (A) sue for specific performance and seek the deed
   (B) rescind the contract and recover all payments less a fair rental amount
   (C) seek damages equal to the cost difference of acquiring a new property
   (D) seek no remedy since no interest was held by the buyer

8. What may happen if a foreclosure takes place and a second mortgage exists on the property?

   (A) The second mortgage is paid out first because it is a lesser amount than the first mortgage
   (B) The second mortgage will be completely satisfied regardless of the balance of the first mortgage
   (C) The second mortgage may not seek expenses in the foreclosure
   (D) The second mortgage may not be completely satisfied if funds from the foreclosure are insufficient.

9. If the mortgagor pays the entire balance due plus any expenses incurred by the mortgagee as a result of a default and filing for foreclosure, the mortgagor has exercised

   (A) right of foreclosure
   (B) right of redemption
   (C) right of eminent domain
   (D) right of seisin

10. Under a deed of trust, when the buyer defaults, the equity of redemption period is

    (A) 90 days
    (B) 120 days
    (C) 60 days
    (D) none

11. When property is sold subject to a mortgage, the lender

    (A) relieves the seller of all liability for the debt
    (B) makes the buyer personally liable for the debt
    (C) still holds the seller liable for the debt
    (D) holds both the seller and the buyer equally liable for the debt

12. A property is being sold by land contract. Under this arrangement, which is true?

    (A) The buyer may get a second mortgage for the established equity
    (B) The buyer gets legal title and the seller has an equitable interest during the period of the contract
    (C) The seller may mortgage the property through a conventional lender during the contract period
    (D) The buyer has no right of possession until the contract is satisfied

13. Under a land contract, which of the following is not the obligation of the buyer?

    (A) Payment of taxes
    (B) Property insurance
    (C) Property maintenance
    (D) Deed preparation

14. If the lender is willing to accept the buyer of the property as the new debtor on an existing mortgage, what has occurred?

    (A) Satisfaction
    (B) Novation
    (C) Equity of redemption
    (D) Rescission

15. Under a deed of trust, when the obligation is repaid

    (A) the trustee deeds the title to the property to the lender
    (B) the trustee deeds the title to the property to the borrower
    (C) the trustor deeds the title to the property to the trustee
    (D) the trustor deeds the title to the property to the lender

16. If the proceeds of a foreclosure sale are insufficient to repay the debt, the lender

    (A) must file a second mortgage

    (B) may pursue other assets of the borrower for the deficiency
    (C) must be satisfied with the funds
    (D) may exercise the right of redemption

17. If there are excess funds after a foreclosure sale and repayment of all debts and expenses, these funds will be paid to the

    (A) lender
    (B) sheriff who conducts the sale
    (C) court and auctioneer
    (D) defaulting borrower

18. When the borrower has completely repaid the loan secured by a mortgage, which of the following is **not** true?

    (A) The borrower is entitled to a formal release
    (B) The lien is no longer enforceable against the title
    (C) The borrower regains equitable title
    (D) The lender no longer has an interest in the property

19. When a first mortgage is unrecorded and a second mortgage lender, without actual notice of the prior mortgage, extends credit and records the second mortgage,

    (A) the second mortgage will now have priority of repayment in case of foreclosure
    (B) the borrower is liable only for the recorded mortgage
    (C) the first mortgage will have no effect on the title
    (D) the first mortgagee may not pursue foreclosure

20. Which of the following is **not** true of the sale of vacant land by contract that is not going to be occupied by the buyer?

    (A) The sale is valid
    (B) The contract should be recorded
    (C) Third parties will not have actual notice of the sale
    (D) The buyer does not obtain an equitable interest without possession

# Chapter 11

# Real Estate Finance

THE uniqueness of real estate as an economic commodity is due in large part to the magnitude of the investment required in each real estate transaction. In most instances the prospective purchaser does not have the funds required by the sales contract and consequently must obtain funds through some source of credit. Although most purchasers invest *equity funds* in the property through a down payment, they also have to rely on *debt financing* for additional funding.

Most customers of a real estate agent have had little experience in purchasing real estate and are, therefore, not fully aware of the credit options available to them. For this reason the sales agent who serves as an adviser is an essential element in the transaction. Many potential buyers have the desire to purchase a particular parcel of real estate, and this is commonly called *demand*. But simple demand is not enough. A prospective purchaser must be able to meet the purchase price by obtaining the financing that, combined with the down payment or equity monies, gives the purchaser *effective demand*.

Successful salespersons and brokers need complete knowledge of lending institutions, their loan requirements, and their current operations if they are to advise buyers on all the forms of financing available to them. Furthermore, they must frequently turn to alternative and more creative forms of financing that will allow the potential buyer to purchase the real estate.

## THE MORTGAGE

### Legal Aspects of a Mortgage

The most common form of financing is the mortgage loan. A mortgage is a legal instrument that allows the borrower to pledge the real property to secure the debt with the lender. Used correctly, the term *mortgage* refers to two documents used to secure a loan: the mortgage agreement (or deed of trust) and the promissory note (or deed of trust note).

## Promissory Note

The promissory note, given by the borrower (*mortgagor*) to the lender (*mortgagee*), makes the mortgagor personally responsible for the debt. Under the promissory note, the borrower is obligated to the lender for repayment of the principal and interest. To be valid evidence of the existence of the debt, the note needs to be in writing. The note must state the borrower's promise to repay the debt and be executed and delivered by the borrower to the lender. The existence of the mortgage or deed of trust must also be indicated if it is security for the debt.

## Mortgage Agreement

The mortgage agreement pledges the real property as security for the loan and sets forth whatever terms the parties to the contract desire. The mortgage on a property creates a lien on the property, and it must therefore conform to the statutes of the local jurisdiction.

## Mortgage Theory

The mortgage agreement determines the mortgage theory being followed by the lender. The practice varies from state to state. When the mortgagor keeps possession of the title and the mortgage acts as a lien, this is said to be *lien theory*.

Under lien theory, the lien is recorded by the mortgagee in the county (or similar governmental unit) where the property is located. When the loan is repaid, the mortgagee gives the mortgagor a satisfaction of the mortgage, and upon recording of the satisfaction, the lien is removed from the property title.

Under the title theory, the mortgagor transfers title by a *deed of trust* to a third party trustee. When the conditions of the mortgage are met, the title to the property is returned to the borrower by the use of a *deed of reconveyance*. In case of default, the trustee can deed the title to the property to the mortgagee or sell the property.

In some states a special form arises, called *intermediate theory*, whereby the title remains with the mortgagor but is automatically transferred to the mortgagee upon default.

## Mortgage Clauses

Each mortgage agreement contains a number of clauses or provisions that are necessary for the proper execution of the mortgage agreement.

☐ The *assumption clause* allows a buyer to assume a loan and to agree to be primarily liable for the pay-

ment of the loan. The seller still remains ultimately liable but is now in a secondary position. This is referred to as "subject to and agreeing to pay."

☐ Under the *subject to the loan,* the buyer acknowledges the existence of the loan but does not become a party to the note. The seller is held primarily responsible for the loan and any deficiency upon default and foreclosure.

☐ The *late charges clause* in the loan describes what will happen if payments are late and what penalties will be assessed.

☐ The *prepayment penalty clause* or *privilege clause* tells whether the mortgagor may repay the loan faster than scheduled or how any penalties will be calculated if the loan is repaid earlier than the scheduled maturity date.

☐ The *defeasance clause* provides for the release of lien when the obligation under the note has been satisfied.

☐ The *due-on-sale clause (alienation)* makes the balance of the loan due upon the sale of the property. It makes the loan nonassumable.

☐ The *release clause* is for mortgages that cover more than one piece of property; it allows for the release of the lien from the individual properties.

☐ The *subordination clause* makes an existing mortgage secondary to a mortgage that is recorded later.

☐ An *acceleration clause* is any clause that can advance the due date of the loan. A due-on-sale clause is a type of acceleration clause.

## Foreclosure

In the event that the borrower defaults on the obligations of the mortgage, the lender may have to take the property to foreclosure. Each state has its own set of foreclosure rules that have to be followed.

A *judicial foreclosure* is one that follows the state statutes concerning the foreclosure process. The property may be subject to a *nonjudicial foreclosure* whereby the process is defined in the mortgage agreement. Or, the property may be subject to a *strict foreclosure,* whereby the lender must be satisfied with the title to the property.

In any foreclosure a *default* must be present. A default most often consists of the failure of the borrower to repay the debt, but it may occur for other reasons. The mortgagee then files a suit, and notice of foreclosure is given. The mortgagor usually has a period of *redemption* to repay the debt before the property is taken and sold.

## TYPES OF MORTGAGES

### Amortized Mortgages

The increased demand for mortgages in the 1940s led lending institutions to offer *amortized mortgages.* In this type of mortgage, lender and borrower work out the essential terms of the loan, setting the interest rate, the term (or length of the repayment period), and the principal amount to be borrowed.

*PI Constant*

The amortized mortgage requires that the borrower make periodic repayments of a stated *constant* amount to reduce the balance of the loan. These payments, usually due on a monthly basis, include the interest payment and a part of the principal amount. (Sample calculations of the use of constants are provided in the following section.) The interest accrued on the unpaid portion of the debt is deducted from the constant, and then the balance of the payment is applied toward reducing the outstanding principal balance. Interest due is always calculated on the remaining balance of the principal, not on the original loan amount. The monthly payments continue until the entire amount of the mortgage is amortized, or paid off.

The amount of the monthly payment is determined by the amount of the loan, the term of the loan, and the interest rate. As the outstanding principal decreases, the amount of interest drops correspondingly. Therefore, larger and larger portions of the equal monthly payments are applied to the remaining balance of the loan. Tables are available that give the required monthly payment for certain rates of interest, term, and loan amount. The constant payment is exactly that—the amount of the monthly payment remains the same throughout the life of the mortgage. It is simply allocated to principal and interest in differing portions each month. This is known as the *principal and interest constant (PI constant)*.

Over and above the constant amount for the principal and interest payments, an additional sum is often collected to pay property taxes and hazard insurance. Such funds are placed in *escrow accounts,* the amount set aside usually being one-twelfth of the annual charges for taxes and hazard insurance. These collections, which can either be placed in separate accounts or combined in a single account, are available when payments are due, so no tax liens or uninsured damage can result. Thus the monthly payment includes payment of the principal, interest, taxes, and insurance and often is called the *PITI payment,* and the mortgage is called a *budget mortgage.*

## Sample Amortized Calculations

The following examples represent situations that salespersons and brokers encounter. Only partial tables are presented here; more complete tables for computing constant payments for an amortized loan can be found in financial reference books or derived with the use of a calculator.

*Example* What are the monthly payments for a $60,000 loan at 12% interest for 30 years?

*Solution* Figure 11-1 gives the constant monthly payment required to amortize a $1,000 loan. Select the line for the 30-year term and read across to the 12% column. A monthly payment of $10.29 per $1,000 is required to amortize a 30-year, 12% loan.

$60,000 / $1,000 = 60
$10.29 × 60 = $617.40

Thus, $617.40 would be required to amortize the loan.

**Constant Payment Table**
**Monthly Payments Required to Amortize a $1,000 Loan**

| Years | 8% | 10% | 12% | 14% | 15% |
|---|---|---|---|---|---|
| 1 | 86.99 | 87.92 | 88.85 | 89.79 | 90.26 |
| 5 | 20.28 | 21.25 | 22.25 | 23.27 | 23.79 |
| 10 | 12.14 | 13.22 | 14.35 | 15.53 | 16.14 |
| 15 | 9.56 | 10.75 | 12.01 | 13.32 | 14.00 |
| 20 | 8.37 | 9.66 | 11.02 | 12.44 | 13.17 |
| 25 | 7.72 | 9.09 | 10.54 | 12.04 | 12.81 |
| 30 | 7.34 | 8.87 | 10.29 | 11.85 | 12.65 |

*Figure 11-1—Constant payment table.*

A remaining balance for amortized loans is often needed, and there are tables that provide the necessary information. Figure 11-2 is an example of a partial loan progress table.

*Problem* For a 30-year loan of $40,000 at 10% interest with a remaining life of 25 years, what is the remaining balance? The loan is 5 years old.

*Solution* From Figure 11-2, a $40,000 loan after 5 years has a remaining balance of $38,640 (40 × $966).

**Loan Progress Table—10%**
**Dollar Balance Remaining on a $1,000 Loan**

| Age of Loan | Original Terms in Years | | | | |
| | 10 | 15 | 20 | 25 | 30 |
|---|---|---|---|---|---|
| 1 | 939 | 970 | 983 | 991 | 994 |
| 2 | 871 | 936 | 965 | 980 | 988 |
| 3 | 796 | 899 | 945 | 969 | 982 |
| 4 | 713 | 858 | 923 | 956 | 974 |
| 5 | 622 | 813 | 898 | 942 | 966 |
| 10 | — | 506 | 730 | 846 | 909 |
| 15 | — | — | 454 | 688 | 817 |
| 20 | — | — | — | 428 | 664 |
| 25 | — | — | — | — | 413 |
| 30 | — | — | — | — | — |

*Figure 11-2—Loan progress table—10%.*

## Priority of Mortgages

### Junior and Senior Mortgages

It is essential in the financing of real estate to establish the priority of a mortgage in the case of default and foreclosure. The recording process generally establishes which mortgage takes precedence over the other obligations. The mortgage with the greatest priority is referred to as the *senior mortgage* or *first mortgage*. Unless it is subordinated or gives up its position to another mortgage, it is paid out first. A *junior mortgage* is any mortgage in position behind the senior mortgage. This could be a second or third mortgage placed on the property. These mortgage priorities are also established by the order in which they were recorded unless they are subordinated to other mortgages.

## SOURCES OF FINANCING

Real estate buyers can obtain financing from various sources. Mortgage arrangements, the most widely used technique of financing, can be made through (in decreasing order of importance) savings and loan associations, commercial banks, mutual savings banks, credit unions, life insurance companies, loan correspondents, individuals and organizations, pension funds, and real estate investment trusts.

## Savings and Loan Associations

Most mortgages are obtained from savings and loan associations and commercial banks; fewer are obtained from mutual savings banks, credit unions, and life insurance companies. Although the other institutions provide funds for mortgages, they are not readily accessible to the general public.

Savings and loan associations are privately managed and owned financial institutions that are governed by state and federal regulations. They supply the greatest number of single-family mortgage loans in the United States. In the past, the associations have concentrated their efforts on this type of loan; more recently they have begun to diversify into loans for home repair, construction, and multifamily housing projects.

The basic function of the association is to provide mortgages for the community. The funds are obtained from time deposits made with the institution, and interest earned on the mortgages goes to pay the interest on the time deposits. Statutes and federal regulations affect the interest rate, as does competition in the market. The regulations that govern federally chartered institutions are set by the Federal Home Loan Bank Board, under which all federal savings and loan associations are incorporated.

Under the Federal Home Loan Bank System, the associations need not rely solely on local funds. The system was devised in 1932 to solve the problems caused by dependency on local funds. The major element of the system is the ability to transfer funds from one bank to another to meet local needs. The system provides for 12 regional banks to assist local savings and loans in times of tight money. The main intention of the federal involvement in savings and loan associations was to develop a national mortgage market. Savings and loan associations are also subject to the statutes of the particular state where they are located, and state-chartered associations come under the auspices of the state banking commissioner.

Savings and loan associations concentrate their efforts on residential construction and usually avoid large commercial projects. In lending for single-family residences, the associations require a down payment on any mortgage. The size of the down payment fluctuates, depending on current economic conditions and the degree of risk involved. Down payments usually range from 15 to 25 percent of the sales price. The maximum loan-to-value ratio is .95, which allows a down payment as small as 5 percent.

Savings and loan associations offer four major types of loans:

☐ New home construction loans
☐ Home purchase loans
☐ Loans for other purposes, such as home improvements
☐ Equity line of credit loans

### New Home Construction Loans

New home loans are generally made directly to a builder, usually of single-family housing. The associations place strict controls on the loans and pay the builder in installments as specific phases of construction are completed, from the footings to the finishing work. The associations verify that the builder is paying the subcontractors so that no *mechanic's liens* can be placed on the title. (A mechanic's lien is used when builders fail to pay subcontractors for completed work.)

### Home Purchase Loans

Savings and loan associations allot approximately 60 percent of their available funds to mortgages that allow people to move from their present homes to homes that are more appropriate for their family size or living style. The home mortgage allows more upward mobility in society and thereby stimulates new housing. This trend is known as *filtering,* a process that passes the existing housing through different economic levels of society.

### Home Improvement Loans

As society has had to shift from an unlimited growth and resources philosophy to a more conservative growth and limited resources approach, a similar shift has occurred in the mortgage market. When the economy began to feel the effects of the oil crisis, double-digit inflation, and energy shortages in the mid-1970s, lending institutions experienced an increase in demand for home improvement loans. Consequently, savings and loan associations today are making greater efforts to offer competitive rates for loans that cover improvements ranging from painting to roofing to remodeling.

Today approximately 30 to 35 percent of the total loans from savings and loan associations are in this area. The associations are usually willing to extend such credit, realizing that improvements increase the value of the property and reduce the risk of the original loan. Improvements also help to maintain the neighborhood, and this has a positive effect on the value of the property. The loans are usually short-term (5 years), but the range is from 3 to 20 years. If the loan is incorporated into the first mortgage, the maturity date can be extended to as much as 30 years.

*Home Equity Loans*

As a result of the 1986 Tax Reform Act, loans based on the equity people have established in their home have become more popular. The lender appraises the property for market value then subtracts any outstanding mortgage balances from 85 percent of the appraised value to determine the available equity line of credit. This is secured with a second mortgage on the property.

| *Example* | $100,000 | appraised value |
| | $\times$ .85 | |
| | $ 85,000 | basis for loan |
| | − 60,000 | existing mortgage balance |
| | $ 25,000 | available for equity loan |

This type of financing has become increasingly popular with the phasing out of the federal income tax interest deduction for consumer credit. The interest on this loan or equity line of credit is fully deductible for federal tax purposes.

## Commercial Banks

The commercial bank is another major source of mortgage money. Banks often have separate departments or mortgage companies to handle mortgages when they are interested in this type of investment. Most commercial banks traditionally have concentrated on short-term loans for construction and other types of loans, but they are now expanding rapidly into residential mortgage lending.

Banks are regulated by federal and/or state authorities, depending on their charter. Regulations may govern the ratio of the loan to the appraised value of property or the term of the loan. Other requirements concern mortgage terms and interest rate ceilings. Due to federal and state restrictions, banks may find it difficult to compete with other lending institutions for long-term residential loans.

Commercial banks have traditionally played their most significant role in real estate financing through short-term construction loans, home improvement loans, and, more recently, equity line of credit loans.

## Mutual Savings Banks

Like savings and loan associations, the mutual savings banks' objective is to encourage personal savings. The first such institution, the Philadelphia Savings Fund, was founded in 1816 to encourage factory workers to save. Since that time, mutual savings banks have spread to 18 states, although they are concentrated most heavily in the Northeast. New York and Massachusetts have three-fourths of the total assets of all mutual savings banks. The banks are chartered and regulated by the individual states.

Mutual savings banks are similar to savings and loan associations in that they are operated for the benefit of the depositors and managed by a board of trustees. Similarly, their basic objective is to pool deposits to provide mortgages and funds for potential single-family homeowners.

## Credit Unions

The credit union has recently entered the residential lending area and is able to make first mortgage, second mortgage, equity line of credit, and construction loans.

## Life Insurance Companies

In the past, life insurance companies have been conservative investors because the major source of their investment funds is their policyholders. Government regulations state the percentage of total assets that life insurance companies can invest in mortgages due to their limited liquidity and relatively high risk. All insurance companies are regulated by the state in which they are chartered. Usually they specialize in large, long-term loans on major real estate projects, such as shopping centers, office buildings, and multifamily projects.

Due to the nature of the life insurance companies' funds, there is usually less fluctuation in the availability of their monies to lend for real estate projects. The placement of a loan with a life insurance company is usually accomplished through a *mortgage broker* or *mortgage banker*. Very few loans are made by a life insurance company directly to a borrower.

## Pension and Trust Funds

Increased interest by private investors has recently made pension funds an excellent source of mortgage funds. Many of the large funds have invested in the secondary market by buying FHA or VA loans from financial institutions. (For an explanation of secondary markets, see the discussion of federal involvement in real estate financing later in this chapter.)

## Loan Correspondents

Many times the larger lending institutions do not have the facilities needed to make various kinds of mortgage loans. Instead of funding loan departments in the individual institution—an insurance company, for example—the institution goes to a local agent or *loan correspondent* to make the mortgage loan for them. In circumstances where the institution does not have a branch office in the area, it will use a loan correspondent to take advantage of his or her knowledge of the local real estate market, neighborhood, special characteristics, and local economic conditions. Loan correspondents are either mortgage brokers or mortgage bankers, depending on the type of loan required.

### Mortgage Brokers

The role of a mortgage broker is to channel mortgage funds from the large investor to real estate developers and owners. The broker serves as an intermediary between the lender and borrower and receives a fee for the services performed. Lending institutions ask the mortgage broker to find and screen both the property and the applicants for their mortgage dollars. The closing is done in the name of the lending institution, and the mortgage broker receives a fee based on a percentage of the mortgage value. The loan is then serviced by the lender or a separate servicing company.

### Mortgage Bankers

Although mortgage bankers and brokers provide the same basic service of finding and matching applicants and mortgages, one basic difference exists: Mortgage bankers use their own funds to make mortgage loans. After they have originated a number of mortgages that are closed in their name, they sell the mortgages as a package to a large financial institution, transferring the mortgages to that institution. However, unlike the mortgage broker, the banker continues to service the loan for the investor. For this servicing, which includes collecting monthly payments, paying taxes, and maintaining escrow accounts, the banker charges the institution a fee in addition to the origination fee.

## Other Sources

Other sources of funds include the various syndications and real estate investment trusts (REIT) that provide first-mortgage capital.

## METHODS OF FINANCE

After learning about the different sources of financing that are available, the borrower must be aware of the alternative types of financing. One of the jobs of the real estate professional is to familiarize the buyer with the principal types of financing. The three major areas are conventional loans, government-backed loans, and the assumption of loans already in existence.

## Conventional Loans

The conventional loan, which is made directly to the buyer without government guarantees or insurance, has few regulations to govern it, so the terms and conditions of the mortgage fluctuate with market conditions. As the demand for money increases, the yield on conventional mortgage loans may be increased by increasing interest rates. During such periods, it is to the seller's advantage when the buyer acquires a conventional loan, because government loans during these periods have high discount points that the seller may have to pay. (Discount points are discussed later in this chapter.) Consequently, conventional loans play an important role in financing during times of tight money because their terms can change rapidly to reflect market conditions.

Today most conventional loans are for 80 percent of the sales price and mature in 15, 25, or 30 years. Loans written for more than 80 percent of the sales price usually require private mortgage insurance.

### Private Mortgage Insurance

Private systems of mortgage insurance have grown in importance, and this new aspect of financing is being used in many parts of the United States. Private companies insure mortgages under conditions similar to those of the Federal Housing Administration (FHA). Under this system of lending, institutions have a partial guarantee of payment. The lender might then loan 95 percent of the sales price of a property but require the buyer to insure the top 15 to 20 percent of the loan through a private mortgage insurance company.

*Example*

| | |
|---|---|
| $100,000 | sales price |
| −80,000 | lender's usual 80% loan-to-value ratio |
| $ 20,000 | additional funds needed |
| −5,000 | down payment |
| $ 15,000 | additional 15% loaned and covered by private insurance |

*Private mortgage insurance* allows a higher loan-to-value ratio and helps stimulate the growth of the mortgage market. The concept originated with the Mortgage Guarantee Insurance Corporation (MGIC) and has grown in popularity. The insurance is paid through a one-time premium of one-half of one percent of the loan amount, collected at the time of closing, and an additional premium that is part of the monthly payment paid by the purchaser until that part of the loan has been amortized. At present, private mortgage insurers insure more housing debt than the FHA.

### Government-Backed Loans

The two basic types of government-backed loans—Federal Housing Administration (FHA) insured loans and Veterans Administration (VA) guaranteed loans—have tight restrictions on the type and conditions of the mortgage involved. The federal government has had a continuing interest in real estate and has played an important role in increasing the growth of home ownership since World War II.

#### The FHA and Its Programs

The FHA, established under the National Housing Act of 1934, principally insures lending institutions' loans that are made for financing mortgages, thereby stimulating the housing segment of the economy.

The objective of the FHA is to encourage lenders to make loans by insuring them. Lenders are then more willing to accept lower down payments, thereby extending to more people the opportunity to obtain mortgages. The FHA only insures loans; it almost never lends money directly to individual purchasers of single-family dwellings. To finance its operation, the FHA charges a mortgage insurance premium (MIP) of one-half of one percent, payable at the time of closing by the borrower. The FHA is a unit of the U.S. Department of Housing and Urban Development.

The FHA places restrictions on the type of mortgage it will insure. These restrictions cover the terms and the amount of the mortgage loan and establish minimum property standards (MPS) for the physical property. To insure that such standards have been met, each property must be appraised by an FHA-approved appraiser before the loan is made. The term of the loan under FHA insurance must be a multiple of five years up to a maximum of 30 years. Under Title I, 203(b), the amount may vary, with an upper limit specified for single-family housing. All FHA-insured mortgages must be in multiples of $50. Mortgages must be paid according to an amortization schedule, and escrow accounts must be established for taxes and insurance premiums. Certain closing costs may be included in the amount of the mortgage.

The agency also has certain guidelines for loan-to-value ratios. The guidelines for residences vary depending on the age of the property and the number of dwelling units. These are subject to change, but ratios are usually below those for conventional loans.

Consider two examples of loan values using the FHA guidelines. The percentages are computed on the appraisal or the sale amount, whichever is lower, and the final product is adjusted downward to a multiple of $50.

*Example* What is the amount of a loan on a single-family, one-unit property selling for $32,000 if it is FHA-insured?

*Solution*    97% of the first $25,000 = $24,250
95% of the amount
over $25,000 =    7,125
_____
Total = $31,375

The loan amount of $31,375 must be adjusted downward to a multiple of $50, so the FHA-insured loan would amount to $31,350. The required down payment for this property would be $1,150 ($32,500 − $31,350).

*Example* Determine the amount of an FHA-insured loan on a property selling for $45,000.

*Solution*    97% of the first $25,000 = $24,250
95% of the amount
over $25,000 = $19,000
_____
Total = $43,250

The total of $43,250 is already a multiple of 50, so no adjustment is necessary. The down payment required for the loan is $1,750.

Discount points under the FHA are now negotiable between the buyer and the seller. The regulations have placed limits on the number of points that can be paid by the seller. These regulations are subject to change and should be reviewed constantly.

FHA loans are assumable, and many buyers and sellers find this to be an attractive feature. The assumption does not require FHA approval. FHA loans do not have the prepayment penalties conventional loan programs may have. The insurance premium can be paid at closing or included as part of the amount financed.

#### VA-Guaranteed Loans

After World War II, the government recognized the need of returning veterans to obtain housing. Consequently, the Servicemen's Readjustment Act of 1944 authorized the Veterans Administration to guarantee veterans' loans. The act has been updated several times to include the veterans of more recent American military conflicts.

The guarantee program protects lending institutions against loss on loans to veterans. Unlike the FHA-backed loans, the VA loans provide that the full amount of the guarantee be paid after reasonable efforts are made to collect after a default by a veteran. Obviously, the financial institution must attempt to satisfy its claim through foreclosure proceedings before applying to the VA for any deficiency.

The following persons are eligible for VA-guaranteed loans; their eligibility does not expire until the privilege has been used:

☐ Any veteran serving for 90 days or more in World War II between September 16, 1940, and July 25, 1947

☐ Veterans of the Korean conflict serving for 90 days or more, any part of which falls between June 27, 1950, and January 31, 1955

☐ Veterans of the Vietnam era serving on active duty 90 days or more between August 5, 1964, and May 7, 1975

☐ Any veteran who has served on active duty 181 days or more after January 31, 1955

☐ Unremarried widows and wives of veterans missing in action or captured, and those meeting certain other conditions

☐ Those who qualify for restoration of previously used eligibility

Under current law, eligibility for VA benefits can be reestablished after an initial property mortgage under a VA loan has been paid in full if no other liability exists on the property. The law also allows eligibility to be restored when another veteran willingly assumes the obligations associated with a mortgage by using his eligibility. The VA issues a certificate of eligibility stating how much of the loan it will guarantee.

Since October 1, 1980, the law has limited the maximum percentage of a guarantee to 60 percent of the loan or $27,500, whichever is less. As in the case of the FHA, a VA-approved appraiser must appraise the property prior to the loan. Interest rates are controlled by the VA. The Certificate of Reasonable Value (CRV) constitutes the ceiling that the VA will guarantee on any mortgage.

VA-guaranteed loans may not require a down payment if the veteran and the property qualify. The lender may require a small down payment. The loan may not exceed the reasonable value of the home.

VA-guaranteed loans carry no prepayment penalties. Discount points may be charged, but these points are the obligation of the seller. The VA loan is assumable by either another veteran or a nonveteran.

## Types of Mortgages

Many different types of loans are now available for mortgage purposes:

### Amortized (Constant) Mortgage

An even, periodic payment (a constant) is applied against both interest and principal so that by the end of the term, both interest and principal are fully paid, or amortized.

### Straight-Term Mortgage

Repayment of the principal is made in one lump sum at the date of maturity. Interest only is paid on the principal during the term of the loan; payments to principal are not made during the term.

### Balloon Mortgage

In the balloon mortgage, also called the *partially amortized mortgage,* an amortization schedule is selected that sets up a relatively low monthly payment.

> *Example*   A 30-year loan of $40,000 at 10% interest would result in a monthly principal and interest payment of $351.20. (See Table 11-1 to calculate this amount.) The lender may be unwilling to make such a long-term commitment at a fixed rate of interest, but it might be willing to do so for five years. A balloon payment of the total amount still owed on the loan at that time is therefore required at the end of the fifth year. This amount will be $38,640, calculated using Figure 11-1. This entire amount must be paid at the end of the fifth year.

### Flexible Payment Mortgage

The terms enable borrowers to adjust their payments on a long-term schedule related to anticipated increases in income. Usually the borrower will have to renegotiate at whatever interest rates prevail at that time, giving the lender the opportunity to adjust the rate. This scheme shifts to the borrower the risk that rates will rise and protects the lender. If interest rates fall, the borrower has the advantage.

### Adjustable Rate Mortgage

The interest rate fluctuates with changes in market conditions, thereby allowing the lender to cover expenses better.

### Renegotiable Rate Mortgage

The interest rate is adjusted periodically by negotiation between lender and borrower, but the rate remains fixed between negotiations.

### Buy-down Mortgage

The interest rate is reduced by the lender for the first several years of the mortgage.

### Adjustable Mortgages

Adjustable mortgages have caused a revolution in banking that may eventually eliminate the long-term, fixed-rate home loan and replace it with mortgages that have no constant interest rate.

### Adjustable Mortgage Loan (AML)

This loan has only one limitation under federal law—its maximum term is 40 years. Its interest rate rises or falls according to whatever money-market or lending industry index is selected as the guide by the borrower and lender. (See Figure 11-3). The frequency with which the interest rate gets adjusted is negotiated or determined by competition among lenders. The Federal Home Loan Bank Board insists that AMLs offered at federal savings and loan associations have no prepayment penalties and that the borrower not be charged a fee for rate adjustments.

### Variable Rate Mortgage (VRM)

The interest rate of a VRM is pegged to an index of lending costs and can rise or fall, depending on the movement of the index. The rate is refigured once or twice a year, and if an increase is justified, the bank gives the borrower notice that it is going to charge more for the next period. The borrower can avoid the increase by extending the terms of the VRM or by getting other financing and prepaying. The VRM's interest rate is not allowed to go higher than a specified amount over the

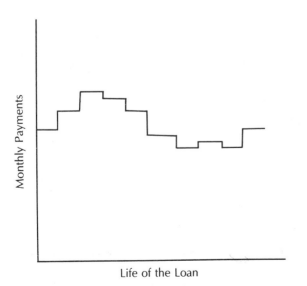

*Figure 11-3—Adjustable rate mortgage graph.*

life of the mortgage. There is no limit to how low it can drop.

### Graduated Payment Mortgage (GPM)

The monthly payments of a GPM increase from year to year, starting much lower than those for a conventional loan for the same amount, then leveling off (after 5, 7, or 10 years) at a fixed payment somewhat higher than that for conventional mortgages. (See Figure 11-4.) The GPM borrower gets a break in the crucial early years of the mortgage term, and this often makes it possible for a potential first-time buyer to become a homeowner.

### Renegotiated Rate Mortgage (RRM)

Also known as the "roll-over mortgage," the RRM offers borrowers the possibility of a lower interest rate in the future. The RRM is actually a short-term loan secured by a 30-year mortgage. The term can be three to five years, with renewal at no charge to the borrower guaranteed at the end of each term. However, the interest rate at each renewal is determined by a national index of mortgage costs or money-market trends. If the index shows an increase is warranted, the bank can boost its rate by that amount for each year of the term. If a decrease is in line, the bank must drop its rate accordingly.

### Adjustable Rate Mortgage (ARM)

Though the term "adjustable" is generally applied to most of the loans under discussion, the official ARM is offered by national banks. The changes in interest on an ARM must be made according to a specified national or money-market index, and there is no interest ceiling. Increases must occur at least six months apart, and each increase can be for no more than 5 percent. However, six months after an increase, the ARM can be increased again, and by as much as 5 percent if the indicators warrant.

### Growing Equity Mortgage (GEM)

The purpose of the growing equity loan is to allow the borrower to make increased payments, with the increases going directly to principal reduction. This type of mortgage has increasing payments, which often double in amount, and the mortgage is paid off in a shorter time. For example, a 30-year mortgage may be paid off in as little as 17 years with the increases.

### Reverse Annuity Mortgage (RAM)

By far the rarest of the four federally approved loans, the RAM is an arrangement devised for mature homeowners who want to cash in the equity on their home without having to sell or move. With the RAM, the home is put up as collateral. The mortgage is not one lump sum,

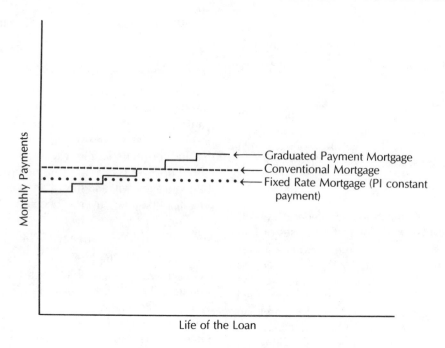

*Figure 11-4—Graduated payment mortgage graph.*

but an annuity paid to the owner, who remains in the house. After the owner's death, the bank owns the property. It is a complicated arrangement, and most banks do not bother with it.

### Buy-down Mortgage

The concept of buying down interest rates for mortgages was introduced several years ago by builders of new homes, and the device was originally called a "builder's buy-down." The basic idea is to induce the mortgage lender to accept a reduced interest rate for a number of years. The lower payments would then induce buyers to purchase homes even in times of high interest rates. This is accomplished by paying the lender a lump sum at the time the mortgage loan is made. The lump sum will pay the lender the amount of income the lender will lose during the early years of the mortgage. Of course, the reduced amount of interest is not being lost by the lender all at once. Instead, the lender is forgoing some amount of interest each month for a number of years.

To determine the amount to be paid to the lender at the time of the buy-down, one must calculate the present value of the right to receive the income that will be lost in the future. This is done by using present value calculation tables.

*Example*   Assume a $75,000 mortgage would be made for 30 years at 18%. The builder or seller is willing to buy down the rate to 13% for the first

five years. The difference of 5% results in $300 per month less to be paid to the lender. The present value of the right to receive $300 per month for 5 years, using the 18% discount rate, is $11,813. This is the amount that must be paid to the lender to reimburse it in advance for the lost interest income. The lower payments will save the buyer $21,000 over the first five years. At that time the rate increases to 18%.

Buy-downs may be used by anyone willing to pay their cost, whether it is the buyer or the seller. Clearly, the seller must recognize that the payment of this amount must come out of the proceeds of the sale and, therefore, represents a discount of the sales price. See Figure 11-5.

### Blanket Mortgage

The *blanket mortgage* allows more than one piece of real estate to be used as security for a single loan. Typically such a mortgage is used in developing a subdivision, where large expenditures are needed for engineering, surveying, platting, streets, and utilities. The mortgage is structured so that as each lot is sold, all or most of the proceeds from the sale go to the lender, who then releases the mortgage on that particular lot. The "blanket" is lifted so that one lot may be released, but the mortgage continues to be in effect for the remaining lots. This process continues until all the lots are sold or until the entire loan has been paid.

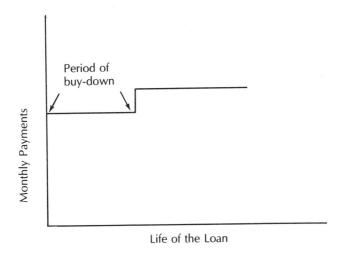

Figure 11-5—Buy-down mortgage graph.

## Package Mortgage

Traditional concepts of residential mortgage lending have been changed by the trend toward the use of built-in appliances. Many of them are clearly fixtures—that is, personal property that has been attached to the real property and has become part of the real estate. Such appliances typically have shorter life expectancies than the house itself. The *package mortgage*, which includes such items, represents a change from traditional residential mortgage lending practices, which do not include such items. Although a package mortgage is useful in many cases, particularly where the home buyer would have insufficient funds to purchase such items separately, it should be noted that many appliances will wear out long before they have been paid for. The long-term mortgage financial obligation may generate a great deal of interest expense that could instead have been allocated to the purchase of these items.

## Open-End Mortgage

Under a true *open-end mortgage*, the lender agrees at the outset to advance additional funds to the borrower, using the original mortgage as security for the later borrowings. Theoretically, the first lien of the mortgage lender is sufficient to protect the total advances made to the borrower, even if they exceed the amount of the original loan. The purpose of this device is to avoid the expenses involved in writing a new mortgage whenever later advances are made.

## Wraparound Mortgage

The *wraparound mortgage* is a type of second mortgage that provides attractive financial alternatives for both the buyer and seller of a property.

Frequently called the *Canadian wraparound*, this type of mortgage is aimed at preserving the benefits of an existing mortgage that has a more favorable interest rate than is currently available. Although the wraparound mortgage was designed for large commercial transactions, the concept has gained popularity in the residential area.

*Example* A owns a property that has an existing FHA mortgage of $50,000 at 9% interest. A sells the property for $100,000, taking a $15,000 cash down payment. To aid in financing the sale, A also takes a $85,000 wraparound mortgage at 10% interest. The borrower has a mortgage loan on the new property at a very attractive rate, and A, as seller, is able to meet the original 9% payment each month with the payment from the 10% wraparound. This process allows A to earn 10% on $35,000 and an additional 1% on the differential on the underlying $50,000 loan. This is a very attractive investment for the person making the wraparound, even though he or she is lending $35,000 at a preferential rate.

Caution is urged in the use of this device. It needs to be reviewed by a skilled attorney and a CPA with tax experience to determine that the tax consequences do not eliminate the economic advantages of the wraparound.

## Shared Appreciation Loans

*Shared appreciation loans* allow the lender to participate in the realized appreciation of the property upon sale or when the loan comes due. In return for this participation, the lender sets favorable loan terms. The monthly payments are constant over the loan period.

### Summary

It should be apparent that the potential for flexibility in mortgage financing is limited only by the goals to be achieved and the ingenuity of the parties involved. For those in the real estate brokerage field, it is important to be aware that there are many ways to structure the financing of a particular transaction.

## SPECIAL FORMS OF FINANCING

### Second Mortgage

Prospective purchasers of real estate, particularly purchasers of homes, have always been short of capital with which to make substantial down payments. Thus it was necessary to bridge the gap, and the *second mortgage* became popular as a means of providing money for the down payment.

When a property purchased for $40,000 has an assumable $34,000 first mortgage against it, and the purchaser has $2,000 cash to make a down payment, the purchaser then needs a $4,000 second or *junior* mortgage.

Traditionally, second mortgages are short-term loans that carry a higher rate of interest than first mortgages. They usually include a series of large paybacks rather than following a form of amortization.

The second mortgage reads like the first mortgage except that it is expected to make reference to and accept the priority of the first mortgage. Even when it does not, however, it is junior in priority to the first mortgage. The priority is key in the case of a foreclosure and sale of the property for repayment of the lenders.

Some situations in which a second mortgage can be used are:

☐ To make up the difference between the available down payment money and the amount needed to purchase real estate.
☐ A very short second mortgage might be used when the buyer has another house on which a sale is pending or when the buyer is certain of receiving funds in a short time from other sources.
☐ To leverage current real estate in order to invest in other real estate or to make other investments.

## Swing Loans

*Swing loans,* which are generally secured by a mortgage, are usually based on the borrower's credit reputation and on the equity in an existing residence. They are used to borrow money for a down payment on a new house. The same result is achieved as if the blanket mortgage, as discussed earlier, were used; however, less formality is involved.

*Example*  The buyer owns property *A,* which is valued at $50,000 and has a mortgage balance of $25,000; the buyer has an equity of $25,000. The buyer needs $20,000 to make a down payment on property *B* to enable her to obtain favorable mortgage financing. A bank lends her $20,000 on an unsecured basis, but looking to the equity in her old house as a source of repayment. The buyer purchases property *B,* and when property *A* is sold, she repays the loan—which "swings" on the equity she had in the property.

The borrower in this case must have a very good credit reputation to qualify for such a loan, and he or she usually must be well known to the lender. If one or the other of these factors is lacking, the swing loan may still be made, but the lender may require an *indemnifying mortgage,* which is, in substance, the same thing as a second mortgage.

## Sale and Leaseback

*Sale and leaseback* is a financial vehicle that has developed in recent years to permit business and industry to free capital that is normally tied up in real estate for use in their own business or manufacturing operations. The user of real estate sells to an investor and simultaneously leases back the property for a desired period. The user may also have an option to repurchase the property at the end of the lease.

## Construction Loan

A form of *interim financing,* the *construction loan* is paid out in installments during the period of construction to provide temporary financing. At the end of that period, a traditional type of mortgage replaces the construction loan. The permanent mortgage is usually arranged at the time the construction loan is negotiated.

## Purchase Money Mortgage

A method of financing commonly used during periods of tight money or for purchasing property that in normal circumstances could not be financed through a conventional lender is the *purchase money mortgage.* The seller lends to the purchaser. The title is conveyed and the seller becomes the mortgagee. This is a common form of second mortgage.

## Land Contract

The *conditional sales contract (land contract)* is sometimes used in place of financing the sale of real property through a conventional lender. This is a two-party arrangement between the buyer and seller whereby the seller retains title to the property as security for the buyer's promise to pay the contract. The buyer gets the responsibilities of ownership during the contract period. In many states, contracts do not have to follow the same stringent foreclosure rules that mortgages do in case of default.

## CONCERNS AND CONSIDERATIONS OF THE LENDER

The concerns of the lender go beyond the repayment plans discussed so far in this chapter. The term and the borrower's qualifications are also of great importance in determining the attractiveness of a loan.

Upon receiving a request for a loan from a potential home buyer, the mortgagee must give careful consideration to the request. Institutions usually look at the suitability of both the property (the physical security) and the applicant (the borrower security).

## Terms

The *term* of a mortgage is the time period extending from the original date of the mortgage to the date of its maturity. The majority of mortgages are long-term loans, ranging from 20 to 30 years. Terms vary from mortgage to mortgage; they depend on the type and characteristics of the property and on the borrower's qualifications, which are contingent on factors such as age and income. Mortgage institutions usually follow their own lending guidelines in addition to the state and federal regulations imposed on them.

## The Property as Security

The lending institution must examine the property being acquired by the applicant to determine its suitability as security for the loan. In deciding the property's value, the lender looks at the economic life of the property. This is determined by its

- □ Location
- □ Age
- □ Physical condition
- □ Structural soundness
- □ Future marketability

On some types of loans, the mortgagee must also look at the income-producing ability of the property. Therefore, the use of the property is one of the major considerations of the lender.

## Appraisals

All lending institutions require appraisals when considering loan applications. Appraisals are estimates of the value of property. The three main methods of appraisal are the income approach, the market approach, and the cost approach. (Note: See Chapter 12, "Real Estate Appraisal," for a fuller explanation of this important aspect of the real estate business and real estate transactions.) These appraisals provide the information on which lending institutions rely in making investment decisions. The amount of the loan is based either on the sales price or on the appraised value, whichever is lower. Buyers often find themselves paying more than the appraised price, and consequently they must pay the difference between the appraised price and the selling price.

Although several reasons exist for doing appraisals, in general the appraiser is most concerned with estimating the value of the property for loan purposes. The established value is used by a loan committee to determine the maximum amount of principal to be loaned. In doing this, the committee employs a *loan-to-value ratio*.

*Example*   When a property is valued at $100,000 and the financial institution has a loan-to-value

ratio of 80%, the institution will not lend more than $80,000. Thus a down payment of $20,000, or 20%, would be required.

## Borrower Qualifications

Having examined the quality of the property, lenders turn to the potential buyer and consider his or her ability to pay. This is done for the benefit of the buyer and the lender and is intended to lessen the chance of default.

### Credit Analysis

The credit analysis considers the following aspects of the borrower's situation:

- □ Net worth
- □ Income
- □ Job stability
- □ Type of employment
- □ Future economic status
- □ Number of dependents
- □ Age
- □ Other obligations
- □ Expenses

All these factors are examined to determine the applicant's financial and personal stability. In this process, lending institutions tend to give most weight to the borrower's income, which can come from various sources.

Lending institutions are now paying more attention to the income of spouses. Consequently, lenders are currently using the income of both husband and wife to determine loan applicant acceptability. The combined incomes have made it possible for more families to qualify for housing loans than ever before.

### Primary Income

Primary income, usually the buyer's monthly net income, is an important factor. From this monthly net amount, expenses (food, clothing, medical bills, house maintenance, automobile payments, etc.) are deducted. Then the lender (mortgagee) looks at the primary income that remains for the borrower to spend on housing. Lending institutions vary on the level of income that can be spent on housing, but most lenders approve loans that require 20 to 25 percent of the applicant's net income to be spent on housing. Due to rising construction and housing costs, these figures are changing. In periods of high inflation, for example, a figure of 30 percent might be allowed.

### Secondary Income

Although primary income is of major importance to lenders, secondary income has become increasingly important. This income can come from several sources, including stocks, other real estate, or part-time jobs. In the past, lenders have not relied on the total amount of secondary income, but only on a percentage of it, allowing for fluctuations.

## Loan Discounts or Discount Points

Often lenders cannot obtain mortgage interest rates that are competitive with other types of investments in the market. In some states *usury laws* place upper limits on mortgage interest rates and thereby limit the rate that mortgagees can obtain on their mortgage investments.

*Points* are a *rate adjustment factor* that increases the yield of the mortgage to a satisfactory level that will allow the mortgagee to make the loan. Points may be called a rate equalizing factor.

Having decided the yield that is needed, the lender determines the number of points needed to make up the deficit. Using a rule of thumb, lenders have decided that each one-eighth of one percent of yield needed is equal to one discount point. One point is equal to one percent of the loan amount.

*Example* Assume that the lender wants to obtain a 10% yield on a regular mortgage. Using the above rule of thumb, the lender charges 8 discount points to accept the loan at 9%.

*Example* In the same situation, upon closing the lender disburses the face amount of the loan, minus the amount of the discount points. For a $20,000 mortgage at 9% interest with 8 discount points, the actual payment to the seller is

$20,000 − (.08 × $20,000) = $20,000 − $1,600 = $18,400

(The .08 is based on each discount point equaling one percent.) The lender, however, will hold the mortgage note for the full sum of $20,000, thereby obtaining a yield of 10%.

The borrower typically pays the discount points under conventional financing, whereas the points are negotiable between the buyer and seller under FHA. Under VA regulations, usually only the seller can pay the points. In most circumstances the purchaser must pay one percent of the loan amount to the lender as a loan origination fee. This is not a discount point but a fee for placing the loan on the books of the lender—*the loan origination fee.*

## FEDERAL INVOLVEMENT IN REAL ESTATE FINANCE

In times of tight money and credit crunches, the federal government feels an obligation to help lending institutions and the public. To do this, a *secondary money market* has been created, in which federal agencies buy primary mortgages from lending institutions, thus generating funds for further mortgage development.

These agencies are the Federal National Mortgage Association, the Government National Mortgage Association, and the Federal Home Loan Mortgage Corporation. These institutions comprise the major money part of the secondary market and help balance the money policies of the Federal Reserve that might be detrimental to the well-being of the lending institutions.

### Federal National Mortgage Association (FNMA)

Commonly referred to as "Fannie Mae," this association was originally government sponsored and is now a private corporation. Established in 1938, its main purpose is to establish a secondary mortgage market. FNMA buys existing FHA, VA, and conventional mortgages and allows the seller to continue to service the mortgage. FNMA provides a service by attracting private capital into the housing market.

### Government National Mortgage Association (GNMA)

This association purchases, services, and sells mortgages insured or guaranteed by the FHA or VA. Under Section 305 of the National Housing Act, GNMA, commonly referred to as "Ginnie Mae," is authorized to provide financing for selected types of mortgages. The association also provides assistance through the purchase of home mortgages, generally as a means of retarding or stopping a decline in mortgage lending and home-building activities that might threaten the stability of the national economy. GNMA got its start as a part of FNMA and was split off in 1968.

GNMA has specific guidelines to follow when purchasing mortgages, and these are similar to those for FHA-approved and VA-guaranteed mortgages. When buying mortgages, GNMA stipulates that payment of the mortgage must be current. One of the primary goals of GNMA is to provide a secondary market for loans that otherwise would not be bought because of their high risks. The activities of GNMA are conducted through the sale of securities by the U.S. Treasury.

### The Mortgage Money Market

Mortgage terms and interest rates are not uniform; they vary from locale to locale. Many different factors influence the mortgage money market, but federal fiscal policy has an extreme effect on the overall cost of borrowed funds.

The supply of and demand for money determine the basic mortgage interest rate at lending institutions. General economic conditions and the degree of risk involved, added to the basic rate, determine the actual interest rate that is charged for a particular mortgage loan. This supply of mortgage funds depends to a large extent on the level of savings in financial institutions, but it is influenced as well by government monetary policies. The demand for mortgage funds depends on personal income and the terms on which the available funds will be loaned.

The forces that influence the money marketplace have caused a significant fluctuation in interest rates over the past several years. The combination of inflation and credit policies has affected the *effective demand* for luxury items. Real estate, as it is known in the United States, constitutes a luxury. The effective demand is a result of the desire for borrowed funds, coupled with the borrower's ability to obtain them. This ability includes the income and creditworthiness of the borrower.

## Truth in Lending

Consumer concern about underlying mortgage terms and conditions spurred passage of the Consumer Credit Protection Act in July 1969. This included the Truth-in-Lending Act, which granted the Federal Reserve Board the power to implement the regulations. The board, using this power, established *Regulation Z*. The regulation applies to anyone who grants credit in any form. Although it does not regulate interest rates, the board assures consumers that information about the cost of the credit is made available in simple language. Another major purpose of Regulation Z is to standardize credit procedures, allowing consumers to shop around for the cheapest form of credit. The main emphasis of the act is on complete and full disclosure.

## Effects of Regulation Z on Real Estate Transactions

The purpose of Regulation Z is not to set or regulate interest rates, but to standardize the procedures involved in credit transactions. It requires that the consumer be fully informed of all aspects of a credit transaction. It also applies to all of the seller's advertising.

All credit for real estate is covered under Regulation Z when it is for an individual consumer.

☐ *Disclosure.* The lender must disclose what the borrower is paying for credit and what the credit will cost in total percentage terms. (Exception: The total finance charge in dollars paid by the parties in the transaction need not be stated.) However, the lender must still indicate the total annual percentage rate. This is done only in the sale of first mortgages on single-family dwellings. The finance charge includes interest, loan fees, inspection fees, FHA mortgage insurance fees, and discount points. Other fees should not be included.

☐ *Right to rescind.* Regulation Z provides that the borrower has the right to rescind or cancel the trans-

action if it involves placing a lien against real estate that is his or her principal residence. This right must be exercised before midnight of the third business day after the transaction, which allows a three-day "cooling-off" period during which the borrower can reassess the transaction. In the case of a first mortgage on a residence, the act specifically states that transactions to finance the construction or the purchase of the dwelling are not included in the right of rescission.

☐ *Advertising.* Real estate advertising is greatly affected by Regulation Z. General terms may be used to describe financing available, but any details that are given must comply with the regulations. Any finance charge must be stated as an annual percentage rate. If any other credit terms are mentioned, such as monthly payment, term of loan, or down payment required, then the following information must be given: cash price, annual percentage rate required, down payment, and amount and due date of all payments.

☐ *Effect on real estate personnel.* Regulation Z does not indicate that brokers or salespersons should refrain from making direct contact with lenders on behalf of prospective purchasers. Of prime importance, however, is that the lender must be the one who decides if the loan should be made.

☐ *Enforcement of Regulation Z.* A lender who fails to disclose any of the required credit information can be sued for a specified portion of the finance charge. The lender, under some circumstances, may be fined up to $5,000 or sentenced to one year in jail or both.

Figure 11-6 illustrates a notice to the customer required by Regulation Z.

## The Real Estate Settlement Procedures Act (RESPA)

This federal legislation, originally passed in 1974 and amended thereafter, applies to all settlements on loans that are "federally related" for residential purposes. Most important, it applies to all loans secured by a first mortgage on a single-family to four-family residential property by any lender regulated by the federal government and those lenders whose deposits are insured by a federal agency. Some other lenders are also covered by the act, but the above broad category includes most residential mortgages made in the U.S. today. In all such mortgage settlements, the uniform settlement statement prescribed by HUD or its equivalent must be used. The form is complex, so many brokers also prepare their own simplified closing statements to clarify the transaction for their clients.

NOTICE TO CUSTOMER
as required by Federal Reserve Regulation "Z"                    LOAN NO. _____

will lend to the borrower(s) in this transaction the amount below indicated. Interest computations on this amount will be at the contractual rate of _____% on the outstanding balance. The **ANNUAL PERCENTAGE RATE** which includes with the contractual rate those costs listed below as **PREPAID FINANCE CHARGE** is _____% and will begin to accure on _____. Beginning on the _____day of _____ 19_____ and due the _____ day of the month thereafter payments for Principal and Finance Charge, will be due in _____ monthly installments of _____.

A.   **AMOUNT OF LOAN** committed in this transaction .......................................................        $_____

B.   Less **PREPAID FINANCE CHARGE** costs due at time of closing
     1. Loan Discount..........................................................................        $_____
     2. Loan Processing Fee................................................................        $_____
     3. Interest Thru...........................................................................        $_____
     4. Private or F.H.A. Mortgage Insurance.....................................        $_____
     5. _____        $_____
     6. _____        $_____
     7. _____        $_____

                         Total **PREPAID FINANCE CHARGE**     $_____

C.   Equals **AMOUNT FINANCED** in this transaction.....................................................        $_____

D.   Other costs not included in **FINANCE CHARGE:**           PAID BY CASH          PAID FROM LOAN
                                                                                     PROCEEDS

     1. Title Insurance or Abstract ........................................        $_____        $_____
     2. Opinion on Title .........................................................        $_____        $_____
     3. Appraisal....................................................................        $_____        $_____
     4. Credit Report.............................................................        $_____        $_____
     5. Survey........................................................................        $_____        $_____
     6. Tax Escrow.................................................................        $_____        $_____
     7. Insurance Escrow.......................................................        $_____        $_____
     8. Hazard Insurance Premium........................................        $_____        $_____
     9. Recording Fee............................................................        $_____        $_____
     10. _____        $_____        $_____
     11. _____        $_____        $_____

                                    Total Charges Paid From Loan Proceeds     $_____

E.   **NET PROCEEDS** ...........................................................................................        $_____

F.   This Institution's security interest in this transaction is a _____ on property located at_____
     _____ also specifically described in the documents furnished for this loan.
     The documents executed in connection with this transaction cover all after-acquired property and also stand as security for future advances, the terms for which are described in the documents.

G.   Late payment formula:
         In event of default a late charge of 5% of the Principal and Interest payment will be charged for each installment not received by the Association within 15 days after the installment is due.

H.   Prepayment formula:
         When amount prepaid equals or exceeds 20% of the original loan, not more than 90 days interest on the amount prepaid may be charged beyond the date of payment.

I.   Rebate formula:
         None

J.   Miscellaneous disclosures:
         This Mortgage also secures the payment of any additional loans up to but not exceeding $5000.00 at the Mortgagee's option.

*K.  **FINANCE CHARGE** includes:
     1. Total Prepaid Finance Charge (from B)......................................        $_____
     2. Total Interest to be Earned over life of Loan................................        $_____
     3. _____        $_____
     4. _____        $_____
     5. _____        $_____

                                    Total **FINANCE CHARGE**     $_____

     TOTAL PAYMENTS on this transaction (Principal and Interest) will be ......................        $_____

INSURANCE

PROPERTY INSURANCE: Property insurance, if written in connection with this loan, may be obtained by borrower through any person of his choice, provided however, the creditor reserves the right to refuse, for reasonable cause, to accept an insurer offered by the borrower. If borrower desires property insurance to be obtained from or through the creditor, the cost will be $_____ for the _____ year term of the initial policy.   OTHER INSURANCE: Credit life, accident, health or loss of income insurance is not required to obtain this loan. No charge is made for such insurance and No such insurance may be provided unless the borrower signs the appropriate statement below. _____ is available at a cost of $_____ for the _____ year term of the initial policy.          (TYPE OF INSURANCE)

I desire_____ insurance coverage.                    I DO NOT desire such insurance coverage.

_____                    _____
DATE                          SIGNATURE                              DATE                          SIGNATURE

                         I hereby acknowledge receipt of the disclosures made in this notice.

                                              _____
                                              BORROWER                              DATE

BY_____        _____
                                              BORROWER                              DATE

* Not required for 1st mortgage purchase loans.

*Figure 11-6—Regulation Z notice to customer.*

*Provisions of RESPA*

☐ The lender must permit the borrower to inspect the closing statement one day prior to the closing. This statement must disclose the anticipated closing costs to the extent they are known at that time; the costs are precisely determined at the time of closing.

☐ The lender must provide to the borrower a booklet, "Settlement Costs," within three days after taking an application for a mortgage loan, and the lender must also provide a good faith estimate of the anticipated closing costs.

☐ The lender's escrow account requirements are regulated. Generally, the maximum that may be required is the sum of the amount that normally would be required to maintain the account for the current month plus one-sixth of the total estimated expenses for real estate taxes and insurance for the following 12-month period.

☐ Kickbacks and unearned fees are prohibited. Partic-

ular emphasis is placed on the relationship between the regulated lender and the title insurance companies. The lender may not, as a condition of the loan, specify the title insurer to be used.

☐ The identity of the true borrower must be obtained by the lender, and the lender must make this information available to the Federal Home Loan Bank Board on demand.

☐ No fee may be charged by the lender for preparation of all of the forms required by RESPA.

☐ The act requires the secretary of HUD to establish economical model land recording systems in selected areas of the country.

Although RESPA is directed at mortgage lenders, it obviously has an impact on those engaged in the real estate brokerage business because of the industry's dependence on the easy availability of mortgage funds. Familiarity with the specified closing statement seems to be essential, if only for explanation to the buyer.

## REVIEW QUESTIONS

1. Which of the following loans allows the borrower to use the equity in one property to fund the equity requirement for another until the first property is sold or closed?

   (A) Package mortgage
   (B) Open-end mortgage
   (C) Swing loan
   (D) Construction loan

2. If a borrower wishes to pledge certain fixtures and personal property as security for the debt as well as the real estate, he or she would use a

   (A) wraparound mortgage
   (B) sale-leaseback
   (C) blanket mortgage
   (D) package mortgage

3. A mortgage that is repaid in equal installments that contain both principal and interest is a

   (A) balloon mortgage
   (B) straight-term mortgage
   (C) package mortgage
   (D) amortized mortgage

4. The dollar value of a loan discount point is equal to

   (A) one percent of the down payment
   (B) one percent of the sales price
   (C) one percent of the amount to be loaned
   (D) one percent of the appraised value

5. Loan discounts for FHA and VA loans are paid to the

   (A) buyer          (C) salesperson
   (B) seller         (D) mortgagee

6. The amount of interest that can be charged for a loan is controlled by

   (A) Regulation Z   (C) usury laws
   (B) RESPA          (D) HUD

7. A financing arrangement between the buyer and the seller whereby the seller takes a mortgage and gives the buyer title to the property is a

   (A) land contract
   (B) purchase money mortgage
   (C) sale-leaseback
   (D) swing loan

8. The truth-in-lending statutes cause lenders to

   (A) limit the number of discount points being charged
   (B) charge only a specified interest rate for each type of loan
   (C) disclose in a meaningful fashion the costs of the credit
   (D) make loans only in certain geographical areas

9. A construction loan is considered

   (A) a permanent form of financing
   (B) a method of self-financing

(C) an interim form of financing

(D) none of the above

10. The primary reason lenders discount mortgage loans is to

(A) meet federal requirements for the sale of the mortgage in the secondary market

(B) increase the yield on the mortgage to the lender

(C) meet regulations and requirements

(D) avoid disclosure on the RESPA statement

11. Discount points are considered

(A) rate equalization factors

(B) police powers

(C) origination fees

(D) none of the above

12. In repaying an amortized loan

(A) the loan is repaid entirely in one payment

(B) each payment includes portions of principal and interest

(C) interest only is paid until the last payment

(D) the interest is computed periodically on the original amount of the loan

13. In making a $15,000 loan, how much will the lender charge if the mortgage is to be discounted 5 points?

(A) $450          (C) $750

(B) $500          (D) $600

14. Truth-in-lending statutes require disclosure of all of the following EXCEPT

(A) the finance charge as an annual percentage

(B) the number, amount, and due date of all payments

(C) the method of computing unearned finance charges

(D) attorney's fees for closing

15. The VA

(A) guarantees loans      (C) discounts loans

(B) insures loans          (D) sells loans

16. Which type of loan may contain prepayment penalties?

(A) An FHA loan

(B) A VA loan

(C) A conventional loan

(D) None of the above

17. When a consumer has both the monthly earning power and the credit to purchase property, there is

(A) demand

(B) supply

(C) effective demand

(D) effective supply

18. If an advertisement lists the monthly payment required to purchase real estate, then it must also state all of the following EXCEPT

(A) cash price to be paid

(B) annual percentage rate (APR)

(C) down payment amount

(D) provider of insurance

19. If a borrower wishes to preserve the advantage of a lower interest rate on a prior loan, he or she might use which of the following to refinance the property?

(A) Wraparound mortgage

(B) Package mortgage

(C) Swing loan

(D) Blanket mortgage

20. When the borrower pays the balance of the loan in advance of the due date, he or she may be subject to

(A) acceleration penalties

(B) loan discounts

(C) prepayment penalties

(D) none of the above

# Chapter 12
# Real Estate Appraisal

---

## VOCABULARY

*You will find it important to have a complete working knowledge of the following terms, concepts, and abbreviations found in the text or glossary.*

| | | |
|---|---|---|
| AIREA | economic obsolescence | net income |
| appraisal | functional obsolescence | physical depreciation |
| appraisal process | gross rent multiplier | plottage |
| assessed value | highest and best use | recapture rate |
| capitalization | income method | return of capital (ROC) |
| comparables | insurable value | return on investment (ROI) |
| competitive market analysis (CMA) | loan value | subject property |
| cost approach | market comparison | value |
| depreciation | market value | |

---

ALL real estate transactions require a determination of the value of land and any improvements found on it. The need for appraisals can typically be found in the different types of transactions that involve real property. The appraisal process is critical to understanding how real estate values are determined.

### REASONS FOR APPRAISALS

Appraisals are commonly required for any of the following reasons:

☐ *In transferring ownership:*
To aid prospective buyers in determining an offering price
To aid prospective sellers in determining a selling price
To establish the value of an estate's assets
To establish the value of property being exchanged or merged through some form of reorganization
☐ *In obtaining credit for financial purposes:*
To arrive at the value of the security offered for a proposed mortgage loan
To provide a sound basis for real estate decision making for the mortgagee
To establish a basis for insurance and the value of the property
☐ *In establishing just compensation in condemnation proceedings:*

To estimate the value before the act of condemnation
☐ *In establishing a basis for taxation:*
To estimate applicable depreciation rates on buildings and to value nondepreciable items such as land
To determine gift or inheritance tax

### THE LANGUAGE OF REAL ESTATE APPRAISAL

Like a foreign language, the terms used in real estate appraisal must be mastered before a person can have a basic understanding of the topic. The following key terms build the framework for the appraisal.

#### Appraisal

An appraisal is a written estimate or opinion of value. The fundamental purpose of any appraisal is to estimate the value of a particular property for a defined purpose at a particular time—and to support that in writing with a logical approach.

#### Value

Value can have many meanings, especially from the viewpoint of the appraiser who must know what kind of value is to be reported in the appraisal.

Several factors must be considered to understand the meaning of value:

☐ A property must have *utility;* that is, it must be useful to a potential buyer before it can have value.

☐ The *scarcity* of the property is important. The greater the demand for a property, the higher its value will be.

☐ *Effective demand* must exist for the property. That is, a buyer must have the purchasing power to buy the property.

One major problem in determining the value of real property is the fact that the benefits—either *value in exchange* or *value in use*—are projected over the years to come and, therefore, are difficult to estimate without considering the influences that economic, social, governmental, and environmental forces have on the property.

*Market Value*

The definition of market value, according to Byrl N. Boyce in *Real Estate Appraisal Terminology,* is:

The *most probable* price in terms of money which a property *should* bring in competitive and open market under all conditions requisite to a fair sale, the buyer and seller, each acting prudently, knowledgeably, and assuming the price is not affected by undue stimulus.

Note that this defines *market value,* not *market price,* which would be the actual sales price of the property.

Implicit in this definition is the consummation of a sale as of a specific date and the passing of title from seller to buyer under conditions whereby

☐ Buyer and seller are typically motivated.

☐ Both parties are well informed or well advised, and they are acting in what they consider their own best interest.

☐ A reasonable time is allowed for exposure in the open market.

☐ Payment is made in cash or its equivalent.

☐ Financing, if any, is on terms generally available in the community at the specified date and typical for the property type in its locale.

☐ The price represents a normal consideration for the property sold unaffected by special financing amounts and/or terms, services, fees, costs, or credits incurred in the transaction. Changes in any one of these conditions could cause a difference between market value and actual market price; therefore, each transaction must be reviewed to determine the conditions present in determining the price.

Numerous definitions of market value have been devised over the years by professional organizations, government bodies, courts, etc. The Supreme Court of many states has handed down definitions of market value for use in the respective state courts that are subject to frequent change.

Market value might be most clearly defined as the price at which a willing seller would sell and a willing buyer would buy, both being informed and knowledgeable and neither being under duress.

It is important that value, price, and cost not be used interchangeably, for they are not always the same. Price and value may, for example, appear to be the same when two similar properties in the same neighborhood are compared. However, if different plans are used to purchase each property, the actual prices might vary greatly because of the types of financing used. Usually cost and value are likely to be similar only when the improvements are new and the property is being used for its highest and best use.

## ECONOMIC PRINCIPLES

Valuation theory is based on the following economic principles.

### Principle of Supply and Demand

The principle of supply and demand runs through all aspects of business and can easily be seen in real estate. If the demand for housing in a specific area increases and the supply is stable or decreases, the real estate values increase. If an area or type of housing is overbuilt, then real estate value declines due to excess supply.

### Principle of Substitution

When two or more like properties with substantially the same utility become available, the one with the lower price attracts the greatest demand. In the case of market value, the principle indicates that the informed buyer will not pay more than what is paid for comparable properties, nor will the seller sell for less than what is paid for comparable properties. A buyer will not pay more for an existing property than the cost to produce new. Obviously, the principle of substitution holds true through all three approaches to value outlined in the appraisal process.

### Principle of Change

Economic, social, governmental, and environmental forces all have present and future effects on real estate and its value. Most properties and their neighborhoods have a four-stage life that embraces, in turn, growth, stability, decline, and renewal. This is known as the principle of change.

## Principle of Conformity

Conformity implies that homogeneity exists between land use and the structures built on the land. It does not imply total uniformity. Property values are often protected by zoning and deed restrictions that specify setback requirements, minimum square footage, building requirements, and amenities packages.

## Economic Life

The economic life of an improvement is the period over which it is depreciated, or the period during which the property can be expected to generate a *return of capital (ROC)* invested. For example, if a property had an estimated economic life of 20 years and the owner wanted to receive a 100 percent return of the capital during its economic life, the owner would need to have a 5 percent return each year for 20 years to receive a total of the 100 percent of capital returned (100% divided by 20 years = .05 per year).

## Highest and Best Use

The concept of *highest and best use* can best be defined as: That use that at the time the property is appraised is the most likely and most profitable use of the property. The existing use of the property may not be the highest and best use.

An appraiser who is considering highest and best use can view a plot of land in two ways: *as if vacant* or *as improved.* Each yields a different value. To attribute value to an improvement, the improvement must add value to the land. It is conceivable that a lot might be worth more with the improvements removed.

In determining the highest and best use, it is essential to remember the *theory of consistent use.* A property in transition from one use to another cannot have one value based on the use of the land and another value based on the improvements. In such a case, the cost of demolition of the improvements must be subtracted from the value of the land as if vacant.

The final step in the determination of the highest and best use of the property is to be certain that the use is legally possible under existing government regulations.

## Principle of Progression

Properties that have higher value tend to increase the value of a property of lower value in the vicinity.

## Principle of Regression

Properties that have lower value tend to decrease the value of a property of higher value in the vicinity.

## Principle of Diminishing Returns

This principle applies when additional increments of money placed in improvements in a property are more

than can be justified for resale purposes. Such property would be considered to be "overimproved."

## Principle of Anticipation

Value can increase or decrease based on the expectation or anticipation that a future event will occur, causing the property to increase or decrease in value. For example, agricultural land might suddenly increase in value when a major industrial firm is seeking a plant site in that area.

## THE APPRAISAL PROCESS

An orderly procedure must be used when the appraiser determines value. Before the appraiser can give an *opinion of value* in written form, the appraisal process must be implemented.

The appraisal process allows the appraiser to consider the property on a step-by-step basis, gathering all the relevant data required to support the final opinion of value. This is necessary because appraisal is an art, not an exact science, and the appraisal process provides the only logical approach to establishing real estate value.

The most detailed approach to the appraisal process has been developed and refined by the American Institute of Real Estate Appraisers (AIREA). The process as outlined by the institute has several steps, as shown in Figure 12-1.

## Definition of the Problem

The first step in the appraisal process is the development of a concise statement of the problem the appraiser is to consider. This prevents any later questions regarding the objective of the appraisal.

Five basic factors are considered in this first step:

☐ *Identification of the real estate.* This includes both the legal description and the street address of the property.

☐ *Identification of the property rights.* An appraisal includes an opinion of the value of the rights the owners have in the ownership or use of the land and improvements.

☐ *Date of the value estimate.* The date of value is not necessarily the date on which the appraisal was completed; rather it is the effective date on which the value is based or was determined. This might be anytime during the past or possibly even in the future. Different types of appraisal call for different dates of value. An estate appraisal would have a date in the past (date of death), whereas an appraisal for financing would be for a present date.

☐ *Purpose of the appraisal.* A statement must be made as to the purpose or objective of the appraisal,

## THE VALUATION PROCESS

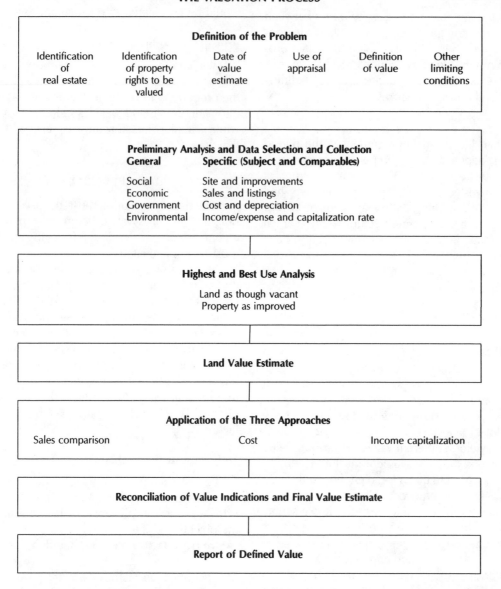

Figure 12-1—The valuation process. (Reprinted by permission from The Appraisal of Real Estate, 9th ed. © 1987 by the American Institute of Real Estate Appraisers, Chicago.)

thereby allowing the appraiser to define the objective of the report.

☐ *Definition of value.* A precise, written definition of the value sought must be included at this point in the appraisal.

### Preliminary Survey and Appraisal Plan

The preliminary survey and appraisal plan involves a number of items that the appraiser must consider:

☐ Data required
☐ Sources of the data
☐ Time schedule for the report

☐ Personnel required to complete the report
☐ A flow chart showing steps of completion for all elements of the report

An appraiser should quote a firm fee in advance of receiving a commitment for the assignment. The fee itself is usually part of a fee proposal indicating what work steps and schedules will be used to complete the appraisal assignment. The proposal is submitted to the owner of the property, who then determines whether the appraiser will receive the assignment. Obviously, the real estate appraiser never quotes a fee as a percentage of the determined value, as such an arrangement could affect the appraiser's judgment.

## Data Collection and Analysis

The collection of data for specific real property should include general data on the economic background of the region, the city, and the neighborhood in which the property is located. Such data include elements that affect the property's value but are found outside the property itself, for example, population characteristics, employment statistics, and economic trends. Specific neighborhood data would include zoning controls, utilities, shopping facilities, schools, and typical land use within the immediate area.

### Economic Data

A second collection of data concerns economic factors such as population, construction costs, current interest rates, and future trends.

### Subject Property Data

Specific data collected for the appraisal can be divided into two areas: data on the subject property itself and data on properties comparable to the subject property used for the market data approach.

Data collection for the subject property would include the title, the site of the subject property, and the improvements on the land. The appraiser looks at such title items as type of ownership, identity of ownership, easements, zoning regulations, and any other restrictions on the use of the property. Data relating to the physical structure would include a complete description of the improvement and analysis of its style, design, and layout, along with information regarding the site such as its size, shape, and topography. The final step in this stage is the determination of the highest and best use of the site, a judgment that is critically important to the determination of the value of the property.

### Comparable Data Information

Specific data gathered on comparable properties includes information similar to that gathered for the subject property. However, it also includes data on sales prices of comparable properties and perhaps the income derived from the rental of properties that may be reasonably compared with the subject property. No two properties are identical, and for that reason the appraiser must determine what adjustments need to be made to reflect the differences among the properties and the effect that such differences would have on their market values.

## THREE APPROACHES TO VALUE

In the majority of assignments, the appraiser uses three approaches to determine the value of a property: cost, market data, and income. On occasion the appraiser may believe that the value indication from one approach is more significant than that from the other two, yet the careful appraiser uses all three as checks against one another and as a test of his or her own judgment. Obviously, in some appraisal problems all three approaches cannot be used. A value indication for vacant land cannot be obtained through the cost approach; nor can a value for a specialized property such as a school be reached by the market data approach; nor can a value for an owner-occupied home usually be found by the income approach. Each appraisal problem requires a complete review to determine the applicability of the three approaches.

Although each approach uses a different method to determine value, the appraiser can determine that one approach is superior for a particular assignment.

## Cost Approach

In the cost approach, the real estate is broken down into a value for the land and a value for the improvements, adjusted for depreciation. The two are then combined to form the value under the cost approach.

The cost approach includes five steps:

☐ Estimate the site's highest and best use as if vacant.
☐ Estimate the current cost of replacing the existing improvements.
☐ Estimate economic depreciation from all causes.
☐ Deduct economic depreciation from current replacement costs (current building costs).
☐ Add the site's value and the depreciated replacement cost of improvements.

The cost of the improvements is based on *replacement cost*, which indicates what a structure that is very similar in size, design, use, quality, and so forth (but not an exact replica) would cost to build today. *Reproduction cost* would reflect the cost of building an exact duplicate of the structure at today's prices.

The appraiser typically uses a published cost manual to provide average building costs for the locality. The average per square foot costs are then used, after any adjustments, to compute the replacement costs of the improvements.

The economic principle of substitution provides the basis for using the replacement cost approach because it states that the maximum value determined would be no more than the cost of acquisition of a different property having equal desirability. The value of the land is determined by the appraiser, using market comparison data that support this theory.

This also assumes that a newly constructed building would have advantages over the existing building, so the appraiser must also evaluate disadvantages or deficiencies of the existing building as compared with the new building. The measure of this deficiency is called *economic depreciation,* that is, the loss in value of improved real estate for any reason.

### Economic Depreciation

Three primary forms of economic depreciation can be evaluated:

- [ ] *Physical depreciation.* The physical wearing out of the property; usually curable.
- [ ] *Functional obsolescence.* Lack of desirability in terms of layout, style, and design as compared with a new property serving the same function; may be curable or incurable.
- [ ] *Economic obsolescence.* A loss of value from causes outside the property itself; usually incurable.

The *curability* of the cause of depreciation is important in determining the amount of depreciation to calculate. Curability is determined by the cost-effectiveness of replacing or repairing a particular problem. If it is not feasible to replace or repair a problem, the form of depreciation is considered to be incurable.

The concept of economic depreciation helps determine the value of real estate for appraisals. It should not be confused with the accounting classifications of depreciation designed to allow the property owner to recover the cost of an income-producing property. Such accounting concepts are critical to the understanding of real estate finance and taxation and are covered in those chapters.

### Depreciation Methods

Because the cost approach uses the "cost new" estimate of cost less economic depreciation, it is necessary to be able to calculate the depreciation. The following cost approach problem illustrates the manner in which economic depreciation is computed.

*Example*  A fourplex has 5,000 square feet of building area and would cost $47 per square foot to replace today. The property has an economic life of 50 years and an effective age of 8 years. The lot has been valued at $26,000 by a market comparison. The appraiser would value the property in the following way:

5,000 square feet $\times$ $47 = $235,000
50-year life = 2% per year straight line
        depreciation
8 years $\times$ 2% = 16% depreciation
$235,000 $\times$ .16 = $37,600 accrued depreciation

| | |
|---|---|
| $235,000 | cost to replace |
| − 37,600 | accrued depreciation |
| $197,400 | present value of building |
| + 26,000 | land value |
| $223,400 | total value of the property |

## Income Approach

In using the income approach, the appraiser is concerned with the present worth of the future potential income from the property. This is generally measured by the net income that a fully informed person is warranted in assuming the property will produce during its remaining useful life. After comparison with investments of similar type and class, this net income is capitalized into a value estimate.

### Capitalization

*Capitalization* is the process of reflecting future income in terms of present value. Selecting the capitalization rate is one of the most important steps in the income approach. A variation of only one-half of one percent can make a difference of many thousands of dollars in the capitalized value of the income. The difference between an annual income of $27,500 capitalized at 5 percent and at 5½ percent is $50,000. In other words, it takes a capital investment of $550,000 to produce $27,500 worth of income at 5 percent, but only $500,000 at 5½ percent.

When an investor purchases a property, he or she expects to earn income on the money invested. Because real estate investment generally carries higher risks than savings accounts or government bonds, the investor expects to earn a higher rate of return from the real estate investment.

### Capitalization Rate

To determine how much income a property should earn (or how much should be paid for a property when you know what income it generates), the investor must determine a *capitalization rate.* The "cap" rate is derived after calculating the return on investment and the recapture rate. These two factors comprise the rate of return of the original capital invested in the property.

### Income Approach Procedure

The work to be done in assembling and processing income data includes the following:

- [ ] Obtain the rent schedules and the vacancy rate for the subject property and for comparable properties for the current year and for several years in the past. This information provides *gross annual income* data and shows the trend in rentals and occupancy.

These data are then related and adjusted by the comparative method to determine the estimate of gross annual income that the subject property should produce to attract investors in the market.

☐ Subtract vacancy loss to obtain effective gross income.
☐ Obtain expense data, such as taxes, insurance, and operating costs being paid for the subject property and for comparable properties; these are then deducted from the gross to determine the *effective gross income*.
☐ Deduct annual operating expenses of the property from the effective gross income. (Note: The figure derived is the *net income*.) Mortgage reduction expenses are not considered operating expenses, although expenses such as management fees, utilities, maintenance, and so on are used.
☐ Select an appropriate *rate of return on investment* as well as a *recapture rate*. Together these form the *capitalization rate*.

### Return on Investment (ROI)

The *return on investment (ROI)* is a percentage derived by dividing net income received from a property by its cost. For example, if a property costs $100,000 and generates a yearly net income of $15,000, the return on investment is 15 percent.

### Return of Capital

The *return of capital (ROC)* or *recapture rate* is a depreciation factor. Depreciation is necessary to compensate an owner for the decline in economic value of a property over a period of time. The recapture rate is determined by dividing the remaining economic life of an improvement into 100.

*Example* A building with a remaining economic life of 20 years has an annual recapture rate of 5% (100 divided by 20). If the building had cost $100,000, the ROC would be $5,000 per year.

The basic income approach uses a simple formula that can be used in a number of ways. The three factors of the formula are income, rate, and value, which may be used in the following ways:

Value × Rate = Income
Income / Value = Rate
Income / Rate = Value

To understand the workings of the income approach, it is necessary to memorize these formulas.

The following example provides an in-depth look at the income approach applied to the same property used in the cost approach example.

*Example* The same fourplex used in the cost approach problem rents for $650 per month per unit. The operating expenses are 30% of the effective gross income. The vacancy rate is 5%. The capitalization rate of 10% to be used includes a 2% recapture rate and an 8% risk rate. The appraiser would value the property in the following manner:

$650 × 4 units × 12 months = $31,200 potential annual gross income
$31,200 × .05 vacancy rate = $1,560 vacancy loss

$31,200 potential gross income
−1,560 vacancy loss
$29,640 effective gross annual income

$29,640 × .30 expenses = $8,892 expenses
$29,640 effective gross annual income
−8, 892 operating expenses
$20,758 net operating income

Value = net income / capitalization rate (V = I/R)
$207,480 = $20,748 / .10

### Gross Rent Multiplier

The *gross rent multiplier (GRM)* is also an income approach to estimating real estate value. When applied to single-family residences, it is most useful in markets with large numbers of rental properties. Because income from a residential property is usually received on a monthly basis, value is usually calculated using the *gross monthly rent multiplier (GMRM)*; it may also be done on an annual basis.

The gross monthly rent multiplier requires the use of rental houses that have recently been sold and that are comparable to the subject property. The sales price of each property is divided by its own monthly rental; the result is a GMRM for each property: sales price / gross monthly rental = GMRM. Finally, the GMRMs for all properties are examined to find the best composite GMRM. (Note that the GMRM is not an average.)

Once the GMRM has been established, it may be adjusted in relation to the fair economic rent (what the market will bear), which may require further study of the subject property and comparables. The final GMRM can then be multiplied by the estimated rental income of the subject property to determine the sales price, as shown in Figure 12-2. Only gross figures are used to determine the GMRM. No allowance is made for expense items. The GMRM is normally used as a "rule of thumb." It is not recognized as being as accurate as the capitalization process.

The resulting multipliers shown in Figure 12-2 are utilized to arrive at the gross rent multiplier (GRM).

| Sales Price | Gross Monthly Rent | Gross Annual Rent | Monthly Multiplier | Annual Multiplier |
|---|---|---|---|---|
| $17,500.00 | $175.00 | $2,100.00 | 100 | 8.33 |
| 18,900.00 | 180.00 | 2,160.00 | 105 | 8.75 |
| 17,750.00 | 180.00 | 2,160.00 | 99 | 8.21 |
| 18,000.00 | 185.00 | 2,220.00 | 97 | 8.10 |

*Figure 12-2—Gross rent multiplier. (From Faculty Guide, Approved Real Estate Salespersons Course. Published by the Real Estate Certification Program, © 1987. Reprinted with permission of the Real Estate Certification Programs, Inc., Bloomington, Indiana.)*

With the market data illustrated, we might conclude that properties in a certain neighborhood are selling for 100 times their gross monthly rent.

After finding the multiplier, comparable rentals should be obtained and compared (adjusting for differences) to develop an estimate of market rent for subject, that is, market rent estimate. Subject's actual rent, if any, may or may not be market rent.

If subject property is renting for $182.50, then $182.50 times 100 equals $18,250.00, which is the estimated value using the GRM.

## Market Data Approach

The market data, or *direct sales comparison,* approach is essential in almost every appraisal of value of real property. The value estimated by this approach is frequently defined as "the price at which a willing seller would sell and a willing buyer would buy, neither being under abnormal pressure." This definition assumes that both buyer and seller are fully informed with respect to the subject property and the market for that type of property, and that the property has been exposed in the open market for a reasonable time.

The application of this approach produces an estimate of value of the subject property by comparing it with similar properties of the same type and class that have been sold recently. (See previous example.) The process used in determining the degree of comparability between two properties involves a judgment as to their similarity with respect to many factors, such as:

☐ Location, to compensate for the difference in physical location
☐ Date of sale, to allow for economic fluctuations in the market
☐ Financial terms of the sale, to compensate for price, special financing, and so forth
☐ Physical characteristics, adjustments made for size, age, plottage, and other items affecting value

These factors are reviewed and adjustments are made by adding or subtracting values for each factor by comparing each to the subject property. For example, if the subject property had a two-car garage and the comparable property had only a one-car garage, the value of the additional garage would be added to the comparable property.

The sales prices of those properties deemed most comparable tend to set the range in value of the subject property. Consideration of the comparative data indicates a figure representing the value of the subject property, that is, the probable price at which it would be sold by a willing seller to a willing buyer as of the date of the appraisal.

### Market Data Procedure

The market data approach has four steps:

☐ Compile and verify comparable sales and listings (such properties are known as *comps*).
☐ Analyze each comparable property or "comp" to compare it with the property being appraised. Elements of the comparison include date of sale, location, condition of sale, description of land, improvements on the property, and physical condition.
☐ Adjust for differences between the comps and the subject property.
☐ Compute the indicated value for the subject property by comparing it with the adjusted selling prices of comparable properties.

In Figure 12-3, the appraiser, using the same fourplex that was used in earlier examples, selected three comparable properties and made adjustments to the comparables to establish an estimate of value.

## Use of the Three Approaches

The cost approach is frequently used where a lack of data prevents the other approaches from being used. It is commonly used for post offices, libraries, schools, and other public buildings that are not income producing or readily marketable.

The income approach is used for properties for which information such as rent rolls and expense items is readily available. Through the use of capitalization, it is possible to determine the amount of risk involved in the real estate investment. The income approach must be used cautiously, however, because it is confronted by many variables.

Perhaps the most commonly used of the three, the market data approach, is employed when recent information is available on comparable properties. Although this concept is relatively simple to use and can provide a quick analysis of the data, caution must be exercised because of the potential error introduced by subjective use of comparables.

**Market Approach Comparison of Three Properties**

| Variable | Subject | Comp 1 | | Comp 2 | | Comp 3 | |
|---|---|---|---|---|---|---|---|
| Sales price | — | $220,500 | | $190,000 | | $200,000 | |
| Location | Average | Good | −2,500 | Average | 0 | Average | 0 |
| Date of sale | Present | 3 mo. | +1,000 | 1 mo. | 0 | 6 mo. | +2,000 |
| Size of lot | 100' × 150' | 100' × 175' | −1,000 | 100' × 100' | +1,000 | 90' × 100' | +1,000 |
| Age | 5 years | 5 years | 0 | 8 years | +2,000 | 5 years | 0 |
| Quality | Good | Good | 0 | Average | +2,000 | Good | 0 |
| Condition | Good | Good | 0 | Average | +2,000 | Good | 0 |
| Square footage | 5,000 | 6,000 | −5,000 | 4,000 | +5,000 | 5,000 | 0 |
| Rooms | 5/2 br | 5/2 br | 0 | 5/2 br | 0 | 5/2 br | 0 |
| Baths | 1½ | 2½ | −1,000 | 1½ | 0 | 1½ | 0 |
| Air condition | Central | Central | 0 | Central | 0 | Central | 0 |
| Garage | Carport | 2 car/unit | −10,000 | Carport | 0 | Carport | 0 |
| Financing | Conv. | Conv. | 0 | Conv. | 0 | Conv. | 0 |
| Total adjustments | — | | −18,500 | | +12,000 | | +3,000 |
| Indicated value | $202,500 | $202,000 | | $202,000 | | $203,000 | |

Figure 12-3—Market approach comparison of three properties.

## RECONCILIATION, FINAL ESTIMATE, AND THE APPRAISAL REPORT

The final step in the appraisal process is the correlation of the three indications of value produced by using the cost, income, and market approaches. In correlating these three to create a final estimate of value, the appraiser takes into account the purpose of the appraisal, the type of property, and the adequacy of the data processed in each of the three approaches. These considerations influence the weight to be given to each approach.

The appraiser does not obtain a final estimate of value by averaging the three individual indictions of value using the three approaches. He or she takes the three preliminary value estimates and examines the spread between minimum and maximum figures. The greatest emphasis is placed on the approach that appears to be the most reliable as an indication of the answer to the specific appraisal problem. The estimate is then tempered according to the appraiser's judgment as to the degree of reliance to be placed on the other two indications of value.

The form of the final report might be a completed standardized form, a one-page letter, or a large volume in a narrative form.

All appraisals must include the data and purpose for which the appraisal was conducted, the value estimate derived, a description of the property, and qualifying statements affecting the property, and a certificate signed by the appraiser.

An *appraisal report* is a verbal portrayal of the property, the facts concerning the property, and the reasoning by which the appraiser has developed the estimate of value. The best report is the one that, in the fewest words, permits the reader to follow intelligently the appraiser's reasoning and to concur with the conclusions reached. As every report is an answer to a question from a client, it should show the facts considered and clearly outline the reasoning employed by the appraiser in arriving at an answer.

### Valuation for Listing Purposes

The process a real estate professional uses when attempting to calculate an appropriate listing price is known as *competitive market analysis (CMA)*—not appraisal. It only indicates the possible market *price*, not the market *value*. It includes many of the same elements used in the market data approach, but it does not include all the elements of an appraisal.

# REVIEW QUESTIONS

1. A capitalization rate includes

   (A) a recapture rate for land only
   (B) return on investment in both land and improvements
   (C) a recapture rate for improvements only
   (D) a return on investment for land only

2. Depreciation can be attributed to

   (A) economic obsolescence
   (B) functional obsolescence
   (C) physical deterioration
   (D) all of the above

3. If a building has an estimated remaining economic life of 35 years, the appropriate recapture rate would be

   (A) 28.5%          (C) 2.86%
   (B) 33.3%          (D) 3.33%

4. Real estate salespersons and brokers most commonly use which appraisal approach in their day-to-day business?

   (A) Cost           (C) Market
   (B) Income         (D) Capitalized residual

5. The most accurate approach to use in appraising an old public library building is

   (A) market         (C) GMRM
   (B) income         (D) cost

6. A real estate appraisal provides the owner of the property with

   (A) an estimate of the value of the property
   (B) a stated definition of the value estimated
   (C) the effective date of the appraisal
   (D) all of the above

7. Real estate appraisers are paid

   (A) on the basis of the value determined
   (B) on a commission basis
   (C) on a fee basis by the broker representing the seller
   (D) on a predetermined fee basis

8. The method used by a listing salesperson to determine the asking price for a single family house is

   (A) income method
   (B) gross monthly rent multiplier
   (C) cost approach
   (D) competitive market analysis

9. Ethically it is permissible for an appraiser to

   (A) hold a disclosed interest in the subject property
   (B) hold an undisclosed interest in the subject property
   (C) charge a percentage fee for the service
   (D) use sales data several years old

10. The period when a property is believed to be functional is its

    (A) functional life
    (B) economic life
    (C) depreciation period
    (D) amortization life

11. A woman owns a building valued at $103,000 using the income approach. She wants a 12 percent return on her investment. What net annual income must be generated by the building to meet this requirement?

    (A) $858,333       (C) $90,640
    (B) $12,360        (D) $1,030

12. Using the cost approach, if a site is valued at $10,000 and the improvements have been depreciated 40 percent and have a remaining value of $60,000, what was the cost of the improvements when new?

    (A) $110,000       (C) $150,000
    (B) $100,000       (D) $160,000

13. The information required for each comparable property used in the market approach includes all EXCEPT

    (A) date of the sales contract
    (B) sales price
    (C) location of property
    (D) the name of the seller's agent

14. In appraising a special-purpose structure, the most reliable approach to valuation is the

    (A) market data approach
    (B) cost approach
    (C) income approach
    (D) gross monthly rent multiplier

15. Economic obsolescence is caused by

    (A) factors within the subject property
    (B) lack of maintenance of the structure
    (C) factors external to the property
    (D) poor design of the structure

16. The process through which a property is capitalized involves

    (A) conversion of present net income into present value
    (B) the manipulation of one known factor to derive a second unknown
    (C) conversion of future net income into present value
    (D) all of the above

17. The income approach could best be applied to

    (A) a church
    (B) a new single-family residence
    (C) an apartment complex
    (D) all of the above

18. The appraisal process includes which of the following steps?

    (A) Making a preliminary survey and planning the appraisal
    (B) Defining the problem and applying the approaches
    (C) Writing the appraisal report, correlating the data, and making a final estimate of value
    (D) All of the above

19. Which of the following would yield a 10 percent capitalization rate?

    (A) Gross income of $8,000; sales price of $80,000
    (B) Net expenses of $8,000; sales price of $80,000
    (C) Net income of $8,000; sales price of $80,000
    (D) Gross expenses of $8,000; sales price of $80,000

20. If the established GMRM is 105 and a property has a gross income of $6,000 annually and monthly expenses of $200, what is the estimated market value using the GRM method?

    (A) $630,000          (C) $882,000
    (B) $73,500           (D) $52,500

# Chapter 13

# Real Estate Investment and Taxation

REAL estate is an important investment area that generates both current and future income. Investment properties such as apartment and office buildings, shopping centers, and stores return cash on a current basis. Other properties, such as vacant land, may generate income in the form of appreciation in value over a short period of time. However, to obtain that income, the property must be sold to realize the gain in value (the *capital gain*).

Even the typical owner-occupied, single-family residence may be viewed as an investment. Although the only current benefit a residence may produce is the pleasure one derives from living in it, it may very well appreciate over a period of years and can then be sold at a profit to produce a capital gain. Of course, the true value of this gain when it is realized will depend in large part on the degree of inflation that has occurred during the period of ownership.

Although the prospect of profit, whether in the form of current income, capital appreciation, or both, is by no means a sure thing when one invests in real estate, any profit that does result will be subject to taxation. The profit will be subject to ordinary federal income taxes as would any earned income, even though it is earned in the form of a capital gain.

In the discussion that follows, two important facts should be kept in mind:

☐ Federal income tax laws are in an almost constant state of change. Rates of taxation vary with federal spending, and the rules and regulations governing the application of the laws are subject to interpretation by the courts and the IRS. As a result, this analysis is limited to fundamental rules and concepts.
☐ State income taxes also affect the profitability of a real estate investment. However, because there is no uniformity among the states in the area of tax law, local sources must be consulted.

## HOME OWNERSHIP

The owner-occupied, single-family residence does not generate current income in the form of dollars that may be spent for other purposes. Because a home is not business property as defined by tax law, the income tax benefits that home ownership generates are essentially negative—they are valuable only when there is income from other sources, such as wages, against which the homeowner may take certain deductions.

Two important deductions result from home ownership:

## State Real Estate Taxes

State real estate taxes paid by the property owner are deductible in determining *net taxable income.* That is, the gross income of the owner may be reduced by the amount of the real estate taxes paid, thereby reducing the amount of income that will be taxed at ordinary income tax rates.

Real estate taxes are not a *credit* to be taken against federal income taxes; there is no dollar-for-dollar reduction in the homeowner's actual federal income taxes. Direct credits are rare under federal income tax law. When they occur, they are usually designed to favor some current federal policy. For example, the installation or adaptation of an energy system may be rewarded by a limited direct credit for the system's use of energy-saving features or materials.

## Interest on a Home Mortgage

The interest paid on a home mortgage is the other important deduction that results from home ownership. The homeowner may deduct from gross income the *interest* portion of all payments made against the mortgage debt. (The entire monthly payment under the standard amortized mortgage loan is *not* deductible; only the interest portion may be deducted.) In the early years of the mortgage the interest portion of each payment is very high, but it declines as the mortgage balance is reduced.

This benefit, too, is only a deduction, not a direct credit against the income taxes of the homeowner. Often the value of this deduction is used to argue the merits of home ownership over those of home rental, for rent paid for residential space is *not* deductible for federal income tax purposes at the present time.

## Maintenance, Repairs, and Improvements

Because the taxpayer's residence, by definition, is not a business property (for which repairs and maintenance expenses would be deductible), the costs of normal maintenance and repairs are not deductible. The income tax law views such maintenance as being made for the owner's comfort, not for the production of income.

The expense of a major improvement, such as an addition of a family room, which increases the value of the home, may not be deducted in the year in which the expense is incurred; however, it will produce a benefit at the time of the sale of the house. That expense will be deducted from the amount of the capital gain that results if the house is sold for a price greater than the original purchase price. (See the next example.)

*Example*

| | | |
|---|---|---|
| June 1987 | | |
| Net sales price | | $60,000 |
| June 1978 | | |
| Purchase price | $40,000 | |
| August 1979 | | |
| Major addition | 10,000 | |
| Tax cost basis | | 50,000 |
| Capital gain realized | | $10,000 |

## Capital Gain on Sale of Residence

When the homeowner sells a residence for more than the price originally paid, there is a *capital gain.* Establishing the amount of the gain, however, is not simply a matter of subtracting the original purchase price from the selling price. The *tax cost basis* on which the capital gain is calculated includes not only the original price but any major (capital) improvements. Since December 31, 1986, this capital gain has been taxed at ordinary income tax rates.

A key feature of the federal income tax law is that there is no corresponding deduction for a capital loss. If the home in the example had been sold for $40,000, the loss of $10,000 could not have been taken against ordinary income because the home was used for personal purposes only.

## Deferring Payment of Capital Gains Taxes

It is important to recognize the difference between two technical terms in the tax law: the *realization* and the *recognition* of a long-term capital gain on the sale of one's residence. A gain is *realized* by the taxpayer when it is received. However, it is not necessarily *recognized* for tax purposes until such time as the tax laws require that it be reported and the tax be paid. In the typical case, one would expect realization and recognition to occur at the same time. But the sale of a primary personal residence is singled out for special treatment in several respects.

When the taxpayer reinvests the proceeds of sale in another primary residence within a specified period of time (currently two years before or after the sale of the first residence), the gain need not be recognized by the taxpayer. The taxpayer may continue this process for many years and many houses, so long as the cost of each new residence is at least equal to or greater than the sales price of the last one. However, the capital gains continue to accumulate, and they must *all* be recognized when there is no such reinvestment.

Over a period of years, this may add up to a substantial liability to be met in one year. Consequently a form of relief has been provided to favor older persons. At present there is a once-in-a-lifetime *election* to exclude up to $125,000 of gain on the sale of a current residence for those over 55 years of age. (There are technical rules that must be met to qualify for this benefit, and it should only be done with the advice of qualified tax counsel.)

Even an apparently straightforward sale of a residence, then, may have important tax consequences. Although it is not the salesperson's or broker's function to advise on how such transactions should be structured, a working knowledge and awareness of the potential problems is important—if only to minimize one's exposure to liability for giving erroneous advice to clients.

It is also important to recognize that one should not, either expressly or by implication, guarantee that there will be a capital gain from home ownership. In spite of continued inflation, the economic fact is that when one sells in periods of very high mortgage interest rates, the market may sometimes dictate a price lower than the owner's original cost.

Finally, the capital gain realized from a profitable sale may be largely or entirely a consequence of inflation. When this is the case, the seller may find that even with more dollars to spend for another residence, it may not be possible to buy *more* house—even equivalent housing may not be affordable.

### Minimizing Taxes by Installment Sales

One way that the seller can minimize the amount of capital gains taxes on a sale is to use the installment method of sale. This method spreads the receipt of the purchase price over several years and recognizes (for tax purposes) only a pro rata share of the gain each year. The land contract (contract for a deed) is an ideal vehicle for this purpose (see Chapter 10). It is also possible, by stipulation in the terms of the contract, to schedule payments in a year sometime after the sale takes place. In this way payment can be received in a year when the seller's income tax rate might be lower.

To qualify a sale for installment reporting of the capital gain, the seller must receive less than the full purchase price in the year of sale and must report on that year's tax return only that portion of the gain actually received. It is not necessary to make a formal election to utilize installment reporting.

If for some reason the seller chooses not to utilize this method (perhaps he or she expects to have greater income and thus a much higher tax rate in the coming years), it is possible to elect formally *not* to take advantage of installment reporting. In this event the tax on the entire gain would be payable in the year of sale even though the full payment might not be received for several years. Although this flexibility is helpful to sellers of appreciated property, the decision as to which approach

is the more beneficial should be made only after consultation with a capable tax advisor.

## COMMERCIAL INVESTMENT PROPERTY

Almost every kind of real estate asset, other than the single-family dwelling occupied by the owner as a personal residence, may be classified as investment property. Different income tax rules apply to different types of properties, and although the rules that apply to investment property are complex and technical, some fundamental concepts must be understood. (Again, this discussion covers only federal, not state, income tax rules.)

One difference in the tax treatment of home ownership and investment properties occurs in how expenses relating to the property are treated. In the case of income-producing properties, federal income taxes are applied against *net operating income,* that is, the income that remains after the expenses incurred to produce the income have been deducted. Thus deductions from the ordinary income earned by investment properties are worth one dollar for every dollar spent.

### Property Taxes and Mortgage Interest

State real estate taxes and the interest on mortgage indebtedness to the extent of net income are deductible in the case of income-producing residential properties. The owner of an apartment building, for example, may take these deductions because they are necessary costs for the production of income. Under current tax law, these deductions are available only to the landlord; they cannot be taken by the residential tenant even though the expenses are obviously included in the rents of all the apartments.

However, the payment of taxes may be shifted under a lease to a commercial tenant. In such cases the increase in the property taxes is paid to the landlord in the form of higher rent. In effect, the two items cancel each other out: The payment of the increased taxes is additional rental income, but that is offset by the higher income tax deduction to which the landlord will be entitled. This element in the negotiation of leases can be critically important to the landlord who is leasing vacant ground for a very long term to a commercial tenant who intends to construct expensive improvements on the property. The improvements will greatly increase the real property valuation for property tax purposes.

### Maintenance, Repairs, Operating Expenses, and Insurance

Although maintenance and repair expenses are not deductible by the homeowner because they are considered to be for personal comfort, the contrary is true with commercial investment property. Assume that the owner of a single-family residence decides to rent it instead of live in it. The repair that was nondeductible on the residence now entitles the owner to a deduction. The difference is the *purpose* for which one holds the property.

One similarity between the two kinds of properties exists in the area of capital improvements: They may not be deducted directly from income *(expensed)* as a current cost but must, as with the homeowner, be treated as capital improvements *(capitalized)*. Other expenses of operation may be deducted as long as they are related to the production of income. Such expenses can be as broad as necessary for the particular property: trash removal, security guards or alarm systems, janitorial services, and the cost of professional management fees. Property insurance is also a legitimate business expense.

## Depreciation Deductions

Economic depreciation is discussed in the chapter on appraisal; this chapter considers *depreciation allowances* for tax purposes.

Depreciation is recognized for income tax purposes as though an actual loss of money has taken place as the result of the wearing out of an income-producing asset. Of course, land does not depreciate or wear out, and, therefore, only the improvements may be depreciated for tax purposes. The taxpayer is entitled to an allowance each year for the economic loss that is presumed to be taking place. This is true even though there is, in fact, no cash outlay by the taxpayer. It is also true even if the buildings, in fact, go *up* in value as the result of market conditions or inflation.

The way the deduction works is that it permits the taxpayer to reduce the net income earned by the investment property by the amount of depreciation that is allowed for that year. Because no cash is really spent, a certain portion of the net income will go untaxed because it is *sheltered* by the depreciation deduction. More important, even if the real estate does not earn enough income to use up the deduction, it is not lost. The deduction is available to the taxpayer to use to shelter income from other sources, such as income from a professional practice or the like. It is for this reason that it is sometimes suggested to high income tax bracket taxpayers that they invest in real estate even if it earns little or no net income.

Because of the ability of depreciation to shelter actual earned income, taxpayers historically have sought ways to maximize their depreciation deductions. Two basic approaches have been taken. The first is to establish a short useful life for the property so that the greatest deduction is available each year. For example, a $100,000 building depreciated over 40 years on a *straight-line* basis generates a $2,500 per year depreciation deduction. If depreciated over 25 years the same building would generate a $4,000 per year deduction. The problem with

this approach is that one has to negotiate with the IRS the question of what the useful life is and prove that the life selected was proper.

The other approach is to elect some form of *accelerated depreciation* rather than straight-line. A variety of such devices have been developed and used over the years. Most recently the tax laws have been manipulated by Congress to encourage certain types of investment (most notably the construction of new apartments) by permitting the use of accelerated depreciation. One form used was the double declining balance method, which permitted depreciation to be taken at *twice* the rate of straight-line, at least in the first year, and well above straight-line for the immediately following years. Of course, the taxpayer cannot depreciate beyond the cost of the improvements, so that in later years the deduction becomes quite modest. Nevertheless, the early years were quite attractive to investors.

Considerable change has occurred in recent years, first with the enactment of the 1980 tax law that introduced the *accelerated cost recovery system* (ACRS). This concept provided a common depreciation plan for all investment real estate and was, in fact, a form of accelerated depreciation. By simply adjusting the permitted length of time over which such property could be depreciated, Congress was able to manipulate the benefits of the depreciation deduction for substantially all investors.

The 1986 tax law drastically modified all earlier schemes and substituted a straight-line deduction based on 27.5 years for residential investment property and 31.5 years for nonresidential property. This approach is the *modified accelerated cost recovery system.*

Ultimately, the price that must be paid for the depreciation deduction advantage is the taxability of the *gain* or profit at the time the investment is sold. As noted earlier, the amount that is taxable is the difference between the selling price and the adjusted (reduced) basis, which will substantially increase the amount taxable. To the extent that depreciation has been taken, that difference is *recaptured* (taxed) at ordinary income tax rates.

## Capital Gains and Losses

Because commercial investment property may be depreciated for tax purposes, and because this benefit is of value in determining current income taxes, the owner's *tax cost basis* is reduced by the accumulated amount of depreciation taken. If the property is later sold at a price that exceeds the tax cost basis, there will be a taxable capital gain.

*Example*   Assume an original cost of $100,000, a useful life of 31.5 years, straight-line depreciation for 10 years at 3.17 percent (100 percent divided by 31.5) per year ($3,170), and a sales price of $85,000.

| Cost | $100,000 |
|------|----------|
| Depreciation taken | 31,700 |
| Adjusted basis | 68,300 |

When this property is sold at $85,000, a $16,700 capital gain will be realized and recognized. It will be taxed at ordinary income tax rates.

### Tax-Deferred Exchanges

To avoid the recapture of depreciation and the additional taxable ordinary income that results, the owner may elect instead to exchange or trade property rather than sell it. The mechanics of and the technical rules that govern such a transaction are beyond the scope of this book. Indeed, only a small number of practicing brokers are qualified to structure such a transaction without sophisticated tax accounting and legal advice.

Two points are important:

☐ The owner's existing tax basis is transferred to the new property. Therefore, it is not a *tax-free* exchange but a *tax-deferred* exchange, and sooner or later the investor must face up to the accumulated tax liability. There is no once-in-a-lifetime exclusion, as in the case of the homeowner.

☐ Any such exchange must be for "like kind" property. That is, property for which the investment property is exchanged must also be investment property. Although there is some latitude in the definition of what constitutes investment property, it is dangerous to generalize on this point.

### Installment Sales

The information provided earlier about installment sales of appreciated residential real estate applies as well to investment real estate. However, with investment properties it is important to remember that because of the practice of depreciating investment properties, the amount of the capital gain may be much higher. It is not unusual in practice to encounter commercial investment property with a zero or near-zero tax cost basis. This means that the entire sales price could be capital gain. The practicing broker should be alert to this possibility in advising clients when the price and the terms of a proposed sale are being established. For sales of investment property over $150,000, the use of the installment sale is severely limited under the 1986 Tax Reform Act. Brokers should insist that their clients seek professional tax advice before entering into such sales. It is possible that the entire amount of gain will be taxable in one year, even though it is not received in that year.

### EVALUATING REAL ESTATE INVESTMENTS

The foregoing discussion, which emphasizes the income tax consequences of real estate investing, illustrates the fundamental tax rules. However, a tax shelter for other income is not the primary goal of most real estate investors; they invest in real estate to earn money. Therefore, the discussion must now consider the merits of real estate as an income-producing investment. How much can a particular real estate investment be expected to earn?

### Rate of Return

When dealing with a simple savings account, it is relatively easy to establish the rate of return on a cash investment. If a person places $1,000 in an account at the beginning of the year and finds $1,060 in that account at the end of the year, it is clear that the investment has earned $60, or 6 percent interest. Furthermore, the amount that the investment will earn is easily predicted at the beginning of the year; the risk involved is easily evaluated; there are no management headaches; and the investment can be liquidated (perhaps at some sacrifice of interest income for early withdrawal) at any time during the year.

None of the preceding benefits exists with real estate investment:

☐ Earnings cannot be predicted with precision at the beginning of the year because of such variables as possible vacancies and unexpected repair costs.

☐ The risk is not easily evaluated because of the same variable and because local and national economic conditions may drastically affect the rent that can be commanded by the real estate investment.

☐ The real estate investment must be actively managed—renters must be found, rents must be collected, and maintenance must be attended to—either by the investor or a paid manager.

☐ The real estate investment is nonliquid; the owner cannot decide to sell it and be certain of selling it the same day, even at a loss.

The establishment of a rate of return on a real estate investment is not an easy task, nor is it an exact science. A relatively high degree of risk is involved in attempting to forecast the future for any given real estate investment. This fact, coupled with the high degree of nonliquidity, indicates that the rate of return on investments in real estate must be higher than that on other, less risky and more liquid investments to attract investors.

Many methods exist by which a rate of return may be forecast, but each method produces only an educated guess as to the future rate of return on the investment as well as the ultimate rate of return of the investment itself. For a savings account, one can predict with accuracy not only the earnings (the rate on the investment) but also the return of the investment. For real estate the ultimate return of the investment requires another educated guess as to the price at which one can sell the investment at some point in the future.

## The Factor of Inflation

The preceding section did not mention the long-term trend of inflation in the economy. If one assumes an inflation factor of 12 percent per year, one finds that a savings account investment loses some of its appeal. Not only is the $60 earned subject to reduction by the income taxes that must be paid on it, but the dollars received are worth 12 percent less than they were when they were deposited. The investor actually loses money and pays a premium for the safety of the investment.

Investments in stocks *might* be a better hedge against this erosion in the value of the dollar, even if one has to accept a lower rate of return on the investment, but "might be" requires extensive study, knowledge, and careful selection of the stocks chosen.

For many years an investment in real estate has been an excellent hedge against inflation because the market value of real estate tended to increase at a rate that was reasonably close to the rate of inflation and often exceeded it. Nevertheless, in determining the attractiveness of a particular real estate investment, one must remember that the inflationary factor is a built-in cost of that investment and one that will have the same impact that it has on a savings account.

When inflation is running at 12 percent per year, does a real estate investment that yields a 10 percent rate of return look attractive? It would be if it were not for the risk factors discussed above. When combining the factors of risk and inflation, assuming a 12-percent rate of inflation and 10 percent as a reasonable rate of return in light of the risks involved, it would appear that a real estate investment at anything less than 22 percent is not as attractive as it may appear at first. The saving grace is the hope that one will at least keep pace with inflation, rather than lose money or purchasing power.

## Determining the Rate of Return

In a typical real estate investment, it is necessary to use borrowed money, assuming it can be obtained at reasonable rates. This is the concept of *leverage.* The rate of return can then be determined by the "cash-on-cash" method.

For example, if one invests $100,000 cash in an apartment building and the net cash earned during the year is $10,000, then there is a 10-percent rate of return, cash on cash. Note that in the cash-on-cash method the rate of return is calculated only on the actual cash invested. In this case the total cost may be $1 million, of which $600,000 is represented by an existing mortgage that is assumed and $300,000 by a second mortgage that the seller agrees to take back. Note, too, that this return has not been factored to account for inflation—but neither has the increased value of the investment been taken into account, which hopefully will result from the same inflation factor.

## SUMMARY

This chapter does not attempt to cover in depth the many factors required to determine the precise rate of return on a real estate investment or the price that should be paid for such an investment. In practice, the "rule book" approach is often discarded and the investment made using a "seat of the pants" method. In spite of the income tax benefits and all its advantages as a hedge against inflation, real estate investment still carries a relatively high degree of risk, and the rate of return should reflect this fact.

# REVIEW QUESTIONS

1. A homeowner may deduct which of the following home-related items from ordinary income in computing his or her personal income tax?

   (A) Depreciation on the property
   (B) Insurance premium costs
   (C) Repair expenses for the property
   (D) Interest on the mortgage

2. The homeowner's expenses that are allowable in the reduction of income tax liability are treated on the tax return

   (A) as a direct reduction of the tax liability
   (B) as a deduction in determining net taxable income

   (C) as an addition to net taxable income
   (D) as an addition to adjusted gross income

3. In investing in real estate, the down payment reflects the investor's

   (A) equity position
   (B) debt position
   (C) residual position
   (D) capital gains position

4. The costs of capital improvements have what income tax advantages for the homeowner who improves his or her property?

   (A) They are a credit against ordinary income taxes in the year the costs are paid

(B) They are deductible in calculating net taxable income in the year they are paid

(C) They may be added to the initial cost of the property to establish the owner's tax cost basis when the property is sold

(D) They may be depreciated over their estimated useful life and deducted on a straight-line basis each year

5. A homeowner who sells his or her property has what period of time to reinvest in another property to defer paying taxes on the gain on the sale?

(A) 12 months          (C) 24 months
(B) 18 months          (D) 36 months

6. *J* received a piece of property as a gift. When *J* wishes to sell the property, what value will be used to determine the basis of the property for tax purposes?

(A) Market value of the property at the time of the gift
(B) The basis of the donor at the time the gift was made
(C) The basis of the donor plus an increment for inflation
(D) Market value less depreciation at the time of the sale

7. The maximum amount allowed for the over-55 exemption is

(A) $62,500          (C) $100,000
(B) $75,000          (D) $125,000

8. Which of the following is **not** considered to be a capital improvement?

(A) Painting the house
(B) Replacing the roof
(C) Installing a new furnace
(D) Adding a tennis court

9. The expenses deductible by the owner of investment property in determining the net taxable income for that property are

(A) only casualty insurance and maintenance and repairs
(B) only maintenance and repairs and property management fees
(C) only casualty insurance, maintenance and repairs, and property management fees
(D) casualty insurance, maintenance and repairs, capital improvements, and property management fees

10. *P* buys an apartment building in 1988. Over what period of time may *P* depreciate the building for tax purposes?

(A) 15 years          (C) 19 years
(B) 18 years          (D) 27½ years

11. After 1986, how much gain on the sale of a property may be excluded in computing the taxes from the sale?

(A) 0                 (C) 50 percent
(B) 40 percent        (D) 60 percent

12. An investment property purchased three years ago for $45,000 is sold today for $78,000. Depreciation deductions totaled $4,500 on a straight-line basis, and inflation has increased the value of the property by $10,800. How much of the sales price is subject to federal income tax?

(A) $33,000          (C) $37,500
(B) $27,780          (D) $25,080

13. As long as a homeowner keeps reinvesting in homes of equal or greater value, the tax on the gains is

(A) reduced by 40 percent with each purchase
(B) avoided by the owner
(C) deferred until the owner no longer reinvests
(D) deferred until the owner reaches 55 years of age

14. Land cost is $40,000. The commercial improvements on it cost $120,000 and will be depreciated over 31.5 years using straight-line depreciation. What is the first year's depreciation on the property?

(A) $1,270          (C) $5,080
(B) $3,810          (D) $7,250

15. A commercial building is purchased for $30,000 cash plus assumption of an existing mortgage of $180,000. The net income to the investor after making the mortgage payments is $1,200 per year. Using the cash-on-cash method, what is the investor's rate of return?

(A) 14 percent          (C) 4 percent
(B) 1 percent           (D) .6 percent

16. A homeowner has the following expenses in a given year: maintenance, $1,600; capital improvements, $8,000; real estate taxes, $450. Mortgage payments are $6,500, of which $4,200 is interest. How much may be deducted on the owner's personal income tax return?

(A) $6,250          (C) $4,650
(B) $6,950          (D) $5,800

17. Using the information in question 16, if the homeowner is in the 28 percent tax bracket, how much tax is saved?

(A) $4,650          (C) $2,625
(B) $1,953          (D) $1,320

18. On an investment property, how is the depreciation on land calculated for tax purposes?

    (A) 15-year ACRS method
    (B) 18-year double-declining balance method
    (C) 27½-year straight-line method
    (D) Land is not depreciated for tax purposes

19. The purchase price less the depreciation is equal to

    (A) taxable gain on the sale
    (B) book value

    (C) before-tax cash flow
    (D) after-tax cash flow

20. Which of the following is **not** deductible when computing taxes on investment property?

    (A) Mortgage equity
    (B) Property taxes
    (C) Depreciation
    (D) Mortgage interest

# Chapter 14

# Contracts

---

### VOCABULARY

*You will find it important to have a complete working knowledge of the following terms and concepts found in the text or the glossary.*

| | | |
|---|---|---|
| acceptance | execution | mistakes of law |
| age of majority | express contract | novation |
| assignment | fraud | offer |
| bilateral contract | illegality of purpose | rescission |
| communication of acceptance | implied contract | specific performance |
| communication of offer | impossibility of performance | statute of frauds |
| compensatory damages | incompetent | statute of limitations |
| condition | infant | undue influence |
| conditional acceptance | legal capacity | unilateral contract |
| consideration | legality of purpose | valid contract |
| counteroffer | liquidated damages | valuable |
| damages | minor | void contract |
| duress | misrepresentation | voidable contract |
| earnest money consideration | mistakes of fact | |

---

THE law of contracts is fundamental to all phases of the real estate business because almost all transactions result from formal and detailed agreements between the parties. Essentially all agreements in real estate must be in writing—for legal and practical reasons. Real estate transactions tend to be rather complex because of the many details. The written agreement formalizes the promise made by each party and eliminates disputes that might arise if the parties would simply depend on their recollection of an oral agreement.

It is helpful in considering the law of contracts to start with a simple working definition and then to add the details later.

A *contract* is an agreement which the parties intend to be legally enforceable.

Details about contracts that qualify this definition are added throughout this chapter.

## CONTRACT REQUIREMENTS

Any contract must begin with a "meeting of the minds"—an offer and an acceptance of that offer that results in an acceptance.

☐ An *offer* must be made to start the negotiation or formation process.
☐ An *acceptance of the offer* is required to form the agreement of the parties—or, the meeting of the minds.

More than simply an agreement is required; to form a legally binding contract, other elements must be present (see Figure 14-1). These are:

☐ *Consideration.* Something of value must be either promised or actually given by both parties before their agreement can become a legally binding contract.
☐ Once these conditions are established, it is necessary to establish that no other facts exist that would contradict the apparent formation of a contract. These include matters that would excuse the parties from keeping their agreement.
☐ *Legal Capacity.* Both parties must be legally competent (have the mental power) to enter into contracts.
☐ *Validity.* Neither party can be subjected to duress or force, fraud, undue influence, or mistake of fact.
☐ *Illegality and Impossibility.* The purpose of the con-

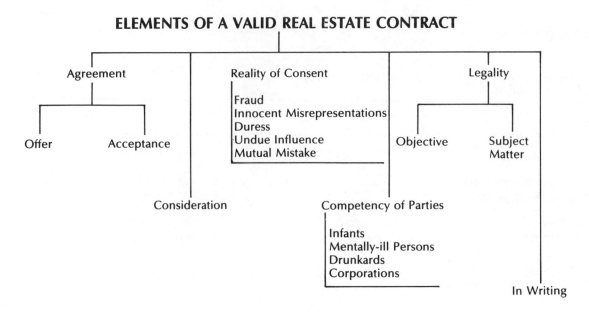

Figure 14-1—Elements of a valid real estate contract.

tract must be legal, and it must be possible to be performed.

### Offer

The *offer* is the initial step in the formation of a contract. The offer is usually made by the person who offers to purchase for a specified amount and under certain conditions. In the absence of an offer, no contract can result because the party who is alleged to be the offeror has not defined what responsibility he or she is willing to assume or what will be accepted in return for the offer.

The offer, to be effective, must be reasonably certain. While the offeror may clearly understand what is meant by his or her offer, this is not the legal standard by which the offer is measured. The law provides an arbitrary standard by which the clarity and certainty of the offeror's term are measured, the standard of the so-called reasonable person. That is, if the offer is clearly intelligible to a reasonable person, it is sufficiently clear and definite in its terms to satisfy the standards required by contract law. Unless it is reasonably certain, any resulting agreement cannot be an agreement at all because of the basic inability to define the terms of the agreement.

The offeror is in complete command of the terms of the offer. At this stage of the negotiating process, the offeror is under no obligation of any kind. That is, the offer is a free and voluntary act on the part of the one who makes it. He or she cannot be compelled by any rule of law to make an offer on terms that will be acceptable to the owner of the property or even an offer that makes any economic sense. The offeror is free to make the offer on any terms or conditions he or she chooses. The offeree—the person who receives the offer—is not under any compulsion to accept the offer, and the offeree's remedy in the event that the offer is unacceptable is simply to decline to act on it.

The offer may be withdrawn at any time before it is acted on. It is the free and voluntary act of the offeror. The offeree is not injured by the withdrawal unless and until the offeree has acted upon it. This rule is true even though the offer, by its terms, specifies that it will be open for a stated period of time. It may be arbitrarily withdrawn until acted on. See Figure 14-2.

The offer must be communicated to the offeree. In the real estate business, this technical requirement is satisfied by the execution of an offer to purchase the property and the delivery of it either to the property owner or to the broker who represents the owner, who is the owner's agent. Delivery (or communication) to the agent is the same, legally, as delivery to the principal (the owner).

Under state statutes of fraud, all contracts for the sale of real estate must be in writing to be enforceable in court. In addition to this technical legal requirement, important practical reasons require that the offer be written: Real estate sales transactions include many details. The written offer is essential to prove what the final agreement of the parties is on all points.

Proper execution of the offer is important. When dealing with individuals, it is generally a simple matter to see that the offer is properly executed; the signature of the individual on the written offer is sufficient. However, entities other than individual persons must have clearly

## TERMINATION OF AN OFFER

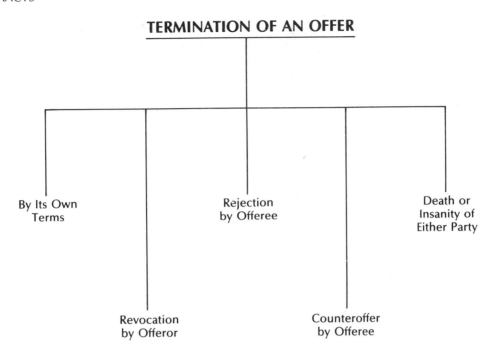

Figure 14-2—Termination of an offer.

established authority to act. It is not enough, for example, that an individual be an officer of a corporation; he or she must be authorized by the corporation to enter into a contract, whether it relates to real estate or any other subject matter. The offer is not complete unless it is signed.

### Acceptance

The second step in the formation of a contract is the acceptance of the offer. The offer by itself is meaningless unless and until the one to whom the offer is made indicates that it is satisfactory and that he or she is willing to enter into an agreement under which he or she will receive the fruits of the offer and will be willing to do what the offeror demands in return. The acceptance of the offer is a simple assent to the terms of the offer and an expression of intent to be bound by the terms of the resulting agreement.

The acceptance of the offer must be absolute, without rejection of any of the terms included in the offer. If not, it is not an acceptance and the contract will not result. The point is that one cannot accept an offer that has not been made. One can only accept the offer that was in fact made by the offeror. Therefore, the entire offer must be accepted, not just part of it. Anything less is a rejection of the offer and clearly is not sufficient to constitute an agreement.

The acceptance of the offer, to be legally effective, must be unequivocal. That is, it must be without any exceptions or any additional terms. In terms of the legal effect of the reaction of the offeree, only two alternatives exist—the offeree either accepts every term of the offer without exception or rejects the offer. The addition of any terms to the offer in the acceptance destroys the acceptance of that contract; it is, in legal effect, a counteroffer or new offer, not an acceptance.

The acceptance of the offer must be communicated to the offeror. Positive action must be taken by the offeree to bind the offeror to the terms of the offer. The offeree may not simply decide that he or she accepts the offer; the law requires positive evidence of the decision that is calculated to reach the offeror. The statute of frauds demands that an acceptance of the offer be in writing to be enforceable in court.

In most cases, the offer will dictate the method by which it must be accepted. For example, the offer might provide that written acceptance must be received by the offeror by a specified time. In such a case, it is the responsibility of the offeree to use whatever means necessary to see that the acceptance is actually delivered to the offeror by the stated time. Nothing less than this makes the acceptance valid.

The typical language encountered in standard offers to purchase real estate is not quite so specific. These standard offers usually provide simply that the offer must be accepted "on or before" a specified time. If such an offer is mailed to the offeree, the offeree is entitled to assume that the mailing of his or her acceptance by the time specified will result in a binding contract, since the offeror has by implication indicated that the mails are an acceptable agency for communication. If, however (as is typically the case), the offer is delivered to the broker as agent for the seller, the acceptance must be delivered to the offeror. Delivery to the agent (broker) is legally the same as delivery to the principal (seller). But because the broker is not the agent for the purchaser, the delivery of the acceptance to the broker does not constitute delivery to the offeror. It must be delivered by either the offeree (seller) or the agent (broker) to the offeror to be a legally effective acceptance.

Frequently the offeree finds that most of the terms of the offer are acceptable, but not all of them. For example, the seller may be willing to accept all of the conditions specified in the offer except the price. The seller may respond by saying, "I accept your offer except that the price is to be increased to $XX,XXX." This is not an acceptance, because it is not absolute and unequivocal. It really is a rejection of the buyer's offer and a new offer to sell that incorporates all of the terms of the buyer's offer except the price. Now the roles of the parties have been reversed—the seller has become the offeror, and it is up to the buyer to accept or reject the new offer to sell.

The steps in an agreement are shown in Figure 14-3.

## Consideration

Consideration is a technical requirement of contract law that is necessary to make the agreement of the parties enforceable.

The concept of consideration is not only one of the most difficult notions to define in the area of contract law, but it is also one of the most difficult to justify. It would seem to be sufficient that the two parties to a contract intend it to be legally enforceable, without imposing the technical requirement that there be some consideration to make their commitments binding. Although the general trend in contract law is to place more emphasis on the intent of the parties to be found to keep their promises, it is not safe to conclude that a court would so rule in any given case.

Simply defined, consideration is something of value that is committed by each party to a contract. The com-

mitment to pay or to do something of value constitutes consideration and makes the promises of the parties enforceable.

*Example*   The buyer offers (promises to pay) $10,000 for the seller's property. The seller accepts and agrees (promises) to convey the property for $10,000. A binding contract results because there is consideration to support each promise—the promise of the other party.

In this example, the buyer does not tender or hand over $10,000 at the time of the offer, nor does the seller tender the property or surrender it to the purchaser. However, each has promised to perform an act of substantial value. Consideration need not be money paid; a promise to perform an act of value to the other side is sufficient. The promise itself is valuable.

The value that must be given to constitute legally adequate consideration has no relationship whatsoever to actual value. As long as something of value is given, the requirement is satisfied.

In the above example, the promise to pay $10,000 is adequate consideration to support and permit enforcement of the seller's promise to convey the property—even if the fair market value of the property being bargained for is $20,000. The law of contracts does not require that full or market value be offered to make the contract binding on the seller. The reverse is also true: If a property has a fair market value of only $5,000, the promise of the seller to convey it is still adequate to bind the purchaser's offer to pay $10,000 for it. The law does not make the contract for the parties, but when they have made it in good faith, the law enforces it.

An *earnest money deposit* is not essential to make the contract for the sale of real estate binding on the parties. It is made binding by the mutual promises of the two parties, and the earnest money deposit adds nothing to its binding nature. The true function of the earnest money deposit is to serve as a source for payment of damages to the seller in the event that the purchaser breaches the contract and does not keep his or her promise.

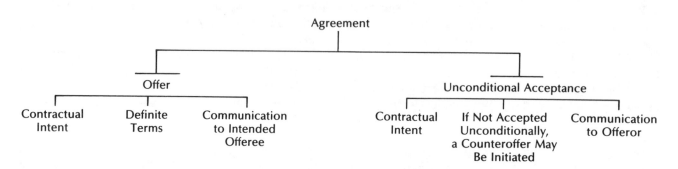

*Figure 14-3—Steps in an agreement.*

## Defects

When a defect occurs in the formation of a contract, that contract—although it is supported by consideration and may appear to be valid—may not be legally binding. Figure 14-4 lists various defects that can make a contract *voidable* (capable of being set aside by one of the parties) or *void* (of no force and effect, not a contract at all).

## LEGAL CAPACITY OF CONTRACTING PARTIES

Each party to a contract must have the legal capacity or power to enter into that contract and to commit himself or herself to the performance of its terms. Technically, this requirement has nothing to do with the actual formation of a contract; however, it is an underlying requirement that cannot safely be ignored in any business transaction. That is, a contract with a person who has no power or capacity to enter into it is not a contract at all.

The law here is quite technical. It is designed to protect the incompetent from his or her own improvident acts and to protect a business entity from the unauthorized acts of one of its members. It is important to be aware of the legal limitations of various persons and organizations.

## Contracts with Persons

Individuals who enter into a contract must be of age and must be mentally competent.

Contracts entered into by insane persons, minors (sometimes referred to as *infants*), or those intoxicated are generally not considered binding contracts. Contracts entered into by such persons are either void or voidable by those individuals but not by the other party to the contract. Generally, the parties must have the mental ability to understand the nature of their contract and the obligations they are assuming.

### Minors

Minors (those less than 18 years old, generally) may enter into contracts prior to reaching majority, but they have the option to avoid them if they choose to do so when they reach majority. This is true for all contracts except those for necessities. While housing might fall into this category, the minor may retain the right to disaffirm or avoid the contract upon coming of age or at any time prior to attaining majority. The safest course is to deal with a minor on transactions involving significant value only through a legally appointed guardian.

### Mentally Incompetent Persons

A mentally incompetent person can pose a serious problem in the brokerage business because his or her affliction may be difficult to recognize and because there is no effective way to avoid the problem except through the exercise of good judgment.

There are two possible cases: The person who is actually incompetent at the time of the transaction but has not been adjudged incompetent by a court, and the adjudged incompetent who has been placed under formal guardianship.

☐ *The adjudged incompetent* has been placed under a guardianship through a court proceeding, and this fact is a matter of public record and, therefore, one that the public is obliged to know. Once the guardianship has been established, the incompetent (the ward) has no capacity to enter into contracts, and there is no effective way to deal with such a person except through the guardian. The incompetent's contracts are absolutely void and cannot be enforced.

☐ *The actual but not adjudged incompetent* is frequently more difficult to recognize because such a person may not always exhibit evidence of incompetence. Many incompetents are never adjudged as such. Their contracts may be voidable if they were incompetent at the time the contracts were entered into. They are not void and it takes affirmative action to void them, but it is quite possible that such contracts can be set aside later.

## Contracts with Entities Other than Persons

Organizations may suffer from a form of legal incompetence. That is, since they are artificial persons, they generally must meet local legal requirements to handle their affairs effectively. When dealing with them, one must be sure that their actions are "competent" in the sense that they are legally binding upon them.

☐ *Partnerships* may be dealt with through any general partner and in the partnership name. Under the Uniform Partnership Act (UPA), it is not necessary that all partners join in the execution of documents relating to real estate transactions. Each general partner has the authority to bind the firm, and third persons dealing with a partner are entitled to rely on the partner's representations that he or she has such authority.

| Voidable (Can be avoided) | Void (No contract to begin with) |
|---|---|
| Duress | Illegality |
| Undue influence | Adjudged incompetence |
| Misrepresentation | Partially void |
| Fraud | |
| Mistake of fact | |
| Actual incompetence | |
| Impossibility of performance | |

Figure 14-4—Defects rendering a contract voidable or void.

☐ *Corporations* can be bound only by the acts of those who have actual authority or those who appear to the general public to have authority by virtue of the office they hold in the corporation. As far as real estate transactions are concerned, the safe course to follow is to obtain a resolution from the board of directors authorizing a specific officer to buy or sell real estate. It may even be necessary to obtain approval of the stockholders in the event that the corporation is the seller and the real estate being sold represents substantially all its assets. It is recommended that an attorney be consulted when dealing with corporations because of the limitations on the authority of various officers.

☐ *Associations* that are neither formal partnerships or corporations do not have a clearly recognized status. The only safe way to deal with them, as far as real estate transactions are concerned, is to treat them as a group of individuals selling individual interests in the property. Each member of the association (or syndicate or other designation) must have the capacity to deal with his or her own property. Legal counsel is always recommended.

☐ *Governmental units* are strictly controlled by statutes or ordinances and have no capacity to conduct business of any kind unless they are specifically authorized by statute to do so. It is very important in dealing with any governmental unit to verify its authority to buy, to sell, or to enter into a contract to do either. An attorney should always be consulted in such transactions.

☐ *Court officers,* such as receivers and commissioners, must have specific court authority to enter into contracts that will be binding on the subject property. Court officers do not have authority to buy or sell real estate simply because they have been appointed court officers. Formal approval of the court is essential for each transaction. Again, an attorney should always be consulted in connection with transactions with court officers.

☐ *Fiduciaries* generally must have specific authority to deal with real estate, and the authority must be in proper form to be made a matter of record if necessary. The term fiduciaries as used here includes executors, administrators, trustees, and agents. In considering the question of capacity to enter into contracts involving real estate, it is important to be aware that none of them has inherent authority and in each case the authority must be verified. An attorney's opinion should always be obtained, because by definition a fiduciary deals with someone else's property.

### Reality of Consent

Contracts may be *invalid* (not binding) when their formation is tainted by the existence of facts that make in-telligent and deliberate agreement impossible. One who is physically forced to sign a contract cannot be said to have agreed, legally, to do so. Nor can one who has been misled as to the facts essential to intelligent decision making. A variety of reasons may exist that justify the conclusion that the agreement was not entered into freely or intelligently. Those that are discussed below are well established factors that will excuse one from performing a contract which appears to have been willingly entered into. In these cases, action must be taken to set the contract aside. There is a contract, but it can be set aside under certain circumstances.

☐ *Duress.* If one is physically forced to enter into a contract, he or she may avoid the contract or set it aside. The same is true when force is threatened rather than actually applied. The term *duress,* therefore, includes both the use of force or the threat of its use.

☐ *Undue Influence.* In any case in which one of the parties has taken unfair advantage of the other because of the existence of a relationship of influence, the contract is voidable by the party who was taken advantage of. This excuse for nonperformance is based on the notion that one party has sufficient control or influence over the other to cause him or her to agree to something that is not in his or her best interest. The relationship of ward and guardian is frequently used as an example, but this is not much help because, by definition, the ward has no capacity to make contracts. Perhaps the relationship between attorney or accountant and client is more helpful. Conceivably, it could be the relationship between a real estate broker and a seller of property.

☐ *Misrepresentation.* Misrepresentation might best be described as an innocent misstatement of fact. In other words, one of the parties had indicated something regarding the contract to be true when in fact it was not.

    *Fraud* exists when the misstatement of fact is deliberate and made with the intent that the other party rely on its truth. A fraud has been committed on the innocent party. This is sometimes called *fraudulent* misrepresentation to clearly distinguish it from *innocent* misrepresentation or misstatement of fact.

☐ *Mistakes.* Two types of mistakes can occur in the formation of contracts: *mistakes of fact* and *mistakes of law.* Only mistakes of fact permit a contract to be set aside.

    A *mistake of fact* occurs when one or both parties assume something to be a fact that is incorrect and this error, in turn, is included in their agreement. An erroneous description of real estate in a purchase agreement is an example. Such a mistake can be corrected by the process of *reformation (correction)* of the contract if it is a minor error. However, if the error is so substantial (for example, 10 acres of land as opposed to 20 acres) that there is no "meeting of the minds," the contract is voidable and can be set aside by one of the parties.

A *mistake of law,* however, occurs when one party has an erroneous notion of the legal obligations assumed by entering into the contract. For example, the purchaser of a home might conclude that there is no obligation to complete payment for it on the date of closing. Contract law compels completion of the promise (or requires payment of damages for breach of contract), since there was no material factual mistake. The buyer is presumed to know the legal consequences of entering into a binding contract. The fact that the buyer did not know the legal consequences is immaterial.

## Legality

A contract that requires the performance of a criminal act by one of the parties would be in violation of the law at the outset, and no court would entertain a lawsuit to compel performance by either party. In addition, a wide variety of objectives are illegal in the sense that they would violate public policy, would be in restraint of trade, would be injurious to third persons, would violate usury statutes, would constitute gambling contracts, and so forth.

In the area of real estate transactions, two examples illustrate the impact of the general contract law.

*Example*   A enters into a lease with B for the use of property for the purpose of operating a gambling casino in a state where gambling is illegal. Because the purpose of the lease violates a criminal statute, it is void and cannot be enforced by either party.

*Example*   A leases real estate to B for use solely as an office, which use would violate existing zoning ordinances. The lease is void and cannot be enforced by either A or B.

The point to be noted in this connection is that the illegal purpose need not be criminal in nature to make the contract voidable (unenforceable as to the legal condition), but that a contract for a criminal purpose is totally void.

## Impossibility

Occasionally parties enter into otherwise binding contracts that, for one reason or another, prove to be impossible to perform. The question then arises as to whether relief is available to the party who promised to do the impossible. The answer hinges on the definition of "impossible" as it has been developed under contract law.

It may be impossible for one party to keep a promise but not impossible for someone else to keep the promise.

*Example*   A promises to sell a farm to B, but it is impossible for A to do so because A does not own the farm. Is A excused under the doctrine of impossibility? No. It may be impossible for A to deed the farm, but it is not impossible for anyone in the world to deed it to B. A is liable for breach of contract to B. To have the benefit of the defense of impossibility of performance, A would have to prove that no one could deed the property.

There may be unforseen difficulty or unanticipated expense in keeping a promise.

*Example*   Suppose a contractor agrees to dig a basement for a house in land that he believes to be sand and gravel and has priced the job at $1,000. Upon beginning the excavation work, the contractor finds that solid granite lies below the topsoil and that the excavation will cost at least $10,000. Is he relieved from performing his contract? No. Extreme or extraordinary difficulty of performance does not relieve him from his obligation.

In this case the doctrine of impossibility will be of no avail because it is not impossible to perform the contract; it is merely very costly and difficult.

## Breach of Contract

A number of possible consequences may result from the failure to perform a valid contract when there has been a *breach of contract.*

### Compensatory Damages

Every breach of contract entitles the injured party to sue for the *damages* that result from that breach. This is true even though there may be other options available to the injured party. It is fundamental to this right, however, that there must be proof of just what the damages were and that they could not have been reasonably avoided. That is, there is a duty to mitigate (minimize) the damages that flow from the breach of contract. The injured party may not sit back and permit damages to accumulate without making a reasonable effort to stop them. The effort required will depend on the circumstances of the case.

The purpose of *compensatory damages* is to put the injured party in as good a position, so far as money damages can do, as would have been the case had the contract been fully performed. Generally, in a sales contract the measure of compensatory damages is the difference between the contract price and the market value at the time and place of delivery. The best evidence of that market value is, of course, a sale of the property to someone else.

*Example*   If the buyer breaches a contract to pay $40,000 for a house, the seller is not entitled to $40,000, because he still has the house.

Proof of his true damages would be shown by the sale of the house to someone else for, say, $35,000. Then he can clearly demonstrate his loss of $5,000, plus the additional expense of reselling the property.

## Liquidated Damages

The parties to a contract may stipulate in the contract that a certain sum will be paid by a party who breaches the contract. This stipulation is called a *liquidated damages clause*. Such a stipulation by the parties may be determined by the court to be a penalty clause and not a liquidated damages clause and, therefore, unenforceable as payment for a breach.

Generally, a provision in a contract fixing the amount of damages payable for a breach must meet two requirements for it to be considered an enforceable liquidated damages clause:

☐ The harm caused by the breach must be very difficult to determine precisely.
☐ The amount so fixed must be a *reasonable* estimate of compensation for the harm that might result from the breach.

When a true liquidated damages clause exists, the injured party must accept the amount of damages agreed to and may not sue for damages in excess of that amount even if additional damages actually result from the breach. In the example used in the preceding section on compensatory damages, if the seller had agreed to accept $3,000 for a breach by the buyer, then that would be the limit of his recovery, even though the ultimate sale resulted in a loss of $5,000. Forecasting such a loss would be pure speculation.

## Forfeiture

When a clause fixes the amount of damages payable for a breach at an excessively high amount, the clause may be unenforceable because it is, in fact, a *forfeiture* or penalty clause. When there is a good faith effort to determine damages in advance, courts enforce the agreement, but they do not do so if the clause is an economic club that bears no relationship to the foreseeable damages.

## Rescission

A party to a contract who has performed his or her side of the agreement and is injured by the complete failure of the other party to perform has a remedy available in *rescission* of the contract and restitution of his or her performance. Under this remedy, the injured party may elect to treat his or her duty under the contract as discharged (rescission) and, further, receive damages that pay for part performance, thereby returning him or her to the position occupied before entering into the contract.

For example, a buyer of goods who has paid the full price for an item (or any part of it) may rescind the contract and recover the payment where the seller has materially failed in performance by failing to deliver on time or by delivering the wrong goods. Or, where a seller of land wrongfully repossesses the land, the buyer may elect to rescind the contract and demand restitution of payments.

## Enforcement of Real Estate Contracts

Generally, the enforcement of contracts is limited to the collection of money damages for any breach of contract that may occur. That is, contracts are enforced by the implied threat of a suit for damages. The parties know, or are presumed by the law to know, that if they fail to keep a promise that is enforceable under contract law principles, the injured party may maintain a lawsuit for the breach and can obtain a judgment entitling that person to recover whatever damages he or she can show have resulted from the breach.

## Specific Performances

Although the general remedy is always available, the law recognized early that in certain situations an award of money damages is not really a satisfactory remedy and that in certain situations the injured party can receive real justice only by the performance for which he or she bargained. This is the doctrine of *specific performance*. It is considered an extraordinary remedy, and its availability is quite limited.

In most states today, it is limited to contracts for unique chattels (one-of-a-kind art works, for example)— situations in which a judgment for money damages would be meaningless and contracts for the purchase of an interest in real estate, on the theory that each piece of real estate is unique and different from any other piece of real estate. The inclusion of real estate as a matter of course in this area is significant.

The law today still considers each parcel of real estate to be absolutely unique and different from any other parcel of real estate, no matter where it is located. This is true even though the parcel may be a lot in a subdivision in which hundreds of other lots have precisely the same dimensions, face the same street, and are seemingly alike as "two peas in a pod." In many cases, the buyer of such a lot may, in fact, be quite easily satisfied with another lot or money damages for the loss of the bargain. The point is that legally the buyer does not have to be satisfied with anything other than the lot or parcel for which he or she bargained. If the buyer chooses the remedy of specific performance, he or she is favored with a conclusive presumption that nothing else will be satisfactory.

A judgment for money damages is simply a conclusion of the court that the plaintiff is entitled to so many dollars from the defendant. The court does not compel the defendant to pay the money; this is accomplished by formal execution of the judgment, under which the sheriff may seize assets and sell them when the defendant fails to pay the judgment. There may be small satisfaction to the plaintiff if no assets are found, and further action to enforce the judgment may be cumbersome and expensive.

A decree of specific performance is an order from the court to the defendant to perform. This is a different matter entirely. Failure to obey is contempt of court and is punishable by severe measures, including confinement in jail until the defendant does as ordered.

### Statute of Frauds

Each state has a statute of frauds that dictates the types of contracts that must be in writing. Such a statute is intended to produce certainty in the obligation and to eliminate the possibility of proving a nonexistent undertaking by perjured evidence.

All contracts for the sale or purchase of real estate must be in writing and signed by the parties involved.

Any contract for the lease of real estate for a period of more than one year must be in writing and signed by the parties involved to be enforceable (some states vary).

Some states go beyond the requirements of the statute of frauds by placing additional requirements on the writing of contracts. Under common law, writing was never necessary for the formation of a contract; today, in the absence of statutory requirements, an oral contract is as enforceable as a written contract.

For the written requirement of the statute of frauds to be satisfied, most states specify that the written memorandum disclose certain information:

☐ The identity of the contracting parties, either by name or description
☐ An identification of the subject matter of the contract
☐ Consideration

Generally the statute of frauds is a device that renders oral contracts that should have been in writing unenforceable. The contracts remain valid between the parties but are not enforceable if taken to court. The statute does not prevent the existence of a valid contract, but it does make written evidence necessary to establish it. In 18 states, the statute of frauds says that the contract is void or invalid unless in writing.

### CONDITIONAL CONTRACTS

Just as the parties are free to establish price and other terms of a contract, so also are they free to place conditions on their agreement. It is quite common for parties to a real estate contract of sale to agree that it should not bind them if certain events do not happen or cannot be made to happen.

*Example* The buyer and seller may agree that a parcel of land will be purchased for $X,XXX if, and only if, it can be rezoned for a particular use. If the rezoning cannot be obtained, the condition on which the contract is based is not met and the contract fails.

There has been no breach by either party in such a case. The most common condition in real estate contracts is the availability of financing on reasonable terms. Some typical conditions that may be encountered are:

| *Buyer* | *Seller* |
|---|---|
| No financing | No title |
| No sale of present house | No survey |
| Destruction of | No zoning |
| improvements | Defects cannot be |
| Defects not corrected | corrected |

There is a possible solution to the problem that arises when a condition cannot be met. There can be a *novation*, a new contract between the parties that is then enforceable according to the new terms.

*Example* The sale may be conditional upon a survey showing that there are 10 acres of ground, with the price to be $10,000. The survey shows only 9.5 acres. The parties might agree to change the contract to provide for 9.5 acres at a price of $9,500. This is a new contract—or a novation. The seller could not arbitrarily reduce the price and force the buyer to complete the sale. The buyer must agree to the change. Because it is a new contract, it must meet all requirements discussed.

### CLASSIFICATION OF CONTRACTS

A number of ways exist in which to classify contracts. The following categories are frequently used.

### Valid Contract

A valid contract possesses all the required elements of a contract, is for a legal purpose, legally binds all parties involved to the agreement, and is enforceable.

## Void Contract

Any agreement that has no legal status (i.e., never formed a legal contract and was therefore never binding on the parties) is considered a *void contract.* For example, an agreement made with a person who has been legally declared incompetent is void from the outset. It lacks an essential element of a void contract—legal capacity.

## Voidable Contract

In a *voidable contract* one party or the other may take action to have the agreement declared void. The parties capable of avoiding the contract change under different circumstances. For example, a contract made with an infant is voidable at the option of the infant.

## Bilateral Contract

In a *bilateral contract,* both parties make promises to each other.

*Example*  A says to B, "I will pay you $10,000 if you will promise to sell me this land." If B agrees, A has promised the payment of $10,000 and B has promised to sell A the land.

## Unilateral Contract

In a unilateral contract, one party gives a promise to another party in exchange for some actual performance by the second party. The promise made by the first party is not legally binding until the actual performance by the second party.

*Example*  An insurance company, in return for payment of a premium, promises to pay for a loss that the policy holder suffers. When the loss occurs, the insurance company's promise is binding.

## Express Contract

In an express contract the agreement is stated in words, either oral or written.

*Example*  A says to B, "I will pay you $100 if you promise me to plow this field." B says, "It's a deal."

## Implied Contract

In an implied contract, the parties' agreement can be inferred from their conduct alone, without spoken or written words.

*Example*  A contractor mistakenly begins to build a house on a vacant lot that A owns. A is aware that the house is being built on his lot but says nothing. When the house is completed, A finds that the law will imply A's promise to pay the fair value of the house from his conduct, even though there was no formal agreement between A and the contractor.

## COMMON REAL ESTATE CONTRACT PROVISIONS

In addition to the legal requirements of a contract, most agreements for real estate must contain certain other provisions:

☐  *Date.* The date of agreement is the date on which the parties entered into the agreement or contract. Some states require this item to appear in all contracts for the sale of any interest in land.
☐  *Signatures.* In most states the statute of frauds requires that the contracting parties be identified and that they sign the contract. In some contract forms for the sale of land, the broker or agent for the buyer and/or seller must also be identified.
☐  *Description of Subject.* A contract for the sale of land should contain a legal description of the property being sold. Such a description should define the location and give the dimensions of the property to be conveyed in the agreement, or it should enable the parties to obtain that information.
☐  *Consideration.* A contract for the sale of an interest in land must include, under the statute of frauds in nearly all states, some statement of consideration to be exchanged for that interest.
☐  *Terms of Payment.* The contract should state how much is being paid in cash and when it is to be paid. If the buyer is taking over an existing mortgage or obtaining a new mortgage from a lending institution or receiving a partial financing from the seller, the terms of financing (such as acceptable rate of interest, amount to be borrowed, and repayment schedule) should also be detailed in the contract.
☐  *Conditions.* Any special contingencies or conditions for the fulfillment of the contract should be written into the contract. The most common contingency is the ability of the buyer to obtain financing.
☐  *Time of Performance.* A contract for the sale of land should include a provision naming the date and place of closing. The date of closing may be simply an approximate date to give the buyer time to obtain financing and inspect the title. The place of closing should be clearly specified.

### Assignment of Contracts

Most real estate contracts can be assigned. The party who sells a contractual right that he or she possesses is the assignor. The party to whom the contractual right is sold by the assignor is the assignee.

*Example* A and B have a contract by which B owes A $100 for services performed. A assigns her contractual right to the $100 for services performed to C. A is the assignor; C is the assignee.

## SUMMARY

Basic contract law requires that parties be competent to enter into binding agreements. It further requires that a provable agreement exists and that it is supported by consideration before it can be enforced in court.

Real estate sales contracts must meet the further test of the statute of frauds and, therefore, must be in writing to be enforceable.

Essential fairness must surround the transaction as evidenced by the rules against fraud, duress, undue influence, and misrepresentation. Remedies of damages, rescission, and specific performance are available in the event of a breach of a valid contract.

Contract rights are valuable property rights that may be bought and sold by assignment. Contracts can be amended and changed by the parties if they choose to do so through the concept of novation.

Finally, conditions may be established that must be met before the parties are obligated to perform an otherwise valid contract.

## REVIEW QUESTIONS

1. A contract of sale is executed by the

   (A) buyer and broker
   (B) seller and lender
   (C) buyer and seller
   (D) seller and broker

2. A contract signed voluntarily by a person who is drunk is

   (A) void
   (B) voidable
   (C) valid
   (D) illegal

3. Mr. Smith did not agree with all the terms of an offer submitted to him. He made a counteroffer. The counteroffer

   (A) need not be executed by the buyer
   (B) would also lower the rate of commission charged
   (C) results in a new contract of sale if accepted
   (D) may not be used in residential sales

4. The concept of duress is based on

   (A) deception
   (B) fear
   (C) abuse of power
   (D) the commission of a crime

5. Consideration in a contract is

   (A) not essential
   (B) an exchange of promises
   (C) more than 10 percent of the purchase price
   (D) more than 25 percent of the purchase price

6. The statute of frauds requires contracts for the sale of real estate to be

   (A) in writing to be enforceable
   (B) in outline form
   (C) reviewed by the county recorder
   (D) reviewed by a real estate commissioner

7. If a purchaser has signed a contract under duress, it is generally

   (A) voidable by the seller
   (B) voidable by the buyer
   (C) valid
   (D) void

8. A contract is generally void if

   (A) it was entered into with a minor
   (B) it requires an illegal act for performance
   (C) undue influence was used to gain the contract
   (D) duress was used to gain the contract

9. A contract involving an exchange of promises between the parties is a

   (A) unitarian contract
   (B) binary contract
   (C) unilateral contract
   (D) bilateral contract

10. Which of the following does **not** terminate an offer to sell real estate?

    (A) Lapse of reasonable time
    (B) Rejection of the offer by the offeree
    (C) Death of the sale agent
    (D) A revocation of the offer

11. Once the contract for the sale of real property has been signed, the purchaser has

    (A) legal title to the real estate
    (B) the right to possess the real estate
    (C) nothing until he or she receives the deed
    (D) equitable title in the real estate

12. Which of the following may **not** be a contract?

    (A) A deed
    (B) An option
    (C) A mortgage
    (D) None of the above

13. The provision in a purchase contract that the seller will pay $75 per day for each day after closing that the buyer may not have possession is

    (A) liquidated damages
    (B) punitive damages
    (C) compensatory damages
    (D) none of the above

14. The assignment of a contract

    (A) removes the assignor of all liability for the duties under the contract
    (B) makes the assignor primarily liable for the performance of the contract
    (C) may be done freely if the contract does not prohibit the assignment
    (D) requires a novation to be completed

15. Your declaration that the execution of a document by you is a voluntary act is

    (A) a notarization
    (B) an affirmation
    (C) an acknowledgment
    (D) a reversion

16. The seller signed the contract of sale while under duress. The transaction is

    (A) void
    (B) voidable by the seller
    (C) voidable by the buyer
    (D) valid upon recording

17. In presenting an offer to purchase a property,

    (A) the offeror is in complete command of the offer
    (B) the additional terms may be added by the offeror
    (C) the document must be recorded to be effective
    (D) the offer will not die if countered

18. The element of a contract that is essential to make the promises enforceable is

    (A) earnest money
    (B) exclusivity of purpose
    (C) consideration
    (D) mutuality of consent

19. All of the following are essential to a valid contract of sale EXCEPT

    (A) offer to be made
    (B) acceptance by the parties
    (C) consideration for the contract
    (D) earnest money deposit

20. A buyer made an offer on December 2, and allowed five days for acceptance. The buyer

    (A) could withdraw the offer prior to December 7, if it is not accepted
    (B) must wait until December 7 to withdraw the offer
    (C) may change the terms of the offer only after December 7
    (D) may not be countered by the seller until after December 7

# Chapter 15

# The Brokerage Relationship and Responsibilities

## VOCABULARY

*You will find it important to have a complete working knowledge of the following terms, concepts, and abbreviations found in the text or the glossary.*

| | | |
|---|---|---|
| agreeing and assuming | gross income | release of liability |
| cash flow | habendum clause | remainder |
| consideration | indefeasible | reversion |
| contingent proposition | IREM | severalty |
| conveyance | joint tenancy | special agency |
| CPM | lessee | special warranty deed |
| debt service | lessor | subject to the mortgage |
| deed | listing contract | sublease |
| estate for years | merchantable title | surety |
| estate from period to period | net lease | tenancy at sufferance |
| exclusive agency | net operating income | tenancy at will |
| exclusive right to sell | offer to purchase | tenancy by the entireties |
| fiduciary | open listing | tenants in common |
| fiduciary deed | percentage lease | title insurance |
| general agency | proposition | universal agency |
| general warranty deed | quitclaim deed | |

Every broker and salesperson must have a working knowledge of the legal documents involved in the transfer of property rights. The discussion that follows is to some degree a review of material covered earlier. However, it adds a new dimension to several of the topics. This chapter discusses certain principles relating to the contracts and options involved in real estate practice, and also covers some fundamental aspects of deeds, mortgages, settlement statements, and property management. Settlement statements, which are of great importance, are discussed in detail in Chapter 17.

The broker and salesperson will discover that in real estate practice they must be knowledgeable about the following types of contracts: agency contracts, listing contracts, propositions, and conditional sales contracts. The parties involved in each of these relationships are shown in Figure 15-1.

## AGENCY RELATIONSHIPS

The basic contract found in the brokerage business is that established between the principal and the agent. Different levels of responsibility can exist in an agency, depending on the authorization the agent has from the principal. There are three basic categories: universal agency, general agency, and special agency.

The universal agent is allowed to perform all lawful acts for the principal, the general agent performs specific types of activities, and the special agent performs a specific type of action. A special agency is the one most commonly found in the brokerage business: A seller authorizes an agent to find a purchaser for a specific piece of property. It is important to note that the agent is the broker for whom the salesperson works; the seller is the principal. The salesperson is not actually a party to the agency agreement.

## REAL ESTATE TRANSACTIONS

### The Parties Involved and Their Actions

| The Maker or the Doer of the Action | The Action | The Recipient of the Action |
|---|---|---|
| Principal (owner) | Listing of real estate (a listing contract) | Agent (broker) |
| Offeror (one who originates an offer) | An offer (to sell or to buy or to lease, etc.) | Offeree (one to whom an offer is made) |
| Grantor (owner/seller transferring ownership) | Deed (transferring ownership) | Grantee (recipient/purchaser receiving ownership) |
| Vendor (seller) | Sale of real estate (contract of sale) | Vendee (buyer) |
| Optionor (owner of property, prospective grantor, or lessor) | An option (to purchase or lease real estate) | Optionee (prospective grantee or lessee) |
| Lessor (landlord or owner) | Rental real estate (lease agreement) | Lessee (renter or tenant) |
| Assignor (one who makes an assignment) | Assignment of contract | Assignee (recipient of an assignment) |
| Lienor (claimant or party aggrieved) | Lien (court judgment, mechanic's lien, unpaid taxes, mortgages, etc.) | Lienee (formal debtor) |
| Mortgagor or trustor (borrower) | Loan on real estate (mortgage or deed of trust) | Mortgagee or trustee (beneficiary (lender), trustee holding title for tender) |
| Condemnor (public agency) | Condemnation (exercise of the right of eminent domain) | Condemnee (property owner) |

*Figure 15-1—Real estate transactions. The various real estate transactions and parties involved: Who originates an action, what the action is, and who receives the action.*

In most states an agency relationship created for the purpose of the sale of a property must be in writing. Termination of the contract can come about by an act of the parties or by the operation of law.

*Termination by act of the parties* can occur as a result of:

Mutual consent
Completion of the contract

Expiration of time as found in the contract
Revocation of the principal
Refusal by the agent to continue with the contract

*Termination by operation of law* can occur as a result of:

Insanity of either party
Death of either party

Destruction of the object
Bankruptcy of either party

## Fiduciary Relationship

An agency contract creates a relationship in which the agent must exercise great caution in his or her actions for the principal. The agent's actions must be reasonable and prudent.

Such a fiduciary relationship also obligates the agent to a high level of loyalty, obedience, and performance of the task contracted for. If the agent does not fulfill these obligations, the principal might have just cause for a lawsuit against the agent.

An agency relationship is created when the principal gives a *power of attorney* to the agent. This allows the agent to act on behalf of the principal. The agent is known as the *attorney-in-fact.*

## Agent's Compensation

Because of the large number of agency relationships created, many disagreements over when commissions have been earned seem to arise. In general, the agent has earned a commission when a purchaser—ready, willing, and able to meet the terms of the listing—has been brought to the principal. Should the principal fail to complete a sale under such circumstances, the agent would nevertheless have earned, and thus would be eligible to collect, the commission.

When the actual commission is earned can usually be determined by the language in the agency agreement (listing contract).

## Independent Contractor

Another role that the broker or salesperson can fill is that of an independent contractor, that is, a person who is hired to achieve a specific result and who performs that act without direct control by the principal. While an independent contractor may be an agent, he controls his own use of time and effort, paying his own expenses and making his own business decisions.

A relationship with an independent contractor can free the principal from many of the legal liabilities that may be incurred with an agent. Whether a relationship is that of independent contractor or agent is especially important in determining tax responsibility.

## LISTING CONTRACTS

A listing contract is the basis of most real estate transactions. It is the instrument whereby the owner of real estate lists property for sale with a broker.

There are several types of listing contracts that create the agency relationship:

- [] *Open listing.* The principal contacts as many brokers as desired to represent the property but is liable for payment of a commission only to the broker who actually sells the property. No restrictions are placed on the seller's right to sell the property him or herself without paying a commission to anyone.
- [] *Exclusive agency.* The owner appoints the broker with whom he or she has listed the property as the exclusive agent for procuring a purchaser during the term of the listing. The owner thus becomes obligated to pay a commission to the listing broker if the property is sold during the term of the listing by the broker or by any other person. But the owner retains the right to sell the property to a buyer procured by his or her own efforts without being liable for a commission to the listing broker.
- [] *Exclusive right to sell.* The owner is obligated to pay the broker the commission if the property is sold, regardless of who procures the purchaser. This type of contract is most advantageous to the broker, and therefore it is the one most often used by the industry. It is also most advantageous to the seller because it motivates the broker to expend the time and funds to market the property since the broker is assured a commission even if the owner sells the property.
- [] *Multiple listing.* Brokers who have procured exclusive right to sell listing contracts from owners cooperate with other broker members of the Multiple Listing Service (MLS) to provide a larger market for their listed properties. The listing broker will share a previously negotiated portion of the sales commission with the broker who finds the purchaser for the property.

### Requirements of Valid Listing Contracts

The following principles are applicable to listing contracts:

- [] State statutes typically require certain employment contracts (especially those that include payment of commissions) to be in writing. As such, listing contracts generally must be in writing.
- [] State statutes of fraud—and/or state license laws—require that listing contracts be signed by the owner or owners to be valid and enforceable. A listing contract which involves real estate that is owned by a husband and wife, for example, should be signed by both parties. If four persons own the real estate as tenants in common, the listing contract should be signed by all four parties.
- [] Listings without a specific termination date are improper. Thus a listing should be given for a specific or computable period of time, such as "until July 5, 198X," or "for a period of 90 days from this date."

☐   The owner must be given a copy of the listing contract.

Under the usual form listing contract, the broker is entitled to payment of a commission if he or she produces a purchaser ready, willing, and able to pay the purchase price on the terms stipulated in the listing contract.

## THE PROPOSITION (OFFER TO PURCHASE)

The proposition, or the offer to purchase real estate, is the instrument whereby a prospective purchaser offers in writing to purchase real estate on certain specific terms. Since it is the foundation of the particular real estate transaction, it must be carefully drawn so that there may be complete agreement between purchaser and seller. It must be definite, specific, and certain. It must clearly establish the rights, obligations, and duties of both parties with respect to the sale and purchase. A proposition containing ambiguities may well lead to the failure of the transaction.

It should be remembered that the proposition is simply an offer until such time as it is accepted without condition by the seller. Since it is only an offer, it may be withdrawn at any time by the purchaser prior to its acceptance by the seller. This is possible because no consideration is paid for the offer, and consideration is a requisite element of every enforceable contract.

When the offer has been accepted unconditionally by the seller, the contract ripens into existence. The legal consideration is found in the mutual promises of the parties—the promise of the purchaser to purchase on specific terms, and the promise of the seller to sell on the same terms. The mutual promises support each other and provide the legal consideration for the contract.

If the seller attaches any condition to his or her acceptance, such conditional acceptance immediately terminates the offer. The conditional acceptance becomes in effect a *counteroffer* by the seller. If the counteroffer is unqualifiedly accepted by the purchaser, the contract will ripen into existence, for there is a "meeting of the minds."

### The Legal Description

The proposition must first contain a description of the property to be sold. This description must be so specific and so certain that there can be no doubt as to the property for which the offer is being made.

In the case of residential property, ordinarily a street and number description is sufficient. However, the careful broker or salesperson will give not only a proper street address but also an accurate legal description. Such a description is ordinarily obtainable from the owner's deed or from a local title company.

Farm acreage can generally be described adequately by the number of acres and by the location (street, road, and township). Again, however, careful draftsmanship of the proposition will employ a specific legal description by metes and bounds.

A more difficult problem arises when a certain portion of a larger tract is being sold. This problem may readily be solved by obtaining from a surveyor a specific legal description so that no doubt may arise as to the boundaries of the property being purchased.

A word of warning: Tax duplicate descriptions, which in many cases are inaccurate and incomplete, should never be used in preparing a proposition.

### The Terms of Sale

Following the description of the property in question, the specific terms of the sale are set forth in the proposition. In general, the terms of sale may be grouped into five general categories.

#### The Cash Sale

Drafting the terms of the cash sale, free and clear, ordinarily presents no difficulties. It is written: "The purchaser hereby agrees to pay for said property the sum of $10,000, upon the following terms: cash."

#### The Sale Subject to an Existing Mortgage

The proposition may be made subject to the existing mortgage on the premises. The language used is ". . . upon the following terms: purchaser shall take title to said real estate subject to the existing mortgage upon the same, the balance of the purchase price over and above the balance due upon said mortgage at the date of closing to be paid in cash."

In the sale subject to an existing mortgage, we should understand two important considerations. First, the seller is not relieved from liability; he still remains liable for his personal obligation on the mortgage note he has signed. Second, the purchaser does not assume personal liability on the mortgage. Thus, in the event of foreclosure, the mortgagee may secure a personal judgment against the seller (who signed the mortgage note). But where the purchaser is concerned, no personal judgment may be obtained; only the property may be subjected to sale to satisfy the judgment obtained by the mortgagee. Any deficiency resulting from the sale may be enforced against the seller who signed the mortgage note. No such deficiency may be enforced against the buyer who took title subject to the mortgage and who therefore assumed no personal liability.

#### The Sale Subject to the Assumption of a Mortgage

There are important differences between a sale subject to an existing mortgage and a sale subject to the assumption of an existing mortgage.

Where the mortgage is assumed by the purchaser, there are several consequences. First, as in the case of the sale subject to an existing mortgage, the seller is not relieved from liability; the seller remains liable for the personal obligation on the mortgage note the seller has signed. However, the purchaser assumes personal liability on the mortgage note. Thus, in the event of foreclosure, the mortgagee may take a personal judgment against both the original seller and the purchaser, subject to the sale of the property, and enforce any deficiency resulting from the sale against both parties.

In the assumption situation, the purchaser becomes the principal primarily liable for the debt, and the seller becomes a *surety*. Under the general principles applicable to the law of suretyship, when the principal (the purchaser) defaults in payment, the surety (the seller) may pay the deficiency and then has the right to sue the principal (the purchaser) for the amount so paid.

In drafting a proposition calling for the assumption of a mortgage, we use language similar to that used for a sale subject to a mortgage, except that a clause is added providing that the purchaser shall "assume and agree to pay the unpaid balance due upon said mortgage at the date of closing." This language is also incorporated in the deed at the closing of the transaction.

Remember, in both situations, the seller who signs the original note and mortgage is not relieved from personal liability by reason of the sale of the mortgaged property. His or her personal liability in this regard can be terminated in only two ways: (a) by execution of a *release of liability* agreement, entered into by seller, purchaser, and mortgagee, by virtue of which the seller is fully released and the mortgagee agrees to look solely to the purchaser for payment of the mortgage, or (b) by payment in full.

## The Sale on Conditional Sales Contract

The conditional sales contract is effective for use where the purchaser in question does not have a sufficient down payment to complete the purchase of the property by securing adequate mortgage financing. In this type of sale, in addition to the down payment, the purchaser makes stipulated monthly payments, with interest, and legal title remains with the seller until the purchase price is fully paid, at which time the deed of conveyance is executed. In the event of default, the seller is entitled to secure immediate possession and to retain the down payment and all subsequent payments as liquidated damages for the purchaser's default. (See Chapter 10 for recent developments in this area.)

## The Purchase Money Mortgage

A purchase money mortgage is a mortgage taken back by the seller from the purchaser upon the sale of real estate. This situation may arise when the seller is willing to finance the purchaser in an amount over and above the down payment that the purchaser has available. Here again, the terms should be carefully spelled out in the proposition, with particular reference to the amount of the mortgage, the rate of interest, how the interest is computed and payable, the amount of the monthly or installment payments, the grace period, and any provision with reference to prepayment privileges.

## The Contingent Proposition

The purchaser may wish to make an offer contingent on the occurrence of a certain event. Generally, these contingencies fall into five categories.

☐ *Subject to the purchaser's ability to obtain a conventional mortgage loan.* The purchaser may require conventional mortgage loan financing to supply the funds necessary to complete the purchase price. In this case, such a contingency should be spelled out specifically in the proposition:

This proposition is specifically contingent upon the purchaser's ability to obtain a firm commitment for a conventional first mortgage loan upon said premises in an amount not less than $26,000 with a rate of interest not to exceed 8½ percent per annum, amortized monthly over a period of not less than 25 years. Should the purchaser fail to obtain such a commitment within a period of 30 days following acceptance of this proposition, then this proposition shall become void, and the earnest money deposit made this date shall be refunded to the purchaser.

☐ *Subject to the purchaser's ability to obtain an FHA mortgage loan.* When an FHA loan is needed by the purchaser, similar language may be used. In such cases, the rate of interest need not be stipulated, as it is fixed by law. All other details should be stated in the contingency language, including the number of discount points the seller will pay.

☐ *Subject to the purchaser's ability to obtain a VA mortgage loan.* The language of contingency is similar to that for the FHA loan. No rate of interest need be stipulated, as it is fixed by law. In the case of FHA and VA mortgages, more time should be allowed for obtaining the commitment, including the number of discount points the seller will pay.

☐ *Subject to the purchaser's ability to sell his or her existing property.* The purchaser may be unable to complete the purchase of the property in question unless and until he or she has sold and disposed of currently owned property. In this situation, the contingency should include a minimum sale price and a time limit for final consummation of the sale of the purchaser's present property.

☐ *Subject to zoning for an intended use.* The purchaser may wish to purchase the property in question only if it can be zoned for an intended use. The proposition must therefore be drafted subject to this contingency. The drafting of this contingency is difficult, as provision must be made for the possibility that the zoning order may be appealed—and final disposition may be delayed over a considerable period of time. Such propositions generally provide that, if an appeal is made, the proposition shall become void.

## Rents and Insurance

After the terms of sale and any contingencies are spelled out, the proposition generally makes provisions for the proration of rents, where rental property is involved. Rents are prorated between seller and purchaser as of the date of closing.

The proposition also provides for the proration or cancellation, as the case may be, of existing hazard insurance. In case of a proration, the unearned portion of the insurance premium is charged to the purchaser at the time of closing. If the insurance is cancelled, the seller will generally receive a short-rate premium refund directly from the insurance company. This is usually less than a pro rata premium refund.

## Taxes

The proposition should provide for the handling of real estate taxes at the time of closing. This may be done by two methods, the installment method and the proration method.

☐ *The installment method* provides for the purchaser to assume a certain subsequent installment of taxes and all taxes payable thereafter: "The purchaser shall assume all taxes upon said real estate beginning with the installment due and payable in May 198X, and all installments due and payable thereafter."

☐ *The proration method* provides for the apportionment of taxes between seller and buyer on a calendar year basis. With this method, the seller pays all taxes assessed for the prior calendar year and remaining unpaid, as well as all taxes assessed for the current calendar year apportioned to the date of sale.

## Assessments

The property sold may be subject to assessments for municipal improvements such as streets, sewers, and curbs. The improvements may be in various stages, with the contract let and the work not started, or the work in process, or the work completed. The broker should be thoroughly familiar with the status of any such as-

sessments, and the proposition should specifically state whether payment should be the seller's or the purchaser's responsibility.

## Abstract of Title and Title Insurance

The proposition contains a clause providing for the furnishing at the seller's expense of an abstract of title showing a merchantable title to the real estate in question. A *merchantable title* is one acceptable to examining attorneys of experience in the particular community. The proposition generally further provides for the securing of a title insurance policy if the title is not merchantable. If the title is neither merchantable nor insurable, the purchaser should be released from the terms of the proposition and his or her earnest money refunded.

## Deeds of Conveyance

Provision is made in the proposition for execution by the seller to the purchaser of a deed of conveyance at the closing of the transaction. Usually a general warranty deed is provided for, although a special warranty deed or a quitclaim deed may be indicated.

## Personal Property

The sale of real estate includes all fixtures attached thereto. Generally speaking, a fixture is personal property that has become real property by reason of its adaptability to the real estate and its being permanently affixed to the same. However, the distinction between personal property and fixtures may be a shadowy one. Therefore the proposition should specifically spell out what is included with the property. A careful broker knows what the seller intends to sell and what the buyer intends to buy, and these items should be specifically mentioned in the proposition, in order that there will be no misunderstanding at the date of closing.

## Default Clause

The obligations of the purchaser upon default of his or her obligations without a legal excuse should be spelled out in the proposition. Many propositions provide that upon such default the purchaser shall forfeit his or her earnest money deposits as liquidated damages in lieu of all other remedies available to the seller. In the absence of a liquidated damage clause, the purchaser may be liable to respond in actual damages for failure to perform.

## Signatures of Purchaser and Seller

The proposition should be signed by all the purchasers. Because the proposition becomes a legal contract only when it is accepted without condition by the seller, all owners and their respective spouses should sign the acceptance.

## THE CONDITIONAL SALES CONTRACT

The conditional sales contract is widely used in the sale of real estate. It is used to purchase real estate on a time or installment basis, and it is an effective method of making the purchase of real estate available to a buyer who does not have sufficient funds to make the necessary down payment over and above mortgage financing. Let us consider now the essential features of the conditional sales (or land) contract.

### Title

Under the conditional sales contract, legal title does not pass to the purchaser until the balance of the contract, both principal and interest, has been paid in full, at which time the seller executes and delivers to the purchaser the deed in satisfaction of the contract.

The purchaser, however, becomes vested with an equitable title and for many purposes is in effect the owner of the real estate, with certain rights and obligations as outlined in the contract. In the event of default, this equitable interest may be lost to the purchaser.

### Payments

Most conditional sales contracts provide for an initial payment in cash, stipulated money payments, and interest on the unpaid balance. The rate of interest is always stipulated, and the computation and payment of interest is handled as outlined in the contract. Interest is frequently computed in advance, either monthly or semiannually, and is included in the monthly payments. Another method provides for payment of interest in addition to the monthly principal payments. Most forms of conditional sales contracts give full prepayment privileges to the purchaser so that he or she may make additional payments at any time. (Any such additional payments will result in interest savings to the purchaser.)

### Improvements

With respect to the improvements on the real estate, the contract usually provides that the purchaser shall keep such improvements adequately insured and in a proper state of repair. There is generally a provision that requires the purchaser to secure the written consent of the seller before making any additions or improvements or doing any remodeling of the premises.

### Assignability

Most conditional sales contracts contain a stipulation that the purchaser has no right to sell or assign the contract without the owner's written assent. However, this does not prevent the sale of the purchaser's interest to a customer who can pay cash, for the purchaser can use the cash proceeds to pay off the contract in full, secure a proper deed, and then deed the property to the new purchaser.

### Default

Upon default of the purchaser under the conditional sales contract, and upon the continuance of this default after any grace period stipulated in the contract, the owner may bring action to eject the purchaser from the premises and to cancel the contract. In such cases the purchaser forfeits the down payment and all monthly payments as liquidated damages for the default. Such a liquidated damages clause prevents the seller from enforcing any other claim against the defaulting purchaser. The forfeiture clause will usually be held to be a liquidated damages clause if the amount of payments received by the seller amounts to a small percentage of the total contract price.

### Escrow

The concept of escrow is used in several different ways in the real estate business. *Escrow* is a deposit, by a party to a transaction, of documents, money, or other things of value with an impartial third party who upon the meeting of specified conditions delivers the deposited item(s) to another party to the transaction.

The party holding the items is called the *escrow agent*. (As an agent, he may receive a fee for his services.) Real estate may be closed through escrow with the parties never meeting face to face. In such a case the agent simply waits for all the documents to clear and for the financing to be approved before closing the loan and disbursing the appropriate items.

Other forms of escrow include the type of account maintained by a mortgagee for deposit of that portion of the monthly payment intended to pay real estate taxes or insurance premiums. The mortgagor maintains these funds until the actual bill comes due and then pays it on behalf of the mortgagee. This is commonly referred to as an *escrow payment*. Some states allow interest to be paid on such accounts.

When the escrow account contains excess funds, they are refundable to the depositor. When a shortage occurs, the lender normally requests a lump sum payment to bring the funds up to date. Frequently the portion of the principal, interest, taxes, and insurance *(PITI)* payment attributable to taxes and insurance will be increased to prevent a deficit from occurring.

## OPTIONS

An option is an instrument whereby an owner of real estate, for a valuable consideration, gives and grants to another person the right and privilege for a stipulated period of time to purchase the real estate at a certain price.

In our discussion of propositions, we saw that the proposition, duly accepted, contained mutual promises—a promise of the seller to sell and a promise of the purchaser to buy—and that these mutual promises supported each other and provided the legal consideration necessary for the contract. The accepted proposition is therefore a *bilateral contract*.

The option, however, is a *unilateral contract*. That is, it is an instrument under which only one party is bound. This party is the seller, who is obligated to convey the real estate if the purchaser exercises the option and tenders the purchase price. The purchaser is under no obligation to purchase, but he or she has the right and the option to do so as desired. For this reason, there are no mutual promises in an option, as there are in an accepted proposition. Since there are no such mutual promises, the legal consideration for the option must be found elsewhere. Usually it is found in a cash payment made for the option by the prospective purchaser to the owner.

The payment for the option may be only nominal in nature, or it may be substantial. Where a substantial payment is involved, the option generally provides that such payment shall be credited toward the purchase price if the option is exercised.

If the option is not exercised, the down payment is retained by the owner as payment for the option.

Options always contain a time limitation for exercise by the purchaser. If not exercised within a given time limit, the option automatically expires.

The option is an effective instrument in land assembly operations. For example, a broker who is employed to assemble numerous tracts of land for a manufacturing concern secures options on all such tracts. The broker does not use the proposition method of purchase because then the broker might be unable to purchase one or more of the tracts and yet be bound to purchase the others.

One very important observation must be made about options. Since a possible or probable purchase of land is involved, the option should be just as carefully drawn and as specific in detail as the proposition, with reference to the legal description, terms of sale, rents and insurance, taxes, assessments, abstract of title, deed of conveyance, and inclusion of personal property contemplated by the purchaser.

For reasons already discussed with reference to the acceptance of propositions, options should be signed by all owners and their respective spouses in order to be valid and effective. That is, the option itself must be a legally binding contract.

## DEEDS

The deed is the instrument for the conveyance of a title to real estate. In this section we examine several types of deeds and then the structure of the deed of conveyance. This material should provide a useful review of information presented in earlier chapters.

### Types of Deeds

#### General Warranty Deed

Most propositions call for the execution by the seller of a *general warranty deed*. As the name indicates, the deed contains several warranties and covenants on the part of the seller. In executing such a deed, the grantor (seller) makes the following warranties:

☐ That the grantor is possessed of an *indefeasible fee simple absolute title* to the real estate. (A fee simple title is the highest title under the law, involving full and complete rights of ownership, to the exclusion of all others.)

☐ That there are no encumbrances against the real estate other than those specifically expressed in the deed.

☐ That the grantee (purchaser) shall have quiet enjoyment of the real estate *and* that the grantor (seller) will warrant and defend the title to the real estate against any and all claims, from the beginning of time to the execution of the deed of conveyance.

Where there is an unbroken chain of general warranty deeds, each grantor in the chain may be liable to all subsequent grantees for any claim arising prior to the date of conveyance by that particular grantor. Where the chain is broken by the execution of a deed other than a general warranty deed, subsequent grantees may not look for redress to any grantors who may have executed warranty deeds prior to the date when the chain was broken.

#### Special Warranty Deed

The *special warranty deed* is a deed of limited warranty, and the warranty contained therein is limited to any claim arising out of the period of ownership of the grantor executing it. Thus, if an owner held title from January 1 to October 31 and was willing to warrant the property only for that period, he or she would execute a special warranty deed with warrants against any claims arising out of that particular period only. The warranty would not extend back to the beginning of time.

#### Quitclaim Deed

The *quitclaim deed* is a deed of release. It conveys without warranty whatever right, claim, title, or interest the grantor may have in the real estate conveyed. If the grantor has a fee simple title, the quitclaim deed will convey the same. If the grantor has no title, nothing will be conveyed by the quitclaim deed.

Quitclaim deeds are generally used to convey lesser interests in real estate, such as life estates or minor interests. They are also widely used to correct prior conveyances that have been improperly executed.

### Judicial Deeds

Many titles to real estate are conveyed by *judicial deeds,* which, as the name implies, are deeds executed pursuant to a court order. Examples of such conveyances are deeds of executors, administrators, guardians, and trustees; sheriff's deeds executed by virtue of foreclosure proceedings; and commissioner's deeds executed in partition proceedings. Such deeds, assuming that the judicial proceedings in the particular case have been legally pursued, are effectual to convey good title to the real estate—but *without* warranties.

## Essential Elements of a Deed

The essential parts of a proper deed are the granting clause, the legal description, the statement of encumbrances, the signature clause, and the acknowledgment. In addition, the deed must usually be duly recorded.

### The Granting Clause

The granting clause contains the names of the grantor and the language of conveyance. For example: "*AB* and *BB,* husband and wife, of Any County, Your State, convey and warrant to *CD,* of Any County, Your State . . . ."

Many old deed forms also include a *habendum clause* that leading authorities believe is no longer necessary since it adds nothing to the granting clause. (A habendum clause would normally begin, "To have and to hold.")

Here we stress again that the marital status of all grantors must be shown, such as "*AB* and *BB,* husband and wife," or "*AB,* an unmarried adult." (We outlined the reasons for this in our discussion of the acceptance of propositions.)

Note that the granting clause also contains the name of the grantee (purchaser). In the example given above, there is a single grantee. When there is more than one grantee, a question arises as to the type of estate that is taken. Estates may fall into several categories.

The first category is an *estate by the entireties.* This estate exists only between a husband and wife and is created by the execution of a deed to two people who are in fact husband and wife. For example: "to *AB* and *BB,* husband and wife." This estate has the following characteristics:

☐ *Full right of survivorship.* On the death of one spouse, the surviving spouse succeeds to the full title, free of all claims of the creditors of the deceased spouse. Any other heirs of the deceased spouse have no interest in the real estate.

☐ *Immunity from individual judgments.* A judgment against one spouse alone cannot be enforced against the real estate during the joint lives of husband and wife. Only joint judgments against both spouses may be so enforced.

☐ *Nonseverability.* So long as both spouses live, neither can convey said real estate without the consent of the other spouse.

The second category is a *joint tenancy.* A joint tenancy, though recognized under the law, is not favored by the law, and therefore it must be spelled out with certainty. It is generally created in this language: "to *CD* and *EF,* as joint tenants and not as tenants in common." This estate may be created in two or more persons; it may also be created in a husband and wife, where the instrument clearly indicates that they are to take "as joint tenants and not as tenants by the entirety." The joint tenancy has the following characteristics:

☐ *Full right of survivorship.* As in the case of tenants by the entireties, discussed above.

☐ *Nonimmunity from individual judgments.* A judgment against one joint tenant may be enforced against his or her undivided interest in the property, and such interest may be sold to satisfy the judgment. Such action in effect destroys the joint tenancy, and the purchaser at a judicial sale becomes a tenant in common with the other joint tenant.

☐ *Severability.* One joint tenant may destroy the joint tenancy by conveying his or her interest to a third party, who then becomes a tenant in common with the other joint tenant.

The third category is *tenancy in common.* This type of tenancy is created by a conveyance to two or more persons, with no language indicating that another type of estate is created. For example: "to *AB, BC,* and *CD.*" In a tenancy in common, there are no rights of survivorship. For example, upon *AB's* death the interest passes to the heirs by law or to the devisees under his will. It does not pass to *BC* and *CD* (unless they are the heirs or devisees). In addition, the undivided interest of each tenant in common is subject to individual judgments against him. Also, an interest may be conveyed to a third person. Here again, a tenancy in common may be created in a husband and wife, as tenants in common and not as tenants by the entirety.

A fourth category is a *life estate with a reversion.* A grantor who owns the fee simple title may convey an estate to another person for and during the natural life of the other person. This creates a life estate and gives the life tenant the use and occupancy and the rents and profits of the real estate during the life of the tenant. However, the grantor who owns the fee has conveyed a lesser estate than full ownership. Thus the grantor is vested with a reversion, which comes into enjoyment upon the death of the life tenant. Thus, when *AB* conveys to *CD* "for and during the period of his natural life," *CD* has a life estate and *AB* has a reversion.

A fifth category is a *life estate with a remainder*. By proper conveyance, a grantor may create a life estate in one person, and then provide that, upon the death of that person, another person shall take title. The other person has a remainder interest, that is, the interest remaining after the life estate. Thus, when *AB* conveys "to *CD* for and during the period of her natural life, remainder on her death to *EF*," *CD* has the life estate and *EF* has the remainder. Nothing remains to the grantor *AB*.

The granting clause also contains an expression of the consideration for the conveyance. This can be expressed as "one dollar and other valuable considerations."

## The Legal Description

The deed must contain an accurate and specific legal description of the property conveyed and indicate the county where it is located. We have seen in our discussion of propositions that a street address may suffice for residential properties. But this is not true in the case of a deed, in which an exact legal description must be used. This is generally obtainable from the abstract of title or a proper survey.

## Statement of Encumbrances

Following the legal description, the deed generally contains a statement of existing encumbrances, indicating that the property is conveyed subject to such encumbrances.

Some examples:

☐ Subject to the unpaid balance of a mortgage in the original principal sum of $25,000 executed to the Last National Bank of Anytown on April 1, this year, and recorded in Mortgage Book 1, page 1. (If an assumption of the mortgage is involved, the language "which unpaid balance grantee herein assumes and agrees to pay" would be added.)

☐ Subject to taxes for this year due and payable in next year and subject to taxes due and payable thereafter.

☐ Subject to the unpaid balance of a certain sewer assessment, Municipal Assessment Record 2, page 2, which unpaid balance grantee herein assumes and agrees to pay.

☐ Subject to all covenants and restrictions of record.

☐ Subject to all easements of record, and subject to all legal highways and rights of way.

## Signature Clause

The signature clause in the deed contains the date of execution and the signatures of the grantors. All grantors and the spouses of those who are married must sign exactly as their names appear in the granting clause.

## Acknowledgments

Most states require that all conveyances be acknowledged before a public official, such as a notary public, if the individuals desire to record the deed. The grantors appear before such an officer and acknowledge the execution of the conveyance to be their voluntary act and deed. The officer certifies this fact on the instrument, signs it, attaches his or her seal, and states the date of expiration of his or her commission.

The acknowledgment is almost always necessary to entitle the deed to be recorded.

## Recording

A properly executed deed is effectual between the parties without recording, but in order to be effectual against all the world, it must be recorded in the proper office. When it has been so recorded, its existence is known to all the world. For example, if *AB* conveyed to *CD*, who failed to record the deed, and later *AB* conveyed to *EF*, who recorded his deed, *EF*'s title, assuming that *EF* had no actual knowledge of the prior deed and paid a valuable consideration in good faith, would be superior to *CD*'s title. *CD* would be left with a remedy against *AB*, the original grantor, for fraud.

## PROPERTY MANAGEMENT

Another area in the real estate industry that works with contractual agreement is property management. It uses two types of contracts, the lease and, in most cases, a second contract that establishes a principal and agency relationship.

Property management includes the management of any property occupied by a tenant rather than the owner alone. Such properties range from farmlands to the largest high-rise, commercial-residential centers being constructed today. The property manager's job includes leasing, the collection of rents, and coordinating the services and maintenance the tenants require.

### Licensing Requirements

The leasing and management of real estate for others has become a specialized aspect of the real estate business, and the professional property manager performs an important function quite apart from the brokerage business. This function has become important enough that most licensing statutes now require a broker's or salesperson's license for those who are engaged in the management and leasing of property belonging to others.

A fine distinction is usually drawn, however, to exempt from the real estate licensing law provisions those who are full-time employees of the owner of a particular apartment or shopping center complex. Also exempt are employees of corporations, such as oil companies, which own many pieces of real estate used in connection with their primary business. Since the full-time employee of such a property owner is not engaged in offering property management services for a fee to the general public, he or she may be exempted from the licensing requirements. The theory here is that the full-time property manager is subject to all the normal employer-employee rules, and incompetence can be dealt with by discharge from employment. Presumably, the owner of properties substantial enough to require in-house management is sophisticated enough to make the protection of mandatory licensing procedures unnecessary. So far as the general public is concerned, however, the performance of property management services for a fee is regulated, just as brokerage services are regulated.

## Professional Qualifications

When one undertakes to perform property management and leasing services for the general public on a fee basis, local real estate licensing laws generally come into play. More important, so does the law of principal and agent. One who manages property for a fee is represented to the public as an expert or professional in the field, and the law requires several qualifications and imposes some sanctions on his or her conduct.

The qualifications required of the property manager by the law are similar to those required of real estate brokers and other professionals who purport to have the necessary qualifications to represent others. Quite simply, when one purports to be a professional property manager, the law requires that one *be* a professional. That is, the property manager must have a certain level of expertise in the field, and the failure to have it does not relieve the manager from liability for losses suffered by the owner as a result of incompetent management. The law recognizes this requirement in an appropriate lawsuit charging mismanagement by the professional property manager.

While the trend in property management is toward specializing in specific types of buildings, the property manager must have certain basic skills to be able to perform the job well. The manager must be familiar with local economic conditions and must have the necessary business connections to be able to provide information to clients as requested.

## The Fiduciary Relationship

More important than the question of competence is the fact that the property manager is an *agent* of the owner and has therefore assumed the responsibilities of a fiduciary. The fiduciary relationship that exists between agent and principal is jealously protected by our legal system, for it is based on mutual trust and confidence. The agent owes a high duty of loyalty to the principal and may not deal with the principal as a stranger.

As a result, the property manager is under strict requirements to account for all funds, to refrain from accepting unrevealed rebates (kickbacks) from suppliers and contractors, and to refrain from making personal profit on transactions entered into on behalf of the principal. This is not to say that the fee arrangement between the principal (property owner) and the agent (property manager) is not flexible enough to permit incentives and rewards for better than average performance. Quite the contrary—such arrangements are common. Nevertheless, the total compensation of the property manager must be made known to the employing property owner.

## Functions of the Property Manager

Among the principal functions of a property manager are:

- [ ] Securing desirable tenants at attractive rates through proper marketing of the property
- [ ] Collecting rents
- [ ] Overseeing appropriate maintenance functions of the property, including the purchase of supplies and goods required for repairs
- [ ] Maintaining good public relations
- [ ] Maintaining complete and accurate accounting, including the issuance of periodic reports

### Preparing the Income Statement

The professional property manager prepares a budget, reviews it with the owner, and, upon their mutual agreement, must then live with this forecast, managing the property within the budget. The periodic statement of receipts and disbursements is matched against the budget and usually appears in this form:

*Income*
Rental income (apartments, stores, offices)
Parking fees
Other income (vending machines, washers, dryers)
Gross possible income
Less: vacancies and collection losses
Total actual income collected

*Expenses*
Payroll
Supplies
Maintenance and repair fees (plumbing, electric, carpentry, painting and decorating services)
Utilities (electricity, water, gas, fuel)
Administrative (management fees, other)

Taxes and insurance (insurance, real estate taxes, other taxes)

Total operating expenses

*Net operating income*

In addition to the statement of receipts and disbursements, an *operating statement* (profit and loss) might be prepared to interpret expenses. This statement is prepared on an accrual rather than a cash basis and may include accrued taxes, depreciation, and amortization of certain expenses.

The manager will also report such *nonoperating expenses* as a mortgage payment, which is called *debt service*. After deduction of all expenses and debt service from the income from all sources, the amount left over for the owner is called *cash flow*.

*Determining the Level of Rent*

The level of rent to be paid may be determined by any one of several different types of leases:

☐ *Fixed rate.* A type of rental payment that requires that the same amount of rent be paid each period throughout the lease. The typical apartment lease might be written this way.

☐ *Step-up rate.* A type of rental payment that allows for a graduated increase in the rate over the life of the lease. Many office leases are written on this basis.

☐ *Percentage rate.* A type of lease that allows for a base rate of rental income plus an additional increment based on the tenant's gross or net sales. Many merchant leases are written this way.

☐ *Reappraisal basis.* A lease with a reappraisal clause that allows the lessor to have the property reappraised periodically and to adjust the rent based on the value of the property determined by appraisal. Many automobile showrooms are leased on this basis.

A successful property manager is one who selects tenants carefully from those who will be able to meet the financial obligation being entered into in a lease. From the collection of rents, the manager must be capable of maintaining proper financial controls and records for reporting to the owner of the property.

**Certified Property Manager**

The Certified Property Manager (CPM) is a REALTOR® who specializes in property management and is a member of the Institute of Real Estate Management (IREM). IREM, along with other professional real property management authorities, indicates that the following points should be included in management contracts:

☐ A complete and accurate description of the property to be managed
☐ Definite beginning and ending dates for the duration of the contract
☐ A statement of the compensation to the manager and the method to be used for its calculation
☐ A listing of the duties the property manager is to perform during the contract, including limitations on authority
☐ Types of reports required and the frequency of such reports

Property management is a complex topic, but it can be broken down into three basic functions the property manager must perform: (1) to market the property so as to secure tenants who provide income; (2) to maintain financial records for the property, indicating what controls have been placed over income and expense items, and (3) to provide basic services, such as maintenance and security, for tenants. Above all, it must be remembered that the basic goal of the property manager is to provide the highest possible net return to the property owner while seeing to it that the investment is preserved.

## REVIEW QUESTIONS

1. The difference between exclusive right to sell and exclusive agency is

   (A) the agent's promise to pay all promotional expenses
   (B) the principal's reservation of the right to sell his or her own home
   (C) the principal's reservation of the right to pay the agent no commission
   (D) the principal's reservation of the right to pay the agent no commission if the principal should sell the property

2. When an agent has produced a buyer who is ready, willing, and able to buy under the conditions of the listing contract, the agent has generally

   (A) consummated the sale
   (B) established his or her personal competence
   (C) earned a commission
   (D) accounted to the principal

3. An agency agreement may be terminated by all of the following EXCEPT

   (A) revocation by the principal

    (B)  reciprocity
    (C)  renunciation by the agent
    (D)  mutual consent

4.  When a salesperson dies, his or her listings

    (A)  become unenforceable and have to be relisted
    (B)  remain in force because they belong to the principal broker
    (C)  become part of the salesperson's estate and must be probated
    (D)  revert to the real estate commission for relisting

5.  A real estate listing contract is

    (A)  a list of all property owned by one person
    (B)  a list of all property for purposes of taxation
    (C)  the employment of a broker by the owner to sell real property
    (D)  a universal agency agreement

6.  The relationship of a licensed real estate broker to the principal is that of a

    (A)  salesperson    (C)  superior
    (B)  beneficiary    (D)  fiduciary

7.  A salesperson may receive a commission directly from

    (A)  a co-broker
    (B)  the owner
    (C)  another salesperson
    (D)  his or her principal broker

8.  An authorization to a person to act for and on behalf of another in a real estate transaction to purchase a lot creates a

    (A)  special agency    (C)  general agency
    (B)  universal agency    (D)  escrow agency

9.  An attorney-in-fact is the holder of

    (A)  a power of attorney
    (B)  a law degree
    (C)  a listing
    (D)  a decree from a court

10.  When a buyer does not have enough money for the earnest money deposit requested,

    (A)  the broker should lend the difference to the buyer from the escrow account
    (B)  the broker may take a postdated check and hold it for deposit in the escrow account later
    (C)  the broker should take a check, not deposit it, and attach it to the offer
    (D)  the broker can take less money than requested and deposit it in the escrow account

11.  Once an agreement of sale is signed by both parties, the purchaser has

    (A)  legal title    (C)  real title
    (B)  equitable title    (D)  blind title

12.  A seller of real estate is also known as a

    (A)  grantee    (C)  vendee
    (B)  vendor    (D)  broker

13.  When the contract for sale of real property includes personal property as well, the seller should provide which of the following?

    (A)  Bill of sale
    (B)  Chattel mortgage
    (C)  Estoppel certificate
    (D)  A registered mortgage

14.  An option contract differs from a contract of sale in that the

    (A)  contract of sale requires consideration
    (B)  option needs no consideration
    (C)  option need not be consummated
    (D)  contract of sale is enforceable by either party to it

15.  An option without valid consideration is

    (A)  valid    (C)  revocable
    (B)  void    (D)  enforceable

16.  The clause in a deed that sets forth the interests being conveyed is the

    (A)  habendum clause
    (B)  testimonium clause
    (C)  indenture clause
    (D)  demure clause

17.  A legal document that transfers legal possession of real property but does not transfer ownership is a

    (A)  deed    (C)  deposition
    (B)  mortgage    (D)  lease

18.  The act of taking private property for public benefit is called

    (A)  condemnation
    (B)  eminent domain
    (C)  police powers
    (D)  none of the above

19.  The deed must be executed by

    (A)  grantor only
    (B)  grantee or grantor
    (C)  lender, grantor, and grantee
    (D)  grantee only

20. Which of the following is **not** a function of the property manager acting for the owner?

(A)  Securing desirable tenants

(B)  Collecting rents

(C)  Maintaining good public relations

(D)  Reinvesting profits from rents

# Chapter 16
# Real Estate Mathematics

THIS chapter reviews the mathematical skills necessary for success in the real estate business and in the uniform examinations. The exam problems are presented in narrative or story format, and you must be able to read the problem and supply the correct answer based on your interpretation of the information. The problems cover fractions, decimals, percentages, area, volume, perimeter, and the proration methods needed in settlement problems.

## FRACTIONS

A fraction is a quotient of two numbers. (It need not be the quotient of two *whole* numbers.) The top number of a fraction, called the numerator, represents the dividend. The bottom number of the fraction, called the denominator, represents the divisor. Thus $3 \div 4 = 3/4$ where the 3 is the numerator and 4 is the denominator. A fraction of this form, where the numerator is less than the denominator, is called a simple fraction and always has a value less than one. So 1/2, 19/32, 52/100, 191/231 are all simple fractions. If the numerator is larger than the denominator, the fraction is called an improper fraction. For example, 4/3 is an improper fraction. If the division were completed, it would result in a mixed number ( a whole number plus a simple fraction: $1\frac{1}{3}$).

Each fraction should be reduced to the lowest possible terms or converted to a mixed number upon the completion of each problem.

### Addition and Subtraction of Fractions

Before two or more fractions can be added or subtracted, each must be put in terms common to the other. This is called finding the common denominator. The simplest way to find a common denominator is to multiply both the numerator (top) and denominator (bottom) of one fraction by the denominator (bottom) of the other fraction. Then repeat the process on the second fraction, using the denominator from the first.

After the common denominator is found, the addition or subtraction may be performed by adding or subtracting the numerator. Finally, the fraction should be reduced to its lowest terms.

*Example (Addition)*

$1/7 + 3/8 = ?$
$1/7 \times 8/8 = 8/56$
$3/8 \times 7/7 = 21/56$

Now add the numerators:

$$\frac{8}{56} + \frac{21}{56} = \frac{29}{56}$$

*Example (Subtraction)*

$7/9 - 1/4 = ?$
$7/9 \times 4/4 = 28/36$
$1/4 \times 9/9 = 9/36$

Now subtract the numerators:

$$\frac{28}{36} - \frac{9}{36} = \frac{19}{36}$$

When more than two fractions are to be added, multiply the numerator and denominator of each fraction by the denominators of the other fractions and then add the numerators over the common denominator.

*Example*

$1/4 + 3/5 + 7/9 = ?$
$1/4 \times 5/5 \times 9/9 = 45/180$
$3/5 \times 4/4 \times 9/9 = 108/180$
$7/9 \times 4/4 \times 5/5 = 140/180$

Now add:

$$\frac{45}{180} + \frac{108}{180} + \frac{140}{180} = \frac{293}{180} \text{ or } 1\frac{113}{180}$$

## Multiplication of Fractions

To multiply two or more fractions, place the product of the numerator over the product of the denominator and reduce to the lowest terms.

*Example*

$3/4 \times 2/3 = ?$

$$\frac{3 \times 2}{4 \times 3} = \frac{6}{12} = \frac{1}{2}$$

*Example*

$9/10 \times 3/5 \times 4/7 = ?$

$$\frac{9 \times 3 \times 4}{10 \times 5 \times 7} = \frac{108}{350} = \frac{54}{175}$$

## Division of Fractions by Fractions

In the division of fractions, the first fraction is the dividend and the second is the divisor. In order to divide a fraction by a fraction, invert (turn upside down) the divisor and multiply the two numbers as you did in multiplying two fractions.

*Example*

$5/12 \div 2/3 = ?$
$5/12 \times 3/2 = 15/24 = 5/8$

## Cancellation between Fractions

Cancellation is the taking out of factors (numbers) common to both numerator and denominator before multiplying or dividing. This is done by comparing the numerator of one fraction to the denominator of another and dividing out the common factor.

*Example*

$$\frac{35}{84} \times \frac{21}{25} = \overset{7}{\underset{4}{\cancel{35}}}{\underset{}{84}} \times \overset{1}{\underset{5}{\cancel{21}}}{\underset{}{25}}$$

$$= 7/4 \times 1/5 = 7/20$$

The common factors were 5 and 21.

## DECIMALS

A decimal is merely the numerator of a fraction following the decimal point when the denominator of the fraction is 10, 100, 1000, etc. If the numerator is one place to the right of the decimal point, the denominator of the fraction is 10; if it is two places or two numerals to the right, then the denominator is 100, and so on.

*Example*

$.3 = 3/10 =$ three tenths
$.03 = 3/100 =$ three hundredths
$.003 = 3/1000 =$ three thousandths

## Converting Fractions to Decimals

To change a fraction to a decimal, simply divide the numerator (top) by the denominator (bottom) and express the answer in decimal form.

*Example*

$3/5 = 3 \div 5 = .60$

*or*

$$5 \overline{\smash{\big)}\ 3.00} \quad \overset{.60}{}$$

If in dividing the last number a series or a repeating number occurs, round off the third digit. If the third digit is less than 5, drop the number. If it is greater than 5, raise the second digit to the next highest number.

*Example*

$$1/3 = 3 \overline{\smash{\big)}\,1.000} \overset{.333}{} = .33$$

$$2/3 = 3 \overline{\smash{\big)}\,2.000} \overset{.666}{} = .67$$

## Adding or Subtracting Decimals

Place the numbers in the proper columns, always keeping the decimal points aligned one above the other, and perform the function.

*Example*

$$\begin{array}{r} 1.075 \\ + .18 \\ \hline 1.255 \end{array} \quad or \quad \begin{array}{r} 1.075 \\ - .18 \\ \hline .895 \end{array}$$

## Multiplying Decimals

Multiply decimals just as you would whole numbers. Once the product is obtained, begin at the right of the decimal point and count the total number of digits to the right contained in all numbers being multiplied. This will tell you how many digits are to be to the right of the decimal point in the product.

*Example*

$$\begin{array}{r} 6.3 \\ \times 2.11 \\ \hline 13.293 \end{array}$$

(1 digit to right of the decimal point)
(2 digits to right of the decimal point)
(3 digits to right of the decimal point)

*Example*

$$\begin{array}{r} 6.7 \\ \times .002 \\ \hline .0134 \end{array}$$

In the last example there were not enough whole numbers to fill the four columns to the right of the decimal point, so a zero was inserted to fill the spot.

## Dividing Decimals

It is easiest to divide by moving the decimal point of the divisor to the right until it becomes a whole number. The decimal point of the dividend must then be moved the same number of places to the right. Then perform normal division by whole numbers.

*Example*

$$5.5 \overline{\smash{\big)}\,31.36} \quad becomes \quad 550 \overline{\smash{\big)}\,3136.0} \overset{5.7}{}$$

## PERCENTAGES

*Percent* or a percentage sign (%) indicates that a whole number or quantity has been divided into 100 equal parts, and the given percentage represents the number of parts to be used. To convert a percentage to a decimal, move the decimal point two places to the left. To convert a decimal to a percentage, move the decimal point two places to the right and add the percentage sign.

*Example*

25% means 25 one-hundredths
*or*   25/100   *or*   .25

*Example*

30% = .30
3.5% = .035

## PRACTICE PROBLEMS: FRACTIONS, DECIMALS, PERCENTAGES

### Fractions

Add the following fractions.

1.  1/6 + 1/8 =
2.  3/7 + 4/9 =
3.  19/20 + 3/5 =
4.  1/8 + 5/12 =
5.  3/4 + 1/16 =

Subtract the following fractions.

6.  1/6 − 1/8 =
7.  4/7 − 4/9 =
8.  19/20 − 3/5 =
9.  5/12 − 1/8 =
10.  3/4 − 1/16 =

Multiply the following fractions.

11.  1/8 × 1/4 =
12.  1/9 × 11/12 =
13.  3/4 × 7/16 =
14.  4/5 × 8/9 =
15.  5/12 × 1/5 =

Divide the following fractions.

16.  1/8 ÷ 1/4 =
17.  1/9 ÷ 11/12 =

18.   3/4 ÷ 7/6 =
19.   4/5 ÷ 8/9 =
20.   5/12 ÷ 1/5 =

## Decimals and Percentages

Add the following decimals.

1.   .5 + .075 + .125 =
2.   .073 + 1.25 + .93 =
3.   .82 + .73 + 2.584 =
4.   .0016 + 1.043 + .3 =

Subtract the following decimals.

5.   1.25 − .075 =
6.   .073 − .0016 =
7.   1.4874 − .896 =
8.   2.043 − 1.0012 =

Multiply the following decimals.

9.   .075 × 1.257 =
10.   .342 × .0017 =
11.   .7589 × 1.2 =
12.   .346 × 3.476 =

Divide the following decimals.

13.   .34 ÷ .516 =
14.   1.25 ÷ .07 =
15.   .78 ÷ .4 =
16.   1.29 ÷ .432 =

Change the following percentages to decimals.

17.   75% =
18.   125% =
19.   27.56% =
20.   43.2% =

Change the following decimals to percentages.

21.   .0025 =
22.   .567 =
23.   .493 =
24.   3.475 =

*(Answers: page 256)*

## RATIOS

A fraction that is used to show comparison is called a *ratio*. To say that ⅔ of the buildings on a block are single-family residences means that two of every three buildings on that block are single-family homes. This may be expressed as a ratio by comparing the smaller number to the larger or the larger number to the smaller.

*Example*

The ratio of single-family homes to the total number of buildings is 2 to 3, or 2:3.

*or*

Of every three buildings, two are single-family residences, a 3:2 ratio.

## GEOMETRIC FORMULAS FOR REAL ESTATE

Before studying geometric formulas, we must refresh ourselves about the concepts of squares and square root and cube and cube root.

### Squares and Square Roots

When a number is multiplied by itself, it is said to be squared.

Thus, in the equation $3 \times 3 = 9$, the number 9 is said to be 3 squared. The number 3 squared is usually written $3^2$. Thus

$$3 \times 3 = 3^2 = 9 \quad or \quad 5 \times 5 = 5^2 = 25$$

Just as 9 can be thought of as 3 squared, 3 is the square root of 9. In equations, the concept square root is designated by the symbol $\sqrt{\phantom{x}}$ .

Thus the square root of 9 is written

$$\sqrt{9} = 3 \quad and \quad \sqrt{25} = 5$$

We can easily discover the square of a number; we simply multiply the number by itself.

The square roots of numbers are harder to determine. Some we know intuitively. For example,

$$\sqrt{100} = 10 \quad and \quad \sqrt{81} = 9$$

But what is the square root of 85?

$$85 = ?$$

We know that the answer is a number larger than 9 but smaller than 10. There are mathematical formulas that allow us to compute square roots, but they are cumbersome. If your real estate work requires that you use square roots, you should obtain a table of square roots. Such tables appear in many math books.

### Cubes and Cube Roots

When a number is twice multiplied by itself, it is said to be cubed. Thus

$$3 \times 3 \times 3 = 27$$

Note that 3 cubed may be written $3^3$. Similarly, 5 cubed is

$$5^3 = 5 \times 5 \times 5 = 125$$

Just as 125 is 5 cubed, 5 is the cube root of 125 and 3 is the cube root of 27.

We can easily discover the cube of a number by appropriate multiplication. But we should turn to a table if it is necessary to obtain cube roots.

## The Measurement of Area

The real estate agent must often determine the area of a flat or plane surface. The area of a particular lot or the total amount of floor space in a house may become an element in the property negotiation. The shapes of lots and other spaces may be infinitely complex, but most spaces can be broken down into three basic shapes for which it is possible to compute areas: quadrilaterals (four-sided shapes), triangles (three-sided shapes), and circles.

Area is expressed in "square" units; we refer to square inches, square feet, and square yards. A square foot is a unit of area that is one foot long by one foot wide, or 12 inches on each side, or the equivalent. A square yard is a unit of area that is one yard, or 36 inches, on each side, or the equivalent. One square yard is equal to 9 square feet, as can be readily seen in this diagram:

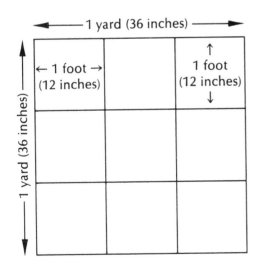

One square foot equals 144 square inches.

## Rectangles

The most common form of quadrilateral is a rectangle. The opposite sides of a rectangle are of equal length, and the sides of the rectangle are parallel; that is, all the interior angles are equal to 90 degrees. A square is a special form of rectangle in which all four sides are equal.

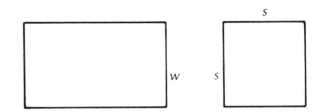

The area of a rectangle may be found by using the formula $A = lw$, where $A$ = area, $l$ = length (the measure of the longer side), and $w$ = width (the measure of the shorter side). By multiplying the length by the width, the area of a rectangle may be found.

When the area of a rectangle is known and the measure of one side is known, the measure of the remaining side may be determined by dividing the area $(A)$ by the measure of the known side.

*Example*

What is the floor space of a building which has a length of 60 feet and a width of 40 feet?

*Solution*

Area = length $\times$ width
$A$   = $lw$
$A$   = 60 feet $\times$ 40 feet
$A$   = 2,400 square feet

*Example*

If we know the area of a building is 2,400 square feet and its length is 60 feet, what is the width?

$A$ = 2,400 square feet
$l$ = 60 feet
$w$ = ?

*Solution*

$$A \div l = w$$
2,400 $\div$ 60 = 40 feet

## Squares

Since the square is a special case of the rectangle, with all four sides equal in length, you need to know only the measure of one side $(s)$ to find the area of the square.

*Example*

Area = side $\times$ side
$A$   = $s \times s$ or $s^2$
$A$   = 20 feet $\times$ 20 feet
$A$   = 400 square feet

## Triangles

The area of a triangle is equal to one-half the measure of the base times the height. The height is measured at a right angle from the base to the apex, which is the point where the two sloping sides of the triangle meet.

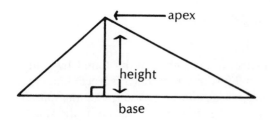

### Example

What is the area (in square feet) of a triangle with a base of 40 feet and a height of 10 feet?

### Solution

Area = 1/2 base × height
$A$   = 1/2 $bh$
$A$   = 1/2 (40 feet × 10 feet)
$A$   = 1/2 (400)
$A$   = 200 square feet

## Right Triangles

The right triangle is unique in that one side is always perpendicular (at a right angle) to the base of the triangle, so the height is equal to the perpendicular side of the triangle.

Another characteristic of a right triangle is that if the lengths of any two sides are known, the length of the third side may be found. This is based on the Pythagorean theorem, which states that the square of the length of the hypotenuse of a right triangle is equal to the sum of the squares of the lengths of the other two sides.

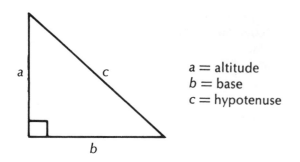

$a$ = altitude
$b$ = base
$c$ = hypotenuse

$c^2 = a^2 + b^2$
The length of side $c = \sqrt{a^2 + b^2}$
The length of side $a = \sqrt{c^2 - b^2}$
The length of side $b = \sqrt{c^2 - a^2}$

### Example

If $a$ = 30 feet and $b$ = 40 feet, what is the length of c?
$c^2 = a^2 + b^2$
$c = \sqrt{a^2 + b^2}$
$c = \sqrt{(30)^2 + (40)^2}$
$c = \sqrt{900 + 1600}$
$c = \sqrt{2500}$
$c = 50$

## Circles

The circumference of a circle is the distance around the outside of the circle. The diameter is the straight-line distance, passing through the center, between two opposite points on the circumference. The radius is the distance from the center of the circle to a point on the circumference.

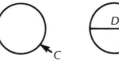  

The value of pi ($\pi$) is needed to compute various dimensions of a circle. $\pi$ is equal to the circumference divided by the diameter, so $\pi$ =3.1416. This value is very close to the fraction 22/7. (For most real estate calculations, the fraction 22/7 will be adequate as a value for $\pi$.)

The circumference (C) of a circle is equal to $\pi$ times the diameter (D): $C = \pi D$.

The diameter (D) of a circle is equal to the circumference (C) divided by $\pi$: $D = C \div \pi$.

The radius (r) is equal to the diameter (D) divided by 2: $r = D \div 2$.

Area (A) is equal to $\pi$ times the radius squared ($r^2$): $A = \pi r^2$.

### Example

A circular lot has a diameter of 20 feet.
1.  What is the circumference of the lot?
    $C = \pi D$
    $C = 3.1416 \times 20$ feet
    $C = 62.832$ feet
2.  What is the radius of the circle?
    $r = D \div 2$
    $r = 20$ feet $\div 2$
    $r = 10$ feet
3.  What is the area of the circle?
    $A = \pi r^2$
    $A = 3.1416 \times 10 \times 10$
    $A = 314.16$ square feet

## Rhomboids

Rhomboids are four-sided shapes (quadrilaterals) in which the opposite sides are parallel but the internal angles are not right angles. Necessarily, two angles are oblique (more than 90 degrees). A special case of the rhomboid is the rhombus, in which all four sides of the shape are of equal length.

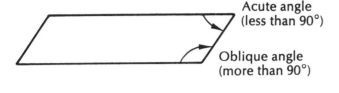

Acute angle (less than 90°)

Oblique angle (more than 90°)

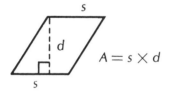

Rhombus

The area of a rhomboid is found by multiplying the length of one of the parallel sides *(s)* by the vertical distance between the parallel sides *(d)*.

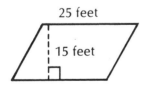

$$A = s \times d$$

*Example*

What is the area of the following figure?

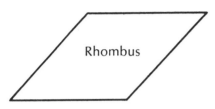

25 feet

15 feet

$A = s \times d$
$A = 25 \text{ feet} \times 15 \text{ feet}$
$A = 375 \text{ square feet}$

## Trapezoids

A quadrilateral that has only two parallel sides is called a trapezoid. Here *a* is parallel to *b*, and *h* equals the vertical distance between sides *a* and *b*.

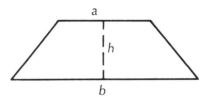

The area of a trapezoid is equal to one-half the sum of the parallel sides times the distance between them.

$$A = \frac{a + b}{2} \times h$$

*Example*

What is the area of the following figure?

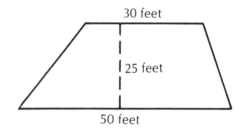

30 feet

25 feet

50 feet

$$A = \frac{a + b}{2} \times h$$

$$A = \frac{30 \text{ feet} + 50 \text{ feet}}{2} \times 25 \text{ feet}$$

$A = 40 \text{ feet} \times 25 \text{ feet}$
$A = 1,000 \text{ square feet}$

## The Area of Odd-Shaped Figures

Quite often the real estate agent must determine the area of a lot that does not have a regular shape. Usually the lot can be broken down into a series of figures for which area can be determined.

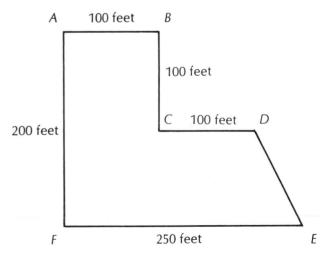

The figure above breaks down into three geometric shapes that are easy to work with:

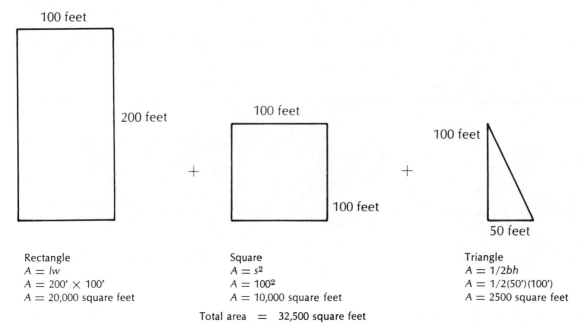

| Rectangle | Square | Triangle |
|---|---|---|
| $A = lw$ | $A = s^2$ | $A = 1/2bh$ |
| $A = 200' \times 100'$ | $A = 100^2$ | $A = 1/2(50')(100')$ |
| $A = 20{,}000$ square feet | $A = 10{,}000$ square feet | $A = 2500$ square feet |

Total area  =  32,500 square feet

## Perimeter

Perimeter is the distance around the outside of a two-dimensional figure. The perimeters of figures with straight sides can be computed by adding up the lengths of the sides.

The perimeter of a circle, or its circumference, is computed by the formula $P = \pi d$, or 22/7 *d*.

*Examples*

Compute the perimeters of the following figures.

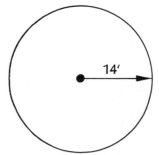

$P = \pi d$

$= \dfrac{22}{7} \times 28 = 88$ feet

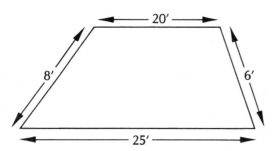

$P = 8 + 20 + 6 + 25 = 59$ feet

## Volume

An area problem is concerned with two dimensions, such as length and width. It yields results in square units—square feet, square yards, etc. A volume problem deals in three dimensions—cubic feet, cubic yards, etc.

*Rectangular Volume*

The volume of a rectangular space, such as the volume of a room, is its length times its width times its height.

$V = l \times w \times h$

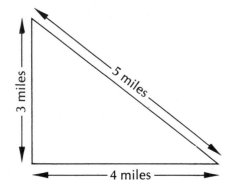

$P = 3 + 5 + 4 = 12$ miles

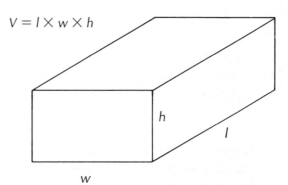

*Example*

Determine the volume of a room that is 15 feet long and 9 feet wide, with an 8-foot ceiling height.

$V = l \times w \times h$
$V = 15 \times 9 \times 8$
$V = 1{,}080$ cubic feet

## Volume of a Triangular Figure

The volume of a triangular area such as an attic space may be readily seen if we understand intuitively that the volume is the area of the triangle times the length of the room.

$V = 1/2 \ (b \times h \times l)$

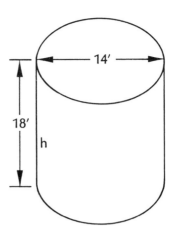

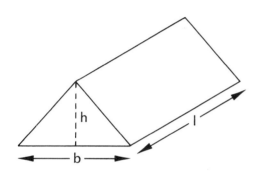

*Example*

What is the volume of a crawl space 4 feet high at the apex, if the floor area is 15 feet long and 9 feet wide?

$V = 1/2 \ (b \times h \times l)$
$V = 1/2 \ (9 \times 4 \times 15)$
$V = 270$ cubic feet

## Volume of a Cylinder

The volume of a cylinder is the area of the circular base $(\pi r^2)$ times the height.

$V = \pi r^2 h$

*Example*

What is the volume of a water tank 14 feet in diameter and 18 feet high?

$V = \pi r^2 h$

$V = \dfrac{22}{7} \times 7^2 \times 18$

$V = 2{,}772$ cubic feet

## Basic Formulas for the Solution of Math Problems

| | |
|---|---|
| Area = length × width | $A = L \times W$ |
| Interest = principal × rate | $I = P \times R$ |
| Interest = mortgage × rate | $I = M \times R$ |
| Cost = selling price × rate | $C = SP \times R$ |
| Tax = assessment × rate | $T = A \times R$ |
| Percentage = base × rate | $P = B \times R$ |
| Value = income × factor | $V = I \times F$ |
| Income = value × rate | $I = V \times R$ |
| Selling price = rent × gross rent multiplier | $SP = R \times GRM$ |
| Net income = gross income − expense | $NI = GI - E$ |
| Commission = selling price × rate | $C = SP \times R$ |

Circumference of a circle = 3.1416 × diameter

Diameter of a circle = 0.31831 × circumference

Area of a circle = 3.1416 × square of radius, or .7854 × square of diameter

## Area Equivalents

| Area | Acres | Metric Area (square kilometers) |
|---|---|---|
| Township | 23,040 | 93.312 |
| Section | 640 | 2.592 |
| 1/2 section | 320 | 1.296 |
| 1/4 section | 160 | .648 |
| 1/8 section | 80 | .324 |
| 1/16 section | 40 | .162 |
| 1/32 section | 20 | .081 |
| 1/64 section | 10 | .0405 |

## Linear Equivalents

Pole = 5.5 yards = 5.03 meters
Furlong = 220.0 yards = 201.168 meters
Perch = 5.5 yards = 5.03 meters

Broad = 22.0 yards = 20.12 meters
Hectare = 2.47 acres = 9,995.72 square meters
Degree = 69.167 miles = 111.359 kilometers
Minute = 1.153 miles = 1.856 kilometers
Second = 101.376 feet = 35.635 meters

## Area Conversion Table

| To convert from: | to: | multiply by: |
|---|---|---|
| Square inches | square centimeters | 6.452 |
| Square feet | square meters | 0.093 |
| Square yards | square meters | 0.836 |
| Acres | square meters | 4,046.849 |
| Square miles | square kilometers | 2.592 |

## Examples of One-Acre Equivalents

| | | | | |
|---|---|---|---|---|
| 10 | rods | by | 16 | rods |
| 8 | rods | by | 20 | rods |
| 5 | rods | by | 32 | rods |
| 4 | rods | by | 40 | rods |
| 5 | yards | by | 968 | yards |
| 20 | yards | by | 242 | yards |
| 10 | yards | by | 484 | yards |
| 40 | yards | by | 121 | yards |
| 220 | feet | by | 198 | feet |
| 110 | feet | by | 396 | feet |
| 60 | feet | by | 726 | feet |
| 120 | feet | by | 363 | feet |
| 300 | feet | by | 145.2 | feet |
| 400 | feet | by | 108.9 | feet |

## Other Conversions

320 rods = 1 mile
144 square inches = 1 square foot
9 square feet = 1 square yard
272¼ square feet = 1 square rod
30¼ square yards = 1 square rod
7.92 inches = 1 link, 25 links = 1 rod
100 links = 66 feet = 22 yards = 4 rods = 1 chain
10 chains long by 1 broad, or 10 square chains = 1 acre
1 acre = 160 square rods = 4,840 square yards = 43,560
   square feet
30¼ square yards = 1 square rod, perch, or pole
40 square rods = 1 rood
4 roods = 1 acre
2.47 acres = 1 hectare
640 acres = 1 square mile = 1 section
36 square miles or 36 sections = 1 township

## Metric Equivalents

| 1 kilometer (km) | = | 100 decameters (dm) |
|---|---|---|
| | = | 1,000 meters (m) |
| | = | 100,000 centimeters (cm) |
| | = | 1,000,000 millimeters (mm) |

| 1 decameter (dm) | = | 10 meters (m) |
|---|---|---|
| | = | 1,000 centimeters (cm) |
| | = | 10,000 millimeters (mm) |
| 1 meter (m) | = | 100 centimeters (cm) |
| | = | 1,000 millimeters (mm) |
| 1 centimeter (cm) | = | 10 millimeters (mm) |

## Metric Conversions

| To convert from: | to: | multiply by: |
|---|---|---|
| Inches | Centimeters | 2.54 |
| Feet | Meters | .305 |
| Yards | Meters | .9144 |
| Rods | Meters | 5.03 |
| Chains | Meters | 20.13 |
| Links | Centimeters | 20.04 |
| Miles | Kilometers | 1.61 |
| Centimeters | Inches | .394 |
| Meters | Feet | 3.28 |
| Meters | Yards | 1.09 |
| Meters | Rods | 5.995 |
| Meters | Chains | .0497 |
| Centimeters | Links | .0499 |
| Kilometers | Miles | .621 |

## PRACTICE PROBLEMS: PERIMETER, AREA, VOLUME

1. How many acres in a square mile?
2. How many square feet in an acre?
3. How many square feet in the property below?

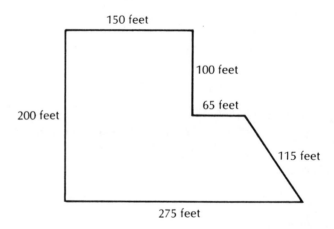

4. What is the price of a lot measuring 373' × 154' at a cost of $1,000 per acre?
5. How many acres are contained in a lot 300' × 450'?
6. If concrete costs $16.50 per cubic yard and labor costs are $.20 a square foot, what would be the cost to build a driveway 28 feet long, 9 feet wide, and 6 inches thick?

7. Building restrictions are such that a 20-foot front yard setback, a 15-foot back yard setback, and a side yard setback of 15 feet are required. How much area on the lot is buildable if the dimensions are 120′ × 150′?

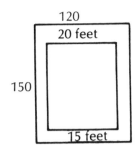

8. Farmer A wants to lease a portion of his farm to Farmer B for cultivation. Farmer B is willing to pay $50 an acre for the tillable land. The area in question has a large pond in the center of it. The outside dimensions are 310 × 240 rods. The pond is circular and has a diameter of 90 rods. How many acres is Farmer B leasing and what is the cost of the lease?

9. How far would a person have to walk to go completely around a circular 1-acre pond with a diameter of 14.28 rods?

10. Compute the cubic content of an industrial warehouse that is 260′ × 340′ and has an average height of 40 feet.

11. A certain lot measures 80′ × 135′ and costs $.63 per square foot. A home is erected on the lot at a cost of $1.85 per cubic foot. The dimensions of the house are 40′ × 60′ × 10′. What is the value of the property?

12. What is the price of a lot measuring 264 feet wide and 660 feet deep at $800 per acre?

13. Compute the proposed cost of the following property:

| Land | 125′ × 100′ @ $ 1/square foot |
|---|---|
| Two-story building | 40′ × 60′ @ $25/square foot |
| Full basement | 40′ × 60′ @ $ 5/square foot |
| Driveway | 10′ × 80′ @ $ 4/square foot |
| Sidewalks | 3′ × 70′ @ $ 3/square foot |
| Yard improvements | $5,000 |

14. A farmer sold a real estate developer three sites of land. Site X had an area twice that of site Y. Site Y was three times larger than size Z. Site Z contained 3 acres. What is the area contained in each site and how many acres does the farmer have left in the original quarter section of land that he owns?

*(Answers: page 257)*

## COMPUTING RATES: SIMPLE CAPITALIZATION

Rate is expressed as a percentage. It is usually related to income or value of an investment. Using the simple rate formula, we can determine the income, value, or rate of return on a property.

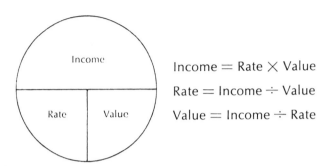

To find the income to be produced from a property with a certain value, we multiply the value by the desired rate. Income is usually a net figure.

*Example*

A man owns a building worth $50,000 and desires a 10% return from his property. What income must the property produce to attain this?

Income = Rate × Value
Income = 10% × $50,000
Income = .10 × $50,000
Income = $5,000/year to produce the desired rate of income

Using the same information, if the man knew his income and his desired rate of return and wanted to find the value of his property, he could do so using the components of the above formula.

*Example*

Income = Rate × Value
Income ÷ Rate = Value
$5,000 ÷ .10 = Value

.10 $\overline{\smash{)}\,\$5,000}$ = 1.0 $\overline{\smash{)}\,\$50,000}$

$50,000 = Value

By dividing the income by the rate, we can find the value of the property when it is unknown.

If the same man knew the value of the same property and knew his net income to be the same, using the same components he could find the rate of return on his property by dividing the income by the known value.

Income                        = Rate × Value
Income ÷ Value                = Rate
$5,000 ÷ $50,000              = Rate
                         .10 = Rate, or
converting to percentage = 10%

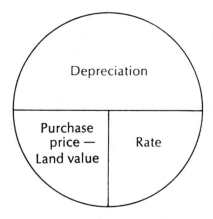

The following formulas will give the annual depreciation:

Depreciation = (Purchase price − Land value) × Rate

Purchase price − Land value = Depreciation ÷ Rate

Rate = Depreciation ÷ (Purchase price − Land value)

### PRACTICE PROBLEMS:
### RATE, INCOME, VALUE, INTEREST

1. What is the indicated value of a stream of income on a yield of $600 per month if similar incomes are yielding 8% per annum return on investment?

2. The value of a house at the end of 6 years was estimated to be $7,650. Based on a straight-line depreciation rate of 2½%, what was the original cost of the house?

3. What is the indicated value of a stream of income on a yield of $1,000 per month with an average annual yield of 13%?

4. How long will it take an investor to recapture her initial investment at a rate of 12% per year return of her money?

5. A person has a property which produces a gross income of $325 per month. Monthly expenses average $155. What is the net income per year on the property?

6. A large barn was converted into 10 apartments with the following rentals: four @ $200 per month, three @ $175 per month, and three @ $150 per month. The total expenses were $10,000, and the debt service was $6,000. What is the yield on the owner's equity if $50,000 is invested in the property? Give both the dollar figure and rate.

7. The monthly interest on a $23,000 loan is $300. What is the annual simple interest rate?

8. What is the quarterly interest payment on a loan of $40,000 with an annual interest rate of 9%?

(Answers: page 257)

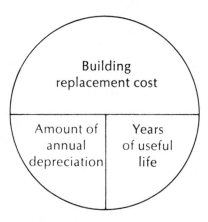

Building replacement cost = Amount of annual depreciation × Years of useful life

Amount of annual depreciation = Building replacement cost ÷ Years of useful life

Years of useful life = Building replacement cost ÷ Amount of annual depreciation

*Example*

A building has a replacement cost of $200,000 and an estimated useful life of 15 years. What is the annual depreciation?

$$\frac{\text{Replacement cost}}{\text{Years of useful life}} = \frac{\text{Amount of annual}}{\text{depreciation}}$$

$$\frac{\$200,000}{15 \text{ years}} = \$13,333 \text{ year}$$

### DEPRECIATION

Depreciation may be considered the loss in value suffered by the improvements to a property, or it may be considered also as a means of recovering the cost of those improvements for tax and investment purposes. A commonly used method of calculating depreciation is the straight-line method, which allocates the total depreciation in equal installments over the economic life of the improvements. Under the Tax Reform Act of 1986, the economic life of the real property was determined to be 27.5 years for residential and 31.5 years for commercial properties under the straight line method.

Often the straight-line depreciation rate is expressed as a percentage. To find this rate:

$$\frac{100\%}{\text{Years of useful life}} = \text{Depreciation rate}$$

$$\frac{100\%}{15 \text{ years}} = 6.67\% \text{ year}$$

Therefore, the first 5 years of depreciation under this method would be as follows:

| Year | Computation | Annual depreciation | Remaining value |
|------|-------------|---------------------|-----------------|
| 1 | $200,00 × .0667 | $13,333 | $186,667 |
| 2 | 200,000 × .0667 | 13,333 | 173,334 |
| 3 | 200,000 × .0667 | 13,333 | 160,001 |
| 4 | 200,000 × .0667 | 13,333 | 146,668 |
| 5 | 200,000 × .0667 | 13,333 | 133,335 |

### PRACTICE PROBLEMS: DEPRECIATION

1. Compute the remaining value of a building that has a 35-year life after four years, using the straight-line method of depreciation. The value is $75,000.
2. A building has a remaining value of $50,000. When new, it had a life expectancy of 45 years; now it is eight years old. What was the value of the building when new if straight-line depreciation was used?
3. Using straight-line depreciation for a commercial property with a life of 31.5 years and a value of $275,000, what would be the depreciation for the seventh year?
4. Using the information in question 3 above, how much depreciation would accumulate during the first four years of ownership?

(*Answers: page 258*)

### PROFIT AND LOSS

Profit or loss is measured by the sales price against the cost of the property. If the cost is less than the sales price, a profit will be made. If the cost is greater than the sales price, there will be a loss.

Profit or loss = Sales price − Cost

*Example*

Profit = $10,000 − $8,000
Profit = $2,000

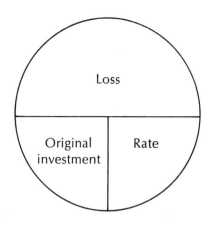

Loss = Original investment × Rate
Original investment = Loss ÷ Rate
Rate = Loss ÷ Original investment

Profit and loss may be expressed as a percentage; it is usually a percentage of the cost.

*Example*

Profit of $2,000 and cost of $8,000
$2,000 ÷ $8,000 = ¼ = 25% profit

To find the cost, divide the sales price by either (1 + profit) or (1 − loss).

*Example*

Sales price = $10,000
Profit = 25%
Cost = ?

$$C = \frac{SP}{1 + P}$$

$$= \frac{\$10,000}{1 + .25}$$

$$= \frac{\$10,000}{1.25}$$

$$= \$8,000$$

### PRACTICE PROBLEMS: PROFIT AND LOSS

1. A man bought two lots side by side that measured 50 feet (*w*) × 100 feet (*l*) and 100 feet (*w*) × 100 feet (*l*). He paid a total of $4,500 for them. He later divided them into three lots of equal frontage and sold them for $2,000 each. What is the percent of return on his original investment?
2. If a house sold for $35,000 at a loss of 6%, what was the original cost of the house?

3. A person buys a lot for $5,000 and sells it at a 15% profit. What was the sales price?
4. A person buys a property for $43,500 and sells it for $65,000. What was the percentage of profit?
5. A woman bought a house for $23,750 and sold it at a $3,400 loss. What was her percentage of loss?

*(Answers: page 258)*

## COMMISSION

The salesperson's and broker's commissions are generally based on a percentage of the gross sales price of the property.

Commission = Sales price × Rate
Sales price = Commission ÷ Rate
Rate = Commission ÷ Sales price

*Example*

Sales price $30,000
Commission fee 6%

$30,000 × .06 = $1,800 commission

## PRACTICE PROBLEMS: COMMISSION

1. As a salesperson, you realize that it takes an average of 10 showings to sell a house. You calculate that each showing has an average cost of $20. If you are paid one-half of the 8% commission for selling a $50,000 property, what is your net income on this sale?
2. The commission rate for selling an apartment building is 6% of the first $10,000 and 5% of anything over that. Broker Jones received a commission of $760. What was the sales price of the apartment building?
3. An 80-acre tract was listed for sale at $400 per acre but was sold for $27,500 with the condition that the purchaser pay the broker's commission of 8%. What was the net gain for the purchaser?

4. If you are a salesperson for a $95,000 property, the brokerage fee is 8%, and you will receive 50% of the total fee, what is the dollar amount the brokerage firm will net from the sale?
5. A broker keeps five-eighths of an 8% commission. The salesperson sold the property for $48,500. How much does the salesperson receive for selling the property?

*(Answers: page 258)*

## SETTLEMENT STATEMENT MATH METHODS

### Mortgage Balances

1. Beginning principal balance × Interest rate = Annual interest
2. Annual interest ÷ 12 = Monthly interest
3. Constant monthly payment − Monthly interest = Amount to principal reduction
4. Beginning principal balance − Principal reduction = New principal balance

Repeat the process for as many months as needed. For example, the process would be repeated 300 times for a 25-year loan.

*Example*

25-year loan, 8% interest for $50,000, $475 constant.

1. Beginning principal balance × Interest rate = Annual interest
   $50,000 × .08 = $4,000
2. Annual interest ÷ 12 = Monthly interest
   $4,000 ÷ 12 = $333.33
3. Constant monthly payment − Monthly interest = Principal reduction
   $475.00 − $333.33 = $141.67
4. Beginning principal balance − Principal reduction = New principal balance
   $50,000 − $141.67 = $49,858.33

### Interest Prorated

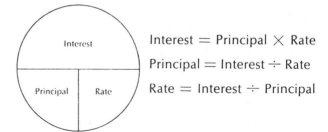

Interest = Principal × Rate
Principal = Interest ÷ Rate
Rate = Interest ÷ Principal

Use the 30-day method for calculations.

1. Compute the annual interest on the mortgage balance by multiplying the rate by the mortgage balance.
2. Divide the annual interest by 12 to obtain the monthly interest.
3. Divide the monthly interest by 30 to obtain the daily interest to the nearest cent.
4. Count the number of days since the last mortgage payment through the closing date.
5. Multiply the number of days by the daily interest figure to obtain the amount being prorated.
6. If the interest is computed in advance, the seller will receive the difference between the prepaid amount of interest and the daily amount used to closing.
7. If the interest is in arrears, the seller will owe for the number of days since the last payment until the closing.

*Example*

A $10,000 mortgage balance remains after the last payment at 12% interest. There are 15 days between the last payment and the closing.

$10,000.00 × .12 = $1,200.00 annual interest
$1,200.00/12 = $100.00/month
$100.00/30 = $3.33/day
15 days × $3.33 = $49.95

15 days is equal to ½ month. The difference between one-half month's interest of $50.00 and the $49.95 computed daily is due to rounding off.

## Taxes—Computed and Prorated

For purposes of your examination, taxes are computed annually from January 1 to December 31. Each month is considered to have 30 days, and a year has 360 days. Taxes are computed by multiplying the rate by the assessed value of the land and improvements.

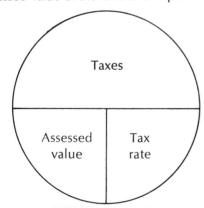

Taxes = Assessed value × Tax rate
Assessed value = Taxes ÷ Tax rate
Tax rate = Taxes ÷ Assessed value

*Example*

Land ($5,000) + Improvements ($12,000)
  = Assessed value ($17,000)
Rate = $9.40/$100 of assessed value

Annual taxes = (Land + Improvements) × Rate
Annual taxes = ($5,000 + $12,000) × $9.40/$100
Annual taxes = $17,000 × $9.40/$100
Annual taxes = $1,598

The rate will be expressed as so many dollars per $100 of assessed value.

To prorate taxes for settlement:

1. Compute the amount of time the seller will possess the property in the year of the settlement through the settlement.
2. Compute the annual taxes.
3. Find the monthly amount of the taxes and multiply the amount by the time of settlement to obtain the prorated amount.
4. If taxes were prepaid, subtract the prorated amount from the prepaid taxes to find how much the seller will receive at the settlement. If taxes are paid in arrears, the seller will be charged the prorated share at the settlement.

*Example*

Assessed value of land ($5,000) + Improvements ($12,000) = Total assessed value ($17,000)
Rate $9.40/$100
Annual taxes = $1,598 due December 31

At closing on June 15:
$1,598/12 = $133.17/month
Seller has held property 5½ months
($133.17)(5½) = $732.44 taxes to be prorated

## Insurance Prorated (30-day Month)

Most insurance is paid either one year or three years in advance. Therefore, upon cancellation or assignment of the policy in force the seller will desire a refund of the prepaid premiums. This amount represents the unused portion of the seller's premium. In order to compute the unused portion:

1. Compute the time remaining on the policy

*Example*

|                 | Day | Month | Year |
|-----------------|-----|-------|------|
| Expiration date | 20  | 8     | NY   |
| Date of closing | 10  | 6     | TY   |
| Time remaining  | 10  | 2     | 1    |

2.  Multiply the remaining time by the rates.

*Example*

Policy has a premium of $360/year paid 3 years in advance

Year = $360
Month = $360 ÷ 12 = $30/month
Daily = $30 ÷ 30 = $1/day

Time remaining × Rate = Amount to seller

| | |
|---|---|
| 1 year × $360 = | $360 |
| 2 months × $30 = | 60 |
| 10 days × $1 = | 10 |
| Amount to seller | $430 |

### Rent Prorated

Rent is usually paid in advance. The purchaser is concerned with obtaining his or her share of the rent at the settlement, when he or she takes possession of the property.

1.  Divide the monthly amount by 30 and round off to the nearest cent to obtain the daily rate.
2.  Multiply the daily rate by the number of days the seller has had possession of the property to closing.
3.  Subtract this amount from the monthly rent, and the remainder is owed the buyer.

*Example*

The monthly rent of $180 is paid in advance; the closing is on the 20th of the month. Prorate the rent:

$180 ÷ 30 = $6/day
20 days seller has possession × $6 = $120
$180 − $120 = $60 to buyer

### PRACTICE PROBLEMS: MORTGAGE BALANCES, RENT, TAX, INSURANCE, INTEREST PRORATIONS

#### Mortgage Balances

1.  Balance after last payment, $38,500; interest rate, 8%; constant payment, $328 per month. What is the balance of the mortgage after the next payment?

2.  Balance after May 15, $24,250; interest rate, 7%; constant monthly payment, $210. What is the mortgage balance after the July 15 payment?

#### Rent

3.  Mr. David is purchasing a four-unit apartment building. The building contains two one-bedroom apartments renting for $180 per month; one two-bedroom apartment renting for $210 per month; and one three-bedroom apartment renting for $270 per month. All rents are due on the first of the month and are current. The closing is to take place on the 20th. Prorate the rents to determine the total amount owed to Mr. David at closing.

#### Taxes

4.  A property is assessed at 40% of its appraised value. The appraised value is $37,500 and the tax rate is $8.27 per $100. Taxes are due January 1 each year in advance. If the sale of the property closed on July 10, how much would the buyer owe the seller for the prorated taxes at closing?

#### Insurance

5.  A home is covered by a three-year fire insurance policy which expires July 11, NY. The premium on the policy was $489.00 and has been paid in full. The home was sold and closing was set for September 23, TY. How much money will be credited the seller at closing if the policy is assumed by the purchaser?

#### Interest

6.  The outstanding mortgage balance after the September 1 payment was $38,500. The monthly PI constant is $328. The interest is computed in arrears at 8¾%. What amount would be debited to the seller if settlement takes place September 20?

*(Answers: page 258)*

## REVIEW QUESTIONS

1.  A $40,000 loan is to be amortized and repaid at a rate of $9.50/month PI per $1,000 originally borrowed. The annual taxes of $480 and the three-year insurance premium of $540 are to be prorated and included. What is the PITI constant?

    (A)  $380.00          (C)  $435.00
    (B)  $420.00          (D)  $465.00

2.  A person who is buying a home is in the 28% income tax bracket. The average monthly interest on the loan is $162. All the interest for that year is deductible from taxable income. How much less will be the income tax bill as a result of that deduction?

    (A)  $1,944.00        (C)  $1,399.68
    (B)  $162.00          (D)  $544.32

3. You desire to sell your house to Ms. Brown for $53,000. The sale is contingent on Ms. Brown's obtaining an FHA loan for $43,500. The discount is $2,175. How many discount points are you paying?

(A) 4        (C) 6
(B) 5        (D) 7

4. You are an apartment manager of a 20-unit complex. You are analyzing two rental options: Option I is to rent each unit for $225 per month with utilities included. Option II is to rent each unit for $185 per month with the tenant paying utilities. The average monthly utility bill for the 20 units is $875. Which option will produce the greater positive cash flow to your principal?

(A) Option I is $275 per month more than Option II
(B) Option II is $75 per month more than Option I
(C) Both options are equal
(D) Neither option produces a cash flow

5. You as a salesperson share commissions with your broker on a 3-to-2 ratio on sales made by you, with the broker taking the larger portion. If you sell a property for $78,500 and the commission rate is 6%, how much more does the broker receive than you as the salesperson?

(A) $942        (C) $2,826
(B) $1,884     (D) $1,056

6. The loan on a property is 75% of its appraised value. The interest rate on the loan is 12% per year. The first quarterly interest payment is $360. What is the appraised value of the property?

(A) $12,000    (C) $18,000
(B) $16,000    (D) $20,000

7. The assessed value of a property for tax purposes is $24,000 and the annual property taxes are $1,200. What is the tax rate per $100 of assessment?

(A) $4/$100    (C) $6/$100
(B) $5/$100    (D) $7/$100

8. On January 1 of this year, Mr. Green paid his annual taxes due in advance for the calendar year in the amount of $720. On April 10, this year, he paid $360 for a three-year paid-in-advance insurance policy. He sold his house and closed on August 15, this year. What is the total prorated amount to be returned to him?

(A) $588.25    (C) $318.25
(B) $450.00    (D) $511.75

9. You can sell houses in a residential development at a commission of 7% of the first $90,000 in sales each month and 9% for all sales over that amount, or can take a straight 8% commission on gross sales. In one month you sell houses for $43,000, $45,600, $48,100, and $56,500. Under which option would you receive more commission for that month?

(A) Option I provides $132 greater commission
(B) Option II provides $231 greater commission
(C) Both options are equal in this case
(D) You will lose money under each option

10. The seller of an apartment house agreed to a commission of 7% of the first $15,000 of the sales price and 4% on any amount over the $15,000. What is the sales price of the property if the commission received was $2,850?

(A) $45,000    (C) $60,000
(B) $50,000    (D) $75,000

11. Mr. Holland takes a home improvement loan for $14,300 at 14½% interest. He sells the home 8 months later and repays the principal and interest in one payment. What is the total dollar amount repaid?

(A) $1,382.32    (C) $15,682.32
(B) $14,300.00   (D) $16,373.48

12. Quarterly interest payments of $562.50 are made on a loan of $15,000. What interest rate is being charged?

(A) 14¾%     (C) 15¼%
(B) 15%      (D) 16¼%

13. Farmer Jones owns a triangular field with the north-south boundary of the field being 1,320 feet in length. The east-west boundary is perpendicular to the north-south boundary and measures 2,640 feet. There is a circular pond with an area of 8 acres in the center of the field. If the field sells for $3,200 per tillable acre, what will be the sales price of the field?

(A) $128,000   (C) $204,800
(B) $256,000   (D) $102,400

14. A warehouse rents for $.057 per cubic foot per year. The monthly equivalent is paid in advance on the first of each month. The dimensions of the warehouse are 75' × 126' × 36'. If the property is sold and closed on the 25th of the month, how much rent will be prorated to the new buyer?

(A) $1,357.25   (C) $269.20
(B) $1,275.25   (D) $54.29

15. Comparable properties have a gross monthly rent multiplier of 105. The property has 10 units, each renting for $2,100 per year with average monthly expenses of $50 per unit. What is the indicated value of the property using the GRM method?

    (A) $220,500          (C) $273,000
    (B) $168,000          (D) $183,750

16. A residential investment has a depreciable life for tax purposes of 27½ years. The property was purchased for $185,000, and the land was valued at $18,000. What is the annual amount of depreciation?

    (A) $7,382            (C) $6,073
    (B) $6,727            (D) $5,872

17. A certain property has gross monthly income of $2,750 and annual expenses of $8,740. The property is valued at $147,000. What is the capitalization rate used?

    (A) 14%               (C) 16½%
    (B) 15½%              (D) 17¼%

18. The owner of a building desires a 14% return on an investment of $130,000. What net income must be generated each month to produce the desired

return if the operating expenses are $12,750 per year?

    (A) $1,516.67/month   (C) $1,897.71/month
    (B) $2,579.17/month   (D) $2,216.76/month

19. You decide to build a two-car garage. The floor of the garage is to be 24′ × 26′ × 6″ and will cost $22.50 per cubic yard for cement and $.53 per square foot for labor. The sides of the garage will be 8′ high and will cost $1.75 per square foot for materials and labor combined. The roof is flat and will cost $2.10 per square foot for materials and $.37 per square foot for labor. What is the total cost to build the garage?

    (A) $2,132.10         (C) $3,532.10
    (B) $3,201.38         (D) $3,272.00

20. If the FHA rate was set at 13½% and the seller paid $3,500 in discount on a $50,000 loan, what was the conventional rate at the time of closing the loan?

    (A) 14¼%              (C) 14½%
    (B) 14⅜%              (D) 14⅝%

(*Answers: pages 259–260*)

## Part III

# Testing Your Understanding of Real Estate Concepts

# Chapter 17

# Listing, Offer to Purchase, and Settlement Procedures

---

**VOCABULARY**

*You will find it important to have a complete working knowledge of the following words and concepts found in the text or the glossary.*

| | | |
|---|---|---|
| agent | debit | offer to purchase |
| bill of sale | deposit | open listing |
| binder | earnest money | PITI |
| broker | escrow | principal |
| chattels | exclusive agency | salesperson |
| counteroffer | exclusive right to sell | vendee |
| credit | multiple listing | vendor |

---

THIS chapter and the ones that follow may well be the most important for students who plan to enter the real estate industry. This chapter will familiarize you with some of the specific problems and procedures of the brokerage business. Particular attention is given to the mechanics of completing listing contracts, offers to purchase, and settlement statements. Careful attention should be paid to the details of preparing these documents so you will be very familiar with them in their completed forms.

The student should totally master the forms involved in these transactions for a basic understanding of all facets of the agreements involved in a real property transaction.

The forms used in this and the following chapters are designed for educational purposes and to point out certain pertinent parts of a transaction. They are not intended for use in the business. The future real estate salesperson or broker should become acquainted with the forms used in the local area, since they vary in format from firm to firm and from city to city.

## EXCLUSIVE AUTHORIZATION TO SELL (LISTING)

See Figure 17-1 for the actual form.

### Section 1

1. *Sales price.* Enter the amount for which the property is listed.
2. *Type home.* Architectural style of the property.

3. *Total bedrooms.* Enter the number of bedrooms.
4. *Total baths.* Enter the number of bathrooms.
5. *Address.* Enter the number and name of street of the property, and the city.
6. *Jurisdiction of.* Enter the county and state where the property is located.
7. *Amount of loan to be assumed.* Enter the loan balance.
8. *As of what date.* The date of the loan balance entered in item 7.
9. *Taxes and insurance included.* Enter "yes" if taxes and insurance are included in the monthly payments, "no" if they are not.
10. *Years to go.* Enter the number of years remaining in the life of the loan.
11. *Amount payable monthly.* Enter the monthly payment on the loan in item 7 and the interest rate being charged.
12. *Type of loan.* Enter the form of financing of the loan in item 7. For example, FHA or conventional; if not otherwise stated, assume it to be conventional.
13. *Mortgage company.* Enter the name of the mortgagee of the loan in item 7 and the address if available.
14. *2nd mortgage (or 2nd trust).* Enter the name of the mortgagee and the address, and the amount of the second loan.
15. *Owner's name.* Enter the name(s) of the owner(s) of the property.

16. *Phones (home and business).* Enter the owner's phone numbers.
17. *Tenant's name.* Enter the name of the person(s) in possession of the property if leased.
18. *Phones (home and business).* Enter the phone numbers of the tenant(s) if the property is leased.
19. *Possession.* Enter the date on which the seller will give possession of the property to the buyer and the type of possession to be given.
20. *Date listed.* Enter the date (day, month, year) the listing is taken.
21. *Exclusive for.* Enter the number of days for which the listing contract will be in effect; for example, 90 days.
22. *Date of expiration.* Enter the date upon which the listing expires; for example, a 90-day listing beginning April 3, this year, expires July 3, this year; a 60-day listing beginning July 27, this year, expires September 27, this year.
23. *Listing broker.* If the person taking the listing is a broker, insert his or her name and the company name, or the company name if the listing agent is a salesperson.
24. *Phone.* Enter the telephone number of the listing broker.
25. *Key available at.* Enter the location at which the key may be obtained in order to show the property; for example, "key in office."
26. *Listing salesperson.* If the person taking the listing is a salesperson, enter his or her name.
27. *Home phone.* Enter the telephone number of the listing salesperson.
28. *How to be shown.* Enter specific instructions as to how the property is to be shown; for example, "by appointment with owners only."

## Section 2

The information in this section is basically self-explanatory, and covers the physical description of the property.

## Section 3

This section includes information to be used for computing the tax for the listed property.

*Land assessment.* Enter the dollar amount for which the land has been assessed.

*Improvements.* Enter the dollar amount for which the improvements to the property have been assessed.

*Total assessment.* Enter the sum of the land assessment and the improvements.

*Tax rate.* Enter the given tax rate. This rate is usually expressed as dollars of taxes per $100 of total assessed valuation; for example, $6.72/$100.

*Total annual taxes.* Enter the product of the total assessment and the tax rate.

## Section 4

Enter any information concerning the schools and public transportation facilities that might affect the property; also, any information concerning the shopping areas near the property.

Under "Remarks" enter any conditions on which the sale is to be contingent or any other vital information not listed elsewhere.

## Section 5

This is a legal section that establishes the contractual agreement between the seller (principal) and the broker (agent).

5-1. Enter the date the contract is entered into.
5-2. Enter the name of the real estate firm taking the listing.
5-3. Enter the date the contract is to begin (day, month, and year).
5-4. Enter the date the contract is to expire (day, month, and year).
5-5. Enter the listing price as you would write it on a check.
5-6. Enter the numerals representing the listing price.
5-7. Enter the sales fee or broker's commission as a percent.
5-8. Enter the date the parties to the contract signed below.
5-9. Enter the name of the listing brokerage firm followed by the agent's name.
5-10. Enter the address as given in Section 1, item 5.
5-11. Enter the telephone number of the seller.
5-12. Enter the name(s) of the seller(s); this is where sellers sign the contract.

### OFFER TO PURCHASE AGREEMENT

This is a document used by the purchaser to convey an offer to the seller. Upon acceptance by the seller, this document then becomes a contractual arrangement setting forth the final details of the transaction and how it is to be executed. See the sample form shown in Figure 17-2.

## Section 1

This section lists the date on which the offer is made along with the names of the various parties involved in the offer—the purchaser, the seller, and the broker.

1. Enter the date on which the offer is taken.
2. Enter the name(s) of the purchaser(s).

# REAL ESTATE LISTING CONTRACT (EXCLUSIVE RIGHT TO SELL)

**Section 1**

| | | |
|---|---|---|
| SALES PRICE __1__ | TYPE HOME __2__ | TOTAL BEDROOMS __3__   TOTAL BATHS __4__ |
| ADDRESS __5__ | JURISDICTION OF __6__ | |

AMT. OF LOAN TO BE ASSUMED $ __7__   AS OF WHAT DATE __8__   TAXES & INS. INCLUDED __9__   YEARS TO GO __10__   AMOUNT PAYABLE MONTHLY $ __11__ @ ___% TYPE LOAN __12__

MORTGAGE COMPANY __13__   2nd MORTGAGE __14__

OWNER'S NAME __15__   PHONES(HOME) __16__ (BUSINESS) __16__

TENANT'S NAME __17__   PHONES (HOME) __18__ (BUSINESS) __18__

POSSESSION __19__   DATE LISTED: __20__   EXCLUSIVE FOR __21__   DATE OF EXPIRATION __22__

LISTING BROKER __23__   PHONE __24__   KEY AVAILABLE AT __25__

LISTING SALESMAN __26__   HOME PHONE __27__   HOW TO BE SHOWN: __28__

**Section 2**

| | | | | |
|---|---|---|---|---|
| ENTRANCE FOYER ☐ | CENTER HALL ☐ | AGE | AIR CONDITIONING ☐ | TYPE KITCHEN CABINETS |
| LIVING ROOM SIZE | | ROOFING | TOOL HOUSE ☐ | TYPE COUNTER TOPS |
| | FIREPLACE ☐ | | | |
| DINING ROOM SIZE | | GARAGE SIZE | PATIO ☐ | EAT-IN SIZE KITCHEN ☐ |
| BEDROOM TOTAL: | DOWN   UP | SIDE DRIVE ☐ | CIRCULAR DRIVE ☐ | TYPE STOVE ☐ |
| BATHS TOTAL: | DOWN   UP | PORCH ☐ SIDE ☐ REAR ☐ | SCREENED ☐ | BUILT-IN OVEN & RANGE ☐ |
| DEN SIZE | FIREPLACE ☐ | FENCED YARD | OUTDOOR GRILL ☐ | SEPARATE STOVE INCLUDED ☐ |
| FAMILY ROOM SIZE | FIREPLACE ☐ | STORM WINDOWS ☐ | STORM DOORS ☐ | REFRIGERATOR INCLUDED ☐ |
| RECREATION ROOM SIZE | FIREPLACE ☐ | CURBS & GUTTERS ☐ | SIDEWALKS ☐ | DISHWASHER INCLUDED |
| BASEMENT SIZE | | STORM SEWERS ☐ | ALLEY ☐ | DISPOSAL INCLUDED ☐ |
| NONE ☐ 1/4 ☐ 1/3 ☐ 1/2 ☐ 3/4☐ FULL ☐ | | WATER SUPPLY | | DOUBLE SINK ☐   SINGLE SINK☐ |
| UTILITY ROOM | | SEWER ☐ | SEPTIC ☐ | STAINLESS STEEL ☐   PORCELAIN ☐ |
| TYPE HOT WATER SYSTEM: | | TYPE GAS: NATURAL ☐ | BOTTLED ☐ | WASHER INCLUDED ☐   DRYER INCLUDED☐ |

| | | |
|---|---|---|
| TYPE HEAT | WHY SELLING | **Section 3** |
| EST. FUEL COST | | LAND ASSESSMENT $ |
| ATTIC ☐ | PROPERTY DESCRIPTION | IMPROVEMENTS $ |
| PULL DOWN STAIRWAY ☐   REGULAR STAIRWAY ☐   TRAP DOOR ☐ | | TOTAL ASSESSMENTS $ |
| NAME OF BUILDER | LOT SIZE | TAX RATE |
| SQUARE FOOTAGE | LOT NO.   BLOCK   SECTION | TOTAL ANNUAL TAXES $ |
| EXTERIOR OF HOUSE | | |

**Section 4**

NAME OF SCHOOLS:   ELEMENTARY _____   JR. HIGH: _____

HIGH: _____   PAROCHIAL: _____

PUBLIC TRANSPORTATION: _____

NEAREST SHOPPING AREA: _____

REMARKS: _____

Date: __5-1__

In consideration of the services of __5-2__ (herein called "Broker") to be rendered to the undersigned (herein called 'Owner"), and of the promise of Broker to make reasonable efforts to obtain a Purchaser therefor, Owner hereby lists with Broker the real estate and all improvements thereon which are described above, (all herein called "the property"), and the Owner hereby grants to Broker the exclusive and irrevocable right to sell such property from 12:00 Noon on __5-3__ , 19 _____ until 12:00 Midnight on __5-4__ , 19 _____ (herein called "period of time"), for the price of __5-5__ Dollars ($ __5-6__ ) or for such other price and upon such other terms (including exchange) as Owner may subsequently authorize during the period of time.

**Section 5**

It is understood by Owner that the above sum or any other price subsequently authorized by Owner shall include a cash fee of __5-7__ per cent of such price or other price which shall be payable by Owner to Broker upon consummation by any Purchaser or Purchasers of a valid contract of sale of the property during the period of time and whether or not Broker was a procuring cause of any such contract of sale.

If the property is sold or exchanged by Owner, or by Broker or by any other person to any Purchaser to whom the property was shown by Broker or any representative of Broker within sixty (60) days after the expiration of the period of time mentioned above, Owner agrees to pay to Broker a cash fee which shall be the same percentage of the purchase price as the percentage mentioned above.

Broker is hereby authorized by Owner to place a "For Sale" sign on the property and to remove all signs of other brokers or salesmen during the period of time, and Owner hereby agrees to make the property available to Broker at all reasonable hours for the purpose of showing it to prospective Purchasers.

Owner agrees to convey the property to the Purchaser by deed with the usual covenants of title and free and clear from all encumbrances, tenancies, liens (for taxes or otherwise), but subject to applicable restrictive covenants of record. Owner acknowledges receipt of copy of this agreement.

WITNESS the following signature(s) and seal(s):

Date Signed: __5-8__                                          __5-12__
                                                              (Owner)

Listing Agent __5-9__

Address __5-10__   Telephone __5-11__
                                                              (Owner)

*Figure 17-1—Real estate listing contract.*

3. Enter the name(s) of the seller(s).
4. Enter the brokerage firm name.

## Section 2

This section describes the real estate being sold based on the legal description and street addresses.

5. Enter the county and state.
6. Enter the legal description.
7. Enter the number, street, city, and state.

## Section 3

This section lists the purchase price and defines how it is to be paid by the offeror.

8. Enter the purchase price, in writing as you would for a check. In the parentheses enter the purchase price in numbers.
9. Enter the manner in which the purchase price is to be paid; for example, new mortgage for 80% of the purchase price, at 13½% for 25 years to be repaid in 300 equal installments of principal and interest, with the balance in cash.
10. Enter the amount of the earnest money deposit received. Again, write it out first as you would for a check, and then repeat it in numbers in the parentheses. *Note:* The earnest money deposit will be a part of the down payment when doing the calculations for the settlement.

## Section 4

Paragraph 3 in this section tells how the property is to be conveyed, when possession is to take place, and who is to pay for the deed preparation.

11. Enter the location at which the settlement will take place.
12. Enter the date on which the settlement is proposed to take place.

Paragraph 5 arranges for the proration of all taxes, interest, and impounded escrow deposits as of the date of settlement.

Paragraph 6 places the risk on the seller for any loss or damage which might occur to the property prior to settlement.

13. Enter the brokerage or sales fee; for example, 6%.
14. Enter any other conditions or remarks pertinent to the sale or on which it may be contingent (inclusion of personal property, separate bill of sale, restatement of financing, possession, etc.).

## Section 5

15. Enter the name of your state.
16. The signature(s) of the seller(s) appears here.
17. The signature of the broker appears here.
18. The signature(s) of the purchaser(s) appears here.
19. Enter the dollar amount of earnest money deposit received.
20. Circle the manner in which the earnest money was conveyed.
21. The signature of the sales agent, broker, or salesperson appears here.

### SETTLEMENT (CLOSING) GUIDE

The following guide to the settlement proceedings in a real estate transaction does not list all the items one might encounter. Debits and credits can vary from one transaction to another because many of the items are negotiable between the seller and purchaser. One must be careful when completing a settlement statement to correctly position each item (see Figure 17-3).

Some simple bookkeeping practices must be followed to complete the settlement statement properly.

☐ The term *debit* is defined as something owed. This pertains to both the buyer's and seller's settlement statements.
☐ The term *credit* is something that is receivable to either buyer or seller.
☐ Since a double-entry accounting system is employed, the sum of the buyer's debits must equal the sum of the buyer's credits, and likewise the seller's debits and credits must balance.

The order in which items appear on a settlement is a matter of choice.

☐ *Purchase price.* The amount to be paid by the purchaser at settlement for the property is entered as a debit to the buyer. Since it is received by the seller, it is entered as a credit to the seller's statement.
☐ *Deposit.* The earnest money amount paid by the purchaser, which is used as part of the purchase price, should be entered as a credit to the buyer. No entry to the seller.
☐ *Sales commission (broker's fee).* The fee charged by the broker for the sale of the property is an expense to the seller and should be debited. No entry to the buyer unless the buyer has agreed to pay the broker a fee to find a property.
☐ *New first mortgage (trust).* If the buyer is obtaining a new loan to purchase the property, enter this amount as a credit since it is the means by which he or she is to pay the sales price.
☐ *Assumed mortgage (trust).* If the loan of the seller is being assumed by the buyer, enter this amount as

## REAL ESTATE SALES CONTRACT (OFFER TO PURCHASE AGREEMENT)

This AGREEMENT made as of _____ 1 _____ , 19_____ ,

among _____ 2 _____ (herein called "Purchaser"),

and _____ 3 _____ (herein called "Seller"),

and _____ 4 _____ (herein called "Broker"),

provides that Purchaser agrees to buy through Broker as agent for Seller, and Seller agrees to sell the following described real estate, and all improvements

thereon, located in the jurisdiction of _____ 5 _____ ,

(all herein called "the property"): _____ 6

_____ , and more commonly known as _____ 7 _____

_____ (street address).

1. The purchase price of the property is _____ 8

Dollars ($ _____ 8 _____ ), and such purchase price shall be paid as follows:

_____ 9

2. Purchaser has made a deposit of _____ 10 _____ Dollars ($ _____ 10 _____ )

with Broker, receipt of which is hereby acknowledged, and such deposit shall be held by Broker in escrow until the date of settlement and then applied to the purchase price, or returned to Purchaser if the title to the property is not marketable.

3. Seller agrees to convey the property to Purchaser by Deed with the usual covenants of title and free and clear from all monetary encumbrances, tenancies, liens (for taxes or otherwise), except as may be otherwise provided above, but subject to applicable restrictive covenants of record. Seller further agrees to deliver possession of the property to Purchaser on the date of settlement and to pay the expense of preparing the deed of conveyance.

4. Settlement shall be made at _____ 11 _____ on or before

_____ 12 _____ , 19_____ , or as soon thereafter as title can be examined and necessary documents prepared, with allowance of a reasonable time for Seller to correct any defects reported by the title examiner.

5. All taxes, interest, rent, and impound escrow deposits, if any, shall be prorated as of the date of settlement.

6. All risk of loss or damage to the property by fire, windstorm, casualty, or other cause is assumed by Seller until the date of settlement.

7. Purchaser and Seller agree that Broker was the sole procuring cause of this Contract of Purchase, and Seller agrees to pay Broker for services

rendered a cash fee of _____ 13 _____ per cent of the purchase price. If either Purchaser or Seller defaults under such Contract, such defaulting party shall be liable for the cash fee of Broker and any expenses incurred by the non-defaulting party in connection with this transaction.

Subject to: _____

_____ 14

_____

8. Purchaser represents that an inspection satisfactory to Purchaser has been made of the property, and Purchaser agrees to accept the property in its present condition except as may be otherwise provided in the description of the property above.

9. This Contract of Purchase constitutes the entire agreement among the parties and may not be modified or changed except by written instrument executed by all of the parties, including Broker.

10. This Contract of Purchase shall be construed, interpreted, and applied according to the law of the jurisdiction of _____ 15 _____ and shall be binding upon and shall inure to the benefit of the heirs, personal representatives, successors, and assigns of the parties.

All parties to this agreement acknowledge receipt of a certified copy.

WITNESS the following signatures:

_____ 16 _____      _____ 18 _____

                   Seller                              Purchaser

_____ 16 _____      _____ 18 _____

                   Seller                              Purchaser

_____ 17 _____

                   Broker

Deposit Rec'd $ _____ 19 _____

Personal Check    20        Cash

Cashier's Check              Company Check

Sales Agent:     21

*Figure 17-2—Real estate sales contract.*

a credit to the buyer and a debit to the seller. The amount is being used by the buyer to pay for the property to reduce the amount owed. The seller will use this amount to reduce the cash he or she will receive. In effect, the assumption is a credit for the buyer from the seller against the purchase price.

□ *Pay existing mortgage.* The seller pays off the existing loan. This amount is debited to the seller, and the property may be transferred free and clear.

□ *Second mortgage (trust).* If a second loan is required to meet the purchase price by the buyer, enter the amount as a credit. No entry to the seller.

□ *Purchase money mortgage (second trust).* If the seller takes a purchase money mortgage for part of the sales price, enter the amount as a credit to the buyer against the sales price and as a debit to the seller against his or her cash receivable.

□ *Land contract.* If the seller sells the property under a land contract, enter the amount of the contract as a credit to the purchaser against the sales price and a debit to the seller against the cash to be received.

□ *Taxes in arrears, prorated.* If the taxes are not yet due and payable, prorate the annual amount of taxes including the day of settlement. Credit the purchaser and debit the seller.

□ *Taxes in advance, prorated.* If the taxes have been paid in advance, prorate the amount, including the day of settlement, and subtract it from the prepaid amount. The remainder should be debited to the buyer and credited to the seller.

□ *Delinquent taxes.* If taxes are delinquent, this amount should be charged to the seller. No entry to the buyer.

□ *Fire insurance, canceled.* Credit the remaining premium balance to the seller.

□ *Fire insurance, new policy.* Enter the cost of the new policy as a debit to the purchaser.

□ *Fire insurance, assigned policy.* If the seller assigns the existing policy to the purchaser, prorate the premium and enter the remaining amount as a debit to the purchaser and a credit to the seller.

□ *Interest in arrears.* If the loan is assumed or paid by the seller and interest is calculated in arrears, prorate to the date of closing the monthly interest and enter it as a debit to the seller. If the loan is assumed, enter the prorated amount as a credit to the buyer.

□ *Interest in advance.* If the interest on a loan is computed in advance and the loan is assumed or paid off by the seller, then enter as a credit. If the purchaser is assuming, then enter the prorated amount as a debit.

□ *Interest on new loan.* Interest may be charged on a newly originated loan. Enter the amount as a debit to the purchaser.

□ *Rent in advance.* Enter the prorated amount as a credit to the purchaser and a debit to the seller.

□ *Rent in arrears.* If rent is collected in arrears, enter the prorated amount as a debit to the purchaser and a credit to the seller.

□ *Title insurance, owner's policy.* Enter as a debit to the seller.

□ *Title insurance, mortgagee's policy.* Enter as a debit to the purchaser.

□ *Deed preparation.* Enter as a debit to the seller.

□ *Abstract continuation.* Enter as a debit to the seller.

□ *Opinion or examination of the abstract.* Enter as a debit to the purchaser.

□ *Appraisal fee.* A negotiable item. It may be charged to the seller if requested by the purchaser, or charged to the purchaser if requested by the lending institution.

□ *Attorney fees, purchaser.* Debit the purchaser for any additional legal fees charged to him or her.

□ *Attorney fees, seller.* Debit the seller for any additional legal fees charged to him or her.

□ *Loan origination fee.* Debit the purchaser for the cost of originating the new loan. In the case of an assumption, a loan assumption fee may be charged.

□ *FHA discount points.* By law are debited to the seller.

□ *VA discount points.* By law are debited to the seller.

□ *Conventional discount points.* Negotiable if charged.

□ *Recording, deed.* Debit to the purchaser.

□ *Recording, mortgage.* Debit to the purchaser.

□ *Escrow balance, assumed.* Debit to the purchaser and credit to the seller for the account balance.

□ *Escrow payoff, existing loan.* Credit to the seller as an offsetting item to the loan balance.

□ *Survey.* May be negotiable but generally charged as a debit to the purchaser.

□ *Prepayment penalty.* Debit to the seller for prepaying loan balance.

□ *Conveyance tax.* Debit to the seller.

□ *Special assessments.* Negotiable.

□ *Settlement fees.* Negotiable.

□ *Credit report.* Debit to the purchaser.

□ *Photo fee.* Debit to the purchaser.

□ *Sale of chattels.* If bought by purchaser, debit to the purchaser and credit to the seller. Such items are sold under a separate bill of sale given by the vendor (seller) to the vendee (buyer).

□ *Balance due from the purchaser.* The amount owed by the purchaser at settlement after subtracting the credits from his or her debits. Enter as a credit, since it is needed to balance the double-entry system.

□ *Balance due seller.* The amount received by the seller at settlement after subtracting the debits from the credits. Enter as a debit if the credits exceed the debits as a balancing item. Enter as a credit if the debits exceed the credits.

# SETTLEMENT STATEMENT WORKSHEET

| | BUYER'S STATEMENT | | SELLER'S STATEMENT | |
|---|---|---|---|---|
| | DEBIT | CREDIT | DEBIT | CREDIT |
| 1. Purchase Price or Sales Price | XX | | | XX |
| 2. Deposit | | XX | | |
| 3. Sales Commission (Broker's Fee) | | | XX | |
| Financing: | | | | |
| 4. New 1st Mortgage (Trust) | | XX | | |
| 5. Assumed Mortgage (Trust) | | XX | XX | |
| 6. Pay Existing Mortgage (Trust) | | | XX | |
| 7. 2nd Mortgage (Trust) | | XX | | |
| 8. 2nd Purchase Money Mortgage | | XX | XX | |
| 9. Taxes in Arrears—Prorated | | XX | XX | |
| 10. Taxes in Advance—Prorated | XX | | | XX |
| 11. Delinquent Taxes | | | XX | |
| 12. Fire Insurance—Cancelled | | | | XX |
| 13. Fire Insurance—New Policy | XX | | | |
| 14. Fire Insurance—Assigned Policy | XX | | | XX |
| 15. Interest in Arrears | | XX | XX | |
| 16. Interest in Advance | XX | | | XX |
| 17. Interest on New Loan | XX | | | |
| 18. Rent in Advance | | XX | XX | |
| 19. Rent in Arrears | XX | | | XX |
| 20. Title Insurance—Owner's | | | XX | |
| 21. Title Insurance—Mortgagee's | XX | | | |
| 22. Deed Preparation | | | XX | |
| 23. Abstract Continuation | | | XX | |
| 24. Opinion of Abstract (Examination) | XX | | | |
| 25. Appraisal Fee | Negotiable | | | |
| 26. Attorney's Fee—Purchaser | XX | | | |
| 27. Attorney's Fee–Seller | | | XX | |

*Figure 17-3—Settlement statement worksheet (page 1 of 2).*

## SETTLEMENT STATEMENT WORKSHEET
### (Continued)

|  | BUYER'S STATEMENT | | SELLER'S STATEMENT | |
|---|---|---|---|---|
|  | **DEBIT** | **CREDIT** | **DEBIT** | **CREDIT** |
| 28. Loan Origination Fee | XX | | | |
| Loan Discount—Points | | | | |
| 29. FHA | Negotiable | | | |
| 30. VA | | | XX | |
| 31. Conventional | Negotiable | | | |
| 32. Recording Deed | XX | | | |
| 33. Recording Mortgage | XX | | | |
| 34. Escrow Balance Assumed | XX | | | XX |
| 35. Escrow Payoff, Existing Loan | | | | XX |
| 36. Survey | XX | | | |
| 37. Prepayment Penalty | | | XX | |
| 38. Conveyance Tax | | | XX | |
| 39. Mortgage Tax | XX | | | |
| 40. Special Assessments | Negotiable | | | |
| 41. Settlement Fee | Negotiable | | | |
| 42. Credit Report | XX | | | |
| 43. Photo Fee | XX | | | |
| 44. Sale of Chattels | XX | | | XX |
| 45. Balance Due from Purchaser | | XX | | |
| 46. Balance Due Seller | | | XX | |
|  | | | | |
|  | | | | |
|  | | | | |
|  | | | | |
|  | | | | |
|  | | | | |
|  | XXX | XXX | XXX | XXX |

*Figure 17-3—Settlement statement worksheet (page 2 of 2).*

## SAMPLE PROBLEM

The following represents a sample problem covering material which might be found in a typical real estate transaction. Refer to Figures 17-4, 17-5, and 17-6.

On August 22, this year, you as salesperson for College Real Estate of Anytown, Your State, listed the property owned by Mr. Jack Nickless and his wife, Margaret, at 2785 Nulsen Drive in Anytown, obtaining a 90-day exclusive authorization to sell listing. The house is a frame Cape Cod with three bedrooms downstairs, two full baths, a full basement, and all built-in appliances in the kitchen, except an automatic dishwasher. The recreation room is 14' × 18' with a fireplace. The home was originally constructed in 1955. It has hardwood floors, with carpeting in the 18' × 22' living room, dining room, and all bedrooms. The house has city water and sewers, electricity, and is heated by natural gas. It also has aluminum storm doors and windows and a two-car attached garage. The lot is 120' × 140' on the west side of the street and has a legal description of Lot 18 in the McCary Addition to the City of Anytown, County of Madison, Your State, as recorded in Plat Book 5, page 26.

The Nicklesses have an outstanding mortgage balance as of August 1, of $10,586. The payments are $125 per month, including principal and interest only, and are due the first of each month. The interest rate is 7 percent paid in advance. The loan is assumable, and the mortgagee is the Anytown Savings and Loan Company. There is a fire and extended-coverage insurance policy that expires April 30, next year, and has been paid in advance at $80 per year. The coverage is for $74,000. The taxes are $8.50/$100, with the property having an assessed value for the land of $4,500 and the improvements of $16,500. The taxes are payable by December 31, this year, and have not yet been paid. The Nicklesses feel they can give possession on or before 10 days after the final closing.

The terms are set at a listing price of $78,500 payable in cash, or cash plus the assumption of the existing mortgage. They will not accept an exchange. They also desire to have the house shown only by appointment between 10 A.M. and 7 P.M., Monday through Saturday. They can be reached for an appointment at 821-5168, and the key will be available at the College Real Estate office. The Nicklesses also agree to the 6 percent brokerage fee.

### The Offer

On September 3, this year, Mr. Charles Vance and his wife, Wilma, are shown the Nickless house. Both Mr. and Mrs. Vance like the house and make an offer of $78,000 that same day. They ask in the offer that the washer and dryer be included in the sales price. The offer is to run until midnight of the next day if it is not accepted prior. The offer is contingent upon the Vances' being able to obtain new financing in the amount of 80 percent of the purchase price for 25 years at a rate not to exceed 13 percent. They also tender $1,000 earnest money by check to you and ask that, if accepted, the closing take place at the College Real Estate offices. You immediately submit the offer to the Nicklesses, and they accept the following afternoon.

### Settlement

With the terms of the contract being met, closing was set for September 30, this year, at the College Real Estate offices. In addition to the purchase price, deposit, new mortgage and insurance proration, and brokerage fee, the following will be charged at the closing:

A title examination fee of $140 will be charged to the purchaser. The recording fee for the new mortgage, $25, will be charged to the purchaser. The appraisal fee, $40, will be charged to the sellers. The mortgagee's title insurance, $75, will be charged to the purchaser. The recording fee, $7.50, and the deed preparation fee, $50, will be charged to the sellers. The loan origination fee, 1 percent of the amount financed, will be charged to the purchaser, and the survey fee, $50, will be charged to the sellers.

## REAL ESTATE LISTING CONTRACT (EXCLUSIVE RIGHT TO SELL)

SALES PRICE $78,500.00                                    TYPE HOME Cape Cod                    TOTAL BEDROOMS 3       TOTAL BATHS 2

ADDRESS 2785 Nulsen Dr., Anytown                          JURISDICTION OF Madison County, Your State

AMT. OF LOAN TO BE ASSUMED $ 10,586.00    AS OF WHAT DATE Aug. 1, TY    TAXES & INS. INCLUDED NO    YEARS TO GO ___    AMOUNT PAYABLE MONTHLY $ 125 @ 7 %    TYPE LOAN Conv.

MORTGAGE COMPANY Anytown Savings and Loan Company         2nd TRUST $ N/A

ESTIMATED EXPECTED RENT MONTHLY $ ___                     TYPE OF APPRAISAL REQUESTED ___

OWNER'S NAME Jack Nickless and Margaret Nickless (H & W)    PHONES (HOME) 821-5168    (BUSINESS) ___

TENANT'S NAME N/A                                          PHONES (HOME) ___    (BUSINESS) ___

POSSESSION On or Before 10 DAFC    DATE LISTED: Aug. 22, TY    EXCLUSIVE FOR 90 days    DATE OF EXPIRATION Nov. 22, TY

LISTING BROKER College Real Estate                        PHONE ___    KEY AVAILABLE AT College Real Estate

LISTING SALESMAN You as Salesman                          HOME PHONE ___    HOW TO BE SHOWN: By Appointment

| | | | | |
|---|---|---|---|---|
| ENTRANCE FOYER ☐ | CENTER HALL ☐ | AGE 22 | AIR CONDITIONING ☐ | TYPE KITCHEN CABINETS |
| LIVING ROOM SIZE 18 x 22 | FIREPLACE ☐ | ROOFING | TOOL HOUSE ☐ | TYPE COUNTER TOPS |
| DINING ROOM SIZE | | GARAGE SIZE 2-car attached | PATIO ☐ | EAT-IN SIZE KITCHEN ☐ |
| BEDROOM TOTAL: 3 DOWN 3 UP | | SIDE DRIVE ☐ | CIRCULAR DRIVE ☐ | BREAKFAST ROOM ☐ |
| BATHS TOTAL: 2 DOWN 2 UP | | PORCH ☐ SIDE ☐ REAR ☐ | SCREENED ☐ | BUILT-IN OVEN & RANGE ☑ |
| DEN SIZE | FIREPLACE ☐ | FENCED YARD | OUTDOOR GRILL ☐ | SEPARATE STOVE INCLUDED ☐ |
| FAMILY ROOM SIZE | FIREPLACE ☐ | STORM WINDOWS ☑ | STORM DOORS ☑ | REFRIGERATOR INCLUDED ☑ |
| RECREATION ROOM SIZE 14 x 18 | FIREPLACE ☑ | CURBS & GUTTERS ☐ | SIDEWALKS ☐ | DISHWASHER INCLUDED no |
| BASEMENT SIZE Full | | STORM SEWERS ☑ | ALLEY ☐ | DISPOSAL INCLUDED ☑ |
| NONE ☐ 1/4 ☐ 1/3 ☐ 1/2 ☐ 3/4 ☐ FULL ☑ | | WATER SUPPLY City | | DOUBLE SINK ☐ SINGLE SINK ☐ |
| UTILITY ROOM SIZE | | SEWER ☑ | SEPTIC ☐ | STAINLESS STEEL ☐ PORCELAIN ☐ |
| TYPE HOT WATER SYSTEM: | | TYPE GAS: NATURAL ☑ | BOTTLED ☐ | WASHER INCLUDED ☐ DRYER INCLUDED ☐ |
| TYPE HEAT Gas | | WHY SELLING | | LAND ASSESSMENT $ 4,500 |
| EST. FUEL COST | | | | IMPROVEMENTS $ 16,500 |
| ATTIC ☐ | | PROPERTY DESCRIPTION | | TOTAL ASSESSMENT $ 21,000 |
| PULL DOWN STAIRWAY ☐ REGULAR STAIRWAY ☐ TRAP DOOR ☐ | | | | |
| MAIDS ROOM ☐ TYPE BATH | | | | TAX RATE $8.50/100 |
| LOCATION | | | | TOTAL ANNUAL TAXES $ 1,785 |
| NAME OF BUILDER | | LOT SIZE 120 x 140 | | |
| SQUARE FOOTAGE | | LOT NO. 18 | | |

EXTERIOR OF HOUSE Frame McCary Addition to the city of Anytown in the County of Madison, Your State/Plat Book 5, pg. 26

NAME OF SCHOOLS: ELEMENTARY: ___    JR. HIGH: ___

HIGH: ___    PAROCHIAL: ___

PUBLIC TRANSPORTATION: ___

NEAREST SHOPPING AREA: ___

REMARKS: The property may be shown by appointment only between 10:00 a.m. and 7:00 p.m. Monday through Saturday. The key is available at the College Real Estate Office.

Date: August 22, this year

In consideration of the services of College Real Estate (herein called "Broker") to be rendered to the undersigned (herein called "Owner"), and of the promise of Broker to make reasonable efforts to obtain a Purchaser therefor, Owner hereby lists with Broker the real estate and all improvements thereon which are described above, (all herein called "the property"), and the Owner hereby grants to Broker the exclusive and irrevocable right to sell such property from 12:00 Noon on August 22, 19 TY until 12:00 Midnight on November 22, 19 TY (herein called "period of time"), for the price of seventy-eight thousand five hundred Dollars ($ 78,500.00) or for such other price and upon such other terms (including exchange) as Owner may subsequently authorize during the period of time.

It is understood by Owner that the above sum or any other price subsequently authorized by Owner shall include a cash fee of 6 per cent of such price or other price which shall be payable by Owner to Broker upon consummation by any Purchaser or Purchasers of a valid contract of sale of the property during the period of time and whether or not Broker was a procuring cause of any such contract of sale.

If the property is sold or exchanged by Owner, or by Broker or by any other person to any Purchaser to whom the property was shown by Broker or any representative of Broker within sixty (60) days after the expiration of the period of time mentioned above, Owner agrees to pay to Broker a cash fee which shall be the same percentage of the purchase price as the percentage mentioned above.

Broker is hereby authorized by Owner to place a "For Sale" sign on the property and to remove all signs of other brokers or salesmen during the period of time, and Owner hereby agrees to make the property available to Broker at all reasonable hours for the purpose of showing it to prospective Purchasers.

Owner agrees to convey the property to the Purchaser by warranty deed with the usual covenants of title and free and clear from all encumbrances, tenancies, liens (for taxes or otherwise), but subject to applicable restrictive covenants of record. Owner acknowledges receipt of copy of this agreement.

WITNESS the following signature(s) and seal(s):

Date Signed: August 22, this year    *Jack Nickless* (Owner)

Listing Agent You as sales person for College Real Estate

Address 2785 Nulsen Drive    Telephone 821-5168    *Margaret Nickless* (Owner)

*Figure 17-4—Real estate listing contract for sample problem.*

## REAL ESTATE SALES CONTRACT (OFFER TO PURCHASE AGREEMENT)

This AGREEMENT made as of _____ September 3 _____, 19 _TY_ ,

among _____ Charles Vance and Wilma Vance (H & W) _____ (herein called "Purchaser"),

and _____ Jack Nickless and Margaret Nickless (H & W) _____ (herein called "Seller"),

and _____ College Real Estate _____ (herein called "Broker"),
provides that Purchaser agrees to buy through Broker as agent for Seller, and Seller agrees to sell the following described real estate, and all improvements
thereon, located in the jurisdiction of _Madison County, Your State_ ,
(all herein called "the property"): ___ Lot 18 McCary Addition to the City of Anytown, County of Madison, Your State as recorded in ___

Plat Book 5, page 26 _____ , and more commonly known as 2785 Nulsen Dr., Anytown,

Your State _____ (street address).

1. The purchase price of the property is __ seventy-eight thousand dollars _____

Dollars ($ _78,000.00_ ), and such purchase price shall be paid as follows:
**80% of purchase price from new mortgage for 25 years at no more than 13% interest; the remainder in cash at the time of closing.**

2. Purchaser has made a deposit of one thousand and no/100————————(by check)———————— Dollars ($ 1000.00 )
with Broker, receipt of which is hereby acknowledged, and such deposit shall be held by Broker in escrow until the date of settlement and then applied
to the purchase price, or returned to Purchaser if the title to the property is not marketable.

3. Seller agrees to convey the property to Purchaser by Deed with the usual covenants of title and free and clear from all monetary encumbrances,
tenancies, liens (for taxes or otherwise), except as may be otherwise provided above, but subject to applicable restrictive covenants of record. Seller further
agrees to deliver possession of the property to Purchaser on the date of settlement and to pay the expense of preparing the deed of conveyance.

4. Settlement shall be made at _____ the offices of College Real Estate _____ on or before

__ September 30 _____, 19 _TY_ , or as soon thereafter as title can be examined and necessary documents prepared, with
allowance of a reasonable time for Seller to correct any defects reported by the title examiner.

5. All taxes, interest, rent, and impound escrow deposits, if any, shall be prorated as of the date of settlement.

6. All risk of loss or damage to the property by fire, windstorm, casualty, or other cause is assumed by Seller until the date of settlement.

7. Purchaser and Seller agree that Broker was the sole procuring cause of this Contract of Purchase, and Seller agrees to pay Broker for services

rendered a cash fee of __6__ per cent of the purchase price. If either Purchaser or Seller defaults under such Contract, such defaulting party shall
be liable for the cash fee of Broker and any expenses incurred by the non-defaulting party in connection with this transaction.

Subject to: __ the washer and dryer being included in the sales price _____

_____

_____

_____

8. Purchaser represents that an inspection satisfactory to Purchaser has been made of the property, and Purchaser agrees to accept the property
in its present condition except as may be otherwise provided in the description of the property above.

9. This Contract of Purchase constitutes the entire agreement among the parties and may not be modified or changed except by written instrument executed by all of the parties, including Broker.

10. This Contract of Purchase shall be construed, interpreted, and applied according to the law of the jurisdiction of _Your State_ and shall
be binding upon and shall inure to the benefit of the heirs, personal representatives, successors, and assigns of the parties.

All parties to this agreement acknowledge receipt of a certified copy.

WITNESS the following signatures and seals:

__*Jack Nickless*__ (SEAL) Seller  __*Charles Vance*__ (SEAL) Purchaser

__*Margaret Nickless*__ (SEAL) Seller  __*Wilma Vance*__ (SEAL) Purchaser

__College Real Estate__ (SEAL) Broker

Deposit Rec'd $ _1000.00_

(Personal Check)        Cash

Cashier's Check        Company Check

Sales Agent:   You as salesperson for College Real Estate

*Figure 17-5—Real estate sales contract for sample problem.*

## SETTLEMENT STATEMENT WORKSHEET

| | BUYER'S STATEMENT | | SELLER'S STATEMENT | |
|---|---|---|---|---|
| | DEBIT | CREDIT | DEBIT | CREDIT |
| Sales Price | 78,000.00 | | | 78,000.00 |
| Brokerage Fee | | | 4,680.00 | |
| New Mortgage | | 62,400.00 | | |
| Nickless Mortgage | | | 10,522.75 | |
| Deposit | | 1,000.00 | | |
| Taxes | | 1,338.75 | 1,338.75 | |
| Insurance | 46.69 | | | 46.69 |
| Title Examination | 140.00 | | | |
| Recording New Mortgage | 25.00 | | | |
| Appraisal Fee | | | 40.00 | |
| Mortgage Title Insurance | 75.00 | | | |
| Deed Recording Fee | | | 7.50 | |
| Deed Preparation | | | 50.00 | |
| Loan Origination Fee | 624.00 | | | |
| Survey Fee | | | 50.00 | |
| Balance Due from Buyer | | 14,171.94 | | |
| Balance Due Seller | | 61,357.69 | 61,357.69 | |
| | | | | |
| | | | | |
| | | | | |
| | $ 78,910.69 | $78,910.69 | $78,046.69 | $78,046.69 |

*Figure 17-6—Settlement statement worksheet for sample problem.*

## Calculations

1. *Brokerage fee*
   $78,000 × .06 = $4,680
2. *New mortgage*
   $78,000 × .80 = $62,400
3. *Nickless mortgage*
   $10,586 × .07 = $741.02
   $741.02/12 = $61.75
   $125.00 − $61.75 = $63.25
   $10,586.00 − $63.25 = $10,522.75
4. *Taxes*
   $4,500 + $16,500 = $21,000

$21,000 × $8.50/$100 = $1,785
$1,785.00/12 = $148.75
$148.75 × 9 months = $1,338.75
5. *Loan origination fee*
   .01 × $62,400 = $624
6. *Insurance*
   $80.00/12 = $6.67/month

| | Day | Month | Year |
|---|---|---|---|
| Expiration date | 30 | 4 | NY |
| Closing date | 30 | 9 | TY |
| Remaining | 0 | 7 | 0 |

$6.67 × 7 months prepaid = $46.69 to seller

## PRACTICE PROBLEMS FOR
## REAL ESTATE TRANSACTIONS

The following problems will provide practical experience in completing a settlement statement worksheet. Blank forms are included at the end of the chapter for your use. Answers are on pages 261–267.

*Guidelines for Completing Listing, Offer, and Settlement Forms*

- ☐ TY = this year.
- ☐ NY = next year.
- ☐ DAFC = days after final closing.
- ☐ All calculations in this text are done using a 30-day month. Therefore:
  10 days = ⅓ month; 15 days = ½ month; 20 days = ⅔ month.
- ☐ Round off all figures to the nearest cent. For ½ cent or more round up; if less than ½ cent, drop.
- ☐ Your answer may differ by a few cents due to rounding; check the examples to see how figures are rounded off.
- ☐ Compute math using either hand calculation or your calculator.

### Problem 1

Mrs. Carolyn Turner has accepted an offer on her house from Mr. and Mrs. Robert David for $97,000. The purchasers will obtain a new deed of trust for $74,000 for a period of 20 years at 12½ percent. The Davids desire to purchase the washer and dryer under a separate bill of sale for $400. The assessed valuation of the land is $8,000, and of the improvements, $21,000. The present tax rate is $7.10/$100. The taxes are computed in arrears and are due December 31, TY. They have not yet been paid. The Davids have given the broker an earnest money deposit in the amount of $1,000. Mrs. Turner has an outstanding mortgage balance of $9,650 after her September 15 payment. The PI constant is $96, with interest at 6 percent in arrears. She has a fire and extended coverage policy with an annual prepaid premium of $144 that expires June 10, NY. The broker will charge a fee of 7 percent.

The closing is set for November 15, TY. There will be a $30 deed preparation fee paid by the seller and recording fees of $31 to be paid by the purchasers. The fee for the new trust is 1 percent. Mrs. Turner will provide an owner's title insurance policy at a cost of $135. The Davids will have to provide a mortgagee's title policy in the amount of $75. The Davids will assume Mrs. Turner's fire insurance policy.

### Problem 2

Mr. and Mrs. John T. Murphy are selling their duplex. The Murphys live in one side and rent the other side for $185 per month, due in advance on the first of the month. The taxes on the property are $9.25/$100 based on an assessment of $3,000 for the land and $12,000 for the improvements. The taxes are due in advance on January 1, TY, but have not yet been paid by the sellers.

The outstanding mortgage balance after the September 1 payment is $28,500. The PITI constant is $450 per month. The taxes are $110 per month and insurance is $12 per month. The interest is 8 percent, payable in arrears. The brokerage fee will be 6 percent.

The property has a fire insurance policy in the amount of $50,000, assessed at a premium of $144 per year, paid in advance. The policy expires August 15, NY.

Mark Jones makes an offer of $51,000. The offer is contingent on Mr. Jones' obtaining financing in the amount of 90 percent of the sales price at 12 percent for 30 years. Also, the Murphys will take back a second mortgage for $2,000 at 12½ percent for five years. Mr. Jones gives the broker a $500 earnest money deposit and the offer is accepted as presented.

The final closing is set for November 10, TY. The rent, taxes, and insurance are to be prorated to the day of closing. The insurance policy is being assumed by Mr. Jones. The seller will have additional closing charges of $25 deed preparation fee, $182.50 owners' title insurance policy, and $75 appraisal fee. The purchaser will have charges of $75 for mortgagee's title insurance, 1 percent loan origination fee, $28 recording fee, and a $75 attorney's fee. The seller will receive back $634 from his tax and insurance escrow account.

### Problem 3

Edward and Mary Smith desire to sell their home, which is owned free and clear. The sales price agreed upon is $74,500, and the commission is set at 6 percent. The Smiths will take a purchase money mortgage for 80 percent of the sales price for 15 years at 12½ percent.

The tax rate is $8.25/$100. The land has been assessed at $6,000 and the improvements at $14,000. The taxes are due in arrears on December 31, TY and have not yet been paid.

The following additional charges are being paid at the closing September 1, TY. The buyer will pay a title examination fee of $175, recording fees of $5, and additional legal fees of $45. The seller will pay legal fees of $50, an appraisal fee of $100, and a well examination and certification fee of $35.

The purchasers will buy the air conditioner, washer, dryer, and lawnmower for $675. They give the broker an earnest money deposit of $500.

### Problem 4

Mr. Otis Brown and his wife, Mary, sold their home to Mr. and Mrs. Charles Joseph for $32,000. The Josephs will obtain FHA financing for $30,550 at 13 percent with the seller paying the five discount points.

The Browns have an outstanding mortgage balance of $25,920 after the April 1 payment. The principal and interest payments are $274/month at 8 percent interest in arrears. The property has an assessed value of $2,500 for the land and $7,000 for the improvements. The tax rate is $8.40/$100, and the taxes are due in arrears by December 31, TY.

The Josephs deposit $500 as earnest money with the broker. A commission of 6 percent is being charged on the sale of the property.

The closing will take place August 10, TY. The Josephs must provide a binder for fire insurance at closing at a cost to them of $182. The lending institution wants an escrow deposit of 2 months' taxes in advance. The loan origination fee is 1 percent. The FHA appraisal fee is $50, the photo fee is $15, and the survey fee is $55. The purchasers will also be charged $75 for a mortgagee's title insurance policy.

The seller will have to provide an owners' title insurance policy in the amount of the purchase price at a cost of $187.50. The taxes will be prorated.

## Problem 5

You as broker sell the residence of Harvey and Lois Jones for $87,750. Also included in the transaction is the sale of an additional lot at $10,000. Both properties are purchased by Mr. and Mrs. William Dallas. The Dallases also purchase from the Joneses a garden tractor for $750 cash due at the closing. You will receive a 6 percent commission on the sale of the real estate.

The Dallases get a new mortgage for 80 percent of the sales price of the residence at 11½ percent. They will purchase the additional lot under a 10-year land contract at 12¾ percent, with 30 percent of the purchase price down. They give an earnest money deposit of $2,000.

The Joneses have an outstanding balance on their mortgage of $10,120 after the August 1 payment. The payments are $175 principal and interest each month. The interest is 7½ percent computed in arrears. There is a fire insurance policy with a premium of $270 for three years, paid in advance, that expires May 1, NY. The tax rate is $7.40/$100. The total land assessment is $8,000, and the improvements are assessed at $20,000, and were due December 31, TY in arrears. The taxes and insurance are to be assumed and prorated.

The closing is to take place August 31, TY. The sellers will have additional closing costs of $75 for the land contract, $100 for an abstract, and $12.50 for recording fees. The purchasers will be charged a $125 abstract examination fee, 1 percent loan origination fee, plus 2 discount points, and $37.50 in recording fees.

## SETTLEMENT STATEMENT WORKSHEET

| | BUYER'S STATEMENT | | SELLER'S STATEMENT | |
|---|---|---|---|---|
| | DEBIT | CREDIT | DEBIT | CREDIT |
| | | | | |
| | | | | |
| | | | | |
| | | | | |
| | | | | |
| | | | | |
| | | | | |
| | | | | |
| | | | | |
| | | | | |
| | | | | |
| | | | | |
| | | | | |
| | | | | |
| | | | | |
| | | | | |
| | | | | |
| | | | | |
| | | | | |
| | | | | |
| | | | | |

## SETTLEMENT STATEMENT WORKSHEET

|  | BUYER'S STATEMENT | | SELLER'S STATEMENT | |
|  | DEBIT | CREDIT | DEBIT | CREDIT |
|---|---|---|---|---|
|  |  |  |  |  |
|  |  |  |  |  |
|  |  |  |  |  |
|  |  |  |  |  |
|  |  |  |  |  |
|  |  |  |  |  |
|  |  |  |  |  |
|  |  |  |  |  |
|  |  |  |  |  |
|  |  |  |  |  |
|  |  |  |  |  |
|  |  |  |  |  |
|  |  |  |  |  |
|  |  |  |  |  |
|  |  |  |  |  |
|  |  |  |  |  |
|  |  |  |  |  |
|  |  |  |  |  |
|  |  |  |  |  |
|  |  |  |  |  |

## SETTLEMENT STATEMENT WORKSHEET

|  | BUYER'S STATEMENT | | SELLER'S STATEMENT | |
|---|---|---|---|---|
|  | DEBIT | CREDIT | DEBIT | CREDIT |
|  |  |  |  |  |
|  |  |  |  |  |
|  |  |  |  |  |
|  |  |  |  |  |
|  |  |  |  |  |
|  |  |  |  |  |
|  |  |  |  |  |
|  |  |  |  |  |
|  |  |  |  |  |
|  |  |  |  |  |
|  |  |  |  |  |
|  |  |  |  |  |
|  |  |  |  |  |
|  |  |  |  |  |
|  |  |  |  |  |
|  |  |  |  |  |
|  |  |  |  |  |
|  |  |  |  |  |
|  |  |  |  |  |
|  |  |  |  |  |
|  |  |  |  |  |

### SETTLEMENT STATEMENT WORKSHEET

| | BUYER'S STATEMENT | | SELLER'S STATEMENT | |
|---|---|---|---|---|
| | DEBIT | CREDIT | DEBIT | CREDIT |
| | | | | |
| | | | | |
| | | | | |
| | | | | |
| | | | | |
| | | | | |
| | | | | |
| | | | | |
| | | | | |
| | | | | |
| | | | | |
| | | | | |
| | | | | |
| | | | | |
| | | | | |
| | | | | |
| | | | | |
| | | | | |
| | | | | |
| | | | | |
| | | | | |

## SETTLEMENT STATEMENT WORKSHEET

|  | BUYER'S STATEMENT | | SELLER'S STATEMENT | |
|---|---|---|---|---|
|  | DEBIT | CREDIT | DEBIT | CREDIT |
|  |  |  |  |  |
|  |  |  |  |  |
|  |  |  |  |  |
|  |  |  |  |  |
|  |  |  |  |  |
|  |  |  |  |  |
|  |  |  |  |  |
|  |  |  |  |  |
|  |  |  |  |  |
|  |  |  |  |  |
|  |  |  |  |  |
|  |  |  |  |  |
|  |  |  |  |  |
|  |  |  |  |  |
|  |  |  |  |  |
|  |  |  |  |  |
|  |  |  |  |  |
|  |  |  |  |  |
|  |  |  |  |  |
|  |  |  |  |  |
|  |  |  |  |  |
|  |  |  |  |  |

**SETTLEMENT STATEMENT WORKSHEET**

|  | BUYER'S STATEMENT | | SELLER'S STATEMENT | |
|---|---|---|---|---|
|  | DEBIT | CREDIT | DEBIT | CREDIT |
|  |  |  |  |  |
|  |  |  |  |  |
|  |  |  |  |  |
|  |  |  |  |  |
|  |  |  |  |  |
|  |  |  |  |  |
|  |  |  |  |  |
|  |  |  |  |  |
|  |  |  |  |  |
|  |  |  |  |  |
|  |  |  |  |  |
|  |  |  |  |  |
|  |  |  |  |  |
|  |  |  |  |  |
|  |  |  |  |  |
|  |  |  |  |  |
|  |  |  |  |  |
|  |  |  |  |  |
|  |  |  |  |  |
|  |  |  |  |  |

# Chapter 18

# Real Estate Licensing Examinations

Over the years, each of the national testing services has made changes in its examination format and content to keep up with the ever-changing real estate industry. This chapter, which reflects the most recent of these changes, presents the most information on the Educational Testing Service (ETS) Real Estate Licensing Examination (RELE), Assessment Systems, Inc. (ASI) Real Estate Assessment for Licensure (REAL) examination, and the American College Testing (ACT) examination.

Each candidate for licensure should contact the appropriate state real estate commission or state licensing agency for complete information on its examination. Tests vary by jurisdiction, and certain state-specific materials are often covered in a unique manner.

Included are sample questions reflecting the topics covered and the testing format used by the different services.

### ETS UNIFORM TEST*

The examination for brokers administered by the Educational Testing Service (ETS) of Princeton, New Jersey, is up to four and one-half hours long and divided into two separate tests—the Uniform Test and the State Test.

The Uniform Test (80 questions) includes questions in the subject areas outlined here. Approximately 20 percent of the questions involve arithmetical calculations. These questions are distributed throughout the test.

1. **Real Estate Brokerage** (35% of Uniform Test)
   a. Listing and Showing Property: The responsibilities of a broker when contracting to list, advertise, and show property for sale, lease, trade, or exchange, including responsibilities under the law of agency, compliance with the Federal Fair Housing Act, and obligations when entering into written listing agreements.
   b. Settlement Procedures: The responsibilities of a broker in arranging settlement or closing, including recordation procedures, closing costs, charges, credits, adjustments and prorations, and compliance with the Real Estate Settlement Procedures Act (RESPA).

   c. Property Management: The responsibilities of a broker managing property on behalf of an owner, including property maintenance, collecting rents and security deposits in accordance with terms of leases and legal agreements, negotiating leases, and advising on current market conditions.
2. **Contracts and Other Legal Aspects** (27%)
   a. Contracts: General aspects of contract law; familiarity with listing contracts, contracts for sales, options, leases, installment land contracts, and escrow agreements; referring clients to legal counsel.
   b. Land Use Controls: Zoning, private restrictions, requirements for subdividing and developing, deed restrictions, and covenants.
   c. Deeds: The general characteristics of various types of deeds and the circumstances under which specific deeds are appropriate.
   d. Property Ownership: The rights and interests that may affect ownership of real property, characteristics of various types of ownership (joint tenancy, timesharing, etc.)
   e. Condominiums and Cooperatives: The requirements for certification of real property as a condominium or cooperative, types of ownership (individual and common), aspects of property conversion to condominium or cooperative.
   f. Other Legal Aspects: The legal implications of public powers over real property (eminent domain, escheat, police powers, taxation, etc.) and special interests in real property (easements, party walls, etc.)
3. **Pricing and Valuation** (15%)
   a. Appraising: The principles of value and approaches to estimating value.
   b. Pricing by Comparative Market Analysis: Pricing real estate for sale, rent, or exchange in the absence of an appraisal report.
4. **Finance and Investment** (23%)
   a. Financing Arrangements: Costs involved in placement of loans, governmental agencies that guarantee or insure mortgages, requirements of the Truth-in-Lending Act regarding advertising financial aspects of a sale.
   b. Financing Instruments: Characteristics of notes

---

*Reprinted by permission of Educational Testing Service, Princeton, NJ 08541.

and mortgages, deeds of trust, installment land contracts, and other financing instruments.

c.  Loans and Mortgages: Characteristics of different types of loans or mortgages (amortizing, term, blanket, package, etc.), essential elements and special clauses of mortgages (prepayment, due on sale clause, variable payment, etc.), sources of junior or secondary loans, conditions and procedures involved in default and foreclosure.

d.  Tax Ramifications: The tax ramifications of home ownership, including interest and property tax deductions, deferred capital gains, etc.; also, the tax ramifications of real estate investments, including depreciation, capital gains and losses, refinancing, etc.

e.  Real Estate Securities: The basic concepts of syndications, how they are formed, and the general federal laws governing securities.

## ETS Salesperson Uniform Test

The Educational Testing Service (ETS) Real Estate Licensing Examination (RELE) for Salespersons is up to four and a half hours long and divided into two separate tests, Uniform and State.

The Uniform test (80 questions) contains questions in the subject areas described here. Approximately 20 percent of the questions involve arithmetical calculations. These questions are distributed throughout the test.

1.  *Real Estate Contracts* (13% of Uniform test)
    Questions in this area cover the general definition and essential elements of a contract and the specific contracts used in real estate, including leases, listing agreements, sales contract (offer to purchase agreements) and options.
2.  *Financing* (24% of Uniform test)
    These questions deal with two major aspects of real estate financing: financing instruments and means of financing.
    Questions in this area cover such topics as basic real estate securities, sources of financing, governmental agencies and acts pertaining to financing (e.g., Federal Housing Administration, Veterans Administration, Truth-in-Lending Act), basic definitions of the major financing instruments, anatomy of a mortgage loan (including types of mortgages, loan fees, loan placement procedures and term loans), junior finance, default and foreclosure.
3.  *Real Estate Ownership* (22% of Uniform test)
    The questions in this subject area cover the following topics:
    a.  Deeds: the definition and necessary elements for recordation and acknowledgment of various types of deeds

b.  Interests in Real Property: estates (extent of title), private rights to real property (ownership), public powers over real property and special interests in real property (easements, etc.)

c.  Condominiums: general information about condominiums, ownership of common and separate elements and the duties and responsibilities of a condominium homeowner's association.

d.  Federal Fair Housing Act: grievances, penalties, practices and procedures with regard to the Federal Fair Housing Act.

4.  *Real Estate Brokerage* (24% of Uniform test)
    a.  Law of Agency: definitions, rights, responsibilities and functions of a principal and an agent
    b.  Property Management: general scope and functions of property management
    c.  Settlement Procedures: title validity, conveyance, settlement charges, credits, adjustments and prorating
5.  *Real Estate Valuation* (17% of Uniform test)
    a.  Appraisal: definition of value, approaches to value, the appraisal process, the valuation of partial interests and appraisal terminology
    b.  Planning and Zoning: public land-use control, public planning and zoning and private subdividing
    c.  Property Description: kinds of property descriptions, plat reading and related terms and concepts
    d.  Taxes and Assessments: real property taxes, special assessments, liens and other tax factors

The question format for the ETS-style Salesperson Uniform Test is the same as that of the Broker Uniform Test. The examinee should review the sample Broker Uniform Test for practice and contact the appropriate state commission concerning the specifics of the state portion of the examination for licensure.

Notes:
1.  For questions involving arithmetic computation, answers involving dollars and cents are given to the nearest dollar.
2.  For questions involving proration computation, unless stated otherwise, the seller is responsible for the day of closing, and a 360-day year is to be used.

### ETS-STYLE PRACTICE UNIFORM TEST

1.  In using the exclusive right to sell listing contract, the broker

    (A)  becomes the agent of the seller
    (B)  is a principal to the contract
    (C)  guarantees the minimum price for which the property may be purchased

(D) submits offers from cooperating brokers only after his own offers have been reviewed by the seller

2. While listing property, the broker notices that the basement wall is severely cracked. The broker has which of the following options?

(A) Disclose the problem to prospective purchasers, even if repairs are made prior to showing

(B) Disclose the problem only if asked by a prospective purchaser

(C) Openly disclose the problem to prospective buyers

(D) Disclose the problem only if the seller will not repair it

3. Which of the following creates a special agency relationship between seller and broker?

(A) An offer to purchase for the listed amount

(B) The contractual agreement to sell any real estate owned by the seller

(C) An offer for more than the listed price

(D) An exclusive right to sell listing on a particular property

4. Under the agency established by the listing agreement, the broker is responsible to do all of the following EXCEPT

(A) present all written offers to purchase regardless of price

(B) tell purchasers the seller will accept less than the listed price

(C) place the principal's interest above all others

(D) account for all monies deposited in the broker's trust fund on behalf of the principal

5. A buyer withdraws the offer before the seller has accepted. The broker has an exclusive right to sell listing on the property. The broker may

(A) split the earnest money with the seller

(B) charge the seller his commission

(C) receive no commission

(D) be reimbursed for his expenses

6. In establishing the price at which a property will be listed, the broker should

(A) always do a formal appraisal using all three methods to estimate value

(B) do a comparative market study before establishing the listing price with the seller

(C) set the price at least 20% higher than the property is expected to bring to allow a margin for negotiation

(D) allow the seller to set the listing price with no input from the broker

7. The breach of contract remedy that would force the seller to complete the transaction is

(A) liquidated damages

(B) recission

(C) specific performance

(D) punitive damages

8. As a broker, you may complete all of the following documents for your principal EXCEPT

(A) leases
(B) options
(C) contracts of sale
(D) deeds

9. If the seller makes a counteroffer, the buyer is

(A) still obligated to the terms of the original offer

(B) required to keep his offer open until the counteroffer is accepted

(C) not allowed to make another counteroffer

(D) relieved of the terms of the original offer

10. A broker may commit an act of discrimination by not paying proper attention to the Federal Fair Housing Law regarding all of the following EXCEPT

(A) religion
(B) race
(C) sex
(D) marital status

11. The written authorization to offer property for sale is a mutual agreement between the broker and principal. This is a contract for

(A) the sale of real property

(B) personal professional services

(C) the sale of personal property

(D) the employment of salespersons

12. A broker who deposits the funds of others that come into his possession in his general account instead of his escrow account is

(A) commingling funds

(B) subordinating funds

(C) alienating funds

(D) investing funds

13. The Joneses are closing the sale of their house on April 10. The 11 percent interest on their mortgage is paid in arrears. The outstanding balance after the April 1 payment is $59,275. What will be the entry for the interest at the Joneses' settlement?

(A) Credit $181
(B) Debit $181
(C) Credit $362
(D) Debit $362

14. The closing date will be July 20, TY. After the June 1, TY mortgage payment was made, the principal mortgage balance was $51,755. The PI constant

is $610. The interest rate is 13 percent in arrears. What is the principal balance at closing?

(A) $51,145      (C) $51,755
(B) $51,706      (D) $51,801

15. If a broker refuses to show a prospective buyer properties listed in certain neighborhoods and only shows him properties in other areas due to his ethnic background, that broker is

(A) panic selling      (C) red-lining
(B) steering           (D) blockbusting

16. The listing contract may be terminated by each of the following EXCEPT

(A) mutual agreement
(B) death of the listing salesperson
(C) lapse of the listing period
(D) acceptance of an offer

17. All of the following must be in writing to satisfy the requirements of enforceability under the Statute of Frauds EXCEPT

(A) offers to purchase    (C) land contracts
(B) options               (D) short term leases

18. On a listing for vacant residential property, the broker is responsible to the principal for doing all of the following EXCEPT

(A) presenting an offer that is low
(B) accepting any reasonable offer for his principal
(C) maintaining and caring for the property according to the listing
(D) marketing the property to the best of his ability

19. The earnest money deposit is

(A) given by the seller to the buyer to show good faith in completing the sale
(B) applied as a credit against the sales price on the buyer's closing statement
(C) used by the broker to cover expenses of sale
(D) forfeited by the buyer if the offer is rejected

20. Under the Federal Fair Housing Act of 1968, it is illegal to discriminate on the basis of all of the following EXCEPT

(A) age               (C) race
(B) national origin   (D) religion

21. Mr. Jones is closing on the sale of his house on June 15, TY. The interest on Mr. Jones' mortgage is 14 percent with interest computed in arrears. The outstanding mortgage balance after the June 5, TY payment was $57,500. What entry will be made for interest on the closing statement?

(A) Credit Jones, $224
(B) Debit Jones, $224
(C) Debit Jones, $447
(D) Credit Jones, $447

22. The closing will take place on June 15. A three-year insurance policy costing $741.29 is to be prorated. The policy was purchased February 1, last year. What entry will appear on the sellers' closing statement?

(A) Credit $340    (C) Debit $340
(B) Debit $402     (D) Credit $402

23. As a managing broker, you receive 1 percent of all that your office sells. If your office charges a 7 percent commission on residential sales and you have four $1 million producers (sales associates) in the office, each of whom receives 3 percent, what is your income based on these four producers?

(A) $40,000     (C) $60,000
(B) $120,000    (D) $90,000

24. A property owner lists his property with a broker and tells the broker, "I want to sell only to a member of a minority group because they have had so many problems in the past." In this situation, the broker should do all of the following EXCEPT

(A) explain to the owner that he cannot legally discriminate against non-minority group members
(B) refuse the listing until the owner agrees to accept offers from any bona fide buyer
(C) list the property, but include in the contract a statement that only offers from minority group members will be considered by the owner
(D) explain to the owner the possible consequences of violations of the Federal Fair Housing Act

25. Mr. Allen asks a broker to help sell his vacant commercial building. The broker contacts Mr. Baker, who is interested in using 75 percent of the building for storage but needs a partner for the remaining 25 percent. Mr. Baker also wants a one-year option to purchase the property. The broker agrees to be Mr. Baker's partner and presents the offer to option the property to Mr. Allen. In this situation, which of the following statements about the option offer is true?

(A) It must be presented with Mr. Baker's signature only, because he is the majority partner
(B) It may be presented with Mr. Baker's signature only, because it is an option offer and not a sales offer

(C) It must be presented with both Mr. Baker's and the broker's signatures as offerors

(D) It may be presented with Mr. Baker's signature only, if the broker explains his interest in the option offer

26. A written contract between an owner and property manager should specify all of the following EXCEPT

(A) the management fee and how it is computed
(B) the rental schedule to be followed by the manager
(C) the tenant responsibilities of the manager
(D) the tax shelter schedule of the owner

27. As the property manager, you are usually responsible for all of the following EXCEPT

(A) accounting for all funds received by the project
(B) the collection of rents from tenants
(C) overseeing the maintenance of the leased property
(D) deeding the units in a conversion to condominium status

28. A property management agreement calls for a leasing fee of 6 percent of the first $50,000 of rental income and 5 percent thereafter. Under these terms, a lease negotiated for $1,200 per month over a 5-year term would result in a payment of

(A) $3,600        (C) $4,100
(B) $3,960        (D) $4,320

29. The broker is drawing up a property management agreement for a property owned by a husband and wife. The contract needs to be executed by the

(A) wife, for both spouses
(B) husband, for both spouses
(C) broker, on behalf of all parties
(D) broker, husband, and wife

30. A buyer has signed an offer to purchase that includes many contingencies. In this situation, the broker must first provide the buyer with a copy of the offer to purchase at which of the following times?

(A) When it is signed and accepted by the seller
(B) After the seller accepts the offer or makes a counteroffer
(C) After all the contingencies are met and the seller accepts the offer
(D) Immediately, before the offer is presented to the seller

31. Which of the following is true of an option on real estate?

(A) It must be in writing to be enforceable
(B) Terms are flexible during the option period
(C) It may not be exercised prior to the date of expiration
(D) It does not require consideration

32. The potential buyer of a property is not exactly sure of the north boundary of the lot. What would be the best means that the broker could suggest to verify the boundary?

(A) Check with the county recorder's office
(B) Read the abstract and opinion of title
(C) Have title insurance issued
(D) Have a staked survey done of the lot

33. For privately owned property to be taken under the right of eminent domain

(A) a partition suit must be filed
(B) just compensation must be paid
(C) escheat proceedings must be filed
(D) patents must be recorded

34. A father and daughter could take title to a property in unequal shares under which of the following?

(A) Tenants by the entirety
(B) Tenants in common
(C) In severalty
(D) Joint tenants with the right of survivorship

35. The owner of shares in the stock of a cooperative building receives what type of lease to a specific unit?

(A) Proprietary lease
(B) Step-up lease
(C) Graduated payment lease
(D) Percentage lease

36. Under a joint tenancy with right of survivorship,

(A) the tenancy may not occur by accident
(B) the creditors have no rights against a tenant's interest
(C) the tenants have unequal shares of ownership
(D) the surviving tenants may not receive a dead tenant's interest

37. Legal title to real estate transfers upon

(A) creation of the deed
(B) acceptance of the offer
(C) delivery and acceptance of the deed
(D) listing the property

38. An easement appurtenant that contains building restrictions to protect the view of the dominant tenement

(A) is considered to be negative to the servient tenement
(B) will not survive the transfer of the property
(C) is a personal right of the dominant tenement
(D) does not have to be placed upon adjoining properties

39. Which of the following deeds should the grantor use if transferring an uncertain interest in real property?

(A) General warranty deed
(B) Special warranty deed
(C) Sheriff's deed
(D) Quitclaim deed

40. Which of the following parties to a real estate transaction would have the most exposure to liability?

(A) The grantor under a quitclaim deed
(B) The grantor under a special warranty deed
(C) The grantor under a general warranty deed
(D) The grantor under a trustee's deed

41. The clause in the deed that defines or limits the quantity of the estate being conveyed is which of the following?

(A) Subordination clause
(B) Habendum clause
(C) Partition clause
(D) Reversion clause

42. For a general warranty deed to be valid, all of the following are true EXCEPT

(A) the grantee must execute the deed
(B) the deed must be in writing
(C) the deed should be properly delivered by the grantor
(D) the deed must be accepted by the grantee

43. If A grants a life estate to B and thereafter to C in fee, C holds a

(A) dower interest
(B) lien interest
(C) curtesy interest
(D) remainder interest

44. The restrictive covenants in a deed

(A) expire upon the sale of a property
(B) encumber the present owner's privileges of ownership
(C) are not to be imposed by the developer
(D) cannot be used in zoned subdivisions

45. If the deed form does not state the extent of the estate being conveyed, it is presumed to convey

(A) an estate at will          (C) a fee simple title
(B) a conditional fee          (D) a determinable fee

46. Which of the following would give title for a limited period of time?

(A) Sheriff's deed          (C) Life estate deed
(B) Warranty deed          (D) Quitclaim deed

47. Under a tenancy by the entirety form of ownership,

(A) the wife owns a 50% interest in the property
(B) the marriage owns the property as an entity
(C) there is no survivorship
(D) the creditors have unlimited rights

48. Which of the following does not go with the sale of a property?

(A) Lease
(B) License
(C) Easement appurtenant
(D) Profit

49. To establish the condominium form of ownership, all of the following must occur EXCEPT

(A) by-laws are established
(B) a master deed is created
(C) unit deeds are created
(D) shares are sold in the corporation

50. Which of the following is NOT a fixture?

(A) Chandelier in a dining room
(B) Showcases built into a wall
(C) Corn growing in a field
(D) Blackboard attached to a wall

51. The assemblage of two pieces of property into one causes the value to become greater than the cost of the individual pieces. This incremental increase is

(A) capitalization          (C) reversion
(B) plottage          (D) depreciation

52. The initial step in the appraisal process is to

(A) inspect the property legally and physically
(B) gather market data from all sources
(C) define the problem of the appraisal
(D) form an opinion of the value to be sought

53. To apply the income approach in the appraisal of an apartment building, the appraiser needs to know

(A) debt service          (C) reproduction cost
(B) tax bracket          (D) vacancy rate

54. A building would cost $550,000 to replace today. It is fully occupied and 17 years remain on a 30-year lease. The net income is $36,000 and the investor desires a 12 percent capitalization rate. The investor would not pay more than what amount for the building?

(A) $257,000    (C) $360,000
(B) $300,000    (D) $550,000

55. Which of the following would NOT be used as a comparable in an appraisal?

(A) A house in another neighborhood that sold in the last three months
(B) A house on a corner lot in the same neighborhood
(C) A house in the same neighborhood that sold 9 months ago
(D) A house in the same neighborhood that sold at a foreclosure auction

56. The analysis of the results of the different approaches to develop a final estimate of value is known as

(A) capitalization    (C) correlation
(B) depreciation      (D) accretion

57. The value of a parcel of land is $15,000. The replacement cost new of the improvements is $60,000. The depreciation was estimated at about 16.6 percent. What is the value of the property under the cost approach?

(A) $65,000    (C) $75,000
(B) $70,000    (D) $80,000

58. Which of the following is NOT used in determining the net operating income in an appraisal report?

(A) Real property taxes
(B) Management fees
(C) Maintenance expenses
(D) Mortgage payments

59. Under the Cost Approach, the appraiser has calculated the current replacement cost of the improvements, which are now 10 years old. The next step is to calculate which of the following?

(A) Capitalization rate
(B) Depreciation
(C) Market value of the land
(D) Gross rent multiplier

60. If the gross annual income from a building is $12,500, the sales price was $100,000, and the net income was $5,000, what is the GRM for the property?

(A) 5      (C) 40
(B) 12.5   (D) 8

61. In appraising residential real estate, the approach relied on as most indicative of value is

(A) income    (C) market
(B) cost      (D) GRM

62. In using the cost approach, the appraiser uses which of the following in estimating depreciation?

(A) Effective age
(B) Actual age
(C) Land value
(D) Net income

63. A mortgage is considered to be

(A) an involuntary lien
(B) a voluntary lien
(C) an encroachment
(D) a subordination

64. Which of the following types of loans is secured by more than one parcel of real estate?

(A) Package    (C) Swing
(B) Blanket    (D) Wraparound

65. Which of the following sources of mortgage money has as its primary purpose the lending on residential real estate?

(A) Savings and loan associations
(B) Federal Home Loan Bank
(C) Commercial banks
(D) Federal Reserve Bank

66. An installment land contract usually provides the buyer with all of the following EXCEPT

(A) the right to income from the property
(B) the right to quiet enjoyment
(C) legal title at closing
(D) possession

67. A primary characteristic of a straight term loan is

(A) a balloon payment with the final payment
(B) lower than market rate of interest
(C) no discount points may be charged
(D) full amortization of the debt and interest

68. In the case of a foreclosure sale, the monies in excess of the judgment amount are paid to the

(A) sheriff    (C) lender
(B) court      (D) borrower

69. The borrower wants a 13 percent rate, and conventional loans are made at 14 percent. How much discount will be charged at the closing of a $57,500 loan to get the rate?

(A) $5,340    (C) $4,600
(B) $5,750    (D) $3,450

70. Which type of loan has the potential of no down payment if both the borrower and property qualify?

(A) FHA    (C) Conventional
(B) VA     (D) Insured conventional

71. If the borrower is forced by the lender to repay the loan prior to the actual due date, the lender is exercising the

    (A) subordination clause
    (B) subrogation clause
    (C) acceleration clause
    (D) prepayment clause

72. Truth-in-Lending requires full disclosure of the

    (A) interest rate in terms of an annual percentage rate
    (B) comparable rates of other lenders
    (C) commission schedules of the real estate brokers
    (D) hazard insurance premium rates

73. Concerning the sale of foreclosed property, all of the following are true EXCEPT

    (A) any monies in excess of the debt and cost of the sale go to the mortgagor
    (B) the buyer of the property at the sale receives a sheriff's deed
    (C) if the proceeds from the sale are not sufficient to satisfy the debt, the mortgagee may levy against the other assets of the mortgagor
    (D) the property is listed with a real estate agent under an open listing

74. A buyer agrees to a financial arrangement that gives her the right to occupy a property and obtain the deed at a later time, after payment of the full purchase price. This arrangement can be which of the following?

    (A) Sale and leaseback contract
    (B) Contract for deed
    (C) Lease from period to period
    (D) Option to purchase

75. To be valid and enforceable, a mortgage must be all of the following EXCEPT

    (A) accepted by the mortgagee
    (B) executed by the mortgagor
    (C) made between competent parties
    (D) oral in nature

76. A house was appraised for $42,250, yet sold for $43,500. The purchaser borrowed $35,913. What was the lending institution's loan-to-value ratio?

    (A) 70 percent     (C) 85 percent
    (B) 80 percent     (D) 75 percent

77. An investment property was purchased for $240,000. The land was valued at 15 percent of the total value. The property has been held for five years and was depreciated on a 40-year schedule. It sold for $300,000. What is the tax liability if the owner is in the 28 percent tax bracket?

    (A) $9,576
    (B) $23,940
    (C) $34,200
    (D) $85,500

78. Which of the following would make a real estate transaction subject to federal security regulations?

    (A) Selling more than 100 units in an in-state condominium project
    (B) Offering for sale portions of a project to people who expect to profit from the efforts of a third party
    (C) Advertising a project for sale in major newspapers
    (D) Offering a project for sale through a national brokerage firm

79. Mr. Smith sold his residence for $120,000. He originally paid $75,000 for the property five years ago. He is in the 28 percent tax bracket. Which of the following is true?

    (A) The depreciation on the property is computed on the $120,000 basis
    (B) 40% of the capital gain is excluded from taxation
    (C) He has 24 months to reinvest in a home of equal or greater value to postpone the tax
    (D) The value of the lot is deducted from the property value to create the basis for depreciating the home

80. Creation of a limited partnership for the purchase of real estate for profit would be subject to federal securities laws because

    (A) any partnership arrangement, limited or general, is considered a security agreement
    (B) the liability of the partners is limited only to losses equal to the amount invested
    (C) the limited partnership agreement is an investment contract since profits are a result of third party efforts
    (D) the tax benefits formulate an investment contract and accelerated cost recovery systems are used

## ETS-Style Practice Uniform Test

*Answers*

| | | | |
|---|---|---|---|
| 1. A | 4. B | 7. C | 10. D |
| 2. C | 5. C | 8. D | 11. B |
| 3. D | 6. B | 9. D | 12. A |

| | | | | | | | | |
|---|---|---|---|---|---|---|---|
| 13. | B* | 30. | D | 47. | B | 64. | B |
| 14. | B* | 31. | A | 48. | B | 65. | A |
| 15. | B | 32. | D | 49. | D | 66. | C |
| 16. | B | 33. | B | 50. | C | 67. | A |
| 17. | D | 34. | B | 51. | B | 68. | D |
| 18. | B | 35. | A | 52. | C | 69. | C* |
| 19. | B | 36. | A | 53. | D | 70. | B |
| 20. | A | 37. | C | 54. | B* | 71. | C |
| 21. | B* | 38. | A | 55. | D | 72. | A |
| 22. | D* | 39. | D | 56. | C | 73. | D |
| 23. | A* | 40. | C | 57. | A* | 74. | B |
| 24. | C | 41. | B | 58. | D | 75. | D |
| 25. | C | 42. | A | 59. | B | 76. | C* |
| 26. | D | 43. | D | 60. | D* | 77. | B* |
| 27. | D | 44. | B | 61. | C | 78. | B |
| 28. | C* | 45. | C | 62. | A | 79. | C |
| 29. | D | 46. | C | 63. | B | 80. | C |

*See also calculations.

*Calculations*

13. $59,275 × .11 = $6,520.25
$6,520.25/12 = $543.35
$543.35/30 = $18.11/day
10 × $18.11 = $181.10

14. $51,755 × .13 = $6,728.15
$6,728.15/12 = $560.68
$610 − $560.68 = $49.32
$51,755 − $49.32 = $51,705.68

21. $57,500 × .14 = $8,050
$8,050/360 = $22.36
$22.36 × 10 = $223.60 or $224

22. $741.29/3 = $247.10/yr.
$247.10/12 = $20.59/month
4 months, 15 days × $20.59 = $92.66
$247.10 + $92.66 = $339.76
$741.29 − $339.76 = $401.53 or $403 credit seller

23. $4,000,000 × .01 = $40,000

28. $1,200 × 60 months = $72,000
$50,000 × .06 = $3,000
$22,000 × .05 = $1,100
$3,000 + $1,100 = $4,100

54. $36,000/.12 = $300,000

57. $60,000 × .8333 = $50,000
$50,000 + $15,000 = $65,000

60. $100,000/$12,500 = 8

69. 14% − 13% = 1% = 8 points
$57,500 × .08 = $4,600

76. $35,913/$42,250 = .85 or 85%

77. $240,000 × .85 = $204,000, value of improvements
100%/40 years = 2.5% depreciation per year
5 × 2.5 = 12.5% depreciated
$204,000 × .875 = $178,500 remaining value
$178,500 + $36,000 = $214,500
$300,000 − $214,500 = $85,500
85,500 × .28 = $23,940

## ASI TEST FORMAT

The ASI examination consists of 80 questions over the general subject areas of real estate for both the salesperson and broker examinations. In addition to the general questions, there are state-specific questions. Since ASI tailors each examination for the individual state, the total number of questions varies. Also, each state determines its own passing standards. Each question on the ASI examination is a four-option, multiple-choice question.

Each state also determines the weighting of each of the content areas covered on the examination for both salespersons and brokers. Those taking the examination should review the REAL Candidate Guide prepared for their state. The subject areas tested are similar to the sample outline shown.

### Content Outline ASI Real Estate Examination

I. Real Estate Law
  A. Contractual
    1. Encumbrances
      a. Priorities of liens
      b. Encroachments
      c. Restrictions/Easements
      d. Mechanic's liens
      e. Attachments and Agreements
    2. Contracts and Agreements
      a. Characteristics of enforceable real estate contracts
      b. Elements of property descriptions
      c. Purchase price
      d. Standard printed clauses
    3. Options
    4. Deeds
  B. General Practice
    1. Nature of real property
      a. Definitions
      b. Methods of legal description

*Content outline reprinted with permission of Assessment Systems, Inc. (ASI), the copyright owner.*

2. Parties dealing with interests in real property
   a. Legal capacity
   b. Individuals
   c. Corporations
   d. Partnerships
C. Fair housing laws

II. Ownership/Transfer
  A. Land titles and interest in real property
    1. Estates in land
     a. Joint ownership
     b. Severalty ownership
    2. Fixtures/personal property
    3. Insurance
    4. Settlement procedures
    5. Lease and leasehold
  B. Voluntary or involuntary alienation of real property
    1. Dedication
    2. Adverse possession
    3. Sheriff's sale
    4. Foreclosure
    5. Escheat
    6. Condemnation
    7. Eminent domain
    8. Inheritance
    9. Gifts
   10. Taxation
  C. Public control
    1. Planning
     a. Urban
     b. Rural
    2. Zoning
    3. Property taxation
    4. Water rights
    5. Health and safety/building codes

III. Brokerage/Agency
  A. Distinction between agency relationships
  B. Agent responsibilities to principal(s) and/or others
  C. Termination of agency
  D. Listing agreements
  E. Property management (residential/commercial)
    1. Management contracts
    2. Rentals and leases
    3. Repairs and maintenance
  F. Investments

IV. Concepts of Appraising
  A. Concepts and purposes of appraisal
  B. Appraisal techniques
  C. Elements of depreciation
  D. Principles of real property value
  E. Approaches to value
    1. Cost
    2. Income
    3. Market data

  F. Economic trends
  G. Neighborhood
    (Broker Examination, Only:)
  H. Site analysis and valuation
  I. Gross rent multiplier
  J. Principles of capitalization
  K. The appraisal report

V. Finance
  A. Methods of financing
    1. Government
    2. Other
  B. Truth-in-Lending and RESPA
  C. Financing instruments
  D. Financing terminology

VI. Mathematics of Real Estate (included as part of other content areas—approximately 20%) Basic mathematics to calculate solutions to the following problem areas:
  A. Financing
  B. Tax assessment
  C. Commissions
  D. Area calculations
  E. Settlement statements
  F. Profit and loss
  G. Tax ramifications
  H. General

## Real Estate Laws, Rules and Regulations, and Other Aspects of Real Estate Appropriate to the Respective State

VII. Duties and Powers of the Real Estate Commission
  A. General powers
  B. Examination of records
  C. Investigations, hearings, and appeals
  D. Sanctions
    1. Cease and desist
    2. License suspension and revocation
  E. Real estate commission membership
  F. Purposes of the license law

VIII. Licensing Requirements
  A. License exempt
  B. Activities requiring a license
  C. Types of licenses
  D. Eligibility for licensing
  E. License renewal
  F. Change in license

IX. Statutory Requirements Governing the Activities of a Licensee (Outlines vary from state to state.)
  A. Advertising
  B. Broker/salesperson relationship
  C. Commissions
  D. Disclosure/conflict of interest
  E. Handling of documents
  F. Handling of monies
  G. Listings and offers to purchase

H.  Place of business
I.  Record keeping
J.  Unfair inducements
K.  Licensee/public responsibility
L.  Incompetent practices

## ASI REAL ESTATE ASSESSMENT FOR LICENSURE PRACTICE EXAMINATION

1.  A power company easement is an example of which of the following?

    (A)  A commercial easement in gross
    (B)  An easement appurtenant
    (C)  An implied easement
    (D)  An expressed easement

2.  The following partial legal description—E¼ of the W½ of the NE¼ of Section 27—contains which of the following?

    (A)  20 acres          (C)  80 acres
    (B)  40 acres          (D)  160 acres

3.  To protect against financial loss due to a recorded but undiscovered title defect, the buyer should request which of the following?

    (A)  A survey
    (B)  An abstract
    (C)  A title insurance policy
    (D)  A private mortgage insurance policy

4.  An example of an involuntary lien is

    (A)  a mortgage          (C)  a property tax lien
    (B)  an easement         (D)  a lease

5.  If Mr. Jones is forced to sign a contract at gunpoint, he is being subjected to which of the following?

    (A)  Undue influence    (C)  Slander
    (B)  Duress             (D)  Libel

6.  If the grantee receives a sheriff's deed, the sheriff warrants which of the following?

    (A)  That there are not liens or encumbrances against the property
    (B)  That the county will compensate the grantee if title fails
    (C)  That the grantee is receiving fee simple interest
    (D)  Nothing to the grantee

7.  A contract involving only a singular promise to perform an act is termed which of the following?

    (A)  Bilateral          (C)  Illegal
    (B)  Unilateral         (D)  Unenforceable

8.  Under an option agreement, which of the following is true?

9.
    (A)  The contract may be oral and still be enforceable
    (B)  The contract may be assigned unless prohibited by the agreement
    (C)  The terms may be altered by the optionee as well
    (D)  The terms have no specific date of expiration for being exercised

9.  The counter-offer will NOT do which of the following?

    (A)  Terminate the original offer
    (B)  Result in a contract of sale if accepted
    (C)  Make the seller the offeror
    (D)  Rescind the listing agreement

10.  A congressional township contains how many square miles?

    (A)  One            (C)  Sixteen
    (B)  Six            (D)  Thirty-six

11.  The absence of which of the following would NOT affect the validity of a general warrant deed?

    (A)  Execution by the grantor
    (B)  Acceptance by the grantee
    (C)  Delivery by the grantor
    (D)  Recording by the grantee

12.  The concept of undue influence in making a contract is based on which of the following?

    (A)  Deception by one of the parties
    (B)  Fear of bodily harm
    (C)  Abuse of a position of power
    (D)  The commission of a criminal act

13.  A limitation placed on the use of real property in the writing of a deed is called which of the following?

    (A)  An acceleration clause
    (B)  A restriction
    (C)  An alienation clause
    (D)  An escalation

14.  The earnest money deposit may be handled in all of the following ways EXCEPT

    (A)  it may be escrowed until the date of settlement
    (B)  it may be applied to the purchase price at settlement
    (C)  it may be refunded to the purchaser if title to the property is NOT marketable
    (D)  it may be used by the broker to pay for secretarial services

15.  The salesperson for the listing broker is

    (A)  the principal to the listing
    (B)  the agent of the seller

(C)  the agent of the buyer

(D)  the subagent of the seller

16. The listing contract contains all of the following EXCEPT

(A)  a legal description of the property being listed

(B)  the terms of the broker's commission

(C)  an expiration date for the contract

(D)  the signature of the cooperating broker

17. If the property being sold is described on the listing contract by lot number, block number, and addition name, the type of legal description is called which of the following?

(A)  Metes and bounds

(B)  Platted subdivision

(C)  Governmental survey

(D)  Rectangular survey

18. If the contract of sale states that the seller "agrees to convey the property to the purchaser by deed with the usual covenants of title free and clear from all monetary encumbrances, tenancies, liens (for tax or otherwise)," the buyer would receive which of the following?

(A)  A general warranty deed

(B)  A quitclaim deed

(C)  A bargain and sale deed

(D)  A sheriff's deed

19. In the conveyance of title by an executor's deed,

(A)  written authority must be present to execute the deed

(B)  the four basic warranties are given

(C)  recording is essential to the validity of the deed

(D)  acknowledgment is required for enforceability

20. An option differs from a contract of sale in which of the following ways?

(A)  The contract of sale requires cash consideration

(B)  The option does not require consideration to be binding

(C)  The option need never be performed on by the parties

(D)  The option is a bilateral contract

21. If a person dies intestate and with no heirs with the capacity to inherit the property, which of the following happens to his/her property?

(A)  It is foreclosed and sold at public auction

(B)  It is condemned and sold under eminent domain

(C)  It escheats to the state

(D)  It reverts to the remainderman

22. When Mrs. Smith moved from her mansion, she removed her crystal chandelier and took it with her. Which of the following is NOT true?

(A)  The chandelier underwent severance

(B)  The chandelier became personal property again

(C)  The chandelier should have been excluded in the contract of sale

(D)  The chandelier was not a fixture before removal

23. If a closing is to take place August 20, this year, and the expiration date on the fire insurance policy is November 30, this year, how much will be received by the seller if the annual premium is $480?

(A)  $120.00          (C)  $133.33

(B)  $150.00          (D)  $123.33

24. Which of the following is NOT a characteristic of the joint tenancy?

(A)  Unity of title

(B)  Created by accident

(C)  Equal interests

(D)  Right of survivorship

25. A buyer gives earnest money to a salesperson. The salesperson deposits the funds in the proper escrow account until closing. What entry will appear on the closing statement?

(A)  Debit buyer; credit seller

(B)  Credit buyer; debit seller

(C)  Credit buyer; no entry to seller

(D)  No entry to buyer; debit seller

26. A profit is all of the following EXCEPT

(A)  less than an estate in land

(B)  assignable interest

(C)  inheritable interest

(D)  corporeal right

27. The liability insurance purchased by a condominium homeowners' association is NOT likely to cover injuries caused by accidents occurring

(A)  in an owner's unit

(B)  by the swimming pool

(C)  in the clubhouse recreation room

(D)  in the parking garage

28. The process used to take private property for the public benefit is called which of the following?

(A)  Escheat          (C)  Eminent domain

(B)  Condemnation     (D)  Seisin

29. The taxes on real property are $960/year. The property was assessed at $24,000. What is the rate per $100 of assessed value?

(A) $12      (C) $35
(B) $4      (D) $8

30. If there is any money remaining after a foreclosure sale, the excess goes to which of the following?

(A) The mortgagee
(B) The financial institution
(C) The county sheriff
(D) The mortgagor

31. The rights to water flowing by ones property are

(A) alluvion rights      (C) profit rights
(B) riparian rights      (D) accretion rights

32. A developer wishes the streets in a subdivision to become the property of the city. How may this be accomplished?

(A) Dedication      (C) Eminent domain
(B) Adverse possession (D) Plottage

33. The leasehold that is characterized by a specified period of time and the potential of automatic renewal is

(A) estate for years lease
(B) period to period lease
(C) tenancy at will
(D) life estate

34. If tenants in common cannot agree on the division of their interests, they would request the court to do which of the following?

(A) Partition the property
(B) Alienate the property
(C) Escheat the property
(D) Condemn the property

35. "M" wishes to leave her property to her brother and niece on a one-third/two-thirds basis. This would require which form of ownership?

(A) Joint tenancy
(B) Tenancy in common
(C) Tenancy by the entirety
(D) Community property

36. A real estate salesperson in selling the listings of another broker, is directly responsible to

(A) his principal broker
(B) the seller
(C) the listing broker
(D) the MLS

37. Which of the following transactions would be considered an investment contract under federal security laws?

(A) The sale of a vacant lot in a subdivision of 150 lots
(B) The sale of a residence to private individual which is mortgaged by a federally-insured loan
(C) The sale of a condominium unit by the developer which has a mandatory rental pool
(D) The sale of a farm to two people on a land contract which has more than five installments

38. If the seller finds the buyer under an open listing, the seller owes the listing broker which of the following?

(A) Only for all expenses incurred while the house was listed
(B) One half of the stated commission
(C) A one percent fee
(D) No commission

39. Which of the following deductions is a tax benefit to a home owner?

(A) Depreciation
(B) Property insurance premiums
(C) Utility expenses
(D) First mortgage interest

40. If a broker found a qualified buyer and the seller defaults on the contract of sale,

(A) the broker has not earned a commission until closing
(B) the buyer must always sue for damages
(C) the seller has no obligation to either party
(D) the listing contract has been breached

41. When listing a home, a seller tells the salesperson that the house is structurally sound. The salesperson later discovers that the house has $1,000 worth of termite damage. The salesperson would be obligated to

(A) protect the seller by not informing anyone
(B) warn potential buyers of the damage
(C) rescind the listing
(D) personally pay for repair of the damage

42. In listing a property, the listing price should

(A) reflect a value at which the property could probably sell
(B) reflect the value the seller feels the property is worth
(C) result only from a formal appraisal from a qualified appraiser
(D) result from an analysis by the lender

43. The listing contract states that the owner has granted the broker "exclusive and irrevocable right to sell" listing. This type of listing contract is which of the following?

    (A) An exclusive listing
    (B) An exclusive right to sell listing
    (C) An open listing
    (D) A multiple listing

44. If a seller should decide to sell only to white Protestants, you, as the broker, should do which of the following?

    (A) Take the listing unconditionally
    (B) Place that restriction in the "further conditions"
    (C) Not take the listing
    (D) Take the listing with reservation

45. The seller received $21,000 after the broker took his/her fee of $1,340.40. What percent of the gross sales price is the brokerage fee?

    (A) 5 percent          (C) 7 percent
    (B) 6 percent          (D) 8 percent

46. A house sold at 91 percent of the original listing price. The seller received $32,475 for the property. What was the original listing price, to the nearest dollar?

    (A) $32,475           (C) $36,083
    (B) $34,184           (D) $35,687

47. A broker received a commission of $2,375 and her fee was 6½ percent. What was the sales price of the property?

    (A) $39,583           (C) $37,853
    (B) $36,538           (D) $35,835

48. All of the following forms of discrimination are covered under the 1968 Civil Rights Act EXCEPT

    (A) sex and religion
    (B) race and creed
    (C) sex and race
    (D) age and marital status

49. In inflationary times, a property manager would not want to give a long term lease with rents based on

    (A) graduated increases in rent
    (B) consumer price index
    (C) cost of living index
    (D) a fixed rental rate

50. Which of the following is true of management agreement provisions?

    (A) The manager may list and sell the property at any time for the principal

    (B) The agreement defines the rights and obligations of the manager and principal
    (C) The manager may place security deposits in the general operating account
    (D) The manager may not check the credit rating of potential tenants

51. The increase in value occurring when two or more parcels of real estate are combined is referred to as which of the following?

    (A) Escheat            (C) Escrow
    (B) Plottage           (D) Remainder

52. If you have a building worth $95,000 and want a return of 14 percent, what net income is needed each month to attain this?

    (A) $13,300           (C) $9,501
    (B) $133,300          (D) $1,108

53. The appraisal of an apartment building would focus on which approach to valuation?

    (A) Cost              (C) Market
    (B) Income            (D) GRM

54. A buyer would consider which of the following as the most important contributor to value?

    (A) Age               (C) Floor plan
    (B) Size              (D) Location

55. The period of time over which a property produces income is

    (A) economic life
    (B) effective age
    (C) actual age
    (D) none of the above

56. Which type of depreciation is considered incurable?

    (A) Economic obsolescence
    (B) Physical obsolescence
    (C) Functional obsolescence
    (D) None of the above

57. The addition of a pool to a single family residence would be governed by the principle of

    (A) change            (C) contribution
    (B) substitution      (D) competition

58. Accrued depreciation is most important under the

    (A) income approach
    (B) cost approach
    (C) market approach
    (D) gross rent multiplier

59. The appraised value of a single family residence under the market approach would be least influenced by

(A) rental income
(B) location
(C) comparable sales
(D) square footage

60. In appraising a home for mortgage purposes, the lender would be concerned with

(A) the amount of the loan request
(B) unpaid assessments
(C) economic changes
(D) purchase price

61. An apartment has $64,000 gross income. The net income is 30 percent of the gross. The investor wants an 11 percent return. What would the investor offer for the property?

(A) $581,818
(B) $831,168
(C) $174,545
(D) $192,000

62. To offer a real estate security for sale, the offeror must do all of the following EXCEPT

(A) provide for a three-day right of rescission in the contract
(B) register the offering with SEC unless exempt
(C) comply with the anti-fraud laws
(D) fully disclose all material facts concerning the offering

63. FHA financing requirements include

(A) second mortgages permitted to meet downpayment requirements
(B) no prepayment penalty
(C) no minimum downpayment requirements
(D) discount points to be paid only by the seller

64. When financing the purchase of real estate with a conventional loan, which of the following is NOT customary?

(A) The seller pays all the discount points
(B) The property must meet the lender's standards
(C) The lender may require title insurance
(D) An appraisal may be required

65. A construction loan is considered to be which of the following?

(A) A junior mortgage
(B) A form of permanent financing
(C) A means of financing personal property
(D) An interim form of financing

66. If the interest rate charged on a loan exceeds the limits established by the state, the lender has violated which of the following?

(A) Truth in Lending statutes
(B) Regulation Z
(C) Statute of Frauds
(D) Usury laws

67. To be valid and enforceable, a mortgage must be all of the following EXCEPT

(A) in writing
(B) between competent parties
(C) recorded by the mortgagor
(D) executed by the mortgagor

68. Mr. Jones has an 11 percent mortgage on his property. The PI constant is $475/month. The outstanding balance after the May 1 payment was $45,795. The settlement is to take place June 20, and all payments are current. What is the outstanding balance of the mortgage at settlement?

(A) $45,695
(B) $45,740
(C) $45,374
(D) $45,325

69. The bank requires two months' interest escrowed in advance on construction loans. If the loan is $65,000 at 17½ percent, how much interest is to be escrowed?

(A) $948
(B) $1,349
(C) $1,574
(D) $1,896

70. A loan that is repaid in equal installments throughout the life of the loan with each installment payment including portions of interest and principal is which of the following?

(A) A balloon loan
(B) A straight term loan
(C) A single payment loan
(D) An amortized loan

71. The loan-to-value ratio is 85 percent. The property was appraised for $42,250 and sold for $43,500. How much could the purchaser borrow?

(A) $35,913
(B) $39,975
(C) $34,800
(D) $35,750

72. The amount a lender will loan uninsured is generally based on which of the following?

(A) The appraised value for loan purposes only
(B) The sales price only
(C) The appraised value for loan purposes or sales price, whichever is less
(D) The appraised value for loan purposes or sales price, whichever is greater

73. The primary difference between an amortized and a straight term loan is which of the following?

(A) The interest rate being charged
(B) The discount points being charged
(C) The method of repaying the principal
(D) There is no difference

74. If the VA rate is 11¾ percent and the conventional rate is 12⅜ percent, how much will the buyer pay in discount at the closing of a $37,500 loan?

   (A) $1,875          (C) $3,750
   (B) $2,145          (D) $0

75. With which type of loan does the lender receive a portion of the profit when the property is sold?

   (A) Adjusted Rate Mortgage (ARM)
   (B) Graduated Payment Mortgage (GPM)
   (C) Shared Appreciation Mortgage (SAM)
   (D) Reverse Annuity Mortgage (RAM)

76. The mortgage type which is subordinate to another mortgage but includes the amount of the other mortgage is

   (A) a land contract
   (B) a wraparound mortgage
   (C) an open-end mortgage
   (D) a purchase money mortgage

77. A two-story building is to sell for $8 per square foot. The first story is 45 feet by 50 feet and has 10-foot ceilings. The second story is 30 feet by 40 feet and has 10-foot ceilings. What will the building sell for?

   (A) $27,600          (C) $276,000
   (B) $53,200          (D) $532,000

78. A drawing of a lot has a scale of ¼ inch = 10 feet. The drawing is 8 inches by 12½ inches. How many acres are in the lot?

   (A) 2               (C) 5.34
   (B) 3.67            (D) 8.21

79. How many gallons of paint are required to paint the walls of a room that is 12 feet by 16 feet by 8 feet, if each gallon covers 96 square feet?

   (A) 2.3             (C) 6.2
   (B) 4.6             (D) 8.4

80. A developer has a 25 acre tract to be developed. He wishes to use 15 percent of the land for roads and 5 percent for a park. He is selling ½ acre lots for $9,500. What is his potential gross from the sales?

   (A) $237,500         (C) $380,000
   (B) $209,000         (D) $475,000

**ASI Real Estate Assessment for Licensure Practice Examination**

*Answers*

| 1. | A | 4. | C | 7. | B | 10. | D |
|----|---|----|---|----|---|-----|---|
| 2. | A* | 5. | B | 8. | B | 11. | D |
| 3. | C | 6. | D | 9. | D | 12. | C |

| 13. | B | 30. | D | 47. | B* | 64. | A |
|-----|---|-----|---|-----|----|-----|---|
| 14. | D | 31. | B | 48. | D | 65. | D |
| 15. | D | 32. | A | 49. | D | 66. | D |
| 16. | D | 33. | B | 50. | B | 67. | C |
| 17. | B | 34. | A | 51. | B | 68. | B* |
| 18. | A | 35. | B | 52. | D* | 69. | D* |
| 19. | A | 36. | A | 53. | B | 70. | D |
| 20. | C | 37. | C | 54. | D | 71. | A* |
| 21. | C | 38. | D | 55. | A | 72. | C |
| 22. | D | 39. | D | 56. | A | 73. | C |
| 23. | C | 40. | D | 57. | C | 74. | D |
| 24. | B | 41. | B | 58. | B | 75. | C |
| 25. | C | 42. | A | 59. | A | 76. | B |
| 26. | D | 43. | B | 60. | A | 77. | A* |
| 27. | A | 44. | C | 61. | C* | 78. | B* |
| 28. | B | 45. | B* | 62. | A | 79. | D* |
| 29. | B* | 46. | D* | 63. | B | 80. | C* |

*See also calculations.

*Calculations*

2.  $1/4 \times 1/2 \times 1/6 = 1/32$
    $1/32 \times 640 = 20$ acres

29.  $960/24,000 = 4\%$ or $4/$100

45.  $21,000 + $1,340 = $22,340
     $1,340/$22,340 = .06 or 6%

46.  $32,475/.91 = $35,687

47.  $2,375/.065 = $36,538

52.  $95,000 \times .14 = $13,300
     $13,300/12 = $1,108

61.  $64,000 \times .3 = $19,200
     $19,200/.11 = $174,545

68.  $45,795 \times .11 = $5,037.45
     $5,037.45/12 = $419.79
     $475 - $419.79 = $55.21
     $45,795 - $55.21 = $45,739.79 or $45,740

69.  $65,000 \times .175 = $11,375
     $11,375/12 = $947.92
     $947.92 \times 2 = $1,895.84 or $1,896

71.  $42,250 \times .85 = $35,912.50 or $35,913

77.  $45' \times 50' = 2,250$ square feet
     $30' \times 40' = 1,200$ square feet
     $2,250 + 1,200 = 3,450$ square feet
     $3,450 \times $8 = $27,600

78.  1 in. = 4 units
     4 × 8" = 32 units
     4 × 12½ = 50 units
     1 unit = 10'
     32 × 10' = 320'
     50 × 10' = 500'
     500' × 320' = 160,000 square feet
     (43,560 square feet = 1 acre)
     160,000/43,560 = 1 acre

79.  (8 × 12 × 2) + (8 × 16 × 2) = 192 square feet
     192 + 256 = 448 square feet
     768/96 = 4.6 gallons

80.  25 × (.15 + .05) = 5 acres
     25 − 5 = 20 acres for development
     20/2 = 40 lots
     40 × 9,500 = $380,000

## ACT REAL ESTATE EXAMINATION SERVICES

ACT Real Estate Examination Services develops both the National and state real estate examinations for brokers and salespersons. In general, if you are an applicant seeking licensure in a state using the National Examinations, you will also take an examination covering the real estate laws of your particular state. The total examination will therefore consist of a National portion and a state portion. The National portion focuses on knowledge and skills practitioners in *every* state will use in everyday practice and is as much a part of local practice in your state as the state portion.

Some of the states using the ACT National Examinations have elected to prepare their own state examinations, while others use state examinations prepared by ACT. The state examinations developed by ACT Real Estate Examination Services are similar to the National Examinations in the format and question types used. Each state examination tests those aspects of real estate law specific to that state. To help ensure the appropriateness of the ACT state examinations, the questions are written principally by real estate professionals in those states. The questions are reviewed by the state licensing agencies to ensure their accuracy and validity.

### Format of the Examinations

All of the tests developed by ACT Real Estate Examination Services contain four-choice, multiple-choice questions.

Although different forms of the National Real Estate Examinations will be administered, all cover exactly the same scope of content; the topics covered in the test are listed below. The state examinations prepared by ACT also have many different versions. Like the National Real Estate Examinations, all versions of a state's examination cover the same scope of content dictated by the state for which the tests are developed. Content outlines for state examinations are available from the licensing authority within each state or can be found in your ACT state Application Folder.

The National Salesperson and Broker Examinations each contain 100 multiple-choice questions, and each question has four alternative responses. To answer a multiple-choice question, you must choose one answer out of the choices given as the correct answer to the question asked. The questions are designed to measure your ability to understand and apply the principles of real estate given in the content outline of the examinations.

Since these examinations are developed with the express purpose of presenting examinees with realistic situations that arise in real estate practice, many test questions contain situational contexts which will require you to apply your knowledge in order to answer the question correctly.

### Content Outline of the National Examinations*

Both the National Salesperson and Broker Examinations are based upon four major content areas. Although the topics included in each of the major content areas are the same for the Salesperson and Broker Examinations, the emphasis devoted to the content areas differs in the two examinations.

Each of the content areas is given below, followed by an outline of the topics it includes. In addition, the approximate percentage of questions devoted to each in the Salesperson and Broker Examinations is indicated for each major content area. Both the National Salesperson Examination and the National Broker Examination are composed of 100 questions. Approximately 10% of the questions in each examination require mathematical calculations. These questions are distributed throughout the examination.

### I.  Property Ownership, Transfer, and Use
Salesperson Examination—36%
Broker Examination—25%
  A.  Nature of real property
      1.  Definitional elements of types of property
      2.  Methods of legal description
  B.  Parties dealing with interests in real property
      1.  Capacity: insane and incompetent persons, minors
      2.  Individuals
      3.  Corporations
      4.  Partnerships

---

C. Land titles and interests in real property
   1. Fee simple, ownership in severalty
   2. Life estate, tenancy in common, tenancy by the entireties
   3. Leasehold interests
D. Special interests relating to real property
   1. Easements
   2. Mortgages and mortgage clauses
E. Special relationships between persons holding interests in land
   1. Fixtures
   2. Priorities of liens
   3. Encroachments
   4. Restrictions
   5. Mechanic's liens
   6. Attachment and transfer of real estate
F. Acquisition and transfer of real estate
   1. Contracts and agreements
      a. Characteristics of enforceable real estate
      b. Elements of property descriptions
      c. Purchase price
      d. Standard printed clauses
   2. Options
   3. Deeds
   4. Adverse possession
   5. Court action
G. Public land use control
   1. Planning and zoning
   2. Property taxation
   3. Eminent domain
   4. Water rights
   5. Health and safety codes in building

## II. Brokerage and Laws of Agency

Salesperson Examination—30%
Broker Examination—30%
A. Real estate agency
   1. Nature of distinctions between types of agents
   2. Creation of agency relationships
   3. Duties of agent toward principal
   4. Duties of agent toward third parties
   5. Duties enforced by licensing authorities
   6. Rights of agent in relation to principal(s)
   7. Termination of agency
B. Federal fair housing laws
C. Federal Real Estate Settlement Procedures Act
D. Property management
   1. Management contracts
   2. Rentals and leases
   3. Repairs and maintenance

## III. Valuation and Economics

Salesperson Examination—17%
Broker Examination—25%
A. Concepts and purposes of appraisal
B. Appraisal techniques
C. Depreciation
D. Principles of real property value
E. The appraisal process
F. Economic trends
G. Neighborhood analysis
H. Site analysis and valuation
I. Gross rent multiplier
J. Principles of capitalization
K. Market data approach
L. The appraisal report
M. Real estate economics and trends in land use

## IV. Finance

Salesperson Examination—17%
Broker Examination—20%
A. Mortgage lending agencies
B. Government mortgage institutions
C. Mathematics of financial practice
D. Federal truth-in-lending legislation
E. Principles of finance

## ACT SAMPLE NATIONAL REAL ESTATE SALESPERSON EXAMINATION*

1. One of the co-owners of a property wishes to have the property sold after bringing an action for partition. That co-owner holds the property under which of the following?
   A. A tenancy at sufferance
   B. A tenancy at will
   C. A tenancy for years
   D. A tenancy in common

2. An acceleration clause in a mortgage instrument permits the lender to:
   F. declare the entire unpaid balance due upon default by the borrower.
   G. require the borrower to pay interest in advance.
   H. increase the size of the monthly payments with thirty days' notice to the borrower.
   J. require the borrower to make equal monthly payments.

---

*The most recent sample examination should be ordered from ACT. Contact ACT Real Estate Examination Services, Box 168, Iowa City, IA 52243.

Copyright 1985 by The American College Testing Program. All rights reserved.

3. An irregularly shaped parcel of land might be best described by a metes and bounds description because:
   A. it accurately places the property between the proper principal meridians so that location inaccuracies are avoided.
   B. its use of sections and miles can describe the exact square footage within the parcel.
   C. it contains enough different types of measurements to accurately describe the parcel.
   D. of none of the above.

4. Baird had given permission to her friend Carr to hunt on her undeveloped forestland. Baird died and her nephew Dole inherited the property. Dole now denies Carr the right to hunt on the land. Is he correct in doing so?
   F. Yes, because a license ceases on the death of either party.
   G. Yes, because an easement ceases on the death of either party.
   H. No, because the land was undeveloped.
   J. No, because an easement does not cease on the death of either party.

5. Which of the following is(are) considered to be real property?
   A. Mineral deposits reserved to the grantor
   B. Airspace over an airport
   C. Newly planted ornamental bushes
   D. All of the above

6. Falk has an easement by necessity and owns the dominant tenement. Grant owns the servient tenement. Because of this easement,:
   F. the value of Grant's property is increased.
   G. the value of Falk's property is increased.
   H. Grant's property has been increased in size.
   J. Falk's property has been increased in size.

7. Which of the following is(are) needed for the creation of an enforceable leasehold agreement?
   I. The type or amount of rental consideration
   II. A requirement that rental payments be made in advance
   III. An adequate description of the property
   A. I only
   B. III only
   C. I and III only
   D. I, II, and III

8. *Ownership in severalty* refers to ownership of:
   F. real property by one person.
   G. real property by two persons.
   H. real property by more than two persons.
   J. homestead property by any number of family members.

9. The owner of an apartment building wishes to purchase an office building. To raise money, the owner secures a mortgage on the apartment building. What is this transaction called?
   A. Wraparound mortgage
   B. Purchase money mortgage
   C. Blanket mortgage
   D. None of the above

10. Which of the following statements about a fee simple estate is(are) true?
    F. It is freely transferable.
    G. It is inheritable.
    H. It is of indefinite duration.
    J. It is all of the above.

11. Baird owes Carr $6,000 for motorcycle repairs done by Carr. Carr owns no real property. Baird owns a house in the center of a subdivision. Which of the following tells why Carr has recorded a lis pendens?
    A. To give constructive notice of the possible future judgment lien in favor of Carr on Baird's house
    B. To obtain an injunction against the sale of Baird's house in the event of judgment denial
    C. To provide for the granting of riparian rights to Carr in the event of judgment denial
    D. To acquire power of attorney which would enable Carr to file for a personal judgment lien on Baird's house

12. Which of the following is(are) true about trade fixtures?
    I. They are legally a part of the real estate.
    II. The tenant may remove them only after expiration of the lease.
    III. They remain the tenant's personal property if appropriately removed.
    F. I only
    G. III only
    H. I and II only
    J. II and III only

13. What is true of the relationship between a judgment lien and a mortgage?
    A. The judgment lien has two real properties pledged as security when the debt is created; the mortgage has one real property pledged at that time.
    B. The judgment lien has at least one real property pledged as security when the debt is created; the mortgage also has at least one real property pledged at that time.
    C. The judgment lien has no real properties pledged as security when the debt is created; the mortgage has at least one real property pledged at that time.
    D. The judgment lien has no real properties

pledged as security when the debt is created; the mortgage also has no real properties pledged at that time.

14. In which of the following circumstances does a mechanic's lien recorded on August 1, 1978, take priority over a state property tax assessment recorded on August 15, 1978?
    F. When the mechanic's lien stems from work done by express contract
    G. When the mechanic's lien was filed within the required statutory period
    H. When the mechanic's lien is an involuntary lien
    J. In none of the above circumstances

15. Which of the following is true of a fixture in a house being sold?
    A. It will pass with the house only if it is conveyed by a bill of sale.
    B. It will pass with the house only if it is mentioned in the deed.
    C. It will pass with the house even if it is not mentioned in the deed.
    D. It will never pass with the house.

16. How is a judgment lien enforced?
    F. By sale of the debtor's property
    G. By writ of execution
    H. By action of the sheriff
    J. By all of the above

17. When the Clear Creek subdivision was built, a deed restriction was written that stated: "The back five feet in depth of each owner's lot shall be designated as a community play area for the homeowners' children." When Carr moved in, he immediately began making plans for a tennis court which would take up the entire back of his lot, sacrificing a tree house, two benches, and part of the sandbox from the community park. A neighbor, Dole, wishes to stop Carr's plans. What should Neighbor Dole do?
    A. Dole may file an attachment lien against Carr's property.
    B. Dole may request a court to enforce the deed restriction.
    C. Dole must wait for the tennis court to be built before he can file an action.
    D. As a private homeowner, Dole has no right to individually enforce subdivision deed restrictions.

18. Which of the following is NOT considered a test of a fixture?
    F. The reason the object was attached to the property
    G. The way in which the object was attached to the property
    H. The way in which the object was adapted to the property
    J. The value of the object attached to the property

19. If a deed restriction is more restrictive than a zoning ordinance, which statement is true?
    A. The deed restriction prevails.
    B. The zoning ordinance prevails.
    C. The deed restriction prevails, but only for the first and second owners.
    D. None of the above is true.

20. When Baird neglected to pay for the newly built dock on his waterfront property, the Submarine Construction Company filed a mechanic's lien on Baird's thirty-foot sailboat. Was Submarine Construction correct in its action?
    F. Yes, because the existence of the dock benefits the boat, thereby making the boat legally attachable.
    G. Yes, because a mechanic's lien covers any property in Baird's possession.
    H. No, because a mechanic's lien is specific only to the real property being improved.
    J. No, because Baird's property fronts a public lake and must be levied against by an attachment lien that includes water charges.

21. A broker was asked by a principal to obtain an offer for a property with a gravel driveway. The broker produced an offer from a third party that, in order to become binding, contained a demand that the driveway be paved. Has a contractual obligation been created?
    A. Yes, because both the principal and third party have offered to enter into a contract.
    B. Yes, because a definite and certain offer has been made by the third party.
    C. No, because the third party has only offered to negotiate with the principal.
    D. No, because the third party has offered to sign an option with the principal.

22. Jane Carr makes a will naming her sons Fred and John as heirs, with each to inherit 100 acres of her farmland and an equal share in the remaining disposable property. Fred wishes to sell his 100 acres while Jane is still alive. Under what condition may he do so?
    F. If the will is delivered to the devisee during the lifetime of the grantor
    G. If the will conforms to all the statutory requirements of the state in which the real estate is located
    H. If the will is witnessed and filed with a court
    J. Under no condition because a devisee has no rights as long as the maker of the will is alive

23. Which statement about a quit claim deed is true?
    A. It carries no covenant or warranties.
    B. It warrants that there are no encumbrances of record.
    C. It warrants against encumbrances known by the grantor.
    D. It warrants against encumbrances known by the grantee.

24. Baird submits earnest money with an offer to purchase Carr's home. Carr doubles the down payment figure on the offer, signs the offer, and has it delivered to Baird within Baird's specified time period. Which of the following is true?
    F. Baird's offer has been accepted, and Baird must now perform according to its terms.
    G. Baird's offer has been accepted but, because of the down payment change, Baird may withdraw one half of the earnest money for closing expenses.
    H. The down payment change in Baird's offer must be notarized before Baird can sign the offer again.
    J. Baird's offer is no longer valid.

25. The essential elements of a valid real estate contract include which of the following?
    A. The signatures of the buyer and the seller
    B. An accurate description of the subject real estate
    C. Competent parties
    D. All of the above

26. Constructive notice is typically given in real estate transactions by:
    I. any telephone conversation witnessed by two or more persons.
    II. a three-day advertisement in a newspaper with a circulation of at least 300.
    III. recording the instrument in the recorder's office.
    IV. filing for judgment three days prior to a writ of execution.
    F. II only
    G. III only
    H. I or II only
    J. III or IV only

27. May a party to a lease include an option to renew in the original leasing agreement?
    A. Yes, if the option to renew also includes an option to purchase.
    B. Yes, if the duration of the option is clearly specified in the agreement.
    C. No, because leases must be renegotiated at expiration.
    D. No, because options may only be used in purchase agreements.

28. A mortgagor defaulted, and the redemption period has passed. Howe bought the affected property at the court-ordered sale and received a deed. Which of the following is(are) true?
    F. The deed Howe received provides no warranties.
    G. The title to the property passes to Howe.
    H. The title to the property is not encumbered by the defaulted mortgage.
    J. All of the above are true.

29. Land may be acquired through adverse possession in a manner similar to the acquisition of land by which of the following?
    A. Easement by prescription
    B. Easement by necessity
    C. Encumbrance through restrictions
    D. Encumbrance through covenants

30. Which of the following terms in a real estate purchase and sale contract can be changed without having the change take the form of a counteroffer?
    F. Purchase price
    G. Identification of fixtures
    H. Closing date
    J. None of the above

31. A zoning law states that no structure on any lot within a subdivision can be constructed within fifteen feet of the lot line. One lot owner obtained approval from the zoning board to build to a point ten feet from the lot line. That owner has obtained:
    A. a building permit.
    B. a variance.
    C. a nonconforming use.
    D. none of the above.

32. Which statement about real estate taxes is always true?
    F. They become delinquent after eighteen months from the due date.
    G. They vary in accordance with the size of the property being taxed.
    H. They are computed by applying the tax rate to the assessed valuation of the property.
    J. Improvement taxes are levied on the same property owners as ad valorem taxes.

33. Riparian rights allow a property owner to do which of the following?
    A. Drill for oil or gas beneath the property's surface
    B. Extract iron ore from beneath the property's surface
    C. Fish from a river adjoining the property
    D. Do all of the above

34. The use of substandard construction materials in a commercial building would accelerate which of the following?

F. Functional obsolescence

G. Physical depreciation

H. Equalization

J. Redemption

35. The power of eminent domain may NOT be used to obtain land for further development of which of the following?

A. Parochial schools

B. Offstreet public parking

C. Railroads

D. Irrigation

36. Falk's tire factory was allowed to continue production in an area newly rezoned for residential use. After Falk's factory burned to the ground, which of the following was true?

F. Falk could build another tire factory on the same lot as long as the city's building codes were met.

G. Falk could build another tire factory on the same lot only if the original design were used.

H. Falk could not build another factory of any sort on the same lot unless granted a variance.

J. Falk could not build another factory of any sort on the same lot under any conditions.

37. Acting as an agent for Seller Baird, Broker Carr negotiated the sale of Baird's real property. If agreed upon, Broker Carr's commission can be paid in the form of:

A. an assignment by Seller Baird of the first monies due her from the buyer on a mortgage note.

B. an assignment of a note.

C. a personal note from the buyer.

D. any of the above.

38. When a salesperson discovers that one of her listings consisting of a house and lot has been rezoned to industrial, which of the following persons must she tell?

I. The owner of the affected house and lot

II. Any prospect who tours the listed property

III. Only those prospects preparing to sign written offers for the property

F. I only

G. III only

H. I and II only

J. I and III only

39. Broker Falk had a listing for Howe's house. Broker Falk conveyed to Howe an offer for the property at the listed price. Broker Falk felt that this offer should not be accepted since the prospective buyer had a poor financial background. However, Broker Falk did not reveal this information to Howe. Has Broker Falk fulfilled the duties of a broker to a principal?

A. Yes, because Broker Falk conveyed the offer to Howe.

B. Yes, because Broker Falk found a buyer for the property.

C. No, because Broker Falk did not make a full disclosure of all of the relevant facts to Seller Howe.

D. No, because Broker Falk did not offer advice about the likelihood of a higher price being offered in the future.

40. A buyer submitted an offer to buy a seller's property on May 15, 1978. The offer was accompanied by a $1,000 deposit. The offer stipulated that an acceptance must be made by May 17, 1978. The offer was accepted by the seller on May 18, 1978. Which of the following statements is true?

F. The buyer may ask that the $1,000 deposit be returned.

G. The seller may sue the buyer for specific performance.

H. The buyer may forfeit the deposit, with one half of it being given to the seller and one half to the broker.

J. None of the above statements is true.

41. A salesperson, employed by a broker, is working to market a seller's property. The salesperson locates a buyer, who wants to make a deposit on the property. In general, who should be named recipient of the check that the buyer will give to the salesperson?

A. The seller

B. The broker

C. The salesperson

D. None of the above

42. A broker found a ready, willing, and able buyer for a house listed with her. However, there were defects in the title that were not corrected so the sale was not completed. According to the laws of agency, has the broker earned a commission on this transaction?

F. Yes, because the house was listed by her.

G. Yes, because she found a buyer on the listed terms.

H. No, because the sale was not completed.

J. No, because there were defects in the title.

43. Broker Baird has obtained a listing for a farm owned by Carr. Owner Carr discharges Broker Baird before the listing contract has expired. Which of the following statements about Baird's agency relationship to Carr is true?

A. Baird is no longer Carr's agent, although compensation may be due Baird for any authorized expenditures.

B. Baird is no longer Carr's agent, although Baird

will receive a partial commission if the farm is sold during the term of the listing contract.

C. Baird remains Carr's agent until the expiration of the listing or until a ready, willing, and able buyer is found, whichever comes first.

D. Baird remains Carr's agent because Carr may only revoke a listing contract because of death or bankruptcy.

44. An owner believes that he is capable of selling his own home but is considering employing a broker. Under which of the following types of listing agreements might the owner personally quote buyers a price lower than that quoted by the broker, and, if accepting that lower price, legally refuse to pay the broker a commission?
  I. Open listing
  II. Exclusive agency listing
  III. Exclusive right-to-sell listing
  F. I only
  G. I or II only
  H. II or III only
  J. I, II, or III

45. A broker shows a prospect a house from the multiple listing service files. The prospect later buys this house through the broker. If this house was NOT listed with the broker's agency, what amount of commission can the broker expect to receive?
  A. All of the commission, because he is the selling broker
  B. One half of the commission, with the other half going to the multiple listing service
  C. The part of the commission to which the selling broker is entitled according to the agreement with the listing broker
  D. The part of the commission to which the selling broker is entitled according to the local board of arbitration

46. Which of the following written agreements indicate(s) an agency relationship?
  F. A listing to sell a property signed by both the broker and the seller
  G. An authorization delegating a broker to transact all real estate business
  H. An agreement stating that a broker has the authority to perform all lawful acts for the principal
  J. All of the above

47. A broker is employed by a seller to sell the seller's cafe. Which of the following would ALWAYS terminate the agency?
  A. The broker's presenting an offer which contained an earnest money deposit of less than five percent of the purchase price
  B. The broker's discovery of the need for major repairs to the listed property

C. The seller's bankruptcy
D. The broker's failure to spend ten percent of the promised commission on advertising

48. Broker Rand obtains his principal's acceptance of an offer to purchase made by Spence. Rand delivers the deed to Spence who refuses to buy. Rand's wife then buys the property at the listed price, but Rand does not disclose the buyer's identity to his principal. Which statement about Rand's behavior is true?
  F. It is legal and ethical because Rand fulfilled his obligations to his principal by finding a buyer at the listed price.
  G. It is legal because the seller obtained the listed price for the property.
  H. It is illegal because Rand must inform the principal that the buyer is Rand's wife.
  J. It is illegal because a broker may not sell property to his wife.

49. A buyer submits an offer to buy a home. One hour later, the buyer discovers the need to recover the earnest money deposited with the offer. Which of the following is true?
  A. The buyer must withdraw the offer before the seller accepts it.
  B. The buyer would be unable to obtain this money until after closing.
  C. The buyer must make a written request so the broker may return this money from his special account.
  D. The buyer may never obtain the money after depositing it with the offer.

50. A broker, employed by a seller, spends much more money than she had anticipated to promote the seller's home, which finally was sold. The broker and the seller had made no agreement concerning the broker's expenses. Which of the following statements would normally be true in this situation?
  F. The seller would have to pay all promotional expenses.
  G. The broker would have to pay all promotional expenses.
  H. The seller and the broker would have to split promotional expenses.
  J. The buyer and the seller would have to split promotional expenses.

51. How many brokers may a seller employ under an open listing agreement?
  A. One
  B. Two
  C. Five
  D. Any number

52. A broker has a listing on an owner's property. The owner has given the broker an option to purchase

the property that runs concurrently with the listing period. What is the biggest danger inherent in this situation?

F. That the owner could receive less than the listing price

G. That the broker's obligations to the owner could be conflicting

H. That the broker could lose money by exercising the option to purchase

J. That the broker's commission could be forfeited

53. Broker Howe listed a luxurious house owned by the Langes who stated that they did not want the house advertised in newspapers or shown by an open house. May the Langes place this restriction on Broker Howe?

A. Yes, because the Langes can place any kind of restriction on the advertisements for the property.

B. Yes, because the Langes are hiring Broker Howe to work for them.

C. No, because Broker Howe has the freedom to advertise the property as Howe sees fit.

D. No, because newspapers and open houses are public media.

54. When should a broker inform, in writing, both a buyer and a seller that the broker will be acting for both parties in the same transaction?

F. Before the negotiations begin

G. Any time during the negotiations

H. Before accepting his/her commission

J. Before the deed is delivered

55. Which of the following statements about the creation of a customary agency relationship is(are) true?

A. Some action or conduct by the principal is necessary to create the relationship.

B. An agency relationship creates obligations for the agent only.

C. The creation of an agency relationship requires that agents have the same obligations to third parties as to their principals.

D. All of the above statements are true.

56. Which of the following statements about a salesperson's rights and obligations when dealing with listing contracts is(are) true?

F. A salesperson can fill in a standard listing contract.

G. A salesperson must make sure that the contract reflects the true intentions of the seller.

H. A salesperson must make sure that there are no indefinite conditions in the contract.

J. All of the above are true.

57. Two different brokerage firms, Baird Realty and Carr Realty, contracted to comarket a listing on a house and to share the commission on a 50/50 basis. Could any circumstances reduce to less than 50 percent the share of Baird Realty, the firm that actually signed the client?

A. Yes, if Baird Realty provided no advertising for this listing.

B. Yes, if Carr Realty showed the listing twice as many times as Baird Realty.

C. No, because the two brokerages contracted for the 50/50 commission split.

D. No, because the concept of sharing this commission renders the Baird-Carr contract void, so Baird Realty must receive 100 percent of any commission earned on this listing.

58. In which of the following circumstances can a listing broker sue and collect the entire commission originally agreed to by both parties to an exclusive agency listing?

F. If the principal waited until after the listing had expired to sell to an offeror whom the broker had procured during the listing period

G. If the principal waited until after the listing had expired to sell to an offeror that had not been procured by the broker during the listing period

H. If the broker had spent over one hundred dollars on advertising and procured a buyer who had signed an acceptable offer to purchase but who had defaulted at closing

J. If the broker had assigned more than one salesperson to the listing and at least one offer had been procured for within one percent of the listing price

59. Which of the following clauses is designed to help a broker who had found a buyer before the listing expired to receive a commission even if the sales negotiations were completed after the listing had expired?

A. An acceleration clause

B. A defeasance clause

C. A protection period clause

D. An alienation clause

60. Can a broker legally charge a constant brokerage fee of $3,000 for every transaction?

F. No, unless the state real estate commission grants special permission.

G. No, unless a majority of brokerages in the same county vote to allow such a program.

H. Yes, because the brokerage fee is completely negotiable between the client and the brokerage.

J. Yes, because Regulation Z provides for constant brokerage fees such as this one.

61. According to federal fair housing laws, which of the following criteria may an owner use in deciding whether to rent to a particular individual?

A. The size of the individual's family
B. The age of the individual
C. The individual's credit standing
D. All of the above

62. For the purchase of a home, Baird is acquiring a first mortgage loan guaranteed by the VA. Because of the Real Estate Settlement Procedures Act, which costs must be listed on the settlement form used by Baird's broker?
   I. Survey fees
   II. Fees for title search
   III. Fees for preparation of documents
   IV. Appraisal fees
   F. I and III only
   G. II and III only
   H. II and IV only
   J. I, II, III, and IV

63. In the usual property management contract, the management fee may be based upon:
   A. a percentage of the gross income.
   B. a percentage of the net income.
   C. a fixed fee.
   D. any of the above.

64. A licensee may be guilty of *steering* if he/she:
   F. shows to a minority prospect, who has asked to be shown ranch-style houses, only those listed ranch-style houses located in the minority prospect's present neighborhood.
   G. refuses to show a three-bedroom, $60,000 house to a minority family of four that has asked to be shown only three-bedroom, $45,000 houses.
   H. tries to persuade a minority family of four that any well-maintained, three-bedroom house would be better for them than any well-maintained, two-bedroom house.
   J. shows to a minority prospect, who has asked to be shown ranch-style houses, those ranch-style houses listed with the licensee's multiple listing service.

65. Which of the following should be included in the employment agreement between a property owner and a property manager?
   I. A statement of the extent of reports to be filed by the manager
   II. A description of the property
   III. A guarantee of time allotted for personal appraisal work by the manager
   A. II only
   B. I and II only
   C. I and III only
   D. I, II, and III

66. An apartment building owner who is using the services of a broker to make rentals prefers to rent to female tenants because the owner thinks that males usually cause more damage to property than do women. What advice should the broker give the owner?
   F. Advertise explicitly for female tenants
   G. Treat all prospective tenants the same
   H. Require a higher damage deposit if male tenants are permitted
   J. Write the owner's preference into the agreement with the broker

67. In appraising a property, which of the following is likely to be affected more by changes in the national economy than in the local city economy?
   A. A dental office building
   B. An apartment building with 16 units
   C. A catering company located near a residential area
   D. An automobile assembly plant employing 5,000 workers

68. In doing a neighborhood analysis of a client's property in Tuxedo Estates, an appraiser notes that the subdivision is exclusive and very large, and the residents are wealthy. If the client's property is at the center of Tuxedo Estates, which of the following is true of the property?
   F. It is more likely to lose value than houses on the perimeter of the subdivision if adjacent neighborhoods begin to decline.
   G. It is less likely to lose value than houses on the perimeter of the subdivision if adjacent neighborhoods begin to decline.
   H. The proximity of public transportation is likely to be an important factor in the valuation of the property.
   J. The property will lose value, because houses in the center of a subdivision decline in value more rapidly than do those on the perimeter.

69. Because of a lack of comparable sales, an appraiser used listed prices in the market approach to estimate the value of a real property. Listings tend to indicate the:
   A. floor of market value.
   B. ceiling of market value.
   C. median market value.
   D. average market value in that neighborhood.

70. Which of the following factors could affect the appraised value of a residential house?
   I. The presence of a river three miles away forming the edge of the residential zoning area which includes this house
   II. The presence of a thousand-foot-tall bluff one mile away
   III. The presence of an industrially zoned area on the far side of a lake which is located four miles from this house
   IV. The presence of a swamp ten miles away

F. I only

G. III only

H. II and IV only

J. I, II, III, and IV

71. A high-rise office building has a gross income of $230,000 every quarter year. Annual expenses are 46 percent of the gross income. What is the approximate annual dollar amount of the net income?

A. $416,600

B. $423,200

C. $496,800

D. $920,400

72. Which of the following is NOT responsible for the increased demand for condominiums?

F. Escalation in construction costs

G. Land scarcity in desirable areas

H. Individuals' desire to rent rather than own property

J. Expenses involved in maintaining a single-family house

73. As part of a neighborhood analysis, an appraiser is analyzing the population composition of an area. Which of the following would NOT be part of the analysis of the area's population?

A. Mass transit facilities in the area

B. Urban-rural balance of the area

C. Size of the households in the area

D. Age distribution of the residents

74. Baird, a professional mountain climber, bought a home built on a cliff and used the cliff to practice climbing. What aspect of value probably caused Baird to offer more for the cliff parcel than the other offeror, a retired farmer?

F. The lack of obsolescence to be derived from the property

G. The absence of depreciation to be derived from the property

H. The amenities to be derived from the property

J. The plottage increment to be derived from the property

75. Appraisals are used to estimate which of the following types of value of real property?

A. Market value

B. Insurance value

C. Investment value

D. All of the above

76. Which of the following is NOT a step in the appraisal process?

F. Definition of the problem

G. Development of a list of possible sources of financing for a purchaser

H. Classification, analysis, and interpretation of data

J. Accumulation of necessary data

77. Which of the following is true of economic obsolescence?

A. It is generally curable because the owner of the subject property can generally invest less money to fix it than what he/she gains in property value by fixing it.

B. It is generally incurable because it results from factors that the owner of the subject property cannot control.

C. It can be caused by a deteriorating foundation under the subject property.

D. It can be caused by a poor floor plan in the subject property.

78. When might a gross rent multiplier be used to estimate the market value of a duplex?

F. When the duplex is being purchased for income purposes

G. When information about recent sales of similar properties is not available

H. When information about recent rentals of similar properties is not available

J. In none of the above circumstances

79. Functional obsolescence of a house may result from

I. construction of a superhighway two blocks away.

II. a lack of bathroom fixtures.

III. uninsulated walls.

IV. zoning restrictions.

A. IV only

B. I or II only

C. II or III only

D. I, II, III, or IV

80. Management expense, electricity expense, and replacement reserves are used in which of the following appraisal methods?

F. Income approach

G. Cost of replacement

H. Market data

J. All of the above

81. Seller Baird offers her house for sale at $36,000. Three buyers who examine Baird's house and the rest of the market find they can obtain similar houses with similar utility for $28,000. Based on the principle of substitution, what is the approximate worth of Baird's house?

A. $28,000

B. $30,000

C. $32,000

D. $36,000

82. An appraiser is hired to estimate the value of a parcel of vacant land. What is the most logical and proper thing for the appraiser to determine first?

F. The listed price of the land

G. The highest and best use of the land

H. What the present owner paid for the land

J. Prices of properties comparable to the land

83. Given the net income of a property, the appraiser can determine an opinion of the value for that property by:
A. multiplying by the rate of depreciation.
B. multiplying by the rate of economic appreciation.
C. dividing by the percent of capital gains.
D. dividing by the rate of capitalization.

84. A straight-term mortgage provides for repayment of what percent of the total loan principal at maturity?
F. 100
G. 75
H. 67
J. 33

85. Dole is buying a home with an FHA-insured loan. The appraisal report states that the value of the house is $7,000 less than the sales price. Which statement is true of this price difference?
A. It can be financed in the form of a junior mortgage.
B. It can be financed in the form of a straight mortgage.
C. It must come out of Dole's personal assets.
D. It forces Dole to obtain a conventional loan instead of an FHA-insured loan.

86. Who signs the mortgage for the amount borrowed under a purchase money mortgage?
F. The mortgagee
G. The mortgagor
H. The beneficiary
J. None of the above

87. According to the federal Truth in Lending Act, the right of rescission guaranteed for the three business days following the transaction applies to:
A. a purchase money first mortgage on a house.
B. a construction loan to build a house.
C. a sale-leaseback on a store.
D. none of the above.

88. The Federal National Mortgage Association buys which of the following?
   I. Lease options
   II. VA loans
   III. FHA loans
F. II only
G. III only
H. I and II only
J. II and III only

89. Howe borrowed $8,000 and gave the lender a straight note secured by a mortgage against the home. Howe made monthly interest payments computed on a 7 percent annual rate for the full term of the note. The total of the interest payments was $1,866.67. For how many months was the term of the note?
A. 40
B. 36
C. 23
D. 16

90. What effect does discounting a loan have?
F. It increases the lender's effective yield.
G. It reduces the amount of the prepayment penalty that can be charged.
H. It increases the cost of the loan in the secondary mortgage market.
J. It reduces the cost of the loan to the borrower.

91. Which of the following is NOT covered by Regulation Z?
A. Real estate loans for household purposes
B. Real estate loans for business purposes
C. Advertisements for mortgage financing that contain the amount of down payment
D. Advertisements for mortgage financing that contain the terms of payment

92. In which of the following cases would the amount applied to the principal of a loan increase while the interest payment decreases?
F. When the principal is paid in a single payment
G. When the loan is repaid in equal monthly payments
H. When the loan is repaid in flexible payments
J. When all payments are balloon payments

93. Gold Savings and Loan agreed to loan Dole 70 percent of the appraised value of a cabin. The loan was secured by a five-year straight note. The interest rate was 11 percent. The first two years' interest combined amounted to $3,080. What was the appraised value of the cabin?
A. $ 8,000
B. $15,000
C. $20,000
D. $28,000

94. Which of the following standard mortgage clauses could best protect the borrower in times of falling interest rates?
F. Acceleration clause
G. Subordination clause
H. Escalation clause
J. Prepayment clause

95. Which of the following best expresses the relationship between the availability of money and the level of loan interest rates?
A. When money is unavailable, interest rates go down.
B. When money is unavailable, interest rates go up.
C. When money is readily available, interest rates go up.

D. When money is readily available, interest rates remain stable.

96. A $40,000 down payment will purchase a home for which of the following sales prices if the local savings and loan will loan an amount equal to twice a family's annual income and the wife earns $30,000 per year while the husband earns $26,000 per year?
    F. $180,000
    G. $152,000
    H. $112,000
    J. $ 96,000

97. A veteran finishes paying off a VA-guaranteed loan and two years later applies for a second VA loan to repair the foundation of his house. Is the veteran eligible for this second loan?
    A. Yes, because the veteran wants the money for a purpose that falls within VA guidelines.
    B. Yes, because the veteran's entitlement allows him to apply for up to two loans in his lifetime.
    C. No, because the veteran did not apply for the loan within one year of the expiration date of the first one.
    D. No, because the VA does not guarantee loans for the sole purpose of home repairs.

98. A seller, who is not in the real estate or real estate finance business, decides to sell her own home and places the following advertisement in the newspaper: "Well-located, 3-bedroom ranch. Owner financing at 11 percent. Substantial down payment required. Call 865-9681 for details." Does the advertisement violate the advertising provisions of the federal Truth in Lending Act?
    F. Yes, because whenever the interest rate is stated, other information about credit costs must also be given.
    F. Yes, because whenever the interest rate is stated, other information about credit costs must also be given.
    G. Yes, because the advertisement is an example of bait advertising since the seller can demand a higher interest rate by simply specifying an unrealistic down payment.
    H. No, because advertisements that contain only one numerical figure about financing charges are not subject to full disclosure.
    J. No, because the seller is not in the business of regularly providing financing.

99. A borrower makes constantly monthly payments of $306.24. The mortgage interest rate is 9½ percent per year, and the current outstanding loan balance is $35,400. What is the amount of principal due in the next monthly payment?
    A. $ 25.99
    B. $ 29.09

C. $ 51.98
D. $280.25

100. The amount of a loan that a veteran can obtain under the terms of the Veterans Administration is decided by the:
    F. Veterans Administration.
    G. lending institution involved.
    H. U.S. Department of Housing and Urban Development.
    J. annual limits issued by the Federal National Mortgage Association.

*Answer Key*

| 1. | D | 26. | G | 51. | D | 76. | G |
|----|---|-----|---|-----|---|-----|---|
| 2. | F | 27. | B | 52. | G | 77. | B |
| 3. | C | 28. | J | 53. | B | 78. | F |
| 4. | F | 29. | A | 54. | F | 79. | C |
| 5. | D | 30. | J | 55. | A | 80. | F |
| 6. | G | 31. | B | 56. | J | 81. | A |
| 7. | C | 32. | H | 57. | C | 82. | G |
| 8. | F | 33. | C | 58. | F | 83. | D |
| 9. | D | 34. | G | 59. | C | 84. | F |
| 10. | J | 35. | A | 60. | H | 85. | C |
| 11. | A | 36. | H | 61. | D | 86. | G |
| 12. | G | 37. | D | 62. | J | 87. | D |
| 13. | C | 38. | H | 63. | D | 88. | J |
| 14. | J | 39. | C | 64. | F | 89. | A* |
| 15. | C | 40. | F | 65. | D | 90. | F |
| 16. | J | 41. | B | 66. | G | 91. | B |
| 17. | B | 42. | G | 67. | D | 92. | G |
| 18. | J | 43. | A | 68. | G | 93. | C* |
| 19. | A | 44. | G | 69. | B | 94. | J |
| 20. | H | 45. | C | 70. | J | 95. | B |
| 21. | C | 46. | J | 71. | C* | 96. | G* |
| 22. | J | 47. | C | 72. | H | 97. | A |
| 23. | A | 48. | H | 73. | A | 98. | J |
| 24. | J | 49. | A | 74. | H | 99. | A |
| 25. | D | 50. | G | 75. | D | 100. | G |

*See also computations.

*Computations for Items in Sample National Examination*

71. Gross income = $230,000 per quarter
    Gross **annual** income = $230,000 × 4 = $920,000
    Annual expenses = 46% of gross annual income
    Therefore, NET INCOME = $920,000 −
        ($920,000 × 0.46) =
        $920,000 − $432,200 = $496,800

89. Loan principal = $8,000
    Interest rate = 7% per annum
    Total interest paid = $1,866.67

Amount on interest paid per year = $8,000 × 0.07
  = $560

Amount of interest paid per month = $\dfrac{\$560}{12 \text{ months}}$

  = $46.67 (rounded)

Number of months in term of loan = $\dfrac{\$1,866.67}{\$46.67}$

  = 40 months

93.  Interest rate = 11%
    First two years' interest = $3,080
    Loan amount = 70% of appraised value
    Yearly interest paid = $\dfrac{\$3,080}{2}$ = $1,540

    Amount of loan = $\dfrac{\$1,540}{0.11}$ = $14,000

    Appraised value of cabin = $\dfrac{\$14,000}{0.70}$ = $20,000

96.  Family income = $56,000 [Wife = $30,000, Husband = $26,000]
    Loan available = $56,000 × 2 = $112,000
    Cash available for down payment = $40,000
    Therefore couple can afford to purchase a home for $152,000

    [Down payment of $40,000 + loan for twice family income]

99.  Outstanding loan balance = $35,400
    Interest rate = 9 1/2% per annum
    Constant monthly payment = $306.24
    Interest paid when $35,400 is outstanding = $35,400 × $\dfrac{0.095}{12}$ = $280.25

    | | |
    |---|---|
    | Constant monthly payment | $306.24 |
    | Interest payment for month | − $280.25 |
    | Principal payment | 25.99 |

# Appendixes

# Appendix A

## Sources of Information

The following organizations are excellent sources of information for individuals seeking information about real estate careers in specialty areas:

**Real Estate Appraisal**

American Institute of Real Estate Appraisers (AIREA) (affiliated with the National Association of REALTORS), 430 N. Michigan Avenue, Chicago, IL 60611
Society of Real Estate Appraisers (SREA), 645 N. Michigan Avenue, Chicago, IL 60611
National Association of Independent Fee Appraisers, 7501 Murdoch Street, St. Louis, MO 63119

**Real Estate Brokerage**

National Association of REALTORS, 430 N. Michigan Avenue, Chicago, IL 60611

**Real Estate Finance**

Mortgage Bankers Association of America, 1125 15th Street, NW, Washington, DC 20005

**Real Estate Counseling**

Society of Real Estate Counselors, 430 N. Michigan Avenue, Chicago, IL 60611

**Land Development and Building**

American Land Development Association, 1000 16th Street, NW, Suite 604, Washington, DC 20036

**Real Estate Property Management**

Institute of Real Estate Management (IREM), 430 N. Michigan Avenue, Chicago, IL 60611
National Association of Home Builders (NAHB), 15th & M Streets, NW, Washington, DC 20005

**Real Estate Planning**

The American Planning Association (APA), 1313 E. 60th Street, Chicago, IL 60637

**Real Estate Syndications**

Real Estate Securities and Syndications Institute, 430 N. Michigan Avenue, Chicago, IL 60611

**Corporate Real Estate**

International Association of Corporate Real Estate Executives, 471 Spencer Drive South, West Palm Beach, FL 33409-6685

**International Real Estate**

International Real Estate Institute, 8715 Via De Commercio, Scottsdale, AZ 85258
International Real Estate Federation (FIABCI), 777 14th Street, NW, Washington, DC 20005

**General Information**

National Association of REALTORS, 430 N. Michigan Avenue, Chicago, IL 60611

# Appendix B

## Answer Keys

### Chapter 3: The Real Estate Business

| | | | |
|---|---|---|---|
| 1. A | 6. C | 11. C | 16. C |
| 2. B | 7. B | 12. C | 17. D |
| 3. C | 8. C | 13. C | 18. D |
| 4. A | 9. D | 14. A | 19. A |
| 5. D | 10. D | 15. A | 20. A |

### Chapter 4: Regulation of the Real Estate Business

| | | | |
|---|---|---|---|
| 1. A | 6. A | 11. C | 16. D |
| 2. B | 7. A | 12. C | 17. A |
| 3. B | 8. B | 13. B | 18. C |
| 4. A | 9. C | 14. C | 19. A |
| 5. B | 10. A | 15. A | 20. C |

### Chapter 5: Legal Aspects of Real Estate

| | | | |
|---|---|---|---|
| 1. D | 6. C | 11. D | 16. D |
| 2. A | 7. B | 12. B | 17. B |
| 3. C | 8. B | 13. D | 18. A |
| 4. C | 9. A | 14. B | 19. D |
| 5. B | 10. C | 15. D | 20. A |

### Chapter 6: Ownership of Real Property

| | | | |
|---|---|---|---|
| 1. C | 6. A | 11. A | 16. D |
| 2. B | 7. B | 12. B | 17. B |
| 3. C | 8. A | 13. B | 18. A |
| 4. D | 9. C | 14. B | 19. C |
| 5. A | 10. B | 15. A | 20. C |

### Chapter 7: Transfer of Real Property

| | | | |
|---|---|---|---|
| 1. A | 6. B | 11. A | 16. A |
| 2. B | 7. A | 12. C | 17. D |
| 3. B | 8. D | 13. A | 18. D |
| 4. C | 9. A | 14. D | 19. A |
| 5. D | 10. A | 15. D | 20. B |

### Chapter 8: Evidence and Assurance of Title

| | | | |
|---|---|---|---|
| 1. C | 6. D | 11. D | 16. A |
| 2. C | 7. A | 12. C | 17. D |
| 3. C | 8. C | 13. D | 18. B |
| 4. C | 9. D | 14. C | 19. B |
| 5. D | 10. B | 15. B | 20. C |

### Chapter 9: Landlord and Tenant Relationships

| | | | |
|---|---|---|---|
| 1. D | 6. B | 11. B | 16. A |
| 2. C | 7. D | 12. D | 17. A |
| 3. A | 8. A | 13. A | 18. D |
| 4. C | 9. B | 14. C | 19. D |
| 5. B | 10. A | 15. B | 20. D |

### Chapter 10: Mortgages, Deeds of Trust, and Land Contracts

| | | | |
|---|---|---|---|
| 1. B | 6. B | 11. C | 16. B |
| 2. C | 7. D | 12. C | 17. D |
| 3. A | 8. C | 13. D | 18. C |
| 4. B | 9. B | 14. B | 19. A |
| 5. B | 10. D | 15. B | 20. D |

### Chapter 11: Real Estate Finance

| | | | |
|---|---|---|---|
| 1. C | 6. C | 11. A | 16. C |
| 2. D | 7. B | 12. B | 17. C |
| 3. D | 8. C | 13. C | 18. D |
| 4. C | 9. C | 14. D | 19. C |
| 5. D | 10. D | 15. A | 20. C |

### Chapter 12: Real Estate Appraisal

| | | | |
|---|---|---|---|
| 1. B | 6. D | 11. B | 16. A |
| 2. D | 7. D | 12. B | 17. C |
| 3. C | 8. D | 13. D | 18. D |
| 4. C | 9. A | 14. B | 19. C |
| 5. D | 10. A | 15. C | 20. D |

*Calculations:*

11. Value × rate = income
    $103,000 × .12 = $12,360

12. $60,000/.6 = $100,000

13. Net income/value = rate
    ($8,000 − $7,200)/$147,000 = rate
    $800/$147,000 = .0054 or .54%

19. Net income/value = rate
    $8,000/$80,000 = .10 or 10%

20. Gross monthly income × GRM = value
    $6,000/12 × 105 = value
    $500 × 105 = $52,500

**Chapter 13: Real Estate Investment and Taxation**

| | | | |
|---|---|---|---|
| 1. D | 6. B | 11. A | 16. C |
| 2. B | 7. D | 12. C | 17. D |
| 3. A | 8. A | 13. C | 18. D |
| 4. C | 9. C | 14. B | 19. B |
| 5. C | 10. D | 15. C | 20. A |

*Calculations:*

14. $120,000 ÷ 31.5 years = $3,810

15. $1,200 ÷ $30,000 = .04 or 4%

17. $4,650 × .28 = $1,320

**Chapter 14: Contracts**

| | | | |
|---|---|---|---|
| 1. C | 6. A | 11. D | 16. B |
| 2. B | 7. B | 12. D | 17. A |
| 3. C | 8. B | 13. A | 18. C |
| 4. B | 9. D | 14. C | 19. D |
| 5. B | 10. C | 15. C | 20. A |

**Chapter 15: The Brokerage Business and Agency Relationships**

| | | | |
|---|---|---|---|
| 1. D | 6. D | 11. B | 16. A |
| 2. C | 7. D | 12. B | 17. D |
| 3. B | 8. A | 13. A | 18. A |
| 4. B | 9. A | 14. C | 19. A |
| 5. C | 10. D | 15. B | 20. D |

# CHAPTER 16: SOLUTIONS TO MATH PROBLEMS

**Practice Problems: Fractions, Decimals, Percentages**

*Fractions*

1. 1/6 + 1/8 = 7/24
2. 3/7 + 4/9 = 55/63
3. 19/20 + 3/5 = 31/20 or 1 11/20
4. 1/8 + 5/12 = 13/24
5. 3/4 + 1/16 = 13/16
6. 1/6 − 1/8 = 1/24
7. 4/7 − 4/9 = 8/63
8. 19/20 − 3/5 = 7/20
9. 5/12 − 1/8 = 7/24
10. 3/4 − 1/16 = 11/16
11. 1/8 × 1/4 = 1/32
12. 1/9 × 11/12 = 11/108
13. 3/4 × 7/16 = 21/64
14. 4/5 × 8/9 = 32/45
15. 5/12 × 1/5 = 5/60 = 1/12
16. 1/8 ÷ 1/4 = 4/8 = 1/2
17. 1/9 ÷ 11/12 = 12/99 = 4/33
18. 3/4 ÷ 7/6 = 18/28 = 9/14

19. 4/5 ÷ 8/9 = 36/40 = 9/10
20. 5/12 ÷ 1/5 = 25/12 = 2 1/12

*Decimals and Percentages*

1. .5 + .075 + .125 = .7
2. .073 + 1.25 + .93 = 2.253
3. .82 + .73 + 2.584 = 4.134
4. .0016 + 1.043 + .3 = 1.3446
5. 1.25 − .075 = 1.175
6. .073 − .0016 = .0714
7. 1.4874 − .896 = .5914
8. 2.043 − 1.0012 = 1.0418
9. .075 × 1.257 = .094275
10. .342 × .0017 = .0005814
11. .7589 × 1.2 = .91068
12. .346 × 3.476 = 1.202696
13. .34 ÷ .516 = .65891
14. 1.25 ÷ .07 = 17.857
15. .78 ÷ .4 = 1.95
16. 1.29 ÷ .432 = 2.9861
17. 75% = .75
18. 125% = 1.25
19. 27.56% = .2756
20. 43.2% = .432
21. .0025 = .25%
22. .567 = 56.7%
23. .493 = 49.3%
24. 3.475 = 347.5%

**Practice Problems: Perimeter, Area, Volume**

1. 640 acres = 1 square mile

2. 43,560 square feet = 1 acre

3.

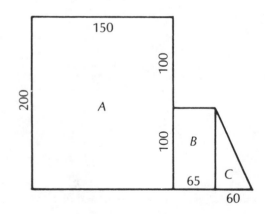

Area A = (150)(200) = 30,000
Area B = (100)( 65) =  6,500
Area C = ½(60)(100) =  3,000

Total                      39,500 square feet

4. $A = L \times W$
   $A = 373 \times 154$
   $A = 57,442$ square feet

   $57,442/43,560 = 1.3187$ acres
   $1.3187\ (\$1,000.00) = \$1,318.70$

5. $A = L \times W$
   $A = 300 \times 450$
   $A = 135,000$ square feet

   1 acre $= 43,560$ square feet
   $135,000/43,560 = 3.1$ acres

6. Labor costs: $28 \times 9 \times \$.20 = \$50.40$

   Concrete costs: $\dfrac{(28 \times 9 \times .5)}{27} \times \$16.50 =$
   $\$77.00$

   $\$50.40 + \$77.00 = \$127.40$

7. $A = L \times W$
   $L = 150 - (20 + 15) = 115$
   $W = 120 - (15 + 15) = 90$
   $A = 115 \times 90 = 10,350$ square feet

8. $A = L \times W$
   $A = 310 \times 240$
   $A = 74,400$ square rods
   $A = 74,400/160$
   $A = 465$ acres

   $A = \pi r^2$
   $A = 3.1416\ (45^2)$
   $A = 3.1416\ (2,025)$
   $A = 6,361.74$ square rods
   $A = 6,361.74/160$
   $A = 39.76$ acres

   | 465 | acres | 425.24 |
   |---|---|---|
   | $-$ 39.76 | acres | $\times$ \$50.00 |
   | 425.24 | acres | \$21,262.00 |

9. $C = \pi d$
   $C = (3.1416)(14.28)$
   $C = 44.86$ rods

10. $V = L \times W \times H$
    $V = 340 \times 260 \times 40$
    $V = 3,536,000$ cubic feet

11. $A = L \times W$
    $A = 80 \times 135$
    $A = 10,800$

    Cost $=$ area $\times$ price
    Cost $= 10,800 \times \$.63$
    Cost $= \$6,804$

$V = L \times W \times H$
$V = 40 \times 60 \times 10$
$V = 24,000$ cubic feet

Cost $= V \times$ price
Cost $= 24,000 \times \$1.85$
Cost $= \$44,400$

$\$44,400$
$+\ 6,804$
$\$51,204$

12. $264 \times 660 \quad = 174,240$ square feet
    $174,240/43,560 = 4.0$ acres
    $4 \times \$800 \quad = \$3,200$

13. | Land | | $125 \times 100 \times \$\ 1 =$ | \$ 12,500 |
    |---|---|---|---|
    | Two-story building | $2 \times\ 40 \times\ 60 \times \$25 =$ | | 120,000 |
    | Full basement | $40 \times\ 60 \times \$\ 5 =$ | | 12,000 |
    | Driveway | $10 \times\ 80 \times \$\ 4 =$ | | 3,200 |
    | Sidewalks | $3 \times\ 70 \times \$\ 3 =$ | | 630 |
    | Yard improvements | $=$ | | 5,000 |
    | | | | \$153,330 |

14. Site Z $= 3$ acres
    Site Y $= 3$ acres $\times 3 = \quad 9$ acres
    Site X $= \underline{9}$ acres $\times 2 = 18$ acres
    $\qquad\qquad\qquad\qquad\qquad$ 30 acres

    160 acres $=$ one quarter section
    $-\ 30$
    130 acres remain

**Practice Problems: Rate, Income, Value, Interest**

1. Let $x =$ Value of stream of income
   $.08x = \$600 \times 12$ months
   $.08x = \$7,200$
   $x = \$7,200/.08$
   $x = \$90,000$

2. $6 \times 2\frac{1}{2}\% = 15\%$ depreciation at the end of six years
   $x =$ Original value of house
   Original value $-$ depreciation $=$ Present value

   $x - (.15x) = \$7,650$
   $.85x = \$7,650$
   $x = \$7,650/.85$
   $x = \$9,000$

3. $RP = AY$
   $.13(P) = (\$1,000.00/\text{month})(12)$
   $.13\ P = \$12,000.00$
   $P = \$12,000.00/.13$
   $P = \$92,307.69$

4. 12%    = return each year
100%   = total amount invested
100/12 = 8.33 years

5. Net income per month = $325 − $155 = $170
$170 × 12 = $2,040

6. Income = 4 × $200 × 12 months = $ 9,600
            3 × $175 × 12 months = $ 6,300
            3 × $150 × 12 months = $ 5,400

Gross income        = $21,300
Less expenses       =   10,000
Less debt service   =    6,000
        Net income  = $ 5,300

$ROI = \$5,300/\$50,000$
$ROI = 10.6\%$

7. $RP = I$
$R(\$23,000) = (\$300 \times 12 \text{ months})$
$R = \$3,600/\$23,000$
$R = 15.7\%$

8. $RP = I$
$.09(\$40,000) = \$3,600$
$\$3,600/4 = \$900$ quarterly payment

## Practice Problems: Depreciation

1. 100%/35 years = 2.8%

4 years × 2.8% = 11.2% depreciated
$75,000 × .112 = $8,400 of depreciation
$75,000 − $8,400 = $66,000 remaining value

2. 100%/45 years = 2.22%/year

8 years × 2.2% = 17.76% depreciated

Value new = Remaining value/100% − Amount depreciated

Value new = $50,000/100% − 17.76%

Value new = $50,000/.8224

Value new = $60,798

3. $275,000/31.5 years = $8,730.16/year

4. $275,000/31.5 years = $8,730.16
$8,730.16 × 4 years = $34,920.64 for 4 years

## Practice Problems: Profit and Loss

1. 3 × $2,000 = $6,000 total sale price of 3 lots
$6,000 − original investment = profit
$6,000 − $4,500 = $1,500 profit
$ROI$ = profit/original investment
$ROI = \$1,500/\$4,500$
$ROI = 33^1/_3\%$

2. Loss = sales price − cost
Cost = sales price/(1 − loss)
Cost = $35,000/(1 − .06)
Cost = $35,000/.94
Cost = $37,234.04

3. Profit = sales price − cost
Sales price = cost + profit
Sales price = $5,000 + .15 ($5,000)
Sales price = $5,000 + $750
Sales price = $5,750

4. Profit = sales price − cost
Profit = $65,000 − $43,500
Profit = $21,500
% profit = proft/cost
% profit = $21,500/$43,500
% profit = .494 = 49.4%

5. Loss = sales price − cost
$3,400 = $20,350 − $23,750
% loss = $3,400/$23,750
% loss = .143, or 14.3%

## Practice Problems: Commission

1. Expenses     = 10 showings at $20 each = $200
Commission = ½ (.08) ($50,000) = $2,000
Net income  = commission − expenses
Net income  = $2,000 − $200 = $1,800

2.                              $x$ = selling price
$.06(\$10,000) + .05(x − \$10,000) = \$760$
$\$600 + .05x − 500 = \$760$
$.05x = \$660$
$x = \$13,200$

3. Original offering = 80 acres × $400    = $32,000
                                              −27,500
Difference between offer and asked price =    4,500
Commission = .08($27,500)                 = −2,200
                                             $ 2,300

4. $95,000 × .08 = $7,600
$7,600/2 = $3,800

5. $SP \times R = C$
$48,500 × .08 = $3,880
⅜($3,880) = $1,455 for the salesperson

## Practice Problems: Mortgage Balances, Rent, Tax, Insurance, Interest Prorations

*Mortgage Balances*

1. $38,500 × .08 = $3,080.00
$3,080.00/12 = $256.67/month

$328.00 − $256.67 = $71.33
$38,500.00 − $71.33 = $38,428.67 after payment

2. $24,250.00 × .07 = $1,697.50
$1,697.50/12 = $141.46/month
$210.00 − $141.46 = $68.54
$24,250.00 − $68.54 = $24,181.46 after June 15
   payment

$24,181.46 × .07 = $1,692.70
$1,692.70/12 = $141.06/month
$210.00 − $141.06 = $68.94
$24,181.46 − $68.94 = $24,112.52 after July 15
   payment

*Rent*

3. 30 − 20 = 10 days remaining
1-bedroom (two)
$180/30 days = $6/day
$6 × 10 days remaining = $60

2-bedroom (one)
$210/30 days = $7/day
$7 × 10 days remaining = $70

3-bedroom (one)
$270/30 days = $9/day
$9 × 10 days remaining = $90

Total $120 + $70 + $90 = $280 owed Mr. David

*Taxes*

4. $37,500
  ×    .4
  $15,000

$15,000 × $8.27/$100 = $1,240.50 annual taxes
$1,240.50/12 = $103.375 or $103.38/month
$103.38 × 6⅓ months = $654.71 charged to seller
$1,240.50 − $654.71 = $585.79 charged to buyer

*Insurance*

|  | Day | Month | Year |
|---|---|---|---|
|  | 41 | 18 | TY |
| 5. Expires | N̶ | X̶ | N̶Y̶ |
| Close | 23 | 9 | TY |
| Remaining | 18 | 9 | 0 |

$489/3 = $163/year
$163/12 = $13.58/month
$13.58/30 = $.45/day
$18($.45) + 9 ($13.58) = $8.10 + $122.22
                      = $130.32 to seller

*Interest*

6. $38,500.00
  ×    .0875
  $3,368.75/year

$3,368.75/12 = $280.73/month
$280.73/30 = $9.36/day
$9.36 × 20 days = $187.20

## Answers to Review Questions

1. (C)
$9.50 × 40 = $380.00 principal and interest
$480/12   =    40.00 taxes
$540/36   =    15.00 insurance
                $435.00 PITI

2. (D)
$162 × 12 = $1,944.00
$1,944.00 × .28 = $544.32

3. (B)
1 point = 1% of amount loaned
$ discount/amount loaned = % of discount
$2,175/$43,500 = .05
.05 = 5% or 5 points

4. (B)
Option I:
20 × $225 = $4,500/month gross income
$4,500 − $875 = $3,625 net cash

Option II:
20 × $185 = $3,700 net cash
Option II yields ($3,700 − 3,625) = $75/month
   more

5. (A)
3:2 = 60% for broker, 40% for salesperson
$78,500 × .06 = $4,710 total commission
$4,710 × .60 = $2,826 to broker
$4,710 × .40 = $1,884 to salesperson
                 $  942 more to broker

6. (B)
4 × $360 = $1,440 annual interest
$I/R$ = value of loan
$1,440/.12 = $12,000
$12,000/.75 = $16,000 appraised value

7. (B)
$1,200/$24,000 = .05, or $5/$100

8. (A)
$720/12 = $60/month
7½ ($60) = $450
$720 − $450 = $270 taxes returned

|      | Y  | M | D  |
|------|----|---|----|
| Exp. | 84 | 4 | 10 |
| Close| 81 | 8 | 15 |
|      | 2  | 7 | 25 |

$360/3 = $120/year
$120/12 = $10/month
$10/30 = $.33/day
2 ($120) + 7 ($10) + 25 (.33) = $318.25
$270 + $318.25 = $588.25

9. (A)
$43,000 + $45,600 + $48,100 + $56,500
    = $193,200
.07 ($90,000) + .09 ($193,200 − $90,000)
    = $6,300 + $9,288
    = $15,588 total commission

$193,200 × .08 = $15,456
$15,588 − $15,456 = $132 more under first
    option

10. (C)
.07 ($15,000) + .04 (sales price − $15,000)
    = $2,850
$1,050 + .04 (sales price − $15,000) = $2,850
$2,850 − $1,050 = .04 (sales price − $15,000)
$1,800 = .04 (sales price − $15,000)
$1,800/.04 = sales price − $15,000
$45,000 = sales price − $15,000
$60,000 = sales price

11. (C)
$14,300 × .145 = $2,073.50 annual interest
$2,073.50/12 = $172.79 monthly interest
$172.79 × 8 = $1,382.32 interest for 8 months
$14,300 + $1,382.32 = $15,682.32 total

12. (B)
$562.50 × 4 = $2,250 annual interest
$2,250/$15,000 = .15, or 15%

13. (D)
$A = ½ bh$
$A = ½ (2,640 × 1,320)$
$A = 1,742,400$ square feet
$A = 1,742,400/43,560$
$A = 40$ acres
40 acres − 8 acres = 32 tillable acres
32 × $3,200 = $102,400 for the field

14. (C)
75 × 126 × 36 = 340,200 cubic feet
340,200 × $.057 = $19,391.40
$19,391.40/12 = $1,615.95/month
$1,615.95/30 = $53.87/day
25($53.87) = $1,346.75 used by seller
$1,615.95 − $1,346.75 = $269.20 to new buyer

15. (D)
$2,100/12 = $175/month
$175 × 10 units = $1,750/month gross income
$1,750 × 105 = $183,750

16. (C)
$185,000 − $18,000 = $167,000
$167,000/27.5 years = $6,072.73/year or $6,073

17. (C)
Rate = net income/value
$R = ($2,750 × 12) − $8,740/$147,000$
$R = $33,000 − $8,740/$147,000$
$R = $24,260/$147,000$
$R = .165$, or 16½%

18. (A)
$NI = R × V$
$NI = .14 × $130,000$
$NI = $18,200$/year
$18,200/12 = $1,516.67/month

19. (C)
24 × 26 × .5 = 312 cubic feet
312/27 = 11.56 cubic yards
11.56 × $22.50 = $260.10 for cement

24 × 26 = 624 square feet
624 × .53 = $330.72 for labor

(24 × 8 × 2) + (26 × 8 × 2)
    = 384 + 416 = 800
800 × $1.75 = $1,400 cost of sides
(624 × $2.10) + 624 (.37)
    = $1,310.40 + $230.88
    = $1,541.28 for roof

Cost of garage:
$260.10 + $330.72 + $1,400 + $1,541.28
    = $3,532.10

20. (B)
$3,500/$50,000 = .07, or 7%
7% = 7 points
1 point = ⅛ of 1% in rate difference
7 points = ⅞% of 1% difference
13½% + ⅞% = 14⅜% conventional rate

### CHAPTER 17: SOLUTIONS TO PRACTICE PROBLEMS FOR REAL ESTATE TRANSACTIONS

#### Problem 1

*See also worksheet on page 263.*

1. *Sales fee*
   $97,000 \times .07 = $6,790.00

2. *Taxes*

   | | |
   |---|---:|
   | Land | $ 8,000.00 |
   | Improvements | 21,000.00 |
   | Total assessment | $29,000.00 |

   $29,000 \times $7.10/$100 = $2,059/year
   $2,059/12 = $171.58/month
   10½ month × $171.58 = $1,801.59

3. *Insurance*

   | | Day | Month | Year |
   |---|---|---|---|
   | Expiration date | 10 | 6 | NY |
   | Closing date | 15 | 11 | TY |
   | Remaining | 25 | 6 | 0 |

   $144.00/12 = $12.00/month
   $144.00/360 = $.40/day
   6($12.00) + 25($.40) = $82.00

4. *Turner trust*

   | | |
   |---|---:|
   | Beginning balance | $9,650.00 |
   | Interest rate | ×.06 |
   | Annual interest | $579.00 |

   $579.00/12 = $48.25/month interest
   $96.00 − $48.25
       = $47.75 reduction after Oct. 15
   $9,650.00 − $47.75
       = $9,602.25 remaining balance

5. *Interest, in arrears*
   $9,602.25 × .06 = $576.14
   $576.14/12 = $48.01

6. *Loan origination fee*
   $74,000 × .01 = $740.00

#### Problem 2

*See also worksheet on page 264.*

1. *Murphy mortgage*
   $28,500.00 × .08 = $2,280.00
   $2,280.00/12 = $190/month
   $328 − $190 = $138

After Oct. 1 payment $28,500 − $138 = $28,362
$28,362.00 × .08 = $2,268.96
$2,268.96/12 = $189.08
$328.00 − $189.08 = $138.92

After Nov. 1 payment
$28,362.00 − $138.92 = $28,223.08

2. *Jones mortgage*
   $51,000 × .90 = $45,900

3. *Interest prorated on Murphy mortgage*
   $28,223.08 × .08 = $2,257.85
   $2,257.85/12 = $188.15/month
   $188.15/30 days = $6.27/day
   $6.27 × 10 days = $62.70

4. *Taxes*

   | | |
   |---|---:|
   | Land | $ 3,000.00 |
   | Improvements | 12,000.00 |
   | Assessed value | $15,000.00 |

   $15,000 × $9.25/$100 = $1,387.50
   $1,387.50/12 = $115.63

   | | | |
   |---|---|---:|
   | $115.63 × 10⅓ months = | | $1,194.80 |
   | or $115.63 × 10 months = | | $1,156.30 |
   | 10 days × $1,387.50/360 | = | 38.50 |
   | | | $1,194.80 |

5. *Rent*
   $185/month/30 days = $6.17/day
   $6.17 × 10 days remaining = $61.70
   $185 − $61.70 = $123.30 to buyer

6. *Insurance*

   | | Day | Month | Year |
   |---|---|---|---|
   | Expiration date | 15 | 08 | NY |
   | Closing date | 10 | 11 | TY |
   | Remaining | 5 | 9 | 0 |

   $144.00/12 = $12.00/month
   $12.00/30 days = $.40/day
   5($.40) + 9($12.00) = $110.00

7. *Loan origination fee*
   $45,900 × .01 = $459

8. *Brokerage fee*
   $51,000 × .06 = $3,060

#### Problem 3

*See also worksheet on page 265.*

1. *Purchase money mortgage*
   $74,500 × .80 = $59,600

2. *Taxes, prorated*
(For calculation purposes, all months have 30 days.)

$6,000 + $14,000 = $20,000
$20,000 × $8.25/$100 = $1,650/year
$1,650/12 = $137.50/month
$137.50 × 8 months = $1,100.00

3. *Sales fee*
$74,500 × .06 = $4,470

## Problem 4

*See also worksheet on page 266.*

1. *Sales fee*
$32,000 × .06 = $1,920

2. *Brown mortgage balance*
$25,920.00 × .08 = $2,073.60
After April $2,073.60/12 = $172.80/month interest
$274.00 − $172.80 = $101.20 principal
$25,920.00 − $101.20 = $25,818.80 after May payment

$25,818.80 × .08 = $2,065.50
$2,065.50/12 = $172.13
$274.00 − $170.76 = $103.24
$25,818.80 − $101.87 = $25,716.93 after June payment

$25,716.93 × .08 = $2,057.35
$2,057.35/12 = $171.45
$274.00 − $171.45 = $102.55
$25,716.93 − $102.55 = $25,614.38 after July 1 payment

$25,614.38 × .08 = $2,049.15
$2,049.15/12 = $170.76
$274.00 − $170.76 = $103.24
$25,614.38 − $103.24 = $25,511.14 after Aug. 1 payment

3. *Interest, prorated in arrears*
$25,511.14 × .08 = $2,040.89
$2,040.89/12 = $170.07
$170.07/30 = $5.67
$5.67 × 10 = $56.70 interest through Aug. 10 closing

4. *Taxes prorated*

| Land | $2,500 |
| Improvements | 7,000 |
| Assessed value | $9,500 |

$9,500 × $8.40/$100 = $798.00
$798.00/12 = $66.50/month
$66.50/30 = $2.22/day
$66.50 × 7 = $465.50
$2.22 × 10 = $22.20
$465.50 + $22.20 = $487.70

## Problem 5. *See also worksheet on page 267.*

1. *Jones mortgage interest in arrears*
$10,120.00 × .075 = $759.00
$759.00/12 = $63.25/month
Seller owes entire month = $63.25

2. *Dallas new mortgage:* $87,750 × .80 = $70,200

3. *Commission: 6%*
$87,750 × .06 = $5,265
$10,000 × .06 = $600
$5,265 + $600 = $5,865

4. *Land contract balance*
$10,000 × .70 = $7,000
$3,000 down payment by buyer

5. *Taxes prorated, owed in arrears*

| Land | $ 8,000 |
| Improvements | 20,000 |
| Assessed value | $28,000 |

$28,000 × $7.40/$100 = $2,072/year
$2,072/12 = $172.67/month
$172.67 × 8 = $1,381.36 to be charged to seller

6. *Insurance, prorated*

|  | Day | Month | Year |
|---|---|---|---|
| Expiration date | 1 | 5 | NY |
| Closing date | 31 | 8 | TY |
| Remaining | 0 | 8 | 0 |

$270.00/3 = $90.00/year
$90.00/12 = $7.50/month
8 months remaining on policy
8($7.50) = $60.00

7. *Loan origination fee:* $70,200 × .01 = $702.00

8. *Discount points:* $70,200 × .02 = $1,404.00

## Problem 1
## SETTLEMENT STATEMENT WORKSHEET

|  | BUYER'S STATEMENT | | SELLER'S STATEMENT | |
|---|---|---|---|---|
|  | DEBIT | CREDIT | DEBIT | CREDIT |
| Sales Price | $97,000.00 |  |  | $97,000.00 |
| Sales Fee |  |  | $6,790.00 |  |
| Deposit |  | 1,000.00 |  |  |
| Turner Trust |  |  | 9,602.25 |  |
| Interest |  |  | 48.01 |  |
| David Trust |  | 74,000.00 |  |  |
| Loan Origination Fee | 740.00 |  |  |  |
| Deed Preparation Fee |  |  | 30.00 |  |
| Insurance | 82.00 |  |  | 82.00 |
| Taxes |  | 1,801.59 | 1,801.59 |  |
| Recording Fee | 31.00 |  |  |  |
| Owner's Title Insurance |  |  | 135.00 |  |
| Mortgagee's Title Insurance | 75.00 |  |  |  |
| Separate Bill Of Sale (W & D) | 400.00 |  |  | 400.00 |
|  |  |  |  |  |
| Balance Due From Buyer |  | 21,526.41 |  |  |
| Balance Due To Seller |  |  | 79,075.15 |  |
|  |  |  |  |  |
|  |  |  |  |  |
|  |  |  |  |  |
|  | $98,328.00 | $98,328.00 | $97,482.00 | $97,482.00 |

## Problem 2
## SETTLEMENT STATEMENT WORKSHEET

|  | BUYER'S STATEMENT | | SELLER'S STATEMENT | |
|---|---|---|---|---|
|  | DEBIT | CREDIT | DEBIT | CREDIT |
| Sales Price | 51,000.00 | | | 51,000.00 |
| Sales Fee – 6% | | | 3,060.00 | |
| Deposit | | 500.00 | | |
| Murphy Mortgage Balance | | | 28,223.08 | |
| Interest Prorated – Murphy | | | 62.70 | |
| New Mortgage – Jones | | 45,900.00 | | |
| Second Mortgage | | 2,000.00 | 2,000.00 | |
| Taxes | | 1,194.80 | 1,194.80 | |
| Rent | | 123.30 | 123.30 | |
| Insurance | 110.00 | | | 110.00 |
| Deed Preparation | | | 25.00 | |
| Owner's Title Policy | | | 182.50 | |
| Mortgagee's Title Policy | 75.00 | | | |
| Seller's Escrow Balance | | | | 634.00 |
| Buyer's Attorney Fee | 75.00 | | | |
| Recording Fee | 28.00 | | | |
| Appraisal Fee | | | 75.00 | |
| Loan Origination Fee 1% | 459.00 | | | |
| Balance Due From Buyer | | 2,028.90 | | |
| Amount Due Seller | | | 16,797.62 | |
|  | $51,747.00 | $51,747.00 | $51,744.00 | $51,744.00 |

## Problem 3
## SETTLEMENT STATEMENT WORKSHEET

| | BUYER'S STATEMENT | | SELLER'S STATEMENT | |
|---|---|---|---|---|
| | DEBIT | CREDIT | DEBIT | CREDIT |
| Sales Price | $74,500.00 | | | $74,500.00 |
| Commission | | | 4,470.00 | |
| Earnest Money Deposit | | 500.00 | | |
| Purchase Money Mortgage | | 59,600.00 | 59,600.00 | |
| Taxes | | 1,100.00 | 1,100.00 | |
| Title Examination | 175.00 | | | |
| Recording Fee | 5.00 | | | |
| Legal Fees | 45.00 | | 50.00 | |
| Appraisal Fee | | | 100.00 | |
| Well Examination & Certification | | | 35.00 | |
| Personal Property | 675.00 | | | 675.00 |
| | | | | |
| Balance Due From Buyer | | 14,200.00 | | |
| Balance Due To Seller | | | 9,820.00 | |
| | | | | |
| | | | | |
| | | | | |
| | | | | |
| | | | | |
| | | | | |
| | $75,400.00 | $75,400.00 | $75,175.00 | $75,175.00 |

**Problem 4**
## SETTLEMENT STATEMENT WORKSHEET

|  | BUYER'S STATEMENT | | SELLER'S STATEMENT | |
|---|---|---|---|---|
|  | DEBIT | CREDIT | DEBIT | CREDIT |
| Sales Price | 32,000.00 | | | 32,000.00 |
| Deposit | | 500.00 | | |
| Sales Fee – 6% | | | 1,920.00 | |
| Brown Mortgage Balance | | | 25,511.14 | |
|     Interest Prorated–In Arrears | | | 56.70 | |
| Josephs Mortgage | | 30,550.00 | | |
| Taxes – Prorated | | 487.70 | 487.70 | |
| Loan Origination Fee – 1% | 305.50 | | | |
| Fire Insurance | 182.00 | | | |
| Title Insurance – Owner's | | | 187.50 | |
| Title Insurance – Mortgagee | 75.00 | | | |
| Tax Escrow – 2 months | 133.00 | | | |
| Appraisal Fee – F.H.A. | 50.00 | | | |
| Photo Fee | 15.00 | | | |
| Survey Fee | 55.00 | | | |
| Discount Points – 5 points | | | 1,527.50 | |
|  | | | | |
| Balance Due From Buyer | | 1,277.80 | | |
| Balance Due to Seller | | | 2,309.46 | |
|  | | | | |
|  | $32,815.50 | $32,815.50 | $32,000.00 | $32,000.00 |

**Problem 5**
## SETTLEMENT STATEMENT WORKSHEET

| | BUYER'S STATEMENT | | SELLER'S STATEMENT | |
|---|---|---|---|---|
| | DEBIT | CREDIT | DEBIT | CREDIT |
| Purchase Price | $87,750.00 | | | $87,750.00 |
| Earnest Money Deposit | | $2,000.00 | | |
| Commission @ 6% | | | 5,865.00 | |
| Jones Mortgage | | | 10,120.00 | |
| Interest | | | 63.25 | |
| Dallas Mortgage | | 70,200.00 | | |
| Additional Lot | 10,000.00 | | | 10,000.00 |
| Land Contract – Lot | | 7,000.00 | 7,000.00 | |
| Loan Origination Fee, 1% | 702.00 | | | |
| Discount Points, 2 pts. | 1,404.00 | | | |
| Insurance | 60.00 | | | 60.00 |
| Taxes | | 1,381.36 | 1,381.36 | |
| Land Contract Preparation | | | 75.00 | |
| Abstract | | | 100.00 | |
| Recording Fees | 37.50 | | 12.50 | |
| Abstract Examination Fee | 125.00 | | | |
| Garden Tractor Bill Of Sale | 750.00 | | | 750.00 |
| | | | | |
| Balance Due From Buyer | | 20,247.14 | | |
| Balance Due To Seller | | | 73,942.89 | |
| | $100,828.50 | $100,828.50 | $98,560.00 | $98,560.00 |

# Appendix C

## Illustrated Structure

As a real estate salesperson, it is essential that you be familiar with all the basic drawings of a residential property, as well as the basic elements of construction involved in a single-family structure.

The materials which follow include all the basics you need to know to be properly informed in dealing with clients interested in single-family purchases.

The following figures have been provided by courtesy of Paul I. Cripe, Inc., Civil Engineers, Indianapolis, Indiana.

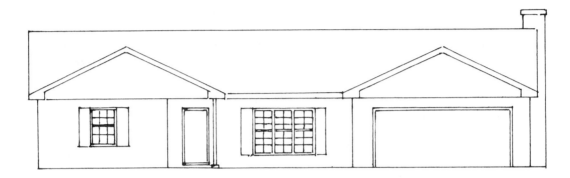

Figure 1—Front Elevation (Figures 2 through 6 generally relate to the structure shown in the front elevation above.)

Figure 2—Several Typical Views Included in A Set of House Plans

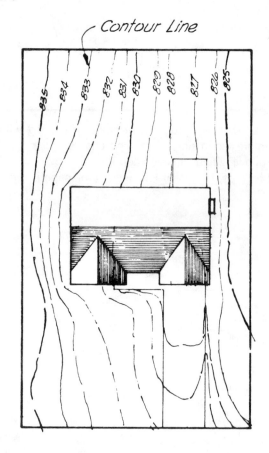

Contour Line

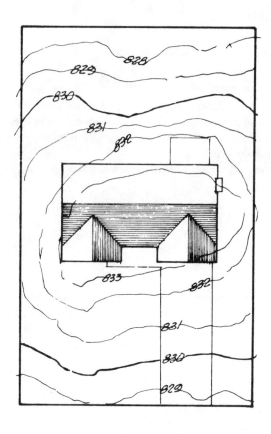

## Plan View
### Construction on a side sloping lot

## Plan View
### Construction on top of a slight knoll

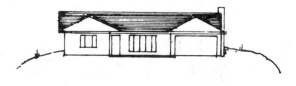

## Front Elevation
### Construction on a side sloping lot

## Front Elevation
### Construction on top of a slight knoll

Figure 3—Topographical Considerations Related To House Construction

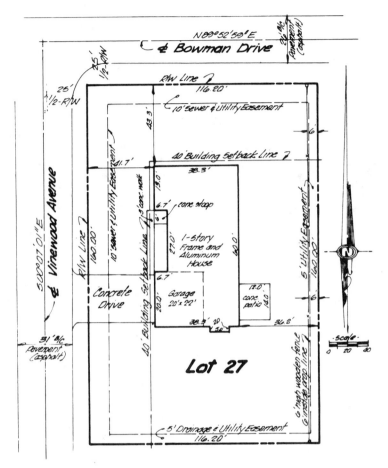

CIVIL ENGINEERING
LAND SURVEYING

PAUL I. CRIPE, INC.
150 E. MARKET STREET
INDIANAPOLIS, IND. 46204
636-5411

SUBDIVISION DESIGN
BUILDING DESIGN

January 21, 19'

Last Federal Savings and Loan Association
700 North Market Street
Indianapolis, Indiana 46204

Gentlemen:

I the undersigned, hereby certify that the within plat is true and correct and represents a survey made by me on the 15th day of November, 19__, of real estate described as follows:

Lot #27 in Willow Creek Addition - Section Five, as per plat thereof recorded October 31, 1977, as Instrument #77-70273 in the Office of the Recorder of Marion County, Indiana.

Based thereon, I further certify that the building situated on the above described real estate is located within the boundaries of said premises. I have shown on said plat the distances from the sides and front of the building to points on the side lines and front line of the lot. I further certify that the buildings on the adjoining property do not encroach on the lot or real estate in question.

The property is improved with a one story frame dwelling, located at 5861 Vinewood Avenue, Indianapolis, Indiana.

*Figure 4—Mortgage Survey*

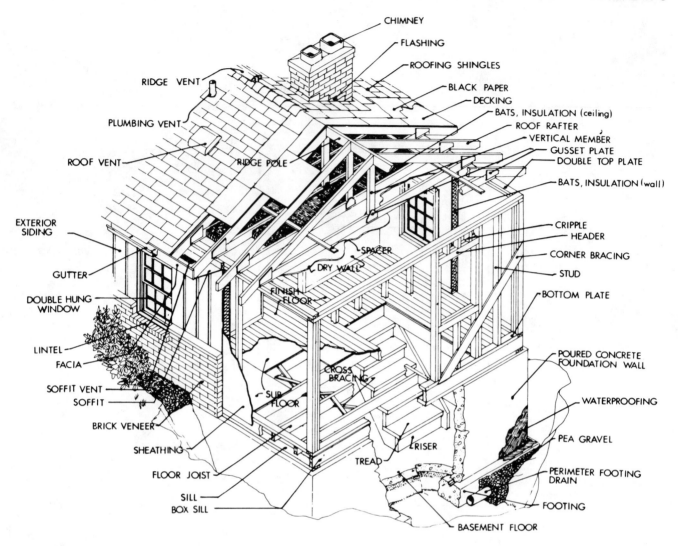

Figure 5—Wood Frame House Construction (Isometric View)

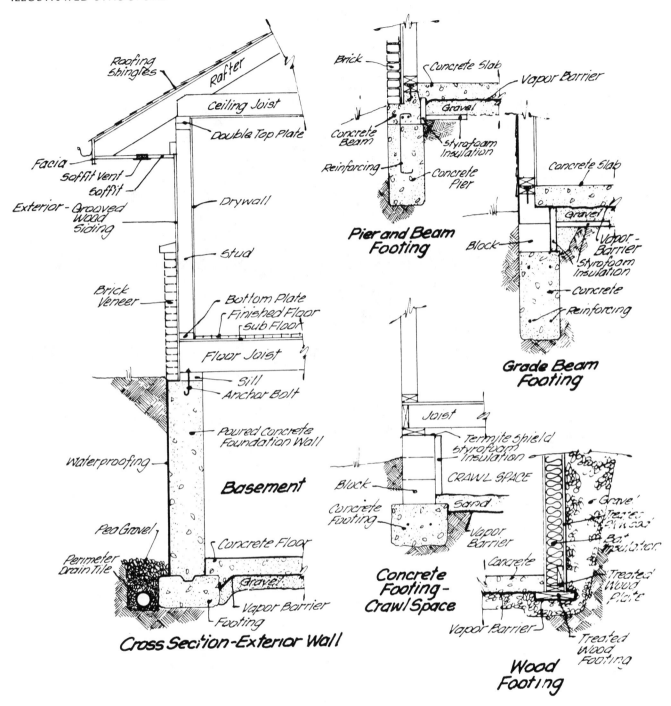

Figure 6—Wood Frame House Construction (Detailed Cross Sectional Views)

*Figure 7—Key Construction Details*

1. Window head frame (header)
2. Wall sheathing, diagonal
3. Verge board
4. Gutter
5. Window jamb trimmer
6. Wall building paper
7. Window sill frame
8. Cripple stud
9. Wall siding
10. Window shutters
11. Corner bracing 45°
12. Corner studs, double
13. Sole plate (bottom plate)
14. Box sill
15. Basement areaway
16. Basement sash
17. Grade line
18. Gravel fill
19. Ridge board
20. Collar beam
21. Roof rafters
22. Interior partition plates
23. Interior studs
24. Cross-bracing
25. Plaster base, lath
26. Gable studs
27. Interior window trim
28. Plaster walls
29. Cross bridging
30. Second floor joists
31. Arch framing
32. Insulation, batts
33. Dining nook
34. Interior door trim
35. Plaster base, rock lath
36. Finish floor
37. Floor lining felt
38. Subflooring, diagonally

39. Sill plate
40. Termite shield
41. Girder
42. Plate anchor bolt
43. Post
44. Foundation wall
45. Frame partition
46. Tarred felt joint cover
47. Drain tile
48. Footing
49. Flue liner tops
50. Chimney cap
51. Brick chimney
52. Flashing and counter flashing
53. Spaced 1" x 4" decking
    (wood shingles)
54. Tight roof decking
    (all other coverings)
55. Ceiling joists
56. Exterior wall plates (double)
57. Lookouts
58. Furring strips
59. Stair rail & balusters
60. Stair landing newel
61. Finish flooring over felt;
    Over sub-flooring on wood joists
62. Book shelves
63. Picture mould
64. Mantel and trim
65. Damper control
66. Base top mould
67. Ash dump
68. Baseboards
69. Shoe mould
70. Hearth
71. Plaster ceiling
72. Boiler or furnace
73. Cleanout door
74. Basement concrete floor

75. Fill-gravel/stone
76. Roof cover (shingles)
77. Roofing felts
78. Soffit of cornice
79. Facia of cornice
80. Vertical board and batten siding
81. Fire stops
82. Ribbon plate
83. Stair wall partition
84. Stair rail or easing
85. Starting newel
86. Cased opening trim
87. Main stair treads and riser
88. Wall stair stringer
89. Face stringer and moulds
90. Starting riser and tread
91. First floor joists
92. Basement stair rail and post
93. Basement stair horses
94. Basement stair treads and risers
95. Basement post (lally column)
96. Facia board
97. Cornice bed mould
98. Leader head or conductor head
99. Belt course
100. Porch rafter
101. Porch ceiling joists
102. Porch ceiling soffit
103. Porch roof beam
104. Porch beam facia
105. Entrance door trim
106. Leader, downspout or conductor
107. Porch trellis
108. Porch column
109. Porch column base
110. Concrete porch floor
111. Concrete stoop
112. Entrance door sill
113. Stoop foundation

Standard N Y B T U Form 8041 •      —Contract of Sale

**CONSULT YOUR LAWYER BEFORE SIGNING THIS INSTRUMENT—THIS INSTRUMENT SHOULD BE USED BY LAWYERS ONLY.**

---

**NOTE: FIRE LOSSES.** This form of contract contains no express provision as to risk of loss by fire or other casualty before delivery of the deed. Unless express provision is made, the provisions of Section 5-1311 of the General Obligations Law will apply. This section also places risk of loss upon purchaser if title or possession is transferred prior to closing.

**THIS AGREEMENT,** made the      day of      , nineteen hundred and
**BETWEEN**

hereinafter described as the seller, and

hereinafter described as the purchaser,

**WITNESSETH,** that the seller agrees to sell and convey, and the purchaser agrees to purchase, all that certain plot, piece or parcel of land, with the buildings and improvements thereon erected, situate, lying and being in the

1. This sale includes all right, title and interest, if any, of the seller in and to any land lying in the bed of any street, road or avenue opened or proposed, in front of or adjoining said premises, to the center line thereof, and all right, title and interest of the seller in and to any award made or to be made in lieu thereof and in and to any unpaid award for damage to said premises by reason of change of grade of any street; and the seller will execute and deliver to the purchaser, on closing of title, or thereafter, on demand, all proper instruments for the conveyance of such title and the assignment and collection of any such award.

**Contract of Sale** (page 1 of 4)

2. The price is

Dollars, payable as follows:

Dollars,

on the signing of this contract, by check subject to collection, the receipt of which is hereby acknowledged;

Dollars,

in cash or good certified check to the order of the seller on the delivery of the deed as hereinafter provided;

Dollars,

by taking title subject to a           mortgage now a lien on said premises in that amount, bearing interest at the rate of           per cent per annum, the principal being due and payable

Dollars,

by the purchaser or assigns executing, acknowledging and delivering to the seller a bond or, at the option of the seller, a note secured by a purchase money           mortgage on the above premises, in that amount, payable

together with interest at the rate of           per cent per annum payable

3. Any bond or note and mortgage to be given hereunder shall be drawn on the standard forms of New York Board of Title Underwriters for mortgages of like lien; and shall be drawn by the attorney for the seller at the expense of the purchaser, who shall also pay the mortgage recording tax and recording fees.

4. If such purchase money mortgage is to be a subordinate mortgage on the premises it shall provide that it shall be subject and subordinate to the lien   of the existing           mortgage of $           , any extensions thereof and to any mortgage   or consolidated mortgage   which may be placed on the premises in lieu thereof, and to any extensions thereof provided (a) that the interest rate thereof shall not be greater than           per cent per annum and (b) that, if the principal amount thereof shall exceed the amount of principal owing and unpaid on said existing mortgage   at the time of placing such new mortgage or consolidated mortgage, the excess be paid to the holder of such purchase money mortgage in reduction of the principal thereof. Such purchase money mortgage shall also provide that such payment to the holder thereof shall not alter or affect the regular installments, if any, of principal payable thereunder and shall further provide that the holder thereof will, on demand and without charge therefor, execute, acknowledge and deliver any agreement or agreements further to effectuate such subordination.

5. If there be a mortgage on the premises the seller agrees to deliver to the purchaser at the time of delivery of the deed a proper certificate executed and acknowledged by the holder of such mortgage and in form for recording, certifying as to the amount of the unpaid principal and interest thereon, date of maturity thereof and rate of interest thereon, and the seller shall pay the fees for recording such certificate. Should the mortgagee be a bank or other institution as defined in Section 274-a, Real Property Law, the mortgagee may, in lieu of the said certificate, furnish a letter signed by a duly authorized officer, or employee, or agent, containing the information required to be set forth in said certificate. Seller represents that such mortgage will not be in default at or as a result of the delivery of the deed hereunder and that neither said mortgage, nor any modification thereof contains any provision to accelerate payment, or to change any of the other terms or provisions thereof by reason of the delivery of the deed hereunder.

6. Said premises are sold and are to be conveyed subject to:

a. Zoning regulations and ordinances of the city, town or village in which the premises lie which are not violated by existing structures.

b. Consents by the seller or any former owner of premises for the erection of any structure or structures on, under or above any street or streets on which said premises may abut.

c. Encroachments of stoops, areas, cellar steps, trim and cornices, if any, upon any street or highway.

7. All notes or notices of violations of law or municipal ordinances, orders or requirements noted in or issued by the Departments of Housing and Buildings, Fire, Labor, Health, or other State or Municipal Department having jurisdiction, against or affecting the premises at the date hereof, shall be complied with by the seller and the premises shall be conveyed free of the same, and this provision of this contract shall survive delivery of the deed hereunder. The seller shall furnish the purchaser with an authorization to make the necessary searches therefor.

*Omit Clause 8 if the property is not in the City of New York.*

*Clause 9 is usually omitted if the property is not in the City of New York.*

8. All obligations affecting the premises incurred under the Emergency Repairs provisions of the Administrative Code of the City of New York (Sections 564-18.0, etc.) prior to the delivery of the deed shall be paid and discharged by the seller upon the delivery of the deed. This provision shall survive the delivery of the deed.

9. If, at the time of the delivery of the deed, the premises or any part thereof shall be or shall have been affected by an assessment or assessments which are or may become payable in annual installments, of which the first installment is then a charge or lien, or has been paid, then for the purposes of this contract all the unpaid installments of any such assessment, including those which are to become due and payable after the delivery of the deed, shall be deemed to be due and payable and to be liens upon the premises affected thereby and shall be paid and discharged by the seller, upon the delivery of the deed.

10. The following are to be apportioned:

(a) Rents as and when collected. (b) Interest on mortgages. (c) Premiums on existing transferable insurance policies or renewals of those expiring prior to the closing. (d) Taxes and sewer rents, if any, on the basis of the fiscal year for which assessed. (e) Water charges on the basis of the calendar year. (f) Fuel, if any.

**Contract of Sale** (page 2 of 4)

11. If the closing of the title shall occur before the tax rate is fixed, the apportionment of taxes shall be upon the basis of the tax rate for the next preceding year applied to the latest assessed valuation.

12. If there be a water meter on the premises, the seller shall furnish a reading to a date not more than thirty days prior to the time herein set for closing title, and the unfixed meter charge and the unfixed sewer rent, if any, based thereon for the intervening time shall be apportioned on the basis of such last reading.

13. The deed shall be the usual

deed in proper statutory short form for record and shall be duly executed and acknowledged so as to convey to the purchaser the fee simple of the said premises, free of all encumbrances, except as herein stated, and shall contain the covenant required by subdivision 5 of Section 13 of the Lien Law.

If the seller is a corporation, it will deliver to the purchaser at the time of the delivery of the deed hereunder a resolution of its Board of Directors authorizing the sale and delivery of the deed, and a certificate by the Secretary or Assistant Secretary of the corporation certifying such resolution and setting forth facts showing that the conveyance is in conformity with the requirements of Section 909 of the Business Corporation Law. The deed in such case shall contain a recital sufficient to establish compliance with said section.

14. At the closing of the title the seller shall deliver to the purchaser a certified check to the order of the recording officer of the county in which the deed is to be recorded for the amount of the documentary stamps to be affixed thereto in accordance with Article 31 of the Tax Law, and a certified check to the order of the appropriate officer for any other tax-payable by reason of the delivery of the deed, and a return, if any be required, duly signed and sworn to by the seller; and the purchaser also agrees to sign and swear to the return and to cause the check and the return to be delivered to the appropriate officer promptly after the closing of title.

*Omit Clause 15 if the property is not in the City of New York*

15. In addition, the seller shall at the same time deliver to the purchaser a certified check to the order of the Finance Administrator for the amount of the Real Property Transfer Tax imposed by Title II of Chapter 46 of the Administrative Code of the City of New York and will also deliver to the purchaser the return required by the said statute and the regulations issued pursuant to the authority thereof, duly signed and sworn to by the seller; the purchaser agrees to sign and swear to the return and to cause the check and the return to be delivered to the City Register promptly after the closing of the title.

16. The seller shall give and the purchaser shall accept a title such as

, a Member of the New York Board of Title Underwriters, will approve and insure.

17. All sums paid on account of this contract, and the reasonable expenses of the examination of the title to said premises and of the survey, if any, made in connection therewith are hereby made liens on said premises, but such liens shall not continue after default by the purchaser under this contract.

18. All fixtures and articles of personal property attached or appurtenant to or used in connection with said premises are represented to be owned by the seller, free from all liens and encumbrances except as herein stated, and are included in this sale; without limiting the generality of the foregoing, such fixtures and articles of personal property include plumbing, heating, lighting and cooking fixtures, air conditioning fixtures and units, ranges, refrigerators, radio and television aerials, bathroom and kitchen cabinets, mantels, door mirrors, venetian blinds, shades, screens, awnings, storm windows, window boxes, storm doors, mail boxes, weather vanes, flagpoles, pumps, shrubbery and outdoor statuary.

19. The amount of any unpaid taxes, assessments, water charges and sewer rents which the seller is obligated to pay and discharge, with the interest and penalties thereon to a date not less than two business days after the date of closing title, may at the option of the seller be allowed to the purchaser out of the balance of the purchase price, provided official bills therefor with interest and penalties thereon figured to said date are furnished by the seller at the closing.

20. If at the date of closing there may be any other liens or encumbrances which the seller is obligated to pay and discharge, the seller may use any portion of the balance of the purchase price to satisfy the same, provided the seller shall simultaneously either deliver to the purchaser at the closing of title instruments in recordable form and sufficient to satisfy such liens and encumbrances of record together with the cost of recording or filing said instruments; or, provided that the seller has made arrangements with the title company employed by the purchaser in advance of closing, seller will deposit with said company sufficient monies, acceptable to and required by it to insure obtaining and the recording of such satisfactions and the issuance of title insurance to the purchaser either free of any such liens and encumbrances, or with insurance against enforcement of same out of the insured premises. The purchaser, if request is made within a reasonable time prior to the date of closing of title, agrees to provide at the closing separate certified checks as requested, aggregating the amount of the balance of the purchase price, to facilitate the satisfaction of any such liens or encumbrances. The existence of any such taxes or other liens and encumbrances shall not be deemed objections to title if the seller shall comply with the foregoing requirements.

21. If a search of the title discloses judgments, bankruptcies or other returns against other persons having names the same as or similar to that of the seller, the seller will on request deliver to the purchaser an affidavit showing that such judgments, bankruptcies or other returns are not against the seller.

22. In the event that the seller is unable to convey title in accordance with the terms of this contract, the sole liability of the seller will be to refund to the purchaser the amount paid on account of the purchase price and to pay the net cost of examining the title, which cost is not to exceed the charges fixed by the New York Board of Title Underwriters, and the net cost of any survey made in connection therewith incurred by the purchaser, and upon such refund and payment being made this contract shall be considered canceled.

23. The deed shall be delivered upon the receipt of said payments at the office of

at                              o'clock on                            19

24. The parties agree that                                                                                    is the broker who brought about this sale and the seller agrees to pay any commission earned thereby.

25. It is understood and agreed that all understandings and agreements heretofore had between the parties hereto are merged in this contract, which alone fully and completely expresses their agreement, and that the same is entered into after full investigation, neither party relying upon any statement or representation, not embodied in this contract, made by the other. The purchaser has inspected the buildings standing on said premises and is thoroughly acquainted with their condition and agrees to take title "as is" and in their present condition and subject to reasonable use, wear, tear, and natural deterioration between the date thereof and the closing of title.

26. This agreement may not be changed or terminated orally. The stipulations aforesaid are to apply to and bind the heirs, executors, administrators, successors and assigns of the respective parties.

27. If two or more persons constitute either the seller or the purchaser, the word "seller" or the word "purchaser" shall be construed as if it read "sellers" or "purchasers" whenever the sense of this agreement so requires.

**IN WITNESS WHEREOF,** this agreement has been duly executed by the parties hereto.

In presence of:

**Contract of Sale** (page 3 of 4)

**STATE OF NEW YORK, COUNTY OF** ss:

On the            day of                        19    . before me

personally came

to me known to be the individual     described in and who executed
the foregoing instrument, and acknowledged that
                    executed the same.

**STATE OF NEW YORK, COUNTY OF** ss:

On the            day of                        19    . before me

personally came

to me known, who, being by me duly sworn, did depose and say
that     he resides at No.

that     he is the

of

                                      . the corporation described
in and which executed the foregoing instrument; that     he knows
the seal of said corporation; that the seal affixed to said instrument
is such corporate seal; that it was so affixed by order of the board
of directors of said corporation, and that     he signed h   name
thereto by like order.

**STATE OF NEW YORK, COUNTY OF** ss:

On the     2     day of                        19    . before me

personally came

to me known to be the individual     described in and who executed
the foregoing instrument, and acknowledged that
                    executed the same.

**STATE OF NEW YORK, COUNTY OF** ss:

On the            day of                        19    . before me

personally came

to me known and known to me to be a partner in

a partnership, and known to me to be the person described in and
who executed the foregoing instrument in the partnership name, and
said                                         duly
acknowledged that he executed the foregoing instrument for and
on behalf of said partnership.

---

Closing of title under the within contract is hereby adjourned to _____ 19 ____ . at

o'clock, at _____ ; title to be closed and all adjustments to be made

as of _____ 19 _____

Dated, _____ 19 _____

For value received, the within contract and all the right, title and interest of the purchaser thereunder are hereby assigned,

transferred and set over unto _____

and said assignee hereby assumes all obligations of the purchaser thereunder.

Dated, _____ 19 _____

*Purchaser*

*Assignee of Purchaser*

---

## Contract of Sale

TITLE No.

_____

TO

### PREMISES

Section

Block

Lot

County or Town

Street Numbered Address

Recorded At Request of

RETURN BY MAIL TO :

Zip No.

STANDARD FORM OF NEW YORK BOARD OF TITLE UNDERWRITERS

*Distributed by*

**CHICAGO TITLE
INSURANCE COMPANY**

---

### THE OBSERVANCE OF THE FOLLOWING SUGGESTIONS WILL SAVE TIME
### AND TROUBLE AT THE CLOSING OF THIS TITLE

The **SELLER** should bring with him all insurance policies and duplicates, receipted bills for taxes, assessments and water rates, and any leases, deeds or agreements affecting the property.

When there is a water meter on the premises, he should order it read, and bring bills therefor to the closing.

If there are mortgages on the property, he should promptly arrange to obtain the evidence required under Paragraph 5 of this contract.

He should furnish to the purchaser a full list of tenants, giving the names, rent paid by each, and date to which the rent has been paid.

The **PURCHASER** should be prepared with cash or certified check drawn to the order of the seller. The check may be certified for an approximate amount and cash may be provided for the balance of the settlement.

**Contract of Sale** (page 4 of 4)

Standard N.Y.B.T.U. Form 8041 *-01 Rev. 11/78   - Contract of Sale

**WARNING:** NO REPRESENTATION IS MADE THAT THIS FORM OF CONTRACT FOR THE SALE AND PURCHASE OF REAL ESTATE COMPLIES WITH SECTION 5-702 OF THE GENERAL OBLIGATIONS LAW ("PLAIN ENGLISH").

### CONSULT YOUR LAWYER BEFORE SIGNING IT.

**NOTE: FIRE AND CASUALTY LOSSES:** This contract form does not provide for what happens in the event of fire or casualty loss before the title closing. Unless different provision is made in this contract, Section 5-1311 of the General Obligations Law will apply. One part of that law makes a purchaser responsible for fire and casualty loss upon taking of title to or possession of the premises.

*Date:*
*Parties:*

**CONTRACT OF SALE** made as of the             day of                    , 19

BETWEEN

Address:

hereinafter called "SELLER", who agrees to sell, and

Address:

hereinafter called "PURCHASER", who agrees to buy:

*Premises:*
The property, including all buildings and improvements thereon (the "PREMISES") (more fully described on a separate page marked "Schedule A") and also known as:

Street Address.

Tax Map Designation:

Together with SELLER'S interest, if any, in streets and unpaid awards as set forth in Paragraph 9.

*Personal Property:*
The sale also includes all fixtures and articles of personal property attached to or used in connection with the PREMISES, unless specifically excluded below. SELLER states that they are paid for and owned by SELLER free and clear of any lien other than the EXISTING MORTGAGE(S). They include but are not limited to plumbing, heating, lighting and cooking fixtures, bathroom and kitchen cabinets, mantels, door mirrors, venetian blinds, shades, screens, awnings, storm windows, window boxes, storm doors, mail boxes, weather vanes, flagpoles, pumps, shrubbery, fencing, outdoor statuary, tool sheds, dishwashers, washing machines, clothes dryers, garbage disposal units, ranges, refrigerators, freezers, air conditioning equipment and installations, and wall to wall carpeting.

Excluded from this sale are:
Furniture and household furnishings,

*Purchase Price:*

1. a. The purchase price is                                                          $
payable as follows:

On the signing of this contract, by check subject to collection:                      $

By allowance for the principal amount still unpaid on EXISTING MORTGAGE(S):           $

By a Purchase Money Note and Mortgage from PURCHASER (or assigns) to SELLER:          $

BALANCE AT CLOSING:                                                                   $

**Contract of Sale—Plain English** (page 1 of 5)

b. If this sale is subject to an EXISTING MORTGAGE, the Purchase Money Note and Mortgage will also provide that it will remain subject to the prior lien of any EXISTING MORTGAGE even though the EXISTING MORTGAGE is extended or modified in good faith. The Purchase Money Note and Mortgage shall be drawn on the standard form of New York Board of Title Underwriters by the attorney for SELLER. PURCHASER shall pay the mortgage recording tax, recording fees and the attorney's fee in the amount of $ for its preparation.

c. If any required payments are made on an EXISTING MORTGAGE between now and CLOSING which reduce the unpaid principal amount of an EXISTING MORTGAGE below the amount shown in Paragraph 2, then the balance of the price payable at CLOSING will be adjusted. SELLER agrees that the amount shown in Paragraph 2 is reasonably correct and that only payments required by the EXISTING MORTGAGE will be made.

d. If there is a mortgage escrow account that is maintained for the purpose of paying taxes or insurance, etc., SELLER shall assign it to PURCHASER, if it can be assigned. In that event PURCHASER shall pay the amount in the escrow account to SELLER at CLOSING.

*Existing Mortgage(s):*

2. The PREMISES will be conveyed subject to the continuing lien of "EXISTING MORTGAGE(S)" as follows:

Mortgage now in the unpaid principal amount of $                                    and interest at the rate of
                              per cent per year, presently payable                         in installments of $
which include principal, interest,
and with any balance of principal being due and payable on

SELLER hereby states that no EXISTING MORTGAGE contains any provision that permits the holder of the mortgage to require its immediate payment in full or to change any other term thereof by reason of the fact of CLOSING.

*Acceptable Funds:*

3. All money payable under this contract, unless otherwise specified, shall be either:

a. Cash, but not over one thousand ($1,000.00) Dollars,

b. Good certified check of PURCHASER, or official check of any bank, savings bank, trust company, or savings and loan association having a banking office in the State of New York, payable to the order of SELLER, or to the order of PURCHASER and duly endorsed by PURCHASER (if an individual) to the order of SELLER in the presence of SELLER or SELLER'S attorney.

c. Money other than the purchase price, payable to SELLER at CLOSING, may be by check of PURCHASER up to the amount of                                                              ($                    ) dollars, or

d. As otherwise agreed to in writing by SELLER or SELLER'S attorney.

*"Subject to" Provisions:*

4. The PREMISES are to be transferred subject to:

a. Laws and governmental regulations that affect the use and maintenance of the PREMISES, provided that they are not violated by the buildings and improvements erected on the PREMISES.

b. Consents for the erection of any structures on, under or above any streets on which the PREMISES abut.

c. Encroachments of stoops, areas, cellar steps, trim and cornices, if any, upon any street or highway.

*Title Company Approval:*

5. SELLER shall give and PURCHASER shall accept such title as a member of The New York Board of Title Underwriters, will be willing to approve and insure in accordance with their standard form of title policy, subject only to the matters provided for in this contract.

*Closing Defined and Form of Deed:*

6. "CLOSING" means the settlement of the obligations of SELLER and PURCHASER to each other under this contract, including the payment of the purchase price to SELLER, and the delivery to PURCHASER of a                                deed in proper statutory form for recording so as to transfer full ownership (fee simple title) to the PREMISES, free of all encumbrances except as herein stated. The deed will contain a covenant by SELLER as required by Section 13 of the Lien Law.

If SELLER is a corporation, it will deliver to PURCHASER at the time of CLOSING (a) a resolution of its Board of Directors authorizing the sale and delivery of the deed, and (b) a certificate by the Secretary or Assistant Secretary of the corporation certifying such resolution and setting forth facts showing that the transfer is in conformity with the requirements of Section 909 of the Business Corporation Law. The deed in such case shall contain a recital sufficient to establish compliance with that section.

*Closing Date and Place:*

7. CLOSING will take place at the office of

at                    o'clock on                                        19

*Broker:*

8. PURCHASER hereby states that PURCHASER has not dealt with any broker in connection with this sale other than

and SELLER agrees to pay the broker the commission earned thereby (pursuant to separate agreement).

**Contract of Sale—Plain English** (page 2 of 5)

**Streets and Assignment of Unpaid Awards:**

9. This sale includes all of SELLER'S ownership and rights, if any, in any land lying in the bed of any street or highway, opened or proposed, in front of or adjoining the PREMISES to the center line thereof. It also includes any right of SELLER to any unpaid award by reason of any taking by condemnation and/or for any damage to the PREMISES by reason of change of grade of any street or highway. SELLER will deliver at no additional cost to PURCHASER, at CLOSING, or thereafter, on demand, any documents which PURCHASER may require to collect the award and damages.

**Mortgagee's Certificate or Letter as to Existing Mortgage(s):**

10. SELLER agrees to deliver to PURCHASER at CLOSING a certificate dated not more than thirty (30) days before CLOSING signed by the holder of each EXISTING MORTGAGE, in form for recording, certifying the amount of the unpaid principal and interest, date of maturity, and rate of interest. SELLER shall pay the fees for recording such certificate. If the holder of a mortgage is a bank or other institution as defined in Section 274-a, Real Property Law, it may, instead of the certificate, furnish an unqualified letter dated not more than thirty (30) days before CLOSING containing the same information. SELLER hereby states that any EXISTING MORTGAGE will not be in default at the time of CLOSING.

**Compliance with State and Municipal Department Violations and Orders:**

**Omit if the Property is Not In the City of New York:**

11. a. SELLER will comply with all notes or notices of violations of law or municipal ordinances, orders or requirements noted in or issued by any governmental department having authority as to lands, housing, buildings, fire, health and labor conditions affecting the PREMISES at the date hereof. The PREMISES shall be transferred free of them at CLOSING and this provision shall survive CLOSING. SELLER shall furnish PURCHASER with any authorizations necessary to make the searches that could disclose these matters.

b. All obligations affecting the PREMISES, incurred pursuant to the Administrative Code of the City of New York prior to CLOSING and payable in money shall be discharged by SELLER at CLOSING. This provision shall survive CLOSING.

**Installment Assessments:**

12. If at the time of CLOSING the PREMISES are affected by an assessment which is or may become payable in annual installments, and the first installment is then a lien, or has been paid, then for the purposes of this contract all the unpaid installments shall be considered due and are to be paid by SELLER at CLOSING.

**Apportionments:**

13. The following are to be apportioned as of midnight of the day before CLOSING:

(a) Rents as and when collected. (b) Interest on EXISTING MORTGAGE(S). (c) Premiums on existing transferable insurance policies and renewals of those expiring prior to CLOSING. (d) Taxes, water charges and sewer rents, on the basis of the fiscal period for which assessed. (e) Fuel, if any. (f) Vault charges, if any.

If CLOSING shall occur before a new tax rate is fixed, the apportionment of taxes shall be upon the basis of the old tax rate for the preceding period applied to the latest assessed valuation.

Any errors or omissions in computing apportionments at CLOSING shall be corrected. This provision shall survive CLOSING.

**Water Meter Readings:**

14. If there be a water meter on the PREMISES, SELLER shall furnish a reading to a date not more than thirty (30) days before CLOSING date and the unfixed meter charge and sewer rent, if any, shall be apportioned on the basis of such last reading.

**Allowance for Unpaid Taxes, Etc.:**

15. SELLER has the option to credit PURCHASER as an adjustment of the purchase price with the amount of any unpaid taxes, assessments, water charges and sewer rents, together with any interest and penalties thereon to a date not less than five (5) business days after CLOSING, provided that official bills therefor computed to said date are produced at CLOSING.

**Use of Purchase Price to Pay Encumbrances:**

16. If there is anything else affecting the sale which SELLER is obligated to pay and discharge at CLOSING, SELLER may use any portion of the balance of the purchase price to discharge it. As an alternative SELLER may deposit money with the title insurance company employed by PURCHASER and required by it to assure its discharge; but only if the title insurance company will insure PURCHASER'S title clear of the matter or insure against its enforcement out of the PREMISES. Upon request, made within a reasonable time before CLOSING, the PURCHASER agrees to provide separate certified checks as requested to assist in clearing up these matters.

**Affidavit as to Judgments, Bankruptcies Etc.:**

17. If a title examination discloses judgments, bankruptcies or other returns against persons having names the same as or similar to that of SELLER, SELLER shall deliver a satisfactory detailed affidavit at CLOSING showing that they are not against SELLER.

**Deed Transfer and Recording Taxes:**

18. At CLOSING, SELLER shall deliver a certified check payable to the order of the appropriate State, City or County officer in the amount of any applicable transfer and/or recording tax payable by reason of the delivery or recording of the deed, together with any required tax return. PURCHASER agrees to duly complete the tax return and to cause the check(s) and the tax return to be delivered to the appropriate officer promptly after CLOSING.

**Purchaser's Lien:**

19. All money paid on account of this contract, and the reasonable expenses of examination of the title to the PREMISES and of any survey and survey inspection charges are hereby made liens on the PREMISES and collectable out of the PREMISES. Such liens shall not continue after default in performance of the contract by PURCHASER.

**Seller's Inability to Convey Limitation of Liability:**

20. If SELLER is unable to transfer title to PURCHASER in accordance with this contract, SELLER's sole liability shall be to refund all money paid on account of this contract, plus all charges made for: (i) examining the title, (ii) any appropriate additional searches made in accordance with this contract, and (iii) survey and survey inspection charges. Upon such refund and payment this contract shall be considered cancelled, and neither SELLER nor PURCHASER shall have any further rights against the other.

**Condition of Property:**

21. PURCHASER has inspected the buildings on the PREMISES and the personal property included in this sale and is thoroughly acquainted with their condition. PURCHASER agrees to purchase them "as is" and in their present condition subject to reasonable use, wear, tear, and natural deterioration between now and CLOSING. PURCHASER shall have the right, after reasonable notice to SELLER, to inspect them before CLOSING.

**Entire Agreement:**

22. All prior understandings and agreements between SELLER and PURCHASER are merged in this contract. It completely expresses their full agreement. It has been entered into after full investigation, neither party relying upon any statements made by anyone else that is not set forth in this contract.

**Contract of Sale—Plain English** (page 3 of 5)

Rider* which may be used with Standard NYBTU Form 8041, rev. 11/78

## SCHEDULE A
### (Description of Premises)

All that certain plot, piece or parcel of land, with the buildings and improvements thereon erected, situate, lying and being in the

*Changes Must be in Writing:*

23. This contract may not be changed or cancelled except in writing. The contract shall also apply to and bind the distributees, heirs, executors, administrators, successors and assigns of the respective parties. Each of the parties hereby authorize their attorneys to agree in writing to any changes in dates and time periods provided for in this contract.

*Singular Also Means Plural:*

24. Any singular word or term herein shall also be read as in the plural whenever the sense of this contract may require it.

In Presence Of:

Closing of title under the within contract is hereby adjourned to _____ 19_____ , at _____ o'clock, at _____ ; title to be closed and all adjustments to be made as of _____ 19 _____
Dated, _____ 19 _____
For value received, the within contract and all the right, title and interest of the purchaser thereunder are hereby assigned, transferred and set over unto _____
and said assignee hereby assumes all obligations of the purchaser thereunder.
Dated, _____ 19 _____

_____
*Purchaser*

_____
*Assignee of Purchaser*

## Contract of Sale

TITLE No. _____

TO

PREMISES

Section
Block
Lot
County or Town
Street Numbered Address

Recorded At Request of
RETURN BY MAIL TO:

STANDARD FORM OF NEW YORK BOARD OF TITLE UNDERWRITERS
*Distributed by*

**CHICAGO TITLE INSURANCE COMPANY**

Zip No.

**Contract of Sale—Plain English** (page 5 of 5)

Standard N.Y.B.T.U. Form 8003–    –    –Warranty Deed With Full Covenants–Individual or Corporation (single sheet)

**CONSULT YOUR LAWYER BEFORE SIGNING THIS INSTRUMENT · THIS INSTRUMENT SHOULD BE USED BY LAWYERS ONLY**

**THIS INDENTURE,** made the                day of                          , nineteen hundred and

**BETWEEN**



party of the first part, and



party of the second part,

**WITNESSETH,** that the party of the first part, in consideration of ten dollars and other valuable consideration paid by the party of the second part, does hereby grant and release unto the party of the second part, the heirs or successors and assigns of the party of the second part forever,

**ALL** that certain plot, piece or parcel of land, with the buildings and improvements thereon erected, situate, lying and being in the

TOGETHER with all right, title and interest, if any, of the party of the first part in and to any streets and roads abutting the above described premises to the center lines thereof; TOGETHER with the appurtenances and all the estate and rights of the party of the first part in and to said premises; TO HAVE AND TO HOLD the premises herein granted unto the party of the second part, the heirs or successors and assigns of the party of the second part forever.

AND the party of the first part, in compliance with Section 13 of the Lien Law, covenants that the party of the first part will receive the consideration for this conveyance and will hold the right to receive such consideration as a trust fund to be applied first for the purpose of paying the cost of the improvement and will apply the same first to the payment of the cost of the improvement before using any part of the total of the same for any other purpose.

AND the party of the first part covenants as follows: that said party of the first part is seized of the said premises in fee simple, and has good right to convey the same; that the party of the second part shall quietly enjoy the said premises; that the said premises are free from incumbrances, except as aforesaid; that the party of the first part will execute or procure any further necessary assurance of the title to said premises; and that said party of the first part will forever warrant the title to said premises.

The word "party" shall be construed as if it read "parties" whenever the sense of this indenture so requires.

**IN WITNESS WHEREOF,** the party of the first part has duly executed this deed the day and year first above written.

IN PRESENCE OF:

**Warranty Deed with Full Covenants** (page 1 of 2)

**STATE OF NEW YORK, COUNTY OF**      **SS:**

On the    day of       19    , before me
personally came

to me known to be the individual    described in and who
executed the foregoing instrument, and acknowledged that
executed the same.

**STATE OF NEW YORK, COUNTY OF**      **SS:**

On the    day of       19    , before me
personally came

to me known to be the individual    described in and who
executed the foregoing instrument, and acknowledged that
executed the same.

**STATE OF NEW YORK, COUNTY OF**      **SS:**

On the    day of       19    , before me
personally came
to me known, who, being by me duly sworn, did depose and
say that    he resides at No.                ;

that    he is the
of
          , the corporation described
in and which executed the foregoing instrument; that    he
knows the seal of said corporation; that the seal affixed
to said instrument is such corporate seal; that it was so
affixed by order of the board of directors of said corporation, and that    he signed h    name thereto by like order.

**STATE OF NEW YORK, COUNTY OF**      **SS:**

On the    day of       19    , before me
personally came
the subscribing witness to the foregoing instrument, with
whom I am personally acquainted, who, being by me duly
sworn, did depose and say that    he resides at No.      ;

that    he knows

          to be the individual
described in and who executed the foregoing instrument;
that    he, said subscribing witness, was present and saw
       execute the same; and that    he, said witness,
at the same time subscribed h    name as witness thereto.

# 𝔚𝔞𝔯𝔯𝔞𝔫𝔱𝔶 𝔇𝔢𝔢𝔡

### WITH FULL COVENANTS

TITLE NO.

**TO**

SECTION

BLOCK

LOT

COUNTY OR TOWN

Recorded at Request of
**CHICAGO TITLE INSURANCE COMPANY**

STANDARD FORM OF NEW YORK BOARD OF TITLE UNDERWRITERS
*Distributed by*
**CHICAGO TITLE
INSURANCE COMPANY**

**Return by Mail to**

Zip No.

RESERVE THIS SPACE FOR USE OF RECORDING OFFICE

**Warranty Deed with Full Covenants** (page 2 of 2)

Standard N.Y.B.T.U. Form 8001 —        Bargain and Sale Deed, without Covenants against Grantor's Acts—Individual or Corporation. (single sheet)

**CONSULT YOUR LAWYER BEFORE SIGNING THIS INSTRUMENT · THIS INSTRUMENT SHOULD BE USED BY LAWYERS ONLY**

**THIS INDENTURE,** made the                  day of                     nineteen hundred and

**BETWEEN**

party of the first part, and

party of the second part,

**WITNESSETH,** that the party of the first part, in consideration of ten dollars and other valuable consideration paid by the party of the second part, does hereby grant and release unto the party of the second part, the heirs or successors and assigns of the party of the second part forever,

**ALL** that certain plot, piece or parcel of land, with the buildings and improvements thereon erected, situate, lying and being in the

TOGETHER with all right, title and interest, if any, of the party of the first part, in and to any streets and roads abutting the above-described premises to the center lines thereof; TOGETHER with the appurtenances and all the estate and rights of the party of the first part in and to said premises; TO HAVE AND TO HOLD the premises herein granted unto the party of the second part, the heirs or successors and assigns of the party of the second part forever.

AND the party of the first part, in compliance with Section 13 of the Lien Law, covenants that the party of the first part will receive the consideration for this conveyance and will hold the right to receive such consideration as a trust fund to be applied first for the purpose of paying the cost of the improvement and will apply the same first to the payment of the cost of the improvement before using any part of the total of the same for any other purpose.

The word "party" shall be construed as if it read "parties" whenever the sense of this indenture so requires.

**IN WITNESS WHEREOF,** the party of the first part has duly executed this deed the day and year first above written.

IN PRESENCE OF:

**Bargain and Sale Deed without Covenant Against Grantor's Acts** (page 1 of 2)

**STATE OF NEW YORK, COUNTY OF** ss:

On the          day of          19     , before me
personally came

to me known to be the individual     described in and who
executed the foregoing instrument, and acknowledged that
executed the same.

**STATE OF NEW YORK, COUNTY OF** ss:

On the          day of          19     , before me
personally came

to me known to be the individual     described in and who
executed the foregoing instrument, and acknowledged that
executed the same.

**STATE OF NEW YORK, COUNTY OF** ss:

On the          day of          19     , before me
personally came
to me known, who, being by me duly sworn, did depose and
say that     he resides at No.
                                                        ;
that     he is the
of
                                   , the corporation described
in and which executed the foregoing instrument; that     he
knows the seal of said corporation; that the seal affixed
to said instrument is such corporate seal; that it was so
affixed by order of the board of directors of said corporation, and that     he signed h     name thereto by like order.

**STATE OF NEW YORK, COUNTY OF** ss:

On the          day of          19     , before me
personally came
the subscribing witness to the foregoing instrument, with
whom I am personally acquainted, who, being by me duly
sworn, did depose and say that     he resides at No.
                                                        ;
that     he knows

                                             to be the individual
described in and who executed the foregoing instrument;
that     he, said subscribing witness, was present and saw
                  execute the same; and that     he, said witness,
at the same time subscribed h     name as witness thereto.

# Bargain and Sale Deed
WITHOUT COVENANT AGAINST GRANTOR'S ACTS

TITLE NO.

TO

STANDARD FORM OF NEW YORK BOARD OF TITLE UNDERWRITERS

*Distributed by*

**CHICAGO TITLE
INSURANCE COMPANY**

SECTION

BLOCK

LOT

COUNTY OR TOWN

Recorded at Request of
CHICAGO TITLE INSURANCE COMPANY

**Return by Mail to**

Zip No.

RESERVE THIS SPACE FOR USE OF RECORDING OFFICE

**Bargain and Sale Deed without Covenant Against Grantor's Acts** (page 2 of 2)

Standard N Y B T U. Form 8002–20M    —Bargain and Sale Deed, with Covenants against Grantor's Acts–Individual or Corporation  (single sheet)

**CONSULT YOUR LAWYER BEFORE SIGNING THIS INSTRUMENT - THIS INSTRUMENT SHOULD BE USED BY LAWYERS ONLY**

**THIS INDENTURE,** made the               day of                              , nineteen hundred and

**BETWEEN**

party of the first part, and

party of the second part,

**WITNESSETH,** that the party of the first part, in consideration of ten dollars and other valuable consideration paid by the party of the second part, does hereby grant and release unto the party of the second part, the heirs or successors and assigns of the party of the second part forever,

**ALL** that certain plot, piece or parcel of land, with the buildings and improvements thereon erected, situate, lying and being in the

TOGETHER with all right, title and interest, if any, of the party of the first part in and to any streets and roads abutting the above described premises to the center lines thereof; TOGETHER with the appurtenances and all the estate and rights of the party of the first part in and to said premises; TO HAVE AND TO HOLD the premises herein granted unto the party of the second part, the heirs or successors and assigns of the party of the second part forever.

AND the party of the first part covenants that the party of the first part has not done or suffered anything whereby the said premises have been encumbered in any way whatever, except as aforesaid.

AND the party of the first part, in compliance with Section 13 of the Lien Law, covenants that the party of the first part will receive the consideration for this conveyance and will hold the right to receive such consideration as a trust fund to be applied first for the purpose of paying the cost of the improvement and will apply the same first to the payment of the cost of the improvement before using any part of the total of the same for any other purpose.

The word "party" shall be construed as if it read "parties" whenever the sense of this indenture so requires.

**IN WITNESS WHEREOF,** the party of the first part has duly executed this deed the day and year first above written.

IN PRESENCE OF:

**Bargain and Sale Deed with Covenant Against Grantor's Acts** (page 1 of 2)

STATE OF NEW YORK, COUNTY OF           SS:

On the      day of        19    , before me
personally came

to me known to be the individual     described in and who
executed the foregoing instrument, and acknowledged that
     executed the same.

---

STATE OF NEW YORK, COUNTY OF           SS:

On the      day of        19    , before me
personally came

to me known to be the individual     described in and who
executed the foregoing instrument, and acknowledged that
     executed the same.

---

STATE OF NEW YORK, COUNTY OF           SS:

On the      day of        19    , before me
personally came
to me known, who, being by me duly sworn, did depose and
say that     he resides at No.                ;

that     he is the
of                   , the corporation described
in and which executed the foregoing instrument; that    he
knows the seal of said corporation; that the seal affixed
to said instrument is such corporate seal; that it was so
affixed by order of the board of directors of said corporation, and that    he signed h    name thereto by like order.

---

STATE OF NEW YORK, COUNTY OF           SS:

On the      day of        19    , before me
personally came
the subscribing witness to the foregoing instrument, with
whom I am personally acquainted, who, being by me duly
sworn, did depose and say that    he resides at No.        ;

that    he knows

                     to be the individual
described in and who executed the foregoing instrument;
that    he, said subscribing witness, was present and saw
         execute the same; and that    he, said witness,
at the same time subscribed h    name as witness thereto.

---

## 𝔅argain and 𝔖ale 𝔇eed
WITH COVENANT AGAINST GRANTOR'S ACTS

TITLE NO.

            TO

> STANDARD FORM OF NEW YORK BOARD OF TITLE UNDERWRITERS
>
> *Distributed by*
>
> **CHICAGO TITLE
> INSURANCE COMPANY**

SECTION

BLOCK

LOT

COUNTY OR TOWN

Recorded at Request of
CHICAGO TITLE INSURANCE COMPANY

Return by Mail to

                          Zip No.

RESERVE THIS SPACE FOR USE OF RECORDING OFFICE

**Bargain and Sale Deed with Covenant Against Grantor's Acts** (page 2 of 2)

Standard N.Y.B.T.U. Form 8004          Quitclaim Deed—Individual or Corporation  (Single Sheet)

**CONSULT YOUR LAWYER BEFORE SIGNING THIS INSTRUMENT — THIS INSTRUMENT SHOULD BE USED BY LAWYERS ONLY**

**THIS INDENTURE**, made the            day of                      , nineteen hundred and
**BETWEEN**

party of the first part, and

party of the second part,

**WITNESSETH**, that the party of the first part, in consideration of ten dollars paid by the party of the second part, does hereby remise, release and quitclaim unto the party of the second part, the heirs or successors and assigns of the party of the second part forever,

**ALL** that certain plot, piece or parcel of land, with the buildings and improvements thereon erected, situate, lying and being in the

**TOGETHER** with all right, title and interest, if any, of the party of the first part of, in and to any streets and roads abutting the above-described premises to the center lines thereof; TOGETHER with the appurtenances and all the estate and rights of the party of the first part in and to said premises; TO HAVE AND TO HOLD the premises herein granted unto the party of the second part, the heirs or successors and assigns of the party of the second part forever.

**AND** the party of the first part, in compliance with Section 13 of the Lien Law, hereby covenants that the party of the first part will receive the consideration for this conveyance and will hold the right to receive such consideration as a trust fund to be applied first for the purpose of paying the cost of the improvement and will apply the same first to the payment of the cost of the improvement before using any part of the total of the same for any other purpose.
The word "party" shall be construed as if it read "parties" whenever the sense of this indenture so requires.

**IN WITNESS WHEREOF**, the party of the first part has duly executed this deed the day and year first above written.

**IN PRESENCE OF:**

**Quitclaim Deed** (page 1 of 2)

STATE OF NEW YORK, COUNTY OF                    SS:

On the          day of          19     , before me
personally came

to me known to be the individual    described in and who
executed the foregoing instrument, and acknowledged that
executed the same.

STATE OF NEW YORK, COUNTY OF                    SS:

On the          day of          19     , before me
personally came

to me known to be the individual    described in and who
executed the foregoing instrument, and acknowledged that
executed the same.

STATE OF NEW YORK, COUNTY OF                    SS:

On the          day of          19     , before me
personally came
to me known, who, being by me duly sworn, did depose and
say that    he resides at No.
                                                        ;
that    he is the
of
                          , the corporation described
in and which executed the foregoing instrument; that    he
knows the seal of said corporation; that the seal affixed
to said instrument is such corporate seal; that it was so
affixed by order of the board of directors of said corporation, and that    he signed h    name thereto by like order.

STATE OF NEW YORK, COUNTY OF                    SS:

On the          day of          19     , before me
personally came
the subscribing witness to the foregoing instrument, with
whom I am personally acquainted, who, being by me duly
sworn, did depose and say that    he resides at No.
                                                        ;
that    he knows

                          to be the individual
described in and who executed the foregoing instrument;
that    he, said subscribing witness, was present and saw
              execute the same; and that    he, said witness,
at the same time subscribed h    name as witness thereto.

# 𝕼𝖚𝖎𝖙𝖈𝖑𝖆𝖎𝖒 𝔇𝖊𝖊𝖉

TITLE NO.

TO

SECTION

BLOCK

LOT

COUNTY OR TOWN

Recorded at Request of
CHICAGO TITLE INSURANCE COMPANY

Return by Mail to

Zip No.

STANDARD FORM OF NEW YORK BOARD OF TITLE UNDERWRITERS

*Distributed by*

**CHICAGO TITLE
INSURANCE COMPANY**

RESERVE THIS SPACE FOR USE OF RECORDING OFFICE

**Quitclaim Deed** (page 2 of 2)

Standard N. Y. B. T. U. Form 8005-A * 12-70-6M—Executor's Deed—Individual or Corporation (Single Sheet)

**CONSULT YOUR LAWYER BEFORE SIGNING THIS INSTRUMENT-THIS INSTRUMENT SHOULD BE USED BY LAWYERS ONLY.**

**THIS INDENTURE,** made the                day of                          , nineteen hundred and
**BETWEEN**

as executor    of                                                      the last will and testament of
                                                                        , late of

who died on the            day of                      , nineteen hundred and
party of the first part, and

party of the second part,

**WITNESSETH,** that whereas letters testamentary were issued to the party of the first part by the Surrogate's
Court,                    County, New York, on                              and by virtue
of the power and authority given in and by said last will and testament, and/or by Article 11 of the Estates,
Powers and Trusts Law, and in consideration of
                                                                                      dollars,
                                      paid by the party of the second part, does hereby grant and
release unto the party of the second part, the distributees or successors and assigns of the party of the second
part forever,

**ALL** that certain plot, piece or parcel of land, with the buildings and improvements thereon erected, situate,
lying and being in the

TOGETHER with all right, title and interest, if any, of the party of the first part in and to any streets and
roads abutting the above described premises to the center lines thereof; TOGETHER with the appurtenances,
and also all the estate which the said decedent had at the time of decedent's death in said premises, and also
the estate therein, which the party of the first part has or has power to convey or dispose of, whether individually, or by virtue of said will or otherwise; TO HAVE AND TO HOLD the premises herein granted unto
the party of the second part, the distributees or successors and assigns of the party of the second part forever.

AND the party of the first part covenants that the party of the first part has not done or suffered anything
whereby the said premises have been incumbered in any way whatever, except as aforesaid.
Subject to the trust fund provisions of section thirteen of the Lien Law.
The word "party" shall be construed as if it read "parties" whenever the sense of this indenture so requires.
**IN WITNESS WHEREOF,** the party of the first part has duly executed this deed the day and year first above
written.

IN PRESENCE OF:

**Executor's Deed** (page 1 of 2)

STATE OF NEW YORK, COUNTY OF ss:

On the      day of      19   , before me
personally came

to me known to be the individual    described in and who
executed the foregoing instrument, and acknowledged that
executed the same.

STATE OF NEW YORK, COUNTY OF ss:

On the      day of      19   , before me
personally came

to me known to be the individual    described in and who
executed the foregoing instrument, and acknowledged that
executed the same.

STATE OF NEW YORK, COUNTY OF ss:

On the      day of      19   , before me
personally came
to me known, who, being by me duly sworn, did depose and
say that    he resides at No.
                                                    ;
that    he is the
of
                              , the corporation described
in and which executed the foregoing instrument; that    he
knows the seal of said corporation; that the seal affixed
to said instrument is such corporate seal; that it was so
affixed by order of the board of directors of said corporation, and that    he signed h    name thereto by like order.

STATE OF NEW YORK, COUNTY OF ss:

On the      day of      19   , before me
personally came
the subscribing witness to the foregoing instrument, with
whom I am personally acquainted, who, being by me duly
sworn, did depose and say that    he resides at No.
                                                    ;
that    he knows

                                        to be the individual
described in and who executed the foregoing instrument;
that    he, said subscribing witness, was present and saw
                        execute the same; and that    he, said witness,
at the same time subscribed h    name as witness thereto.

### Executor's Deed

TITLE NO. _____

SECTION
BLOCK
LOT
COUNTY OR TOWN
STREET ADDRESS

TO

Recorded at Request of
CHICAGO TITLE INSURANCE COMPANY

Return by Mail to

Zip No.

STANDARD FORM OF NEW YORK BOARD OF TITLE UNDERWRITERS
*Distributed by*
**CHICAGO TITLE
INSURANCE COMPANY**

REVERSE THIS SPACE FOR USE OF RECORDING OFFICE

**Executor's Deed**  (page 2 of 2)

Standard N.Y.B.T.U. Form 8011-**10M**          Mortgage Note, Individual or Corporation. (Straight or Instalment.)

**CONSULT YOUR LAWYER BEFORE SIGNING THIS INSTRUMENT — THIS INSTRUMENT SHOULD BE USED BY LAWYERS ONLY**

# MORTGAGE NOTE

$                                                    New York,                                    19

**FOR VALUE RECEIVED,**


promise   to pay to


or order, at

or at such other place as may be designated in writing by the holder of this note, the principal sum of

Dollars on


with interest thereon to be computed from the date hereof, at the rate of _____ per centum per annum
and to be paid on the _____ day of _____ 19 ___ , next ensuing and _____


IT IS HEREBY EXPRESSLY AGREED, that the said principal sum secured by this note shall become due
at the option of the holder thereof on the happening of any default or event by which, under the terms of
the mortgage securing this note, said principal sum may or shall become due and payable; also, that all
of the covenants, conditions and agreements contained in said mortgage are hereby made part of this
instrument.

Presentment for payment, notice of dishonor, protest and notice of protest are hereby waived.

This note is secured by a mortgage made by the maker to the payee of even date herewith, on property
situate in the


This note may not be changed or terminated orally.


_____


**Mortgage Note** (page 1 of 2)

**STATE OF NEW YORK, COUNTY OF**      **SS:**

On the     day of     19   , before me
personally came

to me known to be the individual    described in and who
executed the foregoing instrument, and acknowledged that
      executed the same.

**STATE OF NEW YORK, COUNTY OF**      **SS:**

On the     day of     19   , before me
personally came

to me known to be the individual    described in and who
executed the foregoing instrument, and acknowledged that
      executed the same.

**STATE OF NEW YORK, COUNTY OF**      **SS:**

On the     day of     19   , before me
personally came
to me known, who, being by me duly sworn, did depose and
say that    he resides at No.
                   ;

that    he is the
of
            , the corporation described
in and which executed the foregoing instrument; that   he
knows the seal of said corporation; that the seal affixed
to said instrument is such corporate seal; that it was so
affixed by order of the board of directors of said corporation, and that   he signed h   name thereto by like order

**STATE OF NEW YORK, COUNTY OF**      **SS:**

On the     day of     19   , before me
personally came
the subscribing witness to the foregoing instrument, with
whom I am personally acquainted, who, being by me duly
sworn, did depose and say that    he resides at No.
                   ;

that    he knows

                   to be the individual
described in and who executed the foregoing instrument;
that     he, said subscribing witness, was present and saw
          execute the same; and that    he, said witness,
at the same time subscribed h   name as witness thereto.

# 𝔐ortgage 𝔑ote

TITLE NO

WITH

**STANDARD FORM OF NEW YORK BOARD OF TITLE UNDERWRITERS**

*Distributed by*

**CHICAGO TITLE
INSURANCE COMPANY**

SECTION

BLOCK

LOT

COUNTY OR TOWN

Recorded at Request of
CHICAGO TITLE INSURANCE COMPANY

Return by Mail to

Zip No.

**Mortgage Note** (page 2 of 2)

Standard N.Y.B.T.U. Form 8011—20M— First Mortgage–Individual or Corporation.

**CONSULT YOUR LAWYER BEFORE SIGNING THIS INSTRUMENT - THIS INSTRUMENT SHOULD BE USED BY LAWYERS ONLY**

**THIS MORTGAGE,** made the                    day of                    , nineteen hundred and

**BETWEEN**

, the mortgagor,

and

the mortgagee,

**WITNESSETH,** that to secure the payment of an indebtedness in the sum of

dollars,

lawful money of the United States, to be paid

with interest thereon to be computed from the date hereof, at the rate of _____ per centum
per annum, and to be paid on the _____ day of _____19 ___ , next ensuing and _____
_____ thereafter, _____

according to a certain bond,
note or obligation bearing even date herewith, the mortgagor hereby mortgages to the mortgagee

**ALL** that certain plot, piece or parcel of land, with the buildings and improvements thereon erected, situate,
lying and being in the

**Mortgage** (page 1 of 4)

**TOGETHER** with all right, title and interest of the mortgagor in and to the land lying in the streets and roads in front of and adjoining said premises;

**TOGETHER** with all fixtures, chattels and articles of personal property now or hereafter attached to or used in connection with said premises, including but not limited to furnaces, boilers, oil burners, radiators and piping, coal stokers, plumbing and bathroom fixtures, refrigeration, air conditioning and sprinkler systems, wash tubs, sinks, gas and electric fixtures, stoves, ranges, awnings, screens, window shades, elevators, motors, dynamos, refrigerators, kitchen cabinets, incinerators, plants and shrubbery and all other equipment and machinery, appliances, fittings, and fixtures of every kind in or used in the operation of the buildings standing on said premises, together with any and all replacements thereof and additions thereto;

**TOGETHER** with all awards heretofore and hereafter made to the mortgagor for taking by eminent domain the whole or any part of said premises or any easement therein, including any awards for changes of grade of streets, which said awards are hereby assigned to the mortgagee, who is hereby authorized to collect and receive the proceeds of such awards and to give proper receipts and acquittances therefor, and to apply the same toward the payment of the mortgage debt, notwithstanding the fact that the amount owing thereon may not then be due and payable; and the said mortgagor hereby agrees, upon request, to make, execute and deliver any and all assignments and other instruments sufficient for the purpose of assigning said awards to the mortgagee, free, clear and discharged of any encumbrances of any kind or nature whatsoever.

**AND** the mortgagor covenants with the mortgagee as follows:

1. That the mortgagor will pay the indebtedness as hereinbefore provided.

2. That the mortgagor will keep the buildings on the premises insured against loss by fire for the benefit of the mortgagee; that he will assign and deliver the policies to the mortgagee; and that he will reimburse the mortgagee for any premiums paid for insurance made by the mortgagee on the mortgagor's default in so insuring the buildings or in so assigning and delivering the policies.

3. That no building on the premises shall be altered, removed or demolished without the consent of the mortgagee.

4. That the whole of said principal sum and interest shall become due at the option of the mortgagee: after default in the payment of any instalment of principal or of interest for fifteen days; or after default in the payment of any tax, water rate, sewer rent or assessment for thirty days after notice and demand; or after default after notice and demand either in assigning and delivering the policies insuring the buildings against loss by fire or in reimbursing the mortgagee for premiums paid on such insurance, as hereinbefore provided; or after default upon request in furnishing a statement of the amount due on the mortgage and whether any offsets or defenses exist against the mortgage debt, as hereinafter provided. An assessment which has been made payable in instalments at the application of the mortgagor or lessee of the premises shall nevertheless, for the purpose of this paragraph, be deemed due and payable in its entirety on the day the first instalment becomes due or payable or a lien.

5. That the holder of this mortgage, in any action to foreclose it, shall be entitled to the appointment of a receiver.

6. That the mortgagor will pay all taxes, assessments, sewer rents or water rates, and in default thereof, the mortgagee may pay the same.

7. That the mortgagor within five days upon request in person or within ten days upon request by mail will furnish a written statement duly acknowledged of the amount due on this mortgage and whether any offsets or defenses exist against the mortgage debt.

8. That notice and demand or request may be in writing and may be served in person or by mail.

9. That the mortgagor warrants the title to the premises.

10. That the fire insurance policies required by paragraph No. 2 above shall contain the usual extended coverage endorsement; that in addition thereto the mortgagor, within thirty days after notice and demand, will keep the premises insured against war risk and any other hazard that may reasonably be required by the mortgagee. All of the provisions of paragraphs No. 2 and No. 4 above relating to fire insurance and the provisions of Section 254 of the Real Property Law construing the same shall apply to the additional insurance required by this paragraph.

11. That in case of a foreclosure sale, said premises, or so much thereof as may be affected by this mortgage, may be sold in one parcel.

12. That if any action or proceeding be commenced (except an action to foreclose this mortgage or to collect the debt secured thereby), to which action or proceeding the mortgagee is made a party, or in which it becomes necessary to defend or uphold the lien of this mortgage, all sums paid by the mortgagee for the expense of any litigation to prosecute or defend the rights and lien created by this mortgage (including reasonable counsel fees), shall be paid by the mortgagor, together with interest thereon at the rate of six per cent. per annum, and any such sum and the interest thereon shall be a lien on said premises, prior to any right, or title to, interest in or claim upon said premises attaching or accruing subsequent to the lien of this mortgage, and shall be deemed to be secured by this mortgage. In any action or proceeding to foreclose this mortgage, or to recover or collect the debt secured thereby, the provisions of law respecting the recovering of costs, disbursements and allowances shall prevail unaffected by this covenant.

**Mortgage** (page 2 of 4)

13.   That the mortgagor hereby assigns to the mortgagee the rents, issues and profits of the premises as further security for the payment of said indebtedness, and the mortgagor grants to the mortgagee the right to enter upon and take possession of the premises for the purpose of collecting the same and to let the premises or any part thereof, and to apply the rents, issues and profits, after payment of all necessary charges and expenses, on account of said indebtedness. This assignment and grant shall continue in effect until this mortgage is paid. The mortgagee hereby waives the right to enter upon and take possession of said premises for the purpose of collecting said rents, issues and profits, and the mortgagor shall be entitled to collect and receive said rents, issues and profits until default under any of the covenants, conditions or agreements contained in this mortgage, and agrees to use such rents, issues and profits in payment of principal and interest becoming due on this mortgage and in payment of taxes, assessments, sewer rents, water rates and carrying charges becoming due against said premises, but such right of the mortgagor may be revoked by the mortgagee upon any default, on five days' written notice. The mortgagor will not, without the written consent of the mortgagee, receive or collect rent from any tenant of said premises or any part thereof for a period of more than one month in advance, and in the event of any default under this mortgage will pay monthly in advance to the mortgagee, or to any receiver appointed to collect said rents, issues and profits, the fair and reasonable rental value for the use and occupation of said premises or of such part thereof as may be in the possession of the mortgagor, and upon default in any such payment will vacate and surrender the possession of said premises to the mortgagee or to such receiver, and in default thereof may be evicted by summary proceedings.

14.   That the whole of said principal sum and the interest shall become due at the option of the mortgagee: (a) after failure to exhibit to the mortgagee, within ten days after demand, receipts showing payment of all taxes, water rates, sewer rents and assessments; or (b) after the actual or threatened alteration, demolition or removal of any building on the premises without the written consent of the mortgagee; or (c) after the assignment of the rents of the premises or any part thereof without the written consent of the mortgagee; or (d) if the buildings on said premises are not maintained in reasonably good repair; or (e) after failure to comply with any requirement or order or notice of violation of law or ordinance issued by any governmental department claiming jurisdiction over the premises within three months from the issuance thereof; or (f) if on application of the mortgagee two or more fire insurance companies lawfully doing business in the State of New York refuse to issue policies insuring the buildings on the premises; or (g) in the event of the removal, demolition or destruction in whole or in part of any of the fixtures, chattels or articles of personal property covered hereby, unless the same are promptly replaced by similar fixtures, chattels and articles of personal property at least equal in quality and condition to those replaced, free from chattel mortgages or other encumbrances thereon and free from any reservation of title thereto; or (h) after thirty days' notice to the mortgagor, in the event of the passage of any law deducting from the value of land for the purpose of taxation any lien thereon, or changing in any way the taxation of mortgages or debts secured thereby for state or local purposes; or (i) if the mortgagor fails to keep, observe and perform any of the other covenants, conditions or agreements contained in this mortgage.

15.   That the mortgagor will, in compliance with Section 13 of the Lien Law, receive the advances secured hereby and will hold the right to receive such advances as a trust fund to be applied first for the purpose of paying the cost of the improvement and will apply the same first to the payment of the cost of the improvement before using any part of the total of the same for any other purpose.

16.   That the execution of this mortgage has been duly authorized by the board of directors of the mortgagor.

      This mortgage may not be changed or terminated orally. The covenants contained in this mortgage shall run with the land and bind the mortgagor, the heirs, personal representatives, successors and assigns of the mortgagor and all subsequent owners, encumbrancers, tenants and subtenants of the premises, and shall enure to the benefit of the mortgagee, the personal representatives, successors and assigns of the mortgagee and all subsequent holders of this mortgage. The word "mortgagor" shall be construed as if it read "mortgagors" and the word "mortgagee" shall be construed as if it read "mortgagees" whenever the sense of this mortgage so requires.

**IN WITNESS WHEREOF,** this mortgage has been duly executed by the mortgagor.

IN PRESENCE OF:

**STATE OF NEW YORK, COUNTY OF**          SS: | **STATE OF NEW YORK, COUNTY OF**          SS:

On the          day of          19     , before me
personally came

to me known to be the individual     described in and who
executed the foregoing instrument, and acknowledged that
executed the same.

On the          day of          19     , before me
personally came

to me known to be the individual     described in and who
executed the foregoing instrument, and acknowledged that
executed the same.

**STATE OF NEW YORK, COUNTY OF**          SS: | **STATE OF NEW YORK, COUNTY OF**          SS:

On the          day of          19     , before me
personally came
to me known, who, being by me duly sworn, did depose and
say that     he resides at No.
                                                    ;
that     he is the
of
                    , the corporation described
in and which executed the foregoing instrument; that     he
knows the seal of said corporation; that the seal affixed
to said instrument is such corporate seal; that it was so
affixed by order of the board of directors of said corporation, and that     he signed h    name thereto by like order.

On the          day of          19     , before me
personally came
the subscribing witness to the foregoing instrument, with
whom I am personally acquainted, who, being by me duly
sworn, did depose and say that    he resides at No.
                                                    ;
that     he knows

                                        to be the individual
described in and who executed the foregoing instrument;
that     he, said subscribing witness, was present and saw
                    execute the same; and that    he, said witness,
at the same time subscribed h    name as witness thereto.

## 𝔐𝔬𝔯𝔱𝔤𝔞𝔤𝔢

TITLE NO.

TO

```
STANDARD FORM OF NEW YORK BOARD OF TITLE UNDERWRITERS

Distributed by

CHICAGO TITLE
INSURANCE COMPANY
```

SECTION

BLOCK

LOT

COUNTY OR TOWN

Recorded at Request of
CHICAGO TITLE INSURANCE COMPANY

Return by Mail to

Zip No.

RESERVE THIS SPACE FOR USE OF RECORDING OFFICE

**Mortgage** (page 4 of 4)

Standard N.Y.B.T.U. Form 8035—          Satisfaction of Mortgage—Individual or Corporation

**CONSULT YOUR LAWYER BEFORE SIGNING THIS INSTRUMENT - THIS INSTRUMENT SHOULD BE USED BY LAWYERS ONLY**

### KNOW ALL MEN BY THESE PRESENTS,

*Insert residence, if in-dividual or principal office, if corporation, giving street and street number.*

that

**DO     HEREBY CERTIFY** that the following Mortgage          **IS PAID,** and do     hereby consent that the same be discharged of record.

Mortgage dated the          day of                    , 19     , made by

to

in the principal sum of $          and recorded on the          day of
19     , in Liber          of Section          of Mortgages, page          , in the office of the
of the

*Insert "further" when required.*

which mortgage          has not been          assigned of record

Dated the          day of               , 19

IN PRESENCE OF :

Section 321 of the Real Property Law expressly provides who must execute the certificate of discharge in specific cases and also provides, among other things, that (1) no certificate shall purport to discharge more than one mortgage, (except that mortgages affected by instruments of consolidation, spreader, modification or correction may be included in one certificate if the instruments are set forth in detail in separate paragraphs); (2) if the mortgage has been assigned, in whole or in part, the certificate shall set forth; (a) the date of each assignment in the chain of title of the person or persons signing the certificate, (b) the names of the assignor and assignee, (c) the interest assigned, and (d) if the assignment has been recorded, the book and page where it has been recorded or the serial number of such record, or (e) if the assignment is being recorded simultaneously with the certificate of discharge, the certificate of discharge shall so state, and (f) if the mortgage has not been assigned of record, the certificate shall so state; (3) if the mortgage is held by any fiduciary, including an executor or administrator, the certificate of discharge shall recite the name of the court and the venue of the proceedings in which his appointment was made or in which the order or decree vesting him with such title or authority was entered.

**Satisfaction of Mortgage** (page 1 of 2)

STATE OF NEW YORK, COUNTY OF                    SS:

On the          day of                    19    , before me
personally came

to me known to be the individual    described in and who
executed the foregoing instrument, and acknowledged that
executed the same.


STATE OF NEW YORK, COUNTY OF                    SS:

On the          day of                    19    , before me
personally came

to me known to be the individual    described in and who
executed the foregoing instrument, and acknowledged that
executed the same.


STATE OF NEW YORK, COUNTY OF                    SS:

On the          day of                    19    , before me
personally came
to me known, who, being by me duly sworn, did depose and
say that    he resides at No.
                                                    ;
that    he is the
of
                              , the corporation described
in and which executed the foregoing instrument; that    he
knows the seal of said corporation; that the seal affixed
to said instrument is such corporate seal; that it was so
affixed by order of the board of directors of said corporation, and that    he signed h    name thereto by like order.


STATE OF NEW YORK, COUNTY OF                    SS:

On the          day of                    19    , before me
personally came
the subscribing witness to the foregoing instrument, with
whom I am personally acquainted, who, being by me duly
sworn, did depose and say that    he resides at No.
                                                    ;
that    he knows
                                        to be the individual
described in and who executed the foregoing instrument;
that    he, said subscribing witness, was present and saw
            execute the same; and that    he, said witness,
at the same time subscribed h    name as witness thereto.


### Satisfaction of Mortgage

TITLE NO.

SECTION

BLOCK

LOT

COUNTY OR TOWN

TO

**Recorded at Request of**
**CHICAGO TITLE INSURANCE COMPANY**

STANDARD FORM OF NEW YORK BOARD OF TITLE UNDERWRITERS

*Distributed by*

**CHICAGO TITLE
INSURANCE COMPANY**

**Return by Mail to**

Zip No.

RESERVE THIS SPACE FOR USE OF RECORDING OFFICE

**Satisfaction of Mortgage** (page 2 of 2)

# CHICAGO TITLE INSURANCE COMPANY

in consideration of the payment of its charges for the examination of title and its premium for insurance, insures the within named insured against all loss or damage not exceeding the amount of insurance stated herein and in addition the costs and expenses of defending the title, estate or interest insured, which the insured shall sustain by reason of any defect or defects of title affecting the premises described in Schedule A or affecting the interest of the insured therein as herein set forth, or by reason of unmarketability of the title of the insured to or in the premises, or by reason of liens or encumbrances affecting title at the date hereof, or by reason of any statutory lien for labor or material furnished prior to the date hereof which has now gained or which may hereafter gain priority over the interest insured hereby, or by reason of a lack of access to and from the premises, excepting all loss and damage by reason of the estates, interests, defects, objections, liens, encumbrances and other matters set forth in Schedule B, or by the conditions of this policy hereby incorporated into this contract, the loss and the amount to be ascertained in the manner provided in said conditions and to be payable upon compliance by the insured with the stipulations of said conditions, and not otherwise.

*In Witness Whereof,* CHICAGO TITLE INSURANCE COMPANY has caused this policy to be signed and sealed as of the date of policy shown in Schedule A, the policy to become valid when countersigned by an authorized signatory.

CHICAGO TITLE INSURANCE COMPANY

By: _Alvin W. Long_

President.

Issued by:
EASTERN REGION
Main Office
233 Broadway
New York, New York 10007
(212) 285-4000

ATTEST:

_Chester C. McCullough_

Secretary.

## CONDITIONS OF THIS POLICY

### 1. Definitions

(a) Wherever the term "insured" is used in this policy it includes those who succeed to the interest of the insured by operation of law including, without limitation, heirs, distributees, devisees, survivors, personal representatives, next of kin or corporate successors, as the case may be, and those to whom the insured has assigned this policy where such assignment is permitted by the terms hereof, and whenever the term "insured" is used in the conditions of this policy it also includes the attorneys and agents of the "insured."

(b) Wherever the term "this company" is used in this policy it means Chicago Title Insurance Company.

(c) Wherever the term "final determination" or "finally determined" is used in this policy, it means the final determination of a court of competent jurisdiction after disposition of all appeals or after the time to appeal has expired.

(d) Wherever the term "the premises" is used in this policy, it means the property insured herein as described in Schedule A of this policy, including such buildings and improvements thereon which by law constitute real property.

(e) Wherever the term "recorded" is used in this policy it means, unless otherwise indicated, recorded in the office of the recording officer of the county in which property insured herein lies.

### 2. Defense and Prosecution of Suits

(a) This company will, at its own cost, defend the insured in all actions or proceedings founded on a claim of title or encumbrances not excepted in this policy.

(b) This company shall have the right and may, at its own cost, maintain or defend any action or proceeding relating to the title or interest hereby insured, or upon or under any convenant or contract relating thereto which it considers desirable to prevent or reduce loss hereunder.

(c) In all cases where this policy requires or permits this company to prosecute or defend, the insured shall secure to it the right and opportunity to maintain or defend the action or proceeding, and all appeals from any determination therein, and give it all reasonable aid therein, and hereby permits it to use therein, at its option, its own name or the name of the insured.

(d) The provisions of this section shall survive payment by this company of any specific loss or payment of the entire amount of this policy to the extent that this company shall deem it necessary in recovering the loss from those who may be liable therefor to the insured or to this company.

### 3. Cases Where Liability Arises

No claim for damages shall arise or be maintainable under this policy except in the following cases:

(a) Where there has been a final determination under which the insured may be dispossessed, evicted or ejected from the premises or from some part or undivided share or interest therein.

(b) Where there has been a final determination adverse to the title upon a lien or encumbrance not excepted in this policy.

(c) Where the insured shall have contracted in good faith in writing to sell the insured estate or interest, or where the insured estate has been sold for the benefit of the insured pursuant to the judgment or order of a court and the title has been rejected because of a defect or encumbrance not excepted in this policy and there has been a final determination sustaining the objection to the title.

(d) Where the insurance is upon the interest of a mortgagee and the mortgage has been adjudged by a final determination to be invalid or ineffectual to charge the insured's estate or interest in the premises, or subject to a prior lien or encumbrance not excepted in this policy; or where a recording officer has refused to accept from the insured a satisfaction of the insured mortgage and there has been a final determination sustaining the refusal because of a defect in the title to the said mortgage.

(e) Where the insured shall have negotiated a loan to be made on the security of a mortgage on the insured's estate or interest in the premises and the title shall have been rejected by the proposed lender and it shall have been finally determined that the rejection of the title was justified because of a defect or encumbrance not excepted in this policy.

(f) Where the insured shall have transferred the title insured by an instrument containing covenants in regard to title or warranty thereof and there shall have been a final determination on any of such covenants or warranty, against the insured, because of a defect or encumbrance not excepted in this policy.

(g) Where the insured estate or interest or a part thereof has been taken by condemnation and it has been finally determined that the insured is not entitled to a full award for the estate or interest taken because of a defect or encumbrance not excepted in this policy.

No claim for damages shall arise or be maintainable under this policy (1) if this company, after having received notice of an alleged defect or encumbrance, removes such defect or encumbrance within thirty days after receipt of such notice; or (2) for liability voluntarily assumed by the insured in settling any claim or suit without the written consent of this company.

### 4. Notice of Claim

In case a purchaser or proposed mortgage lender raises any question as to the sufficiency of the title hereby insured, or in case actual knowledge shall come to the insured of any claim adverse to the title insured hereby, or in case of the service on or receipt by the insured of any paper, or of any notice, summons, process of pleading in any action or proceeding, the object or effect of which shall or may be to impugn, attack or call in question the validity of the title hereby insured, the insured shall promptly notify this company thereof in writing at its New York office and forward to this company such paper or such notice, summons, process or pleading. Delay in giving this notice and delay in forwarding such paper or such notice, summons, process or pleading shall not affect this company's liability if such failure has not prejudiced and cannot in the future prejudice this company.

### 5. Payment of Loss

(a) This company will pay, in addition to the loss, all statutory costs and allowances imposed on the insured in litigation carried on by this company for the insured under the terms of this policy. This company shall not be liable for and will not pay the fees of any counsel or attorney employed by the insured.

(b) In every case where claim is made for loss or damage this company (1) reserves the right to settle, at its own cost, any claim or suit which may involve liability under this policy; or (2) may terminate its liability hereunder by paying or tendering the full amount of this policy; or (3) may, without conceding liability, demand a valuation of the insured estate or interest, to be made by three arbitrators or any two of them, one to be chosen by the insured and one by this company, and the two thus chosen selecting an umpire. Such valuation, less the amount of any encumbrances on said insured estate and interest not hereby insured against, shall be the extent of this company's liability for such claim and no right of action shall accrue hereunder for the recovery thereof until thirty days after notice of such valuation shall have been served upon this company, and the insured shall have tendered a conveyance or assignment of the insured estate or interest to this company or its designee at such valuation, diminished as aforesaid. The foregoing option to fix a valuation by arbitration shall not apply to a policy insuring a mortgage or leasehold interest.

(c) Liability to any collateral holder of this policy shall not exceed the amount of the pecuniary interest of such collateral holder in the premises.

(d) All payments made by this company under this policy shall reduce the amount hereof *pro tanto* except (1) payments made for counsel fees and disbursements in defending or prosecuting actions or proceedings in behalf of the insured and for statutory costs and allowances imposed on the insured in such actions and proceedings, and (2) if the insured is a mortgagee, payments made to satisfy or subordinate prior liens or encumbrances not set forth in Schedule B.

(e) When liability has been definitely fixed in accordance with the conditions of this policy, the loss or damage shall be payable within thirty days thereafter.

CONDITIONS (Continued on Reverse Side)

## CONDITIONS OF THIS POLICY (CONTINUED)

#### 6. Co-insurance and Apportionment

(a) In the event that a partial loss occurs after the insured makes an improvement subsequent to the date of this policy, and only in that event, the insured becomes a co-insurer to the extent hereinafter set forth.

If the cost of the improvement exceeds twenty per centum of the amount of this policy, such proportion only of any partial loss established shall be borne by the company as one hundred twenty per centum of the amount of this policy bears to the sum of the amount of this policy and the amount expended for the improvement. The foregoing provisions shall not apply to costs and attorneys' fees incurred by the company in prosecuting or providing for the defense of actions or proceedings in behalf of the insured pursuant to the terms of this policy or to costs imposed on the insured in such actions or proceedings, and shall apply only to that portion of losses which exceed in the aggregate ten per cent of the face of the policy.

Provided, however, that the foregoing co-insurance provisions shall not apply to any loss arising out of a lien or encumbrance for a liquidated amount which existed on the date of this policy and was not shown in Schedule B; and provided further, such co-insurance provisions shall not apply to any loss if, at the time of the occurrence of such loss, the then value of the premises, as so improved, does not exceed one hundred twenty per centum of the amount of this policy.

(b) If the premises are divisible into separate, independent parcels, and a loss is established affecting one or more but not all of said parcels, the loss shall be computed and settled on a *pro rata* basis as if this policy were divided *pro rata* as to value of said separate, independent parcels, exclusive of improvements made subsequent to the date of this policy.

(c) Clauses "(a)" and "(b)" of this section apply to mortgage policies only after the insured shall have acquired the interest of the mortgagor.

(d) If, at the time liability for any loss shall have been fixed pursuant to the conditions of this policy, the insured holds another policy of insurance covering the same loss issued by another company, this company shall not be liable to the insured for a greater proportion of the loss than the amount that this policy bears to the whole amount of insurance held by the insured, unless another method of apportioning the loss shall have been provided by agreement between this company and the other insurer or insurers.

#### 7. Assignment of Policy

If the interest insured by this policy is that of mortgagee, this policy may be assigned to and shall enure to the benefit of successive assignees of the mortgage without consent of this company or its endorsement of this policy. Provision is made in the rate manual of New York Board of Title Underwriters filed with the Super-

intendent of Insurance of the State of New York on behalf of this and other member companies for continuation of liability to grantees of the insured in certain specific circumstances only. In no circumstance provided for in this section shall this company be deemed to have insured the sufficiency of the form of the assignment or other instrument of transfer or conveyance or to have assumed any liability for the sufficiency of any proceedings after date of this policy.

#### 8. Subrogation

(a) This company shall, to the extent of any payment by it of loss under this policy, be subrogated to all rights of the insured with respect thereto. The insured shall execute such instruments as may be requested to transfer such rights to this company. The rights so transferred shall be subordinate to any remaining interest of the insured.

(b) If the insured is a mortgagee, this company's right of subrogation shall not prevent the insured from releasing the personal liability of the obligor or guarantor or from releasing a portion of the premises from the lien of the mortgage or from increasing or otherwise modifying the insured mortgage provided such acts do not affect the validity or priority of the lien of the mortgage insured. However, the liability of this company under this policy shall in no event be increased by any such act of the insured.

#### 9. Misrepresentation

Any untrue statement made by the insured with respect to any material fact, or any suppression of or failure to disclose any material fact, or any untrue answer by the insured to material inquiries before the issuance of this policy shall void this policy.

#### 10. No Waiver of Conditions

This company may take any appropriate action under the terms of this policy whether or not it shall be liable hereunder and shall not thereby concede liability or waive any provision of this policy.

#### 11. Policy Entire Contract

All actions or proceedings against this company must be based on the provisions of this policy. Any other action or actions or rights of action that the insured may have or may bring against this company in respect of other services rendered in connection with the issuance of this policy, shall be deemed to have merged in and be restricted to its terms and conditions.

#### 12. Validation and Modification

This policy is valid only when duly signed by a validating officer or agent. Changes may be effected only by written endorsement. If the recording date of the instruments creating the insured interest is later than the policy date, such policy shall also cover intervening liens or encumbrances, except real estate taxes, assessments, water charges and sewer rents.

F-3415R 10-77

| **Number** | **Date of Issue** | **Amount of Insurance** |
|---|---|---|

Name of Insured:

The estate or interest insured by this policy is                    vested in the insured by means of

## SCHEDULE A

The premises in which the insured has the estate or interest covered by this policy is described on the description sheet annexed.

## SCHEDULE B

The following estates, interests, defects, objections to title, liens, and incumbrances and other matters are excepted from the coverage of this policy.

1. Defects and incumbrances arising or becoming a lien after the date of this policy, except as herein provided.

2. Consequences of the exercise and enforcement or attempted enforcement of any governmental, war or police powers over the premises.

3. Any laws, regulations or ordinances (including, but not limited to zoning, building, and environmental protection) as to the use, occupancy, subdivision or improvement of the premises adopted or imposed by any governmental body, or the effect of any noncompliance with or any violation thereof.

4. Judgments against the insured or estates, interests, defects, objections, liens or incumbrances created, suffered, assumed or agreed to by or with the privity of the insured.

5. Title to any property beyond the lines of the premises, or title to areas within or rights or easements in any abutting streets, roads, avenues, lanes, ways or waterways, or the right to maintain therein vaults, tunnels, ramps or any other structure or improvement, unless this policy specifically provides that such titles, rights, or easements are insured. Notwithstanding any provisions in this paragraph to the contrary, this policy, unless otherwise excepted, insures the ordinary rights of access and egress belonging to abutting owners.

6. Title to any personal property, whether the same be attached to or used in connection with said premises or otherwise.

Countersigned

NOTE: ATTACHED HERETO          ADDED PAGES.

_____
    Authorized Signatory

**New York Board of Title Underwriters Form 100D** (page 4 of 4)

# Appendix E

## Suggested Readings

### Chapter 2

*Real Estate Licensing Examination: Bulletin of Information for Applicants.* Educational Testing Service, Princeton, NJ, most recent edition.

*ACT Real Estate Examination Bulletin of Information.* Iowa City, Iowa, American College Testing Service, most recent edition.

*ASI Real Estate Assessment for Licensing Candidate Guide.* Assessment Systems, Inc., Philadelphia, PA, most recent edition.

Epley, Donald R., and Joseph Rabianski, *Principles of Real Estate Decisions,* 3rd ed. Englewood Cliffs, NJ: Prentice-Hall, 1986.

Gross, Jerome S. *Webster's New World Illustrated Encyclopedic Dictionary of Real Estate,* 3rd ed. Englewood Cliffs, NJ: Prentice-Hall, 1987.

### Chapter 3

Bloom, George F., Arthur M. Weimer, Jeffery D. Fisher. *Real Estate,* 8th ed. New York: John Wiley & Sons, 1982.

Epley, Donald R., and Joseph Rabianski. *Principles of Real Estate Decisions,* 3rd ed. Englewood Cliffs, NJ: Prentice-Hall, 1986.

Gross, Jerome S. *Webster's New World Illustrated Encyclopedic Dictionary of Real Estate,* 3rd ed. Englewood Cliffs, NJ: Prentice-Hall, 1987.

Ring, Alfred A., and Jerome Dasso. *Real Estate Principles and Practices,* 10th ed. Englewood Cliffs, NJ: Prentice-Hall, 1985.

Wurtzebach, Charles H., and Mike E. Miles. *Modern Real Estate,* 3rd ed. New York: John Wiley & Sons, 1987.

### Chapter 4

Bloom, George F., Arthur M. Weimer, Jeffery D. Fisher. *Real Estate,* 8th ed. New York: John Wiley & Sons, 1982.

Epley, Donald R., and Joseph Rabianski. *Principles of Real Estate Decisions,* 3rd ed. Englewood Cliffs, NJ: Prentice-Hall, 1986.

Gross, Jerome S. *Webster's New World Illustrated Encyclopedic Dictionary of Real Estate,* 3rd ed. Englewood Cliffs, NJ: Prentice-Hall, 1987.

Ring, Alfred A., and Jerome Dasso. *Real Estate Principles and Practices,* 10th ed. Englewood Cliffs, NJ: Prentice-Hall, 1985.

Wurtzebach, Charles H., and Mike E. Miles. *Modern Real Estate,* 3rd ed. New York: John Wiley & Sons, 1987.

### Chapter 5

Arnold, Alvin L. *Arnold Encyclopedia of Real Estate.* Boston: Warren, Gorham & Lamont, 1978.

Epley, Donald R., and Joseph Rabianski. *Principles of Real Estate Decisions,* 3rd ed. Englewood Cliffs, NJ: Prentice-Hall, 1986.

French, William B. *Law of the Real Estate Business,* 5th ed. Homewood, IL: Richard D. Irwin, 1984.

Gross, Jerome S. *Webster's New World Illustrated Encyclopedic Dictionary of Real Estate,* 3rd ed. Englewood Cliffs, NJ: Prentice-Hall, 1987.

Henszey, Benjamin N., and Ronald M. Friedman. *Real Estate Law,* 2nd ed. John Wiley & Sons, 1984.

### Chapter 6

Arnold, Alvin L. *Arnold Encyclopedia of Real Estate.* Boston: Warren, Gorham & Lamont, 1978.

Bloom, George F., Arthur M. Weimer, Jeffery D. Fisher. *Real Estate,* 8th ed. New York: John Wiley & Sons, 1982.

Epley, Donald R., and Joseph Rabianski. *Principles of Real Estate Decisions,* 3rd ed. Englewood Cliffs, NJ: Prentice-Hall, 1986.

French, William B. *Law of the Real Estate Business,* 5th ed. Homewood, IL: Richard D. Irwin, 1984.

Gross, Jerome S. *Webster's New World Illustrated Encyclopedic Dictionary of Real Estate,* 3rd ed. Englewood Cliffs, NJ: Prentice-Hall, 1987.

Henszey, Benjamin N., and Ronald M. Friedman. *Real Estate Law,* 2nd ed. New York: John Wiley & Sons, 1984.

Kratovil, Robert, and Raymond J. Werner. *Real Estate Law,* 8th ed. Englewood Cliffs, NJ: Prentice-Hall, 1983.

Ring, Alfred A., and Jerome Dasso. *Real Estate Principles and Practices,* 10th ed. Englewood Cliffs, NJ: Prentice-Hall, 1985.

Wurtzebach, Charles H., and Mike E. Miles. *Modern Real Estate,* 3rd ed. New York: John Wiley & Sons, 1987.

### Chapter 7

Arnold, Alvin L. *Arnold Encyclopedia of Real Estate.* Boston: Warren, Gorham & Lamont, 1978.

Epley, Donald R., and Joseph Rabianski. *Principles of*

*Real Estate Decisions,* 3rd ed. Englewood Cliffs, NJ: Prentice-Hall, 1986.

French, William B. *Law of the Real Estate Business,* 5th ed. Homewood, IL: Richard D. Irwin, 1984.

Gross, Jerome S. *Webster's New World Illustrated Encyclopedic Dictionary of Real Estate,* 3rd ed. Englewood Cliffs, NJ: Prentice-Hall, 1987.

Henszey, Benjamin N., and Ronald M. Friedman. *Real Estate Law,* 2nd ed. John Wiley & Sons, 1984.

## Chapter 8

Bloom, George F., Arthur M. Weimer, Jeffery D. Fisher. *Real Estate,* 8th ed. New York: John Wiley & Sons, 1982.

Epley, Donald R., and Joseph Rabianski. *Principles of Real Estate Decisions,* 3rd ed. Englewood Cliffs, NJ: Prentice-Hall, 1986.

French, William B. *Law of the Real Estate Business,* 5th ed. Homewood, IL: Richard D. Irwin, 1984.

Gross, Jerome S. *Webster's New World Illustrated Encyclopedic Dictionary of Real Estate,* 3rd ed. Englewood Cliffs, NJ: Prentice-Hall, 1987.

Henszey, Benjamin N., and Ronald M. Friedman. *Real Estate Law,* 2nd ed. New York: John Wiley & Sons, 1984.

Kratovil, Robert, and Raymond J. Werner. *Real Estate Law,* 8th ed. Englewood Cliffs, NJ: Prentice-Hall, 1983.

Ring, Alfred A., and Jerome Dasso. *Real Estate Principles and Practices,* 10th ed. Englewood Cliffs, NJ: Prentice-Hall, 1985.

Wurtzebach, Charles H., and Mike E. Miles. *Modern Real Estate,* 3rd ed. New York: John Wiley & Sons, 1987.

## Chapter 9

Bloom, George F., Arthur M. Weimer, Jeffery D. Fisher. *Real Estate,* 8th ed. New York: John Wiley & Sons, 1982.

Downs, James C., Jr. *Principles of Real Estate Management,* 12th ed. Chicago: Institute of Real Estate Management, 1980.

Epley, Donald R., and Joseph Rabianski. *Principles of Real Estate Decisions,* 3rd ed. Englewood Cliffs, NJ: Prentice-Hall, 1986.

French, William B. *Law of the Real Estate Business,* 5th ed. Homewood, IL: Richard D. Irwin, 1984.

Gross, Jerome S. *Webster's New World Illustrated Encyclopedic Dictionary of Real Estate,* 3rd ed. Englewood Cliffs, NJ: Prentice-Hall, 1987.

Kratovil, Robert, and Raymond J. Werner. *Real Estate Law,* 8th ed. Englewood Cliffs, NJ: Prentice-Hall, 1983.

Ring, Alfred A., and Jerome Dasso. *Real Estate Principles and Practices,* 10th ed. Englewood Cliffs, NJ: Prentice-Hall, 1985.

Wurtzebach, Charles H., and Mike E. Miles. *Modern Real Estate,* 3rd ed. New York: John Wiley & Sons, 1987.

## Chapter 10

Brueggeman, William B., and Leo D. Stone. *Real Estate Finance,* 8th ed. Homewood, IL: Richard D. Irwin, 1987.

Epley, Donald R., and Joseph Rabianski. *Principles of Real Estate Decisions,* 3rd ed. Englewood Cliffs, NJ: Prentice-Hall, 1986.

French, William B. *Law of the Real Estate Business,* 5th ed. Homewood, IL: Richard D. Irwin, 1984.

Gross, Jerome S. *Webster's New World Illustrated Encyclopedic Dictionary of Real Estate,* 3rd ed. Englewood Cliffs, NJ: Prentice-Hall, 1987.

Kratovil, Robert. *Modern Mortgage Law and Practice,* 2nd ed. Englewood Cliffs, NJ: Prentice-Hall, 1981.

Levine, Mark Lee. *Real Estate Transactions, Tax Planning,* 5th ed. St. Paul, MN: West Publishing, 1987.

Wurtzebach, Charles H., and Mike E. Miles. *Modern Real Estate,* 3rd ed. New York: John Wiley & Sons, 1987.

## Chapter 11

Brueggeman, William B., and Leo D. Stone. *Real Estate Finance,* 8th ed. Homewood, IL: Richard D. Irwin, 1987.

Epley, Donald R., and James A. Millar. *Basic Real Estate Finance and Investments,* 2nd ed. New York: John Wiley & Sons, 1984.

Epley, Donald R., and Joseph Rabianski. *Principles of Real Estate Decisions,* 3rd ed. Englewood Cliffs, NJ: Prentice-Hall, 1986.

Gross, Jerome S. *Webster's New World Illustrated Encyclopedic Dictionary of Real Estate,* 3rd ed. Englewood Cliffs, NJ: Prentice-Hall, 1987.

Kratovil, Robert, and Raymond J. Werner. *Real Estate Law,* 8th ed. Englewood Cliffs, NJ: Prentice-Hall, 1983.

Wurtzebach, Charles H., and Mike E. Miles. *Modern Real Estate,* 3rd ed. New York: John Wiley & Sons, 1987.

## Chapter 12

American Institute of Real Estate Appraisers. *The Appraisal of Real Estate,* 9th ed. Chicago: American Institute of Real Estate Appraisers, 1987.

Bloom, George F., Arthur M. Weimer, Jeffery D. Fisher. *Real Estate,* 8th ed. New York: John Wiley & Sons, 1982.

Bloom, George F., and Henry Harrison. *Appraising the Single Family Residence.* Chicago, IL: American Institute of Real Estate Appraisers, 1978.

Boyce, Byrl N. *Real Estate Appraisal Terminology,* 2nd ed. Cambridge, MA: Ballinger Publishing, 1981.

*Encyclopedia of Real Estate Appraising,* 3rd ed. Englewood Cliffs, NJ: Prentice-Hall, 1978.

Epley, Donald R., and Joseph Rabianski. *Principles of Real Estate Decisions,* 3rd ed. Englewood Cliffs, NJ: Prentice-Hall, 1986.

Gross, Jerome S. *Webster's New World Illustrated Encyclopedic Dictionary of Real Estate,* 3rd ed. Englewood Cliffs, NJ: Prentice-Hall, 1987.

National Association of REALTORS®. *A REALTORS® Guide to Residential Energy Efficiency,* Form No. 141-03. National Association of REALTORS®, 1980.

Ring, Alfred A. *Valuation of Real Estate,* 3rd ed. Englewood Cliffs, NJ: Prentice-Hall, 1986.

Ring, Alfred A., and Jerome Dasso. *Real Estate Principles and Practices,* 10th ed. Englewood Cliffs, NJ: Prentice-Hall, 1985.

Ventolo, William L., Jr., and Martha R. Williams. *Fundamentals of Real Estate Appraisal,* 4th ed. Chicago: Real Estate Education Company, 1987.

Wurtzebach, Charles E., and Mike E. Miles. *Modern Real Estate,* 3rd ed. New York: John Wiley & Sons, 1987.

## Chapter 13

Allen, Roger H. *Real Estate Investment and Taxation,* 2nd ed. Cincinnati, OH: South-Western, 1984.

Arnold, Alvin. *Real Estate Investment after the Tax Return Act of 1986,* 3rd ed. Boston: Warren, Gorham & Lamont, 1987.

Epley, Donald R., and Joseph Rabianski. *Principles of Real Estate Decisions,* 3rd ed. Englewood Cliffs, NJ: Prentice-Hall, 1986.

Gross, Jerome S. *Webster's New World Illustrated Encyclopedic Dictionary of Real Estate,* 3rd ed. Englewood Cliffs, NJ: Prentice-Hall, 1987.

Levine, Mark Lee. *Real Estate Transactions, Tax Planning,* 5th ed. St. Paul, MN: West Publishing, 1987.

Robinson, Gerald J. *Federal Income Taxation of Real Estate,* 4th ed. Boston: Warren, Gorham & Lamont, 1984.

## Chapter 14

Bloom, George F., Arthur M. Weimer, Jeffery D. Fisher. *Real Estate,* 8th ed. New York: John Wiley & Sons, 1982.

Epley, Donald R., and Joseph Rabianski. *Principles of Real Estate Decisions,* 3rd ed. Englewood Cliffs, NJ: Prentice-Hall, 1986.

French, William B. *Law of the Real Estate Business,* 5th ed. Homewood, IL: Richard D. Irwin, 1984.

Gross, Jerome S. *Webster's New World Illustrated Encyclopedic Dictionary of Real Estate,* 3rd ed. Englewood Cliffs, NJ: Prentice-Hall, 1987.

Henszey, Benjamin N., and Ronald M. Friedman. *Real Estate Law,* 2nd ed. New York: John Wiley & Sons, 1984.

Kratovil, Robert, and Raymond J. Werner. *Real Estate Law,* 8th ed. Englewood Cliffs, NJ: Prentice-Hall, 1983.

Wurtzebach, Charles H., and Mike E. Miles. *Modern Real Estate,* 3rd ed. New York: John Wiley & Sons, 1987.

## Chapter 15

Bloom, George F., Arthur M. Weimer, Jeffery D. Fisher. *Real Estate,* 8th ed. New York: John Wiley & Sons, 1982.

Epley, Donald R., and Joseph Rabianski. *Principles of Real Estate Decisions,* 3rd ed. Englewood Cliffs, NJ: Prentice-Hall, 1986.

French, William B. *Law of the Real Estate Business,* 5th ed. Homewood, IL: Richard D. Irwin, 1984.

Gross, Jerome S. *Webster's New World Illustrated Encyclopedic Dictionary of Real Estate,* 3rd ed. Englewood Cliffs, NJ: Prentice-Hall, 1987.

Kratovil, Robert, and Raymond J. Werner. *Real Estate Law,* 8th ed. Englewood Cliffs, NJ: Prentice-Hall, 1983.

Ring, Alfred A., and Jerome Dasso. *Real Estate Principles and Practices,* 10th ed. Englewood Cliffs, NJ: Prentice-Hall, 1985.

## Chapter 17

Bloom, George F., Arthur M. Weimer, Jeffery D. Fisher. *Real Estate,* 8th ed. New York: John Wiley & Sons, 1982.

Epley, Donald R., and Joseph Rabianski. *Principles of Real Estate Decisions,* 3rd ed. Englewood Cliffs, NJ: Prentice-Hall, 1986.

French, William B. *Law of the Real Estate Business,* 5th ed. Homewood, IL: Richard D. Irwin, 1984.

Gross, Jerome S. *Webster's New World Illustrated Encyclopedic Dictionary of Real Estate,* 3rd ed. Englewood Cliffs, NJ: Prentice-Hall, 1987.

Ring, Alfred A., and Jerome Dasso. *Real Estate Principles and Practices,* 10th ed. Englewood Cliffs, NJ: Prentice-Hall, 1985.

Wurtzebach, Charles H., and Mike E. Miles. *Modern Real Estate,* 3rd ed. New York: John Wiley & Sons, 1987.

# Glossary of Real Estate Terms

**Abandonment**   The voluntary surrender, relinquishment, disclaimer, or cession of property or rights.

**Abatement**   Termination; end.

**Abatement of nuisance**   Termination of a nuisance.

**Abrogate**   To repeal; to make void; to annul.

**Absolute fee simple**   Complete ownership and control without condition or limitation.

**Abstract of judgment**   A summation of the essentials of a court judgment.

**Abstract of title**   A summary of the conveyances, transfers, and other facts relied on as evidence of title, together with all such facts appearing on record which may impair the validity. It should contain a brief but complete history of the title.

**Accelerated depreciation**   A method of depreciation used in the computation of income taxes, which speeds up the write-off of the value of the property at a rate greater than normal depreciation. (See ACRS section in text.)

**Acceleration clause**   A clause giving the lender the right to call all sums owed him immediately due and payable upon the occurrence of a specified event, such as default, sale, etc.

**Acceptance**   Acceptance is determined by the seller's or his agent's agreement to the terms of the agreement of sale; approval of the negotiation on the part of the agent.

**Access right**   The right of an owner to have ingress and egress to and from his or her real property.

**Accessibility**   Ease or difficulty of approach to real property, either via public land or by private property maintained for public use.

**Accession**   In its legal meaning, generally used to signify the acquisition of property by incorporation or union with other property.

**Accretion**   The act of growing; usually applied to the gradual and imperceptible accumulation of land through natural causes, as out of the sea or a river.

**Accrued depreciation**   The difference between the cost of replacement at the date of the original appraisal and the present appraised value.

**Acknowledgment**   A formal declaration of one's signing of an instrument before a duly authorized public official.

**Acknowledgment of a deed**   A form of authenticating instruments conveying property or otherwise conferring rights. It is a public declaration by the grantor that the act evidenced by the instrument is his or her act or deed.

**Acquisition**   Making property one's own; obtaining the ownership of or an interest in property.

**Acre**   A unit of land measure equal to 43,560 square feet.

**Actual age**   The number of years a structure has actually existed.

**Ad valorem tax**   A tax according to a fixed percentage of value.

**Adjacent**   Usually used to designate property which is in the neighborhood of other property but which does not actually touch such property; sometimes used to mean touching or contiguous, e.g., immediately adjacent.

**Adjoining**   Touching or contiguous, as distinguished from lying near or adjacent.

**Adjudged incompetent**   A person who has been declared by the courts to be incapable of handling his or her own affairs.

**Adjusted basis**   *See* Basis, adjusted.

**Administration**   The management of a business, activity, or resource.

**Administration of real estate resources**   The efficient utilization of real estate resources to achieve desired results.

**Administrator**   A person to whom letters of administration, that is, authority to administer the estate of a deceased person who died intestate, have been granted by the proper court.

**Administrator's deed**   A deed used to convey the property of one who has died intestate (leaving no will).

**Advance**   In regard to a construction loan, a periodic transfer of funds from the lender to the borrower during the construction process.

**Advance fee**   A fee paid in advance of service rendered in the sale of property or in obtaining a loan.

**Advancement**   A gift from a parent to a child in anticipation of the share the child will eventually inherit from the parent's estate, which is intended to be deducted therefrom.

**Adverse possession**   The occupation of land under circumstances which indicate that such occupation started and has continued under an insistence of right on the part of the occupant.

**Advertising real estate**   The act of informing the public in order to produce action regarding real estate; public announcements to aid in the sale of real property.

**Affiant**   Any person who has made an affidavit.

**Affidavit**   A statement or declaration reduced to writing and sworn to or affirmed before a public official who has authority to administer an oath or affirmation.

**Affirm**   To confirm or verify.

**Affirmation**   The confirmation of a former judgment or court order; the confirmation by a principal of an agent's acts.

**Affirmative action program**   A detailed plan used to overcome the causes and effects of discriminatory policies in the hiring, employment and/or training of minority group members; the program also investigates complaints made to HUD concerning housing.

**Affirmative Marketing Agreement**   An agreement originated by the National Association of REALTORS® with its local boards regarding the manner in which property is marketed. It promotes the spirit and letter of the Federal Fair Housing Law through the cooperation of the government and the real estate profession.

**After-acquired property**   Property acquired after a particular date or event, e.g., the execution of a mortgage to property not yet owned.

**Agency**   The relationship between principal and agent, arising from a contract wherein the agent is employed by the principal to perform certain acts dealing with third parties.

**Agent**   One who represents another, who is known as the principal.

**Agreement**   A coming together of minds; in contract law, a meeting of the minds.

**Agreement of sale**   A written agreement whereby the purchaser agrees to buy specific real estate and the seller agrees to sell upon specific terms and conditions set forth in the contract.

**Air rights**   Rights in real property to use the space above the surface of the land.

Acknowledgment is made to *The Arnold Encyclopedia of Real Estate* by Alvin L. Arnold and Jack Kusnet published by Warren, Gorham & Lamont, 1978, for the use of some of the material contained in this glossary.

**AIREA**   *See* American Institute of Real Estate Appraisers.

**Alienation**   The voluntary act or acts by which one person transfers his or her own property to another. There can be involuntary alienation as in the event of unpaid taxes, bankruptcy, etc.

**Allodial land**   Land held in absolute independence, without being subject to any rent, service, or acknowledgment to a superior; opposed to "feud."

**Allodial system**   A system of free individual ownership of real property under which ownership may be complete except for government-held rights.

**Alluvion**   Soil deposited by natural accretion, i.e., an increase of earth on a shore or river bank.

**Amenities, amenity return**   Satisfactions received through using rights in real property and not in monetary form.

**American Bankers' Association (ABA)**   A trade association of commercial bankers.

**American Institute of Real Estate Appraisers (AIREA)**   A trade association of real estate appraisers, which conducts educational programs, publishes materials, and promotes research on real estate appraisal. Confers MAI (Member, Appraisal Institute) and RM (Residential Member).

**American Society of Appraisers (ASA)**   The national professional and trade association for appraisers and their firms.

**American Society of Real Estate Counselors (ASREC)**   A national professional and trade association of developers, consultants, and experienced advisors on all real estate matters. Confers CRE (Counselor on Real Estate).

**Amortization**   The process of paying an obligation through a series of payments over time. Generally the payments are made in equal amounts, including principal and interest, and at uniform time intervals.

**Amortized mortgage**   A mortgage in which repayment is made according to a plan requiring the payment of certain amounts at specified times so that all the debt is repaid at the end of the term.

**Annuity**   An amount of money or its equivalent which represents one of a series of periodic payments.

**Apex**   The highest point or peak on a triangle from which the altitude is measured from the base.

**Apportionment**   The division of rights or liabilities among several persons entitled to them or liable for them in accordance with their respective interests.

**Appraisal**   An opinion or estimate of value of property. Also refers to the report setting forth the estimate and conclusion of value.

**Appraisal inventory**   A compilation of all separate items comprising property included in an appraisal report and valued by the appraiser.

**Appraisal report**   A report of the appraised value, together with pertinent information concerning the property appraised and the evidence and analysis leading to the reported value estimate.

**Appraiser**   One who is in the business of making appraisals on the basis of a fee or salary in conjunction with some compensated employment.

**Appreciation**   An increased value in property.

**Appurtenance**   Property that is an accessory to other property to which it is annexed.

**Area**   A two-dimensional measure of surface.

**Arterial highway**   A major route into a prime traffic area.

**Artisan's lien**   A lien given under common law to one skilled in some kind of mechanical craft or art for the reasonable charges for his or her work.

**ASREC**   *See* American Society of Real Estate Counselors.

**Assemblage**   The act of bringing together two individuals or things to form a new whole; specifically, the cost of assembling parcels of land under a single ownership. *See* plottage.

**Assessed valuation**   The process by which a value is placed upon property by a public official or officials as a basis for taxation.

**Assessed value**   The value placed on property for the purpose of taxation.

**Assessment**   A levy or tax imposed on real estate for improvements or taxes.

**Assessor**   An official whose responsibility is to determine assessed values for taxation.

**Assets**   Property of any kind under ownership.

**Assignee**   A person to whom an assignment is made; a successor in interest to the rights of a party to a contract.

**Assignment**   A transfer or setting over of property, or some right of interest therein, from one person to another.

**Assignor**   A person who makes an assignment of interest in a contract.

**Assumption agreement**   The undertaking of a debt or obligation of another by contract.

**Assumption of a mortgage**   The undertaking of a mortgage, by the buyer, which is currently held against the real estate the buyer is purchasing.

**Attachment**   Taking property into the legal custody of an officer by virtue of the directions contained in a writ of attachment; a seizure under a writ of a debtor's property.

**Attachment of property**   A writ issued in the course of a lawsuit, directing the sheriff or law officer to attach the property of the defendant to satisfy the demands of the plaintiff.

**Attest**   To affirm a statement or document to be genuine or accurate.

**Attestation**   The act of witnessing the execution of a paper and subscribing the name of the witness in testimony of such fact.

**Attorney-in-fact**   One who is authorized to perform certain acts for another under a power of attorney.

**Auction**   A public sale of property to the highest bidder.

**Authentication**   Such official attestation of a written instrument as will render it legally admissible as evidence in a law court.

**Avulsion**   The removal of land from one owner to another when a stream, etc., suddenly changes its course.

**Axial growth**   City growth which moves out along main transportation routes, taking the form of fingerlike extensions.

**Backfill**   The replacement of excavated earth against a structure or to fill a hole.

**Balloon mortgage payment**   A large payment during the term of a mortgage, often at the end.

**Balustrade**   A supporting column for a handrail.

**Bargain and sale deed**   A deed which conveys the land described but does so without any warranties.

**Barter**   The exchange of goods or commodities for other goods or commodities.

**Base**   The side or plane upon which the figure is resting, as in the base line of a triangle.

**Base and meridian**   Imaginary lines used by surveyors as a reference to find and describe land location. (Base lines run east and west, meridian lines run north and south.)

**Base line**   A part of the rectangular survey system; a parallel which serves as a reference for other parallels.

**Base molding** Molding used at the top of a baseboard.

**Base shoe** Molding used at the junction of a baseboard and the floor; more commonly known as a carpet strip.

**Baseboard heating** A system of heating in which the radiators or convectors are located in or on the wall, replacing the baseboard itself.

**Basic employment, urban growth employment** Employment in establishments that receive their income from outside the community.

**Basic income** Income received from outside the community.

**Basis, adjusted** The financial interest which the Internal Revenue Service attributes to the owner of an asset for the purpose of determining annual depreciation and/or gain or loss on the sale of an asset; usually the cost of the property plus value of capital improvements less depreciation.

**Batten** Narrow strips of wood or metal used to cover joints; may be used for a decorative effect.

**Beam** A horizontal load-supporting member.

**Bedroom community** A suburban community in which a large number of a major city's workers reside.

**Beltline highway** A limited-access highway which surrounds a city.

**Bench mark** Permanent markers placed by surveyors at important points, upon which local surveys are based.

**Beneficiary** A person having the enjoyment of property of which a trustee, executor, etc., has the legal possession; the person to whom a policy of insurance is payable.

**Benefit-cost ratio** A measure of social benefits to dollar cost.

**Bequeath** Commonly used to denote a testamentary gift; synonymous with "to devise."

**Bequest** That which is given according to the terms of a will.

**Betterment** A property improvement which increases the property value.

**Bilateral contract** A contract under which two parties exchange promises for the performance of certain acts; for example, Mr. A promises to buy Mr. B's house, and Mr. B promises to sell it to Mr. A.

**Bill of sale** A written instrument which evidences the transfer of title to personal property from seller to buyer.

**Binder** A preliminary agreement in writing as evidence of good faith by the offerer; the memorandum of an agreement for insurance, intended to give temporary protection pending investigation of the risk and issuance of a formal policy. *See* title insurance.

**Blacktop** Asphalt paving.

**Blanket mortgage** A mortgage that has two or more properties pledged or conveyed as security for a debt.

**Blight** Decay, as in the case of a neighborhood.

**Blockbusting** The illegal practice of introducing a nonconforming user or use into a neighborhood for the purpose of causing an abnormally high turnover of property ownership in the area.

**Board foot** A unit of measurement for lumber; 144 cubic inches; 1 foot wide, 1 foot long, 1 inch thick.

**Bona fide** Good faith.

**Bona fide purchaser** A purchaser who, for a valuable consideration paid in the belief that the vendor had a right to sell, purchases a particular property.

**Bond** An instrument used as evidence of a debt; also a guarantee of performance.

**Borough** A land division of a city having its own charter.

**Bracing** Lumber nailed at an angle in order to provide rigidity.

**Breach** The breaking or violation of a law, right, or duty, either by commission or omission; failure to meet a contractual obligation.

**Breakeven point** The amount of income needed to just meet the total amount of expenses for a project.

**Breezeway** A covered passage, open on two sides, connecting a house with a garage or other parts of the house.

**Bridging** Small wood or metal pieces used to brace floor joists.

**Broker** An agent who negotiates for the sale, leasing, management, or financing of a property or of property rights on a commission basis.

**Brokerage** The business of a broker; the selling of products or assets of others.

**BTU** British thermal unit; the amount of heat required to raise the temperature of 1 pound of water 1°F.

**Budget mortgage** A type of amortizing mortgage which includes in the monthly payments of principal and interest other costs such as taxes and fire insurance; referred to as a PITI monthly payment.

**Builder** One who improves land by erecting structures.

**Building codes** Government regulations specifying minimum construction standards.

**Building line** A setback line; a line set by law or a deed restriction; a certain distance from a street in front of which an owner cannot build.

**Building paper** A heavy, waterproof paper used as sheathing in wall or roof construction.

**Building permit** Authorization by a local government for the erection, alteration, or remodeling of improvements within its jurisdiction.

**Building restrictions** Limitations on the use of property established by legislation or by covenants or limitations in deeds.

**Built-in** Such features built as part of the house, e.g., cabinets, etc.

**Bulk sales** A sale whereby the entire stock of a business is sold.

**Bundle of rights theory** The definition of ownership based on the concept of combining all possible interests in land into a whole.

**Business-government relations** The framework of laws, codes, regulations, and contracts between business and government within which business operates.

**Buy-down mortgage** A loan on which the interest rate has been reduced for a period of time due to the lender's having received an initial payment from a seller to reduce the rate. In effect, a discount.

**Buyer's market** A market characterized by many available properties and few potential users demanding them at prevailing prices.

**Buying, assuming, and agreeing to pay** Undertaking and promising to pay the seller's personal liability for a debt at the time of purchase.

**Buying subject to** Phrase meaning no personal liability is assumed in regard to a mortgage debt which exists against real estate at the time of purchase.

**By-laws** In reference to condominiums, the day-to-day rules and regulations for operation of the project. They usually appear as an appendix to the master deed and are recorded. Generally, self-imposed rules adopted by a corporation or other group.

**California ranch house** A one-story house having a style similar to that of a ranch.

**Cape Cod architecture** A style featuring a steeply sloped gable roof, dormer windows for second-story rooms, windows with shutters, a square chimney, and usually having Early American decor.

**Capital appreciation** The appreciation accruing to the benefit of the capital improvement to real estate.

**Capital asset** Any asset of a permanent nature used for the production of income (land, buildings, machinery, equipment, etc.).

**Capital gain** Income that results from the sale of an asset and not from the usual course of business. (Capital gains are taxed at a lower rate than ordinary income.)

**Capital improvement** Any structure erected as a permanent improvement to real estate, usually extending the useful life and value of a property. The replacement of a roof would be considered a capital improvement.

**Capital loss** A tax-deductible loss on real property that has been held for more than six months.

**Capital recapture** The manner in which the investment in a property is to be returned to investors; normally stated as a rate or dollar amount per unit of time.

**Capitalism** An economic system based on the principles of ownership of private property, equality, and personal rights.

**Capitalization** The process of reflecting future income in present value; capitalization in perpetuity is capitalization without a time limit.

**Capitalization rate** A percentage made up of the interest rate (return on the investment) plus the recapture rate (return of the original investment).

**Carrying charges** Charges for holding property, such as tax expense on idle property or property under construction.

**Casement windows** Windows with frames of wood or metal which swing outward.

**Cash flow** The net income from a property before depreciation and other noncash expenses.

**Caveat emptor** Let the buyer beware. The maxim expresses the general idea that the buyer purchases at his or her peril, and that no warranties, either express or implied, are made by the seller.

**CCIM** Certified Commercial and Investment Member. A designation conferred by RNMI.

**Central business district** The downtown shopping and office area of a city.

**Central city** The downtown area of a city; also, a city that is the center of a geographic trade area for which it performs certain market and service functions.

**Certificate of no defense** An instrument executed by the mortgagor, upon the sale of the mortgage, to the assignee as to the validity of the full mortgage debt. See estoppel certificate.

**Certificate of sale** A document issued to the highest bidder at a foreclosure sale to indicate ownership.

**Certificate of title** A certificate issued by a person who has examined the record of title of real estate as to the state of the title of such real estate.

**Certificates of beneficial interest** The ownership shares in a trust or mutual fund.

**Certified residential broker (CRB)** Designation granted by RNMI.

**Certiorari** An appellate proceeding for reexamination of the action of an inferior tribunal, or an auxiliary process to enable the appellate court to obtain further information in a pending cause.

**Cestui que use** One who has the right to receive the profits and benefits of the lands or tenements, the legal title and possession of which are held by another person as trustee.

**Chain measures** A series of 100 interconnected wire links each of which is 1 foot in length. A chain 66 feet in length, composed of interconnected wire links each of which is 7.92 inches long (10 square chains of land equal 1 acre.)

**Chain of title** Successive conveyances, or other forms of alienation, affecting a particular parcel of land, arranged consecutively, from the government or original source of title down to the present holder.

**Chancellor** The name given in some states to the judge of a court of chancery (equity).

**Chancery** A court of equity; the system of jurisdiction administered in courts of equity.

**Change** The appraisal principle which describes existence in three states: integration, equilibrium, and degeneration; holds that it is the future not the past which is of prime importance in estimating value.

**Chattel mortgage** A mortgage of personal property to secure a debt. See security interest.

**Chattel personal** An object of movable personal property.

**Chattel real** An item usually considered personal property which is annexed to or attached to real estate.

**Chattels** Items of personal property.

**Chose in action** A right of action for recovery of a debt.

**Circuit breaker** The electrical instrument which automatically breaks an electric circuit when an overload occurs.

**Circulating fireplace** A type of fireplace which is built around a metal form, containing air ducts to distribute heat by convection.

**Circumference** The distance around the exterior boundary of a circle.

**Civil action** Any lawsuit between private parties.

**Clapboard** The boards used for siding, which are usually thicker at one edge.

**Clear title** A title free of any encumbrances or defects.

**Close** A parcel of land, enclosed by a fence, hedge, or visual enclosure; in surveying it has several meanings and could easily be confused with "closing." Close also refers to completing a transaction; when real estate formally changes ownership.

**Closing** The transaction at which the title to real estate is transferred pursuant to a contract of sale.

**Closing costs** The costs of the settlement in the transfer of property ownership, such as recording fees, attorney fees, title insurance premium, etc.

**Closing statement** A listing of the debits and credits of the buyer and seller in a real estate transaction for the final financial settlement of the transaction.

**Cloud on the title** An outstanding claim or condition which affects the title to property and which cannot be removed without a quitclaim deed or court action.

**Cluster housing** A housing arrangement in which units are placed close together to allow for large recreational or common areas.

**Code of ethics** The standards adopted by NAR and the various real estate boards for the business conduct of members.

**Codicil** Some addition to or amendment of one's last will and testament.

**Cognovit clause** The borrower confesses judgment or gives written authority to the lender to secure a judgment that can be attached to the borrower's property as a lien; a waiver of any defense to the claim.

**Cognovit note** A note which authorizes a confession of judgment and admission of the validity of a claim for money.

**Collar beam** The beam that joins together the pairs of opposite roof rafters above the attic floor.

**Collateral** Anything of value that a borrower pledges as security.

**Collateral security** An additional obligation to guarantee performance of a contract.

**Collusion** A secret combination, conspiracy, or concert of action between two or more persons for fraudulent or deceitful purposes.

**Colonial architecture** The traditional design, usually using the characteristics of New England homes; usually two-story houses with balanced openings along the main facade, windows constructed with small panes, shutters and dormer windows on the third floor, with attention to small detail.

**Color of title** A writing upon the face of a document professing to pass title but which does not, either through want of title in the grantor or a defective mode of conveyance; that which appears to be good title, but as a matter of fact, is not good title.

**Combed plywood** A grooved building plywood used mainly for interior finish.

**Combination door** A permanent door that employs a screen panel for summer and glass panel for winter.

**Commercial acre** The remnant of an acre of newly subdivided land after the land devoted to streets, sidewalks, etc., has been deducted.

**Commercial banks** National or state-chartered banks which operate on a basis of stock ownership. The dividends are distributed to the shareholders. The depositors have no share in the management.

**Commercial paper** Bills of exchange or other debt instruments used in place of money.

**Commercial properties** Properties intended for use in business areas.

**Commingle** To mix, as to deposit a client's funds in the broker's personal account.

**Commission** An agent's compensation for the performance of his duties; in real estate, a percentage of the selling price of property or percentage of rentals.

**Commitment** For a mortgage, a statement by the lender of the conditions and terms under which he or she will lend. A conditional commitment is a statement that mortgage funds will be provided if certain conditions are met which permit an owner or developer to begin construction. A firm commitment is a written notification that a financial institution will lend money and on what terms it will do so.

**Common law** Rules developed by usage; judge-made law.

**Common property** Land considered to be public property; also, a legal term denoting an incorporeal hereditament consisting of a right of one person in the land of another.

**Common wall** The wall which serves two dwellings simultaneously.

**Community Association Institute (CAI)** A national association of homeowners' associations.

**Community property** In certain states, the property owned by the "community" or marriage of husband and wife; property owned by the marriage and not in shares.

**Compaction** The act of compressing soil added as fill to a lot so that it will bear the weight of buildings without the danger of their settling, tilting, or cracking.

**Comparables** Properties of like nature which might be compared to one another through careful study, thereby allowing a value to be determined for one of them.

**Competence** Under the law of evidence, being of such form as to be admissible in court for use as evidence.

**Competent** Legally qualified and mentally capable to transact business.

**Complainant** The party who instigates a legal action.

**Compound interest** The interest paid on the original principal and on the accrued interest from the time it became due.

**Concentric circle hypothesis** Transportation is assumed to be the central force in community growth. Therefore the land values are highest where mobility is greatest.

**Concentric circles** Rings around the nucleus, such as rings of neighborhoods or business properties around the center of a city.

**Conclusive evidence** Incontrovertible evidence.

**Condemnation** The process by which property of a private owner is taken for public use without the owner's consent but with the owner's awareness and with payment of just compensation.

**Condition** A future and uncertain event upon the happening of which is made to depend the existence of an obligation, or that which subordinates the existence of liability under a contract to a certain future event.

**Conditional fee** *See* Fee simple conditional.

**Conditional sale** A term most frequently applied to a sale wherein the seller reserves the title to the goods, though the possession is delivered to the buyer, until the purchase price is paid in full.

**Conditional sales contract** A contract for the sale of property specifying that delivery is to be made to the buyer with the title to remain vested in the seller until the conditions of the contract have been fulfilled.

**Conditional vendee** The buyer under a conditional sales contract.

**Conditional vendor** The seller under a conditional sales contract.

**Condominium** The individual ownership of a single unit in a multiunit structure, together with an interest in the common land areas and the underlying ground.

**Condominium conversion** A process by which rental units are turned into individually owned units.

**Conduit** A metal pipe through which electrical wiring is installed.

**Confession of judgment** An entry of judgment upon the debtor's voluntary admission without defense in a legal proceeding. *See* cognovit note.

**Confirmation** The ratification of a transaction known to be voidable.

**Confirmation of sale** A court approval of the sale of property by an executor, administrator, guardian, or conservator of an estate.

**Confiscation** The seizure of property without compensation.

**Conformity** The blending of the use of real estate and improvements upon it with the surroundings so as to appear harmonious.

**Consequential damage** The impairment of value which arises as an indirect result of an act.

**Conservation** The process of saving resources or of using them in such a way that they will not be depleted.

**Consideration** Anything of value given or given up by both parties to a contract and necessary to the enforcement of the contract.

**Constant** The percentage of the unpaid balance of a loan which is represented by the sum of the principal and interest payments for the following year, which is needed to fully amortize the loan.

**Constant payment** A regular, periodic payment which does not fluctuate in amount and which includes both interest and amortization.

**Constant payment mortgage** A loan reduction plan whereby the borrower pays a fixed amount each month, part to be applied to repayment of the principal and the remainder to payment of interest.

**Construction loan (or mortgage)** A form of interim financing in which a lender pays out installments of a loan during the stages of construction; usually three payments are made.

**Constructive eviction** Inability of a tenant to retain possession by reason of a condition making occupancy hazardous or unfit for its intended use.

**Constructive notice** Notice rendered by the public records.

**Constructive trustee** One who is a trustee by operation of law resulting from unlawful possession of property of another.

**Consultant** An advisor on matters who receives a fee for his or her services and advice.

**Consumer goods** Goods used or purchased primarily for personal, family, or household purposes.

**Contemporary architecture** Modern design, as differentiated from the traditional functional design.

**Contiguous** Adjacent; touching or adjoining.

**Contingencies**   Possible future events which are uncertain.

**Contingent fees**   Payment to be made upon future occurrences, conclusions, or results of services to be performed.

**Contract**   A written or oral agreement to perform or not to perform certain obligations.

**Contract for deed**   *See* Conditional sales contract.

**Contract rent**   Rent stipulated in a lease agreement.

**Contractor**   One who has the responsibility for and supervises the improvement of land.

**Contribution**   A payment by each, or by any, of several having a common interest or liability of his or her share in the loss suffered, or in the money necessarily paid by one of the parties in behalf of the others; holds that maximum real property values are achieved when the improvements on the site produce the highest return commensurate with the investment.

**Control data**   The means of using the transactions of real properties to adjust the market data utilized in the comparative approach to valuation. Such control data is necessary in order to segregate certain influences which have caused changes in real estate values, either generally or specifically.

**Convenience factor**   The commonly recognized and easily understood quality offering advantages and values to a particular parcel of real property over that of other properties.

**Conventional home**   A home that is constructed totally at the site. It is the opposite of a factory-built or mobile home.

**Conventional loan**   A mortgage loan made by a financial institution, conforming to its own standards, modified within legal bounds by mutual consent of the parties involved, and without insurance or guarantee by the FHA or VA.

**Conventional mortgage**   A mortgage that is not insured by a public agency.

**Conversion**   A change in the use of real estate by altering improvements but without destroying them; legally, the unlawful taking of possession of the property of another.

**Conversion value**   Value created by converting from one state or use to another.

**Conveyance**   In its common use, refers to a written instrument transferring the title to land or some interest therein from one person to another. Transfer of title or ownership to real estate from one party to another.

**Cooperative**   Ownership form in which a single property is subdivided into several use portions, with each user owning stock in the corporation that owns the property and occupying a portion of it.

**Cooperative apartment**   An apartment complex owned by a corporation or a trust, in which each owner purchases stock to the value of his or her apartment and is given a proprietary lease.

**Cooperative ownership**   Usually a form of apartment ownership in which an occupant acquires ownership by purchasing shares in a corporation. The cooperative property is owned in severalty. The cooperative plan is permitted to place extensive restraints on the alienation of the units as well as their use and improvements.

**Co-ownership**   Ownership of the same property by two or more persons.

**Corner influences**   The effect of street intersections upon the adjoining property.

**Corner influence table**   A statistical table which attempts to reflect the additional value accorded a lot with a corner location.

**Corporation**   A group of different persons or parties established and treated by law as an individual or unit with rights and liabilities, or both, distinct from those of the persons composing it. A corporation is a creature of law with certain powers and duties of a natural per-

son. Created by law, it may continue for any length of time the law prescribes.

**Corporeal rights**   Possessory rights in real property.

**Correction deed**   A written instrument which corrects an error in a recorded deed.

**Correction line**   The line every 24 miles that runs due north and south from the base line in order to compensate for the narrowing of the earth in the rectangular method of survey.

**Cost**   That which must be given up to obtain property. The replacement cost is the cost of replacing real estate improvements with an alternative of like utility. Reproduction cost is the cost of replacing real estate improvements with an exact replica.

**Cost approach to value**   Valuation reached by estimating the cost of providing a substitute for that which is being valued. Depreciation must be deducted in making the valuation.

**Cost of capital**   The amount that must be paid to attract money into an investment project.

**Cost of reproduction**   The normal cost of duplication of a property.

**Counselor**   One who assists clients with advice regarding use and management of assets.

**Counterflashing**   Flashing used on chimneys at the roof line to cover the shingle flashing and to prevent moisture from entering.

**Counteroffer**   A response to an offer to enter into a contract which introduces new or different terms and conditions; acts as a rejection of the original offer.

**County**   A civil division of a territory organized for political and judicial purposes.

**Covenant**   Used in contracts as synonymous with promise; in deeds, it may be a positive or negative undertaking by one or both parties.

**Covenant for further assurance**   An undertaking, in the form of a covenant, on the part of the vendor of real estate to perform such further acts for the purpose of perfecting the purchaser's title as the latter may reasonably require.

**CPM**   Certified property manager; a member of IREM of NAR.

**CRB (certified residential broker)**   A designation conferred by RNMI.

**CRE (counselor on real estate)**   A designation conferred by ASREC.

**Credit**   The power of an individual to secure money, or obtain goods on time, in consequence of the favorable opinion held by the community, or by the particular lender, as to his or her solvency and reliability; a debt considered from the creditor's standpoint, or that which is to be incoming or due to one.

**Credits against tax**   (*See* Tax credit) A direct reduction of the amount of tax penalty owed.

**Crossroad development**   Pattern of city growth characterized by fingerlike extensions moving out along the main transportation routes.

**Cubical content**   The actual space within the outer surfaces of outside walls and contained between the outer surfaces of the roof and the finished surface of the lowest basement or cellar floor; the actual space that lies within the interior dimensions of a structure.

**Cube root**   The root to the third power of a given number. Example: 2 to the third power is 8 ($2 \times 2 \times 2 = 8$); the cube root of 8 is 2.

**Cul-de-sac**   A dead-end street with a widened, circular area at the end to enable a car to make a U-turn.

**Curable depreciation**   Any deficiency that can be cured.

**Curable penalty**   Element of depreciation whose cost of repair or correction is offset by the increase in value of the property caused by the repair or correction. Incurable penalty occurs when the cost of repair adds less than its cost to the property's value.

**Current assets**   Liquid assets such as cash, accounts receivable, and merchandise inventories.

**Current liabilities**   Short-term debts, generally debts due within a year's time.

**Curtesy**   The right a husband has in a wife's real estate at her death.

**Custodian**   One who is responsible for the care of something entrusted to him or her; e.g., a custodian of a public building.

**Custom-built house**   A house sold before construction begins and built to the owner's specifications.

**Cyclical fluctuation**   Variations around a trend in activity that recur from time to time; fluctuations remaining after removal of trend and seasonal factors that recur regularly.

**Damages**   Indemnity to the person who suffers a loss or harm from an injury; a sum recoverable as amends from a wrong; an adequate compensation for the loss suffered or the injury sustained.

**Data assembly**   Gathering, analyzing, and classifying data pertaining to a subject property.

**Data plant**   A collection of information about real properties maintained usually by an appraiser, mortgage lender, and the like.

**Datum**   The horizontal plane from which heights and depths are measured.

**De facto**   In fact or in reality.

**Dealer-builder**   A builder who constructs structures from prefabricated components, usually as the local representative of a prefabricated house manufacturer.

**Debit**   The amount charged as due or owing.

**Debt**   Something which must be repaid or a duty owed, such as a loan.

**Debt capital**   Money borrowed for a particular business purpose.

**Debt service**   Annual amount to be paid by a debtor to retire an obligation to repay borrowed money.

**Debt service coverage**   The requirement that earnings be a percentage or dollar sum higher than debt service.

**Debtor**   The party who owes money to another.

**Decedent**   A deceased person.

**Decentralization**   Dispersion from a center point or figure.

**Deciduous trees**   Trees which do not keep their leaves through the autumn and winter.

**Declining balance depreciation**   A method of depreciating real property for income tax purposes. It involves an accelerated accumulation of depreciation of assets.

**Decree**   The final determination of the rights of the parties to a suit.

**Decree of foreclosure.**   The decree by a court for the sale of property to pay an obligation found to be due and owing.

**Dedication**   An offer of land to some public use, made by an owner and accepted for such use by or on behalf of the public.

**Deductions against income**   Items of expense that can be deducted from income to derive a "net" basis for tax purposes.

**Deed**   An instrument conveying title to real property.

**Deed covenants**   The warranties made by a seller of property to protect the buyer against items such as liens, encumbrances, or title defects.

**Deed money escrow**   An agreement where money is retained by a third party to be delivered to a seller of real estate upon the receipt of the deed to the property sold.

**Deed restrictions**   Limitations placed upon the use of real property in the deed to that property.

**Deed of trust**   An instrument in use in many states, taking the place and serving the uses of a common-law mortgage, by which the legal title to real property is placed in one or more trustees to secure the repayment of a sum of money or the performance of other conditions.

**Default**   Failure to fulfill a duty or to discharge an obligation.

**Defeasance clause**   The clause in a mortgage that permits the mortgagor to redeem his or her property upon the payment of the obligations to the mortgagee.

**Defective title**   A title which would be impaired were an outstanding claim proved to be valid.

**Defects in title**   Imperfections that cast a reasonable doubt on the marketability of title.

**Defendant**   A party sued in a legal action.

**Deferred maintenance**   An existing but unfulfilled need for repairs and rehabilitation.

**Deferred payments**   Money payments which are to be made at some date in the future.

**Deficiency judgment**   A judgment for that part of a secured debt that was not liquidated by the proceeds from the sale of foreclosed real property.

**Delegation of authority**   A transfer of authority by one person to another.

**Delinquency**   A financial obligation which is in default, such as an overdue loan.

**Delivery**   The transfer from one person to another of an item, or a right or interest therein, which means more than physical transfer of possession. However, in the popular sense, in the case of a contract or lease or the like, it implies a transfer of the actual contract or document to the possession of the other party.

**Demand**   The amount of a good or service which will be bought at various prices (and under varying conditions).

**Demand note**   A note which is payable on demand of the holder.

**Demise**   The transfer of interest or conveyance of an estate primarily by lease.

**Demographic**   Pertaining to population structure.

**Demographic characteristics**   Political, social, and economic characteristics of a population of people.

**Density**   The number of units present per unit of area such as dwellings per acre or persons per square mile.

**Deposit, earnest money**   A sum of money or other consideration tendered in conjunction with an offer to purchase rights in real property as evidence of good faith.

**Depositary**   The party receiving a deposit. The obligation on the part of the depositary to keep the item with reasonable care and, upon request, restore it to the depositor, or otherwise deliver it, according to the original agreement.

**Depreciation**   Loss in property value. Accelerated depreciation is a method of reflecting depreciation that enables the owner of an asset to take more of the depreciation during the early years of the asset's life. Contingent depreciation is a loss in property value because of expectations of a decline in property services. Depletion is the exhaustion of a resource such as the removal of a mineral deposit. Economic obsolescence is a loss in property value from events outside the property that unfavorably affect income or income potential. Functional obsolescence is a loss in property value because of a loss in the ability of the physical property to provide services as compared with alternatives. Physical depreciation is a loss in property value due to wearing away or deterioration.

**Depreciation, accrued**   The actual amount of depreciation existing in a property at a given date.

**Depreciation allowance**   The amounts to be claimed or allowed for depreciation.

**Depreciation base**   Cost of an asset that is to be depreciated.

**Depreciation methods**   The methods used to measure decreases in the value of an improvement through depreciation. In appraising, the methods generally used are annuity, sinking fund, and straight-line. In accounting, it relates to various methods by which capital impairment is computed. In addition to the three methods used in appraising, accountants also use declining balance (and variations thereof), weighted rate, and accelerated.

**Depreciation rate**   The periodic amount or percentage at which the usefulness of a property is used up, especially the percentage at which amounts are computed to be set aside as an accrual for future depreciation.

**Depreciation, straight line**   An accounting term showing the reduction of the cost or other basis of property, less estimated salvage value, in equal amounts over the estimated useful life of the property.

**Depreciation, sum-of-the-years' digits**   Annual depreciation computed by applying changing fractions to the cost or other basis of property reduced by estimated salvage. The numerators of the fraction change each year to the estimated remaining useful life of the asset, and the constant denominator is the sum of all the years' digits corresponding to the estimated useful life of the asset. For example, the fraction for the first year's depreciation on a 5-year asset is 5/15. The 5 is the estimated useful life remaining, and 15 is computed by adding together each year's remaining useful life, i.e., $5 + 4 + 3 + 2 + 1 = 15$.

**Depth table**   A technique for real estate appraisal using statistical tables based on the theory that added depth increases the value of land.

**Descent**   The process by which the property of a decedent passes to his or her legal heirs.

**Description**   In real estate, the part of the deed, mortgage, deed of trust, etc., used to locate the boundaries of real property.

**Desist and refrain order**   An order issued by a real estate commissioner to stop an action in violation of the real estate law.

**Deterioration**   A worsening of the condition of a property.

**Determinable fee**   An estate which may last forever is a "fee," but if it may end on the happening of a merely possible event, it is a "determinable," or "qualified fee."

**Developer**   One who prepares land for income production, the making of improvements, and the sale of completed properties.

**Devise**   A testamentary disposition of land or realty. Leaving real property through a will.

**Devisee**   The person to whom lands or other real property are devised or given by will.

**Diameter**   A straight line passing through the center of a circle or a sphere, from one side to the other.

**Direct reduction mortgage**   A mortgage which is to be repaid by periodic fixed amounts plus interest on the unpaid balance.

**Directional growth**   The direction in which the residential sections of a city are destined to expand.

**Disability**   The lack of legal capacity to perform an act.

**Disaffirm**   To repudiate; to revoke a consent once given; to disclaim the intention of being bound by an antecedent transaction.

**Discharge**   The release or performance of a contract or other obligation.

**Discount points**   A fee, usually paid by the borrower, which increases the yield on a loan above the contract rate to the market rate. Usually expressed as 1 point equals 1 percent of original principal.

**Discount rate**   The correlation between dollars transmitted from a lender to a borrower and dollars that must be repaid by the borrower. If a lender advances $960 and the borrower must repay $1,000, the discount rate is

$$\frac{\$40}{\$1,000} = 4\%$$

**Discounting**   A means of converting any cash flow into present value at a selected rate of return; based upon the premise that one would pay less than $1 today for the right to receive $1 at a future date.

**Discretion**   Power or privilege of a fiduciary to act unhampered by legal restrictions or limitations on his normal authority.

**Disintermediation**   An outflow of funds from savings institutions by investors to reinvest their monies elsewhere where the rates of return are expected to be higher.

**Disposable income**   The income left to a household after taxes.

**Disposable field**   A drainage area, not close to the water supply, where refuse from the septic tank is dispersed, being drained into the ground through tile and gravel filtration.

**Dispossess**   To put one out of possession of real estate.

**Distress**   The act of distraining; assuming possession of a tenant's chattels by a landlord in order to satisfy, in whole or in part, a claim for rent in arrears. Another common word for this is "distrain."

**Distributee**   One who receives part of the property of a person who dies intestate.

**Distribution**   The division and transfer of the property of a decedent.

**District**   A city area with a land use different from that of adjacent areas, e.g., commercial, industrial, or residential.

**Documentary evidence**   Evidence supplied by written instruments such as contracts, deeds, etc.

**Documentary stamp**   The revenue stamp issued for payment of a tax on documents such as deeds.

**Documents**   Written records; in real estate, contracts, deeds, leases, mortgages, etc.

**Domicile**   A place where a person lives or has his home; in a strict legal sense, the place where he has his true, fixed, permanent home and principal establishment, and to which place he has, whenever he is absent, the intention of returning.

**Dominant tenement or estate**   That to which a servitude or easement is due, or for the benefit of which it exists. For example, land which includes the right to the use of a right of way over other land.

**Donee**   A person who receives a gift.

**Donor**   The one who makes a gift to another.

**Double, duplex**   Two dwelling units under one roof. A double usually denotes two dwellings side by side, and a duplex, one dwelling above the other.

**Doubling up**   The occupation of a dwelling unit by two or more families.

**Dower**   The legal rights a widow possesses to her deceased husband's real estate.

**Down payment**   Initial partial payment of the total selling price.

**Downzoning**   A public action by which the local government reduces the allowable density for subsequent development (e.g., fewer housing units, fewer stores, etc.) or allowable use from a high to low use (e.g., multifamily to single-family).

**Drainage**   The running off of water from the surface of land.

**Duress**   Unlawful pressure placed upon a person to coerce him to perform some act against his will.

**Dutch Colonial**   The style of architecture that features a gambrel roof, exterior walls of masonry or wood, and porches at the side; especially adapted to flat sites and difficult to fit into a steep slope.

**Earnest money**   Money paid to evidence good faith when an offer of purchase is submitted to a property owner by a prospective purchaser.

**Easement**   The right which ownership of one parcel of land has to use or control the use of another parcel of land owned by another; such rights and obligations run with the land itself and are not mere personal rights of an individual.

**Easement appurtenant**   An easement which runs with the land and is transferred to another in the conveyance of the title.

**Easement in gross**   An easement which does not run with the land and therefore is not transferred through the conveyance of the title.

**"Easy" money**   A financial situation that occurs when lenders have an abundance of funds available for lending. The terms of the loans are favorable to borrowers.

**Eaves**   The lower part of a roof that protrudes over the wall.

**Economic base**   The major economic support of a community.

**Economic base analysis**   A technique for analyzing the major economic supports of a community; analysis as a means of predicting population, income, or other variables having an effect on real estate value or land utilization.

**Economic goods**   Goods that have scarcity and utility; goods that provide desired services but are not in sufficient abundance to be free.

**Economic life**   The period over which a property will yield the investor a return on the investment, over and above the economic or ground rent due to land.

**Economic obsolescence**   Lessened desirability or useful life arising from economic forces, such as changes in optimum land use, legislative enactments which restrict or impair property rights, and changes in supply-demand relationships. Loss in the use and value of property arising from the factors of economic obsolescence is to be distinguished from loss in value from physical deterioration and functional obsolescence.

**Economic rent**   The base rent payable for the right of occupancy of vacant land.

**Economics**   Allocation of scarce resources.

**Economy**   The efficient use of resources with an eye to productivity.

**Effective age**   A statement regarding the amount of depreciation that has occurred on a property. The amount is stated in terms of the number of years that would ordinarily be associated with the degree of depreciation.

**Effective demand**   Desire for property backed by the ability to purchase.

**Effective gross revenue**   A method to determine income less allowance for vacancies, contingencies, and sometimes collection losses, but before deductions for any operating expenses.

**Egress**   A way out; exit; an outlet.

**Ejectment**   Legal action brought to regain possession of property.

**Elasticity**   Ability of the supply of real estate to respond to price increases over a short period of time.

**Emancipate (a child)**   To release a child from parental control for purposes of legal capacity or competency.

**Embezzlement**   A statutory offense consisting of the fraudulent conversion of another's personal property by one to whom it has been entrusted, with the intention of depriving the owner thereof, the gist of the offense being usually the violation of relations of fiduciary character.

**Emblements**   Crops growing on the property which require annual care and usually are the possession of the tenant.

**Eminent domain**   The right of the government to take private property for public use, with just compensation.

**Enabling act**   A state statute used to provide a legal base for zoning codes or other local governmental action.

**Encroachment**   Unauthorized intrusion of real property or its fixtures on the property of another, thereby reducing the value of the property intruded upon.

**Encumbrance**   A claim against a property.

**English architecture**   The design using the characteristics of Elizabethan, Tudor Cotswold, and other English styles; frequently large stone houses with slate shingles on gabled roofs, mullioned casement windows, and wainscoted interiors. Exposed timbers constitute the structural frame of authentic Elizabethan houses, although in modern adaptations, the half-timbering is purely decorative. Between the half-timbers there usually is plaster, although in the original types the spaces were filled with brick nogging.

**Entrepreneur**   One who organizes, manages, and assumes responsibility for a business.

**Equality of economic opportunity**   A state of affairs in which all people have equal chances for the same jobs at equal pay, regardless of race, creed, color, or sex.

**Equitable title**   The right that exists in equity to obtain absolute ownership to property when title is held in another's name. Also, an interest in land that may not amount to fee simple ownership, but is such that a court will take notice of the rights of the holder of such interest.

**Equity**   Justice. Also, in finance, the value of the interest of an owner of property exclusive of the encumbrances on that property.

**Equity funds**   Capital invested to gain a residual ownership interest in property.

**Equity interest**   The amount of the value or total combined worth of a property minus any debts outstanding against it. The amount of the interest may be established through: (1) cash originally put into the property (down payment), (2) the amortization of any debt against the property, (3) any appreciation in the value of the property.

**Equity participation**   That percentage of the income or other return on the investment required by a lender in excess of the normal interest received for financing a real estate project.

**Equity of redemption**   The right to redeem property during the foreclosure period.

**Erosion**   The wearing away of the ground surface.

**Escalator clause**   A clause in a contract providing for the upward or downward adjustment of specific terms to cover certain contingencies, e.g., right to increase interest rates on a loan under special conditions.

**Escalator mortgage**   A loan that allows for a change in interest rate after a specific period of time. Changes in interest rate may be linked to specific money market rates.

**Escheat**   The reversion of private property to the state.

**Escrow**   The arrangement for the handling of instruments or money not to be delivered until specified conditions are met.

**Escrow holder**   The third party who receives a deed or item from a grantor to be held until the performance of a condition by the grantee or until the occurrence of a contingency, then to be delivered to the grantee.

**Estate (several types)**   The degree of interest a person has in land with respect to the nature of the right, its duration, or its relation to the rights of others. Estate in expectancy is a classification of estates by time of enjoyment when possession will be at some future time. An estate in possession is a classification of estates by time of enjoyment when possession is present. Estate in severalty is the ownership in a single individual; a classification of estates by number of owners where the number is one. A freehold estate is a nonleasehold estate such as a fee simple estate, fee tail estate, or life estate. Fee simple estates are the most complete form of estate ownership; the "totality of rights" in real property. A fee tail estate is an estate or a limited estate in which transfer of the property is restricted in that the property must pass to the descendants of the owner. Originally used to insure the passing of land in a direct ancestral line. A life estate is an estate that has a duration of the life of an individual.

**Estate for years**   A leasehold interest in lands by virtue of a contract for the possession for a specified period of time.

**Estate of inheritance**   An estate which may be passed on to heirs. All freehold estates are estates of inheritance, except estates for life.

**Estate at will**   The occupation of lands and tenements by a tenant for an unspecified period terminable by one or both parties.

**Estate in reversion**   The remnant of an estate left in the grantor, to commence in possession after the termination of some lesser estate granted by him or her to another.

**Estoppel**   A legal doctrine under which one is precluded and forbidden to deny his own act or deed.

**Estoppel certificate**   The certificate which shows the unpaid principal of a mortgage and the interest thereon, if the principal or interest notes are not produced or if the seller asserts that the amount due under the mortgage which the purchaser is to assume is less than shown on record.

**Et al.**   And others.

**Et ux.**   And wife.

**Ethics**   The moral principles, such as those owed by a member of a profession or craft to the public, to clients, and to professional associates.

**Eviction**   The ouster from possession of real property of one in possession under a valid lease.

**Eviction notice**   A notice to a tenant to vacate premises because of nonpayment of rent or other violation of the lease agreement.

**Evidence**   That which tends to prove or disprove any matter in question, or to influence the belief respecting it.

**Ex officio**   By virtue of the office; without any other warrant or appointment than that resulting from the holding of a particular office.

**Ex parte**   One side only, or done in behalf of only one person.

**Exception**   An objection; a reservation; a contradiction.

**Excess depreciation**   The amount of depreciation being applied beyond the normal rate allowed.

**Excess rent**   The monetary difference between contract rent and economic rent.

**Exchange**   The process of trading an equity in a piece of property for the equity in another piece of property.

**Exchange brokerage**   The process of bringing two parties together in transactions involving trading of properties.

**Exchange, tax-deferred**   A transaction in which one property, in whole or in part, is exchanged for another. A method of real estate sales used to defer the payment of capital gains tax, in which case the properties must be of "like kind."

**Exchangor**   The broker or salesperson who accomplishes the exchange.

**Exclusive agency listing**   A listing contract providing that the agent shall receive a commission if the property is sold as a result of the efforts of that agent or any other agent, but not as a result of the efforts of the principal; the contract further provides that the agent will receive a commission if a buyer is secured under the terms of the contract.

**Exclusive listing**   The contract to market property as an agent, according to the terms of which the agent is given the exclusive right to sell the property or is made the exclusive agent for its sale. The term is also applied to the property which is listed.

**Exclusive right to sell listing**   A contract between owner and agent giving agent the right to collect a commission if the property is sold by anyone during the term of the agreement.

**Exculpatory clause**   A clause often included in leases that clears or relieves the landlord of liability for personal injury to tenants as well as for property damages.

**Execute**   To complete; to perform.

**Execution**   The act of performing the final judgment or decree of a court; the formal action, usually signing, taken to complete a legal document and make it binding.

**Executor**   The person who is designated in a will as one who is to administer the estate of the testator.

**Executor's deed**   A deed given by an executor of the estate.

**Exempt**   To release, discharge, waive, relieve from liability.

**Exemption**   Something that is exempt; usually refers to a reduction in the amount of tax payable, such as a mortgage exemption.

**Existing mortgage**   The debt contract in which the seller of real estate is the mortgagor, which is to be assumed by the purchaser.

**Exoneration (in suretyship)**   The right which a surety has, on payment of the principal debtor's obligation, to look to the principal debtor for reimbursement.

**Expansible house**   A home created for future additions.

**Expense**   A financial burden or outlay.

**Express contract**   One expressed in words, either written or oral.

**Expropriation**   The act or process whereby private property is acquired for public use, or the rights therein modified by a sovereignty or any entity vested with the necessary legal authority; e.g., where property is taken under eminent domain.

**Extended coverage endorsement**   An addition to a fire insurance policy which extends the coverage to include losses caused by windstorm, hail, explosion, riot, aircraft, vehicle, and smoke damage.

**Extensive margin**   Extra benefits derived from adding increasing amounts of land to a productive state.

**Extinguishment**   The destruction or cancellation of a right, power, contract, or estate.

**Extra use**   Use (or activity) level in excess of a real or normal level of use.

**Facade**   The front or face of a building.

**Factor**   A commercial agent who sells goods consigned to him, for a principal, but uses his own name.

**Fair value**   Reasonable value, consistent with all known facts, at which the purchaser is willing to pay the price and the seller is willing to sell at the price.

**Fannie Mae**   Federal National Mortgage Association.

**Farm and Land Institute**   Brings together specialists in the sale, development, planning, management, and syndication of land to establish professional standards through educational programs for members. Confers AFLM (Accredited Farm and Land Member).

**Feasibility survey**   The analysis of the cost/benefit ratio of an economic endeavor prior to its undertaking.

**Fed**   Federal Reserve Board.

**Federal Deposit Insurance Corporation**   Federal agency that insures deposits at commercial banks and savings banks.

**Federal Home Loan Bank**   A district bank of the Federal Home Loan Bank System that lends only to member financial institutions such as savings and loan associations.

**Federal Home Loan Bank Board**   The administrative agency that charters federal savings and loan associations and exercises regulatory authority over members of the Federal Home Loan Bank System.

**Federal Home Loan Bank System**   The network of Federal Home Loan Banks and member financial institutions.

**Federal Home Loan Mortgage Corporation (Freddie Mac)**   A federal agency established to buy mortgage loans from lending institutions affiliated with the Federal Home Loan Bank System. It forms a secondary market function for such loans. Many condominium loans end up in "Freddie Mac."

**Federal Housing Administration (FHA)**   A federal agency that insures mortgage loans.

**Federal National Mortgage Association**   Federal agency that buys and sells FHA-insured and VA-guaranteed mortgage loans. Popularly known as "Fannie Mae."

**Federal savings and loan association**   A savings and loan association with a federal charter issued by the Federal Home Loan Bank Board. A federally chartered savings and loan association is in contrast to a state-chartered savings and loan association.

**Federal Savings and Loan Insurance Corporation**   Federal agency which insures savers' accounts at savings and loan associations.

**Fee**   An estate of inheritance in real property; compensation for a particular act.

**Fee simple**   In modern estates, the terms "fee" and "fee simple" are substantially synonymous. The term "fee" is of Old English derivation.

**Fee simple absolute**   An estate in real property by which the owner has the greatest power over the title which it is possible to have; an absolute estate. It expressly establishes the title of real property in the owner, without any limitation or end. He or she may dispose of it by sale, trade, or will, as desired.

**Fee simple conditional**   A fee that may terminate upon the occurrence of a specific event, the time of which is uncertain and/or the event itself may or may not ever occur.

**Fee simple determinable**   See Fee simple conditional.

**Fee simple limited**   See Fee simple conditional.

**Fee tail**   A freehold estate of inheritance limited so as to descend to a particular class of heirs of the person to whom it is granted.

**Felony**   A crime graver than those termed "misdemeanor"; the word is defined by several of the statutes and codes of the United States and includes crimes punishable by death or imprisonment in a penitentiary or state prison.

**Feudal system**   A political and social system which prevailed throughout Euope during the eleventh, twelfth, and thirteenth centuries under which ownership of land was vested in the monarch and subjects had only privileges of its use as opposed to private or allodial ownership.

**Feudal tenure**   See Feudal system.

**Feuds**   Grants of land.

**FHA**   See Federal Housing Administration.

**FHLMC**   Federal Home Loan Mortgage Corporation.

**Fidelity bond**   A bond posted as security for the discharge of an obligation of personal services.

**Fiduciary**   One who holds title to property for the benefit of another; or one who holds a position of trust and confidence.

**Filtering**   Upward mobility of people of one income group into homes that have recently dropped in price and that were previously occupied by persons in the next higher income group.

**Filtering down**   In housing, the process of passing the use of real estate to successively lower-income groups as the real estate produces less income or has a lower value.

**Financial institutions**   Organizations that deal in money or claims to money and serve the function of channeling money from those who wish to lend to those who wish to borrow. Such organizations include commercial banks, savings and loan associations, savings banks, and insurance companies.

**Financial intermediary**   A financial institution which acts as an intermediary between savers and borrowers by selling its own obligations for money and, in turn, lending the accumulated funds to borrowers.

This type of institution includes savings associations, mutual savings banks, life insurance companies, credit unions, and investment companies.

**Financial risk**   Possibility of losses created by the amount of and legal provisions concerning borrowed funds.

**Fire stop**   A solid, tight closure of a concealed space, built to prevent the spread of fire and smoke through such a space.

**Firm commitment**   A commitment assumed by the FHA to insure a mortgage of a specified mortgagor; an unqualified promise to make a loan under specified conditions.

**First mortgage**   The mortgage which prevails as a lien over all other mortgages.

**Fiscal controls**   Efforts to control the level of economic activity by manipulation of the amount of federal tax and spending programs and the amount of surplus or deficit.

**Fixity of location**   The characteristic which subjects real estate to the influence of its surroundings and prevents it from escaping such influence.

**Fixture**   A chattel permanently attached to real estate, and becoming accessory to it, and part and parcel of it.

**Flashing**   Sheet metal or other material used to protect a building from water seepage.

**Flexible payment mortgage**   A loan in which the repayment schedule is based on the borrower's financial position. Usually, payments are lower in the earlier years of the mortgage and increase as the borrower's ability to repay the loan increases.

**FLI**   See Farm and Land Institute.

**Floor loads**   The weight-supporting capabilities of a floor, measured in pounds per square foot; the weight, stated in pounds per square foot, which may be safely placed upon the floor of a building if it is uniformly distributed.

**Flow of funds**   An accounting method (used primarily by the Federal Reserve) to describe the sources and uses of the nation's funds in a given period of time.

**FNMA**   Federal National Mortgage Association, the secondary market agency for FHA and VA loans.

**Footing**   The base of a foundation wall or column.

**Forced sale**   The act of selling property under compulsion as to time; frequently the result of legal proceedings ordering the sale.

**Forced sale value**   The price realized at the forced sale.

**Foreclosure**   The legal process by which a mortgagee, after default by the mortgagor, forces sale of the property mortgaged in order to recover his or her loan.

**Forfeiture**   Deprivation or destruction of a right in consequence of the nonperformance of some obligation or condition.

**Forgery**   The legal offense of imitating or counterfeiting documents or signatures in an effort to deceive.

**Forthwith**   At once; promptly.

**Foundation**   The supporting portion of a structure below the first floor construction, including the footings.

**Foundation wall**   The masonry wall below ground which supports the building.

**Franchise**   A specific privilege conferred by government or contractually by a business firm.

**Fraud**   Intentional deception or trickery used to gain an unfair advantage over another.

**Freddie Mac**   See Federal Home Loan Mortgage Corporation.

**Free and clear sale**   A real estate sale that is absolute and unclouded by any encumbrance, such as liens, mortgages, etc.

**Freehold**   An estate in real property with no measurable length of time or termination date.

**French architecture**   Any of several styles originating in France; very common in smaller houses and the perfectly balanced, rectangular formal house with a steep roof, hipped at the ends, its plaster walls one story high, with dormer windows provided for second-floor rooms. The French farmhouse style is informal, of stone, painted brick, or plaster, sometimes with half-timbering used as an accent. Norman French architecture is large in scale, usually distinguished by a round tower.

**Front foot**   A measure (1 foot in length) of the width of lots taken along their frontage upon a street.

**Front foot cost**   Cost of a piece of real estate expressed in terms of front foot units.

**Frostline**   The depth to which frost will penetrate the soil. Footings should be placed below this depth to prevent movement.

**Full face rate of interest**   Rate of interest stated in the debt.

**Functional obsolescence**   Defects in the plan or design of a structure that detract from its marketability and value.

**Functional plan**   The special arrangement of real estate improvements as it relates to property services.

**Functional utility**   The total of a property's attractiveness and usefulness.

**Funds**   Cash or any other resource having value which may be sold in order to buy some other asset.

**Furring**   The strips of wood or metal applied behind a wall or other surface to even it, to form an air space, or to give the wall an appearance of greater thickness.

**Gable roof**   A steeply pitched roof with sloping sides.

**Gambrel roof**   A curb roof having a flatter upper slope and a steep lower slope.

**General mortgage bond**   A document representing an obligation secured by a mortgage.

**General warranty**   A provision that guarantees the quality of title to property conveyed and undertakes to defend that title and to pay damages if the title is defective.

**GI loan**   A mortgage loan granted veterans, which is guaranteed by the VA subject to their restrictions.

**Gift deed**   A deed given without consideration.

**Ginnie Mae**   Government National Mortgage Association (GNMA).

**Girder**   A large beam used to support smaller beams, joists, and partitions.

**GNP**   Gross national product.

**Good faith**   An honest intention to abstain from taking conscious advantage of another.

**Governmental survey**   The process adopted in 1785, also known as the rectangular survey, used for describing land and establishing boundaries. It is used to describe both large and small tracts of land in legal descriptions.

**Grade**   The ground level taken at the foundation.

**Grading**   The process of plowing and raking a lot to give it a desired contour and drainage.

**Graduated lease**   A lease that provides for a variable rental rate, often based upon future determination; sometimes rent is based upon the result of periodical appraisals; used largely in long-term leases.

**Graduated payment mortgage**   A method of repayment of a mortgage loan in which the payment is lower in the earlier years and is gradually increased to cover the total repayment required.

**Graduate Realtors Institute (GRI)**   Educational program for REALTORS® sponsored by NAR. Awards GRI (Graduate, Realtors Institute).

**Grant**   A transfer of real property by a written instrument. A private grant is the transfer of real property from one person to another. A public grant is a government transfer of ownership of real property to a private party.

**Grantee**   One who receives a transfer of real property by deed.

**Grantor**   One who transfers real property by deed.

**GRI**   Graduate Realtors Institute, and that program's designation.

**Grid**   A chart used for the purpose of rating the borrower risk, property, and neighborhood.

**Gridiron pattern**   A layout of streets that resembles a gridiron; a system of subdivision with blocks of uniform length and width and streets that intersect at right angles.

**GRM**   Gross rent multiplier.

**Gross earnings**   The total revenue from operations, before deduction of the expenses incurred in gaining such revenues.

**Gross income**   The total income from property before any expenses are deducted.

**Gross income multiplier**   A technique for estimating real estate value based on some factor (multiplier) times the gross income derived from the property in the past. *See* gross rent multiplier.

**Gross lease**   A lease of property under the terms of which the lessor is to assume all property charges regularly incurred as the result of property ownership, e.g., taxes, maintenance, etc.

**Gross monthly rent multiplier (GMRM)**   A rule of thumb used to estimate the market value of income-producing residential property.

**Gross national product**   The total value of all goods and services produced in the economy in any given period; also, the accounting method used to list the major income and expenditure (product) accounts of the nation.

**Gross profits**   Total profits computed before the deduction of general expenses.

**Gross rent multiplier**   A factor used in arriving at an estimate of real estate value. The factor is obtained by dividing known sales prices of comparable properties by the rental income of those properties. It is usually the average quotient arrived at from the above division (sales price by rental income) of several comparable properties. The gross rental income of a particular property is then multiplied by this factor.

**Gross revenue**   Total revenue from all sources before subtraction of expenses incurred in gaining such revenue.

**Gross sales**   The total amount of sales as shown by invoices, before deducting returns, allowances, etc.

**Ground lease**   A lease for the use of the land only.

**Ground rent**   The earnings of improved property proportionally credited to earnings of the ground itself after allowance is made for earnings of improvements; often called "economic rent."

**Guaranteed mortgage**   A mortgage in which a party other than the borrower assures payment in the event of default by a mortgagor, e.g., VA-guaranteed mortgages.

**Guaranteed sale**   The written commitment by a broker that within a specified period of time he or she will, in absence of a sale, purchase a given piece of property at a specified sum.

**Guide meridian**   A correction line which runs due north and south to compensate for the narrowing of the earth. Used in rectangular survey.

**Habendum**   The second part of a deed following that part which names the grantee. It describes the estate conveyed and to what use.

**Habendum clause**   The "have and to hold" clause which defines or limits the quantity of the estate granted in the premises of the deed. Not essential today per leading authorities unless the estate being granted is a limited one.

**Haec verba**   In the exact words.

**Half-timbering**   A means of construction of house walls with the timber frame exposed, the space between timbers being filled with masonry or plaster on laths; also simulated half-timbering with boards applied on plaster walls as decoration.

**Header**   One beam which is placed perpendicular to joists and to which joists are nailed in framing for a chimney, stairway, or other opening.

**Hedge against inflation**   An investment whose value increases at a rate equal to or greater than the present rate of inflation.

**Height density**   A zoning regulation designed to control the use or occupancy within a certain area by designating the maximum height of the structures.

**Heirs**   Persons appointed by law to succeed to the real estate of a decedent, in case of intestacy.

**Hereditaments**   A larger and more comprehensive word than either "land" or "tenements," and meaning anything capable of being inherited, whether it be corporeal, incorporeal, real, personal, or mixed.

**High-rise apartment building**   An indefinite term used to describe the modern elevator apartment building.

**Highest and best use**   The utilization of real property to its greatest economic advantage; the use that provides the highest land value; the use of land that provides a net income stream to the land that when capitalized provides the highest land value.

**Hip roof**   A pitched roof that features sloping sides and ends.

**Holding period**   The period of time during which a person owns a capital asset.

**Holdover tenant**   A person who remains in possession of leased property after expiration of the leased term.

**Holographic will**   A will written entirely by the testator with his own hand.

**Homeowners Loan Corporation**   A federal agency that refinanced mortgages in default in the early 1930s.

**Homestead**   A dwelling with its land and buildings; a dwelling with its land and buildings protected by a homestead law.

**Homestead exemption**   The interest of the head of a family in his or her owned residence that is exempt from the claims of creditors.

**Horizontal Property Act**   The laws enacted by the various states, which permit creation of the condominium form of real property ownership.

**Housing stock**   The total inventory of dwelling units. This includes forms both owned and rented.

**Housing starts**   Newly constructed housing units. This includes both single-family and multifamily domiciles.

**HUD (Housing and Urban Development)**   A federal department created in 1965 to solve the complex housing problems of the American city by utilization of the vast resources of the federal government in coordination with the various state and local governments. Administrations under HUD include FNMA, FHA, Public Housing, Urban Renewal, and Community Facilities.

**Hundred percent location**   A city retail business location which is considered the best for attracting business.

**Hypotenuse**   The side of a right triangle that lies opposite the right angle.

**Hypothecate**   To pledge something without delivering possession of it to the pledgee.

**Hypothesis of median location**   A theory stating that there is the tendency for businesses and other entities to locate at their lowest time and cost point.

**Identity of interest**   The system whereby the builder and sponsor of a housing project subsidized by the government have ownership interests in each other.

**Illegality of purpose**   The actual purpose of the contract is illegal. In contract law, one of the reasons for avoiding a contract.

**Implied**   Contained in substance or essence or by fair inference but not actually expressed; deductible by inference or implication.

**Implied contract**   One implied by the acts and/or conduct of the parties involved.

**Improper improvement**   Out-of-place improvement; improvement which does not conform to the best use of the site.

**Improved value**   The difference between the income-producing ability of a property and the amount required to pay a return on the investment in the property.

**Improvement**   That which is erected or constructed upon land to release the income-earning potential of the land; buildings or appurtenances on land. An overimprovement is an improvement of real estate in excess of that justifiable to release the earning power of land. An underimprovement is an improvement insufficient to release the earning power of the land.

**Improvements to land**   Publicly owned additions such as curbs, sidewalks, street lighting system, and sewers, constructed so as to permit the development of privately owned land for utilization. (As opposed to improvements on land, which are usually privately owned.)

**In personam**   Against the person. Applied to actions in which the court is to impose upon the defendant a personal obligation to obey the order, judgment, or decree.

**Incentive**   Payment or reward for taking a certain action, usually in excess of fixed compensation and based upon better performance than required by agreement.

**Inchoate dower**   A wife's interest in the real estate of her husband during his life, which may become a right of dower upon his death.

**Income**   A stream of financial benefits generally measured in terms of money as of a certain time; a flow of service. It is the origin of value.

**Income method**   A method of appraising real property basing the value of the property upon the net amount of income produced by it.

**Income/price ratio**   Net income compared to the selling price of the property.

**Income property**   A property in which the income is generated by means of commercial rentals or in which the returns attributable to the real estate can be so segregated as to permit direct estimation. The income may come from several sources; e.g., commercial rents, business profits attributable to real estate other than rents, etc.

**Incompetent**   One who is mentally incapable; any person who, though not insane, is not considered legally competent enough to properly manage and take care of self or property and therefore could easily be taken advantage of by designing persons.

**Incorporeal rights**   Nonpossessory rights in real estate.

**Increment**   An increase. Used in reference to the increases in land values that accompany population growth and increasing wealth in the community.

**Incremental income tax**   The additional income tax caused by a given investment.

**Incurable depreciation**   A defect which cannot be removed or which it is impractical to remove. A defect in the "bone structure" of a building. It is measured by age-life tables or life expectancy.

**Indenture**   Any contract by which two or more parties enter into reciprocal obligations.

**Independent contractor**   A self-employed person, or one employed by another who has no right of control over the employee except as to final results.

**Indirect lighting**  Light that is reflected from the ceiling or other object external to the source.

**Industrial districts**  Areas in which the primary or major improvements to land are in the nature of factory, warehouse, or related property.

**Industrial park**  An area in which the land is developed specifically for use for industrial purposes.

**Industrial property**  In a broad sense, all the tangible and intangible assets pertinent to the conducting of an enterprise for the manufacturing, processing, and assembling of finished products from raw or fabricated materials. Also, in a limited sense, the land, fixed improvements, machinery, and all equipment (fixed or movable) comprising the facilities devoted to such enterprise.

**Infant**  A person not of full age; a minor lacking legal capacity to enter into contracts other than for necessities.

**Infiltration**  Displacement by persons of a lower economic status.

**Inflation**  An economic circumstance that occurs when real purchasing is decreased as a result of rate price increases being greater than the advances in productivity.

**Infrastructure**  The network of public facilities located within the community (e.g., roads, schools, sewers, parks, utilities, etc.).

**Ingress**  A place or means of entering; entrance.

**Inheritance**  An estate in lands or tenements or other things that may be inherited by the heir.

**Injunction**  An order of the court to restrain one or more parties to a suit or proceeding from performing an act which is deemed unjust in regard to the rights of some other party in the suit or proceeding or compelling positive action.

**Input-output analysis**  A technique for analysis of an economy through description of the production and purchases of specific sectors of the economy.

**Installment contract**  An agreement providing for the payment of a specified amount in periodic installments by the buyer as a condition precedent to the performance by the seller.

**Installment note**  A note which provides that payments of a certain sum be paid periodically on the dates specified in the instrument.

**Installment sale**  The sale of real property on an extended payment basis; used to spread the tax consequence of a sale over a period of years.

**Institute of Real Estate Management (IREM)**  National organization to professionalize members who are involved in all elements of property management through standards of practice, ethical considerations, and educational programs. Confers CPM (Certified Property Manager), AMO (Accredited Management Organization), ARM (Accredited Resident Manager).

**Institutional advertising**  Advertising intended to popularize a particular company as opposed to the promotion of its products or services.

**Institutional lender**  A mortgagee who is a bank, insurance company, pension fund, savings and loan association, etc.

**Instrument**  Any formal legal document, such as a contract, deed, or grant.

**Insulation**  A heat-retarding material applied in outside walls, top-floor ceilings, or roofs to prevent the passage of heat or cold into or out of the house.

**Insurable interest**  An ownership interest which an insurer will recognize as a property right, the loss of which will result in true loss of money value to the insured party.

**Insurable value**  The value at which an insurer will recognize any loss.

**Insurance coverage**  The total amount of insurance carried.

**Insurance rate**  The ratio of the insurance premium to the total amount of insurance carried thereby—usually expressed in dollars per $100 or per $1,000—sometimes in percent.

**Insurance risk**  A general or relative term denoting the hazard involved in the insuring of property. The premium or cost of insurance is determined by the relative risk or hazard considered to be involved.

**Insured mortgage**  A mortgage in which a party other than the borrower, in return for the payment of a premium, assures payment in the event of default by a mortgagor, e.g., FHA-insured mortgages, PMI (private mortgage insurance).

**Intangible assets**  The elements of property in an enterprise that are represented in the established organization—doing business, goodwill, and other rights incident to the enterprise—as distinguished from the physical items comprising the plant facilities and working capital.

**Intangible value**  An asset's worth which is not immediately available in dollars but which may be of significant value. An example of this is goodwill.

**Intensive margin**  Extra benefits derived from adding increasing amounts of labor and capital to land.

**Interchange**  A system of underpasses and overpasses for routing traffic on and off highways without interfering with through traffic and for linking two or more highways.

**Interest rate**  The percentage of a sum of money charged for its use.

**Interest rate risk**  The risk of loss due to changes in the interest rate. Earnings, or the value of a property, may be affected as a result of changes in prevailing interest rates in the money market. When interest rates go up or down, properties are generally capitalized at higher or lower rates.

**Interim financing**  A temporary or short-term loan secured by a mortgage, which is generally paid off from the proceeds of permanent financing. *See* construction loan.

**Internal rate of return**  The predetermined earning rate requirement for a project; usually established by comparison with other return opportunities available to the investor.

**International Real Estate Federation, American Chapter**  Promotes understanding of real estate among those involved in the real estate business throughout the world.

**Interpret**  To construe; to seek out the meaning of language; legally, to determine the intent of an agreement between parties.

**Interurbia**  A contiguous urban development larger than a city or metropolitan area.

**Interval ownership**  A form of ownership that creates a sole ownership in a property for a specific part of a year. The buyer purchases a right to use the property—in contrast to time sharing, which creates a joint interest in the property.

**Intestate**  A person who has died without leaving a valid will disposing of his or her property and estate.

**Inventory**  A detailed list of articles, giving the code number, quantity, and value of each; a formal list of the property of a person or estate; a complete listing of stock on hand made each year by a business.

**Inversely related cost**  Cost that declines as volume of activity to which it relates increases.

**Investment**  Monies placed in a property with the expectation of producing a profit, assuming a reasonable degree of safety and ultimate recovery of principal; especially permanent use, as opposed to speculation.

**Investment calculation**  Estimation of value for a particular investor or user.

**Investment credit**  A federal tax law allowance for certain items based on assistance to growth of businesses.

**Investment property**  The property which is within itself a business enterprise consisting of all tangible and intangible assets considered integral with the property, assembled and developed as a single unit of utility for lease or rental (in whole or in part) to others for profit.

**Involuntary lien**   A lien imposed against property without consent of an owner, e.g., taxes, special assessments, and federal income tax.

**IREF**   *See* International Real Estate Federation.

**IREM**   *See* Institute of Real Estate Management.

**Irrevocable**   Incapable of being revoked, modified, withdrawn, or changed.

**Irrigation districts**   Quasi-political districts created under special laws to provide for water services to property owners in the district, an operation governed to a great extent by law.

**Italian architecture**   A style which varies from a completely balanced design to an informal composition with formal treatment and openings. Typical details include completely framed window openings, circular heads over exterior openings, high windows and doors, and S-shaped red tile on the roof.

**Jamb**   The side post or lining of a doorway, window, or other such opening.

**Joint**   The space between the adjacent surfaces of two components connected by nails, glue, cement, or mortar.

**Joint and several**   A duty against two or more, which may be enforced against all jointly or against each individually.

**Joint note**   A note signed by two or more persons who share equal liability for repayment.

**Joint tenancy**   Joint ownership with right of survivorship. All joint tenants have equal rights in the property with the right to automatic succession to title of the whole upon the death of one tenant.

**Joint venture**   An arrangement under which two or more individuals or businesses participate in a single project as partners.

**Joist**   One of the series of parallel beams to which the boards of a floor and ceiling laths are fixed and which in turn are supported by larger beams, girders, or bearing walls.

**Judgment**   The final verdict of a court of competent jurisdiction on a matter presented to it. Money judgments provide for the payment of claims presented to the court.

**Judgment creditor**   The person who has received a decree or judgment of the court against his debtor for money due him for any cause.

**Judgment debtor**   The person against whom a judgment has been issued by the court for monies owed.

**Judgment lien**   The statutory lien upon the real and personal property of a judgment debtor, which is created by the judgment itself.

**Judicial notice**   The doctrine that a court will, of its own knowledge, assume certain facts to be true without the production of evidence in support of them. It is said that the court takes judicial notice of such facts because they are common knowledge.

**Judicial sale**   A court action which serves to enforce the judgment lien; the property is sold under judicial process to pay the debt.

**Junior lien**   A lien granted after the granting of an earlier lien on a different debt against the same property.

**Junior mortgage**   A mortgage having claim ranking below that of another mortgage which preceded it in time.

**Jurat**   The clause written at the foot of an affidavit stating when, where, and before whom such affidavit was sworn.

**Jurisdiction**   A political subdivision with power to govern its own affairs; in law, the power of a court to try specific suits.

**Key lot**   A lot in such a position that one side is adjacent to the rear of other lots. It is considered to be the least desirable of the lots in a subdivision.

**Kiln-dried lumber**   Lumber that was dried in a large ovenlike chamber for a period of time dependent upon its thickness and grade. This reduces the moisture content.

**Knob-and-tube wiring**   A method of wiring whereby the wires are attached to the house frame with porcelain knob insulators and porcelain tubes. Not used very frequently any more.

**Laches**   The established doctrine of equity under which, apart from any question of statutory limitation, courts will discourage delay and sloth in the enforcements of rights and will decline to try suits not brought within a reasonable time.

**Land**   In a physical sense, the earth's surface; in a legal sense, ground and everything annexed to it, whether by nature or by humans.

**Land contract**   A written agreement by which real estate is sold to a buyer who pays a portion of the purchase price when the contract is signed and completes payment in installments made over a specified period of years, with the title remaining with the seller until the total purchase price or a stipulated portion of the purchase price is paid.

**Land economics**   That branch of economics which deals with utilization of land resources in the attainment of objectives set by society.

**Land grant**   A gift of government land to a university, public utility, or railroad, or for a purpose that would be in the best interest and benefit of the general public; also, the original granting of land from the public sector to the private sector commonly used in the early history of the United States.

**Land improvements**   Physical alterations in, or construction of a more-or-less permanent nature attached to or appurtenant to, land, of such character as to increase its utility and/or value.

**Land planning**   The designing of land area uses, road networks, and layout for utilities to achieve efficient utilization of real estate resources.

**Land trust certificate**   An instrument used in financing larger real estate transactions. The investor receives a trust certificate as evidence of his or her share in the trust which is used as the investment vehicle.

**Landlord**   The owner of real estate which is leased to others.

**Landmarks**   A monument or erection set up on the boundary line of two adjoining parcels to fix such boundary.

**Landscaping**   The utilization of a lawn and plantings to improve the appearance of a lot.

**Latent defects**   Physical weaknesses or construction defects not noticeable after a reasonable inspection of the property.

**Lateral and subjacent support**   The right to have land supported by the adjoining land or the soil beneath by the owner of the adjoining property who excavates to the boundary line between the two properties.

**Law**   In a legal sense, an established rule or standard of conduct or action that is enforceable by government. A real estate license law is a law that regulates the practice of real estate brokers and salespersons. Real estate law is the body of laws relating to real estate; generally evolved from the English common law but now including regulations such as zoning, building codes, etc.

**Layout**   The design or floor plans for the arranging of rooms in an apartment or an office.

**Lease**   A transfer of possession and the right to use property to a tenant for a stipulated period, during which the tenant pays rent to the owner; the contract containing the terms and conditions of such an agreement. A graded or step-up lease is a lease with a rental payment that increases over specified periods of time. A ground lease is a lease for vacant land upon which the tenant may erect improvements. An index lease is a lease in which the rental payment varies in accordance with variation in an agreed upon index of prices or costs. A lease with option to purchase is a lease in which the lessee has the right to purchase the real property for a stipulated price at or within a stipulated time. A leasehold is an estate held under lease. A net lease is a lease in which the tenant pays certain agreed upon property expenses such as taxes or maintenance. A percentage lease is a lease in which the rental is based upon a percentage of the lessee's sales income. A tax participation clause (in a lease) is an agreement in a lease whereby the lessee agrees to pay all or a stated portion of any increase in real estate taxes.

**Lease-purchase agreement**   An arrangement whereby a portion of the rent is applied toward a down payment. Upon payment of the down payment the tenant, using borrowed funds, purchases the property and becomes the owner outright rather than a mere lessee.

**Leased fee**   A property held in fee whereby a lease conveys the right of use and occupancy to others. A property which has the right to receive ground rentals over a period of time, and consisting of the further right at ultimate repossession of the termination of the lease.

**Leasehold**   An estate in real property that transfers possession to the tenant for a fixed period of time.

**Leasehold policy**   A form of title insurance taken out by the lessee in order to protect his or her interest in the property. It is commonly used in insuring commercial property because of the value of the fixtures and equipment which are added.

**Legal capacity**   One's capability, power, or fitness to enter into a contractual agreement as determined by law.

**Legal description**   A means of identifying the exact boundaries of land by metes and bounds, by a plat, or by township and range survey system. Metes refer to measures; bounds refer to direction. Metes and bounds descriptions are means of describing land by measurement and direction from a known point or marker on land. A plat is a recorded map of land that identifies a parcel by a number or other designation in a subdivision. A township and range survey system is a system of legal description of land with a township as the basic unit of measurement. A base line is a parallel that serves as a reference for other parallels. Meridians are the north-south lines of survey, 6 miles apart. Parallels are the east-west lines of survey, 6 miles apart. A principal meridian is a meridian that serves as a reference for other meridians. A range is a north-south row of townships; the 6-mile strip of land between meridians. A section is a 1-mile square in a township. A tier is an east-west row of townships; the 6-mile strip of land between parallels. A township is a 6-mile square of land bounded by parallels and meridians and composed of 36 sections.

**Legal rate of interest**   The maximum rate of interest that may be charged in accordance with state law.

**Legality of purpose**   An essential element of every contract is that it be for a legal object. If not so, the contract is automatically void.

**Lessee**   The party who possesses the right to possession of real estate for a limited time under a lease. The lessee is commonly referred to as the tenant.

**Lessor**   The landlord under a lease; one who conveyed a right or estate in realty to another under a lease.

**Leverage**   A financial method applied with the anticipation that the property acquired will increase in return so that the investor will realize a profit not only on his or her own investment but also on the borrowed funds, with the borrowed funds being predominant.

**Levy**   A seizure of property to satisfy a judgment; the imposition of a tax.

**LHA**   Local Housing Authority.

**Liability**   Any debt or obligation; an obligation or duty that must be performed.

**License**   A personal privilege to perform some act or series of acts upon the land of another without possessing any estate therein; a permit or authorization to do what, without a license, would be unlawful.

**License year**   The period of time for which a license retains its validity. Usually specified in the licensing act, it generally differs from a calendar year.

**Licensee**   A person to whom a license is granted.

**Lien**   A charge or claim upon property which encumbers it until the obligation is satisfied.

**Lien theory**   The state law providing a lender a lien against real estate as collateral for a loan. This is less protective to lenders than title theory.

**Lien theory of mortgage**   The mortgage theory under which title to mortgaged property vests in the borrower, with the lender having a lien against the real estate.

**Life estate**   An estate in land held during the term of a certain person's life. The estate terminates upon the death of the holder. The estate may be held by more than one person. The balance of the estate resides in the remainderman who will succeed to the title upon termination of the life estate.

**Limited-access highway**   A highway designed for the constant flow of traffic. The entrance and exit opportunities have been predetermined and set at specific intervals.

**Limited partnership**   A partnership in which some partners make only specified contributions and in return have only limited liabilities.

**Lintel**   The horizontal board over a door or window that supports the load.

**Liquidated damages**   The amount agreed upon as payment for a breach of contract by the parties themselves and in advance.

**Liquidity**   Measurement of the ability one has to sell his or her property quickly.

**Lis pendens**   A pending suit. The doctrine of lis pendens creates a lien against the property of a defendant in a lawsuit pending its final resolution.

**Listing contract**   A written agreement or contract between a principal and an agent providing that the agent will receive a commission for finding a buyer who is ready, willing, and able to purchase a particular property under terms specified in the agreement. A multiple listing is a listing that, in addition to employing the agent, provides for the services of other agents who have agreed among themselves that they will cooperate in finding a purchaser for the property. An open listing contract provides that the agent shall receive a commission if the property is sold as a result of the efforts of that agent or if the agent produces a buyer under the terms of the contract before the property is sold.

**Litigation**   A contest in a court of justice for the purpose of enforcing a right; a lawsuit.

**Livery of seisin**   The delivery of possession of the real estate. Also referred to as investiture.

**Load-bearing wall**   An integral part of the house, which helps support the floors or roof and is relatively permanent in structure.

**Load center**   The electrical distribution center for the structure, either the main center or a branch center. The center is equipped with circuit breaks instead of a main switch and fuse box.

**Loan fee**   The service charge made by the lender for the granting of a loan in addition to required interest.

**Loan maturity**   The life of the loan. The amount of time the loan will remain in existence until the debt is retired. A 20-year loan has a maturity of 20 years.

**Loan origination fee**   The fee charged by the lender to process and create the loan.

**Loan term**   The length of the period of the mortgage loan.

**Loan value**   The basic value which determines amount a lending institution will lend on a property.

**Loan/value ratio**   The amount of mortgage debt and the market or appraisal value of the property for debt purposes, usually expressed as a percentage. For example, an 80% loan/value ratio on a $100,000 property means a mortgage of up to $80,000 may be obtained. The greater the loan/value ratio, the greater the financial leverage available to the purchaser.

**Local Housing Authority (LHA)**   The local body whose major concern is public housing.

**Localization of income** Income production at fixed locations; e.g., from real estate, which has a fixed and unique location.

**Location** Position of land and improvements in relation to other land and improvements and to local or general economic activity.

**Location quotient** An analytic technique using proportionality comparisons, for example, the comparison of the percentage of an activity in a city with the percentage of the same activity in the nation.

**Locked-in period** A period of time during which the borrower of a mortgage may not repay any of the principal. This is written into the contract.

**Loss** The situation that occurs when the cost of the investment or product is larger than the income from operations or the sale of the investment or product.

**Lot** A specific plot of land.

**Louver** An opening filled with a series of horizontal slats set at an angle to permit ventilation without admitting rain, sunlight, or vision.

**MAI** A designation for a person who is a member of the American Institute of Appraisers, a group associated with NAR.

**Maintenance** The keeping up or the expenditures necessary to keep a property in condition to perform the services for which it is designed.

**Maintenance reserve** The sum of money allotted to cover the costs of maintenance.

**Majority age** The age at which an individual is capable of entering into a binding contract; sometimes referred to as "legal age" or "adulthood."

**Malfeasance** The performance of an act that is unlawful or wholly wrong.

**Management contract** An agreement used to define the rights and duties of the contracting parties. It enumerates in detail the method of payment and the rates of compensation of the agent for renting of space and maintaining another's property.

**Management process** A set of guidelines for action, for the implementation of decisions; an orderly means for the accomplishment of objectives.

**Mandatory** Containing a command; imperative.

**Map** A representation of some feature on the earth's surface such as physical features or boundary lines, and the like.

**Margin of security** The dollar differential between the amount of the mortgage loan(s) and the appraised value of a property.

**Marginal land** Land which has returns that barely meet the costs of operation.

**Marginal revenue** An additional amount of revenue resulting from a given business decision.

**Marginal satisfaction** An alteration in the level of satisfaction derived from the occurrence of a given event.

**Marginal utility** The worth of one additional unit of a good or a service that is produced.

**Market** A set of arrangements for bringing buyers and sellers together through the price mechanism. A buyer's market is a market in which buyers can fulfill their desires at lower prices and on more advantageous terms than those prevailing earlier. It is a market characterized by many properties available and few potential users demanding them at prevailing prices. A capital market is comprised of the activities of all lenders and borrowers of equity and long-term debt funds. A money market is a market for borrowed funds, generally short-term. A seller's market is a market in which potential sellers can sell at prices higher than those prevailing in an immediately preceding period. It is a market characterized by very few properties available and a large number of users and potential users demanding them at prevailing prices.

**Market analysis** An estimate of value developed for the purpose of arriving at a selling or market price.

**Market comparison (market approach)** The approach to real property appraisal which compares a certain property to equivalent properties which have sold recently to develop a value.

**Market indicators** Sign posts or indexes of market activity.

**Market price** The price paid for an object regardless of external influences.

**Market rent** The amount charged for rent; established by pricing the rent at a level near that of similar properties in the market area.

**Market value** The price property would command in the market.

**Marketable title** Such a title as is free from reasonable doubt in law and in fact; one which can be readily sold or mortgaged to a reasonably prudent purchaser or mortgagee.

**Market function** The determination of how land will be put to use after the limits are set by zoning and other restrictions both public and private.

**Marketing myopia** A failure to match the needs with the people who have needs.

**Master deed** The title document used in condominium projects, which creates both the fee units and the common interests involved in the projects.

**Master switch** An electrical wall switch which controls several fixtures or outlets in a room.

**Maximum rent** The greatest amount of rent that may be charged as set down in a rent regulation or order.

**Mechanic's lien** A claim created by law for the purpose of securing a priority of payment of the price or value of work performed and materials furnished in erecting or repairing a building or other structure, and as such it attaches to the land as well as to the buildings erected thereon. It is enforceable by foreclosure proceedings.

**Megalopolis** An urban area of great size.

**Merger** In real estate law, the doctrine that a lesser interest is absorbed by a greater estate when both are owned by the same person. E.g., when a tenant buys the fee simple, the leasehold is absorbed into the fee and he is then the owner and no longer a tenant.

**Meridians** The imaginary north-south lines that intersect base lines to form a point of origin for the measurement of land.

**Messuage** The residence and all the adjacent buildings and the land around it.

**Metes and bounds** The boundary lines of land, with their terminal points and angles.

**MGIC** Mortgage Guarantee Insurance Corporation.

**Microeconomics** The science of economic functions from the viewpoint of the individual firm or decision maker.

**Mill** In taxes, equals one-tenth of 1 cent; a measure used to state the property tax rate; a tax rate of 1 mill on the dollar is the same as a rate of one-tenth of 1% of the assessed value of the property.

**Misdemeanor** A criminal offense of lesser grade than that of a felony and usually punishable only by fine.

**Misrepresentation** Transmitting an untruth from one person to another via words or other conduct. Presenting something not in accordance with the facts.

**Mission architecture** The architectural style employing the characteristics of early California missions, generally Spanish in style.

**Mistake of fact** Errors which do not state the true conditions of the contract. If curable, these errors of fact do not generally void the contract.

**Mistake of law** Occurs when a party to a contract having full knowledge of the facts comes to an erroneous conclusion as to their legal effect. The party may not void the contract under a mistake of law based on the erroneous conclusion.

**Mobile home**   A manufactured standardized home which is entirely constructed in a factory and then transported to the site. It is the opposite of a conventionally built home.

**Model house**   A house used for exhibition in order to sell other houses.

**Modern architecture**   The architectural style that employs the principles of contemporary, functional design, intended to combine esthetic quality and utility in a home.

**Modern English architecture**   An architectural design consisting of many elements of the Elizabethan and Tudor styles, but called modern because it is of more recent vintage. Prominent characteristics are the rough plaster or stucco exterior, the steep roof slopes with variegated and graduated slate or red tile, and having no cornices or eaves.

**Modernization**   A process involving the restoration of a structure to its maximum attractiveness and productivity without altering any of its property functions.

**Modular construction**   Prefabrication in three dimensions; i.e., entire rooms of houses or apartments are built in the factory and shipped to their eventual location where very little on-site labor is required.

**Modular planning**   The designing of structures using a designated minimum dimension of length and width such as 4 feet.

**Moisture barrier**   A material used to stop or slow down the flow of moisture into walls.

**Monetary controls**   Efforts by the Federal Reserve to influence the level of economic activity by regulating the availability of money and the rate of interest.

**Monopoly**   An economic condition attained when one party controls the entire market.

**Monuments**   Visible marks or indications left on natural or other objects indicating the lines and boundaries of a survey.

**Moral turpitude**   Conduct contrary to the social duty owed by one person to another, criminal in nature.

**Moratorium**   A temporary suspension, often by statute, of enforcement of the liability for a financial obligation.

**Mortgage (several types)**   The pledge of real property to secure a debt; the conveyance of real property as security for a debt; the instrument that is evidence of the pledge or conveyance. A mortgage bond is evidence of debt secured by a mortgage in favor of individual parties as a group, usually with the mortgage held by a third party in trust for the mortgage bond creditors. A mortgage broker is an agent who, for a commission, brings a mortgagor and mortgagee together. A mortgage company is a firm that, for a fee, brings mortgagor and mortgagee together or that acquires mortgages for the purpose of resale. An open-end mortgage is a mortgage with provisions for future advances to the borrower without the necessity of writing a new mortgage. A package mortgage is a mortgage in which the collateral is not limited to real property but includes personal property in the nature of household equipment. A purchase money mortgage is a mortgage that is given in part payment of the purchase price as security for repayment of funds. Subject to mortgage means the grantee takes title but is not responsible for the mortgage beyond the value of his or her equity in the property.

**Mortgage bank correspondents**   The various mortgage bankers who serve as agents of lenders for the purpose of placing and servicing mortgage loans in a local community.

**Mortgage brokerage**   The business of bringing together the lender and borrower, with additional services such as aiding in the closing of a loan.

**Mortgage commitment**   A notice in writing from the lending institution promising the mortgage loan in the future and also specifying the terms and conditions of the loan.

**Mortgage company**   The private corporation whose principal function is to originate and service mortgage loans sold to financial institutions.

**Mortgage constant**   The percentage of an original loan balance represented by a constant annual mortgage payment required to retire the debt on schedule.

**Mortgage correspondent**   A representative of a lender of money on the security of real property; a representative of a potential mortgagee.

**Mortgage guaranty insurance**   The insurance issued against financial loss. It is available to mortgage lenders from MGIC, a private company organized in 1956, and others who have since entered the field.

**Mortgage insurance premium**   The amount the borrower pays for the insurance on a loan by the FHA.

**Mortgagee**   The creditor or lender under a mortgage.

**Mortgagor**   The debtor or borrower under a mortgage.

**Motivation research**   Analysis of consumers in an attempt to determine why prospective buyers react as they do to products or services or to advertisements used in attempting to sell them.

**Mud entrance**   A vestibule or small room designed for entrance from a play yard or alley.

**Multifamily structure**   A dwelling for (usually) five or more household units.

**Multiple exchange**   Three or more principals involved in the exchanging of various pieces of property.

**Multiple listing**   A cooperative listing arrangement whereby listings are taken and distributed to the other brokers so that they will have an opportunity to sell the property.

**Multiple nuclei**   A theory of urban growth emphasizing separate nuclei and differentiated districts occurring in clusters.

**Mutual savings bank**   A financial institution in which the depositors are the owners. Mutual savings banks are a primary source of home mortgage funds.

**Mutual water company**   A water company created by or for water users in a specific area with the object of securing an ample water supply at a more reasonable rate; stock is issued to users.

**NAR**   National Association of REALTORS®.

**National Association of Real Estate License Law Officials (NARELLO)**   An association composed of real estate commissioners and other officers and officials charged with the responsibility of enforcing the license laws of the various states, provinces, etc.

**National Savings and Loan League**   The national professional and trade association for individual savings and loan associations.

**Necessaries**   An economic term referring to the essential required for existence, such as food and shelter.

**Negative fraud**   The act of not disclosing to the buyer a material fact, thereby inducing him to enter into a contractual situation causing him damage or loss.

**Net income**   That amount of money which remains after expenses are subtracted from income, also termed "profit."

**Net lease**   An arrangement between the lessee and lessor whereby the lessee pays the charges against the property and the lessor nets the rental payments received.

**Net listing**   A listing stating the minimum amount the *seller* will accept.

**Net operating income**   The amount derived by deducting the expenses of operating a business from the gross income.

**Net worth**   The value remaining after all debts and obligations are removed.

**Nominal interest rate**   The rate of interest in the contract.

**Nonbearing wall**   A wall used as a divider and not to carry any load.

**Nonresident**   One who does not reside within the state or is not from that particular state.

**Nonzoning** Not placing any restriction on the use of the land via regulations, etc.

**Note** An acknowledgment and promise to pay a debt. It must be in writing and signed.

**Novation** The substitution of a new obligation for an old one, e.g., where parties to an agreement accept a new debtor in the place of an old one.

**Nuisance** Conduct or activity which results in actual physical interference with another person's reasonable use or enjoyment of his or her property for any lawful purpose.

**Obligee** One to whom a debt is owed.

**Obligor** One who is bound by debt.

**Obsolescence** Loss in property value because of the existence of a less costly alternative that provides comparable or more desirable property services.

**Occupancy** Physical possession.

**Offer** To present a set of terms intended to result in a contract subject to another's acceptance. This is not a contract until accepted by the other party.

**Offeree** The one who receives an offer, such as when the owner of property for sale receives an offer from a potential buyer based on certain terms subject to the seller's acceptance.

**Offeror** The one making the offer.

**OILSR** Office of Interstate Land Sales Regulation.

**Oligopoly** Control of a market by a limited number of participants.

**Open end clause** A clause in a mortgage which provides a method of advancing additional funds against a note after partial payment. To meet new obligations the debt can be quickly restored to its original amount.

**Open end mortgage** A mortgage given to secure future loans made from time to time, usually back up to the original balance after partial repayment has been made.

**Open house** A house that is available for inspection by potential purchasers without appointments.

**Open listing** An authorization given by a property owner to a real estate agent wherein said agent is given the nonexclusive right to secure a purchaser; open listings may be given to any number of agents without liability to compensate any except the one who first secures a buyer ready, willing, and able to meet the terms of the listing, or secures the acceptance by the seller of a satisfactory offer. The seller retains the right to sell directly without payment of any commission.

**Operating expense** Generally any expense occurring periodically which is necessary to produce net income before depreciation.

**Operating expense ratio** The relationship between operating expenses and project gross income.

**Operating profit** Profit arising from the regular operation of a firm engaged in performing physical services (public utilities, etc.), excluding income from other sources and expenses other than those of direct operation.

**Opinion of title** Legal opinion stating that title to the property is clear and merchantable or pointing out defects which must be cured.

**Option (to purchase real estate)** The right to purchase property at a stipulated price and under stipulated terms within a period of time; the instrument that is evidence of such a right.

**Optionee** The one who receives an option, such as the potential purchaser of real estate.

**Optionor** The one who gives the option, such as the owner of the real estate.

**Oral contract** A verbal agreement; one which is not placed in writing.

**Ordinance** A public regulation (usually local laws).

**Ordinary income** Income calculated for tax purposes from ordinary sources, not including items that result from capital gains.

**Orientation** The position of a structure on a site and its general relationship to its surroundings.

**Original cost** The initial cost; the amount paid to build on or acquire the property.

**Overall interest rate** The rate that includes interest on the land, interest on the building, and a recapture of capital.

**Overbuilding** The building of more structures of a particular type than can be absorbed by the market at prevailing prices.

**Overhang** The part of the roof extending beyond the walls, used to shade buildings and cover walks.

**Owner of record** The owner whose name appears on the recorded deed; the one who holds record title.

**Owner's equity** The value of the property in excess of the claims of all mortgages filed against it. In addition to mortgages, other claims, e.g., real estate taxes, would also reduce owner's equity.

**Owner's policy** A title insurance policy taken out to protect the owner's interest in the real estate.

**Ownership of real property** The holding of rights or interests in real estate.

**Package mortgage** A form of mortgage used with new residential sales. Included in the debt is the cost of certain mechanical or electrical equipment. Interest, principal, and equipment are all paid for by means of one equal monthly payment.

**Panel heating** A means of radiant heating, with pipes or ducts built into walls, floor, or ceiling, which serve as heating panels.

**Panic selling** The illegal practice of inducing fear among property owners in a particular neighborhood that an abnormally high turnover might occur as the result of the introduction of a nonconforming use or user into the area.

**Parapet** A low protective wall or barrier built around the edge of a balcony, roof, bridge, or the like.

**Parcel of real estate** A particular piece of land and its improvements.

**Parity** Equality; often used to refer to an equivalence between farmers' current purchasing power and their purchasing power at a selected base period, maintained by government support of commodity prices.

**Parking lot** A parcel of real estate used for the storage of automobiles. Usually about 300 square feet per auto is required for parking space and aisles.

**Parol evidence** Oral or verbal evidence.

**Parquet floor** Hardwood flooring laid in squares or patterns instead of being laid in strips.

**Partially amortized mortgage** A combination of an amortized mortgage and a term mortgage (straight term mortgage).

**Participation loan** A mortgage loan made by one lender with other lenders purchasing interests in the loan.

**Participation mortgage** A loan in which the lender receives debt repayment plus a share of the profits from ownership.

**Partition** A division of real or personal property among co-owners of real estate through a legal proceeding brought for that purpose.

**Partition action** Court proceedings in which co-owners seek to divide the property into individual shares.

**Partition proceedings** A legal procedure by which an estate held by tenants in common is divided and title in severalty to a designated portion given to each of the previous tenants in common.

**Partnership**   A contractual union of two or more parties who share in risks and profits of a business venture.

**Party wall**   A wall located on or at the boundary line between two adjoining parcels, and used or intended to be used by the owners of both properties in the construction or maintenance of the improvements on their respective lots. Quite often it is a perimeter wall of two adjoining houses giving support to both. It is built and maintained under a recorded agreement.

**Pass-through securities program**   A GNMA mortgage-backed security program wherein the principal and interest on the mortgages purchased by the investors are passed through to them as they are collected.

**Patent**   A conveyance from the federal government to a private buyer.

**Payback period**   Period of time necessary for the cash flow from a project to equal the amount of money invested.

**Pennsylvania farmhouse**   An architectural style that employs a Colonial residential type of design with stone walls, sometimes pargeted with plaster and whitewashed, characteristically informal.

**Per capita**   By the head; according to the number of individuals.

**Percentage lease**   A lease under which the lessee pays rent according to the amount of business he or she does, usually a percentage of the gross from the business. There is usually a provision for a minimum rent payment.

**Performance bond**   A bond used to guarantee the specific completion of an endeavor in accordance with a contract, such as that supplied by a contractor guaranteeing the completion of a building or a road.

**Perimeter**   The distance around the outside of an object or geometric figure.

**Perimeter heating**   Any system in which the heat registers are located along the outside dimensions of a room, especially under the windows.

**Periodic tenancy**   A tenancy that continues for successive periods (such as month to month) and continues until terminated by notice of one of the parties.

**Permanent loan**   Long-term financing through a mortgage loan or deed of trust.

**Perpetual easement**   An easement without a time limit.

**Perpetuity**   Without limitation as to time; theoretically, forever.

**Personal property**   The exclusive right to exercise control over personalty; all property objects other than real estate.

**Personal representative**   An executor, guardian, or administrator who represents another party under contract or judicial appointment.

**Personalty**   All property other than realty; chattels.

**Physical depreciation**   Physical deterioration inherent in the property, which impairs its use.

**Pi**   The constant that relates the circumference of a circle to the diameter. The ratio is equal to 3.1416.

**PI constant**   The principal and interest constant used to repay an amortized loan.

**Pier**   A column of masonry, used to support other structural members.

**Pitch**   The incline of a roof.

**PITI**   Stands for principal, interest, taxes, insurance when they are all included in one mortgage payment.

**Plaintiff**   The party who originates an action at law.

**Planned unit development**   A design for an area which provides for intensive use of land often through a combination of private and common areas with arrangements for sharing responsibilities for the common areas. Typically, zoning boards consider the entire development and allow its arrangements to be substituted for traditional subdivisions. An example is a residential cluster development.

**Planning**   The process of formulating a program in advance to achieve desired results. Long-range planning is planning for a period of years in the future. This type of planning is used as a framework for shorter-range planning.

**Plat, plat map**   A map that shows boundary lines of parcels of real estate, usually of an area that has been subdivided into a number of lots.

**Plat book**   A book containing a series of plat maps.

**Plat book designation**   The location of the recorded subdivision of a tract of land. It has a distinguishing name or number so that it can be readily located in the public records.

**Plenum**   The chamber in a warm-air furnace where the air is heated and from which the ducts carry the warm air to the registers.

**Plottage**   The extent to which value is increased when two or more lots are combined in a single ownership or use.

**Plottage increment**   The appreciation in unit value attained by joining smaller ownerships into a large single ownership.

**Plottage value**   Increased value to land created by joining small parcels into large tracts.

**Plywood**   Laminated wood made up in several layers; several thicknesses of wood glued together with the grain at different angles for strength.

**PMI**   Private mortgage insurance.

**Points**   A charge assessed by a lending institution to increase the yield of a mortgage loan so that it is competitive with other investments. Sometimes the loan origination fee is referred to in terms of points.

**Police power**   The right of the state to enact laws and enforce them for the order, safety, health, morals, and general welfare of the public.

**Portico**   A roof supported by columns. It may be part of a building or by itself.

**Power of attorney**   A written authorization to an agent to perform specified acts on behalf of his principal.

**Prefabricated house**   A house with components that are prebuilt and sometimes partly assembled prior to delivery to the building site.

**Prefabrication**   The process of manufacturing component parts of a structure in a factory for later assembly on-site.

**Prepayment penalty**   The penalty levied on the mortgagor or trustor for early payment of the obligation.

**Prepayment privilege**   A mortgage contract clause permitting the borrower to pay loan payments in advance of their due date.

**Prepayment yield**   The sum that may be realized by paying a debt prior to the date due.

**Prerogative**   A sovereign power.

**Prescription**   The name given to a mode of acquiring property rights in land of another by continuous use, without claiming ownership.

**Present value**   The value today, computed by measuring all future benefits of an investment and converting those benefits into terms of today's dollars.

**Price**   The amount of money at which property is offered for sale or is exchanged for at a sale; value in terms of money.

**Price level**   A relative position on the scale of prices as determined by a comparison of prices (of labor, materials, capital, etc.) at one time with prices at other times.

**Prima facie**   Presumptive evidence of fact which is legally sufficient to establish that fact unless rebutted by evidence to the contrary.

**Principal**   One who has another act for him; one who is represented by an agent; also, the amount of a debt.

**Principal balance**   The oustanding amount owed on the original sum borrowed under a mortgage or loan.

**Principal meridian**   Part of the rectangular method of survey. It is a meridian which serves as a reference for the other meridians.

**Principal personal residence**   The primary residence of a person; used for tax purposes.

**Priority**   When two persons have similar rights in respect to the same subject matter, but one is entitled to exercise his right to the exclusion of the other, he is said to have priority.

**Private sector**   The portion of the economy which produces goods and services consumed, in contrast to the portion containing governmental bodies.

**Probate**   A word originally meaning merely "relating to the proofs of wills," in American law it is now a general name or term used to include all matters over which probate courts have jurisdiction, which in many states are the estates of deceased persons and of persons under guardianship as well as trusts and trustees.

**Profit**   The amount in excess of cost realized on the sale of an asset.

**Profit à prendre**   A right to take part of the soil or produce of the land of another.

**Promisee**   One to whom a promise is made.

**Promissory note**   A written promise by one person to pay a certain sum of money to another individual at some future specified time. In real property financing, it serves as evidence of a debt for which a mortgage on the property is held as security.

**Property**   The exclusive right to exercise control over an economic good.

**Property brief**   A folder that presents pertinent information about a property.

**Property management**   The operation of real property, including the leasing of space, collection of rents, selection of tenants, and the repair and renovation of the buildings and grounds.

**Property manager**   An agent for the owner of real estate in all matters pertaining to the operation of the property or properties which are under his or her direction, who is paid a commission for his or her services.

**Property owners association**   An organization with the purpose of administering private regulations affecting residential land uses.

**Property services**   The benefits accruing from the use of property.

**Proportion**   The degree of relationship or ratio between two things.

**Proposition**   An offer to do something; in real estate, an offer to purchase.

**Proprietorship**   A business run by its owner as an individual rather than as a corporation.

**Prorate**   To allocate expenses or income among the parties in proportion to the amount owed or earned. (Noun: Proration)

**Proration of taxes**   The division of taxes equally or proportionately in accordance with time of use.

**Prospectus**   A printed document describing the characteristics of a specific property.

**Public domain**   That land to which title is held by the federal government.

**Public housing**   Housing owned by a governmental body.

**Public Housing Administration**   A unit of the HUD, which administers legislation providing for loans and subsidies to local housing authorities to encourage the development of low-rental dwelling units.

**Public property**   A property, the title to which is vested in the community.

**Public sector**   That portion of the economy which is most affected by governmental bodies and which contains governmental bodies themselves.

**Public trustee**   The public official in each county whose office has been created by law and to whom title to real property is conveyed by trust deed to protect the interests of beneficiaries.

**Punitive damages**   The fine assessed to the wrongdoer in excess of damages actually suffered.

**Purchase and lease back**   A method whereby an investor becomes the actual owner of property through purchase for cash from the original owner-occupant, who continues to occupy and use the property under a long-term lease from the new owner.

**Purchase money mortgage**   A mortgage given concurrently with a conveyance of land, by the vendee to the vendor, on the same land, to secure the unpaid balance of the purchase price.

**Purchase on contract**   The purchase of property on installments with title remaining with the seller.

**Purchasing power risk**   Risk that the value of an investment will decline as a result of inflation (decline in the purchasing power of the dollar).

**Purpose of appraisal**   To estimate the dollar value of the future utility of a parcel of real property for a specific purpose.

**Quadrilateral**   A plane figure with four sides and four angles.

**Qualities of value**   Scarcity, desire, ability to buy, and utility.

**Quantity survey**   A means of determining building replacement cost in which all elements of labor, materials, and overhead are priced and totaled to obtain the building cost.

**Quarter round**   A molding that presents a profile of a quarter-circle.

**Quasi**   Corresponding to, or similar to; having a limited legal status.

**Quasi-contract**   An obligation similar to a contract, which is implied by law.

**Quiet enjoyment**   The right of an owner to use property without interference by others.

**Quiet title suit**   Legal action to remove a defect, cloud, or questionable claim against the title to property.

**Quitclaim deed**   A deed conveying only the right, title, and interest of the grantor in the property described, as distinguished from a deed which guarantees that actual ownership is being transferred.

**Race notice**   The concept used in recordation of a property wherein the first party to register the property becomes the recognized owner.

**Racial steering**   The unlawful practice of influencing a minority person's housing choice.

**Radiant heat**   A form of heating which transmits hot water or air through ducts embedded in the walls, ceiling, or floors; panel heating.

**Radiator**   A configuration of metal tubes, usually cast iron, heated by steam or hot water from the boiler. Heat is transferred to the objects in a room by radiation, and to the air by convection.

**Radius**   A straight line extending from the center of a circle or sphere to the edge. The radius is equal to one half of the diameter.

**Rafters**   The sloping wood components of a roof.

**Ranch style**   A one-story home design, usually with a rambling plan and without a basement.

**Range**   A part of the rectangular system of survey; a north-south row of townships; the 6-mile strip of land between meridians.

**Rate of return (ROR)**   A rate (expressed in percentage) based on the annual net income generated by the property as compared to the invested capital.

**Ratification** The approval or adoption of an act performed on behalf of a person without previous authorization.

**Ratio** A numerical comparison of the degree of relationship between two things, usually expressed as a fraction.

**Real estate** Land with or without buildings or improvements.

**Real estate broker** An agent who negotiates the sale of real property or real property services for a preset commission that is contingent on success.

**Real estate business** A form of business that deals in rights to land and improvements.

**Real estate developing** Preparing land for use, constructing buildings and other improvements, and making the completed properties available for use.

**Real estate financing** The channeling of monies into the production and use of real estate; facilitating the production and use of real estate through borrowed or equity funds.

**Real estate investment corporation** A corporation that sells its securities to the public and has a special interest in real estate or is a builder or developer of real estate.

**Real estate investment trust** A trust designed in a form similar to that of an investment or mutual fund for the purpose of allowing investors to channel funds into the real estate investment market. Special federal law permits pooled investments in real estate and mortgages without exposure to corporate income taxes.

**Real estate market function** The process of placing real properties and their services into the hands of consumers.

**Real estate marketing** The process of putting real properties and their services into the hands of consumers. Brokerage and property management are the two main subdivisions of real estate marketing.

**Real estate operator** Any individual engaged in the real estate business acting for himself rather than as an agent.

**Real estate salesperson** Any person who for a compensation or valuable consideration has contracted with a real estate broker to sell or offer to sell or negotiate the sale of exchange of real estate, or to lease, rent, or offer for rent any real estate, or to negotiate leases thereof, or of the improvement thereon, as a whole or partial vocation.

**Real Estate Securities and Syndication Institute (RESSI)** Provides educational opportunities in the field of marketing securities and syndication of real estate.

**Real estate syndicate** A partnership formed for participation in a real estate venture. Partners may be limited or unlimited in their liability.

**Real estate tax** A money charge levied upon real property for support of local government and for public services.

**Realization of gain** The taking of the gain or profit from the sale of property.

**Real property** The exclusive right to exercise control over real estate.

**REALTOR®** A broker who is affiliated with a local real estate board that is a member of NAR.

**Realtors National Marketing Institute (RNMI)** Provides educational programs for REALTORS® in the area of commercial and investment properties, residential sales, and real estate office administration. Confers CRB (Certified Residential Broker), CCIM (Certified Commercial and Investment Member).

**Realty** Land and all fixtures permanently attached to it.

**Reappraisal lease** A lease having a clause calling for the periodic reevaluation of rents.

**Recapture** A provision for predicting the return of investment. It may be accomplished by inclusion in the capitalization rate in the income approach to valuation.

**Recapture of excess depreciation** The use of excess depreciation against income generated.

**Recapture rate** The rate of interest necessary to provide for the return of the initial investment. Not to be confused with interest rate, which is the rate of interest on an investment.

**Receiver** One appointed by the courts to take control and possession of property pending litigation and some final order by the court.

**Receiver clause** A clause in the mortgage to prevent dissipation of the value of the asset that secures a loan. This clause provides for the orderly appointment of a receiver to take over residential property abandoned by the mortgagor. The receiver rents, manages, and thus conserves the value of the property.

**Reciprocity** The mutual exchange of privileges between groups or states. In the case of real estate it is the automatic recognition of the license of one state in another. Many states do not have reciprocity agreements.

**Recognition of gain** The recognition of the profit received upon the sale of an asset.

**Reconstructed operating statement** Operating revenue and expense figures put into a standard format which permits comparisons with similar properties.

**Recording** The process of entering or recording a copy of certain legal instruments or documents, such as a deed, in a government office provided for this purpose, thus making a public record of the document for the protection of all concerned and giving constructive notice to the public at large.

**Recording acts, registry laws** Laws providing for the recording of instruments affecting title as a matter of public record to preserve such evidence and give notice of their existence and content; laws providing that the recording of an instrument informs all who deal in real property of the transaction and that, unless the instrument is recorded, a prospective purchaser without actual notice of its existence is protected against it.

**Recourse** The right to a claim against a prior owner of a property or note.

**Rectangle** Any four-sided plane figure that contains four right (90°) angles.

**Rectangular survey** The government system of land description, noted for greater accuracy; it is adaptable to the measurement of extensive territory.

**Redemption** The regaining of title to real property after a foreclosure sale. An equity of redemption is the interest of the mortgagor in real property prior to foreclosure. A statutory right of redemption is the right under law of the mortgagor to redeem title to real property before a foreclosure sale for a limited period of time.

**Redevelopment** The process of clearance and reconstruction of blighted areas.

**Red-lining** The refusal to lend money within a specific area for various reasons. This practice is now illegal.

**Refinancing** The negotiation of a new mortgage loan to replace and pay off the unpaid balances of existing mortgages.

**Reformation** An action to correct an error in a deed or other document.

**Regime** A listing of the system of rules or regulations affecting the owners of a condominium project.

**Regional analysis** A process applied to real estate, pertaining mainly to local economies and the surrounding area; for other purposes, the area of a "region" may be defined more broadly.

**Registrar of deeds, recorder** The government officer in charge of a land records office.

**Registration** Recording; inserting in an official register.

**Regression** The appraisal principle that maintains that the value of high-quality properties will be adversely affected by the presence of low-quality properties.

**Regulation Z**  Regulations regarding credit disclosure issued by the Board of Governors of the Federal Reserve System to aid in implementation of the Truth-in-Lending Act.

**Regulations**  A set of rules for controlling activities or procedures. Coercive regulations are regulations which provide penalties for noncompliance. An inducive regulation is a regulation which provides incentive for compliance.

**Rehabilitate**  The process of removing blight by repairing and renovating rather than by destroying improvements.

**Release**  The giving up of a right or claim by the person in whom it exists to the person against whom it might have been enforced.

**Release clause**  The stipulation that, upon payment of a specific amount of money to the holder of a trust deed or mortgage, the lien of the instrument as to a specific described lot or area shall be removed, e.g., from the blanket lien on the whole area involved.

**Remainder**  The right of a person to an estate in land that matures at the end of another estate; a classification of estates by time of enjoyment. A contingent remainder is an interest that will become a remainder only if some condition is fulfilled.

**Remainderman**  One who is entitled to the remainder of the estate after a particular estate carved out of it has expired.

**Remaining economic life**  The future period during which improvements are to be depreciated for tax purposes; usually stated in years.

**Remodel**  To make physical alterations other than keeping the property in repair.

**Renewal**  The process of redevelopment or rehabilitation in urban areas; often used in relation to rebuilding or restoration of blighted areas.

**Rent**  The return on land or real property; the price paid for the use of real property belonging to another.

**Rent controls**  The legal regulation of the maximum rental payment for the use of real property.

**Rent multiplier**  A number used to estimate value by multiplying it by the rent. A rent multiplier may be either a gross rent multiplier or a net rent multiplier. *See* gross rent multiplier.

**Rent schedule**  A plan to estimate the rents to be paid; also, records kept of rentals actually paid in a specific period.

**Rental value**  The value for a stated period of the right to use and occupy property; the amount a prospective tenant is warranted in paying for a stated period of time, e.g., a month, a year, etc., for the right to use and occupy real property under certain prescribed or assumed conditions.

**Replace**  To restore to a former plan or condition.

**Replacement cost**  The estimated cost of building a substantially similar structure as of a certain time utilizing modern materials at present costs and having equal utility.

**Replacement reserves**  Funds allotted for replacement of building components, equipment, etc.

**Replevin**  An action to regain possession of goods.

**Representation**  The principle upon which the issue of a deceased person takes or inherits the share of an estate his or her immediate ancestor would have taken or inherited if living.

**Reproduction cost**  The cost to duplicate at current prices an asset as closely as possible as of a certain time not knowing for corrective measures.

**Rescission**  The annulment or abrogation of a contract and the placing of the parties to it in the positions they were in before the contract was entered into.

**Research and development**  The process of creating new products or new methods.

**Reservation**  A clause in a deed or other instrument of conveyance by which the grantor reserves some estate, interest, or profit in the real estate conveyed.

**Reserve fund**  For multifamily properties, an amount budgeted from income to replace short-lived items such as furniture and equipment; the distinctive feature of a budget mortgage loan on residential property; the monthly payments on such a loan including certain sums which are impounded or reserved to pay taxes and insurance when due; a mortgagee's escrow account.

**Reserves**  Portions of earnings allotted to take care of possible losses in the conduct of business; listed on the balance sheet as a liability item.

**Residence**  The property in which one actually lives as his or her home.

**Residual**  That which remains; an appraisal technique to estimate the amount of net annual income derived from property; that which is left after deduction; the remainder of the income.

**Residual techniques**  Allocation of a portion of income to part of an asset, with the remainder (or residual) flowing automatically to the rest of the asset. Also, the allocation of part of the income to cover debt payments with the balance accruing to the equity being built up in the property.

**Residuary**  Pertaining to the residue.

**RESPA (Real Estate Settlement Procedures Act)**  A federal act passed in 1975 to force disclosure of all aspects of financing to potential borrowers.

**RESSI**  *See* Real Estate Securities and Syndication Institute.

**Restriction**  The term as used in relation to real property means the owner of real property is restrained or prohibited from doing certain things relating to the property, or using the property for certain purposes. For instance, the requirement in a deed that a lot may be used for the construction of not more than a single-family dwelling costing not less than $10,000 is termed a restriction. Also, a legislative ordinance affecting all properties in a given area, requiring that improvements on property shall not be constructed any closer to the street curb than 25 feet is a restriction by operation of law.

**Restrictive covenant**  A clause in a deed in which there is an agreement between the seller and the purchaser in regard to certain restraints as to the use of the property, and which is binding on all subsequent owners.

**Return on investment**  The percentage correlation between the price an investor pays and the stream of income dollars he or she obtains from the investment.

**Revenue stamps**  Stamps issued by the state government, which must be purchased and affixed in the amounts provided by law to documents or instruments representing original issues, sales and transfers of deeds of conveyance, stocks, and bonds; these stamps are evidence that transfer taxes have been paid.

**Reversion**  A right to future possession retained by an owner at the time of transfer of some limited interest in real property.

**Reversion value**  The estimated value of a reversion as of a given date determined actuarially.

**Reversionary right**  The right of a person to receive possession and use of property upon the termination or defeat of an existing limited estate carrying the rights of possession and use and vested in another person.

**Reversioner**  A person who is entitled to a reversion.

**Reverter**  That portion of an estate which returns or goes back to an owner (or reverts) or his or her heirs after the end or termination of an estate such as a leasehold or a life estate.

**Revocation**  A withdrawal; a recall; a repudiation; the taking back of a power or authority that has been previously conferred, such as the revoking of a license; the withdrawal of an offer prior to its acceptance.

**Rhomboid**  A parallelogram that contains oblique angles and whose opposite sides (only) are equal.

**Ridge**  A horizontal line at the joining of the top edges of two sloping roof surfaces. The rafters for both slopes are nailed at the ridge.

**Ridge board**  A board placed on its edge at the ridge of the roof so as to support the upper ends of the rafters; also called a roof tree, ridge piece, ridge plate, or ridge pole.

**Right angle**  An angle of 90° made by the meeting of two straight lines that are perpendicular to each other.

**Right of occupancy**  The privilege to occupy and use property for a specified period of time under the terms of some contract such as a lease or other formal agreement.

**Right of survivorship**  The distinguishing feature of any joint tenancy. It is the automatic succession to the interest of a deceased joint owner.

**Right of way**  A grant serving as an easement upon land, whereby the owner by agreement gives to another the right of passage over his or her land to construct a roadway, or use as a roadway, a specific part of his or her land, or the right to construct through and over his or her land, telephone, telegraph, or electric power lines; or the right to place underground water mains, gas mains, or sewer mains.

**Riparian**  Belonging or relating to the banks of a river, stream, waterway, etc.

**Riparian grant**  The transmittal of riparian rights.

**Riparian lease**  The document defining the terms, conditions, and date of expiration of the rights to use lands lying between the high water mark and the low water mark.

**Riparian owner**  One who owns land adjoining a watercourse.

**Riparian rights**  The rights of a landowner to water on, under, or immediately adjacent to his or her land and its uses.

**Riser**  An upright board at the rear of each step of a stairway. In heating, a riser is a duct slanted upward to carry hot air from the furance to the room above.

**Risk**  The degree of danger of future loss of capital or income.

**Risk evaluation**  The amount of risk involved in an investment as evaluated by the investor; usually related as a percentage of interest.

**Risk rating**  The method by which various risks are evaluated, usually employing grids to develop precise and relative figures for the purpose of determining the overall soundness of a loan.

**RNMI**  *See* Realtors National Marketing Institute.

**ROC**  Return of capital.

**Rod**  The unit of linear measure equal to a length of 5½ yards.

**ROI**  Return on investment.

**Rollover mortgage**  A mortgage that is rewritten or renewed at the termination of a prior loan. The terms may be changed with each "rollover" of the note.

**Row houses**  A series of individual houses having identical architectural features and the presence of a common wall between two units.

**Rules of thumb**  The cost indicators sometimes used to assist in estimating the value of a property. Examples are price per front foot, gross rent multiplier, price per square foot, cost per room, and cost per apartment unit. These are usually guidelines or averages based on experience in the same vicinity.

**Running with the land**  A covenant is said to run with the land when either the liability to perform it or the right to take advantage of it passes to the subsequent grantees of that land.

**Safe rate**  The rate of interest on government bonds, utility bonds, or bank savings.

**Sale-lease back**  A plan that allows for the simultaneous transfer of ownership and execution of the lease—the grantor becomes the lessee and the grantee the lessor.

**Sales contract**  The contract by which the buyer and the seller agree to terms of a sale of property.

**Sales expenses**  Costs incurred in the sale of real property. Broker's commissions, advertising costs, and costs incurred in the preparation of the property for sale are examples of common expenses.

**Sales kit**  A file of information concerning the properties a broker has for sale.

**Salesperson**  One employed by a real estate broker but licensed only as a salesperson.

**Salvage value**  The estimated worth of an item after it is fully depreciated.

**Sandwich lease**  A leasehold interest which is present between the primary lease and the operating lease. In subleasing property, when the holder of a sublease in turn sublets to another, his or her position is that of being sandwiched between the original lessee and the second sublessee.

**Sash**  Wood or metal frames containing one or more window panes.

**Satisfaction**  The written acknowledgment of the release of a mortgage or trust deed lien on the records upon payment of the secured debt.

**Savings bank**  A type of bank which receives savings in the form of the deposits in mortgages and other securities allowed by law. These banks, with the exception of a few in New Hampshire, are mutual institutions and are governed by self-perpetuating boards of trustees.

**Savings and loan association**  A state or federally chartered thrift institution that specializes in making residential mortgages.

**Scarcity**  The amount of limitation of real estate facilities in relation to their demand.

**Scribing**  The fitting of woodwork to an irregular surface.

**Seal**  A particular sign, made to attest in the most formal manner, the execution of an instrument.

**Seasonal fluctuations**  Variations in economic activity that recur at about the same time each year.

**Seasoned mortgage**  A mortgage in which periodic payments have been made for a long period of time and the borrower's payment pattern is well established.

**Second mortgage**  A mortgage made by a home buyer to generate enough capital for the down payment required under the first mortgage. (FHA does not permit this on loans it insures for first mortgages.) Such mortgages are also used to secure borrowings for home improvements or other related purposes.

**Secondary financing**  The loan secured by a second trust deed or a mortgage on real property.

**Secret interest**  Interest hidden or concealed from third-party knowledge.

**Section (of land)**  A portion of land 1 mile square containing 640 acres, into which the public lands of the United States were originally divided; one thirty-sixth part of a township.

**Section 8**  A federal program for leasing housing to lower-income families; sponsored through HUD.

**Sector hypothesis**  A theory stating that sectors of land use arise whereby the highest-priced homes are in the most attractive locations, medium-priced homes follow traffic arteries, and lower-priced homes are near places of employment.

**Sectory theory**  A theory of city growth that considers the city as a circle with wedge-shaped sectors pointing into the center of the urban area.

**Sectors**  Wedge-shaped area pointing to the center of the urban area; a recognized pattern of urban growth and development.

**Secured party** The party having a security interest in property owned by the debtor. Thus the pledgee, the conditional seller, or the mortgagee are all now referred to as secured parties.

**Security** Something of value deposited to make certain the fulfillment of an obligation or the payment of a debt.

**Security agreement** The agreement created between the secured party and the debtor that creates the security interest.

**Security deposits** The funds placed as collateral by a tenant so that the leased property may be restored to its original condition if need be at the termination of the lease.

**Security interest** The interest of the creditor in the property of the debtor in all types of credit transactions. It thus replaces such terms as chattel mortgage, pledge, trust, receipt, chattel trust, equipment trust, conditional sale, and inventory lien.

**Seed money** The money needed to begin a project, such as the funds needed for acquiring or controlling a site, obtaining zoning, making feasibility studies, etc.

**Seised** Possessed of an estate in fee.

**Seisin** In the legal sense, possession of premises with the intention of asserting a claim to a freehold estate therein; practically, the same as ownership.

**Self-liquidating mortgage** A mortgage which, by means of constant periodic payments, will be fully paid off at the end of its term.

**Self-regulating** A system of controls over the conduct of a group, all of whom voluntarily submit to such rules, e.g., the code of ethics adopted by NAR.

**Seller's market** An economic market in which sellers can sell at prices higher than those prevailing in an immediately preceding period; a market in which a limited number of properties is available and there is a large number of users and potential users demanding them at prevailing prices.

**Senior mortgage** The mortgage having a claim preferential to that of another mortgage.

**Separate property** Property owned by a husband or wife which is not jointly owned property; property acquired by either spouse prior to the marriage or by gift or devise after the marriage.

**Septic tank** An underground receptacle in which sewage from the house is reduced to liquid by bacterial action and then drained off.

**Service property** A property devoted to or available for utilization for a special purpose, but which has no independent marketability in the generally recognized acceptance of the term, such as a church property, a public museum, or a school.

**Servicing** The collection of payments on a mortgage. Servicing by the lender also consists of operational procedures covering accounting, bookkeeping, insurance, tax record, loan payment follow-up, delinquent loan follow-up, and loan analysis.

**Servient tenement** Property subject to an easement which benefits another property, called the "dominant tenement."

**Setback** The distance from curb or other established line, within which no buildings may be erected.

**Setback ordinance** An ordinance prohibiting the erection of a building or structure in the area between the curb and the setback line.

**Set-off** A counterclaim or cross-demand charged by a defendant against the claim of a plaintiff in an action seeking money damages.

**Settlement** The process at the closing of a sale of real estate negotiated by a real estate broker whereby the broker accounts to his or her principal for the earnest money deposit and deducts commission and advances by use of a form of settlement statement.

**Severalty** Ownership by a person in his or her own right.

**Severalty ownership** Owned by only one person; sole ownership.

**Severance** The act of removing something attached to the land. For example, the removal of shrubs from the property.

**Severance damage** The reduction in value caused by separation. Commonly, the damage resulting from the taking of a fraction of the whole property, reflected in a lowered utility and value in the land remaining and brought about by reason of the fractional taking.

**Shake** A hand-split shingle, usually edge-grained.

**Sheathing** The structural covering, usually consisting of boards, plywood, or wallboards, placed over exterior studding or rafters of a house.

**Shed roof** A single-pitch roof that slopes from front to back or back to front.

**Sheriff's deed** A deed executed by the sheriff pursuant to a court order in connection with the sale of property to satisfy a judgment.

**Sheriff's sale** A sale of property, conducted by a sheriff, or sheriff's deputy, by virtue of his or her authority as an officer pursuant to a court-ordered sale.

**Shopping center** A planned area for shopping, usually in an outlying location. Typically, stores are surrounded by a parking area. A mall-type shopping center is a shopping center in which the stores face inward toward an enclosed walkway rather than fronting on the parking lot, so that the shoppers can stay inside one building while they visit various stores.

**Sill** The lowest part of the frame of a house, resting on the foundation and supporting the uprights of the frame. The board or metal forming the bottom side of an opening, as a door sill, window sill, etc.

**Simple interest** The interest computed on the original principal alone.

**Simulation** The use of a controlled environment in which to test the effects of a decision.

**Single-family home** A dwelling designed for occupancy by one household only.

**Sinking fund** A fund set aside from the income of a property which, with accrued interest, will pay for replacement of the improvements as they wear out.

**SIR** *See* Society of Industrial Realtors.

**Site** A parcel of real estate that is suitable for improvement.

**Sitting** The placement and orientation of a house in reference to its lot.

**Situs** Location.

**Skylease** A long-term lease on the space above a parcel of real estate; the upper stories of a building to be erected by the tenant.

**Slander of title** A false and malicious statement, oral or written, made in disparagement of a person's title to real property, causing him special damage.

**Slum area** A heavily populated area marked by blight, squalor, or wretched living conditions.

**Slum clearance** The removal of blighted improvements by destruction of the improvements.

**Society of Industrial Realtors (SIR)** Provides educational opportunities to REALTORS® working with industrial property transactions. Confers SIR designation.

**Society of Real Estate Appraisers (SREA)** A trade association of residential real estate appraisers. Awards SRA, SREA, and SRPA designations.

**Social class** A group of people of common social and economic characteristics.

**Social overhead capital** The investments by the government for public betterments such as bridges, roads, schools, and parks.

**Soil pipe** The pipe which conveys waste from the house to the main sewer line.

**Soil pipe and soil stack**   The house sewer transporting waste from the house, and the vertical pipe ending in a vent in the roof, which transports vapors from the plumbing system.

**Sole or sole plate**   The piece, usually a 2 × 4, on which wall and partition studs rest.

**Southern Colonial**   An architectural design that combines both Georgian and New England Colonial, usually characterized by the use of two-story columns forming a porch across the long facade or at the side of the house.

**Sovereign consumer**   The theory that the consumer is the decision maker who determines what goods and services are to be provided within the society.

**Span**   A measure of the distance between structural supports such as walls, columns, piers, beams, girders, and trusses.

**Special assessment**   A legal charge against real estate levied by a public authority to fund the cost of public improvements such as street lights, sidewalks, street improvements, etc.

**Special warranty**   A covenant of warranty in a deed, by which the grantor guarantees the title against the claims of persons claiming "by, through, or under" the grantor only.

**Special warranty deed**   A guarantee only against the acts of the grantor and all persons claiming by, through, or under the grantor.

**Specific performance**   The requirement that a party must perform as agreed under a contract, in contrast to compensation or damages in lieu of performance; the arrangement whereby courts may force either party to a real estate contract to carry out an agreement exactly in accordance with its terms.

**Specification**   As used in the law relating to patents and machinery, and in building contracts, a particular or detailed statement of the various elements required to define the end product and to which it is to conform.

**Specimen tree**   A tree of special interest because of its shape or species, placed in a position of prominence in the yard; often a silver spruce, weeping birch, magnolia, or other unique ornamental tree.

**Split rate interest**   The interest rate paid on property when the rate determined for the buildings differs from the rate determined for the land.

**Spot zoning**   The allowance of a nonconforming use in an area zoned for a specific purpose.

**Spouse**   One's wife or husband.

**Square**   A rectangle in which all sides are equal. The process of multiplying a number by itself.

**Square-foot method**   A means of estimating construction, reproduction, or replacement costs of a building by multiplying the square-foot floor area by the appropriate square-foot construction cost figure.

**Square root**   The number or quantity that, multiplied by itself, will produce a given number.

**Squatters rights**   The rights to occupancy of land created through long and undistributed use but with no legal title or arrangement.

**SRA**   Senior Residential Appraiser.

**SREA**   Senior Real Estate Analyst.

**SRPA**   Senior Real Property Appraiser.

**Stability of income**   The constant annual net income reasonably anticipated over the entire economic life of the property.

**Stagflation**   An economic condition in which there is no economic growth (stagnation) or rapid or large price increases (inflation).

**Stand-by commitment**   An agreement by the lender to make funds available at a future date upon specified terms.

**Standard depth**   The depth chosen as normal, usually the one most common in the neighborhood.

**Standard metropolitan area**   Defined by the Bureau of Census as a county, or a group of contiguous counties, containing a city of 50,000 population or more.

**Standing mortgage**   A mortgage that provides for interest payments only, with the entire principal falling due in one payment at maturity of the mortgage.

**State association**   The association of real estate boards that copes with matters which vitally affect the business of its members within its own state.

**State vet's loan**   A loan made at 4% interest to eligible war veterans upon security of real property located in any state for the acquisition of homes and farms. The program is administered by the State Department of Veterans' Affairs.

**Statement of consideration**   Statement in a deed or other sales contract that confirms the fact that the purchaser actually gave something of value for the property.

**Status**   Standing, state, or condition.

**Statute**   A particular law enacted and established by the legislative department of the government.

**Statute of Fraud**   Legislation providing that all agreements affecting title to real estate must be in writing to be enforceable.

**Statute of limitations**   A statute barring all right of action after a certain period of time from the time when a cause of action first arises.

**Statutory lien**   A lien granted to a party by the operation of a statute, e.g., the lien of real estate taxes.

**Statutory redemption period**   The time allowed to a delinquent borrower to cure his deficiencies before his property is taken permanently from him.

**Statutory warranty deed**   A warranty deed form outlined by state statutes.

**Step-up lease**   A lease that permits increasing rentals at specified times during the lease period.

**Straight-line capital recapture**   The amount of dollar investment recovery in each year that is constant throughout the life of the investment.

**Straight-line depreciation**   See depreciation, straight line.

**Straight term mortgage**   A mortgage in which repayment of the principal is in one lump sum at maturity.

**Strict foreclosure**   The action taken by a court which, after determination that sufficient time has elapsed for a mortgagor to pay a mortgage past due, terminates all right and interest of the mortgagor in the real property. A forced sale of the property is then ordered for the benefit of the creditors secured by the mortgage.

**String, stringer**   A timber or other support for cross-members. In stairs, the support on which the stair treads rest.

**Studs, studding**   The vertical supporting timbers in walls and partitions.

**Subcontractor**   A contractor employed by a general contractor. A subcontractor usually is concerned only with one particular part of the improvement of real estate, such as plumbing, masonry, carpentry, and the like.

**Subdividing**   Division of a large parcel of land into smaller parcels.

**Subdivision**   An area of land divided into parcels or lots generally of a size suitable for residential use.

**Subject property**   The property under consideration; the property being appraised.

**Subject to and agreeing to pay**   The purchaser takes title to the real estate and is also obligated to pay the debt along with the original maker of the note.

**Subject to mortgage**   The purchaser takes title to the property but is not obligated to pay the mortgage. If foreclosure occurs, the purchaser loses his equity and the original mortgagor is responsible for the debt.

**Subjective value**   A value created in the mind. It is the amount people will pay regardless of cost. In appraising, it is used in the income and market data approaches.

**Sublease**   One executed by the lessee of an estate to a third person, conveying the same estate for a shorter term than that for which the lessee holds it.

**Subordinate**   To make subject to, junior to, or inferior to, usually with respect to security.

**Subordination clause**   The clause in a junior or a second lien which permits retention of priority for prior liens. A subordination clause may also be used in a first deed of trust, permitting it to be subordinated to subsequent liens, for example, the liens of construction loans.

**Subrogation**   The substitution of one person in the place of another with reference to a lawful claim, demand, or right by virtue of having paid a claim under an insurance contract.

**Subsidized housing**   Housing for low- and moderate-income families in which rentals are paid in part by the government or in which the government pays a portion of the developer's loan interest costs so that he or she can charge lower rentals.

**Subsidy (two types)**   In real estate, a grant by government that eases the financial burden of holding, using, or improving real property. A direct subsidy is a subsidy which is of direct, visible benefit to the recipient, such as a cash grant. An indirect subsidy is a subsidy whose benefit is felt indirectly, such as tariffs or farm price supports which may affect the land values in a particular area.

**Suburb**   A development of real estate in areas peripheral to the central area of a city.

**Succession**   The legal act or right of acquiring property by descent; succeeding to an asset by will or inheritance.

**Sufficient description**   The real estate which is to be conveyed by the deed can be identified; will stand up in court.

**Sui juris**   Having legal ability to handle one's own affairs; not under any legal disability.

**Summation**   An appraisal method for determining an interest rate; an indicated value derived by estimating the reproduction cost, subtracting depreciation, and adding the value of the land; one method of the cost approach.

**Summons**   A writ directed to the sheriff or other proper officer which requires him to notify the person named in the writ that an action has been brought against him and that he is required to appear, on a day named, and answer the complaint in such action.

**Sum-of-the-years'-digits depreciation**   See Depreciation.

**Sump pump**   An automatic electric pump installed in a basement for the purpose of emptying the sump, a pit serving as a drain for basement water accumulations.

**Supermarket**   A 20,000- to 40,000-square-foot grocery store that is often free-standing.

**Supersession costs**   Costs incurred in scrapping existing improvements in order to make possible new land uses.

**Supply**   Amount available for sale.

**Supply and demand, law of**   A theory that price or value varies directly, depending upon the quantity of units available and quantity of units desired or demanded by the buying public.

**Surcharge**   An additional charge added to the usual charge.

**Surety**   One who undertakes to pay money or to perform any other act in the event that his or her principal fails to do so.

**Surplus productivity**   An appraisal theory whereby net income remains after the costs of labor, coordination, and capital have been paid. This appraisal tends to fix the value of the land.

**Surrender**   The process of cancellation of a lease by mutual consent of lessor and lessee.

**Survey**   The process by which a parcel of land is measured and its boundaries ascertained.

**Survivorship**   See joint tenancy.

**Sustained-yield management**   Selective harvesting of slow-growing crops such as trees to provide for a relatively stable yield every year rather than periodic large yields at irregular times.

**Swing loan**   A short-term loan enabling the purchaser of a new property to purchase that property before having been paid for the equity from the property he or she is presently selling.

**Sweat equity**   Labor or services put into improving real property to gain possession and title in lieu of money.

**Syndicate**   A group of individuals, corporations, or trusts who pool money to undertake economic endeavors. The syndicate can assume the structure of a corporation, a trust, a partnership, a tenancy in common, or any other legal ownership form.

**Syndication**   The process of combining persons or firms to accomplish a joint venture which is of mutual interest.

**Tacking**   The adding together of successive periods of adverse possession of persons in privity with each other in order to create one continuous adverse possession for the time required by statute to establish title.

**Tandem plan**   A secondary mortgage market arrangement whereby GNMA purchases certain original mortgages for resale to FNMA or other investors.

**Tangible property**   Property that, by its nature, may be perceived by the senses. In general, the land, its fixed improvement, furnishings, merchandise, cash, etc.

**Tax**   A charge or burden, usually monetary in nature, levied upon persons or property for public purposes; a forced contribution of wealth to aid in meeting the public needs of a government.

**Tax abatement**   The amount of decrease or deduction of a tax improperly levied.

**Taxable gain**   A profit on a sale of property that is subject to taxation.

**Tax base**   The sum of the taxable property which determines the financial capability of the government to raise funds through taxation.

**Tax cost basis**   The total cost of a property, including purchase price and payments for major improvements; used in determining the basis for capital gains tax.

**Tax credit**   A credit received for a particular item and deducted from taxes owed when preparing the tax return—e.g., a solar energy credit.

**Tax deed**   A deed given upon a sale of lands made for the nonpayment of taxes.

**Tax-deferred exchanges**   See Exchanges, tax-deferred.

**Tax liability**   Simply stated, taxes owed to a taxing authority. Usually real estate taxes, although the term could also refer to ordinary income or capital gain taxes.

**Tax lien**   A claim against property arising out of nonpayment of taxes; the claim may be sold by the taxing authority.

**Tax penalty**   The amount to be paid due to nonpayment of the taxes. Usually expressed as a percent of the unpaid balance.

**Tax roll**   The list describing the persons and properties subject to a particular tax.

**Tax sale**   A sale of land for unpaid taxes.

**Tax sale certificate**   A certificate given to the purchaser of land at a tax sale which transfers the lien but not the title to the purchaser.

**Tax shelter**   An investment motivated primarily to obtain an income tax deduction to apply against taxable income earned from other sources.

**Tax title**   The title transferred through a tax sale.

**Taxable value**   The value upon which the taxes are computed when tax rates have been determined.

**Taxation (several types)**   The right of government to payment for the support of activities in which it engages. A double tax in real estate is the taxation of the property as an asset and the taxation of the property income the owner receives. Estate taxation is the tax imposed by government on property passed by will or descent. A personal property tax is a tax imposed upon owners of personal property. A real property tax is a tax imposed upon the owners of real property.

**Taxing district**   The geographical area over which a taxing authority levies taxes.

**Taxpayer**   One who pays a tax.

**Tenancy**   An interest in real property; the right to possession and use of real property.

**Tenancy at sufferance**   The wrongful holding over by a tenant whose lease has terminated.

**Tenancy at will**   Holding possession of premises by permission of the owner or landlord, but without a fixed term.

**Tenancy by the entireties**   An estate held by a husband and wife, in which both are viewed as one person under common law, which thus provides for ownership by the marriage itself and not by the two parties in shares.

**Tenancy in common**   A holding in one property by two or more parties with interests accruing under different titles, or accruing under the same title but at different periods, or conferred by words of limitation stating that each grantee shall hold a distinct share which need not be equal.

**Tenant**   One who has the temporary use and occupation of real property owned by another.

**Tenant per autre vie**   One who holds lands for the period of another's life.

**Tenant selection**   A process used by property managers to choose rental prospects.

**Tenement**   Everything of permanent nature, such as land and buildings, which may be owned; in a more restrictive sense, a house or dwelling.

**Tentative map**   A map of the subdivision submitted to a local planning commission for study and approval.

**Tenure**   In accordance with the American concept of real estate ownership, this means that all rights and title in and to the land rest with the owner.

**Tenure in land**   The conditions under which an individual holds an estate in lands.

**Termites**   Antlike insects which feed on wood.

**Termite shield**   A shield of noncorrodible metal located on top of the foundation wall or around pipes to prevent the entrance of termites.

**Term mortgage**   A specific type of mortgage loan having a stipulated duration, normally under 5 years, on which only interest is paid. At the expiration of the term the entire principal is paid.

**Terms**   The conditions spelled out in an arrangement or agreement such as a mortgage or a contract.

**Testament**   A will.

**Testamentary**   After death; e.g., a devise of real estate by a will is a testamentary transfer because the will is not operative until after death.

**Testator**   The person who makes or has made a will.

**Tier**   A row of townships running east and west; used in the governmental survey method of land description.

**Time-interval maps**   A series of maps that show land use or some other feature as of different dates.

**Timesharing**   A method of ownership of real property that permits multiple purchasers to buy undivided interests in real property with a reserved right to the use of the facility for a specified period of time.

**Title (several types)**   Proof or evidence of ownership or ownership rights. A search of title is a study of the history of the title to a property. A title by descent is a title acquired by the laws of succession; title acquired by an heir in the absence of a will. A title by devise is a title received through a will.

**Title company**   A corporation whose primary function is to insure titles to real property.

**Title guarantee policy**   The title insurance provided by the owner in lieu of an abstract of title.

**Title insurance**   Insurance that a title is clear or clear except for defects noted; a policy of insurance that indemnifies the insured for loss occasioned by unknown defects of recorded title.

**Title report**   A report, prepared prior to the issuance of title insurance, which states the condition of the title.

**Title search**   The process of checking the public records and legal proceedings to disclose the current state of a real property's ownership.

**Title theory**   A state statute allowing lenders or lending institutions to secure the title to property as collateral for a loan.

**Title theory of mortgage**   The mortgage arrangement whereby title to mortgaged real property vests in the lender.

**Topographical map**   A map that shows the slope and contour of land; a map of the physical features of a parcel of real estate or an area of land.

**Topography**   The contour and slope of land and such things as gullies, streams, knolls, and ravines.

**Torrens certificate**   A document issued by the registrar, in accordance with the Torrens law, which identifies the party who holds the title to property.

**Torrens system**   A system of land title registration in which the state insures the quality of title against certain defects.

**Tort**   A private or civil wrong or injury.

**Township**   A territorial subdivision in the quadrangular survey method 6 miles long, 6 miles wide, and containing 36 sections, each 1 mile square.

**Trade**   Used synonymously with "exchange." A transaction in which owners convey the rights in a particular property for rights in another.

**Trade area**   The geographical area from which purchasers of particular goods and services are ordinarily drawn.

**Trade association**   A voluntary organization of individuals or firms in a common area of economic activity; the organization has for its purpose the promotion of certain aspects of that common area of activity.

**Trade fixtures**   Articles of personal property which have been annexed to the freehold and which are necessary to the carrying on of a trade and which may be removed.

**Trade-in**   A method of guaranteeing an owner a minimum amount of cash on sale of his present property to permit him to purchase another. If the property is not sold within a specified time at the listed price, the broker agrees to arrange financing to purchase the property at an agreed upon discount.

**Traditional design**   The home styling incorporating the ideas of the past, reminiscent of Cape Cod, Colonial, Georgian, and similar architectures.

**Transcript**   A written record of a proceeding which may have been verbal, such as a record of testimony in a trial.

**Transfer book**   A book in which all transfers of real estate within the county are kept. Such books are kept by the county recorder and, usually, the auditor.

**Transfer tax**   The tax required by state law to be paid when real estate is sold.

**Transition**   Change.

**Trapezoid**   A four-sided plane figure of which only two sides are parallel.

**Traverse rod**   An instrument for hanging draperies or window curtains on a rod fitted with slides, pulleys, and cords, by means of which draperies may be drawn.

**Treads**   The horizontal boards forming the stairway.

**Trend**   A prevailing tendency of behavior of some observable phenomenon, such as economic activity, over a long period of time despite intermittent fluctuations.

**Trespass**   Any unauthorized entry on another's property; any person who makes such an entry is a trespasser.

**Triangle**   A three-sided figure.

**Trim**   Finish materials such as moldings applied around openings or at the floor and ceiling such as baseboards, cornices, or picture moldings.

**Trust**   A fiduciary relationship in which an independent party (trustee) holds legal title to property for the beneficiaries of the trust who hold the equitable title during the life of the trust. The trustee may not deal with the property as his own but must deal with it in the best interests of the beneficiaries.

**Trust account**   A bank account held separate from a broker's personal funds, in which a broker is required by state law to deposit all monies collected for clients. (Also see "escrow account.")

**Trust indenture**   A document showing the trust agreement.

**Trust res**   Any property which is the subject of a trust.

**Trustee**   One who holds legal title to trust assets for the benefit of those holding equitable title. *See* trust.

**Trustee's deed**   A device used to transfer property from a trustee to a purchaser. This deed has the same effect as a quitclaim deed.

**Trustor**   The one who conveys title of his property to the trustee to be held as security until he has performed his obligation to a lender under the terms of a deed of trust, or for other purposes, such as management.

**Truth in Lending Act (TIL)**   That portion of Public Law 90-231 (the Consumer Credit Protection Act) which requires that the borrower be informed of true credit costs being charged.

**Turnkey**   A form of housing for low-income families that was originally built by private sponsors to be sold to local housing authorities.

**Ultra vires**   Beyond the power. Applied to the acts of a corporation beyond the powers granted in its charter.

**Unbalanced improvement**   An improvement which does not serve the highest best use for the site on which it is placed.

**Underimprovement**   An improvement which does not serve the highest best use for the site on which it is placed by reason of being smaller in size or less in cost than a building which would bring the site to its highest and best use.

**Undisclosed principal**   One of the parties to a transaction who is unidentified. This might occur when a broker is instructed to keep the identify of his client a secret.

**Undivided interest**   Fractional ownership but without physical division into shares.

**Undue influence**   Taking any fraudulent advantage of another's weakness of mind, distress, or necessity.

**Unearned increment**   An increase in the value of real estate as a result of no effort on the part of the owner; often due to an increase in population.

**Unenforceable contract**   One that is a good contract but for some reason cannot be enforced under the law, e.g., an unwritten contract for the sale of real estate which is unenforceable because of the Statute of Frauds.

**Uniform Commerical Code**   Applicable after January 1, 1965, it establishes a unified and comprehensive scheme for the regulation of security transactions in personal property, superseding the existing statutes on chattel mortgages, conditional sales, trust receipts, assignment of accounts receivable, and others in this field.

**Unilateral contract**   A contract under which one party promises to do something upon the completed act of another.

**Unimproved**   As relating to land, vacant, returned to nature, or lacking in essential appurtenant improvements required to serve a useful purpose.

**United States governmental survey system**   A means of describing or locating real property by reference to the governmental survey; often referred to as the rectangular survey.

**United States Savings and Loan League**   A trade association of savings and loan associations.

**Unities of title**   The particular characteristic of an estate held by several in joint tenancy and which contains the unities of interest, title, time, and possession; i.e., all joint tenants have one and the same interest accruing through the same conveyance commencing at one time and held by each through an undivided possession of the whole property.

**Unit-in-place costs**   A means of estimating building replacement cost in which quantities of materials are costed on an in-place rather than purchased basis and summarized to obtain a building cost.

**Urban plan**   The community facilities that enable the community to function as a unit, e.g., the system of streets, sewers, water mains, parks, playgrounds, and the like.

**Urban planning**   The process of outlining the growth and development of the urban area.

**Urban property**   City property; densely settled property.

**Urban renewal**   The controlled method of redevelopment within urban areas. Although often used to refer to Title I and other public projects, it also encompasses private redevelopment efforts.

**Urban renewal area**   A slum area; a blighted, deteriorated, or deteriorating area; an open land area which is approved by HUD as necessary for an urban renewal project.

**Urban renewal project**   The term applied to the specific activities undertaken by a local public agency in an urban renewal area to prevent and eliminate slum and blight. The activities may involve slum clearance and redevelopment, rehabilitation, or conservation, or a combination thereof.

**Urban size rachet**   The theory that, once a town reaches a certain size, it will continue to grow of its own accord.

**Urban sprawl**   Expansion of a municipality over a large geographical area.

**Usage**   Uniform practice or course of conduct followed in certain businesses or professions or some procedure or phase thereof.

**Use**   A beneficial interest in land under a trust.

**Use density**   The number of buildings having a specific use per unit of area; sometimes calculated by a percentage of land coverage or density of coverage.

**Use districts**   Areas in a city which have land uses that differ from adjacent land uses, e.g., commercial, industrial, and residential.

**Use map**   Map of the municipal area showing important types of land uses.

**User of real estate**   One who has the use of property rights, whether it be through ownership, lease, easement, or license.

**Usury**   The practice of lending money at a rate of interest above the legal rate. This is an illegal practice.

**Utility**   Ability of real estate to provide useful services; usefulness of real property.

**VA**   Veterans' Administration of the federal government.

**VA-guaranteed mortgage**   Veteran's mortgage guaranteed by the VA for an amount not in excess of VA's appraised value of the property.

**VA loan**   A loan guaranteed by the VA.

**Valid**   Having force, or binding force; legally sufficient, authorized by law, or incapable of being set aside.

**Valley**   The internal angle formed as a result of the junction between the two sloping sides of a roof.

**Valuation**   Estimated worth or price; the act of valuing a property by appraisal.

**Value analysis**   Estimation of the present worth of the future benefits to be derived from a property investment.

**Value calculation**   The estimation of the value to be recognized by buyers, sellers, lenders, and renters in the marketplace.

**Value figure**   A figure used to determine how much capital to invest in the property under consideration.

**Value for a purpose**   The theory that in real estate emphasis must be placed on different value factors depending upon the purpose of the valuation; the use for which the property is being considered.

**Value in exchange**   The price an investment asset is predicted to bring based upon comparable market transactions.

**Value in use**   The price an investor would pay based on his or her personal opinion of the investment asset's merit.

**Value of property**   The usefulness of the property relative to its scarcity.

**Variable rate mortgage**   A mortgage that carries an interest rate which may move either up or down, depending on the movement of the standard to which the interest rate is tied.

**Variance**   The authorization to improve or develop a particular property in a manner not authorized by the zoning ordinance; generally granted by a Board of Zoning Appeals.

**Vendee**   A purchaser of property. The word is more commonly applied to a purchaser of real property.

**Vendor**   A person who sells property to a vendee. The word is more commonly applied to a seller of real estate.

**Vendor's lien**   A lien implied to belong to a vendor for the unpaid purchase price of property, when he has not taken any other lien or security beyond the personal obligation of the purchaser.

**Veneer**   Thin sheets of wood of excellent quality glued over wood of lesser quality.

**Vent**   A pipe installed to provide a flow of air to or from a drainage system or to provide for the circulation of air within such a system to protect trap seals from siphonage and back-pressure.

**Venue**   Locality; also, the heading of a legal document showing the state and county to which it refers. Legally, the appropriate forum for filing a lawsuit.

**Verbal**   By word of mouth; spoken; oral; parol.

**Verification**   A confirmation of correctness, truth, or authenticity by affidavit, oath, or deposition.

**Verified**   Confirmed or substantiated by an oath.

**Vested**   Placed in possession and control; given or committed to another.

**Veterans' Administration**   An agency of the federal government that, among other activities, guarantees loans made to veterans.

**Void contract**   That which is entirely null; an agreement that is not binding on either party and is not susceptible of ratification.

**Voidable contract**   An agreement that is capable of being made void but is not utterly null and void; hence it may be either voided or confirmed.

**Volume**   The amount of space that an object occupies in three-dimensional space.

**Voluntary lien**   A lien placed on property with the consent of, or as a result of, the voluntary act of the owner.

**Wainscotting**   Wood lining of an interior wall; also the lower part of a wall when finished differently from the upper wall.

**Waiver**   The intentional relinquishment of a known right. It is a voluntary act and implies an election by the party to dispense with something of value or to forego some advantage or right.

**Wall**   A bearing wall is one that supports any verticle load in addition to its own weight. A cavity wall is a thin, non-load-bearing wall supported by the structure. A foundation wall is below or partly below ground, providing support for the exterior or other structural parts of the building. A masonry wall is a bearing or non-bearing wall of hollow or solid masonry units.

**Warrant**   To guarantee or promise that a certain fact or state of facts, in relation to the subject matter of a transaction, is or shall be as it is represented to be.

**Warranted value**   A term often erroneously used in place of "warranted price."

**Warranty deed**   One which contains a general guarantee of the quality of title being conveyed.

**Waste**   An abuse or destructive use of property by one in rightful possession.

**Water rights**   An aggregate right consisting of the rights to a water supply; guarantee of access to nearby body of water.

**Water softener**   A mechanical device for treating hard water by circulating it through a chemical solution.

**Water table**   Distance from surface of ground to a depth where natural groundwater can be found.

**Waterpower rights**   A property containing the rights to the use of water as a source of power, developed or undeveloped.

**WCR**   *See* Women's Council of Realtors.

**Will**   A written instrument executed with the formalities of law, whereby a person makes a disposition of property to take effect after death.

**Will-cut cruise**   The estimated volume of lumber that can be sawed from the timber in a given area. It is obtained by deducting from the stand cruise an allowance for breakage and other waste. (To cruise is to inspect land to determine possible lumber yield.)

**Without recourse**   An endorser without recourse specially declines to assume any responsibility to subsequent holders for payment of a debt instrument which is transferred by endorsement.

**Women's Council of Realtors**   Provides educational programs and publications for women REALTORS® whose primary interest is in residential brokerage.

**Words of conveyance**   The statement that follows the statement of consideration in a deed to show the intent on the part of the grantor to transfer the property.

**Working capital** Properly, the readily convertible capital required in a business to allow the regular functioning of operations free from financial embarrassment. In accounting, the excess of current assets less the current liabilities as of any date.

**Working drawing** A sketch of a part or a whole structure, drawn to scale and in such detail as to dimensions and instructions as is needed to guide the work on a construction job.

**Wraparound loan** A form of junior mortgage which incorporates the full amount of the loan desired with a higher repayment to retire the existing debt. It is used when it is not feasible or desirable to retire the first mortgage.

**Writ of execution** An order to carry out the judgment or decree of a court.

**X-bracing** Cross-bracing of a partition or floor joist.

**Yield** Income of a property—the ratio of the annual net income from the property to the cost or market value of the property.

**Zone** The area described by the proper authorities for a specific use, subject to certain restrictions or restraints.

**Zoning** Governmental regulation of land use; regulation by local government under police powers of such matters as height, bulk, and use of buildings and use of land. The enabling act is a state statute necessary to provide a legal base for zoning codes. Snob zoning is zoning regulations that require large lots, etc., as a method of excluding those in low-income groups.

**Zoning map** A map showing the various sections of the community and the division of the sections into zones of permitted land uses under the zoning ordinance.

**Zoning ordinance** The use of police powers by the governing body to regulate and control the use of real estate for the health, morals, safety, and welfare of the general public.

# Index

# Index